A Chip
off the
Old Block

To John,
On behalf of Mum.
Josie!

A Chip off the Old Block

Josephine Rundle

Bannister Publications Ltd
118 Saltergate
Chesterfield
Derbyshire S40 1NG

First published in Great Britain in 2011 by

Bannister Publications Ltd
118 Saltergate
Chesterfield
Derbyshire S40 1NG

ISBN 978-0-9566196-8-6

Designed and set in Palatino Linotype by
Escritor Design, Chesterfield, Derbyshire

Printed and bound in the UK by the MPG Books Group,
Bodmin and King's Lynn

Prologue

This is not only my story; it is the story of my Father and my Mother, for without them, there would be no story. They are the history of this country as Drake and Elizabeth, as Churchill and Florence Nightingale. They were ordinary people such as helped to make England great, yet each in their own way as individuals as the sands on the beach.

My Mother was a Saint, yet in no way shy. She had a kind of strength of purpose that sometimes bordered on stubbornness. Her sense of right and wrong was paramount and her conviction that things were planned, that if you always did your best and what you thought were right, everything would be all right. That when things seemed to be going wrong, something would turn up to put things right again. Her faith in life and people was sometimes so unbelievable as to be exasperating. I listened once to her and my Father discussing something just before we left the house, and on the way out he said to her, almost under his breath, "You know your Mother's too good for this world". I knew what he meant. Discuss anything with her; tell her a bit of gossip, and she would always make excuses, never ever a word of criticism about anybody. "You don't know what goes on when they've closed their doors at night", was her usual remark, or "You don't know why". She had her feet firmly on the ground, was always there supporting all the family, especially my Father, completely understanding our problems with a philosophy and wisdom which always seemed right.

My Father was, above all, a patriot. Doing your duty; whether to your country or employer; or your fellow men, was his overriding philosophy. That this sometimes interfered with family harmony was of little consequence. "Did you do your job right? Was your work satisfactory? Were there any complaints?" were the criteria on which he based his judgment. He was a shrewd man, astute in his dealings with fellow men, respected by all for his understanding of their problems, and help in times of need. Two years after his death, a man from the village called at the house and handed my Mother £2.0s.0d, repayment of a loan made two years before his death. "Mr Salt was always good to us at 'pit'" he said. Yet he was ever perceptive of the ways of mean and wary of the scoundrel. "Treat everybody as a rogue lass, until you know he can be trusted, then you can trust him with your life", was his advice to me. A philosophy frowned on by my Mother, who trusted everyone. He was handsome in stature, straight as a ramrod, upright as a guardsman; his sense of humour and twinkling eyes found favour in the eyes of women. He enjoyed flattery, shrived on admiration. This is the material from which I was made.

Introduction

I was born in 1915, the second child of Frances Mary and Isaiah Salt, then resident in the Old School House, Totley, Derbyshire, and so, by birth, I can be classified as a 'Derbyshire Tup'. According to my Mother, the night that heralded my birth was pitch dark, except for the faint glimmer of light reflected from the snow piled high on the walls, and covering the rooftops of the cottages in the lane.

A blizzard had been blowing all day, and, by nightfall the roads were almost impassable. It was bitterly cold as snow swirled in ever more frenzied fury around the old nurse as she fought her way through the deep drifts to the Old School House. Many times that night she had made the same journey, struggling through the drifts, falling constantly into the deep ruts made by farm carts, painfully dragging her aching body in slow progress as she kept vigil on the two Mothers, far in labour, who awaited the advent of their offspring into the light of day. She was weary, and very tired; drenched to the waist, her long black skirts clinging to her body, hindering her boot clad legs as they became heavier and heavier with freezing slush and snow.

It had been a long night since my Father had obeyed the signals from my Mother and set out on his journey, a walk of about two miles, to the little hamlet of Ashfurlong to fetch Nurse Baron, the District Nurse, that there be no danger in this, the birth, of his second child. There were no telephones or buses at such a late hour, and two miles seemed a long way when the reason was urgent, and time precious. As he found his mind wandering, his thoughts went back to the home he had recently left, and the child whose birth he hoped soon to be celebrating. He already had a son, my brother Elijah, now two years old, a sturdy lad, and the apple of his eye, who followed him around the house and his lovely garden, and had been known to follow him up the lane towards the village where he caught the bus to the nearest city of Sheffield. Occasionally, in the early morning when he left to talk to the Strawberry-Lea Mine where he was Manager, the little chap would follow silently until his 'dada' signalled him to turn and laughing, swing him up on to his shoulder to carry him back down the lane and the wide stone steps, through the arched entrance into the building which was home.

As he neared the end of his journey, he thought of his second child; dare he hope for a daughter this time; perhaps a little girl with golden hair like Doris, Mr Turner, his next door neighbour's daughter, whose glorious hair hung down to her waist in shining waves of gold. He'd said to my Mother on more than one occasion "I'd like to have a daughter with hair like that". Hours had passed since he'd knocked on the door of the little cottage where the nurse was ready and quick to leave, telling him of the other call she was expecting that night from another mother far in labour in the same village. She was a large woman and progress through the snow had been slow and difficult as he pushed and pulled, heaved and shoved her and her black bag over the deepest drifts. The blizzard had grown worse as the hours wore on. Somehow they had succeeded in reaching the village, and now, many hours later, as she negotiated the final few yards, at last descending the steps to the old studded door, she thought, and fervently hoped, that this would be her final journey down the lane on that inhospitable and unfriendly night, and that, within the hour, Frances Mary would be delivered of her second child.

She was not wrong in her hopeful prediction, for, at 6.00 a.m. on Thursday morning of the 18th November 1915, I completed the last stretch and burst into this wicked, cruel, beautiful, wonderful world, and cried out lustily in protest.

Chapter 1

A few years before I was born, a travelling theatre visited Dronfield, a small town about two miles from Dronfield Woodhouse, where my parents lived before their marriage. It was made up of a group of actors and actresses who travelled from place to place carrying their equipment, including scenery, with them, calling at small hamlets and communities where they were no other theatres, or provision for the inhabitants to see stage productions, usually staying for only one night.

My Father took my Mother to see the play, a powerful melodrama about the Empress Josephine's divorce from the Emperor Napoleon, called 'The Royal Divorce'. The story told how the unfortunate Josephine could not produce the son which Napoleon so desired, and although he loved her very much, for the sake of his dynasty, he must divorce her. The play was powerful and dramatic, and the actor most convincing when the distraught Napoleon, returning to the Palace to find that Josephine had left, strode on to the stage, hand in coat, and with a dramatic gesture, cried out in an agonised voice, "Josephine, Josephine; where are you Josephine, my guiding star"? By all accounts, my Father was very moved, in fact, according to my Mother, he was completely hooked! So it happens that, three days after my arrival, on the 22nd November 1915, without further consultation, my Father made quite sure that I became entry number 416 in book two of the Dore Registry in the name of Josephine Salt. Always a man to achieve his own way, he returned home in triumph.

On entering the large living room, voices could be heard coming from the bedroom, where an animated conversation was

1

going on to the complicated question of the choice of my name. The two speakers were my Mother and Aunt Ruth; my Father's youngest sister, who was visiting for the primary purpose of viewing the babe. Ruth and my Mother had been friends for a number of years, in fact it was due to their friendship that my Mother had first met my Father, and Ruth was always there whenever the occasion provided an excuse. She was indulged by my Father, who denied her nothing, as we were to find out in later years. This time, however, she had no influence over his decision. "Pauline, I like Pauline", my Mother was heard to say. "Jane", said my Aunt, "or Elizabeth, that's a good bible name, and you know our family's always been fond of bible names". For a minute or two, my Father listened with interest, without speaking, except for a gesture of acknowledgement. Then he interrupted. "She's already got a name". "What's that?" said my Aunt. "She's already got a name", he repeated. "Her name's Josephine". "What do you mean?" said my Mother. "Aye, what do you mean?" echoed my Aunt. "Come on, what do you mean?" "I mean," replied my Father, "Her name's Josephine and she's going to be my guiding star". How I measured up to his expectations, I never knew, but there were moments throughout my life when I felt a closeness which was difficult to define. My Father was a very complex man.

No matter how careful parents are in their choice of names for their offspring, the best laid plans have a habit of going haywire, and there are few odds against someone coming along to change them. This occasion was no exception. A few months before I was born, on the 2nd January of the same year to be exact, another baby girl had made her entry into the lane via Fred and May Ward. Her name was Phyllis, and like all young children, she was fascinated by the new arrival, and with her mother, spent quite a lot of time at the School House. But Josephine is rather a difficult name for a beginner to wrap her tongue around, and before long, my name was whittled down to the last syllable and pronounced 'Dene'.

In the family, in the village, and amongst my friends, for the rest of my young life, I was known as 'Dene Salt'. As an adolescent

I was, very often, grateful to Phyllis, at least to be introduced as 'Dene' did not invite that irritating cliché, 'Not tonight Josephine' from some young 'puppy' trying to be clever. There is an old legend, belief, myth, call it what you will, that was often quoted by the old wives of Derbyshire, and they firmly believed it to be true. It quotes that a new born baby is able to see its whole life stretching before it during the first three months of its life, and its behaviour during that three months is its reaction to the visions. A crying baby was often met with "Aye, it can see what's in store and the poor little mite don't like it". I must have been a miserable child looking into my crystal ball, for I howled for the whole three months. I was weak and puny, wizened and red faced, probably as a result of so much weeping. Whether there was any truth in the fable or not is a matter of conjecture; reflecting on the question, I can only offer, were my tears for the future, or was it just a nappy pin!

By the time I was three years old, my Grandmother was heard to say "You'll never rear that child". Apparently the odds were great but thankfully, her prediction was not proved true. A more important omen, as I have sometime reasoned, was that the nurse who first saw my little wizened face had to spend the night traversing the lanes just because some unreasonable male was trying to leave his watery cave and beat me to it. My life from that moment seems to have been a constant race, against what, or for what, I have never discovered! The male, by the way, was born the day after!

My Mother and Father had moved into the Old School House from their first home to Lemont Road, Green Oak soon after my Grandmother came to live with them. Crippled with arthritis for a number of years, she had gone to live with her youngest daughter Ruth when she married Richard Wheat (Uncle Dick) in their new home at Cowley Bar, Holmesfield. When their first child Jane (Jinney) was expected in 1913, the work of looking after both the babe and the Grandmother was too much for Ruth, and it seemed there was nothing for it but to send her to the geriatric ward at Scarsdale Hospital in Chesterfield, a few miles away. On one of his visits to the hospital, my Father found her far from happy, and

3

asking to be taken out. In floods of tears she cried "They're trying to kill us off". "Of course they aren't" said my Father, "They wouldn't do that." "They are, I tell you" she persisted, "they come round every night wi' that 'Black Jack', it's poison, somebody dies every day." Of course my Father knew this wasn't true, for 'Black Jack' was nothing more than cascara. But he also knew that it was a common belief amongst the elderly and unknowledgeable that it was for the specific purpose of 'bumping them off', possibly because of its effect on the system! Father knew that Grandma was seriously worried.

He returned home and discussed the situation with my Mother. "Do you think we could manage to take her here?" he asked and of course, the answer was "Yes". Even though she also had a young child she rarely denied my Father anything, and she too was concerned for Grandma whom she had known and liked for many years. It was not long before my parents realised that the house at Lemont Road was not big enough for them all, and as the School House was about to be let, they decided to move. The rent was a little more than their present home, and up until now, Mother had paid it out of the housekeeping money. But Father's wages had been raised and he offered to pay the new rent himself. It would be worth it, he thought, Grandma's bed would fit comfortably in the large kitchen where she would have greater privacy, particularly when there were visitors. So, we became a three generation family for, at least, the early years of my life.

Totley Hall was built in 1623 for George Barker, one of the sons of a very old Totley family who owned farms and land, George also owning the local Corn Mill. In 1827, the Hall had passed to the D'Ewes Coke family and, although the present member of the family to own it did not actually live there, he gave a piece of land, and £2,000 to build a school for twelve village children. From the records it would seem that more than this number attended the school for in the 1850's there were eleven boys and 19 girls, one of whom was Emma Hodkin, later wife of Francis Fisher, my great grandfather's brother who remembered paying a penny a week. It may be that the twelve places were free ones, any extra being paying pupils. One might think that Mr D'Ewes Coke was Totley's first known benefactor!

The old School House still nestles comfortably in a corner of the lane, unchanged in its exterior, and altered inside only by the addition of an upstairs bedroom in about 1918 when my Uncle, Arthur Bradley and Aunt Alice moved from there from the Post Office at the corner of Hillfoot Road and Baslow Road (now demolished). Before that date, it comprised one large room, the original classroom, a narrow living room/bedroom, and an 'off-shot' kitchen at the side of the house.

The main living room is very large, approached through a huge studded door leading from a stone porch which has an impressive stone arched entrance, giving the impression of entering a church. The huge Yorkshire Range at the far end of the room was probably included when the house was built, for it was there before my parents moved in, and the mistress would, obviously, require some sort of cooking arrangement.

Lawns, vegetable and flower gardens surround the house within a walled boundary, whilst high mullioned windows to the front and side of the living room add to the impression of a church. A door to the left of the fireplace leads to the 'off-shot' kitchen which at the time of this story, boasted a large shallow stone sink set beneath a window overlooking a small grassed area to the north side of the house, and in one corner, stood a brick built copper, whose little fire door with ash pit beneath, were the instruments for raising heat on washing day and bath night!

Life in the lane was pleasant, if one takes account of my Mother's stories. There were the Marshalls, the Turners, and the Stubbs families in the three cottages built into the bank directly opposite the School House. The Wards lived about fifty yards further up the lane in a small cottage set back from the road, and a few yards further on lived my Aunt Julia and Uncle Walter, and cousins Kay and Albert, who had moved to Totley from Bradway in 1914. Cousins Thomas and Walter would appear later.

Families were much more involved with each other in those far off days; there was no unemployment money or Social Security for those in need, only the 'Parish', and that, to all proud people, was the last straw. The 'Parish' was the small amount of money, about 2s.6d in the 1920s and 1930s, which was allowed each week by the Parish Council to widows and others who had no means of support. There were Friendly Societies, (local clubs to which small amounts were paid each week from workmen's wages, usually no more than 1d, as wages were low). The Societies then paid out small sums in case of illness and a dividend at Christmas, but there was nothing but the 'Parish' for those in real distress. So, neighbours helped each other, and this could lead to some very unusual circumstances.

Mrs Marshall was the second wife of Jim Marshall who, when they married, already had four children, Neville, Fanny, Fred and Hilda. Jim's second marriage brought forth four more in Bessie, Billy, Dennis and Eric. Dennis was the same age as me and it so happened that soon after I was born, when money was a little tight for their large family, Mrs Marshall was offered a job as cleaner at the Fleur de Lys Public House at the top of the lane. Jim worked on the railway, for which, according to my Mother, he received a wage of £1 a week, which he supplemented by working in the evenings as barman at the 'Fleur', and a little extra from a cleaning job would add to the family coffers and be very welcome. "The trouble is," confided Mrs Marshall to my Mother "it's from, 6.00 a.m., and that's when our Dennis wakes up". Never daunted, my Mother came up with the solution. She would listen, she said, for Dennis waking, when she would fetch him across to the School House and put him in the bath with 'Our Dene', "and he can stop here until you come home".

So it was that, at that very early age, I was subjected to the doubtful pleasure of being dunked into a bath with a 'willing' male. Or, perhaps it was a little more discreet, rather more like 'Dene' first, Dennis second! Luckily Dennis' mother returned in time for breakfast. There was no bottle feeding in those days for healthy mums, and so, both mothers sat side by side enjoying the first gossip of the day whilst their respective offspring sucked away happily.

Lambert Stubbs was a great character. He sat in his rocking chair on the short path outside the cottage, swopping stories with passers-by, some a little 'near the bone', always cheerful and ready to help. My Mother recounts the many times he rocked Elijah to sleep when all else failed to do the trick. "Bring 'im 'ore 'ere" he would shout when lungs were being exercised beyond endurance, or if sister was demanding attention at the same time. Lambert would rock and sing to the bairn, 'Nellie Dean', 'Kathleen Mavourneen', 'Farmer's Boy'; he knew them all, and in no time at all, Elijah was peacefully sleeping. "No one," said my Mother "could get him off to sleep like Lambert Stubbs".

Almost opposite the School House was Hall Lane Farm, owned at that time by 'Bill' Unwin. In the yard just outside the farm gates, in another small yard, was a deep well which supplied water to the farm. Every morning, according to my Mother, a horse was harnessed to a frame over the well and left to walk round and round for hours drawing water to the surface. This is still called the 'Well Yard', whilst the adjourning barn had been converted into a house called 'The Well House'.

By the time I was a year old it became obvious that the kitchen was not an ideal place for Grandma. The steam on washing day was considered harmful to her lungs so, another move was deemed advisable. It so happened that the bottom cottage of the row on the main Baslow Road just outside the village at Lane Head had become vacant, (it now has the dubious distinction of being called 320 Baslow Road). There were two downstairs rooms at the front of the house, one with a sink and Yorkshire range would be the living room, whilst the other would become Grandma's bedroom. It was thought to be ideal.

By now Grandma was a complete cripple, and unable to walk. She was a heavy woman, particularly due to her stiff limbs, and as she had to be carried from her bed and returned each evening, rather a burden even for my Father. Soon after the move he commissioned

7

Mr Bradbury, the Blacksmith in the Chemical Yard, Totley Rise, to make two axles and a set of wheels for her Windsor chair. Every morning he lifted her from her bed into the chair, now boasting wheels, and it was easy to transfer from the bedroom to living room. To be returned in the same way in the evening. She had a very confined existence, sitting in her wheelchair all day, but according to my Mother, she was happy and grateful to live with the family.

My Mother was long-suffering. She was very fond of her Mother-in-Law, a kind, over-generous woman, who had not had an easy life and now suffered considerably. But the attention she needed in her daily care, and in toileting, added a very great burden to my Mother, a burden she never criticised, nor even resented, was such her nature.

The migration from Hall Lane to Lane Head was the subject of Elijah's first memory. He was three years old at the time. He told me how he remembered sitting on top of a pile of furniture on a farm cart or dray, probably borrowed from the farm across the road. The ride, in so elevated position was majestic as he rode up the lane, and the main road to the new house, and more dignified than another episode he remembers when he was made to sit on the back step of a Trap (a pony cart), which my Father was driving, he having another man sitting beside him on the driving seat. The Trap hit a bump in the road, and Elijah fell off, landing on his bottom in the middle of the road, until my Father eventually realised that his son was not where he was supposed to be. The dusty road had obviously softened the fall for, after a good dusting down, he was no worse for the experience!

My first memory was a little later, and subject to some doubt as to the actual occasion. I remember my Mother standing at the front door of our cottage holding me in her arms; Elijah stood by her side, and both of us were waving little Union flags whilst we watched rows and rows of soldiers marching past carrying rifles over their shoulders. A band played as they marched past, an indication to her that this was an occasion when the troops were leaving the rifle range in the Bents for the War front. That would be the City battalion leaving for the Somme, when the whole battalion was wiped out. She recalled that although solders came and went regularly to the rifle range, marching past as I had described, she never remembered any other time when a band accompanied them except when the City battalion left. On reflection, I think this could not be right. The Battle of the Somme took place on July 1st 1916 when I was 7½ months old. I think it more likely to be the year after.

My second brother, Geoffrey, was born in December 1917, after which he would have been the 'babe in arms'. As I was the current one, and considering that very few troops left the village in 1918, the last year of the War, and having discussed all the possibilities with Elijah, I feel safe in placing this memory in the summer of 1917, the battalion and the occasion still obscure, unless I have a super, super memory! Nevertheless, an early one by any reckoning!

The birth of my second brother was another occasion for my Father to assert his 'master of the house' authority. It was the current fashion for parents to name their sons after the Generals and heroes of the First World War. The Hancock's of Dore had recently named their son Kitchener after the General who was drowned at the Battle of Jutland and Victor Crookes who can blame the victory of Jutland for his name. Not to be outdone, my Father decided to call his son Joffre, why, we never knew nor understood, for General Joffre was a Frenchman! As on the previous occasion the journey to the Registry Office was made without consultation and, on his return, he proudly broke the news to Mother and Auntie Ruth (yes, she was there this time too), that the baby's name was Joffre. "It can't be," said Auntie Ruth, "there's no such name as Joffre". "Yes there is," insisted Father, "it's here on the Birth Certificate". "That's not Joffre" both women chorused, after perusing the said document, "it's Geoffrey, and we shall call him Geoffrey". And call him Geoffrey they did, whilst my Father persisted in calling him Joffre, for two years until a third son was born, on my Mother's 28th birthday, 14th March, 1920. As on the two previous occasions the routine was the same. An unannounced trip to the Registrar, a more than ever triumphant return home, and the news broke again. Waving the Certificate high in the air he proclaimed, "You'll have to call him Joffre now, 'cos this one's called Jeffrey, and there can't be two Jeffrey's in one house." We learned later that even the Registrar had queried the name Joffre and had taken 'French leave' when he made out the certificate for the first Geoffrey. My Father had not thought to check the spelling on it, and I doubt whether he would have known anyway, the spelling of names was not first priority of parents at that time.

For the first few years of our residence at Lane Head, the road and footpath were just dirt, with a grass verge, about a foot wide down the edge of the footpath, dividing it from the road, but in 1914, the Parish Council requested the Norton District Council to spray the centre of the road with tar to prevent dust flying when cars travelled on the highway, as they were already doing up to Totley Rise and this was done by the end of the First World War in 1918. This left about three feet of dirt at the sides with a grass border dividing the road from the footpath, which at least acted as a simple barrier to dust and dirt thrown aside by the few cars and carts which passed.

The dust was a constant headache for my Mother, rather more than our near neighbours. Our gate was directly in front of the door, whilst that of the third house was set to one side, and our next door neighbours lived in the room below with its entrance from the back yard. Our house was not only always filled with dust, but daughter was obviously obsessed with playing in the dust and dirt of the gutter. On one occasion, dressed ready for a visit to see Mrs Marshall, my Mother found me sitting on the grass verge with feet in gutter, laughing delightedly whilst lifting handfuls of dirt high over my head and trickling it through my fingers into my hair. My hair was my Mother's pride and joy, on which she spent much time and effort to please my Father, so this must have been a severe trial for her as she had to undress and wash me and my hair before we could set off on our visit.

Then there was the time when, having set out the table for a baking session, she couldn't find the half pound of lard which she knew had been put there. She found me again in the gutter with the empty paper, I had eaten the lot! What price cholesterol? Just before Jeff was born, it was decided that Grandma should go to stay with Uncle Teddy, my father's brother, who lived at Newton near Alfreton, about thirty miles away, until the birth was over. The problem was how to get her there. After much discussion, my Father decided to borrow a 'pig cart' from 'Piggy' Hill, a pig farmer who lived at Totley Bents Farm. The cart was little more than a high sided box on wheels, pulled by a horse. A backboard lowered to the ground to form a ramp up which the pigs were loaded. Grandma was safely fastened into her Windsor chair with a clothes-line and wheeled up the ramp into the cart, there to be secured to the shafts of the cart with a second line. The ramp was raised and Dad set off for Newton, a journey completed without mishap, but with no record of what Grandma thought about it. I reckon that, with the sense of humour she was blessed with, she saw the funny side of the situation, and probably felt like a Queen at a Durbar as she sat on her 'throne' so high up in the world.

One very vivid memory stays with me, and remembered by my Mother when I recounted it to her many years later. I was about four years old at the time. It was wash day and Mother was in the cellar-kitchen downstairs, leaving me upstairs in the living room with Grandma, as usual sitting beside the fire in her chair. In my memory, I can see her now, holding the corners of her large white apron which she always wore. It had two huge pockets that held her handkerchief and oddments such as smelling-salts and her purse.

Standing on the top bar of the fire was a huge galvanised tub filled to the brim with small potatoes left there to boil for the pigs which my Father kept in the field at the top of the bank opposite the cottage. "Psst, psst," she hissed, "pass me a potato duck," holding out her apron to receive it. "Come on before thi' Mother comes upstairs." I went to the fireplace and put out my hand gingerly, and was just about to pluck one from the pot when unfortunately, or fortunately as the case may be, Mother did come upstairs and, seeing me so close to the boiling pot, yelled "What on earth are you doing?"

11

I jumped and fled behind Grandma's chair, crouching there before this unusual wrath. "Never do that again," she roared, "she's only four, do you want her to burn to death?" Grandma was sheepish and almost in tears. When my Mother talked about this episode in later years, she was still incredulous at the danger to which Grandma had subjected her granddaughter, but she also had great sympathy for her. "She never could resist pig potatoes" she said, "and, poor lass, she couldn't get 'em for herself."

I was four years old when my youngest brother was born. I well remember sitting on the bed looking at the live doll which lay beside my Mother, and I remember my Father coming upstairs with a large basin of gruel, and watching whilst my Mother scooped it down spoonful by spoonful. When I asked to taste it, it was delicious, made of oatmeal, creamy milk and sweetened with sugar, and cooked to a thick creamy consistency which was easy to digest. It was always given to nursing mothers to help in the production of milk for the babe. I guess all men, just like my Father, could make a good gruel when necessary, for, I am sure, in those days of large families, and delivery of babies at home, they had plenty of practice.

About a year after Jeff was born, in January 1921, when I was five years old, I was playing in the field behind the house when there was a call from my Mother. "Come here, I want you," was all she said, and she was very quiet and silent as she took me into the bedroom where Grandma lay in bed. Auntie Julia stood at the head of the bed. I was intrigued to see how still Grandma was, and a bit puzzled to see the cotton wool in both nostrils. Her face was very white and smooth, not as I usually saw her. "Say goodbye to your Grandma," my Mother said quietly. I looked up at her puzzled. "Your Grandma's dead, give her a kiss goodbye." I was lifted high over the bed and lowered so that I could plant a kiss on Grandma's check. It was cold and left me a bit mystified as to what 'dead' meant. She was buried on 21st January 1921 in Dore churchyard.

Chapter 2

Our row of cottages was built into the side of the hill, the two lowest rooms, the cellar-kitchens, actually being built into the bank. The windows of these two rooms looked out on to a yard which extended behind the first three cottages providing a drying area on washing day and housing the coal-houses of the two neighbouring cottages. Our coal was tipped at the front of the house and pushed, or shovelled down a shoot into one of the cellars. This caused a lot of dust until a corner of the cellar was boarded off from floor to ceiling, making an enclosed coal-place with a door into the cellar. This arrangement was far cleaner, and pleasanter for Mom on washday, and later, as we grew older, on bath nights.

This cellar was always called the cellar kitchen because it was actually like another room with a large window looking out on to the yard. The other called the cellar, had only a small window over a large joiner's bench where my Father did his 'cobbling' and rather primitive joinery. He used to buy leather from the market on Saturday when our shoes were ready for repairing, and, with the 'hobbing-foot' between his knees, after filling his mouth with little nails, would tap them in around the sole to hold it fast against much kicking and climbing which boys tend to do. Sometimes he would add three rows of 'hob-nails' which stood out above the sole, for extra defence against heavy wear. A 'hobbing-foot', for those who don't already know, was an iron contraption in the shape of a foot and ankle, sometimes in a set of three like the Isle of Man three-legged logo. (Forgive me Isle of Man if that's not the right word). The ankle on Dad's was drawn out to a point, which he inserted into a piece of four-by-four wood about two feet long which he could hold tight between his knees for hammering.

Four wide stone steps led down from the back door to the yard, and sometime later, Dad made three steps from the yard up to the field at the back. This was a flat area which extended behind the whole row of seven houses, extending parallel to the road, but much lower, down through the allotments to Hillfoot Road and the Church School. The whole area up to the entrance gate at the side of our house had been used as allotments since the First World War. My Father cultivated one, and later, another two, later still obtaining permission from the Parish Council to create another on the back field. It was hard work turning it into good fertile soil, but eventually it grew some of the choicest vegetables and soft fruits, as well as tomatoes from his home-made greenhouse, and cucumbers from the frame.

My Father prided himself on the quality of his products which, due to its abundance, meant that we never had to buy vegetables, soft fruits or flowers, and there was always plenty left over from immediate requirements for jams, jellies, syrups and bottling. And there was the Village Show every year when the quality of the produce was tested; four white potatoes; four red potatoes; six kidney beans; six pods of peas; a plate of tomatoes; two sticks of celery. Dad entered them all, and proud because he always managed to win one or two prizes. No doubt it was the proximity of the closets which helped him achieve such success, particularly with his celery, for although we were never allowed to witness him in the act, we knew he robbed the 'midden' and used the 'night-soil' in the bottom of the trenches when he prepared them for the young celery plants. My brother Elijah swears he could taste it on the sticks served at Sunday tea, but I was never so discriminating, provided they were succulent and tender. And that they certainly were, deliciously crisp and sweet!

There were two closets for the three families, a tricky situation sometimes, considering there were upwards of 17 bodies to be catered for. The building which housed them was a sturdy stone-built structure in the corner of the back yard, one of its sides being built into the bank created by the cart-road into the allotments. The ground underneath had been excavated to a depth of about four feet to accommodate all the waste produced from the three families, a four foot square door in the field at the back allowing access for emptying

14

by 'Fatty Coates' with his deep horse-drawn covered cart. The two doors to the 'privies' both faced our back door, whilst the fourth side housed the ash-pit and the depository for cans and bottles and the like.

The ashes from the spent fire were removed from the grate every morning, including the cokes and unburned pieces of coal, as well as the waste, all being deposited in the ash-pit, there to be riddled by Mrs Smith who lived next door, retrieving all the large pieces and the residue for banking up their fire. My Mother had no need of riddled ashes, for my Father, Manager of the local ganister mines, from which coal was extracted as a bi-product, was allowed a load of coal every six weeks, or whenever it was required. Our neighbours were not so lucky. The Putrels had only a small family and Father had a good job, so there was no great need. The Smiths were more numerous, and the family certainly benefited from the extra fuel. My Father decreed that the fireplace be cleared every morning, irrespective of how much unburned coal remained from the previous night. There was, of course, the added fact that the fire burned brighter after the clearance, for the coal was not of the best quality, being only secondary in importance to the ganister mined from a lower Strata. Mrs Smith was only too pleased to riddle the contents of the ash-pit every Friday morning, and when she had finished her weekly task, there was an abundant supply of fuel to supplement the family budget.

Great pride was taken by the three housewives in the cleaning of the closets. Although not strictly in competition with each other, they would never dream of letting down their own household in such a communal situation. The seats were constructed from closely fitted floor-boards, the ends around the hole being bevelled and rounded for more comfortable sitting. They were scrubbed as white as butcher's benches. The floors were huge stone slabs, very smooth from much vigorous scrubbing by one of the housewives who took it in turn once every three weeks to accomplish the job. The sides of the floors were decorated after scrubbing, with a broad band of 'donkey-stone', sometimes straight, sometimes with a scalloped edge down the sides and along the front edge of the step, according to the whim of the decorator. I had a burning ambition at a very young age to decorate the closet floors, but my Father put his foot down, "You let her do a lot of things, but she's not doing the 'shitehouses', and that's that" was his final decree!

When dry, the step and floors shone clean and white and woe betide anyone who put a foot on that 'donkey-stone' before it was completely dry. 'Donkey-stone', for those who are ignorant of the fact, was a manufactured soft stone like a very hard greyish-white chalk, which was sold in blocks about 4" x 2" x 2". In use, the block was dipped in water, and the wet face of the block was rubbed backwards and forwards until a sufficiently thick layer had been deposited on the area to the decorated. Another stone, sold by a travelling hardware man was 'rubbing-stone', commonly called 'potmold'. (The man was always known as 'Potmold' because that was his cry as he went along the roads). It was hard, and yellow, or ochre-colour, and sometimes used for areas not considered too important. Closets were important!

They were not comfortable places to dwell unnecessarily long, particularly on a windy night when a blast rose up through the hole surrounding the bare rear. Once my Father, returning upstairs all shivery and blue on a particularly windy night, was heard to say to my Mother, "There's a right gale in't shitehouse tonight, yer shirt's o'er yer 'ead afore yer arse's covered t'hole." In the days of outside toilets there was no item on the shopping list for toilet paper; it would have been considered the highest form of extravagance, even if thought of at all. Pure unadulterated newspaper was the order of the day unless, as sometimes happened, a parcel had arrived in which the goods were carefully packed, then one might enjoy the luxury of tissue paper. Some people cut their newspapers into neat squares, making a hole through the corner of a number of pieces, and threading the bundle on to a string, which was then hung on a conveniently placed nail in the wall at the side of the seat. Nothing so elaborate was seen in our loos. A whole newspaper was deposited on the seat, a strip being torn off to a suitable size for the occasion, or, as often happened, as an insurance against there having been a rush on and no paper left, on the way to the cellar steps, it was the habit to grab a sheet of whatever paper was nearest to hand, and dive down the steps at full speed.

It wasn't the most ideal wiper one could wish for, it was stiff and uncomfortable, dependent on the edition one had grabbed, and the ink which conveyed the messages to the reader was easily transferable, as I heard my Father say "They've been a bit liberal wi' t'ink this week; it comes off on to yer 'ands and arse like soot.". The two closets were not exactly identical; the seat of one, the one we called 'the bottom closet' was lower than that of the 'top closet'. This had, no doubt, been designed for the convenience of children, which would have been a happy situation but for the fact that there was a loose board which none of the fathers had thought fit to repair. This loose board was a source of great distress to me personally, for my little bottom was still too small comfortably to fit the hole without a certain amount of elevation by my little hands pressed firmly on the seat to prevent falling through. Furthermore, when the loose board was disturbed at the hole end, it tilted downwards making the hole even larger, with the distinct possibility that I would sink, bottom first, through it into the quagmire below. Another disadvantage which, in my young mind seemed a little unfair, was that I had to sit on every occasion, unlike my brothers who could stand for, at least some of their bodily functions, for since the birth of my third brother, I had a growing awareness that boys had something that girls had not; furthermore, it seemed to me a very practical appendage for such activities.

No matter how carefully I sat down, when I wanted to rise, that loose board took umbrage, and like a vicious nettle, had a nasty habit of springing up and nipping my bum; and that hurt! One solution was always to use the top closet, even though it was difficult to climb into position, but if someone else had beaten me to it, and waiting was out of the question, there was nothing for it but to 'grin and abide'. Or was there? One day, in sheer desperation, when the top closet was occupied, and I couldn't wait, thinking how unfair it was that I, a girl, could not stand like the boys, it was even more obvious to me that I was never likely to receive any sympathy from my siblings now that there were three in the family. I had no hope.

17

An easier method must be found if I was to preserve my bottom intact. I decided to try.

Down to my ankles went my cotton bloomers, and with an enormous effort I climbed up on to the seat and knelt there trembling, taking great care not to fall into the abyss below. The stinking brown mass rose up in peaks which almost touched the seat, for it was almost time for Fatty Coates to come with his midden-cart to empty it. I could see the great lake of urination which filled the floor of the midden to a depth of about two feet; it would not be a very pleasant experience, I thought as I teetered on my knees looking down. But, having got that far, and the urgency of the situation demanded quick action, there was no turning back if I was to prove my point. Holding my long cotton skirts high in one hand until I could grab them in my teeth, I propelled my lower half forward as I had seen the boys do in the bushes when they were taken short, and hoped for the best. The best didn't happen. I had no sooner started to release the hot amber liquid which was the cause of all this trouble, when I realised that it was not going into the hole I had intended. Instead, it was running down my leg in a steady stream on to the floor which, only that day, had been decorated with its donkey-stone border by one of the neighbours. I panicked, and with the haste of guilt and terror, vacated the seat with a bound almost going head first into the brown peaks, and abandoning my brave attempt. But oh Lord, oh Mom, I hadn't finished, and the flow could not be stopped. By the time I had my feet on the floor, there was a veritable pool. My needlework knickers were soaked; my socks and boots dripped urine and my pride was sorely hurt. With great difficulty, I vacated the closet and made a beeline for the steps to the cellar kitchen in a bow-legged run, legs apart and knees askew, yelling as only a little girl frightened of the consequences, could do. I ran up the stone steps from cellar to living room bawling my head off, dripping urine on every step. I reached my Mother in great trepidation.

I need not have worried. My Mother never hit, nor severely chastised any of her children; that was left to my Father, but only on those occasions when it was 'men's business', and this time it was not. She was none too pleased however, at the prospect of the extra work I had caused her in cleaning the closet again. When I explained that I only wanted to find out if I could do it, she grimaced with great understanding, all the time undressing me and re-dressing in clean clothes, saying in her quiet way "You know, I've told you before, curiosity killed the cat, and if you are not careful, it'll do the same to you." Thus I learned one lesson very early in my young life; there are some things in which girls and boys are not equal, no matter how hard they try.

The word 'shite' should not be misunderstood, it was an expression used in the context of closets by many men in my younger days, and was in no way considered to be swearing, in fact, on reflection; it was a fitting description for such a useful building. One use of the word, however, has always puzzled me. A man from the next village of Holmesfield was always called 'Shite' by the men in all the surrounding villages, and one doesn't always see the relevance of nicknames in the male community.

I remember when either a film cartoon or a comic strip, I don't remember which, showed a trio called 'Pip, Squeak and Wilfred' in a series of escapades which were emulated by the children of the day. There was Wilfred Coates who lived round the corner in Lane Head Road, and for some reason known only to those concerned, Nellie Smith from next door was 'Squeak' and Elijah was saddled with 'Pip'. At least until he left school he was known as 'Pip Salt'.

Shite Barber was a deaf and dumb man who helped formers at busy times like harvesting and hay-time, and at any time in-between when his services were called for. He was a very kind man, a hard worker; I believe he was liked and respected by all the men in the district. It was fun in the hay field, playing hide and seek amongst the haycocks; burying oneself in the hay and lying still so as not to be found first. Or sitting with one's back against a pile of lovely soft, sweet-smelling hay eating sandwiches and drinking home-made Nettle beer out of a bottle, and generally feeling that this was another world, away from that school and housework, and all the hazards of life. It was a veritable heaven for children,

Just as much fun was harvest time, helping, or hindering, the farm workers to stack the sheaves of golden corn, (not the short-stalked varieties of today, but long-strawed ones which stood as high as a ten year old child). The sheaves were built into 'stooks' or, to use the old country word, 'gaites', six or eight stood on end in two rows of three or four leaning towards each other so that the full ears of corn rested against each other in a bright golden row, the space between providing a convenient hidey-hole for another game of hide and seek, or whatever other purpose happened to come to mind! It was in the hayfield that disaster almost struck, and a tragedy prevented only by sheer good fortune. My Father, Mr Smith and Shite Barber were helping to gather in the hay in a field above our house which belonged to Jack Pearson, later, the publican at the Grouse Inn at Totley Bents. The hay was dry and ready for stacking, and it was a glorious day. Children of the helpers were allowed to play in the field provided they kept out of the way of the workers. There were about half a dozen of us, and we all knew the rules. Jack Pearson and Shite Barber were on the stack spreading and levelling the hay as it was thrown by those on the dray. My Father and Charlie Smith were on the dray which had been drawn up to the side of the stack, piled with hay which had been loaded from the haycocks, the two men lifting long hayforks full of hay high over their heads on to the stack, a task for strong arms and the knack of lifting high over the head seemingly without effort.

During the operation, a small heap of hay accumulated on the ground between the stack and the dray as each fork-full shed a few stray pieces, and periodically it was removed by one of the men on the stack whilst the others went for another load. This was the stage of operations on the day in question. We had been playing hide and seek amongst the haycocks until they were gradually taken from us by the workers, but one boy obviously objected to his game being brought to an end. The dray had left and Shite jumped off the stack on to the heap of hay, steadying himself with his hayfork, a deadly weapon with two long, curved, exceedingly sharp prongs, or tines. As he hit the ground, there was a loud yell from below, and out from the pile of hay reared the head of a terrified boy on whom Shite had landed, missing him with the hayfork by a hair's breadth. The boy jumped up and dashed for safety, whilst Shite, unable to speak, yet full of anger, emotion and justified fear of what might have happened, grunted and groaned and made the most frightening noises in an effort to relieve his feelings. The whole episode had a profound effect on me, as it did I'm sure, on the boy. Shite's reaction was much more effective than a tirade of abuse, or a cuff about the ears.

When I was very young, before I started school, one of the treats was when my Mother attended the Mother's Meetings organised by the Misses Dawson. The two sisters lived in a bay-windowed house in Victoria Road, (now called Queen Victoria Road). It seemed a long way to walk, into a different world of larger houses, posh curtains, and carpets all over the floors. They were not exactly religious meetings, although most people who attended were members of the Wesleyan Chapel as, in fact, were most of the villagers. The meetings were, in effect, sewing meetings; you might say the forerunners of the evening classes, which were organised for mothers whose husbands were at work and children at school. And, by no means least, they were a social outing for the mothers.

Any child under school age could attend with the parent provided, as always, they could be seen and not heard! We played around the house and in the road, (there was no traffic to cause danger), and generally got excited doing the things that children do get excited about when they are only occasionally brought together. They were wonderful afternoons enjoyed by everyone, not least for the glass of lemonade, (tea for the mums), and a bun or piece of cake which the mothers had taken as their contribution to the success of the afternoon.

I loved visiting. My Mother used to say I was like an 'ill sitting hen', always wanting to go somewhere. "Mom, let's go to see Mrs Marshall. Mom, can we go to see Mrs Coates? Mom, take us for a picnic to Mrs Siddles." I don't think this was a total reaction to my being the only girl amongst a family of boys, I'm afraid it's a characteristic I have never grown out of. Going places and meeting people has become second nature.

As I grew older, and was allowed to play away from the immediate vicinity of the doorway, I loved the visits to Hall Lane even more, for there was Gladys and Phyllis, who both lived in the lane and we could play together for a couple of hours on our own. Our favourite playground was further down the lane, below the hall gates. The road was just a car-road with a high bank on both sides. A tall wooden fence topped the bank on the right side over which we knew were the hall gardens. On the left side, the road had been cut into the bank, undercutting almost the whole of the root system of a huge oak tree, which now hung way out over the lane, forming a sort of 'den' underneath. The tree had survived in this form for over three generations, for Mrs Stubbs and Mrs Ward, both local women, recounted how they, and their mothers had played in the same way.

The tree was the home of 'Annie Nutty', a little person of the fairy world, who had lived there on her own for as long as anyone could remember. She was immortal and all little girls held her in great awe. If she was alright, you knew that everything else would be alright so, any little girl who happened to be in the lane would climb up the bank at the side and gently knock on the hard root which formed the roof, and call out, "Are you there Annie Nutty?" If there was no reply, the question was repeated when, sure enough there would come a squeaky voice saying "Yes," and we all knew that everything else would be alright. Nobody bothered that it was one of the girls who had produced the squeaky voice, we had the answer, and it was 'magic'.

Sadly, such is the penalty of progress, that the tree was cut down and removed for road widening when the College was built in the 1950s, and poor Annie Nutty was lost to all future generations of little girls. My brother Jeff tells me that Annie Nutty was actually one of the Lancashire witches, who were burned at the stake in the 1700s, so it must have been her spirit which haunted Hall Lane all those years ago. I wonder where she went!

As the only girl, there were times when I had no other girls to play with. Louie Smith, who lived next door, and a year younger than I, was a great friend, but she wasn't always well in her childhood, spending much time in hospital. Consequently, there were times when I was, as one would say, at a loose end. These were the occasions when my Mother, responding to my need, would find a

22

solution. There was little time to play in my Mother's life, but she usually managed to make work into play if the need arose.

I remember clearly one such occasion when I was moping because I had no-one to play with. "I'm going to black-lead the fireplace," she said, "tell you what, why don't you do the fireplace in the room." (The room was the other downstairs room where we sat on Sundays and 'high days and holidays' such as Christmas. You would probably call it the lounge these days, but that was not the word for our cottage). It had a small fireplace, not like the cooking range in the living room, which had an oven at one side of the fire, and a boiler at the other, with lots of fire bars and a tall ash pan to black-lead. The one in the room had just two half circular bars in front of a low fire-hole, with a shallow ash pan in front. It was surrounded by a decorative black iron structure with flower covered tiles set into the recessed sides. This was my challenge. "We'll see who's finished first," Mom said, "and let's see who can get the brightest shine."

Feeling very proud and efficient, I disappeared into my workplace armed with a little pot in which Mom had mixed water with a helping of black-lead scraped from the block she had bought from Mr Gillespie, who came round once a week with a dray covered over like an American 'Surrey' loaded with all the hardware, knick-knacks, and gadgets which a housewife might need, as well as paraffin for feeding the lamps after dark. I had my own special little brush which Mom had found in the bottom of her workbox with which I could apply the black-lead, just as I had seen her do on a number of occasions. There was also a small edition of a polishing brush, a flat, oval affair, with a handle fixed over the top which I could grasp tightly and brush backwards and forwards as fast as little arms could go, until the shine was so great that a sweaty little face reflected from it like the mirror of Snow White's stepmother. And, it was a strange thing, the room fireplace always shone much brighter than the one in the living room, or so my Mother always said! This was not strictly true. My Mother never knew when to stop in the polishing of the living room range. I remember Mrs Smith coming in for a gossip one lunchtime when the polishing was still in progress and, after watching Mom for about ten minutes, she suddenly cried "For goodness sake woman, stop yer' rubbing, you can see your face in it already." Mom put away the piece of velvet she had been using and reluctantly did as she was told.

All my young life and adolescence was spent in the company of my Mother. She was my friend, my confidant, my 'rock of ages'. Everything I did, everything I saw, at school, at play, at work, had to be told to my Mother, and the necessity for her to be there to listen remained with me until the day she died at the ripe old age of 93. If she had not shared an experience, that experience was of no account to me. One day, when I was about twelve years old, there was excitement in the village; King Amanullah and the Queen of Afghanistan were visiting Chatsworth House and were to go past our house on their way to Sheffield about 1.00 p.m. This was convenient, for we didn't return to school until 1.30 p.m. and, as we lived on the road to Baslow and Chatsworth, we were well situated for a good view. There was great excitement as the time drew near, but where was Mom, she must be here? I panicked, rushing to the cellar door shouting, "Mom, Mom, come on quick they'll be here in a minute." But Mom was downstairs washing and she didn't appear. News went around those who were waiting that the visitors were close; here was the first police car. As it swept past, I ran back to the steps bawling, "Mom, come on, they're here, you'll miss them". "Oh, I'm too busy," she said, came back up the steps, "you go and look, or you'll miss them". In tears and desperate, I raced back to the door just in time to see the back of the car as it swept past the War Memorial, and on through the village. Disappointed, yes but I would probably have been more disappointed if I had seen the visitors and my Mom hadn't.

This devotion to my Mother sometimes backfired, as it did one dinner time when I was about ten years old. Mrs Smith, our next door neighbour, was in the habit of coming into our house at dinner time (midday) when we children had returned to school, for the purpose of passing on local gossip. I had the habit of staying at home until the last moment before leaving for the afternoon session. It was easy to see the school yard from the little side window, and the line of children as they answered the teacher's bell. I know that, if I set off when the bell rang, I could run like the wind down the allotments,

24

out through the gates at the bottom, in through the school gate, and still be in the line before the last one had disappeared inside.

On one occasion, I hurriedly kissed my Mother goodbye, and dashed out of the house, but after only a few strides, I realised that my Mother had been busy talking and hadn't actually said 'goodbye'. I ran back wailing, "You didn't say goodbye" running to her and kissing her again. "Aye, yer' silly lass" she said, kissing me, "come here, now goodbye, go on or you'll be late." Mrs Smith sniggered, and as I passed her, she hissed "Yer mardy bitch, yer great babby; get off to school." This wasn't the first, or the last time that I had been the butt of her sharp tongue, and it showed how little some people understood the psychology of the child's mind.

Life was not easy for my Mother, particularly in our younger days, with four children and Grandma to care for. As well as cooking, which all had to be done on the fire or in the coal oven, washing for the family, and housework, not helped by modern gadgets, she also ran a small shop from the cottage doorway and, throughout the summer, made teas and supplied hot water to day trippers from Sheffield.

We were in a direct line for them on their way into the country for the day, either out on to the moors, or into Cordwell Valley, a local beauty spot. Or, sometimes they settled in the village, camping in the fields for the day, playing games, or just enjoying a day away from the smoke and grime. We called them L.M.S. 'Little Mucky Sheffielders'. Unkind, perhaps, yes, I suppose it was, but children are nothing if not honest, and Sheffield in the 1920s was a mucky city.

In the shop my Mother sold drinks, pop, lemonade, Dandelion & Burdock, Sarsaparilla, and any other which happened to be popular at the time. There were toffees, boiled sweets, chocolate and peppermints, in tall bottles or open boxes, and cone shaped bags hung on strings ready for receiving the weighed out goodies. For cheaper brands, or for small quantities, bags were made on the spot from triangular pieces of paper, newspaper, or whatever was available, just as cake-icers made their icing bags. The prices of sweets were very different from our modern day, but then, everything is, isn't it? Chocolates and toffees were two ounces for 1d, Bluebird chocolate toffees were the favourite. They were hard caramels covered with delicious chocolate, and ready wrapped in dark brown papers. There were Milky-whirls, a mixture of white and dark toffee whipped into whirls of colour, Cinder-toffee, which dropped to pieces in the mouth, and 'Marry-me-Quick', a cartwheel of multi coloured sugar confection which was knocked into pieces in the hand with a little hammer, like slab toffee.

When the shop was set out in the cottage window, and the counter was in position, (this was a broad board which rested on the end of the big dresser with the other end suspended on the back of a chair across the doorway), it was a veritable sight for young eyes, and fun ducking under the board to get into the living room. Serving the tea was fun too, at least for me, it meant that there were people about the place; excitement as they came in and sat at the table set in the front room, or if there was an overflow, they would even fill the living room too. It was certainly good value for the customer too. They tended to be of the older variety, some coming year after year and becoming good friends with my Mom.

Tea was homemade bread and butter, with a dish of homemade jam, the favourite being strawberry, and small cake each, or a piece from a larger fruitcake for 6d. Real afternoon tea included a boiled egg, and extra bread and butter, which cost 2d more, 1d for the egg, 1d for the serving. Hot water was served in jugs for those who wanted to picnic outside, for those who had brought their own tea. This was 2d for a large jug, a big white thing which held about three pints, 1d for a small one holding one or two pints. If tea in a teapot was requested, it cost 2d per brewing for two people, a little more for a greater number, and this included the loan of two cups.

The huge black kettle was never off the fire on fine days during summer, for these visits from the dark, dingy streets of Sheffield were the only means for most children and their parents to get away from the smoke of the steelworks and the drabness of living. As we grew older, they became rather an embarrassment, and particularly resented by Elijah. When some particularly nosy group or person gawped, as he described it, into the house through the open door, he would shout "Alright, come in and have a good look, yer nosy buggers." Eventually, he made a rustic archway around the doorway over which my Father trained a Paul Crample, and an American Pillar rose to protect us from the inquisitive stares.

Of course, this was many years after the days of the shop and 'teas', many things were to happen before this. About the time of the shop, however, in fact the same year that my Grandmother died, 16th June 1921, my Father was offered a job as Manager of the Copper Mine in Buenos Aires, a job he dearly would like to have taken, as the prospects were excellent. When he told my Mother, she was adamant, "No, emphatically no," and that was that. "I'm not going to be left with four children while you go all those miles away, and I don't know when you'll be back, no!" He didn't go, but he never quite got over his disappointment. "To think," he once said, "we could have been well-off by now if only she'd said yes. To think, we might have been little Argentineans!"

I have already told you that all the cooking was done on the open fire and in the coal oven, and this applied until 1936 when my Father bought a small electric grill. There was, and still is, no gas at Lane Head, so it was a great relief when electricity was laid on, and to be able to boil an extra pan, or to grill or fry without splashing the fireplace was a great help. But baking still had to be done in the coal oven, and this involved a lot of work in cleaning out flues and regulating air currents. Flues had to be cleaned out at least once a week, usually on Friday morning, to make sure the oven would get hot in the afternoon for bread baking. It was a dirty job. All the soot was drawn from beneath the oven through a slot in the front of the fireplace then, by using a specially made flue brush, (a cylindrical contraption attached to a long flexible wire handle), and feeding it through another slot in the cavity over the oven, the soot and dust could be pushed down the side of the oven into the cavity underneath from where it was drawn out with another specialty designed tool, a coal rake, (like a miniature iron garden draw hoe). After this, black-leading could be completed and the fire built up to raise the necessary temperature for the afternoon's bread baking.

Temperatures were regulated by banking up the fire close to the oven for hot, and drawn away for a lower one, as perhaps for a pudding or cake. When long baking was called for, much as for a Christmas cake, it was a work of art assessing how low the fire could be allowed to go without risking too low a temperature and a spoilt cake. It was a matter of holding the hand in the oven for a few seconds to test for 'cool', or 'hot'; the latter being little more than a quick 'in and out'. If the door couldn't be opened during cooking, then a touch of the oven door would usually suffice.

There was a joke, often repeated by the men folk, that the black-leading was done in the morning, and the bread mixed in the afternoon to clean the hands. The daily removal of the previous day's fire was usually done by my Father, as he rose first to go to the pit and, in order to enjoy a cup of tea and a good breakfast, there had to be a fire to boil the huge black kettle and fry eggs and bacon in the iron frying pan. To get a bright fire quickly, a draw-tin was propped up on the bars. It was a sheet of thick tin with a handle attached, a bit like a policeman's riot shield. When in place, a sheet of newspaper was held over it until the draught going up the chimney held it in place. The same draught drew the flames up the chimney, and quickly produced a bright fire. (It also produced a very sooty kettle!)

The process could be dangerous, for sometimes, the paper caught fire from the hot tin, and our parents frowned deeply on any of us attempting the operation. There was some relief in the 1920s from the laborious task of bread baking for those women who lived nearer the village, particularly in Hall Lane, or during summer when it was hot enough to keep a low fire. The shop at the corner of Hall Lane and Baslow Road, now the Post Office, was run by 'Choppy', or 'Shoppy' Jackson, who was also a baker. At the back of the shop, at the other side of the entrance gate to the rear yard, was the brick building, now demolished, which housed the huge ovens, in which 'Choppy' produced bread and cakes for the shop,. When all the baking was finished, he let the women bring their loaves, at a cost of 1d a loaf, to bake in the ovens, each batch having a card attached for identification. This was a great boon to some women, although my Mother never needed to use the facility as coal was no problem and the family small.

Chapter 3

The two central pivots of village life until 1924 were the Wesleyan Methodist Chapel, and the Church of England School, one might say, the former offered spiritual guidance, the latter, discipline in the community, for it was not unknown for a boy to be chastised, or even punished, for not lifting his cap to an older person in the street, and woe betide misbehaviour out of school if the 'grapevine' carried the message to the Headmaster. Sunday was a day of rest from the usual chores in most households, including ours. In fact, my Father was very strict about observing the Lord's Day. If something had not been done by Sunday, it had to wait until Monday. We were not allowed to play outside on Sunday, no whips or tops, no shuttlecocks, no skipping, and my Father even frowned on us if seen standing outside talking. Button must be stitched on, stockings darned, and all sewing jobs finished before Sunday. If, by any chance, something had been overlooked, it had to wait. Sunday was for Chapel.

Sunday school classes for various ages were held in the morning from 10.00 a.m. to midday, dinner was at 2.00 p.m. and the Children's Service was from 3.00 p.m. to 4.00 p.m. Tea was around 5.00 p.m., after which we were allowed to fetch out our reading books, but only after we had washed our hands and the books were spread on the now cleared table. Books were precious, to be kept clean, not read comfortably on the knee on a sofa. I was two years old when I started attending Sunday school, for the only reason that Nellie Smith asked if she could take me. Evidently, I behaved myself, and so was allowed to continue.

Although primarily a centre for religious teaching, the Chapel was also a meeting house for two Temperance organisations. One of these was the Rechabites, whose origins were connected with Rahab who had a son called Jonadab. Jonadab abstained from all meat and wine, and a Rechabite was a disciple of Jonadab. The Rechabites, therefore, was a society of total abstainers. The other was the Band of Hope, whose members were strictly forbidden to imbibe in any way. This, I believe, was the backbone of the Wesleyan philosophy, and many of the senior members of the Chapel were complete abstainers. Most people supported the Rechabites, not, I think, because they believed in its philosophy, rather for the benefits to its members, for it was the Rechabites who arranged many of the outings from the Chapel. Fewer people belonged to the Band of Hope; it always seemed to me a stricter organisation in which children were seldom invited to join.

The trips organised by the Rechabites were popular, whether all the 'trippers' were members is questionable, no pressure was put on anyone to abstain and one or two had 'pumper's elbow' before the day was out, including the women! One of our earliest outings was to Baslow, six miles from Totley, where we had tea in one of the little cottages near the entrance to Chatsworth Park. We had eaten a picnic lunch in the park and played most of the afternoon with bats and balls. I was a little older when I particularly remember an outing to Darley Dale, near Matlock, a journey of about twelve miles. We parked at the Orchard Café at Darley Dale, later returning there for tea, provided as part of the trip. From the Café we walked to Matlock, on the way leaving some of our party to play in the children's playground opposite the Whitworth Institute. My Mother had risen early, as she always did on outings days, after working well into the night preparing clean shirts, socks and trousers for the three boys, and pressing needlework knickers, petticoat, and frilly dress for me.

There were sandwiches to make, and bags to pack with homemade scones, teacakes, and other goodies for four ravenous children who could gobble through mountains of food after playing in the open air, particularly in competition with their friends. The one who could eat most was the greatest! We were just approaching Matlock when there was an agonised cry from behind, "My sandwiches, I've lost my sandwiches". Poor Dorothy Gascoigne was distraught. She had been happily walking along with the rest of us when, looking down, she realised she was holding only the string, the parcel of sandwiches was somewhere back on the mile of road we had just traversed. Two people offered to go back with her to see if they could find the offending parcel, but without luck. All the other parents had a whip round when we sat down in the park to eat our picnic lunch, but Dorothy could only wail, "My tongue sandwiches." Ours were nothing as grand as tongue, just jam, homemade brawn and potted meat, but Dorothy at least, didn't have to go hungry.

Our transport on these journeys was not the most comfortable. The vehicle was a lorry which Jack Pearson hired out to the football team when they played in the villages in Derbyshire, in the Hope Valley League. For their games two forms were positioned down the sides of the lorry, and after letting down the back-board, a flight of three steps was set in place to enable the players to mount. In wet weather a tarpaulin was drawn over the top, the sides being secured by a looped rope on hooks around the sides, and curtains, or blinds, of thick cellophane sheltered the passengers from driving rain. For our outings, the same system applied, but extra care was taken to secure the forms to the sides of the lorry, not always done for the footballers. Not that they were concerned about such trivialities, they usually stopped on the way home at some Derbyshire pub and were too inebriated to notice, or care, if there was movement of the forms.

Transport improved for later trips, it was more comfortable, and the outings became longer. I remember one to Cleethorpes, whether from Sunday school or the Mother's Meeting, I don't remember; I was six at the time and it didn't matter who organised it, I loved to go, and for once, I asked no questions. Our improved transport was a charabanc, which we always called a charabanc, or more commonly, a 'chara'. It was nothing like the coaches of modern times with its rounded boat-shaped body and high solid wheels, and the uncovered top was open to the elements to be covered over in wet weather by a fabric roof fitted to a metal framework which folded back like a concertina resting along the back of the 'chara'.

The seats were a great improvement on the bare forms. We now had proper seats covered with leather which was arranged in rows across the width of the body, so that now, we could see where we were travelling without too much craning and turning of necks. It was a three hour journey and exciting, not every day did we have chance to ride in so splendid a vehicle, and for me, there were plenty of people to listen to, and children to play with.

Being only a little girl, it was difficult to see out of the side of the motor, but when we were well into the Lincolnshire countryside, there was a chorus of "Oh, look at all those poppies". My Mother lifted me up so that I could see over the side, and what a sight. All the fields were covered with bright red poppies; the glow seemed to stretch for miles as we turned each corner of the road, a sight I have never forgotten, such as the poor soldiers must have seen in Flanders in the First World War.

I remember little of the actual day in Cleethorpes, except that there was a helter skelter on the sands with an iron staircase to the top of the tower where I sat on a mat and sailed round and round to the bottom taking a header into the sand. My Mother remembered the day very well. Summers in those days seemed to be much hotter than the ones we experience today, in fact, it wasn't unusual for my Father, Maurice Johnson and Charlie Smith, to sit on the wall outside our house talking at midnight because it was too hot to sleep, and the day we went to Cleethorpes was no exception. My Mother had made a new dress for me for the occasion, and I remember the excitement of wearing it for the first time. It was made of mauve checked gingham bought from Emily Green's shop at the end of Summer Lane. It had a fitted bodice with a Peter Pan collar, short puff sleeves and a full gathered skirt, which I loved to pirouette in, seeing the skirt billowing round like a fully opened umbrella.

My Mother was very pleased with her handiwork, it was greatly admired. All mums liked to be appreciated by their friends, and they all took pride in the smart turn-out of their children, no less than the smartness of their husbands. But, woe for the hot day at the seaside, for by the time we arrived home, it was obvious that the sea air had taken its toll and had removed the entire colour from my pretty dress. It was now bleached white.

As we grew older, there were trips without our parents, from Sunday school, Day school, and for the boys after 1924, the Church choir. On these occasions, we always brought back a present for Mom, and the trip to Blackpool was no exception. We had been saving for the occasion from our weekly spending money. Mom gave us 1d on Friday night after Dad had given her the housekeeping money, and Dad gave us 1d on Saturday dinner time, usually when he was getting changed for his weekly visit to Sheffield. At the same time, for the lucky one, there was an extra 1d for the one who cleaned and polished Dad's shoes for the visit, 1d well-earned for he was very particular, I suspect, partly because we were always drilled to do a job well, and partly because it was another occasion for teasing.

By the time we set off on our trip, we had at least 6d each, although Geoff always had more than the others. Geoff was very thrifty; if by an unlucky chance you needed to borrow 1d from him, he reminded you every day until it was returned. However, he never demanded interest which was probably as well; I'm sure it would have ruined the system. He was content to have all the debts called in when he needed them. Presents from Geoff had to be sensible and useful; nothing so frivolous as the little green cruet like to baskets of flowers which I chose, for something pretty was what I thought most appropriate for my Mom. No! Geoff thought differently; Geoff was practical. He looked long and hard, and when on the way home we compared purchases, he opened his parcel and drew out a serviceable white basin. It had cost, he said, all of 2d. I had 'blown' my wealth, namely 6d on my cruet; I came back broke, but Geoff was wiser, as he always was on holiday, he came back with cash still in his pocket, seed to sow towards saving for the next trip.

But Chapel was not all fun and outings, there were more serious things to make children more conscious of the needs of the rest of the world, and one I shared with two or three friends was collecting the Methodist Missionaries. My Missionary box sat on the end of the big dresser in the living room where it collected a few coppers according to the generosity of our visitors, and once a year I went around the village collecting ready for the great 'unsealing' day when we competed with each other for the highest amount.

There were two highlights in the Sunday school year; one was Whitsuntide, the other the Anniversary Sermons. On Whit Sunday, every little girl wore white, and it was the custom to have something new for that day, if it wasn't a dress, or new white shoes, it might be a pair of socks or a new white hair ribbon. There was nothing so sure in the folklore of Whit Sunday, that if you didn't have something new to wear, the birds would shit on you, and that would be bad luck indeed!

The custom amongst the community at Lane Head and I've no doubt, in all other parts of Totley, was to visit the neighbours to show off your new clothes. After parading a little to show them off, a discreet penny was slipped into a convenient pocket or into the hand if no pocket was available, just for good luck. The custom was not confined to Whitsuntide, all new suits and dressed were acknowledged and perused with the same reward until the age of embarrassment, or when you felt you could be independent of the small reward.

I remember the day I put on my special new white dress. It was all needlework and Broderie Anglaise from neck to hem, little flower sprays scattered about, the groups getting larger as they reached the scalloped hem. It had a short bolero made entirely of needlework to match the dress, fastening at the sides with bows of blue ribbon. Under it, I wore a needlework skirt to match, a petticoat of flannel, a wool vest, and my corset. A pair of long legged knickers made of cotton, with four inch deep needlework frills on each leg, came down to the knees and put the finishing touch to my ensemble. I was truly grand, and very proud, I knew I would be the best dressed girl on parade!

We went to Chapel on Whit Sunday morning, but instead of the usual Sunday school, we practised the hymns which would be sung around the village next day. In the afternoon there was the usual children's service when the adults and soloists joined us for another practice. On Whit Sunday we all met at the Chapel after dinner, when we were formed into a crocodile, two by two, ready to walk around the village, stopping at chosen vantage points. (I suspect where more money could be collected). One stop was always at Lane Head. The singers stood in a half circle on the road facing the houses, the children in front where they could be seen, everybody raising their voices in resounding notes of rejoicing on this day of celebration. At the end of our recital, the collecting bag was taken round by Jim Green, whilst Mr Elliott, the Superintendent, diplomatically talked to the parents and those who had been watching and listening. This was the opportunity for us to nip into the house and grab a piece of cake or bun as a 'putting-off' until teatime.

The last stop was the lawn at Totley Hall. We sang our repertoire for Mr & Mrs Milner, after which we were allowed to play around the gardens for about half an hour whilst the officials politely talked to our hosts and, I'm sure, accepted a nice little monetary gift as well, then it was back to Chapel where tea was provided. In later years, we all went down to Uncle Joe's fields to play until dark! Incidentally, the fields where part of the Council Estate had been built in the last few years; the path passing behind my house. The Anniversary Sermons was the most important occasion in the Chapel year. Tiers of open seating were erected on the platform at the pulpit end of the main rook, and the sliding screens dividing the two sections of the room were drawn back to make one large room. The highest tier of the seating was about 3ft from the ceiling and the youngest children had to climb up and sit on the top row, legs dangling in mid-air. I dreaded the climb; every time I lifted a leg to the next row, I felt myself falling through the gap in between, seeing myself sprawled on the floor beneath. I was terrified when I had to get up to sing, feeling the pull of that space on my legs, and when I had to sing a solo verse, it was a miracle that any sound issued at all. I longed for the day when I would be old enough to sit on one of the lower rows of seats.

This was, you might guess, an occasion for white dresses with all the accompanying accessories. Emily Green did a roaring trade in white socks and ribbons. Shoes were blancoed as white as driven snow, for they could be seen very clearly between the white dresses on the row below, and white ribbon like a host of butterflies winged around the heads of the little angels on the top row. It was considered an honour to be chosen to sing a solo verse of one of the hymns, one which came my way on two occasions. I remember how nervous I was in case my voice didn't come out of my mouth. I knew Gertie Trusswell had a better voice than mine, and she too was to sing a verse.

I kept calm as my Father had told me, opened my mouth and let my voice rip. It was wonderful; how I loved showing off.

All the villagers attended Chapel for the sermons, including a very eccentric woman and her husband. They were a very old couple who drove from Totley Rise every Sunday in a brougham pulled by a small bay pony, which was left tethered outside in the Chapel yard. They always sat in a corner on the back row and, as soon as the sermon started, rustlings could be heard as a paper bag was brought out from under a voluptuous skirt, and for the rest of the service Mrs sat munching cold peas and potatoes left from their Sunday dinner. Faint rustlings could be heard every time she helped herself to another pea.

There were folks who swore that she sat on the back row because she brought a bottle, wore no breeches, and when caught short, just peed into the bottle. How true, we shall never know, rumours are so easy to invent and prolong, particularly in a country village!

Chapel would not be complete without Harvest Festival, and everybody in the village looked forward to it, not least the children. Pyramids of potatoes scrubbed clean as new pins, celery, beans, tomatoes, marrows and peas, piles of home grown apples, red, green and russet, oranges and lemons, plums, gooseberries, raspberries and bananas. Leeks competing with flowers of every hue, and framing the whole display, two giant sheaves of corn fashioned into fan shapes of fat golden ears of grain by a generous farmer. But the biggest attraction for the children was, without doubt, pomegranates.

On Monday night, all the produce was sold by auction for Chapel funds, or charity. I never knew, nor was I interested enough to find out. Every child went with at least 1d; sweets were forfeited on Saturday in order to save the 1d for the Harvest Festival sale. Patiently we all waited until everything but the pomegranates was auctioned and sold, and then there were shouts as the first fruit was held high. Cries of "I want one", give me one, save one for me," rang out as never a hymn had done in the whole of the harvest service. Eager arms were held aloft, pennies thrust forward, as feet climbed on seats for better vantage points. It was no holds barred, anything was allowed in the name of pomegranate. Pennies were pushed into

36

the auctioneer's hands and the luscious fruit grabbed in grateful thanksgiving.

Then the pins came out. As fathers and mothers produced knives to cut the delectable morsels in two, one by one the succulent seeds were picked out, chewed to extract every drop of delicious juice, and mouthfuls of pips were spit out as we happily trudged our way home. Such happiness was rare indeed! As the year neared its end, Christmas was the next time of rejoicing, as in all churches but before Christmas, about the middle of November, it was the time for the annual concert. Casting was completed about six weeks before the time of performance, items ranging from songs or duets, recitations, short plays, or whatever the performer might be best at.

Rehearsals were held once a week until the last week when two or three were held as necessary and, of course, the dress rehearsal was held the night before the concert. For the first two or three years, because I was so young and fair, I was always a fairy, until I was old enough to be the Fairy Queen in a play called 'Discontented Peggy' and the way she was cured. Dressed in a white tutu I boasted a splendid pair of wings and a magic wand with a beautiful shining star on the end, which transformed Peggy into the good girl she was from then on. I had a few words to say, something like "I am the Fairy Queen", a statement so obvious that it was difficult to go wrong, but enough to raise my prestige to the glittering heights of my imagination.

I never sang on a concert, although Aunt Alice was heard to say I had a 'nice little voice', I doubt whether I would have been very successful as a concert performer. But Gertie Trusswell did have a good voice, powerful enough to sing 'One Alone' from 'The Desert Song', with someone else dressed as the Sheik of Araby. I disliked the song intensely, and still do, but it went down well. As I grew older, my forté was more in acting, and I usually had a part in whatever play was included. The most successful and the most hilarious was a 30 minute sketch called 'Washing Day', written for two people, Sally Slops and Jane Binks. It was a washday scene which told the tale of a pair of socks belonging to Mr Binks. Mrs Binks was a wealthy lady whose washing was done each week by Sally Slops. She was fashionably dressed for the play in a long black and white silk dress, a feather boa around her neck, and a hug black hat with flowers around the brim. Louie Smith was Jane Binks. As Sally Slops, my skirts were also long, or would have been had they not been scraped up and pushed through an apron string, showing the old decrepit boots I wore on my feet. I was unkempt, hair untidy, sleeves rolled up and generally looking like the old washerwoman I was supposed to be.

The props were a zinc Peggy tub borrowed from my Mother. Peggy legs and a few assorted clothes were strewn around the floor, and washed during the play. The action was brisk, opening in the middle of a hot argument about the offending missing socks. Words flew backwards and forwards fast and furious, in rapid succession towards the climax. Louder and louder came the abuse, one trying to be dignified, the other not caring a jot for protocol, until near the end, when the socks were eventually found, I had to shout "Get out, or I'll chuck a can o' watter o'er you". Can in hand, I dipped it into the tub, pulled it out full of soap water, and in my excitement, and enthusiasm for authenticity, let fly. Louie was drenched, and the stage was deep in suds, not what had been rehearsed, but the uproar that followed was well worth it. To make matters worse, I had worked up a good imitation of rage, only given vent to by vigorous twisting and turning of the Peggy legs; every splash downwards splashing even more soap water around the stage. In the middle of the splashing, as if to give credence to the performance, a cry came from the audience "Sithee, she knows how to use 'em an all."

I wasn't the only one of our family to perform at the Chapel concerts. There was the time when Jeff who was about 18 months old, was standing on Mom's knee in order to see better. Elijah walked on to the stage, when immediately there was a cry from the audience, "Dat my Dida, dat my Dida". Jeff was jumping up and down excitedly, pointing to Elijah; bending to look into Mom's face to make sure she had seen, and waving to attract the audience to make sure they too had seen his 'Dida'. Another time was when my Father was particularly keen on poetry and tried to persuade us all to learn a poem each from his book 'A thousand and one gems of poetry'; Elijah opted out, emphatically refusing. Jeff and I learned one, but only half-heartedly, eventually both dropping out of the contest. Then Dad made an offer; 6d for anyone who did recite. This was the incentive Geoff couldn't resist, and he entered into the task with vigour. On the night of the concert, he was word perfect in his rendering of 'The Sweep'. It was a pathetic tale of a little boy who was forced to climb chimneys with a brush to clear out the soot, and Geoff was very serious in his interpretation. The 6d shone out brightly as his reward, and he duly appeared on stage recounting the sorry tale word perfect. Dad was a very proud man!

Preparation for the concerts and Sunday school was a somewhat painful operation for me. It was the custom every Saturday night, for Mom to bring up the tin bath from the cellar kitchen and fill it with boiling water from the big iron kettle always at the ready on the fire-bar. For the first body, this was supplemented with more from a huge iron pan, cooling it of course with cold from the tap. I was always first in the bath, partly because I was a girl, the theory being perhaps that a girl would not be as grubby as boys, but mainly because my hair took a long time to dry sufficiently for my Mother to put in the curl-rags that I had to suffer in the name of ringlets.

As each body was scrubbed clean with lots of soaping, squealing and squirming, and lifted out and dried, the bath was replenished with another kettle of hot water. Bath time was the only time I ever saw my Mother frustrated, and not often at that. After a tiring week of housework and cooking, with no respite or relaxation, the prospect of four bodies needing washing and polishing, hair shampooing, and all corners explored for a week's grime on Saturday night must have been the last straw. This was not helped by the frivolous hanky-panky of Jeff the playful clown of the family. Jeff was always looking for some prank to play on bath night. From an early age, one of his favourite pursuits was dressing up in Father's clothes. After trying to pour water over Mom's head in the bath, pretending to be ticklish whilst she tried to dry him, his next trick was to disappear upstairs whilst Mom emptied the bath and prepared for my hair do, reappearing minutes later in Dad's trousers, jacket and trilby set at a rakish angle like Al Capone, finishing the picture with a pipe and an adult impersonation which had us in tucks of laughter.

As soon as my hair was dry, it was time for the curlers. These were strips of cotton cloth torn from an old sheet or pillowslip, each about 15 inches long by about one and a half inches wide. After combing my hair and making a straight parting, the hair was divided into small sections from the front to the back of the head. A strip of cloth was laid over my head and grabbed by the end and held tight by me whilst my Mother, holding the other end tight, wrapped the section of hair around the cloth in close spirals. When the end was safely tucked in, the end which I held was wrapped over the curled hair, and the two ends were tied tightly together at the bottom. The operation was repeated until all the hair, wrapped in its curl rags, hung from my head like a lot of lamb's tails. My head must have been pretty hard in those days for I slept in those curlers every Saturday night, and every night before a concert, a day trip, a sports day, or any other when I was expected to look my best and be a credit to my Mother, and my Father. I think the latter was important, for my Mother always tried to do things to please him, or so it seemed. She knew how he liked my fair hair (a throwback to Doris Turner) and did everything she could to keep it fair. For shampoo she bought pure Castile soap from the Chemist, grating a quantity into a jug, and adding boiling water to melt it. She then whipped it into lather before pouring it over my head, and lathering well to make it shine. My hair was almost white when I was born, as can be seen from early photographs. By the time I was 17, it was still fair but tempered to pale and deep gold, gradually deepening, but still fair until the age of about 45 when the first grey hairs appeared. My hair always seemed important to my Mother, even when she could no longer see clearly, and probably could only see an outline, she knew and often said "Your hair looks nice today". On such occasions, I'm sure her thoughts were with my Father.

As we grew older, bath times were a little more private. The same tin bath was brought out, now rather a tight fit, for it was only about 3 ft x 2 ft; big enough for the completion of the necessary ablutions, but hardly adequate for luxuriant soaking. Instead of by the kitchen kettle, water was now obtained via the copper tub. This was the usual brick contraption built into the corner of the cellar

40

kitchen, where Mom did the washing every Tuesday. There was a little iron door set in the front beneath the round bottom of the iron copper tub, and beneath that was the hole where the ashes fell when the fire was poked. Geoff was the best stoker, as I remember, using lots of newspapers screwed up and stuffed into the fire cavity, where they were set alight, and replenished with a few sticks and pieces of coal as necessary to keep up the blaze and stir up the heat.

Baths were still once a week, but not always on Saturday. Many was the time when, after Mom had finished washing and the fire still hot, she would fill the copper again for whoever fancied using it. When all had gone to bed, it was her turn, and I'm sure she enjoyed every minute of it. My Father liked to go to the Turkish Baths on Glossop Road on Saturday, he said it fetched out all the coal dust from his pores and 'limbered up' his joints. He was fair skinned with a fresh complexion, and when he returned from the baths he looked as if he had been scrubbed clean.

In 1924, Totley boasted the luxury of a brand new Church, which was built on ground given by Mr & Mrs Milner, next to the School House in Hall Lane. It replaced the 'Tin Tabernacle', a corrugated tin building attached to the Church school, which with the school had been used for church services, under a Lay Preacher, Mr Foulstone. The advent of the Church into the village was to bring about a big change in the life of its residents. First, a choir was needed, and Elijah, who always had an excellent voice, left Chapel and was one of the first to sit in the new choir stalls. Ronnie Steer, and Ernest Pearson, both older, also joined, both acting as Servers, carrying the cross in processionals. Geoff joined later, and Jeff later still.

My Father was one of the first Sidesmen, along with Mr Lake, husband of one of the day school teachers; Mr Billy Wise, the man who gave the cut glass butter dish I won at the Bowling Club Ladies Day in 1925; Mr Coven the tailor, who supplied the cloth for my new coat in 1934 and Mr Herbert Crowther, father of Herbert who married Connie Tym, sister of Laurie, Arthur's Godfather.

I remained at Chapel, attending Sunday school and the evening service, hoping one day that I might be able to join the choir. (Women were not allowed in the Church choir.) In 1928, when I was twelve

41

years old, my Father said I could transfer to the Church Sunday school. A new girl had come to live just down the road from Lane Head who, being the same age as me was in the same standard, and we became firm friends. Margaret's family was not Chapel goers, a good reason for my Father giving way. But, before I left Chapel, I was asked to do something I had never foreseen, nor was prepared for.

The regular organist, Jessie Fox, was ill and unable to play one Sunday night, and I happened to be the only one at the service who could play the piano. But I knew nothing about organs, and said so. Furthermore, I wasn't a brilliant pianist. However, in the absence of an alternative, I was persuaded to have a shot at it, as otherwise there would be no music at all. (I think, perhaps, that might have been a better arrangement!) Nevertheless, always ready for a challenge, and after all, my Father always said there wasn't such a word as 'can't', I approached the organ, sat down, and stared at all the stops. Knowing nothing about them, except that they altered the tune in some way. Not knowing what to expect, I pulled out 2 or 3 likely ones, put my fingers on the keys, and started to play. One thing I hadn't reckoned with was that I had to pedal at the same time. There was silence for a second or two, then getting the message, my feet tried to keep up with my fingers, up and down like my Mother's sewing machine. I was just getting used to the two opposing movements when, thankfully, the service came to an end. I can only say that the congregation kept on singing, I kept on playing, wrong notes and all, and it ended without undue trouble.

I hadn't been long at the Church Sunday school when the Church organ was being overhauled and repaired, and the Children's Service, which was held in the afternoon, was in danger of having no music. A harmonium (a portable organ), had been borrowed for the evening service and it stood just in front of the Chancel steps, a stool in front ready for the player. Miss Oakes, the senior Teacher, suggested I have a go, "After all" she said, "you play for hymns at school don't you?" To this there was no answer, but I was even more nervous of this contraption than I had been of the chapel organ. However, pride, heaven help me, would not let me refuse, and once again voices were raised to the accompaniment of my very questionable performance.

Chapter 4

I was four and a half years old when I started attending day school. The age of compulsory education was five, but if there was room in the reception class, any child nearing five years was allowed to go. The school was built in 1877 as a Church of England Denominational school, as prescribed in the Education Act 1870, which decreed that, all children between the age of five and eleven years old should have full time elementary education. As a voluntary school it was controlled by Managers, later called Governors, who were appointed, not elected, and funded partly by grants from the Government, not by the rates.

The alternative to the voluntary schools were the board schools. These were empowered by the Government and funded by money from the rates in addition to a Government grant and school fees. It was laid down in the Act that fees were not to exceed 9d per week, and only if the parents could afford to pay. A School Board was set up by election in each district with power to appoint Attendance Officers who could enforce the attendance of all children between the ages of five and twelve years old. In the 1920s, the Attendance Officer at Totley school was respected with a certain amount of awe by both teachers and parents, and truancy was soon reported and dealt with, even to the point that he was known to stop a child in the street during school hours and question him (it was usually a him), on the reason for his absence.

Both Dore and Totley were Denominational/Voluntary schools set up by the Church Authorities. The one at Dronfield Woodhouse was set up as an elected group of rate payers, and was always known as a 'Board school'. Penny Acres School at Holmesfield was established well before that date with legacies from various people,

43

which probably accounts for the Church Authorities not setting up a new school there, whereas there was no Church at Dronfield Woodhouse, nor an established school, so one assumes that this was the reason for setting up one of the new Board Schools there.

As written in the Act, religion is not compulsory in the Board Schools, and if any religious education was offered, it must take place at the beginning or the end of the day, to enable pupils to opt out. The practice of holding such education at the beginning of the day has continued ever since, now limited to 'assembly'. Of course, Church Schools were free to give whatever religious education they wished, and sometimes the local Vicar visited the school for that purpose, as at Holmesfield but, although we periodically saw the Vicar at school after 1924, I don't remember him ever giving instruction. This may be because at the time of establishment of the school, there was no Vicar, and therefore no custom of teaching by him.

My earliest memory of schooldays was the day that Dr Parsons came to examine all the new intake of children, a compulsory operation ordered by the Education Department. It was very thorough, as I remember it; nothing seemed to be left out. I was made to stand on one of the low chairs used by the pupils in Standard 1, whose room was being used for the occasion. My Mother stripped off my dress, cotton skirt, flannel petticoat, (yes we wore two), my long legged cotton knickers with their needlework frills, and the garment my Mother called my corsets. This was a straight button fronted bolero type garment made from layers of flannel stitched together like square quilting, and fastened down the front with cotton covered buttons which were used on all underclothes and men's shirts, as they could withstand washing and mangling without breaking. It was an elaborate and superbly warm garment.

Dr Parsons felt my legs and arms, bent them; pinched them; raised them; and turned them; everything except break them, and pronounced that they were in good order; although very thin, they were nevertheless very strong. He ran his fingers up and down my spine, tapped my back, and listened through a contraption which he put in his ears and pressed to my chest while I breathed in and out as he ordered. My ears were examined, and eyesight tested, and finally he looked at my tongue and teeth, and here was the reason why I remember the occasion so clearly. I was, up to now, short tongued, in effect, I lisped! This, decided Dr Parsons, could be rectified. "Open your mouth," came the order, (Doctors never said 'please', even to parents). I obeyed. "Ah yes, that clack wants cutting." The clack is that little piece of membrane which fastens the tongue to the base of the mouth, and if it is too short, the tongue will not move away from the teeth, allowing the 'S' to sound through the teeth. It is the source of that expression 'keep your clack shut, meaning shut up!' Rummaging in his black bag, the good doctor brought out a very small pair of scissors. "Open," came the command again, and I duly opened. "Now, don't move," and I didn't, for that matter, after a command like that, I wouldn't dare. With mouth wide, apprehensive at the sight of this vicious little weapon, I stood petrified as he proceeded to clip my 'clack' and, operation over; I was no longer short tongued. For days, so I am told, I practised every word I knew which contained an 'S', just to prove that I could now 'talk proper'. My Mother always said he had cut it too far because I had never stopped talking since. Had he done so, of course, my tongue would have slipped down my throat, and I would speak no more!

In the early 1920s most girls had long hair, the fashion for bobs and Eton crop came in the later 1920s, and there was always the danger of catching head lice, which produced young called nits. Nits clung to the hair and were only removed with a very small toothcomb. There was one girl in my class who came from a poor area of Totley. Sitting behind her, lice could be seen crawling up her neck, but strange to say, she was so used to them that she was very seldom seen to 'furk', (the name given to furtive scratching). Not so with me. If I lifted my hand once in the direction of my head, my Mother would cry "What are you furking for?" and before you could say 'Jack Robinson', out would come a large sheet of newspaper and the 'nit comb' and I was made to bend over and have every inch of my head carefully scraped to the scalp where the little blighters may be hidden. For many days after, the routine was the same every dinner time and before going to bed, until Mom was sure there were none lurking there. This is the origin of the saying 'Going through it with a fine toothcomb'.

The 'Nit Nurse' came to school once a month to examine the heads of all the girls. If lice were found, the sassafras soap was produced from her black bag, and the offending head was scrubbed, a cap put on until it was 'cooked', then it was washed again to remove the offending animals. A visit to the parents relieved the situation for a time, but little notice was really given by the worst offenders. The School Nurse visited once a term for any minor ailments, not serious enough for the Doctor. If anything warranted investigation, the child was usually referred to the Clinic at Dronfield.

The Dentist visited twice a year, once to cover the new intake, a second to check all school leavers. I remember in my last year, I had to attend the Clinic twice; once to have four teeth filled, when my Mother went with me, no great trauma, and more like a day out. I still have two of those teeth, one with the original filling, after 62 years, it must have been good stuff! The second visit was to have my tonsils out, and this time I went alone, catching the bus to Dore Station, then the train to Dronfield, a little apprehensive in case I had forgotten where the Clinic was, and my nerves were a little strained by the time I arrived there. Patients were kept at the Clinic only until they had recovered from the anaesthetic sufficiently to return home, and I worried in case I hadn't 'come round' before I had to walk back to the Station. I had a horrible feeling that I might act like a drunken man and be 'run in' by a policeman. I needn't have worried, everything went well, and I returned home in pain, wanting nothing to eat, and with a letter for my Mother describing diet and aftercare. This entailed only one day in bed to prevent haemorrhage, and lots of lemon jelly, which just slipped down and presented little difficulty or pain. Lemon jelly was the standard food for the first three or four days; I doubt whether any child who had said goodbye to his tonsils ever liked lemon jelly again.

There wasn't much serious illness in the village, and the District Nurse, Nurse Jessop, knew everyone. All children at some time had Chicken Pox, Measles and Whooping Cough, and mothers knew exactly what to do, only calling the Nurse or Doctor if absolutely necessary. Of course Doctors had to be paid by men, but wives and children were treated free of charge. My Mother told me of the days earlier in the century in Totley when children with Whooping Cough were taken down to the Chemical Yard at Totley Rise where charcoal was produced. News went around the village when the vats were to be opened, and all children with Whooping Cough were held over the vat. The fumes made them 'gip' (catch their breath) and this stopped the spasm which caused the 'whoop'.

Ringworm was rather more common than it is now. It was a common sight for children to be daubed with gentian violet and, in more severe cases, particularly when the ringworms were in the head, for victims to have X-Ray treatment, losing all their hair in the process. I remember Geoff wearing a cap even in school when he had X-Ray treatment and lost his hair for the same reason. The dreaded illnesses were Scarlet Fever and Diphtheria. Scarlet Fever could be nursed at home if the room could be given over to the patient, and a wet blanket could be hung over the door to prevent the spread of the infection. Otherwise, they were taken to Lodge Moor Hospital. Diphtheria was usually treated at home, unless it became dangerous, with possible choking, when they also were sent to hospital. Meningitis was not common, but I remember when I was about six years old, a sad event at Lane Head when Annie Smith died from Meningitis when she was twelve years old. The coffin was not allowed in to the house, (the custom with all deaths from fever); Annie's face could be clearly seen through the glass panel in the lid of the coffin when it was resting on the low wall outside the cottage.

My earliest memory of actual school work was about six months after I started, when we returned to school after the Christmas holidays. Miss Marsden, the infant teacher, had given us all a sheet of paper on which we were to practise 'pot hooks' and 'h's' as a step towards writing the letters of the alphabet neatly. Pot hooks were to train control of the pencil; 'h's' if made correctly could be turned upside down when they became 'y's'. Miss Marsden told us to write the date in the top corner of the paper, and I picked up my pencil and wrote 8th January 1921. The last number fascinated me, probably the reason why I remember it so well. I gazed at it; another year; it seemed to me at that moment how wonderful it was to be a year older, and to live in a brand new year. I have never, in all my life, lost that feeling of wonder and expectancy when the bells ring out at midnight on New Year's Eve. It is a feeling of sadness for days past, as if saying 'goodbye' to old friends, and one of apprehension and excitement for what is to come.

I remember nothing more from my first year at school, certainly not the 'sand trays' which Elijah, Jeff and cousin May remember. These were wooden trays about 12" x 15" and about 2" deep which contained a layer of silver sand about 1" deep. Letters and numbers were traced with the finger, then by shaking the tray, they could be erased and another set of letters, or simple sums imprinted. Sand trays were still in use in 1936 when I was a Sunday School Teacher at the Church Sunday school which was held in the day school. My class of the youngest children was held in the infants room and I found the sand trays ideal for illustrating the stores of the dividing of the Red Sea and Mount Sinai in the flight of the Israelites from Egypt; by piling up the sand creating mountains, and dividing it to imitate the dividing sea.

Little cowrie shells, most of them cream colour, but a few with brown markings, were used to represent the Israelites fleeing across the desert, the browner ones being the soldiers; the 'baddies' who chased them and drowned in the sea. Such imagination; rewarded by intense interest, and wide-eyed wonder; even cowboys and Indians couldn't compete! Going to a Church school had certain advantages. As well as statutory holidays at Easter, Whitsuntide, Christmas, Empire Day and the long summer holiday, we had a half day on Ascension Day, when we went to Church, or a service at school before 1924, in the morning, after which we were free for the rest of the day. Then there was a half day on Shrove Tuesday which, as it was Pancake Day, was a good thing as dinner took rather longer than usual while Mom made pancakes, one at a time for us all. She used the large iron frying pan resting it on a grid on the top bar of the fire. It made pancakes about ten inches in diameter and not too thin either, or should have been making them until eternity. I could manage only one, but the boys, especially Elijah, could scoff them as fast as Mom could make them She made the batter in a large yellow bowl, and tried to save sufficient for a couple for Dad; as she said, "If your Dad doesn't get his pancake on Shrove Tuesday, he'll cry his eyes out."

All schools had a holiday on Empire Day when flags were flown from bedroom windows (why is that illegal now, I wonder?) and bands played in celebration. One holiday which we country children enjoyed, which town children missed, was the week at the beginning of October. It was called 'potato picking week' and it enabled school children to work for local farmers, not only helping them but earning a few coppers for their own pockets. Some boys worked for farmers regularly in the evenings and at the weekends for regular pocket money. Elijah worked for Wakefields in Hall Lane when he was nine years old and, when he was twelve, until leaving school, for Creswicks on Moorwood Lane. Geoff then went to Wakefield's, delivering milk, and helping on the farm, whilst Jeff, like many other boys, earned his coppers by delivering newspapers night and morning for Wesley's who had a newspaper shop at Green Oak.

School started at 9.00 am each morning; playtime, lasting 15 minutes was at 10.30 a.m. An hour and a half was allowed for dinner, with an afternoon playtime at 2.45 p.m., the day finishing at 4.00 p.m., or 3.30 p.m. for infants. Playtimes were times for games, the younger children getting 'scatty' over games like 'tiggy' or an appropriate one for a Derbyshire school, 'ring-a-ring-o-roses' which originated from the Plague at Eyam. Older pupils played more complicated games. I remember joining in a circle for 'In and out the windows' and 'Oh Mary what are you weeping for?' (A story of a girl who had lost her lover), and forming two teams for 'Here we come gathering nuts in May'. And, of course, playtimes were a time for gossip, much as schoolgirls might indulge in. Games in the boys' schoolyard were rather more boisterous. 'Cops and Robbers' was a favourite, when the cops congregated at the top of the yard, the robbers half way down wearing their caps turned back to front. The stampede started when, with whoops and yells, the cops chased the robbers down and round the yard, until all were captured, when the roles changed and the stampede started all over again.

Then there was 'Rusty-bum-Ben', when one boy bent down against a wall and another boy jumped on his back at the same time raising either a finger or thumb, He shouted "Rusty bum Ben, finger or thumb?" and the bending boy had to guess which. If he was right, the boy jumped off, and bent down behind the first boy, and another jumped on to his back, then on to the first. If he was wrong, the boy stayed on, the game continuing until all the boys were either bending and taking the load, or were sitting comfortably up above. It would be impossible to leave the boys' yard without mentioning football. They all had their favourite teams, but the favourite combination was United and Wednesday. As usual one team played up the yard, the other played downhill, reversing at half time. A game like this could last for days, being continued every dinnertime and playtime, until a result could be achieved.

Shrove Tuesday was the day for whips and tops, in both school yards, with shuttlecocks and battle boards coming a close second for the girls. The older boys played clever with 'peg tops', cleverly wrapping the long string around the top and flipping it sideways in a deft movement which set it spinning and humming for a considerable time, We all played with chalk, drawing rings of many colours on the surface of the tops, watching the colours converge as they spun round. For a while the school yards were filled with whip cracks and flying shuttlecocks until the novelty wore off.

Soon after the end of the First World War, the centre of the road was covered with tar macadam, and on Shrove Tuesday it really came into its own, and was wonderful to play on with whips and tops, shuttlecocks and rims made by Mr Bradbury the blacksmith, which were controlled by a long iron hook. The very rare occasions when we heard a car approaching there was plenty of time to get out of the way, for no vehicle went so fast that the driver could not see us in time as he rounded the bend, and by the time we heard one approaching, we had plenty of time to move out of the way.

In the schools of the 1920s and early 1930s pupils did not graduate to the next Form automatically or by age as they do today. The different classes were called 'Standards' and a Standard meant the standard of the pupil. At Totley School there were seven Standards, plus the infants' class. Standard One was one of my favourite Standards, not particularly for the work I did, or lessons learned, for I remember little of them, only that life was very pleasant, and that I worshipped the teacher, Miss Crookes. I wasn't alone in this; almost all the class would have done anything for Miss Crookes. She was kind and understanding, very seldom raised her voice, even to the dullest children, and she was pretty, a fact which goes a long way towards the popularity of teachers I would say. She had the most beautiful black hair taken up in a roll around her head in the fashion of the day, her eyes were brown and kindly, and when she walked between the rows of little desks, her long, ankle length skirts rustled very expensively, or so we thought!

One day Miss Crookes had a headache, it was very bad she said, and asked us all to sit quietly for a few moments. We were all very concerned, and when she asked if anyone had a clean handkerchief as she would like to put some eau de cologne on her forehead; how glad I was that my Mom always made sure I had a clean handkerchief whenever I went to school. Hands stretched forward, eager that mine would be the one chosen and, as Miss Crookes came to my desk and chose my handkerchief I was the proudest, happiest person in the whole world, as if I alone was going to cure that awful headache that was troubling my idol. The handkerchief was one from a box of half a dozen I had received from Father Christmas a few months before, and was very precious to me. They were white with coloured edges, and in one corner of each was a quotation for the day of the week. 'Solomon Grundy born on Monday', 'Christened on Tuesday' and so on for the seven days of the week.

A few days later, when Miss Crookes gave back my hankie, beautifully laundered, she gave me a box of new ones too, and I vowed I would never use them; they would remind me of her forever and ever. I still have them upstairs with about another dozen boxes given at various times as presents. Pretty things in those days were not easily or regularly come by, and when they did, they were treasured like jewels. When my Mother was a young girl, this was even more so; a piece of silver paper wrapped around a toffee was considered too pretty to throw away, so it was carefully straightened out and put in between the pages of a cookery book or the bible, lovingly to gaze on every time the book was opened.

One of my vivid memories of Standard One had really nothing to do with my own schooling, yet it proved interesting in my knowledge of the world outside school. One day, just after lunch, we heard a mild commotion outside the sliding doors which divided our classroom from that of the older groups in the big room. As the doors opened a 'crocodile' of children walked two by two through them, turned and walked into the infants' room next door. As we turned to look, Miss Crookes said "Say 'Good Afternoon' children," and we dutifully did her bidding. All the girls were dressed alike in navy blue gym dresses and white blouses, grey knee length stockings and black shoes. The boys wore grey jackets and trousers, navy blue ties, grey socks and black shoes. One of the older boys was crying as he walked beside a smaller boy who was obviously his brother, whom we learned later were the Hill brothers, Cecil the elder of the two, Leslie who was about my age. They were the younger brothers of two older boys, Graham and Eric Hill who were both in the Navy. Or Merchant Service, I'm not sure which. Both the younger boys joined when war broke out, the three oldest all lost at sea.

The new intake was the children from Cherry Tree Orphanage in Mickley Lane, now a Cheshire Home. Two of the girls, Mary McDougal, whose sister was in a higher standard, and Mary Shaw became my good friends, although both the girls and boys tended to stay in their own groups during playtimes. Two sisters, Susie Taylor, a year younger than I and her sister Evelyn about two years old, had come from Australia, and I remember hearing how Susie had cried the first time she saw snow. My geographical knowledge was greatly enhanced to hear that snow didn't fall in Australia, at least where the girls came from.

The orphanage children seemed very happy, at least they never gave the impression that they were unhappy with their lot, perhaps they were just resigned, having no alternative, for although everything was done for their care and comfort, we all knew it was not like being at home with parents. They were much disciplined, and a little reticent sometimes in joining in games and other activities. This, I think was partly due to restrictions and rules of the orphanage, which were, of course, essential to the efficient running of the place, and even wearing uniform set them apart from the rest of us.

I thought it was wonderful to wear a uniform, in fact when reading about girls at boarding school, I would have settled for a gymslip, so smart they looked with a neat blouse and tie. The nearest I came to wearing a uniform at school was in my last year when the Governors, or whoever was responsible, decreed that there should be a uniform cap for boys, and a beret for girls. I was so proud when my Father said I could have a red beret, with the school badge on the front, a very simple logo with no crest or motto, just a shield shaped badge with T.C. of E.S. on it, but it was enough to raise the prestige of the few who took up the offer. Sadly, I think it died a natural death, probably because money was not very plentiful, and perhaps not everyone wanted their prestige raised anyway.

The one and half hour dinner break was essential for many of the children; there were no school dinners in those days, although if for any reason it was necessary to take sandwiches, we were allowed to sit in our classrooms when one of the teachers would make some sort of drink for anyone without one. On the two occasions that I stayed at school with sandwiches I loved the novelty of it and often asked if I could do it again.

The orphanage was about a mile away, but every dinner time and end of day, the orphanage children formed into a 'crocodile' with one of the older girls walking at the side of the youngest child at the front; the others bringing up the rear. Even though it was a two mile round trip, with another mile both night and morning, I don't remember any of them being late for lessons. It was equally hard for many of the other pupils. Totley School had a large catchment area. The nearest Board Schools were Dronfield Woodhouse and Abbeydale. The nearest Church School at Dore, so all children between five and 14 not in their areas had to attend Totley School. (The age for leaving school had been raised from 12 to 13 in 1899, although any child who passed a test could leave at the age of twelve. In 1918 the age was raised to 14, unless there was a special reason for leaving at 13, particularly necessary during the First World War when children were needed to earn money whilst their fathers were away). It was hard for those who lived at Totley Rise, the Chemical Yard and Grove Road, which were all in Totley Parish, for they too had a two mile walk twice a day, and 'woe betide' anybody who was late.

For those of us who lived at Lane Head, dinner times were often interrupted by running errands, one of them not resented; in fact it was a veritable 'God send' and competed for. About 50 yards up the main road from the corner of Hillfoot Road where the old Post Office stood, was a row of three cottages built at a right angle to the road, approached by a short flight of steps. The first one was occupied by Mr & Mrs Thomas and their two grown up sons Archie and Ernie. Almost every day at dinner time, Mrs Thomas was in need of something from Evans' shop in Hillfoot Road, when she stood at the door waiting for the first child to make an appearance round the corner. There was great competition, and a stampede to be that first one, for there was always a reward of 1d for the lucky one. It took only a few minutes to nip back to the shop, return with the purchase, and receive 1d for the trouble.

There was another errand none of us welcomed, but had to be done before we could have a cup of tea. The Water Board had a nasty habit of turning the water off without notice, be it wash day, or any other. As we were at the end of the piping system, when it was turned on again, it was brown and unfit to drink for some time. One of us, usually the first one home, had to take the big jug from Mom's washstand and run down to the spring at Moneybrook at the bottom of Lane Head Road and fill it with water from the pipe which came out of the bank bringing pure spring water from the moors above the brickyard. It wasn't running down the hill, which took time and effort, but walking up again with a gallon of water which became heavier and heavier with each step and flopped over the rim so that by the time it reached the kettle, there was little more than a half left. Little recompense that tea made from it was so good to drink.

During this time, we had a dog called Jock; a cross between an Alsatian and a Sheepdog. On Sunday afternoons when the weather was fine, the older boys of the village, Dick Wortley, and his brother Stanley; Elijah, Cyril Wortley and George Johnson, were in the habit of taking their weekly exercise walking through the Gillfield Wood, accompanied by Jock, who was a popular member of the gang. He needed only a slight bidding to jump over the highest field gate with the grace of a Grand National racehorse. He could run and retrieve and follow instructions as meticulously as a 'Trials' competitor. If Mom, needed anything from the shop at dinner time, one of us would take him on the way to school, buy whatever was required, put it in Jock's mouth and say "Take it home Jock," and he would set off, in a direct line, never looking to right or left, disregarding other dogs or distractions, until he could see Mom waiting to relieve him of his burden. On one occasion, he carried a pound of lard without putting his teeth through the paper. Sometimes, more than one article was required, we then took a wicker shopping basket, putting the purchases in it, and Jock would carry the basket anywhere he was told. He was a wonderful companion. One Saturday, when I was 17, I decided to walk over the moors to Hathersage to visit some friends and relations; a walk of about seven miles. One of the friends walked back with me to the beginning of the moors near Padley and Fox House, and I walked the rest of the way alone, except for Jock. It was 10.30 p.m. when I arrived home, but I knew I was perfectly safe with Jock beside me. Sadly, times have altered; I wouldn't like to walk over the moors today, even with Jock.

In the house, Jock was ready for anything, wherever he happened to be needed. My Father had been to the fish market one day and bought cockles for his Sunday starter, but when he went to retrieve them from the low shelf on the cellar head, where they had been placed out of contact with other food, the shelf was bare, the cockles had gone, and this time he couldn't blame the boys! My Mother was in the cellar kitchen the next wash day, when she heard a noise in the 'stick hole', the space under the cellar steps which had an opening but no door into the kitchen, where the stock of sticks for lighting the fire was kept. Mom went to the bottom of the steps and shouted Jock downstairs and, pointing to the stick hole said "After it Jock". She went in herself, carefully moving the sticks to one side to give Jock a clear run, and then as the last few were removed, she could see the cockles in a heap close to the back wall and a huge rat looking

55

out at her. She backed out fast. "Come on Jock," she called. "Get it Jock," as he dashed past her and with a quick dive, and a well-directed nip he had it, backing out with it firmly in his jaws.

Sadly, Jock met his end in a less than dignified way. Dad, being a countryman, had a horror of sheep worrying, and would not stand for a dog which went off for a day, no matter for what reason. Jock developed a habit of taking time off and although there was never any suspicion that he was sheep worrying, he had, so to speak, 'shot his bolt'. Dad took him to the brickyard where there was a deep pond, fastened a brick around his neck, and threw him in. It nearly broke his heart, but no matter how abhorrent the job, my Father never shirked it if he thought it was necessary.

Before Jock, we had another dog, a cross between as Retriever and a Spaniel. She was a beauty, with a shiny black curly coat, and we loved her very much. Sadly, after many years, she suffered the same fate as Jock, for the same reason. But my Father was not a hard man, I once saw him cry when our little tortoiseshell cat got run over a few days after she had given birth to a litter of kittens. He bent over her as she lay wounded and as she turned her head and looked at him, he turned to my Mother and said tearfully, "Look, she's asking me to look after her kittens."

Dinner time for us children was the time for a cooked snack meal, when Mom made things especially for us. Dad came home from the pit about 3.30 p.m. when Mom gave him what he fancied. Many times she cooked for him and when he arrived home he said he would like a tin of crab or lobster instead. She indulged him because he had a Duodenal Ulcer, eventually going on a strict diet for two years until it was cured. About 6.00 p.m. we all had tea, a misnomer really, for during the week it was something cooked, and the main meal of the day. It might be 'hash' made with stewing steak, a sheep's head, or a beast cheek with lots of vegetables and served on a thick slice of bread. Sometimes it was broth, with the meat served as a second course with butter beans or, in winter, dried peas soaked overnight and boiled in a muslin bag, then served with sugar sprinkled over and a nut of butter to add extra flavour. Or on Monday, it would be the remains of the Sunday joint, for it always started as a five or six pound cut of rib or ladder staves, or a good lean piece of corner cut. Dad's favourite, either for cost or flavour, was brisket lap. Unfortunately he wouldn't ever have it steam roasted, and it wasn't the tenderest of meat, but he always said, "Get it chewed, you've got good teeth, that's what they're for." So we chewed and chewed; a good ruse really, for by the time we had finished chewing the first piece, the jaws were tired and the joint went further! Dad believed in chewing, he even told us to chew rice pudding 92 times, and did it himself, either to prove his point or, as I suspect, for fun.

It was washday dinners that I liked the most; something that Mom could prepare and leave to cook whilst she went down into the cellar kitchen to get on with the washing. Things like crisp skinned baked potatoes, or a huge pudding tin full of oven bottom chips served with fried eggs, or sausage, or home pressed meat. There was always a pudding, either rice, which I didn't like very much, or bread and butter pudding, usually made with left-over tea cakes instead of bread which was Elijah's favourite, but which I disliked intensely. I liked tapioca, and didn't mind large sago, which was Elijah's pet hate, 'frog's eyes' he called it. Very often Dad would have a macaroni pudding and I usually 'cribbed' a spoonful or two if he hadn't finished it off by the time I arrived home from school. Later, as part of his diet, Mom made an egg custard for him very day, and I loved a spoonful of that.

Washdays were far from easy, and for someone as particular as my Mother, they were certainly not. The cellar kitchen had a stone flagged floor on which she knelt on a pile of clothes or a small rug to rub the clothes in the galvanised 'Peggy tub'. Some women put the 'whites' to soak in cold water the night before to loosen the dirt they said, ringing them out the next morning before putting into the first washing water. My Mother, as many others did, put them straight into the tub of hot suds, and let them soak for about an hour whilst she got on with the other chores, like preparing our dinner.

The copper fire was lit early, and as soon as the water was hot, it was ladled into the 'Peggy tub' with a large tin ladle. The tub was emptied and refilled in the same way as necessary throughout the day. The 'Peggy tub' had corrugated sides which were used for rubbing the most soiled parts of garments, particularly shirt collars and cuffs, although collars were usually loose ones which were laid out on the bottom of the stone sink and scrubbed with a small scrubbing brush. All articles were rubbed vigorously between the heels of the hands, or in the case of inexperienced brides like me when I did my first wash, between the knuckles, which resulted in bleeding and sore knuckles, much to the amusement of both my parent. When all had been rubbed; the 'Peggy legs' were brought into use.

'Peggy legs', to make the explanation as simple as possible, were in effect, a five legged stool about 12″ high, with a hole in the centre, in which a wooden shaft was fixed. A wooden peg, about 12″ long, passed through a hole in the top of the shaft, which was grasped with a hand on the underside of each side of the peg, the whole contraption plunged into the tub to be rotated round and round, backwards and forwards, swishing the clothes quite violently from one side to the other, until it was assumed that all the clothes in the tub were now rid of dirt and stains.

The next operation was 'mangling'. Our mangle, like all others of the time, was about 5ft tall. An iron frame with lots of scrolls and swirls for decoration, it had a wheel at the top which was attached to a long screw, itself attached to two springs, much like the springs of a car. When the wheel was turned, it either eased, or added pressure to the rollers, causing them to squeeze tighter, or less tight according to the thickness of the article being mangled, or the amount of water to be squeezed out. The rollers were made of wood, about 8″ in diameter, whilst a wheel about 18″ in diameter with a handle attached, was fixed to a large cog, and when the wheel was turned, it turned a series of cogs, which in turn, turned the rollers.

For the first washing, my Mother wrung the clothes out by hand. I was always fascinated at the expertise with which she wrung out the sheets by taking a section from the tub in both hands, twisting it in opposite ways, then flinging that section over her arm before taking the next section, ringing again, and flinging again up the arm, eventually making a spiral of sheet from wrist to shoulder, wrapped round her arm like a snake. All articles were washed twice, and rinsed twice, the water being emptied between each operation. The tub was filled from the copper, and all articles wrung out in the same way until the last rinsing, when the final wringing was done through the mangle.

Moving the 'Peggy tub' to a position under the sloping board which caught and channelled the water as it was squeezed, each article was lifted out of the tub and the end was pushed between the rollers. The handle was turned, and the article was drawn through, to be caught at the other side and dropped into the wicker clothes basket ready on the floor at the back of the mangle. Whites came first, when they were put into the copper to boil with soap powder, later to be rinsed, starched and blued so that they dried snowy white. Then came the coloureds, some put to one side for starching after the whites, then socks and sundries and, last of all, the working clothes, dusters and polishing rags, or anything that might benefit from a dunking. On a fine day, to see a line full of dazzling snow-white washing was my Mother's pride and joy. If by any unfortunate incident, an article dropped to the ground whilst being hung out, it was taken inside and rinsed again in case there should be a grain of dirt on it.

Housewives were proud, and most of them were meticulous in their work, some more than others, and all had their priorities, but they all helped each other. Washday was one time when help was appreciated more than any other. Sheets were made of linen, or unbleached calico, which was very heavy. Nonetheless, they had to be folded neatly before being passed through the mangle. They were not ironed for if they were carefully folded and plenty of pressure put on the rollers, there was not a crease to be seen. In fact, all articles were treated to a turn under the mangle; it took out the creases and made ironing much easier. Mrs Smith washed on Mondays, my Mother on Tuesdays. This was partly so that the clothes-line could be stretched across the back yard, using each other's posts. When the sheets were dry, they helped each other to fold, straight from the line. It was a work of art, one which I learned as soon as I was strong enough to hold the weight. Each person took hold of the ends of a sheet, gathering across the end by crawling the fingers, and then when the centre was reached, the two handfuls of sheet were pulled tight, the two women rocking backwards on their heels, pulling and stretching to straighten the sheet, so that when it was folded end to end, sides to middle, every corner was even, and all sides were inline ready for the mangle. Neither needed asking for much help, it was understood.

My Mother had had enough by the time she had finished washing, so the ironing was left until the next day, My Father often criticised Auntie Ruth for doing both on the same day. "She'll be laid out all next day" he said, "expecting everybody to run round after her." My Mother was wiser, washing was enough for one day, ironing could wait for the next, even thought she might still be going it when my Father returned home from the Cross Scythes at 10.30 p.m. and probably the next night too. It was a mammoth task. Shirts were made of thick cotton and were cut to a peculiar pattern, not easy to manoeuvre an iron around, and starched loose collars needed the pressure of a Chinese launderer to bring them to the stiffness required for smart wear. Then there were my clothes. Cotton dresses were starched, and even the plainest had a certain amount of needlework, each section needing stretching and pressing carefully to preserve the pattern.

Petticoats were little trouble, but cotton skirts were embroidered around the neck and hem with needlework almost as elaborate as the dresses and requiring almost as much care. Last but not least were my knickers, with their long legs ending in a 6" frill of needlework, and my Mother was just as particular about them as she was about all the top clothes. All this laborious work was accomplished with three flat irons. The fire was prepared beforehand to ensure a hot, bright fire with no smoke, and a grid was attached to the front of the bars on which the irons stood with their faces tight up to the fire bars, with great care that there was no danger of smoke to spoil the face of the iron and transferring it to the garment being ironed. As one iron became hot enough, it was removed from the grid, and another was put in its place; in this way being used in rotation, handling them with a thick iron holder, usually made by sewing together two or three layers of flannel, covered with a layer of cotton material to prevent the hands from burns. To test for the correct heat, the iron was held close to the face and, for garments which required a hot iron, a quick 'spit' would double check (if it sizzled, it was hot).

If it didn't glide easily over the fabric, Mom used to rub the surface with 'ironing soap', a form of Castile soap which was very hard, and when rubbed over the surface of a hot iron, which was then passed backwards and forwards over a spare bit of cloth, the surface was like glass, gliding along the garment like a galleon on a calm sea. Our clothes basket was large, always piled high, and overflowing when curtains and cushion covers needed washing. No wonder it took so long.

I think it was about 1933 when Mrs Allott called. She was a 'rep' for washing machines; a dynamic, tall, big and super confident woman. She explained to my Mother how good a washing machine would be, how it would make life much easier. Mom listened, but she never did anything without Dad, he controlled the money, and he wasn't very enthusiastic about labour-saving gadgets. "When will he be home?" asked Mrs Allott. Tomorrow was arranged and about 3.30 p.m. the next day she duly called. Mom had said nothing to Dad and she kept quiet whilst Mrs Allott put her case. "No, no" said my Father. A discussion followed, somewhat one-sided as Dad stuck his heels in and seemed unmovable, but Mrs Allott was a determined 'rep' and an undaunted woman, and when two seemingly unmovable objects are put together, something's got to give, and it wasn't going to be her. "Come now Mr Salt, you aren't proud of the way your wife has to slave over a wash tub are you?" she asked, "A successful man like you wouldn't want that." She really did know how to get round a man, and she was a persuasive woman. Before she left she had an order for Mom's first washing machine, delivered in time for its trial run the following Tuesday.

It was, to describe it in its simplest form, nothing more than a straight sided zinc tub, standing on four legs. A spindle inside attached to the lid with revolving paddles, agitated the clothes when the lid closed. The handle attached to the spindle on the outside was pushed and pulled, backwards and forwards to agitate the clothes and best of all was the small mangle fastened to the top with two inch rubber rollers which were so easy to turn. Probably the greatest advantage was that Mom no longer had to kneel on the flagstones, this new invention could be worked without even bending, no ponching the clothes with the old 'Peggy legs', Mom was delighted. Out went the old mangle, no more turning of the great wheel, and no more rub, rub, rub, on the sides of the 'Peggy tub'. And a final bonus; the new machine had a tap to drain away the spent water; no more ladling; washdays from now on would be a veritable pleasure.

By this time I had said goodbye to the needlework dressed and skirts, for simple tobralco and plain cotton ones so, although the shirts of the boys had not altered a great deal, there was far less ironing to do for me. Mrs Allott became a great friend of many years standing. Mom went to stay with her in Manchester after Dad died, and she came to live with her for a short time in the 1950s. She was divorced, and bringing up two young boys, so it was necessary for her to earn a living. The elder son went to school; the younger one was only three years old. As a rep, transport was essential and a car out of the question so she bought a second-hand motorbike. The three year old was wrapped in layers of clothes and a shawl, and strapped to the pillion of the bike when she went on her rounds. One day the strappings were not secure and, feeling that the bike was lighter than usual, she looked behind her to see the bairn bouncing down the road like a football. Never daunted, she turned round, picked him up none the worse, dusted him down and strapped him on again and went on her way.

There came a time when she needed somewhere to live, and with no money, this was a problem; but not for long. She found a house which would sell quickly when necessary and another one which she fancied for herself. An offer was made on the first, and when it was accepted, she made an offer on the second. Transactions were quicker in those days, and more or less controlled by the purchaser, so she had time to sell the first at a profit, in time to clinch the contract on the second. Now she had her first house, property dealing became a lucrative pastime, with houses made into flats, and others let out room by room to students. She even took a Night School course on plumbing and maintenance so that she could do all the running repairs herself. She really was a remarkable woman.

In the 1920s and 1930s, all women had to work hard by today's standards. Most were confined to the house, with very few who had only one child going out to work, in local households for pin money or like Mrs Marshall, from necessity. In all households, the man was the Master, to a greater or a lesser degree and most women were content with their lot, after all, there was little alternative for the majority of them. A woman's only satisfaction was in her own work; how she kept house; did the cooking for the Lord and Master, and his children, and the pleasure she might derive from seeing a whole family well turned out; perhaps admired a bit, and the satisfaction she earned from them for a job well done. Her own pleasure didn't come into the picture; she had made her bed and she must lie on it, for better or worse, 'till death do us part!

There were, of course, good and bad husbands; those who went out boozing every evening, and sometimes at dinner times too, or even left home for weeks at a time on boozing expeditions, returning home broke and in a bad temper. There were others who tried to make their wife's work easier; who appreciated a clean and polished home, well turned out children, and who was a good moral example to them all. Whatever faults my Father might be accused of, I do believe he came into the latter category. Every Sunday morning he rose first, got a good fire going, and cooked the breakfast for us all. This was usually home-fed ham, or bacon, eggs and tomatoes, or perhaps fried black pudding or oatcakes. When all was ready, he came to the bottom of the stairs and called 'Breakfast'. Mom wasted no time, she appeared at once, but it took a little time for the message to sink in to the rest of us. It took at least two more calls before there was a hint of movement, and if there wasn't, along came a loud banging on the wooden sides of the stairs, and a final call "If you don't want to get up alright, but when you do get up, see as yer wacken." Yawning, at any time of the day was forbidden, especially in the morning.

Sometimes, like all children, there were occasions when the appetite didn't respond to the sight of ham rendered down to a plateful of 'dip' and we 'gypped' at the thought of eating it. This was the occasion for herb treatment. Dad grew his own herbs, except those easily found in the fields and woods and, like his father, was keen on their use for minor ailments. Loss of appetite was one. Next morning a jug of 'Herby grass'/Herb-of-Grace/Rue, it has many names, sat in the middle of the table, and the offending child had to have a good 'swig'. If by any unlucky chance the appetite was still elusive, next morning there was a jug of 'Wormwood' tea waiting on the table, to be taken by the half cup. The Herby grass was taken by the cupful, as it was a weaker brew. On the third day the treatment was drastic. In the centre of the table stood a three pound stone jam jar in which Mom had poured boiling water over the roots of Gentian (obtained from the Herbalist or Herb Chemist, as it was imported). Now Herby grass was acceptable, in fact, after being brought up on the taste, it is possible to drink like ordinary tea. 'Wormwood' was the first stage of punishment. It was bitter, as those who make their own Vermouth will know; it took the breath, and threatened to take the lining from the mouth. Now Gentian; that was the real punishment, if you didn't eat your breakfast after that, there was little hope, there was only starvation. If 'Wormwood' was bitter, then Gentian was 'gall'. It was served in an egg-cup and that was, very often, too much. But Dad was allowed one concession; Mom was allowed to throw in a handful of large raisins; the kind we put in the Christmas puddings. They swelled as they absorbed the juices, and floated like little plums. Provided we gulped down a good mouthful of Gentian, we could pop a raisin in the mouth and hope that its sweetness disguised the bitterness of the Gentian. I told you Dad was shrewd; he knew that by taking the raisin, we took in at least a teaspoonful more of the 'poison'. And, I can assure you that we all ate a good breakfast after that.

Throughout the summer, straight after breakfast on Sundays, Dad went into the garden and picked the vegetables for dinner; it might be a basket of peas which, when he had shelled them, would yield a colander brimming full of the sweetest most delicious peas ever tasted. There was nothing like a 'Little Marvel' or a 'Kelvedon Wonder', ending in autumn with a marrowfat like 'Onward'. There was a continuous supply throughout the summer. Then there were the beans. First little French ones, grown on bushes close to the ground, cooked and served whole. These were followed by kidney/stock or runner beans, a supply which lasted all summer, growing up 8ft high poles, showing their bright red flowers; 'Painted Lady' and 'Princeps'. When these were ready for gathering, out came a sharp knife, helped on by a few strokes on a 'steel' and a cutting board and Dad sat at the table slicing them into narrow slanting pieces which showed the little beans inside. I remember having a boiling of turnip tops when the leaves were young and tender; no doubt Dad picked one or two from each plant so as not to deprive the roots of necessary nourishment. Then, every spring, we were sent out into the fields with a carpet bag and a pair of scissors to harvest the new tender growths of stinging nettles, which were full of iron and, we were told, the best spring tonic. My Father firmly believed that a good helping of boiled nettles and a week on holiday at 'bracing' Blackpool kept the doctor away for the rest of the year. Nettles, for those who have never tried them, are like 'King Henry' a good substitute for spinach.

Mom prepared the potatoes, except for the first in the season. Dad was very fond of little tiny potatoes no bigger than marbles, but Mom drew a line at those, so he stood at the sink for almost an hour scraping enough for his own serving from the supply he had poked from the roots with a trowel, leaving the rest to grow on.

Sometimes Mom would go to Sheffield, perhaps to visit Auntie Annie, or to attend a meeting without Dad, and he would use such occasions to show his prowess at preparing tea. He often boasted that he could keep house as well as any woman, and even baked the bread when Mom was confined to bed with the babies. When Mom arrived home, probably with us children, the table would be set, salad made, cakes brought out of tins, and everything but bread and butter cut ready for us to sit down and enjoy. On such occasions his eyes would sparkle at his accomplishment, and pride in showing us what he could do.

My Father dealt out all the money for everything but food; not the least being clothes. They were adequate, I can't say more than that, for they were not to our own choice, or approval. He kept a pair of corduroy knee breeches upstairs for years, which he had obtained from some source thinking them to be serviceable and hard wearing. When the time came for Elijah to wear them, he hated them, for the other boys teased him at school and laughed at him. But Dad didn't listen; to him if you had clothes to wear, that's all that mattered; there was no room for vanity. From a man who was so particular about his own dress, this may seem strange, except when one remembers that his own working clothes were nothing more glamorous than cord knee breeches.

As we grew older, there were occasions when all of us demanded a bit more freedom of choice; some rather traumatic, but more of that later. We had a comfortable home and, although my opinions may differ from the boys, as girl's opinions often do, I knew that my Father could cope with any situation which might intrude on our security. I knew that I could go to the ends of the earth with my Father, knowing that I would always be safe. But it was really my Mother who kept home on an even keel. She was so undemanding, going about her work with a diligence which was part of her nature. Her philosophy had been taught by her grandmother, "If a job is worth doing, then do it well." There was no room for half measures for her; if the job couldn't be done to her satisfaction at the time, then it was left until it could be done properly. She didn't go round the house every day dusting, 'tickling up' as she used to say. Each room was turned out once a week. Bedroom floors were covered with linoleum which was scrubbed and polished, except under the rugs beside each bed, windows were cleaned and paint washed down. The sitting room was turned out, floor and furniture polished, and fireplace black-leaded whenever there had been a fire in the grate. Before about 1924 the living room floor was bare stone flags with 'clippy' rugs to walk on. They were brutes to scrub on hands and knees, but about that time, thin linoleum was put down and life was made a little easier.

Every day was filled from rising to going to bed, no matter what time that was; there were often dark looks from my Father and, as he got older, from Elijah, on arriving home around 10.30 p.m. to find her still ironing, or dusting or some other task left from the day's schedule, or maybe one to help towards the following day. No matter what anyone said, Mother had a stubborn streak, and there was no end to the day in her book, so long as there was a job to be done, she would do it. And there was always a job!

On Saturday afternoon, Dad was usually in Sheffield, Elijah playing football and Geoff out with his pals. But Jeff was very often at home and ripe for fun. Mom used to leave the dusting until

Saturday afternoon; she had been busy enough all morning putting the final touches to the living room, swilling the front path, and finishing the front step with donkey stone, and she knew that all who might complain were always out on Saturday afternoon. One day she was dusting the mantelpiece, a double-decker about 6ft high. It had two shelves over the top, the top one surrounded by a thick brocade pelmet, which hid the lower shelf where Dad kept his pipes, cartridges for his shotgun, and other personal things. Mom cleared the shelves, placing everything on the table, whilst she dusted and polished the shelves. Jeff saw the pipes, and couldn't resist the temptation. He grabbed one, and also the tin which held Dad's tobacco, and proceeded to fill the pipe as he had seen Dad do. Mom and I thought he would stop there, but no, the temptation was too great; the impersonation must be authentic and complete. He was in the mood, and perfection was on the cards. Taking a box of matches, with a flourish, he struck one and proceeded to light the tobacco, pulling and puffing as he had seen Dad do on many occasions.

Lying back in the Windsor chair, feet stretched out on the fireplace boiler top, he was the picture of complete contentment. He drew on the pipe as had never been drawn before, and slowly his eyes glazed, his face grew to a paler shade and suddenly, with a gulp, he bolted into an upright position, teetered for a second or two, then made a dive for the cellar door. We heard a frantic stamping of feet down the cellar steps, across the floor, and out the back door. He returned a few minutes later a little sheepish, but not in the least subdued.

My Mother loved cleaning out cupboards and drawers, a task I hated. "You never know what you might find." She used to say. To her it was more a pastime than a chore. I was fascinated as a little girl to see her making the decorative shelf papers for the cellar head. In all houses with cellars, the cellar head was the pantry. On the wall opposite the door was a tier of shelves, on which jams, marmalades, treacles etc. in daily use were kept. The top shelf held the lighter pans, colanders, sieves and other cooking utensils too big for a drawer. There was a standing area at the top of the steps, where a smell cupboard with zinc mesh panels, which we called the 'meat safe' stood, and down the side of the steps was another shelf which housed the heavy pans.

About once a month, all the shelves were cleared and fresh patterned paper was put on. Mom chose a newspaper with the last printer's ink on it, and folded a large sheet in half, then in half again, and again, until it was about 2" wide. Then, with the kitchen scissors, she cut a scalloped edge by simply trimming the end of a half-moon shape. Then she cut a hole in the centre of the end, then another, and a smaller one, and sometimes, a little strip was taken out parallel to the edge. Then came the moment when she put down her scissors and opened the sheet, to reveal the most miraculous and wonderful pattern I had ever seen. Needless to say, it wasn't many years before I asked if I could cut the pattern, I even graduated to making doylies from the white shelf paper used in the cupboards, as a change from using Mom's lovely crocheted ones.

Elementary education before the Education Act of 1944 was primarily for teaching the three R's, Reading, 'Riting and 'Rithmatic, plus History, Geography, Sewing and Cookery for girls, and Woodwork, Gardening and a very basic Science and Drawing for boys. Algebra was for boys only, why? I never enquired; I was glad enough that it wasn't in my curriculum. All girls from the first year until leaving school learned to knit and sew, first the basics like hemming, running stitch, different types of seams and a few embroidery stitches, progressing through to the top class when simple garments like nightdresses and underskirts could be made on the one sewing machine. Knitting was confined to stocking stitch, moss stitch and garter stitch, in making kettle holders and scarves, and for the older pupils who wanted to, bobble hats and stockings. I have two nightdress cases made and embroidered when I was ten years old. When I was twelve years old we were initiated into designing, being set the task of designing and embroidering on a piece of linen about 8 " square. My square was hemmed all round and decorated with a basket of flowers, the handle boasting an embroidered bow of ribbon, (I can't help thinking, I must have been flower minded even at that young age). The stitches used were lazy daisy stitch, stem stitch and satin stitch.

Of course, most girls were initiated into knitting and sewing at home, for sheets were often made from unbleached calico bought by the yard, and hemmed by hand before using. Handkerchiefs were made from off-cuts of old sheets which had worn thin, and most housewives turned sheets 'sides to middle' or as it was called 'robbing Peter to pay Paul' by cutting across the width and stitching top to bottom. The latter was usually a last resort, for the seam across the middle could be mighty uncomfortable on the rear. Nothing was wasted; middles were cut out of worn sheets, the sides being made into under slips for pillows; pillows and mattresses were made from 'ticking' bought by the yard, made into bags, and filled with feathers sterilised in a hot oven, or grey 'flecks' bought by the bag from the market or big stores. Small pieces of cotton or linen, too small for anything else were used for the centres of crocheted doyleys, or tray cloths ready for that day when a meal had to be taken in bed. And, of course, clothes were cut down, and the best bits used to make clothes for younger children. Being the old girl I never had to wear 'hand-me-downs' but I do remember having to wear a pair of Elijah's boots for school when he had grown out of them before they were worn out. But, no-one bothered about such things, everybody did it!

Sewing classes were held twice a week, when pupils supplied all their own fabrics. This was a minor restriction on the Orphanage girls, and they never did any sewing. All their time was spent in knitting grey socks for both girls and boys, and they gave us the impression that much of their spare time in the evenings was doing the same thing, although much of this was spent in looking after the younger children, entertaining them until bedtime, putting them to bed, and repairing, darning and patching theirs and the boys clothes. None of them ever came to Cookery classes, I presume because it was difficult to supply cooking materials.

During the nine years at school, Arithmetic progressed from simply numeracy through to simple division, addition and multiplication, to long division, decimals and fractions, percentages, areas, capacities, and circumferences of circles and spheres; calculating areas and volumes of squares, cubes triangles, parallelograms and cones, and the inevitable problem sums as calculating the times of filling and emptying baths and tanks from a given flow of taps and sink plugs, the top standards graduating to square and cube roots, with a little Algebra for boys. Tests were held at the end of each academic year when we were given a foolscap sheet of paper for our answers, the results being marked by a full cross, half cross, a line or a '0' which covered the whole page. I had little difficulty with arithmetic; consequently it was one of my favourite subjects.

English tests and exams consisted of letter writing, composition, punctuations, spelling, and pronouns, suffices and prefixes, verbs and nouns etc. Test papers were given out for the occasion, for text books were unknown, and marking was the same as far arithmetic. My one proud moment was when I won the half-crown.

There was no actual examination in reading; I imagine that progress was record by continuous assessment, for we were regularly pounced upon during the weekly silent reading time to read a section and explain to the class what it meant. Sometimes we were asked to give a résumé of the story we were reading, and I wasn't too good at that. I could read fast, whether silent or aloud, but remembering what I read to give a resume of what it was about other than a broad understanding of the story was almost a non-starter, said to be a measure of intelligence! But then, concentration was my very weak point.

I remember the rapid questions fired during History lessons and 'Treaty of Utrecht' written in big letters on the blackboard. The unending list of dates; of battles; of Kings and Queens, and woe betide anyone who could only remember the six wives of Henry VIII. Geography lessons consisted of learning about rivers and mountains, tributaries and estuaries, towns and cities and countries all over the world. Every so often we were given sheets of paper on which to draw the outline of a certain country to include such features as written on the blackboard. Considering that there was only one atlas in the book cupboard for the whole class, there was little wonder that some weird and wonderful maps were drawn from these remembered from the blackboard; England, France and Finland have never since had such a coastline.

Poetry was part of English lessons, with some of the better known ones learned by everyone. Like 'The Pied Piper of Hamlyn', 'The Quality of Mercy', 'Abu Ben Adam', 'Leary the Lamplighter' and 'Meg Merilees' and many more than I can remember. Poetry was one subject I enjoyed, particularly in the top classes, and Mr Wood was critical about the expression and interpretation put into the reciting of them. I suppose is suited my love of theatricals. There were some pupils, mostly boys, who were embarrassed when called on to recite a poem, when they were brought to a sudden stop by 'Mary had a little lamb' in a whining voice from Mr Wood, which ridiculed the way it was recited. (One girl I rather envied, although she was about two years younger than I, was Marjorie Elliot, daughter of the Chapel Superintendent, when her father sent her to learn elocution. Her rendering of 'Dick Turpin's ride to York' on the Chapel concert was loudly applauded).

After the end of year examinations, if the results were not high enough for a move to the next Standard, the pupil stayed down for another year, or until they had caught up with the rest. Occasionally someone stayed down longer; when I left school at the age of 14, a boy the same age was still in Standard One, sitting in a little low chair in the middle of the six and seven year olds. Everyone knew how hopeless he was at learning, but after leaving school and working on his father's farm, later having a farm of his own, no-one could calculate the weight of a pig like him, nor outmatch his calculations of the cash in his hand, and the transaction he was about to make. Everyone it seemed has his own forté and his was all practical.

Sewing was not one of the most popular lessons for the girls of Standards Five upwards, partly I fear because the teacher, Mrs Lake, was not a popular teacher. She disliked Margaret and me intensely, and we reciprocated. Why she should have been as antagonistic I don't know. She resented us being such close friends, having failed to realise that we were the only two girls of our age who lived south of the village, and we had no other choice. We were both confirmed at Totley Church on the 16th May 1929, and she treated us as though we were lesbians (overhead saying to Miss Foulstone, "Look, they're even walking up the altar together") as if that were a crime. My Mother, who served on the same Committee (Hospitals and Scouts), thought she was a very nice woman (teachers are often very different outside school), but I might add, she was not very popular with any of the pupils, partly due to the fact that the poor woman was not blessed with a very pleasant countenance, and was a little forbidding to us all, very often the butt of jokes.

The girls from all the top four classes went to Mrs Lake for sewing and knitting twice a week. It was on one of these occasions that an unfortunate calamity befell her, not intentional, but a source of great humour to the whole class. Two girls took it in rotation to act as monitors, giving out and collecting in the cloth bags in which we kept our current work. (The Orphanage girls took their knitting home with them after every lesson). On the day in question, the lesson over, the two monitors were collecting the bags and had opened the lid of the huge wooden trunk in which they were stored. One girl was late finishing and Mrs Lake went to her to sort out her problem. Having identified the girl's mistake, she returned to the front of the class and, with her back to the box, sat down to rectify it, not knowing the lid was open. With a wild cry, she fell backwards, legs flailing in mid-air, struggling frantically to get out, without success. The air was electric; horror; apprehension and suppressed laughter, all fighting for supremacy.

The two monitors grabbed her arms, and after a great effort, managed to haul her into an upright position, face red as a beetroot, florid and angry, with a tirade of words issuing from her on carelessness, dangerous practices, and everything which allowed her tongue to rid her of such embarrassment. Both Margaret and I said "Thank goodness we weren't monitors that afternoon".

One winter's day, when the roads and the school yard were covered by about 6" of snow, I set off down the allotments, arriving in time to join the queue before it had disappeared inside. It was sewing day and so, after answering the register call, the girls trouped upstairs to Mrs Lake's class. Almost immediately on arriving in the room, I was confronted by her and charged with throwing a snowball with a stone wrapped inside, which had hit one of the other girls. I emphatically denied the charge, but she insisted "Someone has seen you throw it," she said. "I don't think she did," I replied. I was not yet initiated into 'Police tactics', and was dismayed when she said triumphantly, "So, you don't think so." I was staggered as she went on, "But you're not sure, you might have done." "No", I stammered, "I am sure, I didn't throw a snowball." "Don't tell lies," she cried, now red in the face. "You are a bad girl," and turning to her desk, she fetched out her cane. I was angry. To be accused of something I hadn't done was bad enough, but to have the additional charges of dishonesty cast upon me was too much. "Hold out your hand," she shouted, but I refused, saying I had done nothing. I could have told her I wasn't even in the yard, but that would be worse; we were supposed to be in the yard before the bell went, and to be late was enough for the cane from a teacher who was so inclined. "Hold out your hand," she repeated, making a grab for my arm. By this time I was crying with fury. "Get off, get off, and leave me alone." She made a dive at me, grabbed my arm again, by which time tears were running down my cheeks, mingling with the snot from my nose, and I was wretched. Down came the cane, once, twice, three times, each time catching the tips of my fingers as I tried to pull my hand away. She was furious, like a maniac, ranging blows one after the other, until I finally pulled my arm away, and ran to my seat. That was the one and only time I suffered the cane, and to the rest of my schooldays, I hated Mrs Lake, not for the punishment, but because she didn't believe me.

There is always retribution for a wrongdoing, or so some people believe, and Mrs Lake eventually found her venom bouncing back on to her own shoulders. It was like this. When I was twelve years old, Mr Wood said he would like me to take over from him and play the piano for hymns every morning. We assembled in the big room for prayers and hymns before starting lessons in our own classrooms. (This is now called assembly) then, it was the occasion for fulfilling that part of the Education Act which set down the rules of religion, although, being as Church school, there were lessons on religion at other times. There were two hymns and prayers said by Mr Wood, followed by notices to the pupils. I was very nervous and apprehensive about playing in front of the whole school, but he was very understanding; I was allowed to choose the two hymns, which was as well for although I could 'rattle off' three flats, I wasn't so good on sharps beyond the first two. Sometimes, however, he would express a wish for a certain hymn, and it was then that I was truly sorry that I could play the piano at all, when it landed me in such a job.

She was not even my teacher, except for sewing, and I resented her interference. However, it was not in the nature of children of school age to question adults, and their idiosyncrasies so, at playtime, I went upstairs to her room, accepted the piece of white paper she held out, and set to work, drawing the stave and trying meticulously to copy the notes. I had been working for about ten minutes when Mr Wood came upstairs and, surprised to find me there, asked what I was doing. When I told him, he was furious. "Leave that at once," he shouted. "Get outside where you should be at playtime," and as I put down my pen and got up to go, he roared "Mrs Lake can do that herself if it needs to be done." And, she obviously did; for a day or two later when I opened the book, there, taped inside was a newly written sheet of music which was never played, nor did I ever hear it played. It all seemed a fruitless bit of 'peeve'.

Music was a subject that was enjoyed or just tolerated. It consisted solely of singing traditional songs like 'The British Grenadiers'; 'Where the bee sucks there suck I' and 'Nymphs and Shepherds'. All songs had to be learned by word of mouth; no sheets of music; no song books for reference; just listening and following everybody else. This caused minor problems if one wasn't careful, for children don't have the most perfect diction, always made worse by opening one's mouth to sing. I remember singing 'On Richmond Hill' where there dwelt a lass 'more fair than made ay morn', and I couldn't understand what on earth 'ay morn' meant, and I never asked, partly because pupils didn't question the teacher about what seemed trivial matters, partly and probably mostly, because I didn't want to appear dense, not realising that probably half the class didn't know anyway for they were all singing the same thing. It was many years afterwards that I was sufficiently interested to find out that I should have sung 'Mayday morn', by which time it was too late!

Chapter 5

As soon as I could walk, it was obvious to my parents that there was something not quite right with my ankles, and this was made more obvious when my Father played with me or when out walking, they held my hands and swung me to and fro, as parents often do with their young children. The bones in my wrists and ankles would not stand the strain and, when I started running, my ankles gave way, letting me down badly. Dr Parsons suggested that I wore clogs which would support my ankles and strengthening my feet. So, my Father went to the local shoemaker, I think it was Mr Reville at Holmesfield, and had a small pair of clogs made for me. For the first few years at school I dutifully wore my clogs, not a trial then as it would be by today's standards, for men wore clogs for work and some women wore them for swilling and other times when they would prevent wet feet.

From the day I started school I could run a good race, it didn't matter whether it was a 100 yard sprint, an 'egg and spoon' race, a sack race, a skipping race, or a three legged race, I would always beat the rest. We had the school sports on the side of the Bents and races at the village show in Earnshaw's field (where the Council school is now). My Father was always the 'scratch man', spacing out the competitors according to their ability or on their previous results. He was also the 'starter', firing the gun to start the races.

By the time I was twelve years old, I had gradually been moved back each year, until now my Father put me on the 'scratch line' for the 100 yards sprint, about six yards behind the next person in front. "Oh Dad," I shouted, "It's not fair." "You can do it lass," he answered. "Go on, show 'em you can do it." The gun was fired and I set off, with a quick burst of speed, passed the first girl, then the second and the third, gaining all the time until, with about two yards to go, with a superhuman effort, lungs bursting, I hit the tape first. My Father came striding down the 100 yards stretch, patted me on the back, smiling broadly, eyes twinkling, "You see," he said, "I knew you could do it." I knew he was very proud, and I was happy to know that I had pleased him. But winning was not all sweet; it made a few enemies amongst the mothers of the girls who were usually runner's up, probably made worse because the one who had ousted them was 'Lady Muck' (my nickname).

The worse of these was Mrs Dronfield who lived in Hillfoot Road, who once made sure that I heard when she criticised my Mother for sending me to school on a summer's day in white shoes. "Sithee, white shoes to go to school in, it's bloody daft," she said as I was passing. I hated her for evermore. The last item on the school sports programme was always the skipping competition, when all the girls entered a ring about 40ft in diameter bounded by a rope. It was a test of endurance to see which girl could carry on skipping for the longest time. The competition had been going for some time until there were only two competitors left in the ring, both tired, both determined to win. Suddenly, in a loud voice so that everyone could hear, came Mrs Dronfield's voice "Sithee, it's her again, I wish she'd trip hersen up on 'er bloody rope." She had said the wrong thing, for now I knew I was going to win, nobody but nobody talks about me like that and gets away with it. With renewed energy, I went into battle, stronger than ever and I won, much to her chagrin.

I have never considered that I was the sporty type, but I did like a challenge, and my Father was quick to realise this. He had had a nervous breakdown about 1923 or 1924 and Dr Marshall suggested that he take up some kind of sporting activity as part of a recuperating process, and suggested that bowling might be a good way to start. There was a Bowling Club at the Cross Scythes Hotel and they had an excellent crown green behind the hotel, so Dad followed Dr Marshall's advice and joined, taking the game very seriously. Dad was runner up in the tournament for 'The Shield' in 1926 and in 1926 they won it. In the same year he was elected Captain, an appointment which made him very proud. This was the first year he took me to play on 'Ladies Day' when members took their wives, fiancés, daughters or other ladies to compete for prizes donated by the members. Whether the thought had ever entered his head to take my Mother, I don't know; I doubt it. She was a hard worker on various Committees, but I think she would have been very uncomfortable in that artificial, pretentious, theatrical situation, and was probably not even interested in looking on.

My Father bought a new dress for me; for once a rather 'posh' one made of Rep cloth, with an elaborately pleated front skirt. My Mother had put my hair in curl rags the night before, and combed it into ringlets tied with a ribbon to match my dress. I could see my Father was very proud as we walked on to the green and I was proud to walk beside him when it came to my turn to play, enjoying the remarks of the other members. They had never had such a young competitor before, and were intrigued by my Father's confidence. I knew nothing about bowls, which in my small hands seemed very heavy, but ever anxious to learn, I did everything he told me as well as I could. I liked to please my Father, he was so critical of effort and always said "You must always do your best, and do your work well", so to please him was an achievement.

I walked beside him on to the green with Billy Wise and his wife, who was my opponent for the first heat. He explained what the 'jack' was and pointed to the crown of the green and how the bias of the bowl worked to counteract it. The footpad was thrown into position and I was told I must not step over it or I would be disqualified. Then the game began. I knew all eyes were on me, even though there was another couple on the green playing across the other corner, but I revelled in the limelight. My Father was with me, and I feared nothing. The two tossed for who should start, and Mrs Wise bowled the 'jack' followed by her first bowl. It was my turn. How well I remember my Father's words explaining how to bowl my first bowl. "You see that shrub, the one with a bit sticking up, now bowl for that". I looked mystified, "But." "Do as I tell you lass, bias on the left, and bowl for that shrub." Taking the bowl in my right hand, holding it as I had seen him do, I did exactly as he told me. One foot on the pad, the other behind, with knee bent, and with arm swinging

77

I let roll my first bowl, watching anxiously as he walked after it, arm swinging as if to push it on faster until, turning, he smiled, or rather grinned with satisfaction calling out "Good wood". It was within a foot of the 'jack'; not bad for the first effort.

Due entirely to my Father's strategy, at the end of the day, I was thankful to see the pride and pleasure on his face when it was announced that I had won second prize, a beautiful cut glass butter dish and silver butter knife, donated by Billy Wise. Mine or more honestly my Father's success continued for the next two years when again I won second prize, a silver toast rack and a silver and porcelain jam dish. The fourth year, 1929, it poured with rain and the match was called off, but after some discussion, it was decided to hold a whist drive inside the Cross Scythes, giving the prizes for that. I had never played whist but I had watched my Father and Mother play sometimes with Frank Fox, who came to visit often on Saturday night, so I knew the principles of the game. As I was an official guest, and a contestant for the bowls match, I was expected to join in the amusement I might add, of the rest of the crowd. Making sure I knew what the trumps were at any one time, and being careful not to revoke (I'd seen Mrs Smith's fury when this happened when she came in to our house and joined in, and her reputation for being keen was universal). I played my cards, and hoped I wouldn't look too much of an ignoramus. Lo and behold, at the end of the whist drive I was rewarded with third prize, a fishing basket, which I used for many years as a cat basket for my beautiful silver grey half Persian cat 'Tippy' on our journeys from Whitley Bay to Holmesfield in the 1970s. In fact, I think it was used more than any of the other three prizes, which spent much of their time in a cupboard.

Until around 1927 there was neither gas nor electricity at Lane Head, although gas had reached the Villas about 200 yards down the road. Before it came to Lane Head, all activities after dark such as sewing, reading, card and other games, were done in the light of a paraffin lamp placed in the middle of the table. Ours was a metal one about 18" high, with a glass bowl to hold the paraffin. A wick led down through a hole in the metal burner into the bowl of paraffin, and a very thin lamp glass rested in the burner enclosing the flame and magnified the light. The wick had to be trimmed every day, and fuel checked ready for lighting at dusk; there was nothing worse than a badly trimmed wick which smoked the glass causing an even greater job cleaning it in the dark.

We weren't allowed to read during the day, but when the lamp was lit after tea, we could get out our books, or in later years, one of the Castle's Books of Knowledge that Father had bought for us in an effort to further our education. But first we had to wash our hands, and then bring our books to the table to read by the light of the lamp. Even when we did have electricity, we still had to read only at the table.

We had two comics per week, 'Chips' and 'Comic Cuts' and on Monday and Tuesday there was a stampede home to be the first to grab them. But four people can't read one comic all at once so someone had to wait until the afternoon. If my Father had already arrived home, we had to sneak it out from under the cushion where it had been hidden, and disappear into the room to read. If he had not yet arrived, it was a matter of reading with one ear cocked for his footsteps on the pavement, and trying to concentrate on the story. At some time or another I think we have all said that this habit spoiled our concentration in later years, trying to study, yet reading the same paragraph over two or three times, before it would sink in.

Margaret, my new friend, passed on her 'Schoolgirl's Own' magazine. I loved Betty Barton, Polly Linton, and short tongued Paula, as well as the black Princess Naomi, and I dreamed lovely dreams of going to boarding school myself. Later, I had visions of being a 'cowgirl' in the Wild West of Canada, from reading too many 'Western' magazines; it didn't matter that it could be freezing cold in winter, I just wanted to ride on the range in Stetson and Chaps. Unfortunately, I have never learned to ride a horse.

Sometimes we played cards on winter evenings, a habit which started when Frank Fox started visiting, sometimes he would go next door to the Smiths, sometimes to us. Frank was a keen Chapel goer but, as he was a cripple, he seemed not to have many close friends, although he was a respected member of the community, and liked by all the villagers. It was through Chapel that he became friends with

Nellie and myself, and remained a friend for many years. The favourite game was 'Donkey', a game like 'Rummy' but in 'Donkey' the loser was patted on the back by all the other players to the cries of 'Donkey Donkey', An innocent game, and one where the 'Donkey' was treated gently, with the fun demanded of the game, but in the unlucky chance that I was 'Donkey' my Father couldn't resist teasing. He had a habit of slow timing, a form of teasing whereby he pretended not to understand what a person was saying, blowing up a situation by prolonging a system of questioning which is, at once, both silly and frustrating.

I was the one most often at the receiving end of this silly game, which did not stop until all five males took up the tormenting, and I ended up under the table in tears. Then my Father changed completely, I was 'mardy' I was a 'cry-baby', I was a 'madam', all of which I considered very unfair considering all the hefty slaps my back had endured in the process, instead of the mild ones usually handed out. I am sure it was this unreasonable teasing which made me grown up on the defensive, and irritated by the silly humour of men and boys. Teasing to such an extent breeds resentment, and is cruel to a child if done to excess. It spoils an otherwise congenial nature.

The time we all looked forward to in winter was Christmas. Toys were not readily given to children, and most of us were thankful to receive a toy or a book, as well as the few oddments put in the stocking. We hung up our stockings on Christmas Eve, after writing to Father Christmas and throwing our letters up the chimney, always surprised that the little bird perched on the chimneypot caught them, no matter how hot the fire was. We were hopefully expectant of the article we had asked for, an expectancy which rarely ventured beyond what we reasonably could receive. I remember one year when I had asked for a wrist watch, when I really knew it would cost more than my Father could afford for if I received an expensive present, I knew the boys would have to have one of equal value; that was fair according to my parents philosophy, and funds wouldn't rise to those heights. When I received a stencil set instead, I was still disappointed, money that year obviously didn't stretch to a wrist watch. There was always the traditional apple, orange, a few nuts, a penny in the toe of the stocking, the penny being very welcome; it was half a week's spending money!

One Christmas, when I was about eleven years old, and Elijah was 13, we were both deprived of our Christmas presents. I had asked for a book, 'Hans Anderson's Fairy Tales' and Elijah had asked for a box of paints. On Boxing Day we had visitors, Auntie Ruth and our cousins Jinny, Roy, Ruth, Raymond and Catherine. Roy had recently started attending Dronfield Grammar School and Auntie Ruth wasted no time in telling my Father that he needed a cadet's uniform. (The school had a Military Cadet Corp, of which my Father disapproved; he wouldn't even allow Elijah and Geoff to join the Scouts, saying it was the first step to militarism). But before Auntie Ruth left, she had the cost of the uniform. There was more, Roy had to have some paints for the Art Class, and yes out came Elijah's Christmas paints. In the meantime, Jinny had taken a fancy to my book, and asked if she could borrow it. As usual Auntie Ruth won the day. "Lend it to Jinny," she said, "You can read it when she brings it back." To Elijah she said "Let Roy have your paints, I'll get you another box." Needless to say, Elijah never got his paints, and my book was never returned. Although discreet comments were made by both of us and my Mother, there was never a word of criticism of them from my Father.

There were evenings, even in winter, when playing outside was much better than playing cards or reading, especially on moonlight nights. Skies were clear, and the moon shed enough light to read a newspaper. One of our favourite games was one that all could join in, girls, boys, young and very young, the more the merrier. It was called 'Hare and Hounds' or 'Holler'. Two teams were formed, one being the 'hares' and the other the 'hounds'. The hares were given a good start, usually a slow count up to one hundred, when eyes were kept closed and no one knew which way the hares had chosen to run. When the count was finished, the hounds set off in pursuit calling out "Shout Holler or the dogs won't foller". If there was no reply, the call would go out again, echoing down and around the hillside and across the valley like the yodel of an Austrian cowherd's man. Eventually came the answering cry "Holler," this was a drawn out cry like 'Ho-o-ller-er' on two distinct notes, high and low, which echoed back indicating the direction the hares were running. The hounds chased in pursuit of the call, down the hill (Lane Head Road), on Bents Road, along Penny Lane, or up on to the Moors and Strawberry Lea Lane, up Moss Road on the mountainside on the opposite side of the valley, periodically calling "Shout holler or the dog won't foller", when the answer might come from a different direction altogether, the hares having crossed the Moor and the fields into Gillfield Wood, even as far as Woodthorpe on the opposite hillside.

Hiding was not always as simple as it might sound; there were no street lights, but moonlight lit the whole valley, and the merest shadow could be seen fleeing across a field or down a lane unless the shadows of trees or hedgerows were used for cover. A single game of 'Hare and Hounds' could, and often did; last until bed time and a late one at that.

Winter brought frost, and much keener frosts than we generally experience these days. Summers were hotter, and winters were colder. Even the liquid in the chamber pots were known to freeze, and on such nights, Mom would wrap the oven plate in a piece of blanket and put it in one of the beds, a stone hot water bottle in another, and two fire bricks from the brickyard in the other, after getting hot in the oven for a couple of hours before bedtime. It was on these dark nights that I was particularly nervous of ascending the dark staircase with nothing more than the small light of a candle; holding the candlestick with my fingers wrapped tightly through the handle. I approached with tentative steps to about halfway, then a quick sprint to the top as if the devil were after my last leg. Getting into bed after saying my prayers was worse, for there was always something under the bed ready to grab that same leg before I could get it safely under the sheets.

But frost had other pleasures to offer. Every boy had a sledge, some simply home made efforts, some more elaborate and large. The favourite field was one belonging to Tyms down Hall Lane, where the College Hostel is now built. It had a convenient slope long enough to work up a fast ride, and Norman Taylor's sledge was ideal for the purpose. It held at least five bodies, and Norman was very generous in offering one of the middle seats to a girl who didn't have a sledge, which applied to most girls. I was lucky on a number of occasions, enjoying an exhilarating ride, but once, it was the cause of an injury which might have been much worse. Jeff had gone down the field just before us but had hit something and slewed approximately half way down. He was in a direct line with our sledge which, with five people on board, was a hefty weapon. As we drew closer, Norman and the brake man did their best to guide our sledge away from Jeff but not quite enough and, as we drew level, I put out a foot and pushed him out of the way, sustaining a severely sprained ankle in the bargain. For once, I wasn't called 'mardy' or 'madam' but Geoff couldn't resist a discreet tap on the ankle, accusing me of 'swinging the lead', for which he was severely chastised for once, by Dad.

There was a dam at Old Hay, in the bottom of the valley, just before rising up the opposite hill to Dore. This was a favourite place for those who could skate, and most of the village boys had a good try, especially those who lived near the dam, like Charlie Coates. Those who couldn't skate made slides and sailed round the dam from one slide to another. The atmosphere was like no other activity in the whole year, and one time when young and old, provided they could stand on their two feet, were welcome as to a party.

Summer evenings were not entirely given over to play. Some families sent their children into the wood collecting firewood, even mothers, like Mrs Wortly went 'sticking' during the day, and my Father was a strict taskmaster, who expected everybody to put in a full day's occupation of some sort. There were gardening jobs for the boys, when Elijah wasn't feeding hens, milking goats and chasing horses. Elijah always seemed to 'take the can back' so to speak, for the other two, and he was made to work both morning and night at some job or other, whether at home or on a farm, and if I didn't get out of his way quick enough, he would tell my Mother to find me something useful to do, like darning, or washing dishes, or anything to prevent me from wasting time. However, we managed to find time for some leisurely pursuits, usually in the 'Butts' field at the top of Lane Head Road. There was a flat area just right for the boys to play cricket, emulating Bradman or some other current cricketing hero.

Then there was 'Peggy', a game faintly resembling 'Knur and Spell' of parts of Lancashire. The game was played with a piece of wood about one foot long shaped like a shuttle, pointed at both ends, the 'Peggy' and a long stick with which to strike it. The game was often played on the wall just below our house, or in the field, using a conveniently large stone on which to rest the 'Peggy'. Having put it in place, the tip was struck a sharp blow with the long stick, when the shape of the 'Peggy' allowed it to rock forward and fly into the air, when it was struck a smart blow like a baseball player and the winner was the one who could drive it furthest down the road or across the field.

The field belonged to the Rifle Range in the Bents, and was used by soldiers during the First World War for small arms training. When the war was over, it was a testing range for armour plate by Vickers Armstrong of Sheffield. The testing was done during the day and never at weekends, in fact very little until the Second War seemed imminent when testing started again, so we knew we were quite safe in the evenings, and weekends, although some territorial camps were held occasionally during holidays. The 'Butts' were, and still are, positioned at distances of 500, 750 and 1,000 yards from the targets situated just under the edge of the hill which rises up on to the moorland plateau. When target firing was in progress either from the 'Butts' field or from the shorter 'Butts' on the actual range, we liked to watch the targets rising and turning and the flag signal of the man behind which indicated the score of the firer.

Around the 500 'Butt' was a very wet area. A spring rose in the hillside just above the brickyard, flowing under the road at the top of the field, where it was little more than a trickle, but as it flowed down the bank it created a wet marshy area sufficient to grow an abundance of 'milkmaids' (for the botanists, Cardamine Pratensis) which grew on both sides of the stream. A few cowslips, primroses, rushes and sedges, added to the abundance of daisies, buttercups, which were held under the chine to see if we liked butter, crane bill, ragged robin, water ravens, clovers, vetches and wild pansies, which we all used to gather and take to our respective mothers, to see them lovingly put into eggcups and jam jars, and displayed on the outside

84

windowsill, with the jars of bluebells or tadpoles from the pond or brook. Incidentally, my Father used to gather purple clover flowers (clover knobs) to dry and smoke in his pipe. He said they were good for his chest, which was probably right if the noses of the onlookers could stand the stink!

I couldn't leave the field without mentioning the 'daisy chains'. Every little girl made daisy chains, coming home with coronet, tiaras, circlets and necklaces, with an extra one for Mom's hair, which she dutifully wore, for five minutes, just to show she was willing to play. Making daisy chains was, it seemed to me, the epitome, the embodiment, the essence, the truest symbol of a country girl's life. If we got hungry there was always 'gobbelty guts'. (Sorrel or Rumex Acetosella/Acetosa) a member of the Dock family which has edible acidy leaves, and cultivated to use in salad. We loved to pull the leaves and chew them to extract the acidy juice then spit out the chewed residue in case it gave us stomach ache. According to Frank, my husband, in Durham it's called 'Sour Gob'.

Before the advent of street lights, the road from the village was lonely and very dark, except on moonlight nights. It was on such a night that I was walking home; from where I remember not. The moon was very bright and the little window of our cottage, which faced down the road, sent out a welcoming light. There was a gulley on the right side of the road, formed by the hill falling away as the road wound uphill. A low wall bounded the edge of the road and prevented falling over into the gulley. I had just passed the War Memorial and started up the last stretch of open road when I noticed, way in front, just below the house, a white shape rising up and over the wall of the gulley. I was fascinated as it moved very slowly towards the centre of the road. It seemed to hang there for a few moments before moving slowly and silently down the road. The night was very quiet, there was only a very slight breeze, nothing more than a gentle movement of air. The white shape floated like a zephyr, with no hint of noise, as it drew nearer altering its shape like an amoeba, spreading out and coming together with a gentle rise and fall, all the time getting closer and closer. My steps became slower and slower as I watched, partly in wonder, partly in fascinated terror, growing into one of trepidation. As the apparition drew to within two or three yards of me, I stood petrified.

It didn't waver, slowly and gently it came nearer and nearer, my eyes riveted on it, and as it drew level with me, I stood rooted to the spot in terror, bracing myself ready to run if only I could find the spur, then I saw what it was. The apparition was no more than a double sheet of newspaper, shining white as a ghost in the moonlight, caught in the breeze at the top of the road and carried on the current of air as it moved down the slope. I watched as it passed and as it drew level with the houses below the War Memorial, I saw it float gently down, resting silently on the ground. Finding energy at least, I set off running as if 'Old Nick' himself was after me and didn't stop until I was safely inside the house.

My Father was a man of many interests; he tried his hand at most things over the years. Some were short-lived, possibly because they were not as easy as first thought, others more long lasting, easier, or just more profitable, who can say? Most of them were successful, while they lasted, like the mushrooms which he grew in the little shed erected at the side of the house. He put shelves down the side and filled them with well-turned manure, inserted small pieces of mushroom spawn, kept them in the dark and waited for the result. The mushrooms grew well and were harvested as they reared their heads above the composted manure and were delicious when fried with the home fed bacon which he produced and cured himself after a pig killing. When he stopped growing mushrooms I can't remember, some things tended to fizzle out and disappear without really knowing when. However, the pigs lasted much longer.

One or two people in and around the village, mostly farmers, kept pigs and were allowed in those days to slaughter them on their own premises. More often than not, my Father killed two at a time, one for our own use, one for selling, unless it was a very big pig like Sally the old sow that had produced many a good litter and was now past her breeding days. It wasn't a particularly joyful day when Sally was killed, for she had been somewhat of a pet. Dad would stand leaning over the wall of her sty on summer evenings scratching her back and putting her into a contented mood. He always said "A contented animal always gives more milk." He used to let her out of the sty with her litter and drive her around the field for exercise, but Sally had done her duty and now must go. When anyone decided to slaughter one of their pigs, all the other men knew, so there was never any danger of causing a glut. They were not the 100 pounders of today's market, these were good big, well fed on the best corn; pigs with all the flavour of good corn feeding with plenty of fat around the slices of ham to show just how well they had been bred. There had, of course, to be an 'R' in the month, as everyone knew that pork soon 'went off' in midsummer. There were no freezers, and fridges were thin on the ground so what wasn't needed at the present moment, was preserved in some way for future use.

I was about eight or nine years old when my Father handed me a little notebook and sent me off on my way around the village canvassing for orders for pork joints, pig's fry, trotters and the like. I had a list of all the prices in the front of the book, so all I had to do was to take down the name and address of the customer (Dad knew everybody anyway), and the item ordered. Not forgetting the initial introduction of myself and what I was selling. I was not a shy child by any stretch of imagination so my Father knew he wasn't putting me under any strain in sending me out in this way. OK, say it was my curiosity getting a hold again, wanting to know what's going on, wanting to be 'in the act', under no illusions, I felt important in the role of vendor of pork and offal. I also revelled in the look of satisfaction on my Father's face when I returned with a full order book.

A year or two later my Father decided to expand his customer catchment area and by this time he had a motorbike and sidecar. He loaded me into it and took off for Dore, the village a mile away, there to ply my trade, whilst he went into the 'Devonshire Arms' to pick up a few orders. (That was his story, and pubs were notorious trading places; you could sell anything in a pub when the men had had a drink or two!)

Many years afterwards, whilst talking to a Solicitor's Clerk who had lived in Dore at the time, the conversation turned to those early days when I was a budding salesman. On hearing my maiden name he remembered who I was before my marriage and related a tale which turned my face a bright pink. On arrival home from the office one day, his mother, whilst discussing the events of the day, recounted my visit. " … a girl," she said, "a pretty little thing with long fair ringlets, asking for orders for pork." She continued, "She read out all the prices; loin was so much; pig's fry was so much, leg of pork was a little dearer at so much; then she came to stomach pork." I became horribly embarrassed as the Clerk continued. "My Mother laughed even as she told us," he said. "Go on," I said, "You may as well tell me." He laughed as he continued his mother's story. "Nay love," she said to me, "You mean belly pork don't you?" and continued "My, the poor little mite did blush." Had I known this story at the time, it might have put me off, but I don't really think so, it's not the only embarrassing moment I have experienced and survived.

Killing a pig was a major operation. Sam Mather, who worked for Colin Thompson the butcher, came to kill it in the back yard and Charlie Smith from next door helped to scrape and clean it. The chosen one was brought down the field squealing and grunting, whilst the pig form (in brief, a low wooden platform with handles at each corner for carrying) was brought out of the cellar and put in position in the back yard near the drain. We children were not allowed anywhere near to see the actual killing, a gory operation done by sticking a sharp pointed knife into the pig's throat. The rush of blood which followed flowed into the drain, some being caught in a bucket to be made into black pudding. My Mother filled the copper and lit the fire to get the water boiling, and we were there to see the cleaning and scraping to remove all the stiff hairs around the pig's hide. Copious buckets of boiling water were carried from the cellar kitchen and thrown over the pig to soften the hairs and make them easier to scrape off and clean the carcass in the process. I wasn't particularly squeamish; such things had to be done in the name of good food, and I was particularly fond of roast pork with apple sauce! I did, however, squirm a little when the little hoofs were pulled off with a large hook. It took a strong pull from Mr Smith to release each hoof, and my finger nails felt every pull.

Within an hour, with entrails removed, the carcass was carried to the cellar and hung on a large hook to dry out and set with the inside wedged open with two thick wooden struts between the front and back legs. Next day the cutting up commenced and my Mother's work began. Firstly, there was the leaf fat to cut up into small pieces to be rendered down in the oven in large pudding tins. The resulting white lard was poured off periodically as soon as it had melted into large shallow tins to be stored for use in making pastry, bread and other cooking, and sometimes spread on slices of bread with a dash of salt, as a snack after school when the appetite would not wait for teatime. When the last of the fat had been poured off, the residue was pressed with a saucer or a turnip masher, to extract the last few drops, leaving crisp crunchy scraps which were delicious to eat at teatime with a sprinkling of salt and bread and butter.

In the meantime, the cutting up of the carcass was in progress. At least one of the hams was retained for our own use, as well as one side of belly and loin, both to be cured on the wide stone bench which ran down the whole of one side of the cellar. The cellar was the one beneath the living room; the cellar kitchen was beneath the room. The ham and side of bacon were laid on the bench and spread all over with salt, to which a pinch of saltpetre was added. The salt cured, the saltpetre hardened so that the resulting bacon was firm to cut (not wet and soggy like today's bacon). The salt was pure cooking variety, bought in a large block about 9" x 9" x 16". With a large carving knife, Mother would cut a slice down from one end on to a sheet of paper where it was crushed fine with a rolling pin. It was then ready for use for sprinkling on red cabbage before pickling, for all cooking and for curing the hams and bacon. The salt was rubbed into the flesh and inspected daily, when a little more was rubbed in where necessary, and to prevent putrefaction around the bone cavities, a little saltpetre was sprinkled in between bone and flesh. After approximately one week, they were turned over, and the treatment repeated to the other side. When satisfactorily cured, the salt was washed off and the meat hung up to dry out.

After a few days, both ham and bacon were tied tightly in muslin bags to prevent attack by flies, and hung on large hooks in the wall at the side of the staircase. There were always one or two hams and a flitch of bacon hanging on the staircase between the two living rooms, the wall being protected from grease by hefty sticks which was put behind to prevent them touching. As the cutting up continued, with my order book beside him, Father made them up for delivery, carefully wrapping in greaseproof paper, pricing and labelling them for Elijah and myself to deliver. I helped to deliver the local ones, carrying the lightest in a small wicker basket, whilst Elijah had the larger orders in a large butcher's type basket. I liked delivering, there was a certain pride, even at such a young age, in vending one's own produce, and I gathered many a penny tip in the bargain.

My Father's favourite meals at pig killing time were spare rib 'Sparerib' pie, chitterlings and pig's fry. The pie was made with the ribs which had most of the meat removed, leaving quite a generous amount still attached to them, the trimmed off meat being added to that set aside for the pork pies, which were my Mother's next job. Bones were not, by any stretch of the imagination, the usual ingredient with which to fill a pie, but on the principle that the closer the bone the sweeter the meat, I can well understand why he enjoyed his 'Spare rib' pie. After all, even today, a time of abundance, there are those who enjoy barbecued spare rib. The chitterlings were another matter. No one was allowed to clean the small intestines but Father himself. Running them in copious amounts of cold water; cleaning them with salt very carefully so as to remove every trace of whatever one might call it from the wrinkled inside membranes, turning them inside out until he was quite sure that they were without taint. They were then boiled until tender when their protein content solidified as in all meat, and were eaten with lots of pepper and salt, with a dash of vinegar, accompanied by bread and butter. Chitterlings could also be bought from the pork butcher along with the bag, but Father would never buy them in case they hadn't been cleaned well enough. I must admit to being partial to them myself and, as my Father was heard to say, "What doesn't poison feeds; and strength goes in at the mouth."

Pig's fry was a simple casserole of liver, meat, heart and a piece of veiling, the latter being the membrane of the stomach which had a network of fat in a lacy pattern. Pig's fry for customers was always wrapped in a bit of veiling before being wrapped in paper for delivery. Kidney was never added to our fry, Dad said it wasn't good, it being the filter of the body. Neither did we ever eat fry in the traditional way, my Father preferred it casseroled; saying it went further.

As a side swipe so to speak, Father was good at economising, even though we were blessed with an abundance of food. When frying the ham for Sunday breakfast and we were late rising, every drop of 'dip' had to be eaten and the longer it stood on the hob, the more fat there was in which to dip our bread. Nothing was allowed to be left on the plate, although he always left a tiny morsel on the edge of his own plate. "It's more polite for grownups" he said, "It shows you've had sufficient." To us he said "You work to provide food, don't waste it." Sometimes he would come home with a pocket full of field mushrooms from his before breakfast walk, which he fried after the bacon, and after crisping them in the fat, he poured boiling water over them, reducing it to a gravy consistency and served up a plateful each. It required two or three slices of bread to clear the plate. And, of course, there was the classic Yorkshire pudding. Not the little buns served these days, but good big ones made in a large pudding tin and cut into squares, served with lots of gravy before the meat course in the true Yorkshire tradition. The correct way to cook a traditional Yorkshire pudding was under the joint as it was being rotated on a spit hanging in front of a hot fire. The juices from the meat fell into the pudding, giving it an added flavour and conserved the juices. On occasions I have utilised a grid in the roasting tin and cooked the pudding underneath, but I prefer to have the drippings in the gravy rather than the pudding. Ours at home was always cooked separately because my Father liked very thin pudding with crisp edges, and only baking could produce that.

Of course there were lots of cheap nourishing meals in those days, and people weren't ashamed to admit to economising as the 'Jones' element seems to frown on in the affluent society of today. They need time to prepare, but the result is much more rewarding than the boredom from watching repeat television programmes, and who knows, a dinner party could be greatly enlivened with a good casserole of sheep's head broth, marrow bone soup or good old fashioned hash made with every known vegetable and served on a thick slice of bread rather than dishes from foreign field like goulash, coq-au-vin or pot-au-feu which is, after all, only beast cheek hash under another name. And what's wrong with heart, wrapped in foil and baked very slowly until tender, which used to be served in some of the largest hotels as roast goose? You could feed a family of children for a week on a beast heart; or a good Lancashire Hot Pot, or a tender wild rabbit. My Father had the snickling rights on the moor above the brickyard, selling rabbits for 6d or 1s.0d each to the villagers. If you have never tasted Yorkshire pudding with lashings of jugged rabbit gravy, you've never really tasted Yorkshire pudding.

My favourite breakfast was oatmeal porridge. Mom put a quantity of medium oatmeal into the large stew pot and put it in the oven just before going to bed. In the morning, there was a lovely crusty layer around the pot where it had boiled and risen, and sunk as it cooled. With a large wooden spoon, she stirred it and added a little hot milk to break down the lumps. I loved lumpy porridge and always begged Mom "Don't break all the lumps," so that I could have some of them to chew on. Then there was udder, bought in a chunk from the butcher, boiled until firm and served on Saturday breakfast with bread and butter when cold. But my Mother was wise, she knew that children did not live on bread alone, nor did they thrive without a luxury now and then; filling meals were alright but they could prove a trifle boring if not relieved occasionally with some sweetmeat or other and the long stone bench in the cellar came in handy in the preparation of such delicacies as the spirit moved her to make.

Sometimes two large slabs of short pastry would be seen cooling on racks or large pastry boards, whilst she made thick custard, spreading it over one sheet of pastry to a thickness of about an inch or more, and covering it with the other sheet, like a sandwich. When completely cold, she would sprinkle it with icing sugar and cut it into conveniently sized slices to appear on the tea table later that Sunday for it was usually Sunday when she found time for such work. Then there was the coconut ice. Sweets without buying them was luxury indeed and Mom made a very tasty variety in pink and white by boiling two teacups of white sugar with half a cupful of water and three quarters of a cupful of coconut, melting this slowly then boiling it for about twelve minutes. She would then beat it until it was sugary and well mixed. Then half would be poured into a small bread tin, whilst the other half was tinted pink with a little cochineal. When cool, it was turned out on to a sheet of greaseproof paper and placed on the cellar bench until set enough to cut into slices.

Mom had her own way of doing some things which made them much more acceptable and tasty than the usual method; her apple charlotte for instance. Instead of using fingers of bread as usually advocated, she used breadcrumbs to line the basin, pressing them into a thick wall on to the well-buttered sides and bottom, using a generous layer to cover the top before sprinkling it with sugar and dotting with blobs of butter to make it crunchy. When it was turned out she served it with lots of creamy custard. There was the 'lardy cake' (fat cake she called it), which was made from yeast dough saved from bread making. About half a pound of dough was rolled out and dotted in rows with home rendered lard; then sprinkled with sugar with a layer of currants. It was then folded into three like puff pastry and rolled out; the whole procedure repeated twice more before the final moulding into a round and then set to prove before baking. Sometimes a plain one was made without fruit or sugar, which would later be split and served with a generous layer of butter and eaten with cheese. Not for these days of cholesterol warnings you might think, but then, all good things hold some danger don't you think? And as the saying goes 'a little bit of what you fancy does you good'.

Bread dough came into its own at Christmas too; for making mince pies and tarts. Dad didn't like mince pies that dropped to pieces in his fingers, preferring something that had a bit more 'bite'. "I like to be able to bite 'em" he said. This time Mom worked in a bit more lard into the dough and then let it stand for a while before rolling out. You should try it some time! Of course, we had the usual teacakes, any stale ones being used up in bread puddings or toasted for tea, and Mom was well known for her delicious scones. Her hot cross buns were unconventional, no spices, as nobody liked them, but with extra currants to compensate, and the crosses were made with a sharp knife, not the type seen today with strips of pastry, a custom I had never seen until many years later, when home baking disappeared for the commercially produced substitutes.

There was one other delicacy (I call it that because I was very fond of it; other people might have different ideas). I mean 'beestings custards'. Our milk was delivered every day by Uncle Joe from his farm at Woodthorpe, Holmesfield. He came in a horse drawn milk cart and carried the milk in large urns from which he filled a two gallon can as needed. To serve the milk, he swung the can up and under his arm, tipping it forward to pour out the quantity required into a little gill, half pint or pint measure before tipping it into the waiting jug. Nobody had fridges, and milk was not pasteurised as it is today, so in hot weather, milk was scaled (brought to boiling point and held there for a few seconds without actually boiling). Then it was poured into a jug which had been well cooled under a running tap, and then it was covered with a little muslin cover which had heavy beads stitched all round to weigh it down. (Beads could be bought in little boxes, and any spare piece of muslin was utilised for the milk jug covers). In this way there was little danger of sour milk, but if by some freak of weather and the milk turned sour, Mom would boil it until the whey parted from the curds, when it was strained and the curds mixed with a little sugar, a squeeze of lemon, a few currants, and a pinch of nutmeg. Then filled into little patty tins lined with pastry. Alternatively the sour milk would be added to the scone mix instead of fresh, it was never wasted.

Now, back to the beestings custards. When a calf was born, the first milk was given to the calf because it contained the cholesterol necessary for its survival. The following milkings held progressively less of the substance and about the third milking it was good for human consumption. The chief benefit to the cook was that it would set into firm custard without the addition of eggs and the flavour was slightly different especially with the liberal sprinkling of nutmeg which Mom put on before baking. Before making the custard to test for setting, about a quarter-pint was put in to a dish in the oven, to indicate how much, if any, milk should be added. In the absence of fridges, during hot weather, when the Sunday joint of meat, particularly beef, was received usually on Friday, all housewives would seal it in order for it to keep sweet until Sunday. Against all the modern advice given by so-called experts, that meat should not be cooked twice, it was sealed by putting into a hot oven and heated through until about 1/4" all over was thoroughly cooked forming a crusty layer which prevented putrefaction, when it was put aside to cool until its full cooking on Sunday. I never heard of anyone getting food poisoning through this method, as they certainly would have done had the meat been left under the muslin cover until the surface putrefied.

And now, back to the pig. As cutting up proceeded, there were lots of parings of good lean meat, and this is what Mom used for her pork pies. She made two, one for immediate consumption; the other, which weighed about 3lbs, was stored in the stone bench in the curing cellar for tea on Christmas Day. Although this was about six weeks after the pig was killed in November, the pie kept well in the cold weather, and an almost fridge cold cellar. It amazes me now how we could do justice to the tea we had on Christmas Day after the colossal dinner we had consumed only about three hours before, the time in-between spent in chewing nuts and eating oranges and apples from our stockings.

The pies were made with hot water pastry, the small one raised in the traditional way, adding the filling to support the crust from within whilst easing the pastry upwards with the hands and tying a strong fold of greaseproof paper around the outside to support it whilst cooking. The pies, filled with this luscious lean corn fed pork were deliciously well seasoned but, as I remember, without herbs, although according to my Mother's cookery book, which I still have today, she did recognise that herbs could be added, if desired. The larger pie was, of necessity, baked in a large cake tin with a loose bottom, the tin being lined with a double layer of greaseproof paper to prevent fat oozing out too much. It would be difficult, well almost impossible to raise a pie with hot pastry of such dimensions without support. Nevertheless, it was just as delicious served with winter salad made from Dad's January King cabbage or the tender heart of a freshly cut savoy. Mixed with home grown onions and, if they had ripened in the bottom drawer of the big dresser, the last of the seasons tomatoes from the greenhouse Dad had built in the back garden. There were no tomatoes in the shops in those days during the winter, until the first of the season arrived from the Canaries and, about February, the first of the English and Dutch so any surplus of home grown were bottled for winter use or made into chutneys and pickles. The same applied to cucumbers which were almost unobtainable from October to February, although one could very often obtain one by ordering for a special occasion, when the price was very high.

Vegetables in winter were limited to brassicas, with perhaps a meal of winter spinach or any of the root vegetables, including Swedes, which were grown by the farmer by the acre for cattle feed, and human consumption. However, one year, Dad had a brilliant idea; something he had heard and he would try anything once. A preserving enthusiast had told him how to prepare runner beans, the large ones which grew up poles, which we called kidney beans, by sealing them in a tin and burying them in the garden until Christmas Day. Always ready to try, Father selected a large 4lb biscuit tin and filled it to the brim with beans in order to exclude all air, an important point, he was told. The tin was sealed carefully with tape and buried in a convenient spot in the back garden. Christmas Day arrived, snow covered the ground, but Father was quite sure he could locate the spot where he had buried the tin. He dug there, he dug here, we watched as he continued to dig everywhere. (There was no need for spring digging that year). Tensions grew, all the neighbours came out to watch thinking he was burying a body or something. But, determined not to be beaten; after about half an hour, the elusive beans were found and retrieved from their burial place. He carried the tin triumphantly back to the house where Mom had a pan of boiling water at the ready, for time was getting short if the beans were to be cooked for Christmas Day this year.

We all stood round waiting expectantly as the lid was unsealed and removed, and there, before our eager eyes, lay the beans, a rotten putrefied brown mass of decomposed vegetable matter, and the odour which rose from the conglomeration competed successfully with that from the midden in high summer. Father never tested the same theory twice.

The row of cottages at Lane Head were the last houses between Totley and Baslow, six miles away, and on a direct route from Sheffield to Bakewell, a matter of 16 miles. Consequently, we were in a direct line for tramps that walked from the Workhouse in Sheffield to the next one at Bakewell. Tramps could stay in the Workhouse for one night (I believe they had some work to do whilst there to qualify). When they left, they were given bread for one meal only and, I think, 1s.0d towards the next day and night's lodgings. My Father had a good deal of sympathy for tramps, as his own father, so we were often told, had to leave home looking for work in the 1880s. He told my mother never to turn away a tramp without a crust of bread and if he was at home when one called, the 'traveller' received, not a crust of bread, but half a loaf spread with dripping or jam, sufficient for two or three meals, and probably 1s.0d too. I vow there was a mark on our wall in tramp's language telling all future tramps that this house was a 'good cop' for they never hesitated to call.

My Father was generous to all souls who seemed to be worse off than us; if they were disabled in any way, or just trying to earn an honest living. I remember the chickens he always sent to 'Dicky Fortnight' and his two sisters on Christmas Day every year. The Wainwright's lived in the middle cottage next to Mrs Thomas who gave us the 1d for running errands. All three were behind the door when brains were handed out, two slices short of a whole loaf so to speak, but not exactly with a screw loose. Every year they accepted the chicken with guarded thanks, except on the last occasion when I delivered it. One of the sisters answered the door and, seeing what I had brought, pushed me away with a tart "Get off; we don't want your charity." I was a bit taken aback, but when I told my Father what she had said, he was nonplussed, "Never mind lass, it's alright." He seemed to understand the situation entirely.

There was hardly a day passed without someone earning a living by begging, if that's not too unkind a word. There was the 'Herdy Gerdy' man, who plonked his Herdy Gerdy in the centre of the road, and turned the handle quickly to render a lively tune whilst we were eating tea. And there was the very polite man with a 'club foot' who came once a week, who also stood in the middle of the road playing a selection of tunes on his cornet, and would take requests for favourite tunes if anyone cared to ask. Soon after Mom and Dad had returned from their holiday in Blackpool, when a corner player had played 'Standchen Serenade' outside the Palace Theatre, Mom sent me out to ask him to play it for her. He was, we learned, a trained musician who had hit bad times in the depression and it seemed no tune was beyond his scope. Neither of these men actually came to the house begging for money after playing, they stood for a few minutes when someone from each house would come out with a copper or two, always received with very polite thanks and a touch of the forelock in respect, and then they went on their way to stand before another row of houses.

The umbrella man came round periodically and asked politely if he could repair umbrellas. The rag and bone man came about once a month with a balloon and a little windmill fastened to his horse's head, and we would run to Mom to see if she could find a few rags so that we could have a balloon. It was more for a windmill, and quite a bundle if you wanted a 1d. The scissor grinder came once in a while, but Dad usually sharpened ours as he did all the knives, including those he used for carving and cutting up the pigs. Every Sunday he sharpened the carving knife on the front step before finishing it off on large steel. You could cut the meat thinner with a sharp knife, and Dad knew all the tricks.

Mrs Somerset called round once a week with a huge wicker basket full of fish. She had a shop somewhere in Sheffield and a few more customers were 'grist to the mill' I suppose. Then there was the pikelet man. He called about once a week too, selling muffins and pikelets freshly made in his shop in Sheffield. And there were the gypsies. I imagine there was a gypsy sign on the wall along with that of the tramps, for they called round regularly with their baskets of lace and clothes pegs they had made from branches cut from willow trees. They were simply made by splitting the wood and shaping with a penknife then fixing together again with a narrow piece of tin wrapped around the end. Mom said they were the best; they were springy and never left the line. Mom wouldn't turn away a gypsy, "It's unlucky," she said. We were never short of bits of lace or clothes pegs for she always found a copper from somewhere for a gypsy. I've known Mom search every pocket for a halfpenny when a bill needed paying, but she always found one for the situation. A gypsy once told her she would live to be 92, and she firmly believed it; it must have been correct because a gypsy told her so. Actually the gypsy wasn't far wrong; Mom lived for a month after her 93rd birthday.

I was about seven years old when Dad took us to Blackpool for the first time. My Mother had recently received a small amount of money on an insurance policy and soon after, when they were talking about Mrs Green, an old friend of my Mother's who had taken a boarding house in Blackpool, my Father said "I wish I could take the kids to Blackpool for a week," and Mum said "Well, why can't you. There's my insurance money." "That's yours," my Father protested, but Mom persuaded him to use it. "It's better spent on that than anything else," she said. So, on a windy day in September, we left Central Station at Blackpool, along with the Marshall family, who had decided to have a holiday too, although they stayed somewhere else, and we didn't see them again during the week. But I do remember Mrs Marshall's umbrella turning inside out in the wind, a job for the repairer I guess.

We had left Dore & Totley Station early in the morning on a journey which was comparatively uneventful, except that any journey, especially by train was an exciting adventure. As we neared Manchester, Dad told us to stand at the window and see the children, all with bare feet, scrambling down the embankment and even up to the railway lines. He gave us all a few pennies to throw down to the children as they shouted "penny-down, penny-down". Dad explained that they were begging because their fathers were out of work and they had no money for food. "But," he added, which I couldn't quite understand at the time, "They'll go back home now, and put their shoes on until the next train comes." Cynical or shrewd?

We spent a lot of time on the beach, and particularly liked to watch the Salvation Army Band which played every morning. There was a tiny little woman who went round with a collecting bag while the rest of the Army girls sang 'My cup is full and running over'. Jeff was three years old and although he enjoyed watching the band as much as he did, one day when we were leaving, Mom realised that Jeff was missing. Dad searched everywhere but Jeff could not be found, so after about an hour we went back to the boarding house in Dean Street near the Pleasure Beach at South Shore, all very worried and despondent. When we arrived at the house, there was Jeff safe and sound. He'd seen the boatmen near the central pier hauling the pleasure boats up the beach and had gone to join in. He couldn't see what all the fuss was about. "I knew where we were staying," was all he explained.

We went to Blackpool two or three times after that, taking most of our food with us. Mrs Green charged 3s.6d a night for a double room, and we had two, with two double beds in one of them for the same price. On top of this was 6d for the use of the cruet, and a small cost for potatoes which she supplied so that they could all be cooked in one pan. We had brought peas which Dad had shelled so that we could carry more, kidney beans, lettuce, cucumbers and tomatoes to last us a week, and each morning Mom and Dad went shopping on Bond Street for meat, and something for tea like salmon. Then Mom sat at one of the tables in the dining room along with some other visitors doing the same thing, slicing the beans if that's what we were to have that day. I once went into the kitchen for something whilst the vegetables were cooking. The top of a giant gas stove was full of pans of all sizes, each containing different greens, with one huge panful of potatoes. I wondered how she could remember whose was which, but when I asked Mom she just said "its practice."

Once when we went to Blackpool, when I was about eleven years old, which would be in 1926, we went, as we often did, on to the sand hills on South Shore. There was nothing beyond the Pleasure Beach but sand hills between Blackpool and St Anne's but whilst we were there, a small airfield had been set up and twin-seater biplanes were taking people for short flights around Blackpool for 5s.0d a flight. I asked Dad if I could have a go, expecting him to say "No, it's too expensive," but surprisingly he said I could, and after being told to sit in the front seat, the pilot in the back one, we soared up into the air with the wind nearly taking off my scalp, marvelling at the scene below. "There's the Pleasure Beach," the pilot said, "and there's the Tower," and we were zooming over the piers and circling round over the sea and back again to a thrilling landing. I was the only one in the family who remembered the planes, or thought I was, until one day mentioning it to Jeff he said "I'm glad you've mentioned that, nobody believes me when I tell them I went up as well." It seemed that no-one in Lytham could remember such an event, but both Jeff and I remember it well.

Blackpool was a wonderful place for a holiday in the 1920s, there was the Tower and the Zoo in the basement and Reginald Dixon playing on the huge Wurlitzer organ which Mom loved to listen to; in later years watching Elijah and I dancing on that wonderful mosaic dance floor. There were trips to Stanley Park and tram rides to Fleetwood to watch the boats, and the wonderful illuminations if we happened to be there in September, as we usually were. Then there was the Golden Mile; rows and rows of side stalls, with every known performer appearing during the season, and some characters only Blackpool could produce. Like the Fat Lady in her dark tent which you paid 1d to enter; The Vicar of Stoicey, the notorious Vicar who had seduced one of his female congregation and been de-frocked for his efforts. And the man with the Macura machine, a small contraption like a hand drill with a rubber pad instead of the drill which health enthusiasts used to massage their bodies. The performer was selling something, and to entice a crowd, he ran around bending down and whirring his Macura machine and calling his imaginary rabbit. Crowds collected during his performance only to disperse when he stopped and started the real sales talk.

Best of all was when it rained. Then we went on to the Pleasure Beach, not only to have a go on the coconut shies or Noah's Ark, but to stand under a six sided stand with a roof to repel the rain, and counters all round on which sheets of music were displayed. In the centre was a piano, the pianist playing whatever tune was requested. 'The Isle of Capri', 'When it's moonlight in the Rockies', 'Ramona'. 'When the clouds go rolling by', and 'Josephine' from the new film 'Little Women' there were dozens of them all sung for the purpose of selling the sheets of music. Another man encouraged singing, waving a small baton to keep everybody in tune, whilst they read the words from a black cloth which he unrolled from the ceiling. A whole afternoon was spent singing, returning after tea if it was still raining.

Early in 1927, Dad bought a motorbike and a few weeks later decided to go touring Wales with Jeff, aged seven, as company. They returned a week later having travelled hundreds of miles and thought he rode the pillion as if he had been born to it. A few weeks later, Dad bought a sidecar so that Mom and the rest of us could go for rides, the first one to Hathersage to see Aunt Elizabeth. Aunt Elizabeth was Mom's Great Aunt, her Grandmother's sister. She was a 'canny' little woman, very kind and gentle, in a long black skirt and buttoned up boots; she always wore a black apron during the week and a white one on Sundays. Her hair was scraped back in a bun at the back of her head, as all the ladies of her age, and when she went out, a poke bonnet sat on top of the bun with ribbons tied in a bow under her chin to hold it in place. An ankle length cape, with a small cape over the shoulders put the final touch to her ensemble. She lived in a tiny cottage just off the main street at Hathersage, on a lane which led to Brookfield Manor. When the time came for returning home, it was rather a crush trying to get all the bodies back into the sidecar, when Aunt Elizabeth suggested they leave me behind and collect me the following Saturday. "She can play with Mary and Annie," she told my Father. They were her granddaughters who lived in a cottage on the main street near the Methodist Chapel. I needed no second bidding. Jumping out of the sidecar I stood and waved goodbye and thus started my first of many holidays at Hathersage.

The following Saturday, Aunt Elizabeth suggested that she should come to Lane Head and look after us whilst Mom and Dad spent a week's holiday at Blackpool without us. It was September so we had returned to school, and she said "It'll do you both good to get away on your own for a while." As she lived alone, perhaps she saw it as a change for herself also. Nevertheless, she was very welcome and kept house for us in her own unique way. Edward Dalton, her husband, died about 1990 and left her with four children, the eldest 13, the youngest (Auntie Annie) aged two years old. Samuel the eldest and Reuben Elliott who lodged with them obtained work on the building of Derwent dam and the family moved from Totley to Hathersage for convenience. But, even with one son working and little from Reuben, money was scarce and Elizabeth took in washing and did dressmaking to supplement their income. (She was a dressmaker before her marriage, never going out of 'service' as her two sisters did.) Naturally she developed a thrifty outlook and never wasted a morsel, nor encouraged an expensive appetite.

She looked after us well, although now 80 years old, but our meals were substantial and filling rather than small delicately presented morsels, after which we might be hungry an hour after eating. One economy which stands out in my mind was teatime, when we could have unlimited bread and jam and one cake, or a piece of cake. But it was only bread and jam, no butter on the bread, "If you want butter, then no jam, if you want jam, it's good enough without butter." However, there was one compensation, albeit one instigated by my Father. Every morning, Aunt Elizabeth lined us up at the door ready for school, when she examined us to see if we were clean, turning each hand to make sure, then out of the extremely large pocket of her encircling apron, she pulled out a few pennies, pressing one in each hand, and planting a kiss on each head as we went on our way. We missed our parents, and were glad to see them home again, but even today I still remember the kindness of Aunt Elizabeth.

Our parents said they had enjoyed their holiday, but "Never again," said my Mother, "will we go without the children; it just wasn't the same." They did enjoy one night which would never have happened had we been there; the cost would have been too great. They paid a visit to the Palace Theatre or the Winter Gardens, I'm not sure which, when the play was 'The Battle of Zeebrugge'. "It was magnificent," said my Mother, as she told us about it, "The whole stage was lowered and flooded and the ships sailed on just like on the actual sea. The noise of the guns was deafening." It was very vivid as she related the scene (actually I think this was the Battle of Jutland which occurred in 1916, why it was called the 'Battle of Zeebrugge' in Blackpool, I haven't found out). Nevertheless, it made a profound impression on my Mother, as did the cornet player who played

'Standchen' when they came out of the theatre, for she went straight to the Pleasure Beach stand and bought the music for me to play.

The next time I stayed with Mary and Annie, and their Mom and Dad and two older brothers, Ernest and George. Mom was Auntie Annie, Mom's second cousin. She was always full of fun, until Rueben, her husband, died suddenly two or three years later when all the fun seemed to have drained from her, and she seldom smiled again. But that first holiday with them was exciting. There was the festival and Flag Day when Mary had a big box of the prettiest flags I have ever seen. There were butterflies and bees and all kinds of flowers, cut out of cardboard and embossed in the liveliest colours. And there was the organ at the Chapel. Mr Speed the tuner came from Dronfield to keep it tuned, and someone had to ply the bellows to fill the pipes so that he could play. Usually a man from the village did this job, but he was ill so Mr Speed asked if we two girls could manage to pump hard enough, otherwise he would have to come again. We said we would try and going into the little pump room behind the organ, we took hold of the big shaft and tried our best to push it down. The bellows were large and made of strong material and it took all our strength to move the great bar, the only thing was for one of us to sit on it, the other one adding her weight on the down stroke. In this way we succeeded in keeping enough wind in the bellows for Mr Speed to finish the job, being rewarded by a couple of sweets from his pocket.

One day Mr Smith said that Louis could go to Rotherham for the day to see her Aunt, Mrs Smith's sister, if Dad would let me go to keep her company. Dad agreed but he warned us that there was going to be a big meeting of unemployed at Rotherham that Saturday, which would most likely end in a riot and that if we saw a crowd anywhere, we were not to go anywhere near them. "Now remember," he told us, "if those men get angry, they'll be dangerous, so if you see any crowds you must nip down another road and ask someone how to get to Louie's Auntie."

We promised to do as he said, and taking a bus to Millhouses, then a tram to Fitzalan Square, and another to Rotherham, we alighted at the stop that Mrs Smith had told us. We hadn't walked very far when we saw in front of a big building a few hundred yards away, which we learned later was the Town Hall, a big crowd, who seemed to be doing a lot of waving and shouting. We were just passing a large park, with a railing fence, but a little further back we had seen a wrought iron gate leading into the park. "Look," I said, "that woman back there told us to go round the corner and down the next road to the left didn't she?" Louie agreed. "Then," I suggested, "if we can get through that gate into the park, we should be able to cross to that far corner and find a way out on to the road round the corner." Louie agreed again, "Come on let's try," she said crossing the road in the direction of the gate.

We were a bit worried as there was no-one else in the park and, being country girls, we wondered if people were allowed in on Saturday, or whether it was empty because of the meeting. However, we reached the far corner and finding another gate, we arrived, as we had thought, in the right road and within a few minutes were safe with Louie's Auntie. The streets were quite empty when she accompanied us herself back to the tram to ensure we were safe and when eventually we arrived home, Dad was very pleased. He felt we had shown a lot of common sense saying "It's very important to keep out of trouble rather than to try and get out of it." We read in the paper the following Monday that the crowd was so dangerous that the Riot Act was read and many people arrested. The Riot Act was passed in 1715. It decreed that a crowd of more than twelve people must disperse in one hour of the Act being read, or they would be arrested for murder as felons. The Act was first read in London, Oxford, Norwich and Bristol in the 18th century by a solicitor but after the formation of the Police Force, they took on the responsibility, both for reading the Act and for dispersal of the crowd.

I was about eleven years old when, as a treat, Dad decided to take Elijah, Nellie Smith and me to the pictures at Abbeydale Picture House. I had never been to the pictures before, but I had heard a lot about them, and like my brothers, collected cigarette cards of photographs of film stars like Claudette Colbert, Greta Garbo, Norma Shearer, Bette Davies, Nelson Eddy and Clive Brook, which were given in packets of cigarettes. The films, of course, were silent. Talking films didn't hit the screens until 1927, when 'Showboat' and 'Sonny Boy' came to London and later in the provincial cinemas. The cost of entrance to Abbeydale Picture House was 9d in the 1930s; in 1927 it was probably about 6d. The film was Charlie Chaplin in the 'Gold Rush'. It was exciting; I can remember seeing Charlie sitting in his old wooden hut on the edge of a precipice in a snowbound landscape of the Rockies, cooking and eating his boots and his consternation when the hut was hit by a sudden gust of wind and taken sky high and away, leaving him sitting there in deep snow. It would be many years later before I went to the pictures again, for country children have far too many other things to do, and the expense of travel to Sheffield would be a burden on the budget.

Town children and those nearer to a cinema were more regular visitors. In some districts there were special performances on Saturday mornings at the cost of 1d. It was somewhere for them to go while Mum and Dad did the shopping, or they could get out of the way for other reasons. I remember our cousins, Teddy, Arthur, Ernest, Frank and Jacky who lived at Newton near Alfreton. They went to Tibshelf a few miles away every Saturday when the films were always serials; and ensured they attended the following week for the next instalment. They usually ended on a dramatic moment with the villain in his top hat and heavy moustache leaving the heroine, usually Pearl White, tied to the railway line, missing death by inches as the train approached to within a yard of the poor girl. Just as it reached her, the film was cut and the message on the screen read 'Continued next week'.

Uncle Teddy had a big family and by the mid-1930s he had ten children. I remember my Father chastising him quietly on one occasion when the penultimate child was conceived. "You should think about Florrie you know," he said. I learned later that Auntie Florrie had been my Father's girlfriend before she married Uncle Teddy, and he always had a soft spot for her. We occasionally went to Newton to see our cousins. Unfortunately, poor Jacky, always laughing, worked on the Burma Road and died of tuberculosis in Africa after being rescued after the war. I stayed once for a few days when Arthur, Frank and Jackie took me fishing in a stream nearby.

They threaded worms on to a pin fastened on a piece of string and I learned to do the same. Lying flat on my stomach or kneeling on the edge of the bank and letting the worm sink under the water very gently, I hoped to capture a big minnow. I had already been shown how to tickle trout by Elijah on visits to the brook in Gillfield Road, although I wasn't very successful at it, and of course it was an offence, but we were careful not to be caught.

Uncle Teddy was much more easy going than my Father; he was gentle, and when visiting us, he always had a bag of 'tuffies' in his pocket. Auntie Florrie was not as industrious as my Mother either, except in producing children, and Ethel, the eldest of the family, had a tough time as the family grew bigger for she was the hardest worked in the household. Being such a large family it was impossible for all of them to sit round the table at the same time, but the living room was also the kitchen with the copper at the side of the sink. The copper-top provided a convenient overflow for some of the boys (they were all boys except Ethel and Avis, next to the youngest). Elijah stayed once and he was assigned to the copper-top for his meals with one of the boys. Years after, he said that what he remembered most was the sticky copper-top from previous servings of rice pudding.

Mealtimes at our house were much more formal occasions in comparison to some of my friends. Dad was strict about table behaviour; one sniff and he would say "Get off in the room and blow your nose." We weren't allowed to eat and drink at the same time; if he glimpsed one of us attempting to pick up a cup before our mouths were completely empty, he would snap out "Empty your mouth before you drink." On Sundays I used to look with envy on the Smith's children who were allowed to buy a bottle of Tizer from Mrs Ward's next door who kept a little shop as my Mother had done years before. Mr Smith delivered newspapers on Sunday morning for a few extra coppers for the family budget, earning I think 2s.6d for his morning's work. On his return, the younger children ran to meet him to collect the few coppers for the Tizer to drink with their Sunday dinner. My Father wouldn't let us have even a drink of water. If you were thirsty you had a drink before sitting down and waited until everyone had finished before getting another.

As young children, we all stood at table, Elijah and I being the first to be allowed to sit down. Geoff stood at the back of the table and Jeff, when too old to sit on Mom's knee, stood at the front in between Mom at one corner and Dad at the other. When Jeff was about five years old Dad bought a stool for him to sit on; still between them and in front of the fire. He had a habit of leaning back on the two back legs, for which he was severely chastised, but once he leaned too far and landed in the fireplace. Luckily he was grabbed by Dad before any damage was done. When Jeff went to the war, Arthur inherited the stool and sat in the same place, with the same habit! More of this later.

Another of Dad's aversions was women who whistled. All three of the boys could whistle, but no matter how they tried to teach me, I couldn't get a note out, possibly because every time I tried, my Father happened to be around the corner and packed me off into the house. "A whistling lass and a crowing hen is good for neither mice nor men," he said. Mom loved to hear men whistling, she said they were happy at their work if they were whistling. At 6.00 p.m. every evening, we could hear a man whistling as he came on the flat and down towards the house. "Here's Norman," she used to say, "You can put your watch right by Norman's whistle." Norman worked for Creswicks on Moorwood Lane and he whistled all the popular tunes and some classics, as sweet as any opera tenor.

Bonfire night was second only in importance to Christmas, a great occasion for the whole of Lane Head. The bonfire was made on the back field before Dad ploughed it up to make a garden. We gathered logs from the wood and collected all sorts of waste wood, or anything that would burn, just as children do today, and there was great excitement when it was dark enough and all the fathers came out to supervise the event. Lots of newspapers were stuffed into a convenient hole in the pile of wood where the wind would take the flames into the stack, and a great roar went up when a long stick was set alight and thrust into the hole. We had scrubbed large potatoes and we stuck them on the end of long sticks, poking them into the bottom of the fire when it became red and glowing. Sometimes one fell off, or the stick caught fire, then after a lot of poking around in the embers, one of the dads or an older brother would succeed in pulling it out, badly burned; but that didn't matter, the blacker they were, the more they were enjoyed. Mom made parkin about two weeks before bonfire night and stored it in a large stew pot in the cellar. By bonfire night it had become all sticky and delicious. Dad made bonfire toffee in a small iron saucepan. He put in a pound of sugar and a big spoonful of treacle, a large piece of butter and a tablespoonful of vinegar to make it brittle. He stood over the fire stirring it until the sugar dissolved and kept an eye on it until it bubbled and thickened, then to test it, he filled a cup with cold water and fetched out the large steel that he sharpened the knives on. He dipped the steel into the water and then into the toffee, turning it round to get a good layer of toffee on it, then straight into the cold water again to see how near to setting it had become. We watched as he pushed it up and off the end of the steel like a barley sugar stick. If it was still soft, it was boiled a little longer, and when we all had a tester to chew or crunch and he was satisfied that it was cooked, he poured it into one of Mom's backing trays to set. When quite cold, he tapped the tray underneath with the handle of the steel and broke it into pieces all ready to eat.

Dad was a good provider; every year he went to Mr Stark at the Bents and bought a big carpetbag full of lovely big green eating apples, which he kept under the bed in his bedroom. We only had to ask and we could help ourselves. Straight off the tree they were delicious, all crunchy and spicy, not like some of those he bought during the winter from the market. Dad's trips to the market weren't all with Mom's blessing. When he arrived home with bags full of apples, oranges, grapes and grapefruit, fish and shellfish she responded very quietly, only conceding with a sideways glance as he unpacked his purchases. "If he'd give me half of what he's spent on that I'd make it go twice as far," she said on more than one occasion. For Dad wasn't too generous with the housekeeping money, yet he expected it to cover whatever he happened to fancy, like the tin of crab or lobster he preferred when Mom had already spent money on the meal she had prepared for him. Neither was he generous to us as far as money was concerned; he provided everything we needed, the clothes we wore; the provision was always to his choosing. The only real row I ever had with him when I was 19 years old over my clothes, when his anger or hurt showed in him saying "Haven't I been a good Father to you?" and I couldn't deny that he had, for is the choice of clothes more important than supplying them? Perhaps to a 19 year old, but he couldn't see the argument.

About the same time as the last incident, my Mother had said to me in a quiet moment, that she would like a new hat. I said "Why don't you ask him to buy you one?" "I'm not," she said emphatically, "if he can't see I need a new hat, I'll go without." "That's daft," I said, "if you want a new hat, he should buy you one, or go and buy one yourself out of the housekeeping money and let him whistle for his next tin of crab." But Mother wasn't like me. I was a 'Salt', not a 'Fisher' and my tactics were different from hers. The next Friday when we were setting off on the coal round (more of this later), I said to my Dad "Oh, by the way my Mother wants a new hat." He replied "Your Mother wants a new hat does she?" and before I could answer he added "then why doesn't she say so?" I reminded him that my Mother was independent and he should see that she wanted a new hat without having to tell him. He said no more but the following Saturday he returned from Sheffield with a large bag containing a new hat. My Mother took it without a word, then when she saw what it was, she thanked him (with little grace I might say) and tried it on. The thing about my Father was that he always knew what to do and how to do it and this time was no exception for the damned hat fit, and what's more it suited my Mother, and she liked it! I asked him later how he knew what she would like. He said, "I know what suits your Mother, and I know enough about her to know what size she takes." There was no competing with my Father; he was too damned clever by half.

I remember at least one Saturday when I was about nine years old when he responded to my pestering and agreed to take me to Sheffield with him. The fish market, as it was then called, was the main venue and I gaped open-mouthed to see all the stalls full of every kind of fish, each one described to me according to how good to eat they were, rather than how they had arrived on the slabs. One of his favourites was conger eel, a very white fish with a slimy skin which I thought revolting, but when cooked is firm and satisfying. And there were the shellfish which like him I could eat, not only at mealtimes, but any time in-between. Mussels were favourites to bring home, when he cleaned them of the beards and put them in a large iron pan on the fire with only the water they had been washed in, not white wine and umpteen vegetables and herbs we are told to use today. That is a continental influence, but our home produced mussels, like our meat, need no such additions to make them palatable and delicious. After a few good shakes of the pan, they were tipped out on to the sink, all the closed ones discarded, the rest served up with salt, pepper and vinegar, as a starter to whatever was the meal of the day. But the highlight of the visit to the market was to sample some of the shellfish set out on little saucers on the counters. At 2d a saucer you could choose cockles, mussels, whelks, winkles, all with salt, pepper and vinegar to put on according to your own palate Dad asked if I would like a saucer, and his eyes twinkled when I said I'd have one of the winkle ones. I'd seen a man using a pin to pull them out of the shells, and I wanted to have a go. After that I had a plate of shrimps, while Dad had whelks. He offered me one to try, but I couldn't get my teeth round it, I chewed for what seemed an eternity, without getting even an inroad into the flesh. He laughed and after struggling for some time, let me spit it out.

There came a time when Dad had to curb his likes and dislikes. He had been suffering from severe stomach pains for two or three years, which after an X-ray, proved to be from a duodenal ulcer. For two years he kept to a rigorous diet until it was cured, getting full support from Mom, who made him egg custards daily, with steamed fish of various kinds, and made slippery elm tea to add a lining to his stomach. After a year, he progressed to lean lamb chops and a little mashed potato and gradually, after two years, he returned to a normal diet with no further trouble. As with all diets, it is much easier with support and encouragement isn't it?

When writing about my Father I am writing from my own point of view, and from my own memories. The story might be different if told by any of the three boys, almost certainly it would if

111

told by Elijah himself. He was the eldest and the 'whipping boy' for all the rest. I don't remember my Father hitting either of the younger ones, and he certainly never laid a finger on me, but Elijah has memories of severe beatings at a very young age, it seems he was the 'butt' of my Father's temper, for Mom told me that he had a very hasty temper in his earlier years, tempered later, probably after the nervous breakdown. He wore a wide heavy leather belt over his knee breeches (such belts were worn by many miners to give support to the back in the crouched conditions down the pit, and the heavy work in setting props and shovelling coal). The leather belt was the weapon used in the thrashings of the young Elijah, who told me many years later, that the beatings broke his spirit and made him very unsure in years to come, a totally different reaction from my defiant one from the teasing of my young days.

There was sometimes a funny side, (for me, not for Elijah). I remember one thrashing, this time with a slipper. I had been out playing with the boys, some from the village included. I saw what they were doing, for they were always up to some innocent mischief. This time I feared for the result, for they had broken into the cricket pavilion on the Sic and were playing with the pads and stumps when Paskin, the village policeman appeared. Now the police constables and the sergeant who lived in the police house in Grange Terrace were very lenient with the village lads; Paskin more than the rest, but this time I could see trouble ahead when he eventually called to see my Father, which I knew he would. I rushed home in mild terror for the trouble I saw coming and plonked myself on the sofa waiting for the 'bomb to drop'. My Father had just washed and changed from his pit clothes so he was not wearing his belt, when a knock came to the door. I sat petrified with fear for the wrath I knew would come and when my Mother opened the door and invited P.C. Paskin into the living room, I saw the colour change in my Father's face. "You know Mr Salt; you'll have to control those lads of yours." "What have they done now?" said my Father. "They've broken into the cricket pavilion," said Paskin, "and you know Mr Salt, it won't do." With a mild warning to Father as to what would happen next time, he departed but Dad was in a furious mood, and I sat waiting in fear of what would happen. Eventually, Elijah arrived home, to a tirade from Father, who rushed to him, grabbed him by the scruff of the neck, and forced him over his knee. Off came a slipper and bang, bang, bang on Elijah's backside, whack after whack landed on that rear, making even my bum smart in sympathy. But Elijah, ever defiant, at every stroke, shouted "You're not hurting me, you're not hurting me," which only made Dad hit harder. The strokes and cries continued, Dad getting more exasperated, Elijah getting more defiant, until there had to be a truce.

Dad stopped hitting and Elijah stood up in front of him with hands behind holding his bottom, tears rolling down his face. Then in a final act of defiance, he drew back his shoulders and cried "You didn't hurt me, you didn't hurt me," and he turned yelling out of the door. I must admit, to my shame that laughed to myself at his defiance when it was obvious he had been hurt, very much. Such defiance belies the breaking of the spirit as he professes and his retaliation to situations was often funny (funny in a humorous way and not in a peculiar way). If Elijah accidentally tripped over a chair leg, he'd turn round and take a running punch at it, probably incurring more pain than the original tripping would have done, but with more satisfaction.

Strawberry Lea pit was a foot rill, (called a drift in Yorkshire and Durham), meaning that there was no shaft; entrance being from a hole in the hillside; coal and ganister being brought to the surface by horse drawn tubs. In earlier years, probably before there was sufficient headroom for a pony, a rope was attached to the tub, the other end being fastened to a winch on the surface. (It can still be seen there, although not used for many years). A pony was tethered to the winch, the rope being wound round it as the pony walked round and round in a circle.

When my Father was Manager, there were two pit ponies, one small brown one called Jenny, the other a larger grey one which was broader across the back and who passed wind a lot by the name of Dolly. When the shift was over, Charlie Smith led the brown one and my Father led the grey one to the field at the corner of Hillfoot Road and Penny Lane which belonged to Mr Dungworth, the Licensee of the Crown Inn. A favourite time to go to the pit to meet my Father was Saturday dinnertime, when he let us ride for a while on the back of one of the ponies. I liked to ride on Jenny, for she was more docile and my legs could span her back easier than Dolly's. The field was used by Dad for almost anything that took his fancy; at times he kept fowls in the shed, at other times he stored feeding stuff for goats and pigs and at one time he had two horses of his own.

Elijah carried the brunt of the work in looking after the livestock, including the animals. Before going to school each morning, he let out the fowls and fed them, returning every evening to fasten them in the shed away from foxes. Dad once bought a litter of 'rickety' pigs, which were so weak they just wanted to lie around all day. Elijah's job was to get them on their feet and run them round the field three times a day, morning and dinnertime and after school to strengthen their legs. At one time there were eight goats tethered at intervals down the centre of the field. I remember one nanny tethered at the top. She was very docile for a goat, so much so that Elijah just lay down under her and milked her straight into his mouth. He couldn't resist a bit of fun. One day he altered the length of the tethers, shortening them so that two adjoining billy goats could just reach each other, horns touching. Then he would stand and watch as they ran towards each other, and just as the horns were about to meet in an almighty butt, they were whipped away, head over heels, to land yards away.

The grey pit pony was a regular means of fun-making activities. Elijah used to ride round and round the field like a cowboy, his friend Dick Wortley joining in the fun. Once this nearly resulted in tragedy. Both lads decided to ride tandem but galloping round the field, they both slipped sideways, clinging on upside down as the pony continued galloping until, inevitably they both slipped off beneath the pony's pounding hoofs. Unfortunately for them 'Old Rimmock' (Mr Rimmington), who lived in the little cottage above the field, saw the episode and reported it to Dad. The consequences need not be told here, you might guess what the reaction and result was.

Another hiding resulted when Dad found the cigarettes and matches hidden in the shed where the fowls and feeding stuff were kept. Elijah just would not give up or lie down for long, Rimmock or no Rimmock. One day I watched as he and Dick Wortley chased the grey pit pony around the field to make it pass wind. The faster they chased, the more it did, round and round and round the field, with an occasional kick back with its hind legs, which only made it pass wind more. I was disgusted; how crude lads are I thought, yet I laughed and laughed until tears rolled down my cheeks, mad with myself for being so undignified but unable to help myself and, although I knew this was another occasion for a beating if Dad heard of it, I was so fascinated by the antics, I just couldn't leave.

One day Dad bought two foals for his own use, intending to break them in to use with a plough, and to draw a cart. This was around the time he decided to plough up the back field for a fourth allotment, and one of them was broken-in with a little trouble, taking to the pony plough well and eventually ploughing all four. When they were bought, they were kept on a small piece of land, and in a barn on the rifle range behind Mr Johnson's orchard, after which they were moved to a small area behind the little cottage near the Moneybrook spring. When they were ready for breaking in, they were moved to the big field at Hillfoot, where they had more room for exercise and for breaking in.

The second horse was a maverick. I can remember Dad standing in the middle of the field with a stick in one hand, holding a long rope to which the horse was tethered. Round and round it pranced, kicking and struggling like a bucking bronco at a rodeo. It was stubborn, would not be broken in, even to the long tether. Dad hitched it up to a pit tub, put on a harness, and made it pull the tub on Strawberry Lea Lane and up Lane Head Road, but it pulled on the bit so hard that it bled from the gums. Dad took it down to Mr Bradbury, the blacksmith in the chemical yard to be shoed, but it wouldn't stand still, one shoe was fitted but the blacksmith wouldn't do another that day. So for a while it was on the road with only one shoe. Dad took it again for another try but this time it reared and fought with its hoofs, until the situation became dangerous. Mrs Bradbury had been watching from a bedroom window and even she was alarmed, shouting to her husband "Stop it Bill, let it go, it'll kill you." They all seemed to agree that the horse had won the day. There was nothing more to do but to sell the damned thing. One morning Dad set off with the horse, with only one shoe, for the street market at Chesterfield, where it was sold, presumably to some farmer who thought he could do better than Dad.

Until the World War II, the kilns at the brickyard were open, with the entrance road running alongside. They were covered over when war broke out because the fires in the sides of the kilns were clearly visible from the air; a guide for enemy aircraft. The large office building was built well after the war when Pickford Holland & Co was taken over by General Refractories. The warm kilns were a welcome invitation for the tramps on their way to Bakewell, often spending all night with the night watchman before moving on next morning. The night watchman at that time was Jack Slack, nicknamed 'Black Jack'; I'm not sure why, probably because he had black hair and wore black clothing. He was well versed on herbs and their use, and there was one herb which only he knew where it grew just above the brickyard on the moors. Our Grandfather was a keen herbalist, (more in the family tree), keeping a very comprehensive journal about them, but Black Jack would not tell even Grandfather where to find 'Parsley-Piert', a herb used for stones in the bladder. It is an Alchemilla, (Arvensis) which the women herb sellers of Cheapside called 'Parsley Breakstone'.

Above and behind the brickyard are the remains of the clay mine which Joseph Salt, our Great Grandfather owned and managed. He lived at one of the small cottages just below the brickyard (now demolished), where he died in 1891. His father, another Joseph, who died in 1828 aged 31, was believed to be the owner/manager before his son, but proof of this has so far eluded me.

The men folk of the Salt family must all have been gardeners, for there is still a flat area above the brickyard called 'Salt's' garden. From time to time my Father ploughed it to make a garden, where he grew vegetables. Whether this had originally been Great Grandfather's garden is not certain, but as he lived in the cottage for a number of years, it is very likely.

It is true that my Father was somewhat of a disciplinarian, and sometimes thought to be unreasonable in his dealing with the family, particularly the children, but it is well to remember that these were the times when men were the providers, and consequently the undisputed masters of the household. According to the way they provided was the criterion on which they were judged by their fellow men, and their reputation was enhanced or degraded somewhat by the behaviour of the family outside the home. As I grew older I came to the conclusion that my Father was so strict with Elijah first, because he held him responsible for the two younger boys, and because he was very jealous of his own reputation. Being the proud man that he was, he saw his reputation not only in his achievements, but those of his 'tribe' and anything that remotely interfered with the good name of the whole family could not be tolerated. The least hint of trouble, worse a brush with the law was in his eyes a serious disgrace, although it must be admitted, that he himself had had more than a brush when he was put in the local jail for one night by Gamekeeper Stone of Thickwood Lodge, when he was accused of illegally shooting a grouse, and the next day was fined £1 at Renishaw Court. His defence was "I thought it was a wood pigeon your Honour," but that excuse from a countryman was, as he often laughingly said, so unlikely, they didn't believe him.

However, he was always supportive of his children in the outside world when he thought they needed it, and tolerant of their antics if he thought they were trying to learn or doing a job, like the day he found his nails had been stolen. On one of his Saturday trips to Sheffield, he bought a pound of nails for a job he intended to do during the week. When the time came for him to use them, the bag was empty, the nails gone. He came upstairs where Mom was preparing dinner. "Damn me," he said, "I bought a pound of nails on Saturday, and there isn't a single one left; I bet one of those little devils has been round them." "Well," said Mom, "I did see one of them with a hammer in his hand, ask 'Liga'." He did and found that the whole pound of nails had been used by Geoff to nail boards together to make a trolley. A trolley was nothing more than a length of timber, with two crossbars for axles, on which four wheels were attached, the front one being fastened with a bolt to allow it to pivot, and be guided by a piece of orange rope begged from Mr King the greengrocer. (Oranges were imported in large wooden boxes fastened round with a strong plaited rope). Unlike Elijah's with the large pram wheels, Geoff's had no box attached; he certainly intended it holding together, with a pound of nails!

Elijah's was a more elaborate affair but it was nearly his 'undoing'. He had a lucky find one day in the shape of four large pram wheels, which he attached to his trolley in the hope that they would enable him to travel faster. He also attached a large wooden apple box over the back axle, cutting a piece out of the front to enable him to sit on it with his feet either side the crossbar on the front axle. With pressure from the feet it could be guided in a straight line or turned at will. He took it to the middle of the tar macadam road, sat in the seat and started away down the road. But he hadn't reckoned on just how fast those wheels could go and he whizzed down to the memorial at top speed before he realised that the Bakewell bus was just behind him. Nothing for it but to make for the gutter, hitting the verge so fast that he went 'arse o'er head' on to the path. I bet the bus driver wasn't too pleased!

Elijah played football for Totley, who were in the Hope Valley League and Dad always followed them on away matches. As an ambulance man, he was always conscious of the possibility of accidents and one particularly bad one was when they were playing Bradwell, at Bradway, I think. During an unusually rough tackle, Elijah suffered a severe cut to his bottom lip and Dad was on the spot immediately to render first aid treatment, followed by a trip to the local Doctor to have it stitched. At regular intervals, a knee came out of joint when kicking a ball and Dad usually managed to manipulate it into joint again until, eventually it came out at such regular intervals that the hospital Doctor told him he would have to stop playing or suffer a permanent injury. Of course he didn't, not immediately, but as the hospital visits became more frequent, and physiotherapy of little use, he had to succumb.

Our first wireless set appeared about 1932, when I was 16 years old. A few years before, Dad had brought a strange contraption called a 'cat's whisker', which one of his friends, I think it was Mr Coven the tailor, had loaned him to show us this new and wonderful invention. It was nothing more than a board, about 18" long and 12" wide on which a sort of cylinder framework with wires attached was fastened. When it was plugged into the electricity, a spark could be seen between two wires (the cat's whisker), and when the headphones were put on, a sound came through the wires, a phenomenon which was nothing less than miraculous.

When my Father brought home our first loudspeaker, we were very excited. It was a brown wooden box with a half round top and a fretwork cut out in the front through which the sound issued from the speaker. Dad thought it was a debatable blessing; he liked to hear the news and some of the plays, but at 6.15 p.m. every evening, just as we were sitting down to tea and we had all rushed home from work to hear Henry Hall and his band, he objected, just like parents do today. "What do you want to listen to that rubbish for?" he said, similar remarks being repeated whenever any of the big bands like Joe Loss or Billy Cotton performed. He had been brought up in the era of Kathleen Mavourneen, Nellie Dean, brass bands and hymns, and these new-fangled dance bands and modern tunes were as alien to his ears as 'pop' music was to the parents of the 1950s and 1960s. He did like to go to the pictures occasionally, but only when Alistair Sim was on the programme, or Tom Walls, Ralph Lynn and Roberson Hare, who were the great comedy actors of the day, very often with Yvonne Arnaud, a French anglicised actress with a husky voice and a hilarious sense of humour.

It wasn't unusual for Dad to come home from work, washday no exception, having been told that Tom Walls and the team, or Alistair Sim were on at the Abbeydale Picture House, and announce that they were going that night. No matter that the copper was full of washing, or that Mom might not feel like going out. She might protest that she had too much to do, but she would end up going just the same, although reluctantly.

Chapter 6

In August 1926, I learned the facts of life, all in one 'fell swoop'. No preparing, no gentle lead up, no biological explanation, just 'jump in with both feet', the whole information not wrapped up in diplomatic jargon, given 'straight from the hip'. Why half a dozen girls should be at the corner of the Crescent, the main road into Heatherfield, the new estate, I have no cause to remember. We were on holiday and for once, my Father must have, for some reason, overlooked or just didn't know that I was mixing with the forbidden gang. Vera Marriot lived in the bungalow on the corner, and it was Vera who channelled the conversation around to the subject. There had been some discussion about the new Princess Elizabeth, born on the 21st April that year. (The public were more genuinely interested in the Royal Family in those days of Empire, and held them in great respect). My shock was not on a personal basis; I kept thinking "The Duke & Duchess of York did that." It didn't bother me that my parents did it, in fact they never entered my head, but that the Duke & Duchess of York should do a thing that I thought only prostitutes did haunted me for many nights to come. So, when one morning I rose and found a stain on my nightdress, I wasn't shocked at all.

How my Mother knew to come into the bedroom at that time I never knew, for she usually went straight downstairs in the morning. This morning she came in carrying a bundle of white cloth which she put down as she sat on the bed. "You're a woman now," she said, and started to explain, but soon realised that I knew already. Picking up the bundle of cloth, she opened it out showing me the squares of sheeting which she had made from an old sheet. They were about 15" square, made from double cloth and in two opposite corners were two pieces of tape stitched down at each end to form a flat slot.

She had made a belt about 1″ wide from the same material, with a button on one end, a buttonhole on the other. Two pieces of tape were attached both front and back, leaving ends of about, 8″. She showed me how to fold the cloths so that they formed a pad with twelve layers of cloth in the centre where extra thickness was needed. Then I was shown how to attach the cloth to the belt by passing one of the tapes through one of the slots, using the other end to tie a bow; repeating with the other tape and loop and watched as I put on the first one. Then she gave me a short talk. I must be very careful not to let the boys see anything. I must never talk about it in front of the boys and Dad. I must not wear my skirts short any more, and I must be very careful to keep the cloths from them all. For this, she gave me a cloth drawstring bag in which I had to put the used clothes and, as from now on, I could use her bedroom to dress and undress when I had 'colly wobbles'. I would keep the bag in there, where she would collect it on wash day. The word 'period' was never used; in fact it really was a taboo subject, even among women. I never admitted to even the closet of my school mates that I had 'started', although I guessed from guarded remarks from some of them that each in turn had done so. They all thought I was very late in maturing.

It wasn't a very pleasant job for Mom on washing day, but all Moms had to do the same; there were some commercial sanitary towels at the Chemists but they were expensive and, in our social group, nobody even though of buying them. How Mom managed to dry them was a mystery, they were always dried separately and never, never seen on a washing line.

This then, I thought, was another thing I had to put up with because I was a woman. How the men get away with things. That feeling of inferiority and resentment overwhelmed me once more. It was soon after this that I started having, what were called in those days, bilious headaches, somewhat of a family failing, for my Mother had suffered in the same way when she was young, and Elijah's headaches were worst of all. I remember many times seeing him laid out on the sofa, whilst Mom put vinegar soaked cloths on his forehead. She was always very worried on these occasions, when his face was ashen and he lapsed almost unconscious.

Mr Wood was quick to see when I was not well. "Josephine, have you got a headache?" he would say as my face went whiter. To the answer "Yes Sir," he would tell me to go and sit near the fire, a large tortoise stove in the middle of the room. It had a high square fireguard all around on which clothes were dried on wet days, and on which I could rest my head on my arms. Many times, after about half an hour; he would send me home, where bed was the only cure. Unlike Elijah, who had to sleep with head raised, I needed to lie flat to relieve the sickly feeling. Later the malady developed into migraine with the frightening flashes in the eyes, and tunnel vision associated with it. Dr Parsons was consulted about the headaches and, in my case; he suggested that if I had my hair cut, they might disappear. It was becoming the fashion to have bobbed hair but my Father was very reluctant for me to have mine bobbed. He finally agreed and so I lost my long tresses for the 'flappers half shingle'.

My Mother had jet black hair, falling to her waist in shining waves when she let it down at bedtime. In the daytime she made it into a roll and fastened it around her head in the current fashion for women with a dexterity which used to fascinate me. Some women used a pad made from horsehair to wrap the hair around in order to produce a good roll, but my Mother's hair was so long and thick, she needed no such roll. A few months after having my hair bobbed, Father agreed to Mom having her tresses cut off also. Short hair, we found, was not only more comfortable, it saved time.

Like all girls of that age, I was becoming more conscious of my appearance. Every little blemish, real or imagined, was a catastrophe; blackheads were constantly being searched for, and the watch key at the ready to remove the offending morsels. My Mother only let me use the key, and not often at that, if I first softened the skin by steaming over as bowl of boiling water with a towel over my head. Then I had to splash liberally with cold water to 'close the pores' she said. Make up was only now appearing, very irregularly, in the big stores, but one my Mother and Mrs Smith were very pleased about was Snowfire cream which was sold in small tins holding about a tablespoonful for 2d a tin. Snowfire also produced face powder, also in 2d tins but this was a luxury 'ordinary' women weren't interest in.

A few years before, both women had attended Lady Rachel Cavendish's wedding at Edensor Church on an extremely hot day, when they both returned sunburned and blistered. When the Snowfire cream appeared, my Mother said "What could we have done with this then?" I wasn't allowed to use either cream or powder, but my Mother said I could use a little Mercolised Wax and Prolactum. The wax was for the face to keep the skin soft; the Prolactum was like a red 'lipsyl'. She gave me the money, about 6d each time, and I called at the Chemist at Totley Rise when I went to Colin Thompson for the Sunday joint. Thus I started my beauty treatment. One motherly warning when I always remember was "It's no good putting cream on your face if you don't wash it off before going to bed." I promised I would never go to bed without washing my face.

One dinnertime I came home from school moaning because I hadn't any long stockings. "Even the orphanage girls have long stockings," I wailed. After dinner, Mom went upstairs and rummaged in a drawer, returning with a pair of pale fawn lisle stockings which had been somewhat worn, but otherwise in good condition. "These are all I have," she said, "see if they will fit you." It didn't matter that they were fawn when all the other girls had lovely black or grey ones, they were long stockings, now I was grown up; no matter how they wrinkled round the ankles, as Mom said, I was a woman now, and I rejoiced as I ran down the allotments for the afternoon session.

One morning each week we had to assemble in the boys' yard for drill. This was little more than physical jerks on the level area of the yard, where we could do arms and knees bend, hands on hips, turning to left and right, marching on the spot, stretch upwards then touch the floor; aerobics had nothing on our physical jerks. We had to go through the boys' yard to enter school, but after that it was a forbidden area, as the girls' yard was forbidden to the boys under sufferance of the cane, but there was something a bit teasing through the rails of the dividing gate. At the bottom of the yards was the building which housed the toilets. It was brick built with the wall dividing the yards passing through the middle, the same wall forming the back wall of the girls' toilets, which were really only holes in boards, under which a row of metal containers caught whatever happened to be deposited through the holes. Half the area on the girls' side was an open passage through which an open drain took surface water from the sloping schoolyard. Whether it took any other drainage is a matter of speculation. The same wall on the boys' side formed part of a central store for the cleaners' tools, its other wall being the back wall of another open passage which housed the boys' toilets; in other words, a urinal wall. I suppose they must have had a regular toilet as well, I never went in to see.

Inside the store was a row of let down doors in the bottom of the wall behind the bins for the purpose of emptying and as access to the store was through a door from their yard, they couldn't resist temptation. Ever on the lookout for a prank, when they knew there were bottoms on seats, they used to open the doors and with pieces of stick, had fun tickling the girls' bums. Elijah confesses to being one of the culprits. Not content with that, the bigger boys would line up in front of their wall and see who could 'pee' through the open top, and over into the girls' passageway. There was a regular contest to see who could 'pee' highest and furthest. Luckily not many of them could raise enough power to reach the passageway.

School for me was no hardship, although I enjoyed the holidays, and sometimes wished I didn't have to go, not because I was in any way afraid, although we were all in awe of the Headmaster John Wood, who had come to the school in 1908 in response to a resolution passed at one of the Parish Council meetings following a directive from the Ministry of Education. Mr Wood did not tolerate pupils of either sex whom he thought were not trying their best, or just being apathetic; one reason why if you didn't know something, you had enough sense not to show your ignorance by asking questions. He also 'put the boot in' for other more social reasons. One boy, a member of a family who were considered a bit 'behind the door', 'two slices short of a full loaf', not really 'a screw loose', but just a bit removed from normal, whatever that is, was Cobby Green who lived on Summer Lane, one of the less salubrious areas of the village. Standing behind him during one lesson, I remember Mr Wood suddenly sniff then, grabbing Cobby by the ear, he pulled him up from his seat shouting "Three times round the garden Green and sweeten," and out poor Cobby went, scared stiff and cringing.

News went around the school every morning. "He's got brown boots on." This means 'look out', and all the pupils were on their best behaviour and apprehensive all day rather than be at the receiving end of a 'brown boot temper'. If the cry was "He's got his black boots on," then everything was going to be alright, it would be a good day, and we could all breathe freely. Such was the power of this man who could be held in such awe that all depended on the colour of his boots.

John Wood was always kind to me, in fact I never remember him severely chastising any of the girls, certainly he never hit any of us, although one or two might have been victims of his sarcastic remarks, me included. However, the boys were a 'different cup of tea' so to speak. Those who behaved reasonably well and did their work as well as possible; were left alone and in some cases, were respected. Others were the constant butt of his vengeance and wrath. One particular treatment which was supposed to wake up anyone who appeared to be going to sleep, who looked lethargic and needed livening up was fortunately, reserved for the few. The Headmaster would creep up behind the offender, grab hold of one ear, and with a slow pull, raise the victim clear of his seat, when the chair beneath him was quietly drawn away, and the ear released, letting him fall backwards on to the floor. The treatment was, naturally I think, reserved only for boys. Whether this was because he had a daughter of his own, I wouldn't hazard a guess, but when I heard my Mother talking about her Headmaster at Woodhouse School, I assumed that as they both belonged to the same era and the same school of thought, it was the way they were trained in their College days. I am not surprised that some of the old boys I have spoken to are not so charitable towards Mr Wood; they have different memories from mine. To some he was near to being a despot and an ogre.

I have memories of listening to him reading to the class on Friday afternoons as a change from silent reading. It was, no doubt, a means of us all hearing about 'Oliver Twist' when there was only one copy in the book cupboard. The book cupboard was our library. It was about 5ft high x 4ft wide with 12" deep shelves to hold the books. There were none of the classics, no Brontes, no Jane Austin, no Dickens, except 'Oliver Twist' and a paperback about 'Little Nell' and although at some time we had to recite extracts from Shakespeare, I think they, and other poems were learned by rote rather than by sight. I do, however, remember reading 'Lorna Doone' and the exciting adventures of John Ridd; East Lynne, and books by lesser known authors. Although there were one or two books explaining about the weather, plants and the sea, there were no textbooks for use in lessons. Everything was written on the blackboard during or before the lesson, and rubbed off afterwards ready for the next. Bad luck if you didn't understand or didn't concentrate (like me sometimes) or had a bad memory.

The occasions I loved and remember very clearly, happened about once a month when Mr Wood received a newspaper from France. He sat on a desk at the front of the class reading snippets of news to us, sometimes explaining the finer points of the affairs of France which otherwise we would not understand. I used to listen enthralled, and after these sessions Mr Wood was my hero. How wonderful I thought, to be able to read French and at the same time talk in English, translating from one language to another so quickly. From the first time I heard him, the ability to speak and understand French was the ultimate in education; an illusion brought to an end in the 1960s when I knew people who spoke French fluently but otherwise were 'as thick as two planks'.

About this time, it could have been 1927; Mr Wood informed us that there was to be a total eclipse of the sun which would be visible in our district at about 8.00 a.m. a few days hence. This warranted a lesson on the ways of the earth, the sun and the moon and all the other relevant information necessary to understand the phenomenon. The day before the event, because this was possibly a 'once in a lifetime' opportunity and to add interest to the lesson, we were instructed to make our way next morning to the top of the mountain path instead of attending school; there to congregate with the rest of the villagers and await the awe inspiring occasion. Drawers were rummaged for dark glasses and pieces of glass were smoked over paraffin lamps or a newly lit fire, for we were warned, "If you look at the sun without protection, you will go blind."

There was general excitement on the mountain as the crowd grew, for mothers and some fathers and anybody who could raise the energy for the climb had congregated there. Dead on time there were cries of "Oh look," and "It's wonderful," as the first shadow crossed the face of the sun. Cheers rose from those too moved to keep silent, whilst others were so overawed as to be struck dumb in their wonder. Gradually, the black crescent moved over the face of the heavenly orb, the light gradually fading and growing darker until it was as if night had fallen. Then, like a giant halo, there appeared the wonderful climax we had been told to expect, and explained in some detail by an enthusiastic Headmaster, the corona, a circle of bright fingers of fire shooting out from the edges of the new black sun.

We were overawed and silent for some moments, apprehensive and expectant when suddenly there was a wild cry as one of the company could stand the strain no longer. Poor Annie Green, (Cobby's sister) who, like her brother was known to be 'one note short of a full octave' and extremely frightened, broke away from the crowd and set off running down the mountain path as if the very devil were after her heels. She went down Moss Road, across the 'Sic', along Penny Lane shouting hysterically, "World's coming to an end, world's coming to an end." We all watched, with much laughter and banter, as she ran frantically without stopping, up Chapel Fields to disappear through the stile into Chapel Walk. With much talking and discussion, making use of the occasion for a little local gossip, the crowd dispersed, children racing down the mountain in the wake of Annie, and the classroom, others taking their time for the day was still young and housework could wait.

Miss Marsden, the infant teacher, was very versatile; she taught not only general subjects to the infants, but also sewing and knitting to all pupils up to Standard 4. Drawing and painting were taught to boys of all ages, music and dancing to the whole school. She took us on nature walks, showed us how to identify wild flowers and initiated us into making pressed flower books for reference. By the age of eight or nine we knew all the parts of the flower, the calyx, petals, anthers and stigmas (they were called pistils in those days) and without dwelling on the human equivalent, we learned how the stigma was fertilised by the anthers so that seeds could be produced. My pressed flower book has disappeared over the years, but I found Jeff's amongst other books and I'm sure he has saved it; he even remembered pressing one or two of his specimens.

May Day was the traditional day for dancing around the maypole and for about six weeks before the date, dancing was done in earnest. Both boys and girls in the lower classes learned maypole dancing in the school yard practising 'Cobwebs' 'Plaits' and 'Barber's Poles' in intricate weaving around the pole whilst the older girls perfected 'Shepherd's Hey', 'Bean Sticks, 'Country Gardens', 'Gathering Peasecods', and 'If all the world were paper', until they were perfect enough to dance on the lawn at the hall with an audience of the Milner ilk.

In 1928, Mr Wood decreed that Totley should have a May Queen, a cause of great excitement amongst the girls, who huddled in groups to discuss who the chosen one might be. After all the conferring and discussions amongst the teachers, two names were produced to stand as candidates, my own and that of a girl called Olive King. There were three weeks to voting day and I was fairly confident and well on the way to being favourite; no enemies to speak of, a presentable appearance and intelligent enough to be, in effect, head girl. I reckoned without the debatable system of electioneering and had nothing to offer in lieu of the gifts of fruit and sweets from her father's shop handed out liberally by Olive to prospective voters. On the day she brought hair clips which acted like magic. The girls crowded round to see these modern contraptions sent by an aunt in France. "What are they and how do they stay in?" everybody chorused. "Do they really hold the hair as well as slides?" Questions, questions, questions were followed by demonstrations to show how efficient French trinkets were, and most of them changed hands permanently to the now adoring disciples. For me, the rot had set in, the competition was too great; I had nothing to offer but myself, and if that wasn't good enough, so be it. I would have made a lousy politician. I lost by one vote; you might say 'might as well be a mile.'

The strange thing was that my Father was more disappointed than I was, according to the times he quoted 'Only one vote', in the pub for the next few days, whilst I had the satisfaction of knowing why.

There were eight girls in the dancing team, including myself; Agnes Taylor, Gertie Trusswell, Gladys Cartwright, Isabel Small (now Mrs Reynolds), Margaret Sproson, Thelma Nodder and, I think Nellie Drury. All were dressed in white, with white shoes and socks. In 1929 the team changed, some girls had left school and I had another role. Mr Wood decreed that it should be an 'all pupils' event, and I was to play the piano for dancing instead of Miss Marsden. She was delighted, as it enabled her to oversee the dancers more closely. The upright piano was brought out of the smoke room and positioned on the lawn of the hall where I could see the dancers more clearly. I was sorry not to be dancing, for it was one of my favourite occupations, but I suppose it was another experience.

The maypole was set up in the middle of the lawn with the pole firmly fixed into a decorated barrel, the six small girls in white, the six boys in white blouses and grey or black shorts. The May Queen in 1929 was Thelma Nodder, who lived in Grove Road, Totley Rise. Thelma took over from me as the 'sprinter' of the school. My steam was beginning to run out, and at the Sports Day that year, I was beaten at the tape by her; my scratch position for once was a bit too much. I was in Standard 3, about nine years old, before I gave any thought to life after school. My cousin May, who is seven years older than me, was assigned to Totley School as a Pupil Teacher as part of 'Teacher Training College' education. She was allocated, if that's the right word, to classes two and three, which were taken together by one teacher. She had a wonderful sense of humour and the 'Salt' twinkle in her eyes and the children loved to have her sit on the desk in front of the class reading and occasionally stopping to answer a question about the current book Another Pupil Teacher, Ida Creswick came to school at the same time and was allocated to the infants, or Standard 1, but she was never as popular as cousin May. I remember thinking 'how wonderful it would be to be a teacher' and doubted very much that I would ever realise that dream, so it was dismissed from my mind.

Choice of a career was not the uppermost thought in the minds of girls, and as subjects taught were designed for boys or for girls, a division which fortunately has in the past few years been rectified, there was little encouragement to have high aspirations on leaving school. I remember sitting in a sewing class in Miss Marsden's room where the windows were on the level of the school gardens, and I needed only to turn my head to see the boys at their digging and planting and feeling very envious of them. Even at that young age, I loved growing things, even a teaspoonful of linseed when Mom was making Dad's linseed tea to relieve the tightness of his chest, or the penny packet of mignonette or candytuft bought from Friday or Saturday's pocket money could raise a feeling of satisfaction when the bright blue flax flowers appeared, or the scent of mignonette added to the little bouquet for Mom and to learn more, instead of the inevitable sewing, was an impossible dream.

I remember one day, as I walked up the stairs to the 'big room' for yet another sewing class, this time with Mrs Lake, I looked back to see the Headmaster telling a boy to put some water in a jam jar on the table, and I heard him say to the rest of the boys, "Get out the chemistry things," or something to that effect. When I arrived home that afternoon I asked Elijah, "What did Mr Wood do with that water?" "What water?" he answered. "That water in the jam jar, what did he do with it?" I said. "Oh I don't know," he said. "You must know," I replied. "You should know, I want to know, you should remember then you can tell me." My curiosity about all things should not be put off like that I thought, if boys could know, then so should I.

Drawing and painting was for boys only; Elijah was particularly good at drawing and won prizes at the village shows, but this was another subject I regret not taking, and often thought how much earlier my interest in painting would have developed had such a distinction not been made at school. It was ironic that, in later years, I was to teach horticulture and botany with painting one of my favourite hobbies, when Jeff turned out to be a dedicated and excellent Chef. What would he have done with school cookery? Cookery was taken at the age of eleven. I liked it, and was good at it.

About half a dozen girls from Dore joined us at Totley every Wednesday in the 'Tin Tabernacle'.

Since 1924, when the new Church was built in Hall Lane, it had been used by the Headmaster for the top classes, but on Wednesday, the boys moved out for gardening, leaving the room for the girls. There were two gas cookers at the far end of the room and cupboards for all the utensils. The teacher, Miss Foster, came from Dronfield, about three miles away. The first hour was spent in learning housecraft, things like how to wash a duster; how to keep a dishcloth scrupulously clean, and other important uninteresting things a woman has to do, as well as a little science of cooking; why bicarb and cream of tartar make pastry rise; how yeast works; why the protein in meat firms with heat, and other mysteries one needs to know to be a good cook, or so we were told.

I remember one lesson which, at first had been interesting. It was to do with the menu of the day, which included the use of the pulses, including lentils. We were being told the theory behind the recipe, and the blackboard was becoming filled with notes which we had to copy down, having no text books, as usual. I had a nasty habit of mind wandering, it seemed to work faster than the notes appeared and I suppose I grew bored. Miss Foster, who was young and very popular, had written a sentence about the pulses and had added the symbol of three dots at the end when she must have seen the glazed look in my eyes. Suddenly, she said, very loudly "Josephine, what do they mean?" pointing to the dots. "Peas, beans and lentils Miss," I replied, to the general amusement of the class, and my embarrassment. The three dots were, of course, the symbol for 'therefore'.

Once before I had been caught in the same way; with much embarrassment, when I first came into Standard 6. Elijah was on his last term and in the same room, which made things worse for I got teased, even at home, plus a lecture from my Father for wasting time when I should be learning. The lesson was about adding suffixes to imply something younger, like duck and duckling, and the question asked me was "Josephine, what do you call the young that feeds on sap?" "A baby Sir," was my quick reply from the depths of my reverie. "Sap girl, not pap" he roared, and the class erupted.

Cookery classes were the beginning of my intense interest in cooking. Both Margaret and I took great pains over details, no matter how simple toe recipe, and were always top of the points table at the end of each lesson. As a project, one day we all had to work together to create a dinner for the teachers, and I was assigned the task of making the Yorkshire puddings. With apprehension we set the tables, under supervision of Miss Foster, who checked that we had the entire cutlery in right order, accoutrements in the right place, and table napkins folded into neat water lily shapes. Then came the dishing up. Two girls were assigned the dubious distinction of waiting on, and I was one of them. With great trepidation, we handed round the soup, bowls of vegetables, and plates of meat carved by Miss Foster, being careful to serve from the left, and pick up the used plates from the right; all very embarrassing when our guests were the teachers whom we knew as Gods and Goddesses, or morons as the case may be. The meal over, and everybody satisfied, there were compliments all round, and how I glowed when Miss Foulstone piped up, "Who made the Yorkshire puddings, they were delicious?" Whenever I make Yorkshire pudding, I think of my masterpiece of that day in 1928.

One top scoring pudding, however, was almost my downfall. We had made rice pudding and as usual I had top marks. I didn't like rice pudding, but I was so proud of myself that I wouldn't let anyone else have any; I ate the lot and was immediately sick, to the great enjoyment and ridicule from the lads. "Serves you right" they chorused, to my chagrin.

Learning the English language was not a favourite subject of mine; I could see little sense in predicates, pronouns, subjunctives and all the other tenses. I could speak English, I could understand English, I could write English, or so I thought. Why did I need all these complicating additions to what I thought were perfectly straightforward sentences. I knew what a verb was, I knew a noun when I saw one, an adjective, an adverb, and a clause could be identified, if necessary and I knew sufficient about punctuation to make sure everybody could understand what I wrote; anything else

133

was boring. To make me even more arrogant about the subject of English was my prize for essay writing. Mr Wood offered a prize of half a crown (12s.6d) for the best essay, on any subject we wished. My Father had bought for us a set of 'Castle's Book of Knowledge', which were a source of enlightenment when questioned "What is so and so?", or "Who did that?" and one of them was my source of information for my essay, which I decided should be on photography. I knew nothing about the subject, and don't even know why I chose it, but my winning essay of 500 words as requested was really the undoing of my future English lessons. If I could win a prize, why should I learn anymore? If only I had realised that if one didn't know one's language, it was very hard to learn a foreign one. At that time, I had never heard of plagiarism and had no idea what it meant, but I did feel guilty about the subject when, in my childhood mind I felt I should only write about what I knew and although all the words were my own, nothing directly copied, the feeling did not leave me, not for many years, when I realised that all writers did research, they all 'hashed up' information retrieved from someone else's writing. Only then was I content with my prize.

At the age of eleven or twelve, dependent on the date of birth, children of suitable ability were allowed to sit the scholarship examination, for the chance to attend the Grammar School at Dronfield. Totley, Dore and Holmesfield had three scholarships, the Minor, Fanshawe and Foundation, all of different values. The Major was awarded at the end of the first year as an upgrading from the Minor. It carried a cash award as well as all fees, books, uniform and fares, plus £5 per year. The Minor allowed all expenses. The Fanshawe allowed all expenses, but no cash payment. The Foundation allowed fees for tuition only.

There was an Entrance Examination which was open to children of the area who did not pass the scholarship and children outside the area who could afford to pay everything, including tuition. Those pupils still aged eleven who did not pass first time were allowed to sit again for the Foundation only; their parents paying for everything but tuition. There was never more than one entrant from Totley School, sometimes there were none. In 1927 when

134

I took it I was the only one, and there had been none for a number of years before that.

At eleven years old the journey was exciting but very foreboding for one who had never been so far before alone, and I was nervous; and a little scared at the prospect of finding my own way, with this important exam at the end of it. I reached the school in good time, but still felt very apprehensive, knowing nobody, not even knowing where I was supposed to be. Eventually, I found a cloakroom, took off my coat and hat, and made sure I had my pencil case and a handkerchief. By this time a man appeared directing a few other girls and myself to a classroom, there telling us to find our names on the desks; to sit down quietly until the examination commenced. I felt my stomach descend right down to my shoes when I saw that I had been allocated a desk at the edge of the aisle. I felt very vulnerable with no place to hide, and extremely lonely. There was a huge clock on the wall straight in front of me, with the loudest tick I had ever heard, and a few minutes later a man walked into the room in a flowing gown and a peculiar square hat on his head with a tassel falling over one eye. I had never seen anyone dressed like that before. Nor had I taken an examination before, except the year end tests at school, and I didn't know what to expect. The school test had never worried me, but this was different, more important.

The papers were given out, arithmetic first, my strong point, but when we were told to begin, I couldn't think of a thing, except that man sitting there at the front of the room. When he got up and started walking down the aisle towards me like a great black crow, I panicked and my mind went completely blank, never to recover for the rest of the examination. When I looked at the papers afterwards, I was even more mortified for the questions were so easy. I could have done them all with little effort; but the chance had gone. However, not altogether; for I was just eleven and allowed to sit again; but only for the Foundation scholarship. I shall never know why, even my Mother couldn't shed a light on it, why my Father let me sit for this exam. He hadn't really intended that I should go to the school for he must have known he would have to pay for books, uniform and fares. I travelled this time with the Headmaster and his daughter,

135

who was also taking the examination and there were no nerves; I knew what to expect. When the results were published, Mr Wood was delighted. At the end of the day he came home with me to give my Father the good news. Sitting beside him on the sofa, I was excited, but not a little apprehensive, not for what my Father might say, but what would happen if I did go to Dronfield. The blue and maroon uniform was a signal for cat calls of 'Grammar Bog, Grammar Bog' and my nature was not the type to welcome such treatment. It was bad enough being called 'Lady Muck' as I knew I was, because some of the village girls though I was 'uppity'. (My Father had been called 'Lord Muck' ever since he had come to live in Totley.)

My Father heard the news very quietly, looking first at me, then at my Mother and after what seemed an eternity of deliberating; he said he couldn't let me go because he couldn't afford it. Mr Wood was aghast. "But Mr Salt," he said, "do you realise that Josephine's paper was the top of the whole of Derbyshire?" He asked my Father to please reconsider. Mr Wood went on to say "I am sending my daughter, and she only just got through, with the bottom paper. Education is important for girls as well as boys," he persisted. But it was to no avail, I couldn't go. "I have two more boys to think of, and if they pass, I can't afford to send them if I let Josephine go". That was the end of the discussion. Mr Wood turned to me saying how sorry he was. He bid my Mother and Fathers 'a good afternoon' and went on his way. My feelings were mixed. I would dearly have loved to go to Grammar School to learn French like Mr Wood, but deep down there was that feeling of relief that cries of 'Grammar Bog' would not be directed towards me every time I walked down the road. There was no feeling of resentment for many years. But when I heard that Marjorie had been made Headmistress of a local school whilst I was at that time struggling to build up a business, I did wonder what I would be doing had I gone to Dronfield Grammar School all those years before.

Returning to school after the summer holidays of 1928, we were informed by the Headmaster that a new class was to be formed; it would be called 7X. It was to be an extension of Standard 7 for three boys and three girls. A large table had been introduced at the end of the room, around which the six of us were to sit. There were large drawers in the side, one for each of us, in which to keep our books and personal things. We thought this was luxury as previously we had desks with only very small shallow drawers. We felt very important.

After setting the rest of the class to work, the Headmaster came over to us carrying some books. "There is nothing more I can teach you," he said, "you have all the arithmetic and English you will require, so for this last year, you are going to learn shorthand, and make yourselves familiar with the typewriter keyboard." We were amazed, and not a little excited as he handed to each of us a copy of 'Pitman's Shorthand', a card with the letter as set out on the keyboard of a typewriter, on which we could learn the positions and fingering as explained on the reverse, and a new exercise book for notes. Opening one of the books, he explained a little of the system and after telling us "You will continue with History and Geography and you girls will still go to your sewing classes, but all other times will be spent on this new study," he left us to it adding, "If you get into difficulty I'll try to help you, so don't be afraid to ask."

So, I learned my first typing from a printed card and strange as it may seem, it worked and at least one appetite was whetted. When Margaret and I left school the following year, her Father sent her to Gregg's College in Sheffield for a year and when they left for Elstree the same year, she obtained a job as secretary at Geoffrey de Havillands, the airfield from which Amy Johnson left on her flight to Australia.

During my last year at school, Mr Wood decided to have a school concert to be held in the Labour Hall at Green Oak. Labour had come to Totley in time for the 1926 elections, when a man called Rodgers came to live in a bungalow on the Heatherfield Estate. Most of the children at the school took part in the concert, trained either by Mr Wood or Miss Marsden. I remember Geoff was in a sketch about the 'Ten little Nigger Boys' (not a title allowed these days). It was something like 'Ten Green Bottles hanging on the wall' where one dropped out every so often. My part was, as usual, playing the piano.

The music teacher for both Elijah and I was Miss Harris, a very strict disciplinarian who really did rap knuckles with a ruler. Geoff and Jeff went to Miss Minnie Wild who lived in Lane Head Road, who was much more humane, and let her students play more popular tunes. I remember Jeff playing 'The Isle of Capri' and I was very envious when I was playing some unknown boring tune which was considered good for practice. For the concert, I was to play 'Under the Double Eagle' by Wagner, a piece which I had been learning and which Miss Harris thought I could play well enough to play in public. My turn came, and I mounted the platform, took my seat and started to play. I wasn't particularly nervous and things were going well when suddenly the lights went out; the hall was in darkness. As usual, I had to show what metal I was made of and, instead of stopping, I continued to play. I knew the piece well, good Lord, I'd played it often enough, so I was very sure of myself. I played on, the lights stayed off and the hall stayed dark, and I finished to a cheer that almost raised the roof. Josephine Salt was wonderful, she had saved the day; such was my pride - until my next lesson. As soon as I entered the music room Miss Harris rounded on me in a red faced fury. She wanted to know why I didn't stop and why had I gone on playing? She thought I should have stopped immediately. I was flabbergasted and deflated and felt that indeed pride comes before a fall, and there was worse to come. "You know you'll never make a concert pianist, you're not good enough, you'll be an accompanist, and you could make a successful one," she cried, "but not if you memorise the music." She continued, "If you memorise the music as you did this time, you will either lose your place in the music, or you'll go at your own pace and lose the soloist. Never, ever do that again". I should have been warned about Miss Harris' temper, for I had met it before.

I passed my first exam in 1927 with distinction. The second was passed in 1928, again with distinction, when Miss Harris was very pleased. In 1929 I entered for the third stage, and again passed, but not with a distinction. I was relieved to have passed, for it was a much more difficult exam and I expected Miss Harris to be pleased also, at least I hadn't failed. She was furious. "You had no business to just pass," she cried, and I got a tirade of criticism because I hadn't done better. "You should have got a distinction, if you only get a pass you could have so easily failed." I was flattened, and felt that her reasoning was unfair, and was her pride not mine that had caused all the aggro as she made evident with her final remark. "I have never had just a pass before." She must have conveyed her displeasure to my Father, for he said she had complained that I wasn't practising enough. His answer was to stop me having lessons. "I'm not paying any more, you'd better stop" and I did. He was good at using an occasion to suit his decisions.

One night he came home and said that Elva Scott had come home from London where she had just qualified as a dancing teacher. She was the younger daughter of Mr Scott, the Licensee of the Cross Scythes Inn, and Mr Scott told my Father that she wanted to start teaching in Totley, and was looking for students. I was about twelve years old and Mr Scott knew me from my efforts with the Bowling Club, and my Father knew that I wanted to learn tap dancing. He told me that night, that he had arranged for me to go to Elva's classes which would start just as soon as she could get enough students. I was overjoyed, and so excited I couldn't keep it to myself. As far as that goes, I hadn't been told to keep it to myself, so I never thought I was doing anything wrong when I told Gertie Trusswell about it. A few days later, on his return home from the Cross Scythes, my Father said "Why did you tell Gertie Trusswell about the dancing lessons?" This took me by surprise, and his manner overawed me. "I didn't tell her," I blurted out. "You're telling lies," he said. I fumbled and tried to explain but didn't dare say he hadn't told me not to say anything. "You told her, and her father's letting her go and for that, my girl, you will not go." I was devastated. Something I had dreamed of for years, with little hope of it ever happening, was refused, for what? The trouble really, as I saw later was that Mr Trusswell was a 'nobody'; he was barman at 'The Cross' and if his daughter was going to the classes, it was no place for my Father's offspring.

I had come across this attitude on more than one occasion. My Father noticed me talking to a village girl whose father had once worked at the pit; my Father in effect being his employer. He said that night, "You don't play with Ethel Turner again," and when I protested saying "I like her," he continued, "I've told you, don't let me see you with her again." No wonder I had a reputation of 'Lady Muck'.

One day Mr Wood told us that we were going on a trip to Liverpool. The SS Carinthia had docked there and the top two classes were going to view it. I was very excited, as it meant that I would be able to put on my best dress, a green silk creation which Dad had bought for me to wear under the green coat lined with multi-coloured pure silk which he had bought from Elsie Turner when she had grown tired of it, or grown out of it, I don't know which. I don't really mind wearing second hand clothes, although I envied those who always had new. But this was a lovely coat, the lining made it special and I loved to wear it open so that I could show it off and with my large brimmed green straw hat, I knew I looked older and more sophisticated than I really was. That's what most girls want to do until they reach the age of 21, then its panic time every birthday, wanting to go back instead of forward.

The trip to Liverpool was a great treat. As well as the trip round the Carinthia, we paid a visit to Port Sunlight, the model town built by Lord Leverhulme for his work people at the Sunlight Soap Factory. We walked around the streets, viewing the houses and discussing the architecture as well as learning about the philosophy of the Lever Brothers in their consideration for their workers. It was all very interesting and not marred at all at the thought of returning to school and having to write essays and answer questions about our day.

It was also in this last year that I had my first boyfriend. Jobie and we got to know each other better when he sat beside me at the table doing shorthand. Gordon Lowkes sat at the end of the table, and with Margaret, we sometimes made up a foursome. But Gordon lived the opposite way, on Heatherfield, whilst Jobie and I grew into the habit of walking home together and, after reporting to our respective homes, (Jobie lived in the bottom villa in Lane Head Road). We often walked up to the brickyard or down the hill and up Moss Road; Jobie was my boyfriend, with slight lapses, occasionally, for almost five years. He was faithful; I sometimes grew bored and failed to turn up for a meeting, but I knew that I only needed to walk past his home when I knew he was there, or to hesitate near the farm gate of his brother's farm where he worked, and we would be walking out together again, probably that night. Such was my confidence; you might say justifiably, my conceit.

Like all girls of our age the world over, both Margaret and I had crushes on boys and film stars. Margaret was deeply in love with Clive Brook; she used to dream about him regularly. My heart throb was Nelson Eddy; I could feel my eyes glazing over when I saw him on the screen and heard his voice. The boys of Dore came in for some heartrending too. We went to Dore Church every Sunday night. For the last three months at school, I was seconded to Miss Marsden's classroom, there to help with the new intake of infants. I was very proud, as this was what my Mother had done in her last three months at Dronfield Woodhouse School before she left in 1904.

Life on the other side was great. Miss Marsden was not the most popular teacher with the other teachers, she was brusque and sometimes a bit sharp tongued, but she was kind and understanding and had a sense of humour which matched that of the children in her care. I liked her and enjoyed every minute of my time with her. When Christmas came, she organised a small party, particularly for those children who would be moving up to Standard 1. Presents would be handed out by Father Christmas. I could hardly contain my excitement when she asked if I would like to act as Father Christmas; "Of course I would," I told her, She opened a box which she had brought from home, and took out a crimson coat trimmed with white fur, and helped me to dress in the adjourning cloakroom. A sack was produced, filled with presents (donated by whom, I don't know, probably the other teachers). When my disguise was complete, she left me to await her signal.

I had rehearsed in my mind all the things I would say to the children as I handed out the presents. There were about 20 of them, and when the time came, and I entered the classroom with, as I thought, the dignity and aplomb befitting such a personality, they were awestruck and speechless. Some ingenuity was required to illicit any response from the shyest of them, but its remarkable how the adrenalin triggers off the inspiration which comes with the excitement of the occasion. "Hello, little girl, what is your name? My you are a big boy, and what have you asked Father Christmas for?" came fluently so long as there was some response forthcoming; a bit more ingenuity was necessary for those who remained silent.

The job completed and lots of smiling faces around me when Miss Marsden said "Now children, say thank you to Father Christmas for all your lovely presents", instead of a chorus of "Thank you Father Christmas", one lone voice chimed out from a boy "That's not Father Christmas." "Yes it is," snapped Miss Marsden, "No it ain't" came the response equally as sharp "it's Josephine Salt, I can see her shoes." So much for my disguise for, sure enough, when I looked down; the red robe was a bit too short and my shoes peeped from underneath for all to see.

When the day came for leaving school I had very mixed feelings; excited at the prospect of going out into the world of adults, yet sad that a part of my life had come to an end. It was Christmas 1929, the last day before the holiday, when Mr Wood made his way to the door where the six pupils who were leaving stood in a line waiting. The ritual which followed had been performed before every school leaver since he had been the Headmaster. He shook hands with each of us in turn, wishing each one success in whatever career we followed, at the same time pressing into each hand a 6d piece. "So long as you have this, you will never be without money," he said, followed by "The only advice I will give you is keep on learning." My 6d was my most prized possession, sadly stolen with my purse in which it was kept, when I took my three-week-old son to the Clinic in Orchard Place in Sheffield in 1937.

So ended my formal education. No College, no University to call my 'alma mater'. My education from now on would be through an abundance of experience, the lessons learned from life. "Keep your eyes wide open, listen and pick other people's brains," had been my Father's advice. "Make use of every opportunity and don't be too proud to listen when people want to talk to you about their jobs, and tell you how good they are." Sound advice indeed. The art of picking brains, watching and listening thus taught me by my very shrewd

Father was, I think, the most valuable lesson of my life, for it never failed, never waned; it became a habit so strong that whatever task I observed other doing, my mind absorbed the routine and method of its construction whether or not I had use of it at the moment.

As the year passed, I have on many occasions had cause to bless this habit when some unexpected some unfamiliar task had been expected of me, and out of the depths of my mind has arisen a thought, a suggestion, directing my hand into the right direction for completion of the job in hand. This has tended to make me a 'Jack of all trades' and 'Master of none', for I have not achieved fame in any one field, rather developing into a 'know all' when in the company of others who, by their ignorance, showed they had never tried, or been interested in the work of others.

There have been times, sadly, when I have missed the education I might have enjoyed had circumstances been different and desperately wished that I had been given the opportunity to study languages, literature and the sciences in my younger years when the brain could more quickly absorb all the facts and figures; when the intellect was sharper and memory was laying down deeper paths in the brain. To spend time in study and revision without the distracting and time consuming tasks of daily life which interfere with learning in later years.

Gradually, all these thoughts built up a very large 'chip' on my shoulder, but being of that Scorpio temperament which fights, it probably gave me the incentive necessary to put my whole heart into learning. My Father had sown the seed, my Headmaster had nurtured its roots; it was up to me to bring it to harvest. The consequence is I have never lost my curiosity, never lost the urgency to find out, about matter, about politics, history and religion; about people and the arts. It has been an obsession which has eventually led me to the position I now enjoy, if that's the right word. The 'chip' remained with me for a number of years; which made me cynical, more critical of others, who I felt had wasted their time and opportunities; had taken for granted the education and favours, handed out by a privileged society or a fond 'Daddy'.

143

It took many years to make me realise that my intelligence and ability to learn was at least up to the standard of those who I supposed were better educated than I. The revelation in time, built up a slight feeling of resentment that I had missed out somewhere that by now I could have been much more knowledgeable and confident if fate had not stepped in. Confidence, I think, is the crucial attribute. Not self-confidence, for by anybody's standards, I had plenty of that; my proud upbringing had made sure of that. In personal attributes I was not lacking, never nervous when meeting strangers, no matter how elevated their status and I could hold a conversation with anyone except, and here in the crunch, when and if the conversation developed on a higher plane; when it involved some knowledge of literature, science or mythology or even Shakespeare. I was the ignoramus, the uneducated one, who was wise enough to keep her mouth shut lest ignorance should stand out like the sore thumb that it was.

The first time I really felt this was one of the most embarrassing and disappointing occasions of my life, which I was to be reminded of time and time again as the years went by; a memory of a chance missed. I was 18 years old, a member of the 'Young Conservatives' to which I had been introduced by cousin May. The Annual Garden Party was to be held at Grove House at the bottom of Hillfoot Road, which Mrs Grant, of the Mansion House, Newfield Lane, Dore, was to open. At the committee meeting a few weeks before, I was elected to second the vote of thanks, which would be proposed by another member of the committee, (yes I too was a member of the committee). I was not perturbed at the prospect, I had more than sufficient confidence to stand up in front of a crowd and make a speech, provided, and here was the crunch, provided I had confidence in what I had to say. When I thought more about the event, I realised that I did not have much confidence; in fact, I hadn't a clue about what I should say. Oh I had words, I made up brilliant sentences, thinking of all the ways I could say 'thank you'; I composed a really flowery speech that would have cut Caesar to shame but I hadn't the knowledge to know that it would be right. Was I supposed to say all these complementary things? Was I supposed simply to agree with the proposer and leave it at that?

All the picking of brains I had ever done was of no use to me now, for I had never seen anybody second a vote of thanks. No mock speeches, no mock trials, procedures for committee officers had not been in my school curriculum, and I hadn't a clue how to find out. My Mother was sympathetic, but "I'm sorry lass, I can't help you," was her response, "I've never been asked to do anything like that," she continued "Isn't there anybody you could ask?" Of course I could have asked my Father, with his experience of committee he would have known, but both my Mother and I knew that it would most likely result in a lecture about what he had, or had not, learned at school or at best, a long lecture on what to do, and what not to do, with a third degree after the event as to the outcome; and that was the last thing I wanted to boost my confidence. "Of course," suggested my Mother, "you could ask cousin May, she would know; why not ask her?" Now this is where pride comes before a fall; I was too proud to show my ignorance. (If my Granddaughter should ever read this, I would say this to her, "Beware of false pride; if the only way to find out what you want to know is to ask, then in great haste, ask!")

The day of the Garden Party arrived, and the proposer of the vote of thanks sat down. It was my turn now. Should I give my nice little speech, even though he had said most of the things I had thought of? Should I pick out one or two and agree with them, possible enlarge on them? Or should I play safe and be brief? My mind has never; neither before nor since, circled around a problem, crossing in so many directions, as it did in that ten seconds between the proposer sitting down and me standing up. And out it came.

I played safe, or so I thought, until I saw the look on the faces in front of me when they realised that all I was going to say was "Ladies and Gentlemen, I would like to second the vote of thanks", or words to that effect, and I knew that all these lovely words I had originally thought of would have been more appropriate. But, the die had been cast; the boat had gone out; it was too late, and I had missed my chance. Who knows, I might even have lost, in that ten seconds, the chance of becoming the first Lady Prime Minister.

There may be some virtue in being self-taught, but a self-taught man, or woman, never had the same assurance and confidence in the knowledge he/she acquired as the one who received it from a teacher who is an accepted authority on the subject. Much knowledge is obtained from reading, but at the back of the mind there is always the possibility that the information obtained in such a way, or the interpretation of such knowledge, is not correct. Worse still, the accumulation of knowledge so obtained might lead one to come to a wrong conclusion on many subjects. Not a situation to breed confidence.

None of this worried me on my school leaving day, nor in the early years of my adult life. Expectations for girls at the time did not demand a great deal of academic knowledge; furthermore, they were not uppermost in most people's minds. I had been endowed with sufficient of the attributes of human nature to surmount the usual rigours of life, and so, when my Father decreed that I should not go out to work, but should stay at home and help my Mother, I didn't question his decision nor the reason for it. On reflection, in later years, I think it is no mystery. There was little for girls to do on leaving school, except domestic services; what in those days was called 'being a skivvy', and the most likely place for such demand was in the newly built bungalows and houses of the new Heatherfield Estate, where the occupants were considered no better than the villagers. 'Bread and treacle folk' some people called them since one man lost his attaché case on the bus on the way to the office, and when asked what it contained, admitted to 'bread and treacle sandwiches'. When a piano fell through the floor of one of the bungalows, the episode clinched the reputation.

My Father was a very proud man, Manager of two mines, and employer of some of the village men. He was a sideman at Church, a Parish Councillor, and Captain of the Bowling Club, one of the most respected men in the village. There was no way he would have allowed his daughter to submit to the indignity of domestic service with such people, it was completely against his nature. Snobbery, maybe?

146

Chapter 7

For the first three months of my adult life, I did as decreed and stayed at home, but whether I actually did much to help is questionable. My Mother never forced me to do anything; she was so used to doing everything herself. I think she found it difficult to delegate even those jobs I could do. She had her own routine, and I doubt very much that had I done the ironing, she would have relaxed and sat down in the evening; it was against all she had ever known, even before her marriage.

I spent some time making myself a new dress; very clever of me according to Jobie. I remember making trifles and salads for Sunday tea; radish lilies and roses, cucumber butterflies and celery curls which I loved fiddling with, and I remember my Father bringing in a huge colander full of raspberries for the tea one Sunday and my Mother asking if I could do something nice with them for tea. I said I'd make a Raspberry Fool and set about sieving the raspberries and whipping the cream, blending them carefully with sugar and piling the finished delicacy into one of the best glass dishes, a swirl of cream added for decoration. "Dr Parsons would approve," my Mother said, a remark prompted by a recent event when Mrs Smith had made a batch of blackberry jam, which was still cooling on the table when the Doctor arrived to see one of the children. "What's that?" he said, looking at the jam. "Blackberry jam," said the lady proudly surveying the results of her efforts. In a sharp criticising voice the Doctor cried "Go and throw it in the midden, you'll have me coming for appendicitis next with all those seeds." Mrs Smith was devastated, in fact mortified, that he should so ridicule her handiwork, and as expected, Dr Parsons never set foot in the house again; it would be Dr Marshall in future. One or two of the choicest raspberries saved from the massacre were placed in situ as a final touch to the 'fool' and tea was ready.

Teatime on Sunday was almost as important as dinnertime. Even after roast beef and heaps of home grown vegetables, Yorkshire pudding baked in a large pudding tin in the true Yorkshire way and served as a starter, we could all do justice to a three course tea. There was usually a large tin of salmon, a piece of home boiled ham or bacon, or a basin of brawn, served with a salad of home grown lettuce or, in winter, a hearty savoy or January King cabbage sliced finely and mixed with home grown tomatoes, radishes, spring onions and grated carrots, the whole made delicious with homemade salad cream made from egg yolk, vinegar, cream and mustard, boiled in a double boiler. After this there was trifle, tinned fruit with cream, stewed home grown soft fruit, as the season allowed or, as on this occasion, a concoction of raspberries. As if this was not sufficient to satisfy the most avaricious appetite, there was always a fruit cake, a sponge cake, scones and teacakes, and plates piled high with homemade bread and butter. No one worried about cholesterol, or obesity, the only criteria being satisfaction and a full stomach. And, today it was raspberry fool.

The meal progressed in the usual way and first course over, plates were cleared away; cakes brought to the table, followed by the 'fool'. I watched Dad's expression as he gazed at this strange concoction and waited; I could tell what was about to happen; I knew the signs only too well and braced myself. He took his time, taking a piece of scone, then a piece of sponge cake, but before he sunk his teeth into the last delicacy, Mom rose and reached for a serving spoon and he watched as she lifted the dish ready to serve. Tapping on the edge of his plate he asked, "And what do we have here?" Without a flicker Mom said "It's Raspberry Fool." "Oh," he said pausing, "so it's Raspberry Fool," said in that slow way I knew only too well, with that same quizzical look on his face. "Fool?" (then another pause) "And what's Fool?" "Dene's made it," said Mom. "She made it from your raspberries." Dad's poker face didn't slip, but the signs were there, I knew this would go on until I shed tears of exasperation and anger. "My raspberries, do you mean to say they're my raspberries?" he said. "She sieved them to get the seeds out and mixed them with cream," said Mom, knowing full well what he was up to, but wanting the situation not to get too serious. "Seeds, seeds, do you mean my lovely raspberries have no seeds, my raspberries put through a sieve?" he said. Mom very quickly served him with a dishful and he could see I was very near tears. As the dish landed in front of him, he sunk his spoon into the pink concoction and took his first mouthful, then slowly finished the rest. Without looking at me, he held out his plate and said "I'll have another helping of that."

About two weeks after I left school, Dad came home from the Cross Scythes and broke the news that he had arranged for me to go to Abbeydale Night School for shorthand and typing. The Headmaster of Abbeydale Evening School was a member of the Bowls Team and the conversation had gone the way of discussing children and their futures. I was to start the next day, half way through the terms, but he assured me I'd catch up with my experience from school. This was a poor substitute for the full time course my friend Margaret was enjoying at Greggs Business School but I was thankful for even this small chance of something more than being in 'service', or staying at home.

As usual, Dad had overestimated or misunderstood the experience I had had at school, and he told the Headmaster that I had two years' experience and he had arranged for me to join the third year class and I had never even seen a typewriting machine. Consequently, when on the first night the teacher asked what I could do, she was amazed, but told me to do my best as the lower classes were full. I found it tough going, not helped by my Father's constant enquiries as to how I was getting on, and I dreaded the end of the session when I was expected to take the examination for speed and accuracy typing along with the other prospective secretaries. The test was for 40 words a minute, which I had no hope of achieving with any accuracy, but as usual I did my best and opted for accuracy rather than speed. Naturally, as my expectancy wasn't very high, I wasn't disappointed when I didn't pass; my biggest trial was when I arrived home that night and went through the third degree as to why. I had given my marked paper showing my one mistake, but no matter what explanation I gave, I should not have made it, according to him. "You

149

should be more careful in your exams or you'll never get on," was his final comment. How I envied Margaret and her College Course.

This wasn't the first time my Father had miscalculated in his eagerness to set his offspring on a career course. I remember the first day Elijah started at Walsh's as an apprentice cabinet maker. Arrangements had been made as before, in the pub with Mr Lake, who was a Director at Walsh's. A few days before the starting date, he had been to Sheffield and bought about £5 worth of tools (I suppose he thought he knew what was required from his own efforts at carpentry, although that was rather more rough joinery than professional carpentry). We often kidded him on his methods of taking measure-ments. "A thumb, a hand and an elbow" was the often heard cry, referring to the way he quickly made a calculation for the job in hand. Nevertheless, he did get the jobs done, like the doll's cradle he made for my first birthday out of an ammunition box for the doll (Florence), which was given to me by Florence Glossop, the daughter of the owner of a Coach company who lived on Moorwood Lane, Holmesfield and the cupboard he made from ammunition boxes in 1913 was still in existence, and being used in 1966, probably is so even now.

Elijah set off for work on his first day, no doubt full of expectancy and apprehension as to what silly jobs he was going to be asked to do, as all newcomers were subjected to. Tea was almost ready when I looked out from the door to see him walking up the road carrying the tool bag he had taken so expectantly that morning. "He's coming," I called, "but he's bringing his tool bag back," and so he was, there were the tools just as they were in the morning. Of course, Mom and Dad wanted to know what had gone wrong, but the simple answer was, as usual, apprentices were only tea-makers for the first few weeks. So our prospective cabinet maker was a little subdued for a while, but as the years passed, he proved the best in the region.

Some jobs my Mother gave me to do I didn't like too much, although I didn't mind polishing the room floor, or scrubbing the cellar steps, which I could decorate with donkey stone. But I liked helping with the cooking most of all and one of my most sorrowful memories is the remembrance of coming home from Sunday school one afternoon and finding Mom resting on the sofa. Whether it was the shock of seeing her there, for I had never seen her like that, she was always doing something. When she said "Make us some scones for tea love," I answered, "Oh, I can't be bothered." What a daughter, I thought afterwards, when I had time to think. How thoughtless children can be sometimes.

So passed the months from Christmas to Easter that year of 1930, uneventful and not very promising for that 'keep on learning' philosophy instilled into us at school. Also, there were times when little remarks crept in when one of the boys found a forgotten hole in a sock or Dad arrived home early and found dishes in the sink, probably from a recent batch of baking. "Two women in the house, and my socks not darned. Two women can't sew a button on. What have you been doing all day, pots in the sink?" By Easter time I was growing fed up, with a strong feeling that a net was closing in on me. I was tired of being just a girl, the odd one in the house, sleeping behind a curtain and of little consequence to anybody. I wanted to spread my wings, even into domestic service if that was the only way to escape. But it wasn't the only way, luckily as Mr Micawber would say, "Something else did turn up."

Talking one day to Gladys, my friend from schooldays, she told me of her intention to start work at Photo Finishers of Nether Edge, Sheffield. This was the factory part of Sheffield Photo Company of Norfolk Row, Sheffield where all their processing, developing and printing of commercial photographs were carried out. A collection and delivery service brought work from chemists and shops over a wide area. Grimsby to Worksop, from Rotherham, Doncaster, Scunthorpe and other parts of Lincolnshire to villages in Derbyshire and Yorkshire as well as postal services to seaside places such as Cleethorpes, Skegness and Scarborough.

During the summer holiday season, more seasonal workers were required; and Gladys suggested I apply. I did, and started work with her immediately after the Easter holiday. My Father agreed because it was seasonal work, but he was not very generous when the question of transport was considered. When Elijah had started work two years before, according to Father, walking was good for you, he

151

said he must walk to Dore & Totley Station, two miles away where he could catch a train to the city and walk back from the station in the evening. In fact, Elijah was picked up at the door at 7.00 a.m. every morning by 'Chippy' Fox who drove the brickyard lorry. He only had to walk home in the evening. I wasn't so lucky. My workday varied as the season wore on; at first from 8.00 a.m. in the morning until 5.00 p.m. in the evening, progressing to 7.30 a.m. until 6.00 p.m. and so on to 11.00 p.m. according to the day's work, for everything had to be cleared for delivery next morning, and the holiday season was hectic.

However, my constitution was just as valuable as Elijah's and if walking was good for his soul, then it would be equally as good for mine. So walk I must, not like him to the station, but the three miles to Beauchief, there to catch a tram to Broadfield Road, taking 'shanks' pony' once again up the hill of Sheldon Road to the converted old Chapel at Nether Edge which was now Photo Finishers.

I found the long days very tiring, sometimes arriving home late at night with bleeding thighs through sweating and rubbing together. My Mother was very often shocked to see the state of me, but it never dawned on her to tell my Father. "There's a kettle of boiling water, take it downstairs and bathe your legs," she'd say, "and take this cream and rub some in to soothe them." She was very sympathetic and understanding but in those days such intimate things were not discussed with men, or within men's hearing.

My first wages were 13s.6d (78p in today's money). On Friday my pay packet was handed to my Father unopened, as was the custom of the day until the age of 21. Some children gave it to their Mother, usually if she was the dominant person; but in our house, it was my Father. I received in return, 3d spending money, and as I no longer received 1d a week from my Mother, I was just 1d better off for working.

The most obvious disadvantage of this arrangement was that the parent who received the wages, bought the clothes, and being of the minority group in the house, it was very often difficult to put the case for freedom of choice. In fairness, the boys didn't get much freedom of choice either, but sex understands sex and their needs were more obvious as a rule. There were occasions when Elijah had room to grouse, the other two were more content for a few years yet.

My first job at Photo Finishers was trimming snapshots in the checking room. Each girl sat at a long table in front of a small guillotine fixed to the table. One girl attended the dryer which added the gloss to the snapshot, placing the dry prints in boxes, each print stamped with the number of the order, passing the boxes to the trimming tables. Each trimmer took a box, trimming the edges of each snapshot evenly and neatly, returning them to the box and passing it to a checker facing her on the opposite side of the table. She checked them with the negatives, transported in the same box, also checking for quality, too vigorous, too soft, over or under exposed or other faults. It was surprising how quickly one could work up a speed in twisting a print with the left fingertip whilst lifting and cutting with the guillotine blade with the right and as the season wore on, it became very pleasant, work becoming more automatic, and there was time for singing, or telling jokes with the other trimmers and checkers. I remember one day the boss passed by just when we were in a robust rendering of 'Our Blessed Redeemer' with soprano, alto and myself having a go at descant I had heard the church choir singing. Fortunately, Gordon Christie was a very understanding boss, provided work was not hindered or neglected.

Sometimes I took a turn on one of the driers when Edna who usually operated it wanted a break. The dryer was a large gas-heated drum about 3ft in diameter, the face of which was heavily chromium plated. A canvas conveyor belt passed round other small rollers providing a flat 'table' on which the wet prints were spread, picture uppermost before they passed under the hot drum between the belt and the chromium face. The drum rotated very slowly, as the prints were taken up the back, over the top, to be retrieved as they dropped off on to the canvas table below. Semi-gloss prints were dried naturally; matt ones were printed on matt paper and dried naturally.

The most important occupation for the dryer operator was to keep the drum clean and shining, the merest speck of dust could ruin a glossy print and waste was counted. The drum was polished regularly with metal polish and dusted vigorously before each batch

153

of prints. Sometimes when we were very busy, a call would come from the darkroom downstairs where the spools were unreeled and hung on racks which were then lowered into vats of developer, or from the drying room outside, where the developed spools were transported around a continuous track through a heated cupboard, being cut into negatives when they emerged at the end, quite dry. From here the envelopes of negatives, with their order forms, were sent up to the lift to the printing room.

Sometimes, someone was wanted in the reception area where the post was received and drivers brought in orders collected from contributing chemists. Here the orders were sorted, spools having their order sheets attached with rubber bands before being sent down the chute to the developing room. Repeat orders were sorted and sent to relevant Departments, whether for reprints, enlargements or other processing. At the end of the day, parcels were packed, maybe large prints, framed photographs or a commercial order for some advertising firm. Altogether, this was a satisfactory first season at work, and a little sadness that in September it came to an end.

As a rule, Gladys travelled home by bus, but sometimes she walked home from Beauchief with me. We were walking up the hill from Totley Rise on the last day when, as we came in sight of the Cross Scythes she said, "What are you going to do now Josie?" "I don't know," I answered, "I don't think I want to stay at home, but I don't know what else I can do." After a moment's thought Gladys said, "They want a kitchen maid at Totley Hall." "What does a kitchen maid do?" I asked. "Well, I expect she helps in the kitchen and learns to cook," she replied, adding "and you like cooking." "Oh I don't know", I said, "Do you really think I could do it?" The idea grew on me very quickly and instead of continuing up the road, I crossed over with Gladys, who lived in Hall Lane, and walked down to the Hall, not for a moment thinking of the consequences when I got home.

In my innocence I went to the front door of the Hall and faced the great oak edifice with a certain amount of apprehension. I couldn't see the bell, but at the side of the door was a huge knob, attached to a long rod, fixed to the wall and I assumed it was some kind of gong or bell. It was high and I had to stretch up to reach it, but after a mighty

154

effort, I managed to give it a hefty pull by using both hands, and could hear the sound reverberating inside. After what seemed like an eternity, the door opened and a large grumpy man stood looking at me scowling. He had a huge bandage wrapped around one of his feet and I learned later that he suffered from gout. "What do you want?" came his gruff question; almost a shout. In my nervousness my answer was a bit hesitant, "I understand that Mrs Milner wants a kitchen maid," I stammered, by this time scared stiff and wishing I'd never heard of kitchen maids. "You should be at the tradesman's entrance," this time it was a shout, "go round to the back door." He was just about to close the door when a figure appeared behind him. "What is it Adam?" came the question from Mrs Milner, for she had heard the commotion and came to see what was going on. "This girl here," he started, "should be round the back, she's come for the kitchen maid's job." He still held the door, but Mrs Milner came forward, took the door out of his hand and confronted me herself.

"What do you want little girl?" she asked, much more kindly than her grumpy husband. When I said what I had come for, she invited me inside, guiding me into the drawing room and offering me a chair near the fireplace. Settling herself on a settee opposite, she turned and opened the conversation. "Now, you say you want to work for me as a kitchen maid?" she said, "Do you know what a kitchen maid's duties are?" She seemed very kind and I had no difficulty in replying. "Helping the Cook," I replied, and "learning how to cook and do other jobs in the kitchen." "Do you like cooking?" she asked. "Oh yes," I said enthusiastically, "I was good at cooking at school, and my Mother is a good cook." I was on good ground now and more confident. "Who is your Mother?" she enquired, and when I told her, her attitude seemed to change. "Who is your Father?" this question asked quite sharply as if it was very important. When I told her my Father was Mr Salt she said quickly, "Mr Israel Salt?" I nodded, "Yes". "Would you really like to be my kitchen maid?" she asked, I thought more enthusiastically. When I replied "Oh yes Mm", she rose and held out her hand, "And so you shall be, I'll call and see your Father tomorrow." I was surprised at this sudden decision and just managed to stammer "Thank you Mm." "Let's say you will start on 1st October

155

shall we, will that be alright?" Would it be alright? You're telling me, it will be alright, I thought. "Yes, thank you Mm," I muttered, both delighted that I had got myself a good job, but a little apprehensive about the reaction from my Father when he knew.

My Mother was also apprehensive. "I don't know what your Father will say, you know he doesn't want you to go into service," she said, looking a little worried. "Well, I'm going, whatever he says," I replied. I knew she didn't like the idea of breaking the news to him, but she needn't have worried for Mrs Milner knew exactly how to deal with my Father; after all, she knew the family well, Uncle Arthur was her forester and under-head gardener and I didn't know until years later, that she moved in the same circle of society of friends as our Great Great Aunt Julia Newbry of Cheltenham.

At 3.00 p.m. the next afternoon when she knew my Father would have returned from the pit, he was getting washed at the sink in the living room when the knock came to the door. My Mother opened it and in strode Mrs Milner, coming straight to the point with "Ah, Mr Salt, I'm so pleased and honoured to have your daughter coming to work for me." I can imagine the relief on my Mother's face from the expression when she told me about the visit. My Father was amazed, but Mrs Milner had hit that little nerve in him that tingled at the thought that the Squire's wife should be honoured to employ his daughter. Explanations had to wait, for Mrs Milner took a good hold of the situation as she charged across to the sink. "Does Josephine wash up at this sink?" she asked, and my Mother answered, "Yes, Mm." "And is it the right height for her?" she doesn't have to bend over?" "No Mm," came the answer. "You see, the sink that Josephine will have to use in the scullery is rather high," she explained, "I can put a duckboard there for her to stand on, so I think it will be alright." With little more to say, she bid them good day and left. The questions and discussion then began.

I think my Father was a little mesmerised at the speed of this episode, and it took a little time for him to absorb what it meant. First was the fact that I was, after all, going into domestic service, and on this point my Mother sensible pointed out that this was not ordinary domestic service, it was in a gentleman's house. Furthermore, it would be good training for, she said, "She'll learn to cook more things than I can teach her, and she'll learn how to run a bigger house than this. Furthermore, "the other servants will be different from the usual domestic servant or Mrs Milner wouldn't employ them." This last point, she thought, was one of the decisive reasons for him accepting the situation.

When relating this to me later, she said, "It brought it to his mind what Mrs Milner had said about it being an honour. "You know," she said with the hint of a twinkle in her eye, "your Father was always one for flattery." The second reason for his agreeing to the arrangement was a practical one. There were only two bedrooms at the cottage and although they were a good size, being large enough to take two double beds comfortably, since Jeff had reached the age of a year, old enough to move into a bed, he had slept with me in one of the double beds, Elijah and Geoff sleeping in the other. This arrangement had worked alright until I reached the age of puberty, when it became a bit embarrassing both for me and, I presume, for the boys. Mother suggested I use their room as a dressing room, but communal sleeping was still a problem.

By the time I was 13, my parents thought I should no longer sleep with Jeff. They must have been thinking this was for some time, for I had heard them discussing the possibility of moving to a three bedroomed house. My Father absolutely refused to move nearer the village, and there were no houses beyond ours for another six miles, at Baslow, so here we stayed. I might add that it wasn't unknown for brothers and sisters to sleep in the same room, but to have to sleep together at my age stretched credulity a little.

Elijah had completed his first year's apprenticeship with Walsh's cabinet making firm and had learned sufficient about furniture making to enable him to make a good bed. Dad decided he should make four, one each for the four of us. He obtained a quantity of oak and Elijah cut, carved, polished and produced four beautiful beds such as any handmade furniture company would be been proud of. Of course, Mom had two more lots of bedding to launder each week, but that was of no consideration, it was just 'woman's work'. So, for the past year, I had my own bed, but still had to share a room

157

with my three brothers, not an ideal situation and before long, my Father would have to agree to a move. Now, it seemed, there was a way out of the situation, if I went to the Hall, everybody would be happy.

There were still two weeks before I had to report to Totley Hall, so Mom decided we should spend a day with Auntie Annie as it might be a long time before we could all go together again. Auntie Annie was really my Mother's Aunt, sister of her mother who died when she was five years old. She was a sort of second mother, and the nearest we had to a Grandma. She had worked in domestic service since the age of eight, first with a local farmer at Dronfield Woodhouse. It was common in the 19th century for children to be boarded out at an early age, working for board and lodging, and sometimes a few coppers for spending money (which they often sent home for the rest of the family). She later trained in various gentlemen's houses rising to the job of Cook, twice for the Master Cutler, and once for the Lord Mayor of Sheffield, when Lord Mayors were members of the upper class, if you'll forgive that expression.

Born in 1866, by the time of the First World War, I don't know the exact date; she left domestic service and took a shop and bakery at 61 Neville Street, Pitsmoor in Sheffield where her brother, Uncle Jack went to live with her, after the War. Whilst we were still at school, Mom had taken us to see Auntie Annie during the summer holidays, a real treat and something very different for we weren't used to the city, the rows and rows of houses all joined together in long streets, and the town people seemed very different from our family and friends.

We set off early in the morning, taking a bus to Millhouses and then a tram to Spittle Hill, then walking up Spittle Street, round the bend into the street which eventually led to Neville Street. Women stood at the doors in their 'pinnies' gossiping as we passed, and passing remarks as to who we were. It was all very strange. But all was well when we reached Auntie Annie's shop and felt the welcome from her, and Uncle Jack, if he was at home. Not that Auntie Annie was very effusive in showing her feelings, like my Mother, she kept her own countenance, casting a quirky glance occasionally and saying only what was necessary for the occasion. Uncle Jack worked at Bridehouses Goods Yard since he returned from the War, which must have been a complete change for him. He had been a farmer, being called up late in the War, when he was sent to Kent as a groom, rounded up from all parts of the country vetting the horses ready to ship across the channel, treating and grooming those that had completed a tour of duty ready for their return to the battlefields. He was a solid country man with a basic sense of humour, much more outgoing than his sister whom he loved more than anything or anybody. When Auntie died in 1949, Uncle Jack was devastated. He died five weeks later of a broken heart. The autopsy result showed that his heart was slowed and broken with the stress of grief. But now back to Aunt Annie.

Auntie Annie had retired after working as a cook for many years for Mr & Mrs Hobson of 'Eschscholtz', a large house in Whirlowdale Road, Sheffield, before becoming the offices of Dysons Refractories, owners of the brickworks on Totley Moor. Mr Hobson had twice been Master Cutler, an office which demanded a great deal of entertaining. These were the days before everything could be bought from the supermarket, when all wines were made by the Cook; all salad creams and sauces, jellies from fruit juice and gelatin; baking powder from bicarb and cream of tartar had to be made in the kitchen. (Self-raising flour had not yet been invented). It was the time when Cook was mistress of her kitchen and even the mistress had to beg entry. At the back of the shop was a long narrow kitchen and behind that, another kitchen which held the huge ovens reaching to the ceiling in which she baked bread and cakes to sell in the shop.

The bakery section was closed by the time of our visits, the shop now being a general store selling groceries, sweets, tobacco and cigarettes. One item she had continued to make was ice cream. It was delicious old fashioned ice cream, made in a wooden tub with a zinc container standing inside, leaving about 4″ all round in which she put pieces of ice. The ice was delivered from the ice making factory in Pond Street near the markets, whenever it was required. (As there were no telephones, I assume she had a standing order every so often). One thing that mystified me as a girl was, why didn't the ice melt quicker when she put salt in the container with it? When we put salt on the footpath to melt the snow, it was quicker. It was many years before I sunk my pride to ask, and even then, the answer wasn't a particularly scientific one. "It melts slower," Aunt Annie said in her precise way.

She was always precise. Whenever you asked a question, you always got a precise answer, such as a teacher might explain. I always got the impression that she was fond of children but was at a bit of a loss how to treat them. So, she treated them as adults, with an occasional slightly quizzical quirk of countenance. But she was exceptionally kind, as was obvious only towards us, but towards her customers, and it was obvious that they respected her very much, it was 'Miss Fisher this and Miss Fisher that', no familiarity even after a number of years.

Uncle Jack said, "No wonder she's daft with 'em, if they want summat they can't pay for, she let's 'em 'ave it and pay later, but she don't always get paid." I watched this in action on numerous occasions, most of all I remember the packets of Woodbine cigarettes. It was a poor area and the men, more often than not, couldn't afford a full packet of five, at 2d a packet (less than 1p in decimal currency). Auntie split the cigarettes, passing over the counter two of them for which the customer paid 1d, and his name would be written on the packet. The next purchase would also be 1d, but this time, the customer would receive three cigarettes. It was, in a way, making sure he came back, but I'm sure Auntie Annie never thought like that.

One sale I loved to watch was sweets. The best toffees were 2oz. for 1d but there were many cheaper ones, like Aniseed Balls and Fish Mixtures as well as Tiger nuts, the only place I ever saw them and Cinder Toffee. There was no law that sweets had to be wrapped, although Bluebird and some other toffees were already wrapped. Boiled sweets, mint rock, broken toffee and other loose items had to be sold in bags of some kind. I remember Mom making little cone shaped bags out of triangles of newspaper in our own house window shop, but the speed with which Auntie Annie made them fascinated me; it was nothing short of miraculous. A quick turn of the hand, grasp the corner in finger and thumb, and a neat turn of the point, and hey presto the bag was ready. I longed to have a go, not only at making the bags, but weighing and serving things, but you didn't do that with Auntie Annie, we were not allowed in that wonderful world behind the counter, although we all tried at some time or another.

Tea with Auntie Annie was always the same, and one of the pleasures of our visit. A tin of salmon from the shop served with tomatoes and homemade bread and butter made from the cream she obtained from the Dairy across the road, followed by peaches, again from the shop and Auntie's delicious ice cream. She always used the same two glass dishes for this salmon and peaches which still hold pride of place in my cupboard. Uncle Jack often used to visit us at Lane Head and once he went on holiday to the Isle of Man with my father. (He was the one who brought me the horseshoe brooch, which I will tell you about later). Aunt Annie never visited, I doubt whether she went anywhere except to work and the shop was even open on Sundays. In the early days at Neville Street, she sometimes went to help out at another bakery close at hand, but towards the end of her life her memory failed, and Uncle Jack told how often he caught her with her hat on and an overall in a parcel under her arm, and when asked where she was going, she always said, "I'm just going down to the bakery, they want me to bake a batch of buns." How sad, for the bakery by then had been closed for a number of years. But I've raced ahead; I'll go back a few years.

On one of Uncle Jack's visits, he brought a present for me from Auntie; it was a bail of beautiful Roman satin. My Mother took it to Emily Green, the dressmaker, who made it into a beautiful dress, bright luminous pink, which I wore on Sundays and special days. The first visit after receiving the gift, during a lull in the conversation with my Mother she asked, "And did you like the material I sent for you?" Taken by surprise, and a little guilty that I hadn't succeeded in finding a pause in which to thank her, I blurted out, "Oh thank you very much for sending it," but before I could get any further she cried "Listen to the girl, I ask her if she liked it and she starts to thank me, whatever next?" I looked at her sheepishly and said, "Yes Auntie, Mom had it made into a dress for me and I like it very much." "Oh, that's alright then," she said, and that was the end of the matter.

There wasn't far to go to Neville Street for milk and cream, and it couldn't have been fresher. Across the road from the shop was a dairy. There was a wide high archway through which could be seen a large paved yard with buildings all around it. At certain times, cattle could be seen in the yard at milking times, and when the sheds were being cleaned out. It was the practice for cows to be kept in towns, and there were a number of them in Sheffield. One was Bill Holmes who kept cows in South View Road; another was Jack Helliwell who kept his in a short street off Broadfield Road.

During the winter, many of them were supplied with fresh hay and clover by farmers in country districts. Before his marriage, when Grandma Salt ran a farm at Dronfield Woodhouse, Dad used to mow a load of clover before 5.00 a.m. in the morning when he left for the pit and Uncle Dick (Auntie Ruth's husband, who worked for Grandma before he married) delivered it to a cow keeper in Sheffield. Uncle Walter, May's father, was twelve years old when he took dray loads of hay to Dankels at the bottom of Ecclesall Road, and often to his sheep on the moors. Elijah remembers taking a 'chain horse' to the bottom of the brickyard hill, or to Totley Rise, when Tommy Duddy, the farm man at Creswicks on Moorwood Lane, had taken a load of hay or clover to Sheffield, bringing back a load of grain from a brewery. Wet grain was heavy and it took two horses to pull the load up the steep hills. The relief horse was chained to the shafts as lead horse, taking the strain from the one who had done the double journey.

Some of the cow keepers kept their cows during the summer in fields and open spaces around the city. Bill Holmes kept his in fields in Springfield Road, Millhouses. He took a stool and milked them in the field twice a day. This arrangement was called 'Agistment' ('Gisting' in Derbyshire). A Mr Harrison of Tyzacks Road, Woodseats had an Agistment in Bocking Lane and abbey Lane, and Tom Harrison of Soho Street, where Shaw's Wire Works were later built, milked his cows in fields where Hunters Bar School now stands. Sometimes a cow keeper would keep a 'travelling' herd, buying a newly calved cow, keeping it for one 'note', (the time a cow was milked after calving), at the same time feeding it well in order to put meat on whilst being milked. Brewer's grains left from brewing beer, and bean meal supplied fibre, Indian meal and Ureco (flaked Maize) provided protein, and bran and chop, linseed cake, turnips and swedes, were all fed to the cow and when the lactation period was over and milking stopped, the cow was sold, either for beef or for servicing again.

We hear these days of herds of 200 cattle or more, but in those early days it was possible to make a living with far less. It could, of course, be that expectations were less then or that progress and technology have created a breed that must have more of the perks. Whatever the reason, one man, Mr Hawke, kept only eight cows, which he milked for one 'note', the third then sold them back for servicing again and he retired very comfortably off on the proceeds. The third note, the lactation period after the third calf, was the most productive.

Some milk procedures would buy a cow in calf and after it was born, would sell it immediately at the auctions held every Thursday in the Fairground at Sheffield (held at the bottom of the approach road to the Royal Victoria Hotel under the arches). The cow was then milked for one, two, or three 'notes'. There were, of course, some Dairies where no cattle were kept. Milk was brought in by the milk train from Derbyshire (from Grindleford to Heeley station), where it was sold to and collected by the milk dealers who sold it from home. Sometimes they fell short of milk and it was common for farmers who had their own delivery rounds and often had surplus milk, to be stopped on their way home by the dairymen who relieved them of the surplus. Elijah remembers that Creswicks were often stopped by one dairyman off Broadfield Road for their spare milk. Bookers of Birchett, who also delivered their own milk, took their spare milk to Mr Booker's father in Aberdeen Street. Mrs Booker's father, Reuben Shaw, was a cow keeper in Franklin Street. The last of the cow keepers in Sheffield was Mr Siddall of Aberdeen Street in the 1950s.

On this present visit, just before I went to work at Totley Hall, Auntie Annie was most interested to hear that I was to go into gentlemen's services. The previous Christmas I had taken her the first cake I had ever iced; it had a little mirror to simulate a pond, and lots of scrolls and stars made with the two or three Tala icing tubes my

Mother had bought for me. Auntie Annie was impressed with my effort. After a few minutes discussing exactly how I covered the cake and mixed the icing, she went upstairs, returning with a large cardboard box and a small tin box. Opening the cardboard box she brought out three wooden turntables, and the spindle on which they turned saying, "These are the turntables I always used when I iced cakes." I looked at them closely as she fixed two on the spindle, one for the base, the other for the top, and explained that each could be used for the base as well as the top, according to the weight of the cake. Then, turning to me with that quizzical smile on her face, she surprised me by saying; "Now you are interested in icing, you can have them." I was completely taken aback. I knew she had spent three years at Bell's Confectionary business learning cake icing and decorating and other confectionary, and my Mother had told me of her visits to a French teacher to learn the art of patisserie, and to be given her turntables was pleasure indeed. But there was more to come. She opened the tin box and there were the smallest, daintiest icing tubes I had ever seen. "These are the icing tubes I used," she said, "They are French," and after only a moment's hesitation, added "you can have these too."

There then followed my first real lesson in making icing bags from greaseproof paper. There was a cotton bag inside the tin box but Auntie said, "If you want to be professional, you must use paper ones, professional cake-icers never use cloth bags." It was at these times that Auntie was at her most precise and serious, she had obviously loved her work, and must have been jolly good at training her kitchen maids, for she made quite sure I understood everything she was doing. My next lesson was on this present visit. After questioning me at some length as to what I expected life to be like living in a gentleman's home, she went on to explain that because there was no butler at the Hall, the Cook under whom I would work was head of the staff, and was expected to control and direct them ."So," she said, "as well as training you in the duties of the kitchen, you will have to learn how to behave correctly in that sort of house."

I was beginning to be rather worried, wondering what to expect and, of course, I didn't realise that the type of house she had worked in was much bigger than Totley Hall, a quiet country house, not the busy entertaining house of the Master Cutler. Nevertheless, she assured me that I would have to know how to behave in the company of the upper-class people and this would be learned in the Servant's hall. "Table manners are just as important for staff as they are for the gentry," she said. "When you grow up, you will want to meet 'well-off' people and you must know how to behave."

There followed my first formal lesson in table manners. She went into the shop, returning with a large William pear. "Now, you will have dessert just like the mistress and you must know how to deal with it; do you know the correct way to eat a pear?" I could have said "Put it in your mouth and bite," but not to Auntie. I muttered meekly "No." She produced a plate and a small silver knife and fork with pearl handles. "Now," she began, "take the fork and hold it daintily in your left hand, steady the pear with the knife, and gently push the fork into the pear through the end." (This was the end which had been the flower, not the stalk end). "Now," she continued, "hold the knife daintily and peel down from the stalk end to the fork, and don't touch the pear with your fingers." I obeyed whilst Mother watched patiently. She said she had never been told how to do that, I was lucky that Auntie was so kind.

Peeling the pear proceeded painfully, it wasn't as easy as it sounded, and I sadly wanted to discard the tools and simply take a bite. But, I persevered, and at least could release the pear from the fork, but the job wasn't finished. Now I had to cut it very carefully in half, then in quarters and take out the core. This done, I could now cut off a little from one quarter, impale it firmly on the fork and transfer it to my mouth, at the same time putting the knife down on the edge of the plate, not clinging on to it ready to cut the next piece. Task completed, she said if I practised, I would soon be able to do it like a lady. To be honest, by the time I had finished, I hoped I'd never see a pear at Totley Hall, the feeling of eating it would disappear by the time I had it peeled. Luckily, or perhaps unluckily, things weren't as formal there, so I never had to peel a pear. I did, however, have to peel grapes, but that's another story.

Chapter 8

The day arrived for my departure from home for the new life I would lead from now on. My Mother had packed a large suitcase with the clothes I would need, and one or two trinkets for my dressing table, carrying it for me to the Post Office corner where I would cross the main road to walk down Hall Lane. Here she kissed me goodbye and I walked the rest of the way alone. My feelings were very mixed as I left her, and the tears weren't far away as I waved a last goodbye before she disappeared up the next road again. But the prospect of my new job soon raised my spirits, and the excitement and expectation took the place of sadness.

The latch gate in Hall Lane led into the wooded surrounds of the Hall and the flight of steps up into the courtyard at the back of the house. As I crossed the stone flags to the kitchen door, it opened and Cook stood in the doorway waiting to greet me. A step or two more and she came towards me, taking my case and carrying it into the kitchen where I would spend so much of my time in future. To my eyes, used to a cottage living room which, although a good size, was nothing like the one which now confronted me. It was huge, and almost the whole of one wall was filled by a big black cooking range whose three large ovens each boasted a shining shelf below. The fire hole in the centre was so large I thought it must hold a cwt. of coal all at once, and beneath was the biggest ash pan I could imagine. No wonder, I thought, it was necessary after burning so much coal.

Rising, almost to the ceiling, was the highest of mantelpieces, the shelf on top holding bright brass and copper pans in all shapes and sizes, whilst underneath still hung the 'hook' and 'jack' once used for roasting meat in front of the fire, obviously left from by-gone days. A bright fire shone out in welcome and the aroma of food cooking in one of the ovens filled the kitchen. It was all so homely and I knew I would be happy here. A large bare wooden table, big enough it seemed to me to seat an army, stood against the wall opposite the fireplace. It was scrubbed white, and now littered with the tools of cooking, weighing scales, and a well-used 'Mrs Beaton's' cookery book.

The third wall was almost wholly filled by a cupboard which rose from the floor to within a foot of the ceiling. I was to learn in a few moments that here were kept the many and varied cooking and serving dishes with which I would become familiar as time went by. Immediately opposite, beneath the window, was a long stone sink, at the moment holding a panshon of soap water and an assortment of dishes and pans. There was no need of a 'duckboard' here I thought, for it was quite low and suitable for my height. The floor, with which I could soon become very familiar, was made of black and red earthenware tiles, which thankfully I soon realised, would need no polishing.

Cook took me upstairs and along a short corridor to the bedroom I would share with Annie the under-housemaid, whose first name, explained Cook, was Gladys. When Gladys had joined the staff, the parlour maid's name was also Gladys. To prevent any confusion Mrs Milner asked if she would mind using her second name Annie, and she agreed. Gladys Wragg had now left, but Annie had retained her name.

The bedroom, built over the scullery had a window overlooking the courtyard. It was very large and although holding two single beds, two wardrobes and dressing tables, there was still sufficient space in the centre of the room for a brightly patterned rug. This, I thought, was going to be sheer luxury for me, almost as good as having my own room.

Cook left me to unpack, and went downstairs to continue preparing lunch. I was to join her and the rest of the staff in the Servant's hall when I was ready. It didn't take long to unpack, and having done so, I excited put on the grey dress, white apron, black stockings and shoes which would be my uniform from now on. All the servants wore dresses, except Cook, who wore blue and white stripes, front staff changing after lunch into pale grey. Aprons for everybody were large white ones similar to the ones worn by nurses. They had full skirts set on a waist band which fastened at the back with a large cloth button, a bib covering the chest with straps crossing over the back and fastening at the sides with two more buttons. Kitchen staff changed into similar aprons after lunch, but housemaids and parlour maids changed into less voluptuous ones with bibs which fastened with two small gilt safety pins, the waistbands tying at the back in a huge bow. All three front staff wore stiff cuffs when answering bells or the front door, or serving meals. Neither Cook nor kitchen maid wore caps; others wore caps with broad turned back brim, and a drawstring at the back which could be let out for ironing.

When I was satisfied with my appearance, I went downstairs to the kitchen where Cook was putting finishing touches to the dishes for the Master and Mistress and Edna, the parlour maid, was standing by waiting to take them through to the dining room. Cook introduced me to her, and also to Mary, the head housemaid who was to show me where to find the servant's hall, and to help me with my first setting of table, a job which I would be responsible for from now on.

Before we sat down to our own lunch, I was introduced to Annie, a local girl from Totley Rise, with whom I would become firm friends during my stay at the Hall. This first meal passed pleasantly. Cook sat at the head of the table, with Edna on her right and Mary on her left. Annie took the seat next to Mary; I occupied the seat next to her. Old Nurse Forbes held the honoured position next to Edna with Miss Knott by her side when visiting the household, which was every Wednesday; the seat at the bottom of the table was Mrs Hill's when she came to wash Mr Milner's large white handkerchiefs in the morning, and spending the afternoon carefully ironing.

During the conversation, I learned that the servants ate exactly the same fare as that served to the front of the house, except when special menus were created for visitors, when Cook was free to choose what she cooked for us, unless game was on the menu. Grouse and pheasant were often sent to the household during the shooting season, but this delicacy was not for servants. Not that this was any hardship, for Mrs Milner was most particular about the welfare of her staff and good food was one of the things we had in abundance. When a roast was served, it was carved quickly and brought back to the kitchen to be kept hot. Puddings, if not duplicated, were treated in the same way, so that both front and back of the house ate almost simultaneously. I already knew of the mistress's concern for our personal comfort when she took the trouble to measure the height of the sink at home, and now I realised this went further when Cook said, "If you would like to bring a friend, or your Mother to tea today, just tell me, this is your home your know, and Mrs Milner doesn't mind any of us having visitors." In return for this consideration, I was also to learn that my mistress was a keen disciplinarian and 'woe betide' anyone who didn't do their job well.

Almost immediately after the meal was over, everyone seemed to disappear all at once, leaving me with Cook, who helped me to clear the table, explaining that the servant's hall would be, more or less, my responsibility. She would help me today with the clearing and washing up, then as this was her free time, we would go back to the servant's hall and she would explain exactly what my duties would be. As I listened, I thought they didn't sound too arduous, but I hadn't reckoned on the time factor for although they amounted to straight forward housework, my day would start at 6.00 a.m. in the morning, finishing at 9.00 p.m. at night. The rest of my first day was spent in finding out where things were kept, and getting acquainted with the rest of the rooms where I would work, the most important being the scullery.

The scullery was another very large room with a floor of stone flags. There was a small window in one corner, in front of which stood a pot sink. A duckboard had been placed on the floor in front, but whether this was for my benefit or a regular feature, I don't know. It was a bare room with only a long bench down one side on which a coffee grinder was screwed down for security in use. In an alcove, where a fireplace had been removed, stood a large, very old gas stove, the high mantelpiece above it displaying a row of black iron pans of all sizes. On the far side of the room a wide stable door led into the courtyard where Mr Young, the chauffeur, was putting the final touches to the ablutions of the family Daimler. Beyond the garage, facing us across the courtyard Cook pointed out the small stone building up two steps in which, she said, the garden boy cleaned the shoes of the family and visitors, and where, sometimes, I would pluck poultry and game.

The scullery stood immediately beneath my bedroom, and next to the garage, which had been the old coach house; consequently the original hayloft over the garage and then stables next door adjourned the bedroom, its existence brought home to me with a vengeance on my first night. As this had not been a working day for me, I was allowed to stay up late; in future I would have to retire at 9.00 p.m. every night, except on my day off, when it would be 9.30 p.m.

Annie and I went upstairs together, chattering about 'something and nothing' as new acquaintances are apt to do, still talking when we climbed into bed. The next day would start at 6.00 a.m. for me so, after setting an alarm, the light was put out and we both settled down to sleep. Suddenly, I sat bolt upright, as a loud scurrying and scuttling was heard overhead. I was about to ask Annie what was happening when she called, "Don't worry Josephine; it's only the rats having their village sports." I gasped, "Do they always go on like that every night?" "Yes," she laughed, "but don't worry they can't get through to us, and you'll soon get used to them." At the time I thought this very unlikely, but strangely enough, I did.

6.00 a.m. came all too soon, and half asleep, I dressed in the dark so as not to wake Annie, and finding my way along the corridor, past Cook's bedroom door and the store room next door, both over the kitchen, went quickly downstairs to the back hall and into the kitchen. It seemed even larger than the day before now that I was alone, and very quiet and eerie. But this was no time for dwelling on that for too long; I must make a start if I was to have everything done by 7.30 a.m.

First the tools, coal rake to rake out the ashes from the spent fire in the scullery. Sticks and coal brought in by the garden boy, yes; there they were by the side of the fireplace. First get the fire lit, and hope it will go first time lighting, I'd seen my Father growing frustrated if the sticks were not dry. Thankfully, this time it caught on first time lighting. Soon bright enough for the big black kettle to be filled and stood on the trivet for morning tea. But, as Mary said when I looked worried about whether it was boiling, "Not to worry Jose, there's always the gas stove to fall back on." (Although I was soon to learn that to use the gas stove when there was room on the fire was not good economics).

Next were the brushes and cloths to polish the range before it got too hot; in the scullery again, yes, in the cupboard under the sink, in the box with the handle. The stove was easy, it had been black-leaded the day before, Friday, so needed little polishing, the brass fender required a little more elbow grease, but soon came up shining and bright, only the floor to sweep and a quick wipe over in front of the sink and the table, a flick with a duster over cupboards and mantelshelf, and there was only the big 'clippy' rag to shake when Mary appeared at the kitchen door. All was well as she was the kettle boiling away on the fire grid, and said a boisterous "Morning Joss," proceeding to make the tea. Mary was a bit unpredictable, one minute full of 'beans' and friendly, the next making a mischievous remark or a 'catty' sideswipe at somebody's expense. Fortunately, I was to come into contact with her very little, so I learned to cope with her moods. I took my second wash of the day, rolled down my sleeves, and called Cook with a cup of tea, had one myself, and started on the servant's hall, whilst Mary, having finished hers, filled a glass with hot water, placed it on a silver salver, and went upstairs to call the mistress.

The servant's hall was a long narrow room at the bottom of a sloping corridor leading from the kitchen to the Butler's Pantry, where Edna, the parlour maid cleaned the family silver, washed all dishes from the dining room and supervised the use and laundering of all the table linen and cutlery stored there. A fireplace was situated on one side wall, and there was a high window at the far end of the room. A long polished table and about ten chairs stood in the centre with a large sideboard on the other side wall. Two easy chairs completed the furnishings, leaving a space of about 10ft square in front of the window proving a handy place for a little 'tomfoolery' after dinner in the evening.

As in the kitchen the fire grate had to be cleaned and a fire lit; the floor swept and dusted with a mop and furniture dusted before setting the table for breakfast at 8.30 a.m. Breakfast was the same for mistress and staff, except that nobody in the Servant's hall took porridge, probably because no-one liked that made for the front of the house from oatmeal sent from Scotland every month, and made in the Scottish way with salt. During the week there was bacon, eggs and tomatoes, with brown and white toast and marmalade. (The smell of brown toast even now reminds me of the toast I prepared on the cooker grill in the scullery at Totley Hall). At the weekend we had sausage with gravy on Saturday, and boiled eggs on Sunday.

Breakfast over, table cleared, cloth neatly folded and put away, and fire banked up with coal, I made my way to the scullery to wash and put away the dishes, Edna doing the same in the Butler's Pantry. I must admit that, after my first three hours' work on that first morning, I felt I had already done a day's work, but the real work was yet to come, and curiosity, as well as a willingness to please, kept me sufficiently awake to respond.

Straight after breakfast every morning, Mrs Milner came through to the kitchen door, calling out in a falsetto voice as she strode up the slope past the servant's hall to the kitchen door, "Cook, Cook." As per protocol she never actually came into the kitchen, for traditionally, that was Cook's domain. Cook, having pulled down her sleeves and patted her hair, followed the mistress into the pantry to talk over the day's menus for lunch and dinner.

The pantry was really a room, or rather two rooms. The main one had originally been the 'Stillroom' in the days when all wines were made on the premises, and the diary where milk was stored and cream skimmed off for making butter. Cheese had also been made in here and stored on shelves in the inner room. There was a 3ft steel stone bench down one side of the room, where possibly curing of bacon and hams had taken place, now used to stand the large yellow bowls of milk delivered every morning from the Home Farm (Totley Hall Farm) in a two two-gallon milk cans by Connie Tym, daughter of the farmer. They stood there for the cream to rise, covered by muslin cloths, which were soaked in cold water

173

throughout the day in summer, evaporation helping to keep down the temperature, although with all the stonework and only a small window, it always seemed very cold to me. When cream was needed for some recipe or other, or for after dinner coffee, the cream was skimmed off with a skimmer, like a very high shallow saucer, the skimmed milk being used for regular cooking.

Mrs Milner was thrifty, although not mean, and unless visitors were expected, she would ask if there was anything left from the previous day which could be used today. Sometimes she would request something special, perhaps for a dinner party or luncheon, when she would open her special recipe cupboard in the Butler's pantry, handing the chosen recipe to Cook, who was expected to hand it back immediately it was finished with. There was an unwritten law in the kitchens of that day, that the mistress's recipes were her own and nobody must disclose their content. At the Hall, nobody ever did.

About 9 o'clock Mr Lewis, the Head Gardener came to ask what vegetables were required and to tell Cook what was available, by which time she had returned to the kitchen with the day's menus. In the meantime, I could get on with peeling potatoes which were required for today's luncheon, though baked ones might be ordered for dinner. This was where my cookery training really began for, although we had had an abundance and variety of vegetables at home, I now encountered varieties I had never seen or heard of before, and must learn how to prepare them for any recipe Cook was required to produce. As soon as the vegetables were delivered she would explain if anything special had to be done with them, and that settled I could begin. Cabbage, cauliflowers, sprouts, salsify, artichokes, Globe, Chinese and Jerusalem; seakale and spinach, I learned how to prepare them all and, I might add, every bit of spinach had to be pushed through a hair sieve, not chopped as I notice in recipes these days. Eventually, I had to take charge of all vegetable cooking as well as preparing, so it was necessary that I learn all the ways they could, and would, be served.

As time went on, it was during these times in the scullery and kitchen, for it was my job to keep the sink in the kitchen free of dishes,

174

that a call would come from Cook, (I was told to call her Lily like the rest of the indoor staff instead of Cook, unless the mistress was near, so from now on that's what I will call her). "Joss, come and see this", or "Joss will you come and help me to do this?" and obeying the call, I would be initiated into some intricate method of production or subtle blending of ingredients into a delicious concoction. One day it was Hollandaise sauce, how to add the butter gradually so that it didn't curdle. Another day it was mayonnaise, and the gentle art of adding oil drop by steady drop, all the time whisking it to thicken, always explaining how it would be used and why a particular sauce was used or could be adapted to suit an individual dish.

And there were many of these fiddly little jobs like peeling and de-seeding grapes to be included in the fresh fruit salad, for it was the height of inelegance to have to spit out a mouthful of seeds and chewed skins of grapes. And the days when the mistress decided to have a savoury instead of, or as well as, a sweet course. The savoury was usually sardines on toast, a simple sounding but nevertheless time consuming little job, usually assigned to the kitchen maid. The sardines, the smallest kind like 'Skippers' had every bit of skin removed, then each one would split carefully, the backbone removed, and the whole put together again without even the hint of a crack in the flesh. Crusts were removed from slices of toasted bread, which were then cut into 'fingers' each one buttered to receive a single sardine. After setting under the grill for a second or two they were displayed carefully in sunray fashion on a doyly in an 'entre' dish with space between each to allow for picking up with finger and thumb, or with a small pair of tongues if that was the custom of the house, or whim of the day.

But there were times when the roles were reversed. "Joss, do you know what to do with oysters?" came the call one morning, and leaving what I was doing, I went to the kitchen to see what the problem was. "I can't get the damned things open," the exasperated Lily said, "I've never had to do oysters before; did you ever see your father open oysters?" I had, but not to take a great deal of notice. Oysters had not been on the list of shellfish he had introduced me to. But I had seen him eat them, or I should say swallow them whole, after sprinkling salt and pepper and a dash of vinegar over them. "I think he opened them with his penknife," I told her, then as she picked one up to examine it, "Oh yes, and he did it from the back, there where that bump is in the shell." Not having a penknife handy, the best substitute was the most pointed paring knife and after somewhat of a prolonged struggle, the whole dozen oysters were retrieved for whatever special dish was afoot. A similar call came one day, this time it was mussels. "How did your father clean mussels?" said a puzzled Lily (she wasn't very good on shellfish, except lobster, which we had quite often). I knew that one, it was easy. "You scrub them well, and remove all the fuzz, it's called the beard," I told her. "Then Dad threw out all the open ones, and put the others in the big iron pan with a drop of water and shook them over the fire." "Right," said Lily, "let's do that then." "Now," I told her, "when the sizzling finished, tip them into the sink and throw out all those that haven't opened." That done, Lily grimaced and transferring them to the table said, "Poor little beggars, fancy being boiled alive like that."

Occasionally there were deliveries of groceries and household things, and if Lily was in the middle of a baking session, or other such occupation which tied her to the table, she would ask me to check the order and put things away, being careful to put them in their respective cupboards so they would be used in strict rotation, oldest first. I remember those occasions best when soap was on the order. I said Mrs Milner was thrifty and like many housewives of the day, she was thrifty about household soap. It came in sticks about 18" long and was cut into pieces about 2" with a heavy knife. Then it was flung up on to the top of the kitchen cupboard, there to stay for about three months until it was quite dry and rock hard. It was very difficult to work up lather with it, but that I suppose was why it was so economical.

My work of washing up was made much easier by Lily's methodical approach. Before starting work, a big panshon standing in the sink was filled with hot soapy water and into this, every basin, dish or pan; all cooking tools were put immediately they were finished with. Then when I, having finished the vegetables, or whatever job I was doing, came into the kitchen to start washing up, they were much easier to clean. Very often, if another basin or dish was required, she would lift one from the panshon, rather than fetch a clean one from the cupboard, cutting down my work considerably.

Coffee was served at 10.30 a.m. each morning, and this was a chance for all the servants to congregate in the kitchen for a gossip; or to give a resume about what was happening 'up front'. Both Mr & Mrs Milner were advanced in years, so there was little chance of 'juicy' morsels of gossip as a general rule, but when visitors were staying, stories came thick and fast. Like the morning Edna came in, furious with a male guest, a relative of Mrs Milner, and old enough to have had more sense (or it might have been the frustration of age). Edna had knocked on his bedroom door early in the morning, carrying a glass of hot water which he preferred to tea, and hearing him call "come in," had opened the door to find the randy old man lying back in bed with the bedclothes pushed down to the bottom of the bed, knees wide apart, showing all the parts he had been born with. Now Edna was a very sober person, although having a ready sense of humour was a stickler for protocol and had a strict upbringing as one of a large family of seven girls and two boys. She was not only embarrassed but slightly annoyed, although we all had a good laugh, and a short discussion as to what was missing in the poor man's life to make him so frustrated and in need of a cheap thrill. This was the man who said that coffee should be like the perfect lover; hot, strong and sweet who, on his first visit after Edna joined the staff, when she called in the morning with the customary mug of shaving water and nobody had told her he had thick sideboards and a long beard, had guffawed somewhat embarrassingly for Edna, and revelled in her unease.

I soon learned that service life was not always calm and uneventful. Whether it was the closeness of the community and certain isolation from the outside world, is debatable, but tongues were certainly loosened and stories were sometimes quite lurid from the lady's maids and chauffeurs who lunched and dined with us in the servant's hall, sometimes staying for a week at a time. When two or three arrived at the same time, I do believe they tried to outdo each

177

other with their stories, although I have no doubt that there was a large element of truth in what they said, whether it was the Prince who wheeled the drunken lady back into the party in a wheelbarrow, or the number of offspring in a certain village ascribed to a certain Lord after a particularly virulent weekend visit.

Some of this rubbed off on them I fear, for sometimes it was necessary to make sure one was not alone with some of the chauffeurs, for they had a more than roving eye on the females. The older staff had experienced this before and knew exactly how to deal with it; I was less experienced in their wiles and not sure how to deal with the situation; after all, I was only a kitchen maid and who would believe me if I said anything?

One chauffeur who came regularly with Mrs Milner's daughter, Mrs Wilson of Horsley Gate Hall, was a handsome man, known for his roving eye, a 'ladies' man' indeed, although perhaps quite harmless in effect. On his first visit after I came to the Hall, he noticed that I was new and immediately put on the charm, much to my dismay and disgust. If I dived into the scullery to get out of his way, he followed me there; if Lily left the kitchen to fetch something from the pantry, he immediately made a dive towards me, and I very soon grew irritated when he was around.

However, I didn't have to worry for long. One morning, when we knew that Mrs Wilson was coming to lunch, Mary asked if Mr Rowlands had 'got a bit fresh' with me, and when I said he had, she said, "Don't worry, I'll see to it." Now Mary herself didn't mind a bit of fun and she was old enough and had been in service long enough to gain experience in such situations. I was relieved when, seeing the car arrive from an upstairs window; she came down to the kitchen and stayed until we all went in to lunch. She was very forthright and had probably warned him to 'keep off', for I never had any more trouble.

It was a phenomenon of such a cloistered community that whoever the callers were, whether workmen or visitors, they automatically started flirting and joking with the female staff as of right, and if not flirting, then a certain fluency of tongue. I remember Harry Green, the local joiner and undertaker who was doing some work in the house. For a few days he used the joiners shop down the drive under the Turret room. He came into the kitchen every morning for a cup of coffee and during the afternoon, when he knew there would be a cup of tea. He was a jovial man with a temperament well suited to his later occupation as Landlord of the Fleur de Lys at the top of the lane. He had finished the job and was in the kitchen having a cup of tea one day when there had been a lot of bantering and joking, with stories passed around very fluently. I knew that he kept looking at me, but at the same time I didn't know that he had been one of my Mother's suitors in the days before she had become engaged to my Father. Suddenly, he turned to me and said, "Aye, you're a good looker, but not as beautiful as your mother. She was a real beauty." How subtly does the child learn about the parent?

So passed the days of the week; with a slight variation each day. On Monday, after Lily had sorted out the leftovers from Sunday meals, and the chaos in the pantry had been brought into a state of tidiness, I took over. The stone benches were scrubbed to remove all traces of spilled milk and cream, shelves were washed down and paper covers carefully clipped and replaced and the window cleaned. Finally, the flagged floor was scrubbed not quite the difficult task of scrubbing the front hall floor as those in the pantry were stone and smooth with age and constant walking on. Nevertheless, I was glad when I could rise from my knees and stretch my back for a minute or two.

The pantry and kitchen both opened from the small back entrance hall from which a flight of narrow uncarpeted stairs gave access to the back bedrooms, meeting a large landing from which a door led to the front of the house via a wide balustrade gallery running round two sides of the back hall to the top of the main stairs, doors leading off to the main bedrooms, bathroom, the day and night nurseries, and the bedroom used by the parlour maid and the head housemaid.

The back stairs were the duty of the housemaids, but it was my job to scrub and polish the entrance hall floor and the corridor leading to the servant's hall, both done on Wednesday when the servant's hall received its weekly turn-out. The fireplace was black-

179

leaded and the fire lit before breakfast, the rest of the work being left until later. Easy chairs were brushed, sideboard, table and dining chairs polished, window cleaned and floor scrubbed and polished. For safety's sake, the sloping corridor between the entrance hall and the servant's hall was left unpolished, the morning's cleaning work ending with polishing the entrance hall floor.

One morning, during breakfast, Mary, in a half joking manner, asked if I had seen any mice yet. I was surprised at the question and said I had not. "You will," she said with a grimace, "Now the weather's turned cold, they'll move in." Sure enough, a few days later I saw my first mouse as it scuttled out of the ash pan and made a quick exit behind a cupboard. I reported the sighting to Mary as we ate our egg and bacon. "Tell you what Joss, I'll get up with you tomorrow morning and show you how we catch them," she said. I was intrigued; more so at bedtime when she came through to the kitchen before I went to bed and took the oven plates out of one of the ovens and reared them up against the doorpost out in the hall. "Now," she said, "Don't open the kitchen door until I get here in the morning, and I'll show you what to do."

As arranged, I was at the kitchen door when she arrived at 6.00 a.m. the next morning. "You hold one oven plate and I'll take the other; when I open the door and switch on the light, make a dash and drop the plate on as many as you can." We waited only a second then she flung open the door, switched on the light and my God! There were dozens of them; little tiny mice no more than an inch long trying to scuttle after the parent who had disappeared immediately. Mary dropped her oven plate on one tight group and I followed suit, cringing at the squelching sound that issued from beneath. Mary quickly picked up her plate and massacred a couple more; I wasn't quick enough, I had only four, Mary had seven altogether. "Right Joss," she said with satisfaction, "We'll do that again tomorrow, shall we?" As I nodded she added, "It'll take about four mornings to get them all," so matter of fact, it was unbelievable.

On Fridays the cooking range in the kitchen was black-leaded and this I knew how to do from lessons learned from my Mother. But this was a much bigger range than the one at home; the flues were different and there were more of them. Lily had explained which were the more important ones which must be quite clear for the big oven to raise enough heat for bread making, the rest of them formed a hidden warren behind that great black frontage which required a lot more 'elbow grease' to raise a shine that my Mother would have been proud of. The fender was black, another candidate for black-lead, with brass fittings, all brought to a shine with Brasso polish, pokers and kettles all receiving the same treatment. Also on Fridays, the floor was left until after breakfast and vegetable preparation, for this was the day when it had a good scrub. The black and red tiles were much easier than the stone flags of the pantry and looked bright and welcoming when they were clean.

As time went on, Fridays became unwelcome for other things than black-leading a huge range. Whether it was the result of early rising and long days or more likely, my Mother said, because the close atmosphere of working in the house all day, particularly in and around a hot kitchen, didn't agree with my constitution, was never decided. The fact was that the bilious headaches I had suffered at school, returned with even more intensity and for many weeks, every Friday after scrubbing the floor, Lily would remark on my ashen face, and pack me off to bed to sleep it off. The cynics amongst you might think it was psychological, a self-induced ailment brought on sub-consciously on the busiest day of the week. I too might be tempted to go along with that theory had I managed to 'duff' any work. Far from it, whatever was left of Friday morning's work was finished after dinner if I had thrown off the bug and risen by then, otherwise it was completed on Saturday morning which was not a busy day as a rule and could well accommodate the extra work. This was the time when Lily earned the nickname my 'second mother' for she surely was, ministering to my needs, as kind and concerned as my own Mother was. Mrs Milner too was sympathetic, suggesting to Lily that a hot bath every day might help. The suggestion wasn't very popular, as the mistress had said I could use her bathroom; then it wouldn't interfere with the bath roster of the rest of the staff. A bit embarrassing for me but luckily not for long, for in a few weeks the malady left me and the house was tranquil once more.

Actually, the Friday work which had to be suspended in the name of migraine was cleaning and polishing all the copper jelly-moulds, preserving pan and decorative pans from the mantelpiece, so that by Friday lunchtime the kitchen shone from floor to ceiling, or rather to the top of the mantelpiece. Tuesdays and Thursdays were flexible because other unexpected jobs were inclined to interfere with routine, especially when the house was full of visitors and extra cooking was called for. Or, as occurred twice during my time at the Hall, there were nurses in the house who tended to invade the kitchen, either to prepare a meal or a tray for the patient, or as one nurse had a habit of doing when she was nursing Mr Milner, came into the kitchen after dining with the mistress (as nurses always did), saying she was ravenous, not wanting to make a pig of herself before such an august person. She would help herself to a good chunk of pie, or to several slices of bread and jam or dripping.

Tuesdays was really the day for thoroughly cleaning and polishing the pans used in regular cooking. Potatoes and green vegetables were always cooked in black iron pans with shiny interiors (not like the imported iron ones on sale today, which never really come clean. The old type required only a good scrub-out after use, but all other cooking such as sauce, milk, coffee, chocolate and confectionary was done in copper pans which were kept on a high shelf in the kitchen. A brass jamming pan hung at the side of the fireplace with one or two brass and copper cooking tools. All these were polished on the outside once a week, a rewarding job when they all shone brightly in the firelight.

The scullery was the job I liked least, (apart from the front hall floor). There was nothing in it that raised a feeling of satisfaction when it had been cleaned. The gas stove was a huge black thing with a high awkward shelf on which plates were kept warm when the shelf in the kitchen was full. The long bench looked little better for scrubbing, and the ledges and bars underneath only irritated with their inaccessibility. The walls were bare stone with nothing to relieve their monotony and the shelf over the oven cavity held only black pans in all sizes from 5″ to 15″, the latter being used for boiling bones for stock. There was nothing which shone, although one consolation was that the floor was not scrubbed. Instead, the door was flung wide open and buckets of water were thrown over it and vigorously swept outside with a heavy yard broom. The only thing I hoped for after this was that the weather wasn't too cold when I had to work at the sink whilst the floor dried.

All indoor staff had a half day off each week after lunch was over. My half day was Thursday. Lily took Wednesday after doing as much preparation for dinner as possible, leaving me to finish the dishes and prepare tea. In addition, we all had a half day on Sunday, once a fortnight; Lily and I rotated; the two housemaids rotated; Edna took the same day as me; also the same Sunday, and in her absence, Mary acted as parlour maid. For my efforts, my wages were £18 per year, £1.10s.0d a month, which I took straight home to my Father, receiving 3d per week from him on my day off for spending money. This was more than enough for my needs as there was nothing I really needed to buy. He still bought my clothes, such as I needed, and there was plenty of food, fruit and chocolate desserts which satisfied my appetite.

Nurse Forbes, who I mentioned on my first day, was 24 years old when I first came to the Hall. She was a Scott who had been Nurse to the three children of the master and mistress. Mr 'Billy'/William was married and had one daughter called Mary, about five years younger than I. They lived at Carlton in Lindrick, coming to visit the Hall two or three times a year. Mary found a friend in Jean Shepley of Woodthorpe Hall who tragically was lost on the first ship to be torpedoed during the War, the 'Yorkshire', on her way home from a holiday in the Far East. Mr Roy, the younger son was killed early in the First World War, a sorrow with which Mrs Milner never became reconciled. Marjorie, their only daughter, married Major Wilson of Beauchief Hall, the family who owned, and I believe still do own, the Snuff Mills in Sharrowvale Road, Sheffield.

Mrs Wilson was a brusque kind of person, far from good looking, but like her mother, was very thoughtful and kind to her employees, and to us. On my first Christmas, when she visited on Christmas Eve, I heard her come striding up the passage calling "Josephine," and when I went to see what she wanted, an envelope was thrust in my hand with a 'Happy Christmas' greeting from her. When I opened the envelope I found a 10s.0d note, a veritable fortune for me. With the £1 note already given by Mrs Milner, I was really rich, all good money to save for the holiday in Blackpool the following August with my family.

Before Christmas, however, I had a birthday. Six weeks after I joined the staff, they all contributed to a present for my 15th birthday on the 18th November, a beautiful cut glass powder bowl for my dressing table. This was such a surprise, I nearly wept at such kindness when I had been here for so short a time. It was very precious, the first personal thing I had ever owned for my first dressing table. I took it upstairs and put it where the light would fall on it from the window, reflecting in the sunshine all the colours of the rainbow.

Miss Knott was a teacher at a Boarding school, who without relatives with whom she could stay during the holidays, for some reason was invited to spend them at the Hall. There was little affection between Nurse Forbes and Miss Knott; however, they both spent many hours together walking in the gardens.

During the summer of 1931, after an operation, Mrs Milner went to Bournemouth with Nurse Hicky for a two week holiday. It was customary, I was told, on such occasions, although unofficial, for the indoor servants to move into the front of the house every afternoon. All the usual morning work was carried out but when lunch was over and dishes cleared, all but Lily and Edna doffed their uniforms and sat around in the drawing room or out in the gardens when the weather was kind. Lily remained in uniform as she still had to cook dinner in the evening and Edna had to be ready always to answer the door and receive visitors.

There was a large grand piano, and a harpsichord in the drawing room, one at each end of the room, and I couldn't resist trying out the piano; the harpsichord sounded strange to my ears and was very different to play. I felt really important sitting at the grand piano playing some of the music and songs I found in the music stool. One song we all sang. Some of the older staff and Nurse Forbes remembered it was Mrs Milner's favourite; they told how she opened her lungs wide and let the words zip forth. The song was 'Cockles & Mussels, alive, alive oh'. I must admit, we also 'let it rip'; I wonder the people in Hall Lane didn't hear and think they were listening to a crowd of fisher lasses in Ireland.

Unfortunately, Mrs Milner didn't stay as long as expected. We were all, except Edna and Lily, out in the garden taking photographs when there was an urgent call from the house that she was on her way home. 'Scuttle' was perhaps too mild a word for the speed with which we all made a dash for the house, picking up clothes from the drawing room, plumping up cushions, rearranging furniture and hurriedly donning uniforms. I heard Mary say this had happened a few years before when the staff had enjoyed a steak and onion lunch in the Smoke Room. When Mr Milner came through the door, he shouted, "Good God, the smell of onions pervades the whole house." No-one enlightened him as to the reason.

Afternoons were always relaxed and quiet. When I had finished washing up the lunch dishes, I was free until 3.30 p.m. The housemaids usually sat around in their bedrooms or in the servant's hall and Edna pottered about in her pantry, always ready in case of callers. Lily, like me, was free until time for preparing the tea at 4.00 p.m. It was simply afternoon tea with sandwiches, bread and butter, jam, and two or three cakes, as well as hot scones which were served in a silver dish with a domed lid to keep them hot. The scones were my job; a few minutes in the bottom cool oven, split and covered with plenty of butter. I also had the job of cutting brown and white bread and butter. "Cut it thin Joss," Lily had said the first time I did it, and gradually I managed to cut it wafer thin, 'straight as a die' across the loaf. Mary saw me one day and as usual found an appropriate quip, "As you cut your bread, so does your life lie." In my innocence, or wishful thinking, I must have assumed that if I cut the loaf absolutely straight, I would have a trouble-free life, how wrong I was. It probably owed more to my Father, who considered a badly cut loaf was just slipshod and would say "Get it cut straight or leave it alone." My success in this simple operation was noticed by the mistress as Edna said one day when returning the cakes to the kitchen. "Oh Joss," she said, "Mrs Milner says Josephine's bread and butter is delicious, but will you ask her to cut it just a little thicker?" You can't win can you?

Some of the early holidays of the Milner's had been abroad. Like many families of similar status in society, they had climbed the Matterhorn, visited the major cultural cities of Europe and spent some time in India in the heyday of the British and the Raj where, like so many others they acquired an appetite for Indian Curry. This always had to be served in, what we were told, was the true Indian fashion with little bowls of sliced banana, shredded coconut and mango chutney and for those who liked it hot like the Hindus, one or two chillies floating whole and a pinch of cayenne, not forgetting to include also one or two bay leaves (which were always left in to serve). For those who might find it a little too hot, a plate of dry bread, cut into cubes for popping into the mouth to deaden the effect, were included in the accoutrements of the table.

Every year, according to Mary who had worked at the Hall for a number of years, the family spent a long holiday in Scotland during the shooting season but by the time I arrived, Mr Milner was past shooting. However, they often received game from friends and relatives. Mrs Wilson often brought a brace of pheasants when the Major had been shooting. The Shepley's sometimes brought a brace, as did relatives from Holkham and Lindrick.

It was my job to pluck all the game and poultry. The latter I didn't mind and often they came from Hall Farm ready plucked, needing only to be dressed and trussed for oven or pot. Pheasants were very often somewhat of a nightmare. They were hung for two weeks to mature before being plucked, by which time they were often as 'high as heaven', sometimes maggoty, and the skin was so wafer thin that it required the patience of Job and a great deal of effort to remove the 'pens' without tearing it.

There was one particularly difficult bird on one occasion whose 'pens' seemed to defy all effort to remove them. It was maggoty, and the skin particularly tender. No matter how carefully the 'pens' were removed, the inevitable result was a ½" tear. I carefully eased back the skin, but there was no disguising the offending wound. Of course it could have been stitched back in place with a trussing needle and fine cotton, but obviously Lily had not thought it serious enough for the operation. The morning after, during the briefing in the pantry, the mistress said, "Tell Josephine to take more care with the plucking, it so spoils the appearance of the bird." I felt deflated, and not a little annoyed, as I said to Lily, "I wouldn't mind eating one that had been torn, given the chance."

These times in the potting shed were occasions for gossiping with my cousin Tom Ibbotson, who started work at the Hall on the same day as me, although he was almost a year younger than I, having left school at the end of September. He was a cheerful colleague, always laughing, and being of similar age, we loved swapping tales, me from the house; him from the garden. Feathers flew and shoes shone brighter as the stories got juicier and juicier and imagination ran riot.

I have little recollection of plucking grouse, but Mary told of times past when the master went shooting and a dinner party was being held at the Hall in celebration of the 'bag'. As on first nights of pheasant shooting, some of the 'bag' was cooked, whilst the others were used to decorate the dining table. Braces of birds were set in zigzag fashion down the centre of the table on a bed of heather and bracken, instead of the usual flower or pot plant decorations. A case of pheasants to eat and pheasants to it!

One day one of the gardeners brought in two woodcocks from Gillfield Wood, as well as two snipes, very small birds with long thin beaks. I had the usual job of plucking them but when I watched Lily preparing them for cooking, I was surprised to see that although she drew the entrails from the woodcocks, she didn't bother drawing from the snipes. She had called me in to watch the preparation, and I stood amazed as she seasoned the snipe and stuffed it into the woodcock intact. "You see Joss," she explained, "you leave the entrails in so that as the birds cook, the juices from the snipe flavour the woodcock and provide the basting liquid." At first I was appalled and horrified at what seemed a disgusting habit, wondering about people who would eat such things. But, as Lily pointed out, "We eat liver and kidneys, and you eat chitterlings when your father kills a pig, so what's the difference?" I might have said "The stuff inside the chitterlings," but I guess I didn't think fast enough.

Most meat was hung for a few days before cooking; as all butchers know, freshly killed meat is never tender and the extra hanging time ensures it will cook and eat well. I remember large legs of mutton being hung in the pantry for a fortnight. (It's a pity we can't buy mutton now instead of the much less tasty lamb). There was, of course, some danger of flies and other disease carriers, so meat that was hung for any length of time, as well as all the game, was kept in an outside meat safe on the flat roof of the water cistern which supplied the main bathroom. Access to the safe was via the window of the bathroom, through which Edna would retrieve whatever was required. Smaller joints of meat for more immediate use were kept in a large fridge about 3ft square x 6ft high which stood in the corner of the pantry. It was used regularly for setting jellies and blancmanges and standing puddings and other complicated dishes between different processes. By the late 1920s of course, it was possible to buy jelly squares which required only the addition of boiling water, but such quick methods were not used by professional cooks. Jellies were made of fresh fruit juice and gelatine; piquant sauces and the like were made from tomatoes, onions and herbs from the gardens, salad cream and mayonnaise were made in the kitchen, as required. Heinz Beans had been on the market for some years, and I remember HP Sauce from the day in 1927 in Hathersage when, at dinner time, one of the girls suddenly said 'snot rag' and when we all gaped at her, she pointed to the label on the sauce bottle which read 'Cartons of HP Sauce' and she had read it backwards. But none of the readymade sauces were seen at the Hall, each one was made as the recipe of the dish demanded. Here is a recipe for lemon jelly from one of Mrs Milner's cookery books, now in my possession:-

Take six lemons, rub half a pound of lump sugar on the peel of half of them and squeeze the juice of all six into a basin. Soak two ounces of gelatine in a pint of water, after first washing the gelatine (leaf gelatine, of course). Add to it the sugar and lemon juice and dissolve it in a small enamelled saucepan over the fire, and stir in through a jelly bag. If it is not bright, clear it with the whipped white of an egg, exactly as stock is cleared, and strain again. Add, when nearly cool, half pint of sherry. Pour it into a mould that has been held over some steam so as to get the inside moist. And here's the tip for turning it out. The mould should be held together in both hands, then make a quick but not too violent movement downwards, as if you were going to throw the dish on the ground, and suddenly stop. You will guess, quite correctly that this was a dish made for the front of the house, not for we humble mortals in the servant's hall. Sherry for servants indeed!

Towards the end of May 1932 I was very thankful that I had taken notice of all that Lily had taught me. She had developed a rash on her hands which necessitated a visit to Dr Marshall's surgery. On her return she went immediately to report to the mistress and on returning to the kitchen, said she had to go home for a few days. How long she was away is a matter of discussion between Edna, Lily and me. I have always thought that it was about ten weeks; Lily thinks it was only a few days, and then she returned but was not allowed to cook for some time. Edna falls between the two, opting certainly for a few weeks, for she remembers helping in some of the decision making, and certain events which stand out like landmarks in that period. Whatever the answer was I will recount the events as I, with Edna's help, remember them.

Lily had been up to her bedroom to pack a few things and had been gone a few minutes when Mrs Milner could be heard coming up the passage to the kitchen door, calling out my name. I quickly rolled down my sleeves and went to the door a little apprehensive as to what it was all about. "Josephine," she said rather seriously, but firmly, "Cook has scabies and must go off duty for some time; while she is away you will carry on and do the cooking." (Actually, Lily says it was dermatitis, not scabies, as originally thought). I was staggered at Mrs Milner's order but there was no room for argument, I had been thrown in at the deep end, and it was up to me to sink or swim. However, sink or failure was neither in Mrs Milner's book, nor mine, and after the first shock I felt a certain excitement at the prospect and perhaps, a little silly pride that she should think me capable.

189

One thing that did worry me for a few moments was that there was to be a dinner party that evening, when nine people were invited, including Lady Roberts, Mr Eric Roberts, Sir William Ellis and the Hon. Violet Warde-Aldam, who was already staying at the Hall with her maid. It was to be a six course dinner, and I knew that Lily had made the tomato soup, for she had asked me to keep an eye on it in the scullery. She had also started the sweet, using a recipe from Mrs Milner's private collection, which I had to return when finished with. It was a delicious pudding for which Lily had made a fatless sponge cake a few days before and left it to dry. The day before, she had crumbled the cake finely, passing it through a sieve for an even texture, and mixing it with very strong black coffee and gelatine, pouring the mixture into a jelly mould which had a deep, distinct pattern and leaving it in the fridge to set. This is the point it had reached by the time I took over.

I made a thick coating sauce with arrowroot, using sugar from the jar which contained the vanilla pods and a few drops of maraschino for flavouring. Maraschino was bought by the bottle and kept in the Butler's pantry, being brought out by Edna when it was needed. Turning the mould out carefully, the sauce was poured over it carefully and blanched almonds were stuck all over, picking out the pattern. Needless to say this had to be done very quickly and neatly so as to retain a smooth, shiny surface and before it set and created wrinkles around the almonds. This pudding was never made for staff, but we did get a chance to taste if a little was returned to the kitchen.

Before she left, Lily had reminded me how to finish the sweet, and she confirmed that the soup needed only heating. The vegetables were no problem for I always did them anyway; the real difficulty was having only one pair of hands, no-one to whip the potatoes to a cream whilst I put finishing touches to another dish. As Lily had said recently, "Joss, I do miss having a kitchen maid, cooking's alright, but I detest the clearing up afterwards." I fully understand how she felt, like trying to entertain without a husband to organise the drinks.

The main course presented little trouble, but I almost panicked when I remembered that the 'entree' was a Lobster Mayonnaise. This was served on a huge silver salver about 18" in diameter, on which a salad was arranged in a pattern composed of sections of shredded lettuce, chicory, grate carrot and celeriac, each section divided by rows of neatly laid slices of radish, cucumber butterflies, clipped chives, grated carrot and celeriac, tomato segments and spring onions; the whole being finished with tomato 'lilies', radish 'roses' and lilies and tiny spring onion brushes. When finished, it was a splendid sight. This part of the operation didn't cause any problems for whenever a salad of mayonnaise was asked for, it had been my job to do it, and but for the time factor, I would have enjoyed it just as much this time. But I had never cut a lobster in two, and wasn't sure what to do with the eggs. I had left a space in the decorating of the base to accommodate it in the pattern, but I hesitated at the sight of a large leggy lobster. This is where Edna came in.

During Lily's absence Edna was often my salvation. There were many moments when I was glad of her help in the correct way to finish off dishes, and the correct way of presentation, after all, she was the one who saw every dish in its finished state, and knew what reception to expect. "What's the matter Joss?" she said, "I've never chopped a lobster in two before," I said. "Give me the cleaver," she said very purposefully, "I've seen Lily do this," as she lifted the cleaver high and brought it deftly down on to the unfortunate crustacean. It was severed by the cleanest cut one could hope for and I could finish the job. The flesh was loosened, the eggs arranged in little piles, and claws cracked and returned to their rightful place and the whole settled into the centre of the dish in its regal red shell. It was magnificent.

Edna carried it carefully to the dining room, setting it on the table outside whilst she cleared away the remnants of the previous course. She returned a few minutes later in a fury, her face bright and red with anger. "Edna, what's wrong?" I asked fearful that I had done something radically wrong. "The mean bitch," she exploded, "the mean bitch, you're only 15 and she can't give you credit for your work." I was still worried. "Edna, what did she say about me?" I blurted out. "Nothing, that what's wrong, she said nothing." I was more puzzled than ever until she explained. The silver tray had been put into another tray for handing the dish around to the guests, but instead of placing the servers on the dish, she had put them at the side on the second tray. As was the custom, the dish was first held in front of the mistress, (a sort of approval of satisfaction), and after her acknowledgement, it would be taken to the chief guest, on this occasion Lady Roberts, for her to help herself. This time Edna held the dish for approval, explaining that Josephine had done it and the mistress might like to see it undisturbed and was completely taken aback to see how angry the mistress was at this breech of etiquette, as she plunged the servers into the salad and, with a flourish of the hand, indicated "Get on with serving it." When Edna finished explaining, I said "Edna, you shouldn't have done that, I enjoyed doing it, and it doesn't matter." But Edna was not so easily placated. "I don't care," she said defiantly, "she could have acknowledged it, the mean bitch."

The morning after the dinner party I had finished washing up the breakfast dishes with a little help from Mary, when I heard the usual footsteps striding up the passage. I took little notice until I heard a cry "Cook" in that high falsetto voice, and again from the pantry, "Cook." "That's me," I thought, "my God, that's me." I hurriedly rolled down my sleeves, smoothed my hair and made sure my apron was clean, and quickly made my way to the pantry. I was a little disappointed that there was no mention of the party, but there was nothing said about the fiasco of the lobster so, on the whole, it was a relief.

There were many times in the following weeks when I was glad of Edna's help but there were times when even Edna couldn't help. Like the time when I forgot that baked potatoes had been ordered for dinner, and there was barely half an hour before they would be required. Large potatoes were always used, and I knew they would take at least an hour, probably more. I really did panic. What the hell could I do? (No microwaves in those days). One thing I knew I must do was to produce baked potatoes somehow, anyhow. I couldn't just leave them without potatoes. Hastily, I grabbed one of the copper pans from the shelf and popped it on the gas stove, with a lid on to make an improvised oven. I quickly scrubbed four potatoes, and dropped them in the pan, turned up the heat and hoped for the best. The aroma that issued from that pan was enough to turn off the gastric juices completely, but as one side seemed to be burning too much, they were turned over for the other side to cook. Gradually the outside became softer, but there was no way of knowing what the inside was doing.

The time came for serving. I had made a large 'water lily' with crisp white napkins in a silver serving tureen and I now carefully placed a potato in each cavity and Edna took them to the table. Edna, not knowing what had transpired, came back to the kitchen after serving the course, with a mystified look on her face. "She says, I don't know what Josephine's done to the potatoes tonight, they are quite strange," she said. I told her what had happened and we both had a good laugh. "They looked alright to me," Edna said, "at least they had their potatoes." I wondered what would be said the following morning, but I was lucky, for nothing was said, perhaps I was lucky and the blame was put on the breed of potatoes. Not so lucky with the pan though; it took every spare moment for the next month to bring back the shine, and I fear it always carried a few faint scars.

After a short time, Lily returned but was still forbidden to do any cooking, nor to put her hands in water, but she was around to help with other jobs and a young woman called Isabel came in to help with the cooking. On my first day off after Lily's return, I was at home when my Father came home from the pit. "Hello lass," he said to me as greeting, "so you've finished your stint at cooking," this was more a statement than a question. "Yes," was the only reply I thought necessary. He stripped off his shirt, poured hot water from the kettle into the bowl in the sink and proceeded to wash his hands, still black with coal dust. After scrubbing his arms and swilling his face with as much water as would have filled a reservoir, or launched a couple of ships, he rubbed himself dry before turning to speak to me again.

"And did your mistress say you'd done a good job?" he shot the question at me, taking me off guard. "No," I replied, in what I suppose was a surprised voice, for it never entered my head that she

193

should have done. "Oh, so she didn't tell you you'd done a good job," he persisted. I didn't answer this and he continued. "Did she have any complaints?" "No," I said, again surprised at the question. "So, she didn't complain, but she didn't say she was satisfied." By this time I was getting exasperated, in fact a little angry when he persisted with "That's funny, she had no complaint, but didn't say you'd done your job well." He knew I was very near to tears, not hurt tears, just sheer frustrated ones because I knew what he was trying to do. The seed had been sown. Why hadn't something been said? After all, I'm only 15. She could have said whether I had managed alright, couldn't she? Such thoughts only made me feel weepier, and by now by Father could see his treatment had worked. The tears were overflowing and the happiness I had felt at coming home had changed to wretchedness. He looked hard at me; saw how upset I was and his mood changed. To him it had only been a joke, a way for him to give me another lesson in life, as he saw it. "Mrs Milner came to see me last night," he blurted out and when I looked at him surprised and a little apprehensive, he continued, "and she's very pleased with the way you coped." At this, I was flabbergasted. "You mean she came here?" I managed. "Aye lass, she came to tell me," he paused then said "I'm proud of you lass." I burst into tears, floods of them. How unfair. Why couldn't she have told me, why did he have to tease me? After all, I'm only 15, she could have said something. My Father listened until my tears subsided enough to listen, then he delivered the lesson that this episode was all about. "Let this be a lesson lass, never expect praise. Do your jobs well so you get no complaints, but never, never expect praise."

One day during that first summer, Mr Lewis told Mrs Milner that the large cactus plant would be flowering at 12.30 p.m. that morning and she sent word through to the kitchen that if we would like to see it flower, we were to go to the conservatory at midnight in time to see it open. The conservatory was built against a 12ft high wall facing south, which extended westwards from the house. It housed all kinds of exotic plants, including a large banana plant which rose to the roof, and produced small bananas.

The cactus was a type that flowered only once every seven years, a huge plant which rose to the top of one wall. It would be in full flower for only 20 minutes, so we could not afford to be late. We all trooped into the conservatory at midnight, there to be met by Mr Lewis and some of the other garden staff (there were five of them including cousin Tom). Mrs Milner arrived a few minutes later. There, pointed out by Mr Lewis, was the object of our viewing, a resplendent plant, now in the process of producing its very rare offspring. The plant itself was magnificent, even without the flower for which we were waiting. And then it appeared, like a butterfly emerging from its cocoon, slowly unfurling before our eyes. We were entranced; the colours could already be seen developing as each petal opened. Then in a sheer burst of glory, it was wide open, red and gold and luminous in its beauty. The anthers and stigmas stood out like a bright yellow sunburst from its throat, the pointed petals stretching about 8ft across the wall, like a radiant fire. We all stood transfixed, waiting to see whether Mr Lewis had forecast not only the rise of this gorgeous beauty, but also its decline. Sure enough, after 20 minutes, the luminosity faded, the brightness declined and slowly and petals turned in on themselves, the anthers wilted and in a few seconds more, it was over. After the anticlimax there was an air of despondency as Lily thanked the mistress for letting us see this miracle, and we all trooped back to bed.

In January 1931, Mr Milner had been taken ill and for a few weeks there were two or three nurses in the house, which made more work for the housemaids and extra cooking too. Their hours were erratic, as they were, between them, on duty for the full 24 hours. One of them, Nurse Hickey, was older than the other two and it was she who came to the kitchen most. They were superior beings, or tried to be, and rather 'ruled the roost', even in the front of the house; after all, they had the master's life in their hands and that gave them the excuse. However, at the end of January, Mr Milner died of cancer, and for a long time the whole household was very subdued.

That wasn't the last we saw of the nurses. Before the master's death, Mrs Milner found that she had breast cancer, but she refused to have anything done about it as she didn't want the master to be worried. However, by the time he died it was becoming urgent, and an early operation was advised. After some consultation, it was decided that the operation should be performed at home and the Blue room next to the mistress's bedroom was disinfected and set out as an operating theatre. (Mr Milner's had been done in the Smoke room). The surgeon, (possibly Mr Finch), came from Sheffield to perform the operation and he visited each morning to see his patient and consult with Nurse Hickey. Fortunately, the operation was a success and after a few weeks, and the holiday in Bournemouth, she returned to full health and we were free from nurses once more.

Soon after this came the event which was to change the pattern of my life once more. Early in September, my Father decided to take us to Blackpool once more and as on previous occasions, we caught the train at Dore & Totley station about 6.00 a.m. that morning. The journey still took about three and a half hours and there were still hoards of barefoot children shouting "Penny down" as we neared Manchester. The journey was uneventful and reasonably pleasant, if one can call it pleasant to be cooped up sitting facing each other across a narrow carriage on seats not blessed with thick padding; when there was no toilet for those unfortunate enough to be caught 'short', and cups of tea could be bought only when the train stopped at a station large enough to have a tea bar. We still took all our home-grown vegetables, except potatoes but we were all nearer adulthood with equally adult appetites, the load was greater. However, to compensate, muscles were stronger and the occasion compensated for the effort. We had been at Blackpool about three days when my Father received a telegram from Mrs Milner which read "Josephine returning as housemaid, please buy uniform." Dad was a bit taken aback, one doesn't go on holiday with a family of children expecting to buy working clothes, but after some discussion with Mom, it was decided to go to Bond Street, which crossed the bottom of Dean Street where we were staying, and known as the best shopping street in Blackpool.

After looking in a number of shops, it was clear that they were more used to selling waitresses uniforms than those for housemaids in gentlemen's houses and everywhere the prevailing colour seemed to be brown; nowhere could we find a grey dress, or the type of apron and cap as worn by Totley Hall maids. By the end of the afternoon, I had a brown dress, a 'nippy' cap and an apron which covered little more than the waist, with a lacy frill around the base and bib. I fear Mrs Milner thought she had been deposited into Lyon's a corner Café when she first saw me for I looked exactly like one of their waitresses. I can't remember whether brown shoes and stockings were included, but I rather think I still wore the black ones I already had.

So, I returned at the end of the week as under-housemaid, working alongside Annie. The mistress did look 'askance' at my attire the first afternoon, but I came in contact with her very little and my usual kitchen uniform was still worn in the morning, with a cap passed on from Annie until I could make one for myself.

For a while there was a mystery as to the reason for a change in housemaids, all I knew at the time was that Mary had left in a hurry, and that Annie Fisher, daughter of one of my Mother's second cousins, was coming as kitchen maid. I knew there had been a row between Mary and Edna, the reason, Mary's sharp tongue, a little jealousy, Edna's strict father and a mediator in Mrs Milner. Mrs Milner told me of the dispute between the two as the reason for me being 'upgraded' and that sufficed. It took me many years to learn the whole story, in fact only recently, from Edna herself.

After the master died, the mistress must have been very lonely, for she often came to the kitchen door saying, "Put your hat on Cook and come with me, I want to talk." This put Lily on the spot so to speak. She sometimes said, "But Mm, I have cooking to do," and as she says now, "It was a bit embarrassing Joss, after all she was the boss." On reflection, I think it shows how little difference there was between Mrs Milner and her servants, certainly we were treated as employees, but her humane treatment displayed more than just an employer.

It was obvious that my routine would change the main advantage; to me it seemed that I always seemed to be dressed up. No more dirty black-leading, except for the small fire bars in the bedrooms, no more washing up and sadly no more cooking. There were, however, many jobs which took a lot of elbow grease and much more chance of reprimand from the mistress, who always seemed to be close at hand, in an elusive way. One such occasion was soon after I began working in the front of the house. Each bedroom had a small fireplace where, except in the middle of summer, a fire was lit during the late afternoon, in time for the occupants to change for dinner. It was my job every morning to remove the ashes, polish the grate, wash the hearth and lay the fire ready for lighting. A large Hoover cleaner was used once a week by the Head housemaid but only first thing in the morning downstairs or in the bedrooms when Mrs Milner came downstairs or had gone out. On all other occasions, the carpets were brushed on hands and knees with brush and dustpan; first sprinkling water to allay the dust.

It was whilst brushing the carpet in the mistress's room one morning that I noticed the end hook of the curtains had slipped off its ring and on closer inspection, saw that the little eyelet had broken from the large wooden curtain ring. The room, including the window, was about 12ft high and there was no way I could do anything about it. I decided to tell Annie but this was her day off, so it had to wait for the next day.

Just after breakfast the following day, the bell rang on the kitchen board. "It's for you Joss," Lily called. I hurriedly left the servant's hall and went upstairs to see what the mistress wanted, smoothing my apron as I waited for her answer to my knock. "Come in," came the loudest call I had heard, for usually I had difficulty in hearing her, and I was warned that something serious was wrong.

"Haven't you seen that curtain?" she shouted and as I stood staring helpless continued, "Come girl, haven't you seen that curtain?" "Y-yes Mm," I stuttered. "Then," she shouted again, "Get it put right." "B-but Mm," I stammered, "I can't reach up there." She looked exasperated and I was decidedly nervous. "Girl," she said impatiently, "use your common sense, of course you can't reach it." For a second I was relieved, but she went on, "Get Lewis to bring a ladder, he'll put it right." "Yes Mm," I muttered and as I turned to go she added, "And remember, it's your job to see that all these things are done and to find out how." "Yes Mm," I said again, my ego sorely hurt and a bit aggrieved that the one person who could have

198

explained the routine was off duty. Just my luck, another lesson learned the hard way!

I soon found that although a very fair employer, she was a strict disciplinarian when it came to training, and did not pull any punches if and when criticism was called for. She was crafty in her methods of finding out whether jobs had been correctly carried out. Every morning, except Wednesdays, all work downstairs had to be finished before she came down to breakfast at 8.30 a.m. Annie swept and dusted the drawing room whilst I lit the smoke fire, brushed the carpet, then dusted the stairs and the back hall. The stairs wall was hung with family portraits in thick carved frames which were first brushed with a small soft brush before dusting. I heard some strange stories about how easily one could be caught out with them, so I was particularly careful to go into all the corners.

One morning there was a cry "Jose-ph-i-ne" and I rushed to see what had gone wrong. There was the mistress standing on the stairs with a white handkerchief in her hand. As I crossed the hall she held it out, and in the most deprecating voice said "This picture; you haven't dusted it this morning." I started to stammer that I had, but before the words could usher forth, she had reached the bottom of the stairs and as she passed said, in her quietest voice, "See that it's dusted immediately." Annie appeared from the drawing room, having heard all that went on. "You're not the first to be caught like that," she said explaining "She has a clean white handkerchief every morning, just to wipe down all the picture frames as she comes downstairs." I was flabbergasted and cross that I had been caught out so craftily. "Don't worry," Annie said, "You'll not be caught out again, and she'll soon stop."

I knew from past experience that Mrs Milner knew the short cuts in housework, from the day when Uncle Arthur died two years before. He was Forester and Deputy Head Gardener at the Hall, and when he hadn't turned up for work one morning, she had found him dead behind the outside toilet door and had sent for my Mother to help her. On her arrival at the School House Mrs Milner suggested that they tidy the room a little before the Doctor arrived. My Mother smiled when she told me about it. "She swept round the fireplace,

199

but couldn't find a shovel," she explained, "so she lifted the edge of the rug and swept the crumbs underneath," adding, "she said nobody would find them there."

I thought back to this occasion one morning when I had been late and hadn't been careful in spreading the newspaper before removing and polishing the fire bar and a small stain was left on the carpet at the edge of the paper. I hadn't worried unduly at the time, thinking I'd ask Annie how to remove it. But with the detecting ability of Mrs Milner, she knew what had happened. "I guess I wasn't the first to do that," I said to Annie. "Oh yes she knows everything. Do you remember Joss; she lifts the edge of the rug every morning to see if the carpet's been brushed underneath."

The Smoke room was a nightmare to dust. There were pictures covering the walls and standing on every cupboard and side table. It was a very personal and cosy room where the mistress had breakfast and spent much of her time. There was a 'dado' around the walls on which all sorts of little drawings, childish poems, homemade birthday and Christmas cards and snapshots of her grandchildren stood on the ledges, filling every space between those standing on the bookshelves. Fortunately dusting in here could be left until after breakfast when the mistress always went out for about an hour with Peter, her French poodle.

The back hall held no problems; it had been built, with the dining room, as an extension in 1884 when the Milner's first moved into the Hall. Before that, the house had changed little since it was built in 1623. The large stained glass window, designed by Mrs Milner, rose to the ceiling and covered the whole of one wall; the ornate carved staircase rising from the back hall had been removed from Thornbridge Hall at the time of the extension and the floor was almost covered by a beautiful carpet, designed by Mrs Milner and made by Mr Milner. Many people remembered seeing him sitting under the loggia outside the drawing room window with a rug over his knees, prodding the canvas with a large hooked needle. All the rooms held samples of his work, done over the years.

The front hall was part of the original building, with a cream sandstone floor, and oak panelled walls. There was a large stone fireplace over which were the arms of the Barker family who built it. On the opposite side stood a large oak chest and a side table on which trays were put during lunch and dinner and doors led off from each corner to the drawing room, the Smoke room, the dining room and up two steps to the Butler's pantry and the rear of the house. Mrs Milner could be seen every Friday morning doing the flowers, either on the back hall table or in as little room under the stairs, approached through a door outside the entrance to the dining room, where she stored her flower containers.

The drawing room was usually decorated with huge banks of flowering plants on each side of the window. Mr Lewis supervised the display but it was usually carried out by one of the other gardeners and the garden boy. The display in summer was spectacular with calceolarias, cinerarias, schizanthus and ferns with geraniums and primulas substituted as they came into bloom, the whole display sorted and rearranged each week.

The sandstone floor in the front hall was the subject of the most unpleasant job in the whole house, for it had to be scrubbed every Wednesday morning as soon as the mistress had left for her morning walk. The problem was that in order to preserve the pale colour, the cleaning had to be done with cold water without soap, and even in summer it was never so warm that cold water was a pleasure. To make matters worse, water had to be slopped profusely over each flagstone, immediately scrubbed hard to loosen the dirt and more water swilled on to stop it going back into the surface. Large cloths were used frantically to mop up before it could soak in. My right hand is bigger than my left and I swear it was caused through gripping that oversized scrubbing brush and I bet my life on blaming those rough tiles for the hoofs I still carry on my left hand through resting them hard on the flags whilst scrubbing. But there are hazards and penalties to all worthwhile jobs, or so they say.

Another advantage of being housemaid was the end of early rising. My day began at 7.30 a.m. like Annie and Edna, and I soon found the benefit by the disappearance of the migraine headaches which had dogged me for so long and the extra time off in the afternoon was very welcome to the longer day's work. For now,

Annie, the new kitchen maid had taken on the responsibility of thin bread and butter. After lunch we changed uniforms and caught up on personal tasks like hair-do's and refurbishing clothes, or even taking a nap if that's how we felt. I had changed my day off to Tuesday as Edna continued to have Thursday, when Annie took over as parlour maid and I had responsibility for all housemaids' work. Annie's day off was still Monday, so for these two days it was my job to lay out the evening clothes for Mrs Milner and any female guests, whilst the parlour maid did the same for the males.

These were the days before the luxury of washbasins in every bedroom, instead a piece of furniture called a washstand was part of all bedroom suites, on which a set of toiletries stood on the marble top. A soap dish, a powder bowl and a large deep bowl and a matching fancy jug were standard, all decorated with flowers, or birds according to fancy. And of course, although not a vital part of this story, nevertheless decidedly important was the matching 'potty' which lived under the bed ready for those who might be caught short during the night, and was emptied by the housemaid in the morning. Just as my Mother had to do and every housewife of the day, I took a bucket with a lid, emptying the contents of the 'potty' washing that receptacle with the jug of water I had armed myself with. Sounds abominable doesn't it? But it was no worse than emptying bedpans by hospital nurses, or has technology progressed beyond that necessity?

The large washstand jugs were filled with cold water every night and hot water was carried from the kitchen in small cans like those used for watering gardens, but having a hinged lid to keep the water hot. Every morning, and about 6.00 p.m. in the evening, just before the mistress and her guests retired to dress for dinner, a can of hot water was taken to each room, when the fire was replenished and evening clothes laid out ready for dressing. Whilst dinner was being served, the rooms were tidied, curtains drawn, if not already drawn in winter, beds were turned down and night clothes laid out, either on beds, or draped over a chair-back before the fire in cold weather. At 9.30 p.m. a can of hot water and a hot-water bottle were taken to each room and the fire replenished for the last time.

I was always nervous when I reached the door of Mrs Milner's room, for I often had difficulty in hearing her answer my knock, particularly in the morning when the voice came from the depths of the bedclothes, or as happened on one embarrassing occasion. I had knocked twice and hearing no reply, thought the mistress must not be awake, so I carefully opened the door, to be confronted by the rear of a figure wearing combinations, the split parted to reveal a bare pink bottom, as she bent to retrieve some garment from the bottom drawer of the wardrobe. As I put my foot out to cross the threshold, she spring upright and turned in a fury. "My God, girl, why didn't you knock?" she roared. "I, I did Mum," I stammered, "but you didn't answer." "Then knock again until I do answer," she went on, which I thought was pretty unreasonable, considering I was supposed to wake her. She'd no business to get up so early I told myself as a salve to my conscience. She had the last word, of course, "Never do that again," she rapped as I put the glass of hot water on the bedside table, and the can of water on the floor near the wash handstand, making a discreet exit.

I wasn't the least bit nervous when it fell to me to service the rooms of Mr Billy, Mrs Milner's son and his wife and daughter Mary when they were staying for a week and using the Turret room, and the room next door round the corner at the end of the corridor, usually called the Pink Room. However, I had mixed feelings about the last named since Edna and I, whilst the mistress was away, had tested the rumour that the room was haunted.

It was during dinner one night that Mary had told us of the haunted room and we had a heated debate as to whether we believed the story. Mary assured us that it was true. "There had been a ghost in that room for years," she said, whilst Edna argued, "I don't believe it, and to prove it, I'll go and sleep in there tonight if somebody will come with me." No-one offered, but Edna persisted, "Will you come with me Joss?" and never let it be said that I shirked a challenge; I said I would.

Edna made up the bed and we retired around 10.00 p.m., talking for a long time, afraid to go to sleep. Eventually, we both drifted into oblivion, our fears, for a time, forgotten. Suddenly, we both shot upright, terrified. "Something rang across my feet," gasped Edna. "Mine too", I cried. "What was it Edna, was it the ghost, or could it be a rat?" Even a rat would be better than a ghost I thought. By now we were both scared stiff. "I don't know," she almost screamed, "I know something ran across my feet, I couldn't have imagined it." She jumped out of bed and switched on the light, "What's more, I'm not waiting to find out, come on, we're getting out of here," and with that she made a dive for the door, followed closely by me at speed as if the ghost was making a grab at the hem of my nightdress, across the landing and into our own room. Annie looked up sleepily as I dived into bed, "What's the matter?" she mumbled drowsily, "did you see the ghost?" "I don't know," I muttered from the depths of the bedclothes, "but I'll never sleep in that room again." Of course Mary swore it was the ghost, "There have never been any rats inside this house," she said firmly; which wasn't quite true.

Mary Milner, Mr Billy's daughter was about four years younger than I, but as she was a guest, I had to pay as much attention to her needs as to her mother and other guests. I took a can of water to her bedroom and put coal on the fire before turning my attention to her evening clothes. They had already been unpacked and put into drawers, one dress left hanging on the wardrobe door. I carefully laid out the dress on the bed, with its matching underskirt by its side, and then turned to the chair to drape the rest of the underclothes over the chair-back in front of the fire. Then came the stockings! I thought the dress was very pretty, so lovely and fine and floating, with tiny embroideries over the bodice but the stockings! I had never seen anything so fragile and delicate in all my life. I couldn't believe how they could be drawn on to the legs without tearing. I looked at them hard and long, of the purest silk, the finest most ethereal gossamer as I reverently laid them beside the dress, the little silver slippers waiting to accept two very fortunate feet. I could only think "All this luxury, and she's not even as old as I am," as if age were any criterion for wearing such gorgeous things.

Sometimes the routine was a little different. Mrs Milner's nephew, Mr Eric Roberts, was a member of the Playhouse in Sheffield and occasionally he was given a small part in one of the plays. On such occasions he, his mother, Lady Roberts and Mrs Milner would have high tea at 6.00 p.m. instead of dinner in order to leave in time for the performance. When this happened, Lily was free to cook whatever she liked for the staff; usually served immediately they had departed, leaving us with a welcome long evening.

We all enjoyed the time after dinner when all work was over for the day. Some sat at the table sewing, knitting or writing letters; Lily often sat in one of the easy chairs reading. And sometimes the call would come, "Give us a dance Joss." There was a lot of fun and joking and I needed no second bidding. Grabbing a scarf, or even an antimacassar from a chair-back, I would float around the room just like Isadora Duncan, arms and scarf waving whilst I twisted and turned sweeping down to the floor, then floating the scarf up to the ceiling, pirouetting round on one shoe clad toe, with the other leg bent like the most elegant skater. Or, I would go all Grecian, or Egyptian, doing a most impressive sand-dance with hands pointing and head nodding like a figure from an Egyptian tombstone.

At one time I had a fancy for writing a short story and spent my evenings trying out my skills in that direction. Having little experience away from the village, it was very parochial, the story of a kitchen maid and a garden boy in a large country house and all that happened to them in their love for one another and the intrigue that went on the 'big house'. It called on all my imagination, sometimes so far-fetched that Lily and Mary wondered how I had picked up my information, particularly about the behaviour of the 'ladies'. Every night there was the call "Let's read it Joss," or "What's happening tonight Joss?" and they all ready what I had written, sometimes laughing, sometimes questioning about what was going to happen next.

When it was finished, they persuaded me to send it to 'Pearson's Weekly'; a popular weekly tabloid type newspaper which published jokes, snippets of news and short stories. I did as they suggested, and in a few weeks' time received a letter to tell me that it had been received but at the present time they had no immediate plans to use it. It was no great disappointment, I knew it wasn't good enough but a few weeks later, we were all surprised to read a story so similar, but without the writer's name, that Annie, after reading it said "That's just like your story, except for the names." There was more difference than just names, but so much that was similar that we all had suspicions that it had been 'hashed up' for publication, a system we knew was practised and probably still is.

Our complete freedom to have visitors meant that I was not surprised one day when my Mother came through from the front of the house where she had been having tea in the drawing room with Mrs Milner and one of the village Committees. It could have been a meeting to organise a series of sewing meetings for some charity, or a meeting of the Hospital Committee. Both my Father and Mother were on the Hospital Committee and, as President and a member of the Hospital Board; the mistress periodically invited the ladies of the Committee to tea, as thanks for all their work. It was probably one such occasion on the day in question. Mom was in time to have another cup of tea with us, and as usual, I cleared the table and folded the cloth before putting it in the sideboard. I noticed how intrigued she was to see me meticulously folding it in the original creases so as not to crease it more; a habit once learned, never forgotten. She was glad she said that I was learning to do things neatly and properly.

But my Mother could still tell me a thing or two about correct procedure and manners and one was the simple one of entertaining and serving tea. She described how Mrs Milner had donned her hat and worn it throughout the meal as a mark of respect for her guests, explaining that it was a custom practised by all hostesses which was intended to show that there was no distinction between hostess and guests. Because they were in outdoor clothes, the hat was a symbol.

A great deal of work was done in the community for the upkeep of the Voluntary Hospitals before the creation of the Health Service in 1948. In April each year, an egg collection was made around all the villages and sent to the hospitals for preserving for winter use. Patients in hospital were given sufficient food, but little variety. Rice pudding was a joke because it was served every day. If fresh eggs were required by the patient for boiling, they were supplied by the patient or by relatives and kept in the patient's bedside locker. When required, the name of the patient was written on the shell before it was taken by the nurse for boiling in the little kitchen at the end of each ward. There was always plenty of bread and butter (Margarine was almost unknown, and used only by the poorest people for cooking). For other delicacies like cake, jelly, or fruit, the patient relied on relatives and friends.

Large earthenware pots were used for preserving eggs by the housewife and by the Institutions, the eggs first being washed or wiped, then laid down carefully in closely packed rows so as not to crack them. A solution, or rather a suspension of either lime and water isinglass or water glass, was poured gently over them.

Heaps of quicklime was tipped in the fields by the farmer for weathering and later spreading on his fields, and it required only a word to the farmer to obtain a large lump of preserving eggs, or for lime washing. It was prepared in the same way for both jobs and it was usual for Mom to whitewash the cellars and closets as part of spring-cleaning at the same tune as our surplus of eggs was laid down. Quicklime was simply a piece of limestone which had been subjected to great heat in a kiln, when it was turned into a chalk-like rock. During the process, it absorbed a great deal of heat and when put in water, it literally boiled. When my mother 'slaked' lime for white-washing, she warned us all not to touch it for fear of being scalded. As the bubbling subsided and the liquid cooled, it was given a good stir and was ready for use. Isinglass was bought from the chemist for a few coppers. It was dry, like spun fibreglass. When put into water, it dissolved and when stirred, was ready for pouring over the eggs. Water glass was very similar, but was already dissolved and concentrated. Sold in tins, it only required having water added to the contents of the tin and it was ready for use. Eggs preserved in this way lasted for a year for cooking, baking and making scrambled eggs.

Whilst the glut lasted, most children and many adults around the villages collected them in dozens, half dozens or even single eggs. Everyone gave willingly, farmers being particularly generous; it was not considered a burden in those days to help in the running of the hospitals. Whist Drives were held regularly and a dance was held every year to raise funds, when all refreshments and prizes were given and the Committee worked very hard in serving them and organising. Jumble Sales were particularly popular, whether for hospitals, Scouts or any other worthy cause, one of the main attractions being Mr Crowther, who always manned the hat stall. He had a great sense of humour, trying on all the hats and holding mock sales auctions throughout the afternoon, to everybody's delight and entertainment.

Throughout the summer, from the early rhubarb to the late plum season, it was 'jamming time' when the collection for hospitals changed from eggs to jam jars and we all went round the villages again with our baskets. At one time I remember 1d being paid for empty jam jars for the hospitals when fruit was especially plentiful, but usually they were saved by householders and given freely. Fruit for jam was also given. Almost all households had an allotment or garden where, amongst other things, they grew soft fruit and could spare a little. But mostly, money was collected so that fruit could be bought in large thrifty lots from the market or growers when bulk production was undertaken in the hospital main kitchens.

I have often heard adverse comments about the hospitals before the creation of the National Health Service that treatment was extended only to the favoured few who could afford to pay. This assumption is quite wrong according to my knowledge of the situation at the time. Certainly, up to the First World Ward, specialised treatments such as that for arthritis and other ailments carried out at Buxton and in Spa towns was usually obtained by special recommendations from a J.P., who was usually one of the Governors of the local hospitals, for payment would be made through the Board of Governors to the hospital undertaking the treatment.

In the late 19th century Mr Milner, the Local J.P. gave me one of the two recommendations for my Great Uncle to take treatment at Buxton Devonshire Hospital and my Great Uncle Arthur was granted a recommendation by Mr Milner along with a second one from the Vicar of Holmesfield, also to attend Buxton Hospital just after the turn of the century. Recommendations were also given for other matters. When my Father wished to join the Sheffield Police Force in 1907, he had to obtain a reference from a J.P. to whom he was familiar. Mr Milner, knowing the family so well was the obvious choice. But Dad reckoned without the J.P.'s eccentric way of reasoning and when he admitted to being the brother of Joseph William Salt who had married a week before, the reference was refused. Why? Because Joseph William's father, Edward Abraham Salt, had been buried only the week before; the marriage was unseemly as the family was in mourning. Any member of the same family was not fit to be a policeman. Such was protocol where power was invested.

In the 1920s no-one was refused treatment at the Voluntary Hospital. Casualties and short-term patients were treated as today, without question, and essential physiotherapy was given as a matter of course. But, for chronic ailments and those of a non-urgent nature there was a type of 'means test', not very rigorous and even those like my father who had a well-paid job, was not asked for contributions no matter how long hospital treatment was required. Every hospital had an Almoner, usually a woman, who saw and questioned every patient, or relative of a minor on admittance and after assessing the ability to pay for treatment, they were asked to pay towards the cost, or let off completely.

It was as convalescents that some hardship was experienced, after operations and long treatments, where rest and rehabilitation was advised. Many hospital patients were manual workers who had no reserves to tide them over this period, let alone funds for a convalescent home. Certainly there were holiday homes and convalescent homes for miners and some other factory workers, financed from Union funds but there was a tight system of payment for those run by the Hospital Services, usually entered only by recommendation. It was in this respect that the Hospital Committee did their most valuable and regular work in collecting for the 'penny in the pound' scheme. This was a system whereby each member paid one penny in every pound he earned into the scheme each week and should any of his family and particularly himself require convalescence, the whole cost was met out of the funds.

As members of the Hospital Committee, with other villagers such as Mrs Lake, Mrs Colin Thompson and Mr Lake, both my Father and Mother were collectors of the 'penny in the pound' subscriptions. My Mother once told me that no-one paid more than 2d per week; such were the wages of those days. Of course many people helped in hospitals as they do today. Doctors and Surgeons were volunteers, on a roster basis, nurses did the cleaning as well as nursing and even the cleaning was not of today's labour-saving variety, so all help was very welcome.

'It's an ill wind that blows nobody any good', or so the old adage tells and for once, a little breath of the wind blew my way. When Mr Milner's Will was published in 1931, Mrs Milner informed us, through Lily, that he had left us all £1 for each year of service. Whoever decided on the final sums was generous. Lily had joined the staff in August before I joined in October and Edna arrived earlier in the same year, yet we all received £2 each. Nurse Forbes, although having been retired for a number of years; returning to the Hall only as a safe haven for the rest of her life, received £1 for each of the years since she first joined the household as nurse to Mr Billy, altogether £45.0s.0d, a nice little windfall. Mine was more than a windfall, it was a veritable godsend. I had never owned so much money in all my life and to be left a 'legacy' made me feel very important.

The master's death brought a sad day for the mistress, for nor only did she lose her husband but before long she was to lose the home she had known for almost 50 years. Death duties were a drain on many estates and so they were at Totley Hall. By September we knew that the Hall was to be sold and some of us would be redundant. Archie Thomas told me recently that the Hall was not sold, but after death duties depleted Mrs Milner's funds, there was insufficient left for its upkeep. The theory is that the move to a smaller house at Baslow enabled her to let the Hall and live on the proceeds. How true this is I have no comment, at the time we all assumed that the sale of household contents at the end of the year was the prelude to the ultimate sale of the house. It made no difference to our position; Lily and Annie were moving to Baslow with the mistress, along with

Lewis who would take charge of the gardens, the rest of us would find employment elsewhere.

It was a busy time, men all over the place, visitors coming and going, the only anchor being the usual routine of mealtimes and service to the mistress. The valuers were under the feet all day and every day, examining furniture and pots and pans, marking them and pricing for the eventual auction. Many small items were put to one side for the Church Jumble Sale held as usual before Christmas, a few of the items being bought there by my Father, including the scales always standing on the kitchen table, and used by Lily for measuring ingredients, later used by my Mother until she came to live with me, and since, to the present day by me. Now over a hundred years old, I reckon they have almost earned retirement!

One day, towards the end of the valuation, after consuming innumerable cups of tea, one of the valuers approached me, as I learned he had the other members of the staff who were leaving. "What are you going to do when you leave the Hall?" he said. I told him "I haven't given it a thought." "I can find you a job if you want one," he said. "I know a woman who wants a Cook General." I hadn't a clue what a Cook General was, nor what she was supposed to do. I could only assume from the name that there was cooking to do, so I said I might be interested. After all, I still didn't fancy remaining at home all the time and November wasn't the time when Photo Finishers took on extra staff. He made arrangements for me to go to a large house on Ecclesall Road South, a suburb on the southern outskirts of Sheffield. There was no mention of an interview, or of references. I suppose my new mistress took the valuer's word, or that they weren't necessary, after all she couldn't question Mrs Milner's judgment could she? I was told to report for my new job on 4th December 1921 and having left the Hall on the 27th November, I had a few days to prepare my clothes and pack my bag. I had little idea of what to expect, knowing only that I would be the only serving maid, just what my Father had avoided almost three years before.

211

Chapter 9

A few weeks before I started my new job my Father had exchanged his motorbike and sidecar for a little two-seater car. It was very low and bright red; we called it the 'Red Bullet'. On 4th December he loaded my suitcase into the tiny boot and a few minutes later deposited me at the gate of the house in Ecclesall Road South where I was to spend at least one month on trial, on both sides. I felt little excitement as I reached the door and my heart sank when it was opened by a tall, thin, tight-lipped woman, whose miserable face was set in the most depressing downward curves which had frozen into position beyond the efforts of a host of angels to unfreeze. Her manner was forced in a great effort to be pleasant which didn't quite work; it was so artificial as to be embarrassing.

With few preliminaries, she showed me to my room. It was small, no bigger than a box room with a window overlooking the side of the house and the garage. A single bed stood against one wall, a small dressing table and a travelling trunk, which served as a seat, the only other furnishings. But it was the colour which hit me right between the eyes and made my heart sink, for everything in the room was covered with violet drapes. All were beautifully tailored and much effort had been put into the fitting, but the pleated frill surrounding the dressing table did nothing to make me want to sit before it. The curtains rose to the ceiling and hit the grey carpet below, whilst the covers of the large travelling trunk and the single bed, both meticulously pleated to match the dressing table, did nothing to raise my spirits, everything was so funereal and depressing.

I quickly unpacked and changed into the uniform I had worn at Totley Hall and went downstairs where I could hear someone preparing tea. A small cloth had been spread on one end of the kitchen table and a plate of bread and butter, a small dish of jam and another plate on which was a piece of cake were set for my meal. As I entered, the mistress poured out a cup of tea, indicating that it was for me, explaining that as it was Saturday, no dinner would be cooked that night, but a cup of cocoa and a sandwich would be served before bedtime. She then left me to my first meal. A little bewildered at the sparseness of the meal and with that awful depressing feeling, I drank my tea and ate the piece of cake.

The few dishes were brought out of the dining room by the daughter of the house, a rather nice looking girl of about 19 years old, who acknowledged me not unpleasantly, then left me to wash them. Her mother followed a few minutes after I had finished and took me on a conducted tour of the kitchen cupboards and drawers. I soon realised it was the occasion for a series of excuses for someone's careless housekeeping. "Don't look too closely in here;" as she opened a cutlery drawer, "I haven't had time to clean it out. I'm afraid the pans aren't as shiny as they should be," she said lifting one from the shelf, "I really haven't got around to doing all these little jobs." And so on, etc. etc. I wondered where I could begin and what my job really was. There was no mention of cooking so far, and I got the impression that my job was really back to being a kitchen maid.

There were three children in the household, a son of about 24, whom I saw only once, the daughter whom I have already mentioned and a son aged almost 16 who went to a public school in Sheffield. I was surprised to hear that one of my jobs was to see that he had a bar of chocolate in his schoolbag every morning for break time. Showing me where they were kept, his mother opened the door of the high kitchen cupboard to show me a large box covering half the bottom shelf which was overflowing with bars of milk chocolate. I wondered why he couldn't be trusted to help himself and I wasn't surprised when I first met him to see a pasty faced thin individual with even less personality than his mother. By the time the tour was over, I still wasn't sure what I was really supposed to do but decided that there was another day tomorrow and being dismissed for the night, I went to my room.

When the door of that little room was closed to the world that night, I was devastated, quite alone, and very, very lonely. There was no Annie to talk to until sleep overtook me, no prospect of anyone with whom I could pass a remark or two; the future looked very grim. Once in bed I cried tears of sheer loneliness. Whatever I looked like in this morning, tonight was given over to uncontrollable sobbing, until at last I managed to fall asleep.

I rose next morning about 7.30 a.m., feeling jaded, but hopeful that today would be better than yesterday. How wrong I was. I had been told that there was no hurry on Sunday morning, so was a little surprised to find the mistress was already in the kitchen cooking breakfast. I assumed it would be served in the dining room, so the first job was to set the table. This done, and breakfast served, I sat down at the kitchen table to eat my own, feeling sick with nostalgia for the servant's hall. I had never in my life had a meal alone and it didn't go down very well. As soon as I thought everyone would have left the dining room, I cleared the dishes and washed up and, as all was silent and not knowing what I was supposed to do next, made my way upstairs, made all the beds and tidied the rooms, assuming that, being Sunday, no extra cleaning was expected. Having done everything I could think of upstairs, I returned to the kitchen, realising at once that someone was around, for I could hear a sizzling sound coming from the oven and on opening the door a little, saw that it was a joint of beef.

I was even more confused. The mistress had cooked the breakfast, now someone had started preparing dinner and there was no-one around to ask what I was supposed to do next. I went back upstairs, tidied the bathroom, dusted down the stairs, the dining and sitting rooms, and was about to start on the hall when I heard voices in the kitchen, at first in conversation, then raised as if in anger. Going through to the kitchen, the fury which met me knocked me back pretty quickly. The mistress was bending over the roasting tin looking at the piece of beef of frizzled condition which she had just

215

lifted out of the oven and, face as red as a turkey cock, was raving and shouting my name as fast as the words could splutter out of her mouth. "Look what you've done, it's ruined," she shouted. "Why didn't you look after it?" but before I could say a word, she continued "Where are the vegetables? You've not even peeled the potatoes." I was flabbergasted. "I don't even know where the vegetables are, you never thought to tell me where they are," I shouted back. "And how should I know it was my job to do them if you don't say so, you cooked the breakfast, you put the meat in, how would I know I had to look after it?" and so it went on.

The job of Cook General had been a bit of a mystery; now it was even more confusing. Had I been told that I had to keep the house clean, cook all the meals and do every other job to keep the household on an even keel, life would have been much simpler but in this house the routine was far from simple and more bewildering every minute. I shouldn't have made the beds, they all made their own in their own good time, I certainly shouldn't have been in the 16 year old's bedroom except to clean when he was at school, although he looked quite incapable of committing the slightest indiscretion and I took umbrage at the hint, and said so. Monday was no better. Returning to the kitchen from making my bed I was rather disconcerted to see the mistress and her daughter doing the weekly wash. A zinc Peggy-tub stood in the centre of the floor, the daughter threading clothes through the mangle rollers whilst her mother turned the handle. The following week I was told to bring down my own to be washed with the rest. I was completely baffled by the system; no wonder my Father hadn't wanted me to work for such people.

The final straw was when the mistress lifted an old pan from a high shelf which obviously had not been used for generations and I was accused of putting it there without it being cleaned. By this time I no longer sat back and took the punishment. I had been at the house for ten days, in which time I had met the master and the chauffeur. The master was a kindly man but a bit subdued when he asked how I was getting on, and how he hoped I would stay. The chauffeur enlightened me on the latter remark, "Oh aye," he said,

"he'll want you to stay, he's fed up with the trouble over maids."
Surprised, I asked "Why?" "Oh, they had one for two years but she
left to get married and they've had about 17 in three months since
she left," he answered with a grimace.

I thought this was rather an exaggeration but it did confirm
that the mistress was a difficult person to deal with, which boosted
my confidence a little, after it had been rapidly draining away. I told
the chauffeur I was going to leave and that I'd had enough. "Don't
do that," he pleaded, "stick it out a bit longer, the Boss is alright, he's
bloody fed up with her neurotic ways, but you'll get used to her."
Then he added, rather wryly, "He's worked hard in the scrap
business and can afford a good life, but she can't keep up with it,
she's never been used to this sort of life, I think it gets her down a
bit."

I had no intention of getting used to a woman who, I thought,
was ignorant of the correct way to run a household and wasn't even
capable of training a servant; and that in my book, just what was I
there for. My mind was made up, I would leave tonight. I had been
here just two weeks during which all the drawers had been washed
out and cutlery cleaned, shelves and cupboards cleaned and covered
with clean papers and pans were all polished and shining, except the
one from the high shelf which I refused to do, so now was the time
for exit.

Immediately after washing the dishes from supper, I made a
beeline for my bedroom and packed my case, fastening it ready to
leave. Then I noticed that in my hurry, I'd forgotten a pair of shoes,
so tying them in a piece of brown paper, I tied them to the suitcase
handle. Then I spotted an apron just back from the wash and into a
second parcel it went. I ended up with five parcels tied to the handle
of the case by the time I left that awful bedroom.

The mistress was in the kitchen when I entered, and to say
'the lid came off the kettle with the force of the steam' was an
understatement. "Where do you think you're going?" she burst out.
"I'm leaving," I answered defiantly, "I've had enough, and I'm going
home." "You can't walk out like that," she almost screamed, "you're
here for a month, take that coat off at once. "Oh yes I can," I shouted

back, "I'm going; I'm not stopping here any longer." "You won't get any wages," she cried, trying to bar my way, "I'll see to that." "You can keep my wages in lieu of notice," I called back as I made a beeline for the door. She made a dive and grabbed my suitcase handle, screaming abuse that a respectable lady wouldn't even know, but the parcels prevented her taking a good hold and I was able to pull and drag the case free, making for the door as fast as possible.

Outside the door, I met the master just alighting from the car after attending a meeting. "Hello Josephine, where are you going at this time of the night?" he said, surprised. I told him what had happened and his face fell. "I can't stand her anymore," I told him, "I don't know when I'm doing right for doing wrong, and she's never satisfied, and always so miserable and depressing." "I thought at last we had somebody to stay," he said "you don't know what a relief it has been," but he could see I was determined. "Let me have a talk to her," he pleaded, "I'm sure she'll be better if I explain." But all his pleading and offers of help wouldn't change my dislike for the woman, so I said my excuses and started down the drive.

It struck me like a thunderbolt as I turned into the main road. How was I to get home? There were no buses to Totley and I couldn't walk the three or four miles carrying this damned suitcase. And how much money had I in my purse? Then I remembered. When Dad had bought his car a few weeks before from his cousin Tom Bradley, I had met Tom and remembered that he lived in Dore, and there was a bus to Dore from the terminus at the top of Ecclesall Road, about 300 yards away. I had a few pence left from last week's spending money, that should be enough for the fare to Dore, about two miles. I knew his address and if I could find the house, he would probably take me to Totley, I reasoned, and resolved to catch the next bus out of the terminus.

I started walking, dragging the suitcase with its five parcels dangling from the handle and occasionally banging against my shins. It was a slow, weary progress helped only by the mood of determination which swept over me, that I wouldn't be beaten; I wouldn't be a skivvy for anyone anymore. So far I hadn't given a thought to what I would say to my Father, or what he would say to me, for that matter I think I was past caring, I'd pushed the boat out and if I were left in deep water, my back was broad enough to take the punishment.

I arrived at Lavender Cottage in Town Head Road about 9.30 p.m. and to say Tom was surprised was an understatement. He had met me only once and then only briefly on my day off from Totley Hall when he delivered the car. I could understand his surprise when he opened the door so late at night to find a comparative stranger standing there asking for help. I explained my predicament and how I'd arrived on his doorstep ending "You've got a car Tom, will you take me to Totley please?"

"Of course I'll take you home lass, but what's your Father going to say?" I told him I neither knew nor cared, I was tired and just wanted the day to end, "I only hope he understands," I said miserably. "Well," said Tom briskly, now in charge of the situation, "it's no good going yet, we may as well wait until he comes home from the pub, he'll be in a good temper then anyway." I agreed that would be wise, he was usually in a good mood when he arrived home, although like all men who had had enough to make them merry, his good humour could easily change to bad temper if something upset the equilibrium. Not that my Father ever got drunk, he said "A man who can't hold his beer shouldn't drink," and my Dad could always hold his beer. So, as Tom suggested, we had a cup of tea, and I met Floss, his wife, and we all got to know each other better whilst we waited.

We set out about 10.20 p.m. and by the time my Father appeared, I had explained to my Mother, who was a little apprehensive, and I was sitting nervously on the horsehair sofa beside Tom when he walked in. "Hello lass," he said cheerfully, his eyes twinkling, "what brings you home?" Before I could explain he caught sight of Tom, and was even more surprised. "Hello Tom," he greeted him as he looked from one to the other. "I just gave her a lift home," Tom said meekly; there was little more he could say, so I thought I had better come clean.

My Father's face changed completely as he listened. It was a very different situation finding his daughter sitting on his sofa unexpectedly, from another when there was doubt as to the reason. "Why have you come home?" was his first question. "I've left," I said as defiantly as I could, although by now I felt far from defiant. "You've left your work?" he said in a voice which showed he was not going to be pleased. "Yes," I said quietly, now feeling very subdued. "Why?" he said, very firmly this time. I told him everything that had happened since the last time I was at home. He already knew about the uncertain start, the untidy drawers and the unpolished pans, but this was more serious, this had to be got to the bottom of, (if you'll pardon the grammar) and the third degree started, questioning, slow-timing. "So you think there was no reason to complain about your work?" he said. I nodded. "You're sure you did your work right?" he said. I had told him about the dirty pan and he had accepted my explanation. "When I knew what I had to do," I replied, as he looked quizzically at me, not unkindly.

The slow-timing went on for another 15 minutes, my Mother and Tom sitting silently, until he could see I was getting really upset. "So, you left your wages in lieu of notice you say." "Yes," I agreed meekly. "But they were my wages, what am I going to do without my wages," he said. At this, I burst out "You can keep my spending money until I've paid it off," I told him, very near to tears. He looked at me for a long time, the tension weaving its way under my skin until I felt I must scream. "Alright lass," he said at last, "you'll pay it off with your spending money." My spending money was still only 3d a week, and my wages were the same as at Totley Hall, 7s.6d a week, so this was going to be a stiff sentence I thought. Christmas was only a few days away and I had the princely sum of a halfpenny in my purse, so the outlook was dismal.

Nevertheless, always too proud to show any weakness, especially in front of my Father, I accepted the sentence and was happy to return home, the dye had been cast and I had to live with it. Christmas came and went without any undue trauma, it was a time to be home and there was little reason or opportunity to spend money and the week between Christmas and New Year passed uneventfully until the afternoon of New Year's Eve.

There was always a dance at the Labour Hall every Saturday night, (now Green Oak Hall and the Conservative Club). When I was 16, Dad had been allowed me to go, provided Elijah saw me safely home. Since then, he had relented a little and, when I was at home had allowed me to go with Ida, my closest friend, who was six years older than I. We had often laughed about our lack of money but it had never interfered with our enjoyment of the dance. No-one in those days had an abundance of money, so we never felt inferior and we both had a strong sense of humour, much in the forefront one night when we were both particularly hard up. "We walk in all our finery like two bloody Queens, and we can't raise 6d between us," she quipped. We did, of course, have the requisite 6d to get into the dance but, as she said, "Thank goodness there's always some lad with 2d who will buy us a cup of coffee." There was to be a dance this New Year's Eve, but of course, I couldn't even raise the 6d to get in.

My Father came downstairs ready to go for his usual pint. "Aren't you going out tonight?" he asked. "No," was the obvious response. "Why?" he said, isn't there a dance tonight?" "Yes," I answered a little exasperated. "Then why aren't you going?" he persisted. "You know why I'm not going," I answered again rather shortly. He knew why I wasn't going, and as usual was tormenting. "Isn't Ida going?" he asked. "I don't know, I haven't seen her," I replied. "Why haven't you seen her?" he said. "There was no point, I wasn't going anywhere, and she doesn't even know I'm at home," I said. I thought this would be the end of the teasing but it continued as usual; I was in a mild temper. It was bad enough not having any money; it was even worse having to stay at home on New Year's Eve and having it rubbed in the bargain, and this bantering was the last straw.

I jumped up, intending to run upstairs out of the way, when he put a hand out and grabbed my arm and pushed me back in my chair saying "Not so fast lass." With one hand on my shoulder, he put his hand in his pocket and drew out two half crowns (5s.0d)/25p in today's currency. Putting them on the table, he said, now very serious, "Here, get off to your dance, I will say this, you stick to your convictions, you're a chip off the old block and I admire you for that," and as an afterthought he turned to go out saying "I'm proud of you lass."

At this change of fortune and sign of a truce, I immediately subsided into a torrent of hysterical sobbing and uncontrollable tears of relief. My Mother came and put her arms around me saying quietly, "Come on lass, you'll not be fit to go to the dance," and for a moment this made me worse. She continued "Come on, dry your eyes and get ready, before it's too late." I had never had so much money in my purse since my windfall at Totley Hall and to add to that pleasure, the following Saturday, my spending money was raised to the princely sum of 1s.0d (5p today), a veritable fortune.

Early in January my Father received another visit from Cousin Tom, probably something to do with the car, and during the conversation about various topical matters, Tom talked about his recent venture. Until the Depression which had hit most countries since the fall of Wall Street in 1929, Tom had been the senior salesman at Brocklehursts, the local car salesrooms but about three months before Christmas 1932, he had been made redundant as had many more men. Not to be outdone and ever resourceful he decided to put his considerable talents in salesmanship to another use and had set himself up in business as a salesman of 'produce' rather than cars. As he said to me at a later date, "People will always want to eat no matter how poor they are." During his conversation with my Father he said he could do with some help, but money was tight and he couldn't pay a wage. I'm sure you can guess what came next. Yes, Josephine could go and live at Lavender Cottage and help Tom to get his business off the ground, and I wouldn't require any wages, he would still give me spending money.

I needed no second bidding, Tom was handsome; ten years younger than my Father, with a very strong resemblance to Maurice Chevalier, the French film star with a personality to match, and I loved him. My Father drove me to Dore a few days later and I began my education in salesmanship, more than that, I had fun. Life was certainly not dull at Lavender Cottage, although I was expected to put in a good day's work, paid or unpaid. Tom's philosophy on

222

business was not exactly by direct approach, he was subtle and crafty. "You see Joss, we're not going to bang on the door, we're going right under the kitchen door and come up in the kitchen." This; with a movement of the hand which went down almost to the ground and then curved upwards about 1ft in front; presumably in the kitchen.

He had already started the business by buying a small Bradford van painting it bright yellow with no name in sight. (It wasn't illegal at that time not to show the trading name and address on the side of the vehicle). Again came his explanation. "Women are curious," he said, "when they see a strange van in the street, and they'll not miss this bright yellow one, they'll ask questions." He warmed up and became more animated as he spoke and I was intrigued. "You'll see them peeping from behind the curtains to see what's going on and they'll gossip and ask each other what we're selling, and they'll not know unless they buy some."

He was warming to the whole idea and taking pleasure in telling me how it was to be done, "and before you know it," he said, "we shall be right in the kitchen, then we'll be able to sell them whatever we like." He was so confident and sure of himself. The produce we were going to sell was 'ready peeled potatoes'; not an unusual commodity in these 'pre-packaged', 'pre-prepared', 'pre-cooked' and every other 'pre' one can dream up days, but in 1932 no-one had ever done anything like this before and anything labour-saving was not considered necessary for housewives. It was revolutionary; and it worked!

Tom had ordered a quantity of cans, similar to the milk delivery cans which were used by farmers. They had wide bases with narrower tops to prevent water splashing whilst carrying, and were made in different sizes to hold one, two or three pounds of potatoes as necessary. The potatoes were peeled by hand, a mammoth task, but fortunately there was plenty of free help. Both Tom and Floss, his wife, were popular and Floss, although 'fiery' had a sense of humour which pleased the young men who came every evening to help. Another girl, Bessie Marshall from Hall Lane, had been helping for about a month for a small wage and was still there for the first week after I started, when she left having had, as she said, "Enough."

After tea each evening, two tin baths were brought in and set in front of the hearth and filled with water. Tom, Floss, Bessie and I sat around them, with Claude Wragg and Aden Taylor adding a third pair of hands to each bath. Tom would dip a bag of potatoes into the bath and three potato peelers were wielded with great dexterity, peel falling in regular showers to form a thick carpet on the bottom of the bath (a bit like an Army life). As each potato was peeled, it was put or thrown into the other bath where the other three workers waited with knives at the ready to relieve them of the eyes. In this way we ploughed our way through three bags (cwts.) every night for the first two weeks, working to a very late hour.

The work was not considered a chore. Instead it was time for fun and jokes and stories, particularly from Claude and Aden, both village lads who had been family friends for years. They travelled around the Clubs and performed at all the local concerts as a double act impersonating and singing the songs made famous by Flannagan and Allan, of 'Underneath the Arches' fame. The stories they told were hilarious, their jokes of the Club type. When they were present there was never a dull moment.

Next day, Tom would load the little yellow van with the 'ready for the pot' potatoes now transferred to tall 'Peggy tubs', each one two thirds filled to allow for the inevitable swishing of the water as we travelled the bumpy roads. Floss sat in the seat beside Tom, whilst I crouched just inside the back door hanging on to one of the tubs in case the door flew open, a position not too uncomfortable whilst the van was at a standstill. However, at the first movement, water spilled to and fro and following the line of least resistance, created a wonderful wave action that not only soaked me from above, my lap holding a veritable pond but the river effect from front to back of the van caught my behind in the fold. By the time we reached our first stop I was the archetype of natural accidents. "Are you alright back there?" would come from Tom, as we rounded a particularly acute bend. "Hold on Joss, I'm turning left," and as I braced myself for a right swerve, he'd change his mind, "We'll go down this road today," and take the right turn instead. "Let some more see the 'yellow peril'" was his excuse with the reasoning that the more women who saw the van, the more new customers we would get.

Business was brisk; in a few weeks the van was too small and the quantity of potatoes needed to supply new customers so great that Tom bought a potato rumbler and there was no more peeling by hand. He ran a hosepipe out on to the front path of the cottage to supply it with water and within a couple of hours, five or six bags were peeled, requiring only eyes removed. So, the production line changed. With the advent of new machinery, productivity increased and C.N.P. rose accordingly.

The original intention, as Tom had already explained, was to get into the kitchens and then drop the product which caused all the work. That meant dropping the peeled potatoes and selling them as other greengrocers did, straight from the sack, introducing other vegetables and fruits and building up a regular greengrocery round.

Hawkers, as they were called, could be seen in almost every street during the Depression, when men did anything to earn a living, as dole money could be claimed for only 26 weeks. But Tom had been right; he had found a way into the kitchen and made a profit from the first moment, without the hassle of knocking on every door in the hope of an order. Before two months were over, the business was thriving and making a good living for Tom and his family.

Nevertheless, his ambitions didn't stop there. When Elijah was made redundant from Walsh's cabinet making firm, my Father bought a quantity of timber to build two or three poultry houses which now stood in the field at the top of the bank opposite the cottage alongside the pig sty's housing a hundred or more of laying pullets, young chickens being raised in incubators for follow on. By the time Tom was ready to expand into new products, there were several fowls to grub out and arrangements were made between the two men for Tom to buy them live, as and when necessary, to supply orders which he was confident would be forthcoming.

It was at this point that I commenced my lessons on the art of canvassing. How to persuade the housewife to buy something she hadn't given a thought to that day, didn't even need and that your product was the best and the best value for money. I learned how to knock on a door confidently, how to introduce myself and the goods I had to sell, even though all I had was a notebook and the goods weren't even there for her to see. I learned to smile a confident smile which would disarm, "Use your natural charm," said Tom, "You've got plenty of it. Take it for granted you'll get an order, and you will."

After the first nervous session I found that what he said was true; I could talk people into giving orders with little effort. Provided the product was reliable, I could sell it and we gathered orders as fast as we could prepare them. Our daily routine was heavy. We had extended the rounds to include not only the village, but Dore Road, Devonshire Road, Rushley, Ecclesall Road South and Park Head and Knowle Lane, spending the mornings selling in one of these areas, home for a light lunch, spending the afternoons canvassing a new street or group of houses, and home again for dinner about 5.30 p.m.

After tea, Tom would drive to Totley to collect as many fowls as we had orders for bundling them into the van live and depositing them in his garage which was a little way further up Town Head Road from Lavender Cottage. This gave me a little respite whilst Floss bathed Peter, their three year old son, and I fed him with 'pobs' (bread and hot milk sweetened with golden syrup, or sometimes with sugar). It was a lovely relaxed way of spending an hour after the hectic pursuits of the earlier part of the day, but I didn't and couldn't relax for long.

As soon as Tom returned with the livestock, we both ensconced ourselves on upturned orange boxes with squawking fowls running around our ankles. Tom could ring a neck in a split second and this he did, tossing the still squawking and struggling cadaver over to me whilst he grabbed and rung another for himself. "Get it between your knees," he cried, as the first one came flying towards me. But I had plucked game before and needed little telling how to do the job. As soon as one was done, another followed, and it was often near midnight by the time the plucking was finished.

"Can you dress a fowl?" said Tom on the first occasion. Like a fool I said "Yes." "Take my advice, never say you can do anything, you'll always get the job." I did. All the now bare carcasses were transported to the cottage and after a quick cup of tea, Tom went to bed and I turned to the little kitchen to commence the drawing and trussing. This needs no explanation to those cooks who regularly have to accomplish the same task, but after seeing the entrails of a dozen or more fowls being extricated from the still warm cadavers, seeing them drop straight out of the arse end into an already full bucket, whilst almost dropping from sheer fatigue, I can only say that some days I wished that fowls had never been given the breath of life.

Floss knew that Tom was fond of the ladies to put the matter mildly and made no secret about what she thought about it. One day she was in such a fury because he had gone out and she suspected the worse, that she went to the garage, took a brick and broke every window in the van. On Easter Sunday my Father and Tom had gone on a fishing trip to Flamborough Head and Floss couldn't contain her temper. On Monday morning, she rose, still furious. "If they've gone away, then so are we," she shouted. "But," I said, "We've got to finish the potatoes ready for Tom to load on Tuesday morning." "To hell with the potatoes," she screeched, "he can do his own potatoes." Nothing I could say would calm her temper as she packed sandwiches for the journey and prepared Peter's food for the day.

"Come on, let's get going," she said, "there's a trip to Blackpool today, we'll go there." A few minutes later I found myself in a local hire car on the way to Dore & Totley Station where we caught the train for bracing Blackpool. The journey was uneventful, taking about three and a half hours. Sight of the sea was a delight, even though the day was not one of the brightest. In fact, by early afternoon, it was snowing fast and growing quite cold. We strolled on to the Central Pier hoping to find shelter from the wind but the snow turned into a blizzard and after pausing only long enough to take a couple of photographs. We returned to the promenade and very soon left for the station to return home. So much for our day of protest!

Needless to say, Tom was not pleased. Floss refused to help with the potatoes and encouraged me to follow suit, so poor Tom paid dearly for his weekend off. It was inevitable that this arrangement could not last. Gradually I realised that almost all the work rested on my shoulders. Floss had given up the rounds and Tom spent a number of afternoons with his lady friend in Petre Street, Sheffield when he was supposed to be canvassing with me. He would drop me off at Knowle Lane or other point convenient to the new area or road he wished to explore, saying "I'll pick you up at 5.00 p.m.," or whatever time suited. Since we had stopped selling peeled potatoes his work on the potato rumbler had ceased and but for wringing the fowl's necks, he did little else except drive the van and weigh out orders whilst Floss and I did all the running to houses for orders and delivering when complete.

Before long I grew very disillusioned and one day confided to my Father, "I'm doing all the work; I could be running my own business." "In that case," he said, "You'd better leave lass, if he's using you unfairly, I'll not have that." "It's such a pity," I told him, "it's a damned good business, but he won't have the work."

So, once more I left a job and returned home, although I often returned to visit Floss and Peter. It was on one of these visits that a little bit of history came to my notice. Floss' parents and her younger brother Thomas lived next door to Lavender Cottage from where Thomas ran the general shop opposite the Church which had been started by his father or his grandfather, I'm not sure which. In November 1933 he came into the cottage with a large 'patty tin' in his hand. "I've brought something to show you," he said, "what do you think of these?" He held out the tin for us both to take a sample. "Taste them," he said, obviously enjoying the mystery.

"Where on earth did you get them?" asked Floss, for we both thought they were garden peas. But in 1933 garden peas couldn't be bought out of season and frozen foods had not yet been invented. "They're nice aren't they?" Thomas said laughing, "you know where I got them, out of a tin." "Good Lord," exclaimed Floss, "out of a tin, who ... ?" Before she could say more, Thomas pulled a tin out of his smock pocket saying "Batchelors have started putting peas in tins; I've just been to the wholesalers and bought a box full. We could, of course, buy many things in tins, such as Heinz beans, salmon, crab and lobster and some fruits from South Africa such as peaches, apricots and pears, but vegetables were strictly a seasonal food, preserved only by drying and to be able to buy peas in tins almost as good as fresh ones was, as one would say, 'A nine days wonder'.

On 4th November 1933, I was bridesmaid for the one and only time in my life, when cousin May and Laurie were married at Totley Church. The four bridesmaids wore velvet, two in gold, and two in deep red. We carried sheaves of autumn leaves and wore headdresses to match. My gold dress was to become my favourite dance dress, for you must realise, long dresses were worn to all dances, even local hops, although there wasn't exactly strict competition (we couldn't afford that). We were all very careful to make the most of whatever assets we had been blessed with. My hair and teeth were my most outstanding assets and the gold dress was just right. As Jim, my current boyfriend always called me "my golden girl."

An added bonus on returning home was that I could now attend the dances every Saturday night and it was a luxury for me to have a real dance dress, after many years of 'making do'. My first had been a pale blue taffeta which my Father bought for me to attend my first dance when I was just 16. It was made in the current fashion, reaching the knees in front, and dropping down to ankle length at the back. The sleeveless bodice and the back train were heavily embroidered.

I cringe now to think of the day Edna invited me to go home with her to Whittington as our Sundays off coincided. I said "Yes," but what was I to wear? I hadn't a dress suitable to go visiting, particularly as I knew that Edna had a big family, most of who would be at home. "Why not put on your new dress on?" Edna suggested. "I can't do that," I said, "it's an evening dress." "Of course you can," she persisted, "it's nice, put it on." So I decked myself in my new dance dress and wore the short coat from the costume my Father had bought when I left school two years before.

We set out for the bus and train to Old Whittington and from there walked the short distance to Edna's home. I was embarrassed, but Edna kept assuring me that I looked nice, and that everybody would like me. The latter was, I believe, quite true. I met some of Edna's sisters on later dates and they made this quite clear, but I'm sure they had a laugh over my dress.

On one of my days off, I complained to my Mother that I didn't have a change from the blue taffeta for a special dance to be held the following Saturday. After listening and sympathising for a while, she disappeared upstairs, returning with a deep blue silk taffeta bedspread which she had washed only once. "Can you manage to make one from this?" she asked, "there's enough to make a dress if you're careful cutting it out." I needed no second bidding, out came the scissors and cutting out began. Before the day was out, I had a new dress for Saturday nights. This was the first of many home-made creations, except for the dress I had made when I was 14 years old, when Jobie thought I was very clever but Mom was cross with me wasting time when she wanted some chores doing.

In 1932 many articles had been sent to a Church Jumble Sale from Totley Hall during the sorting out for removal. Amongst these were the spring scales which used to stand on the kitchen table and probably dated from the time that the Milner's first came to Totley. There was a large porcelain jug and the crimson robe which Mr Milner wore when he was High Sheriff of Derbyshire. My Father bought all three. I still use the scales, the vase stands in the landing window and the robe? Well the robe was made of the thickest most luxurious satin, heavy royal crimson. It was too good to be wasted so after some discussion as to how it could be used to best advantage, both Mom and Dad agreed that I could have it to make a new dance dress. This time I didn't risk making it myself. Mr Father agreed to pay for it to be made by Mrs Emily Green, who had made my Roman satin dress with the material given by Auntie Annie a few years prior. I felt really important in my first real dance dress and to think it had been worn on such stately occasions on the shoulders of the High Sheriff filled me with pride; I was the most important person on the dance floor. But, after the wedding, the gold velvet took first place, the others fading into insignificance. Yet even gold velvet can become boring if worn every week and before long the sewing machine came out once more for new creations.

One of cousin May's bridesmaids periodically sold off-cuts and remnants of fabrics at very cheap prices. They were all types of crepes, elephant crepe, which was quite bulbous and bouncy and other medium, small and very find versions of all colours, tints and shades and I treated myself to samples of them all. A grey dress in the medium type was trimmed with a plaited band in maroon and grey on the neckline, a dance dress in heavy crepe had an inset panel of blue smocking from waist to knees, flaring out to the hemline and finished at the waist with a huge blue bow. My favourite was a deep blue day dress in the finest crepe with a gathered bodice and lots of ruching on waist and sleeves, but the one most admired, and the most useful, was an ensemble in pale grey medium crepe, the neckline and the short split sleeves piped with blue, with a belt to match. With it I wore a long loose coat in the same material and colour, which fastened at the neck with a large 'artist's bow' and a fashionable blue beret. By this time it was approaching the end of 1934 and I must go back to November 1933 when I returned home for the last time from Lavender Cottage.

After being away from home for the best part of three years, it was clear that I had to be housed rather more privately; if only for appearances sake. In fairness to my parents, my situation was not very different from that of many other girls. Families were large and accommodation often limited. But, I was the only girl and something could be done about it. Dad suggested that Elijah rig up a framework in one corner of the room, to which a curtain rail could be fitted. When a curtain was hung, the bed would be discreetly hidden when the room was being used for sitting in. It was a reasonable arrangement so far as sleeping was concerned, but it held no privacy for dressing or getting changed. My clothes were all kept in my parents' room and I still used that night and morning, but there were times when I wanted a little privacy for more intimate operations, and this caused problems, always with Geoff.

There had always been extra electricity between Geoff and I, call it 'second child syndrome' or in this particular case, 'middle children syndrome'. Either way, sometimes there was friction. Geoff particularly resented the fact that I had, as he said, 'taken over the room, and that he should knock before coming in'. Actually, there was little reason for anyone coming into the room except on high days and holidays, but Geoff found reasons. He flatly refused to knock, or give any other indication when he was going to 'barge in'. He caught me in some very embarrassing situations over the next three years. I've often wondered how much the situation influenced me in getting married when I did; the promise of a real bedroom must have been a physiological 'pull'. But that's another story.

At Easter 1934 I went back to Photo Finishers. Now 18 years old, I had been away from the firm for three seasons. It had changed little and most of the people I had known before were still employed there and I settled in quickly, this time to a change of job. I was assigned to the printing room, where snapshots were printed from negatives sent in by customers and from newly developed spools. It was a dark room with a series of 6ft high square enclosures, a bit like the old Stock Exchange, inside each of which a high powered electric light bulb provided the light for printing. On each side was an opening and a box-like contraption which pivoted up and over, allowing light to come through the opening when it was done and shutting it off when in an upward resting position. A small door at the front of the shutter allowed the negative and printing paper to be held in position whilst working the shutter, and on the bench underneath, stood another box divided into compartments, which contained printing paper, vigorous, extra vigorous, soft and extra soft.

As each order was received, a negative was inserted in the shutter, the correct paper for the intensity of the negative was placed over it, the door closed and counting began. This was the secret of obtaining a good print without entailing a lot of waste. One second too long or too short, too vigorous or too soft a paper and the print would be thrown out by the Developer. She sat at a lower level than the printer, at a low, shallow sink which held hypo, the developing liquid, whilst a smaller sink held the fixing solution. Overhead hung a small powered red electric light bulb, the only light in the room except for the little which came from the interior of the printing boxes as they tilted forward.

Outside the wall, in line with the Developers, were large sinks which actually went through the walls, half on each side. The developed and fixed prints were tossed into the sink of water, which was constantly being replenished from running taps in the room outside, where they were washed until there was no trace of fixed left in the water. A numbered slip of paper accompanied each batch and was matched to the negatives by the checker when received from the dryer.

Every Printer had a number, which was included in the number on the back of the order and on every print; consequently there was little chance of cheating on the amount of waste any one printer had created during the day. If caught trying to 'snitch' a few out of the waste dish, it was instant dismissal, so very few tried it. All waste was counted by one of the accounting staff at the end of the work shift and above the limit allowed; a fixed amount for each piece was deducted from the wages at the end of the week.

This was my job for the whole of that season and when September arrived, I expected to leave with the other seasonal workers. However, Mr Christie, the Manager, informed me that I was to be kept on to become a member of the permanent staff, when I would be allowed one week's paid holiday each year and a rise in wages. This was good news indeed; I now had a job for as long as I wanted. When I first went to Photo finishers in 1930, my wages was 13s.8p (about 69p). When I returned in 1934, I started at 15s.0d (75p). Now I would get the princely sum of 17s.0d (85p), plus overtime and, in season, there would be plenty of that.

Another 'perk' attached to the job was the free films we were allowed for our holidays. Taking photographs was encouraged as it produced pictures for the show cards and posters which were sent round to all the customers. We all competed in the production of pictures which might be accepted by the Manager and Directors and after the holidays, there was a lot of excitement whilst we waited to see if ours had been selected. For those which were accepted, we were paid 15s.0d each, a week's wages! It was a common sight to see our own faces looking back from a chemists shop window in Sheffield, Rotherham and Doncaster or, if we went that far, in Grimsby or Goole, or Nottingham.

For a short time, I worked at the developing sink, but I wasn't too keen on that and it was through working in the dim red light which caused me to need my first spectacles for astigmatism, thankfully checked when I came out into the light again. For before long, I landed the job of picture framer, working alone in the balcony which stretched the whole length of the Chapel, reached via a flight of stairs near the reception area at the front door. I enjoyed working up there, with a glue pot on a little gas burner, framing photographs, paintings, engravings, in every sort of frame. There was a technician whose job it was to mitre the frames, but the guillotine was upstairs and I often had to cut my own, usually for the cheaper frames; I seldom risked the very heavy expensive kinds.

It was whilst I worked on the balcony that the Commercial Department received an order to photograph a quantity of hats for a local millinery firm. We had a Commercial Department where all sorts of articles were set up and photographed for various trades. Occasionally, models were chosen from the staff, either to wear the articles or to assist in displaying them. My most successful attempt was after the Director in charge of the department sent his secretary round all the female workers to find someone with photographic fingernails. The order was for a series of photographs of table knives for a local cutlery firm. In those days I had respectable hands and good nails, so I was very pleased with myself when my hands were chosen. All I had to do was hold a single knife out of each batch in one hand, with fingers curled around the back of the blade, each fingernail in line one above the other, showing the blade and the nails to advantage. Both elbows rested on the table, the thumb of my right hand straight down from the bottom of the handle. That was the nearest I came to being a model.

The occasion of the hats saw me modelling a large brimmed Gainsborough type set at a rakish angle, myself peeping from beneath in a coy pose. The Director liked it; I had a presentable photographic face, but the Manager thought it would require too much 'spotting' to hide a small mole at the side of my mouth and every additional process meant additional cost. So, my career as a modeller of hats never got off the ground.

In 1933 when I left Dore, I was able to attend the dances every Saturday night at Green Oak Hall, and it was here that I came to know the man whom, if I hadn't been such a 'prig', I might have married. His name was Jim, ten years older than me with a reputation for the ladies. I was very wary of him at first and not a little rude. However, he said he wasn't as bad as he was made out to be and challenged me to test him by letting him take me out to tea at Longshaw Lodge where, he said, they made a good afternoon tea. The gauntlet was down and I couldn't resist picking it up, either to prove or disprove. That was the challenge.

The following Saturday afternoon we walked over the moors to Longshaw, had a lovely tea and set off to walk home via the main road across the top of Froggatt Edge, to Owler Bar and home. We hadn't gone far when he started to sing, songs I knew and some I had never heard before. Soon his arm went around my waist, and with a humorous song or two and a little tickle occasionally, I was getting 'hooked'. He had a strong sense of humour and many tales to tell; all clean. Before we arrived home at Lane Head arrangements had been made to meet again during the week and a date for the dance every Saturday.

For many years, Jim had belonged to a cycling club in Sheffield, whose members held rallies periodically, meeting at Robin Hood's Stride or other popular meeting places. He no longer went on all day rallies, for a reason explained later, but usually attended in the afternoon on his motorbike. Inevitably, the question arose, "Would I like to go too?" I hadn't a clue what rallies were all about but agreed, as much out of curiosity as enthusiasm. "But," said Jim, "I can't have you riding pillion; I'll buy a sidecar and it will be safer and more comfortable." After the first meeting, I doubted the wisdom of this; I could see immediately that a woman being helped out of a sidecar in best Sunday clothes didn't fit in with half-dressed sweaty men and an odd equally sweaty wife. In fact, I stood out like a sore thumb and felt very uncomfortable. "You'll enjoy it better next time," said Jim, but I didn't, "I'll get you a bike," he said, and before long he bought a frame and the bits and pieces with which to build a bike and duly delivered it for me to practise. He would make another for himself then we could cycle to the rallies and I would feel more comfortable.

I had never ridden a bike but this magnificent Raleigh was tempting and Jeff said he would teach me. The following Saturday afternoon, he wheeled it out from the back yard and propped it beside the wall waiting for me to pluck up enough courage of start. One foot was put gingerly into a stirrup and, with Jeff holding tight, the other foot made contact with the one on the opposite side and slowly we set off up the road. "We'll go down Lane Head and round the Bents," I suggested and reaching the top of the lane, turned carefully to the right. Everything was fine at first; I could feel Jeff hanging on to the seat and my confidence began to grow, but not for long. The hill got steeper; the bike went faster and soon Jeff was left far behind. Down I went, past the houses, nearing the bend at Money Brook Farm, round the bend and still in the saddle. I could steer alright but how the hell can I stop? I hadn't a clue, which was probably as well for at that speed had I known where the brake was, no doubt I would have shot 'arse over tip' into the road. Luckily, the slight incline beyond the farm slowed my speed a little and then the road was straight on towards the Grouse Inn. Now, I was enjoying myself, the wind in my face and the exhilaration of success, blinded me temporarily to the fact that the next bend was an acute angle and if I didn't make it, the odds were I would land in the farmyard with 'Piggy' Hills pigs. Jeff was far behind; he had given up way back up the hill; I was on my own. Lord help me, how do I stop? Only one thing for it and luckily the long straight had slowed me so that I could make a supreme effort and jump off. The bike went one way, I went the other. No damage done, but I decided that biking was not for me.

My Mother was party to one situation over Jim, which showed she had, after all, a bit of romance in her. I had returned from work at dinner time one day suffering a very bad attack of migraine (that's what bilious attacks were now called). I needed to go to bed to sleep it off. Unfortunately, I had arranged to meet Jim that evening and it wasn't in my book of ethics to let a man down, or anybody else for that matter; if a promise had been made, by hook or by crook, I kept it. But what to do about Jim; I told my Mother and she was very understanding. "Will you go down to the 'phone and tell him I can't come?" I asked her. My Mother wasn't fond of telephones, but she agreed to go down to the village and 'phone from the box inside the 'Top Shop'. I called after her, "Tell him I'll write," then with relief, made my way into the room and healing sleep.

Tea was over when I rose and Mom was alone doing the washing up. "Did you manage to talk to him?" I asked. "Yes," she answered, "he understands and hopes you'll soon be feeling better. And," she added, "he says he'll look forward to your letter." "That's the trouble," I told her, "I don't know what to say." She looked at me hard, with a knowing look on her face and I wondered what her mind was cooking up. When she did voice her thoughts, I thought she was joking "Go to the garden and fetch a pansy; send him that." Seeing my confusion she continued, "Its pansies for thoughts they say." I looked at her in amazement, not knowing whether she was joking or not, but although she had that quizzical look on her face that showed there was humour beneath, I could see from her expression that she was serious.

Hesitating only for a moment, I ran into the back garden and, after plucking the biggest, bluest face in the border, returned with it into the house. Mom had a piece of paper at the ready and she produced a roll of Sellotape. The pansy was spread in all the glory of its petals, the shining face fixed there very carefully so that it would travel safely through the post. Underneath, in the most carefully designed handwriting was the message, "Pansies are for thoughts." The letter was posted and I returned home satisfied that I had done everything to satisfy my obligation.

Jim and I were friends for nine months, but I grew ever more anxious as the months went by. He was getting very serious and the relationship too complicated for my 18 years. I knew this was a different situation from the ones I had been told about before I started going out with Jim and he assured me that, if anything went wrong, we could get married. But there was too much to lose as well as freedom and girls who went 'off the rails' were frowned upon, in many ways outcasts. Also, my Father was strict; I knew I would never dare to go home if anything did go wrong, nor if I had done anything to lower his opinion of me. There was always the thought present at the back of my mind that I would be letting him and the family down.

He often said to us all on our way out, "Remember whose house you come from," or "Remember who your Father is," implying that you must not let him or his household down in any way.

The situation grew more serious. One night, after a particularly trying evening, we were arguing outside the house after my parents had gone to bed and their window was open, allowing them to hear some of the argument. According to my Mother, my Father was exasperated. "Listen to the two of them arguing again, why don't they get married, or call it a day?" he said. Had I known this at the time, perhaps I wouldn't have been so apprehensive, but I didn't and just assumed that he would think the worse.

One day Jim had arranged to take me to Bridlington for the day, but at the last minute, I couldn't face another day of argument, so when he called I was still in bed. My Father came downstairs to answer the knock at the door; I could hear voices and realised who it was. Dad was very angry, "You promised to go; get your clothes on and get off," he told me. "I don't want to go," I started, "I've changed my mind." "Then you shouldn't promise, if you don't want to go," he persisted. I told him I had written a letter to tell Jim I didn't want to go, but after asking Jim if he had received it, and he hadn't, Dad said I still should go.

At this stage, my Mother came downstairs and joined in, having heard the commotion and wondering what was happening. "Go on love, it'll do you good, a day at the seaside," she said. This, and the fact that George, Jim's young brother had also come long, decided me to go. There is a photograph in the album which shows the serious faces of us both as we went down the steps of the quay at Bridlington to board the 'Yorkshireman' leaving George on the quayside. There was time on board to clear the air, to make Jim realise how worried I was about the seriousness of the relationship. He understood and in future, he assured me, there would be nothing to worry about, and the day ended with everybody in good spirits.

My attitude to personal relationships may seem strange in these enlightened days and in the early 1930s there were girls who risked the wrath of their parents. One 16 year old had an affair with her dancing teacher, and on a trip to Blackpool illuminations, they locked themselves in a compartment to the disgust of everybody on the trip. They were married before the baby was born and as far as I know, lived happy ever after. On the other side of the coin was the 16 year old girl who was seduced whilst drunk after a day's outing by one of a group of village boys and she was kept in the attic by her mother for nine months, then sent away for the birth of the baby, such was the considered disgrace. The age of majority was 21 years and until then, children were vulnerable and in many ways defenceless.

I wasn't exactly fair to Jim. He was a very industrious man, whose one aim in life at the time I met him was to look after, feed and clothe his mother and his brother George, who was a semi-invalid. He had one sister who was married and caused him no trouble. He had been a furniture shop Sales Manager before opening his own General Stores where his family lived in the house at the back. He was very concerned about his widowed mother who was crippled with arthritis, as I saw one day when I visited.

Any extra money which could be earned was a bonus and to this end, every Sunday when the shop was closed, he filled the sidecar with cigarettes, sweets and drinks and a folding trestle table which he set up on the moors on Stanage Edge near the footpath used by ramblers. I looked down my nose at this, not only because it was Sunday for by then Sunday had become more liberalised for most people. It was, I thought, degrading to stand on the moors selling things. Snob that I was!

But Jim's answer was simple. "I can make £5 in one morning on the moors, as much as I make all week in the shop," and I could see the sense of the argument, although it stuck in my craw to say so. At the time I was a Sunday school teacher and rather an over-pious one at that. When he suggested that I go with him one day, I refused, as I even refused to go any more on Sunday trips to the seaside and he, sensibly said "If you won't go out, then I might as well make some money."

After a week or two he said he wouldn't go anymore, furthermore, he would try not to be such an atheist, to please me. He was bitter about his mother's plight, said there was no God; if there were, he wasn't a good God, or he wouldn't allow his mother to suffer so much. I put on my best Evangelical argument for a loving God, whose plan is for our good in the long run and one day, when he said he believed what I said, that he wouldn't be bitter about it and yes he believed there really was a God, I felt like Billy Graham, (although at the time I'd never heard of him). A convert and I'd done the converting. How vain and ridiculous can one be?

Soon after this, my holiday was due. I had never been away without the family, when Ida asked my Father if I could go with her for a week to Scarborough. She had been before with another friend and had enjoyed it very much. My Father said I could go but Ida would be responsible for me. She was six years older than me, but we had been close friends since the previous winter, when we started going to the dances together. The day came for departing and my Father asked how much money I had for my board and lodgings and spending money. With so little weekly spending money, it was obvious I had very little, and said so. He put his hand in his pocket and with a satisfied look on his face, handed to me the princely sum of £2.0s.0d. I stared at it unbelievingly, as I took it and put it in my purse. "Just be careful lass, and do as Ida tells you," was his parting shot.

I had collected my free film from the office and, armed with the family camera, which my Mother had obtained from the 'John Bull' newspaper in exchange for coupons, I was ready to go. It had taken dozens of photographs already, although it was nothing but a box with a shutter which opened to let in the light when a lever was flicked. It worked overtime on our holiday but sadly none of the pictures were worth selling.

The journey to Scarborough was exciting, it wasn't every day one had the opportunity for such luxurious travel and I sat very upright in one corner revelling in every moment, although Ida wriggled and squirmed all the way. "I don't know how you can sit so straight all the time," she said, "I get so uncomfortable, I can't sit still." Speaking of comfort, it was, of course, relevant to that day and age. They were single carriages with seats facing along the full width. It was before the days of corridors, so ladies could occupy a carriage and feel safe, at least to the next stop. There was a mirror above the seats on each side and lovely pictures of seaside places to whet the appetite for further holidays. We carried sandwiches for the journey, 'whetting the whistle' with a cup of tea bought from a small trolley on one of the platforms on the way, arriving more or less none the worse for the three and a half hour's journey.

We went on visits to Whitby and Robin Hood's Bay, and south to Filey, bathing in the pools on Filey Brigg. Unfortunately, not understanding how quickly the tide came in there, we were caught near a cave with no hope of reaching dry land, but before we had time to panic, round the corner came a little boat with two men on board looking for just such a situation; we weren't the first silly buggers to be caught by the tide. We were each hoisted up into one of the men's arms and carried to the boat, later to be deposited on dry land.

We stayed with Mr & Mrs Dalby, where Ida had stayed before. They were a marvellous old couple who fed and watered us well, but the ablution arrangements were a bit primitive. The bedrooms were small and there was no bathroom, so a small triangular washbowl had been fixed in the corner of the square landing on the turn of the stairs; not exactly luxury, but then neither Ida nor I were used to luxury. She lived in the middle cottage at Money Brook in the Bents, where there was only one full bedroom over the living room, with a much smaller one over the little back kitchen. There were three girls and one boy, and to make matters a bit more difficult, her mother and father hadn't spoken to each other for a number of years, all contact between them being through the children, so father slept on the landing, leaving the bedrooms to the rest of the family.

It was whilst we were at Scarborough that my thoughts came into better focus, with the help of Ida, who knew the situation very well. Jim's friend was Frank Nunn, the owner of the Redgates Toy Shop at the top of the Moor in Sheffield. We were always a foursome at dances, although Ida and Frank never met on other occasions. But, she had known Jim longer than I had and could see the problems only too well, although as she said "There's only you can solve them." So, we returned home with my mind more or less made up.

On 6th October, about three weeks before our last meeting, I had met another man, and Jim had heard about him. On 23rd October, he was waiting once more. "Is it serious?" he wanted to know. "Yes," I replied, not knowing whether it would be serious or not; all I knew was that I didn't want Jim to waylay me anymore. "I'll not bother you again," he said. "I love you very much, but I'll not bother you again." Two weeks later, I decided to send back the presents he had given to me, they were few; presents were not exchanged too freely, food and clothing were more important. A small pearl handled penknife which had belonged to his mother, a silver propelling pencil, and the 'bike'.

Jeff volunteered to ride the bike to Heeley where Jim lived so he took the other articles as well, returning somewhat later, without the bike, but bringing back the penknife and the pencil. "He wouldn't take them," said Jeff, "Says they were presents and you have to keep them. And," he added, a bit mystified, "He says he's going to keep the pansy, says it's the most precious thing he has." Who says men are not romantic?

On Saturday 6th October 1934, the Saturday night dance was cancelled for cleaning and decorating Green Oak Hall, so Ida and I decided to go to Sheffield to the pictures. It was a rare treat, if that's the right word, for we were not too fond of Sheffield. We decided on the Cinema House in Barkers Pool, where Norman Shearer and Nova Pilbeam, the child star were appearing in the film about the eternal triangle. There were two houses at all the picture houses during the week, but at the weekend, the performances were continuous, as a few people came out, a few more went in.

The house was full so we had to wait until there was a break in the programme, when some people would leave and there was plenty of time to pass remarks and a few jokes with the rest of the queue during the half hour wait. There was a real joker just behind, and then behind him, a group of young men, about eight in all. The jokey chappie shot out a particularly funny mouthful which turned the heads of most of the queue, Ida and I amongst them. One of the young men behind told me later that when I turned round, laughing, he said to his nearest companion "See that girl in front; I'm going to marry her."

We entered the Cinema at last and sat in the back right hand corner of the circle. In the back left hand corner sat the group of men. As we entered there was a shout across the circle, "See you later." Now Ida and I were country girls, and although country girls have a reputation of being well up-to-date in the facts of life, they are a little reluctant to flaunt themselves in front of the 'townies' and Ida and I responded coldly. The picture over, we all left the Cinema, Ida and I to catch a bus for Totley but awaiting for us were two of the young men, one a round, red-faced specimen wearing a bowler hat, the other a tall slim poker type man wearing a peaked cap.

"Oh God," said Ida, "they're waiting for us; I don't like the fat one." "Neither do I," said I. "We'll keep together," continued Ida, and lose them down the hill (to Pond Street). The decision was taken out of our hands; the tall one started walking by the side of me, and the fat one by the side of Ida. Soon, we were split up in the crowds on the street, ending up at Pond Street, with the decision from both men that they would ride on the bus with us to see where Totley was. When we arrived at Totley, we still had them in tow. They proved to be Police recruits, spending three months in the School at West Bar, and had been in Sheffield for only three weeks.

Part of their training was to be given an assignment to find a certain place in the city, with nothing to help but a map, and with limited time to find the place and report back with proof. That was the immediate excuse for wanting to go to Totley; other reasons were disclosed by degrees. Although Ida was not very enthusiastic, when they left Totley, we arranged to see them again one night during the week, and on the night in question, we all went for a walk round the Bents and the village. By the time they had boarded a bus back to Sheffield at around 9.00 p.m., I had arranged to see Frank the following Sunday.

At the dance on Saturday night, Ida was none too pleased and tried to persuade me not to carry on seeing him. But, having promised, when Sunday came, I kept the appointment and met him at the bus at 6.00 p.m. I told him I was going to Church and was dressed for the occasion in one of my creations, the grey dress, with the loose coat to match with the artist's bow and the blue beret to match. I said he could come if he liked, and was very surprised when he said he would. I thought it would have put him off and let me off the hook. I was so wrong; we walked sedately down Hall Lane and into Church as if we were an old married couple, not two comparative strangers on their first date.

Much against Ida's wishes, I continued to meet Francis Rundle. She was upset that our close friendship was in danger of coming to an end, so agreed to meet Bob twice more to keep us together. But, never the type to beat about the bush, she finally protested. "It's no good Josie," she said, "He tries to be funny, but he's just daft." I said I was sorry she felt so strongly about him but plenty of sympathy with her when she added "I can't stand him any longer, he's got big feet, his face is always so damned bloated as if he's going to blow up, his daft jokes are so childish and I can't stand going out any longer with that bloody bowler hat."

I was very sad to think that our friendship was in such danger, even though we still managed to go to many of the dances on Saturdays when Frank was on duty, and two years later, when Frank and I were married at Totley Church, Ida was my chief bridesmaid, with Frank's sister Kitty and another family friend.

The night that I met Francis Rundle I was wearing a coat made for me earlier in the summer from a piece of material bought from Mr Coven, the tailor, who lived in Sunnyvale Road, Totley. But my Father never understood that with a new coat went a new hat, and possibly new shoes. This time was no exception; I had a coat that was enough. Mr Coven had sent a small bundle of spare fabric left over from the coat and after considering for a while, I reckoned I could make a respectable hat myself. Prince George, later Duke of Kent, had just married Princess Marina of Greece, who had introduced a new fashion in 'pill-box' hats which earned the name 'Marina' hats. Mine was based on the same idea and it was this creation I wore on that fateful night. Before long, I wanted a proper hat and a dress and more fashionable shoes. Courting had made me very conscious of clothes and now there were many more occasions for dressing up.

Soon after joining Sheffield Police, Frank had been enlisted into the Police Band which, throughout the year, gave concerts at various venues both in the city and further afield. Whenever they were playing at the Victoria Hall, or Endcliffe Park, or sometimes at the Pavilion Gardens, my Mother and I liked to go for the afternoon or evening, and I soon grew tired of appearing in the same coat and homemade hat, and rebelled.

My Father wouldn't listen to my continuing requests for something new and more fashionable, one request resulting in a hot argument and a blazing row. I had never rebelled before so he was taken completely off guard. "Aren't I a good Father then?" he shouted, very angry that I should question his judgment. "Yes," I shouted back, "but you don't understand girls, you think they only need two pairs of knickers, one for wearing, one in the wash, and you think women are like men wearing the same suit year in and year out until it's worn out and shiny." By this time I knew I had sunk my boats, so a final thrust wouldn't hurt. "I want more," I screamed, "I don't want to be ashamed, I want to be smart like everybody else." He was angry, angrier than I had ever seen him and turning on me in a rage he shouted, "Then keep your money, buy your own clothes, I'll have nothing more to do with it."

Up to now I had done as all other children did until the age of 21 and handed over my pay packet to my Father intact. At least it was intact and unopened until a few weeks before when I had been put in charge of the Framing Department, when I told my Father I was going to ask for a raise in wages. "You'll do nothing of the sort," he said, "If your employer think you're worth more, he'll give you a raise without asking." Now my Father was a good Boss, who did do that sort of thing, but he wasn't in the real world of business and I took no notice. I heard other girls asking; town girls had no inhibitions, and neither would I. I asked, and received a raise of 2s.0d a week (10p). The first week I opened the packet and removed the 2s.0d before handing it over, muttering something like "We've been told to check immediately in case of mistakes," God forgive me, but "when needs must, the devil drives", or so they say. Whether he believed me or not, I don't know, it didn't particularly worry me at the time.

Now I had all my wages and knew exactly what I was going to do. My closest friend at Photo Finishers was Marjorie, who lived in Belper Road, off Abbeydale Road and she knew the Misses Robertson who had a gown shop at the corner of Belper Road, where she often bought her own clothes, paying 1s.0d in the pound for twenty weeks until they were paid for. She approached the Misses Robertson who agreed to let me do the same. I went the following Saturday lunchtime and chose a brown velour coat with a fluffy white collar, which cost £5.0s 0d, a hat in matching velour, with a turned back brim at 4s.11d; a pair of brown court shoes for 7s.11d and a dance dress for £1.14s.11d, for all of which I had to pay 7s.6d per week for twenty weeks. A sum I knew I could pay and still give my Mother something for my board.

Since the row with my Father, we had not spoken to each other, and it was clear to me that he had no intention of breaking the silence and if that was how he felt, then neither had I. But, as usual, he had his own way of punishing me, as I found out the following Friday night. Here I must divert for a little explaining.

During the Depression of the early 1960s, my Father had been asked by a large Coal Distributor, 'Hallamshire Coal Supplies', if he could do anything to relieve the financial situation of the unemployed in the way of setting up a credit system whereby they could obtain coal by the ton, and pay for it weekly; a thing that had never been done before. Not only were the coal firms concerned, but all those who had dealings with the poor and, as a Parish Councillor, my Father was one of them. Some small suppliers delivered in bags at so much a bag, which helped, but it was an expensive way of purchasing. It was suggested that my Father test the ground, so to speak, first in Totley and then in Dore and this being a success, he eventually migrated to the farms over the moors; Overstones and Hathersage, where the bigger users filled up during the summer when prices were lowered and business slack for winter use when the weather was bad. By 1933 when I returned home, it was a thriving small business, with a reasonable commission, my Father doing all the collecting and keeping the books himself.

Now, he said he would like me to help him on his regular Friday night round and to save time, he called for me outside Photo Finishers in the Wolseley car which had replaced the little red bullet and after tea, we set off. I enjoyed the evening especially as I always met him at the Devonshire Arms at Dore for a drink with his friends and popular Landlord Johnnie Thorpe. If by any chance I particularly wanted to with the girls from work, he never questioned it and did the collecting alone.

On Friday nights, after work during summer, some of the girls liked to go to Millhouses Park to play tennis or swimming in the pool, although I couldn't swim, nor could I play a good game of tennis (I'd never had chance to learn), but I did like to go sometimes for the fun.

The Sunday after my shopping trip, I came downstairs in my new clothes. My Father was in the house, but he said nothing to me. When I had gone out, he said to my Mother, "Where did she get the clothes?" Mother told him and also told him how I was going to pay for them. "Keep your eye on her, and see as she does pay for them then," he told her. And that, for the time being, was that. After 20 weeks he mentioned them again; he was shrewd and quite capable of keeping an eye on things himself without the aid of Mom. "Has she paid for those clothes yet?" he fired at her one night. "It's the final payment on Friday," she said, and he didn't mention it again.

For the past five months neither had spoken to the other. He met me as usual outside Photo Finishers and drove me home. We had tea and both set off in the car in silent defiance; he dropped me off at the top of Town Head Road, Dore and I dutifully collected the 'shekels' for the coal company but it was the end of the Port & Lemon. As soon as I appeared at the Devonshire, Father rose and left, without a word, either to me or to those he had been drinking with.

On the first Friday, after I had cleared my debt, I knew I had to break the silence. My Mother had said to me a few weeks before, "Isn't it time you spoke to your Father?" "Why?" I had answered, "My Father doesn't want to speak to me, so why should I?" "You know it's breaking his heart, you not speaking," she said. "Well," I answered, "he shouldn't have gone all silent first; it's his fault, not mine." But I hadn't been happy and neither had Elijah.

One of my friends at Photo Finishers was Madeline, a refined girl whose elderly parents had obviously come from better stock than the usual working girl. Madeline's pet hobby was playing the violin in a small orchestra which met in a hall in Ecclesall. One day she suggested I join too, as they had a piano but no piano player. I was a bit dubious, as I'd never played with anybody before, but after the first night I enjoyed the experience and looked forward every Wednesday to having tea at her home and going to the hall together.

The arrangement worked well, until the argument. My Father had always met me at Ecclesall terminus about 10 o'clock and had been interested to know how I was progressing. But the first night after the argument, Elijah was there instead, disgruntled at having to fetch his sister and angry with me for getting into such a situation. "You've no business to treat him like that," Elijah said. "You should speak to him; it's your place to speak first." I naturally had my little say but he counted, "Don't think I'm coming to meet you every Wednesday, because I'm not." So, without a chauffeur, that was the end of my orchestral career.

Now the time had come for repentance and reconciliation. "How much do you want me to give Mum for my board?" I asked as we set off on that Friday evening. Dad showed no emotion or surprise at my question, nor that I had broken the ice and was silent for only a second then he said, "You don't need to pay your Mother anything, I'll see to that." I was a bit surprised but on his next words I really knew how he could hit where it hurt. "You'll come with me every Friday from now on, no more going out with the girls." And that was the end of the question so far as he was concerned. I never went to Millhouses or anywhere else on Friday night again.

Facilities in the dining room at Photo Finishers were very good, a small oven for warming pies, roasting potatoes or anything we fancied and no questions were asked if any of us wished to disappear for a couple of minutes to prepare. A gas stove provided boiling rings for heating Heinz beans or soup and kettle, cups and saucers were supplied by the firm. Consequently, there was time after dinner/lunch for sitting outside sunbathing, or taking walks up Lyndhurst Road or taking photographs and hoping for a winning negative.

One of the lunchtime activities was the dubious enjoyment of trying to contact the spirit world. Marjorie's mother was a 'medium' and Marjorie herself a bit psychic. Every dinner time a few girls congregated on the balcony near one of the arched windows around an Ouija board (Marjorie called it a 'planchette board'), and a little glass which was supposed to move under supernatural influence around the board spelling out a message from the letter around the rim. By the middle of the summer of 1935, I had moved once again, this time to the basement, to take charge of the Enlargement Checking Department. There was a steep flight of wooden steps from the main floor to the basement down which Mr Christie ran with such speed that everyone scurried about as if shot. I hadn't been down there long before I realised I could do the same, and just for fun and devilment, sent bodies scurrying to the shouts of "Oh Salty!"

One day, other feet came rushing downstairs during the dinner hour. "Salty, you've got to come upstairs, you're wanted on the board," said the messenger. "What do you mean; wanted on the board?" I queried. Marjorie's got a message, it keeps repeating "Get Josephine," the girl said. I sniggered, "Go on, I'm busy, you're just having me on," I told her. "No," she persisted, "that's all we can get, it just keeps repeating get Josephine." For peace and quietness I went upstairs.

There they were all anxiously waiting. "Come on Josie," cried Marjorie, "it's asking for you." I was sceptical but obeying instructions, I placed my finger over the glass without touching it, and kept an eye on Marjorie's finger to see she wasn't touching it either. The glass started to move. Slowly it spelled out a message. "Give your money to your Father, he needs it." I was astounded, nobody knew about me keeping my wages except Marjorie herself. We looked at each other and she shook her head. "I didn't move it Josie," she said, "honestly I didn't."

We tried again. "Will you repeat the message?" she asked the invisible spirit and whilst we all kept an eye on her finger to make

249

sure she wasn't moving the glass, it spelt out the message again, exactly as before. "Who is speaking?" asked Marjorie. At first there was no movement, then after a second request "Who is speaking?" the reply was spelt out "ISRAEL". Now my Father's name was Israel, at least that was the name he was known by, although even Marjorie didn't know that, and in any case, he was very much alive. I was mystified, particularly as the board carried on working quite normally, if that's not too profane a word.

On arriving home that night I asked my Mother "Who is Israel?" "Your Father of course," she replied. "No," I said, "another Israel," and I told her why I wanted to know. She grimaced a bit then "You shouldn't dabble with such things," she warned, "You'll hear something you don't want to know." "But, who is Israel?" I asked again. "Oh that'll be Israel Newbry, Aunt Newbry's husband," she said, explaining that she was my Fathers Great Aunt and Israel was a Sea Captain and that they had lived at Cheltenham. "But is my Dad short of money?" I asked. "Why should Israel tell me to give my Father my money?" "Well, he's not very well off at present," she answered, "but I don't think it's desperate." I left it at that, more curious as to why my Father needed my wages than I was about the message from the Ouija board. It did bring to mind another occasion, which I thought had been a bit of fun borne out of curiosity.

Earlier in the year, Marjorie had suggested we paid a visit to Mucky Emma, a spiritualist who lived in a little hovel in Little London, an area between Broadfield Road and Chesterfield Road, approached by a short road under the railway bridge from Broadfield Road. One evening about half a dozen of us arrived at the door of Mucky Emma's little cottage and, after knocking and hearing a call "Come in," we gingerly made our way into a square entrance and through the door into what could, with a stretch of imagination, be called a living room. It was very dark, but as our eyes became accustomed we could see, in the dimness, a filthy little old woman sitting in a chair beside the fireplace. Ashes from the fire filled and overflowed from the ash pan, even reaching the worn out hearthrug. A crystal ball stood on the table and, as we entered, Emma pulled out a filthy pack of cards from her apron pocket. Marjorie went through the door first, as she was the more accustomed to such phenomenon and was braver than any of the rest of us. I followed her, ducking under the curtain which hung over the door, presumably to keep out the draughts. I had just straightened up and faced her when she stuck out her arm and pointed a finger at me shouting "He's there." I turned, wondering what she was pointing at, when she said again, "He's there and he's got his hand on your shoulder." She could see that I didn't understand, nor did any of the others, so she continued. "There's a man with his hand on your left shoulder; he's touching that brooch you've got on." I put my hand on the brooch made of gold in the three legged symbol of the Isle of Man which Uncle Jack had brought back for me from a holiday there with my Father a couple of years before. "He's your guide," Emma said again, "he'll always watch over you so long as you wear that brooch."

I felt it again, disbelieving what she said, whilst the other watched open mouthed. I didn't know whether to be afraid, or just cynical about what seemed to be usual fortune-teller spoof. "But," she repeated, "I tell you love, as long as you wear that brooch, Israel will see it shining and he will be with you wherever you are." With that, she picked up the crystal ball and said "Who's first?" I don't remember anything she told me about the future and when everyone had heard their own prophecy and paid the requisite silver, I was glad to get out of that dark filthy house.

Nothing really wonderful happened during my work as an enlargement checker, but I was a bit 'miffed' one day when the Manager asked how I had costed the packets of orders waiting in the tray for delivery to the Dispatch Department.

Chapter 10

Life in Totley in the 1930s was much the same as in all the small villages in Derbyshire, although modified to a certain extent by its proximity to a city. The working day commenced at 8.00 a.m. for those lucky enough to be in work and most men in Totley found work of one kind or another, if they wanted it. The day finished at 5.00 p.m., except on Saturday, when 12 noon was normal, except in the retail trades where closing time was usually 9.00 p.m.., the assistants having a half day during the week in lieu.

By the time tea was over in winter and a possible nap in a chair by the fire, many men took themselves off to the pub about 9.00 p.m. provided they had a 'sneck-lifter'. Tommy Duddy, the farm man at Creswick's was the man associated with the 'sneck-lifter' more than anyone else. He always said, "If I have a 'sneck-lifter', I can get in and somebody will buy me the rest." A 'sneck' by the way, is a door handle, where a curved piece of metal passed through a hole in the door, the other end having a flattened piece where the thumb fits, whilst the rest of the hand holds the handle underneath. When pressed, the metal fitting raises another flat rod which usually rests in a metal hook on the door jamb when the door is closed. All old doors have such a catch and some new ones which simulate old ones.

This was, of course, when Totley proper ended at the Cross Scythes Hotel for although one or two houses had been built near Green Oak on what would later become the Heatherfield Estate, it was not until around 1927 that Mr Melling started building those further up and on the main highway. There was no Laverdene Estate, no Marstone Estate and that wonderful avenue of horse chestnut trees which, lined the road in front of Mrs Earnshaw's house from Cross Scythes to the hexagonal Lodge where the old gardener Mr Weston lived with his daughter Muriel, had not yet been partly demolished when the big house was demolished for the sake of that new estate. New Totley had houses down one side with two only at the top of the other side, the fields between them and Miss Harris's house at the bottom, still farmed by Colin Thompson. Pearson's Nursery filled the land between, when Mickley Lane was really a lane, winding and tree-lined from Lemont Road to Mickley at the top of the hill, with only the Matchbox House and the two villas at the end of Glover Road and Cherrytree Orphanage in between.

Below Green Oak, a high wall held back the bank of Mr Thompson's fields where he kept his cattle before slaughtering for sale and the high wall of the Monkey Gardens on the opposite side hid the grounds which were then used by Mr Gledhill for growing rhubarb. The absence of a Church until 1924 was probably the reason why Totley didn't have an annual festival like the other villages, for the Feast, as it was called, was held on or around the Church Saint's day. Neither did we have Well Dressings, although there were the remains of a well in Hall Lane. Consequently, the residents were less insular than those of the more isolated villages, even though there was a certain jealous loyalty and competition between them all. Dore & Totley were always in competition with each other and much bantering and friendly rivalry was practised, not only in sport, but any other way where an argument could be started.

There were, in all villages, and Totley was no exception, various social evenings and dances arranged by the hospital and Scout Committees and Harvest and pea and pie suppers organised by the Chapel. In 1930 Miss Foulstone, one of the school teachers and daughter of the Lay Teacher of the Church, organised the first Youth Club which was held in the school. I remember little about the activities, except that she asked one or two of the girls to teach the boys how to dance, whilst she organised the music from a gramophone. I had never learned ballroom dancing but, like the other girls, I could understand the rhythm of music and had seen people dancing at Barlow Feast and Abbeydale Gala, so it was easy to pick up the steps of the waltz and quickstep and guide a body into a semblance of a glide rather than a jerky walk.

We went to Sheffield only when necessary and to the pictures even less often, even after the 'talkies' came in 1928 and it was not until about 1932 before we became interested in films and film stars. But by that time, film stars were almost worshipped by adolescent girls and very popular even by the older members of the community, for they were glamorous and publicised by the film makers into Gods and Goddesses. Even so, the reverence of such bodies was expressed more in collecting their portraits on cigarette cards rather than spending hard earned money on seeing them on the screen. The cards were issued in sets of 50 and much swapping went on with the duplicates that were inevitable. Of course, the girls had to rely on brothers and fathers for their supply, for girls didn't resort to smoking, expect in secret. Ida and Dorothy, another friend of hers, used to buy a 2d packet of Woodbines, smoke one between them and hide the packet in the wall at the bottom of Lane Head Road, near the bridge at the bottom. Sometimes they took rather a lot of puffing to keep them alight after spending a few nights in the secret hiding place on rainy nights. But, like stolen apples, which always taste best, secret cigarettes were always the most enjoyable.

There were, of course, the weekly football matches and cricket in the summer, both sports arranged by the Sports & Social Club, which was held in an upstairs room originally used by the British Legion over Mr Evans' disused cow house, then a store room. The main pastime for members of the Sports & Social Club was snooker. There were two three quarter sized tables for those who could afford to play. The older man had the monopoly, for the charge for a game was 2d a game, or 20 minutes as the case may be, and spending money for most boys wouldn't stretch that far every evening, particularly if they were also members of the football team and had to pay the cost of travel to away matches. Elijah was in the football team until the age of 21, when he became a man and kept his wages, he was given 10s.0d (50p) a week by my Father. 20 minutes, by the way, wasn't arbitrary, it was checked carefully by an alarm clock and Archie Thomas, the long-time Secretary, told me of one frustrated player, Dan Reynolds, who once flung the clock through the window when he hadn't finished his game.

There were other activities like dominoes and pontoon, no doubt with prices fixed according to the players, for I never knew a man who could resist a bit of a gamble. There were Whist Drives at regular intervals and the Saturday night dances of the later 1930s in the Labour Hall were organised by the Club but it was mainly a Club for men rather than women. It was probably due to the influence of Mr Foulstone, a devout Church man, that the Club never had a licence, hence there was no drunkenness on the premises.

I never had any inclination to join the Sports & Social Club. Occasionally, I went to football matches on the 'Sic' in the Bents, but I grew a little nauseated at the antics of some of the other village girls, who went only to ogle the players, particularly the visitors. "Oh, look at those thighs," one would say. "By gum, he's well-built isn't he?" said another, or "I'd let him do me any time." As the match went on, the cried got worse. "Kick 'im where it hurts." "Grab 'im by the nuts." And once when a poor player got his trunks ripped open, there was almost a stampede on to the pitch to get a closer look. Once Elijah got blood on his shorts when a ball hit him in the loin and he recalls the lasses jumped up and down frantic with excitement shouting "Sithee, he's got blood on his pants." I'm sure none of the girls understood the first thing about football and certainly didn't consider a 'good match' one where the footballer had been good.

Cricket was more decorous. Many of the players were married men, like Billy Ramsell, our next door but one neighbour, Archie Thomas, the Club Secretary, Frank Taylor the wicket-keeper, Jim Green and Maurice Johnson both from Lane Head. This was village life at its best; a summer's day, an idyllic setting, men in glistening white and refreshments organised and served in the pavilion by their wives and sweethearts.

One day in 1932 the men decided to organise a cricket match for the women. There were one or two good players amongst the older girls, the rest were girls from my school days, either the same age, or a year older. I liked playing cricket, but this was different. For one thing, the committee decided that our opponents would be the 'Bing Boys', the female section of the Hallamshire Harriers Cricket Club of Bramall Lane, Sheffield, the most successful Sheffield team at the time. Then, we had to play with a hard cricket ball and I was scared stiff. The Bing Boys turned up in white, like male players, with black peaked caps to add to their professionalism and they were very forbidding to our 'one off' team. But we had the support of the men. "Come on Gertie", "Catch it Isabel" and "Knock it for six Vera," rang round the field. The Bing Boys won the toss and decided to bat first. I was scheduled to be one of the three bowlers, something I had no experience of at all, except in our own games at school, when I had bowled underhand with a soft ball. (Bear in mind that the original bowling in the 19th century was underhand, but it was now considered 'sissy').

My turn to bowl came round and amid cries of "Come on Josephine," I let fly with my first ball. I had made up my mind to bowl overhand and had done a bit of secret practice, just to show we weren't pathetically parochial, but that first ball got distracted on its way to the wicket and went wide. The second was better, but the stumps were in no danger as the batter landed out at it and scored two runs. "Come on Josephine, let her have it," came from Frank Taylor, and I did. By this time I had got the measure of the pitch and the technique and the next one was near enough for the batter to land out. But, it must have developed a bit of spin, (not intended, I'm sure); for she missed it and the stumps were flying. The crowd roared, and adrenalin rose and I had the bit firmly between my teeth. My arm was beginning to ache, it wasn't used to the particular type of swing and I decided to revert to underhand bowling, feeling more confident and having a good eye from my days of bowling at Cross Scythes.

The first ball caught the batter completely off guard. Expecting another dubious overhand, this was, to say the least, a surprise. My underhand proved to be much more direct, with more speed than I could hope to muster overhand. To her complete surprise, she was bowled out. My appetite was whetted. Now confident, with careful aim I sent down the next ball, now to a new player. None of them were used to underhand bowling and this player looked decidedly nervous. The cries from the men were deafening. "Make it a hat trick Josephine," "Come on Joss, let's have a third." I bowled a beauty, slow and straight for the stumps, which hit the ground with a little bounce and too near the wicket for a good swipe. The poor girl was mesmerised by the change of speed. She missed, the stumps went flying to an uproarious shout and I had succeeded in getting a hat trick.

By the end of the match, we had lost by a large margin; the Bing Boys soon got our measure and almost wiped the floor with us; not altogether unexpected. My batting was not so successful. I was shit-scared of that hard ball and already visualised myself in a hospital bed. The speed of the delivery from their bowler made me very glad that I was out for a 'duck' first ball, eyes shut and all. Following this, the men thought it would be a good idea to have a Ladies Football match. Who our opponents were, I don't remember. I knew nothing about football, except that one team kicked the ball one way into the goal, and the other kicked it the opposite way. I was assigned the position of Centre Forward and told that my job was to kick the ball into the goal. I remember very little about the game, except that it was messy and that there seemed to be a lot of running about for nothing. I fear my opinion has changed little. Needless to say, we lost.

My Father always followed the Totley team on their away games; he felt he should be there in case of accident. This was fortunate on at least one occasion when the match was at Dronfield Woodhouse between Totley and Earl's Cement team from Bradwell, in the Hope Valley League. Elijah was 17 at the time. After a particularly bad confrontation, he emerged with a severely cut lip and Dad diagnosed that it needed stitching. Hospital was not necessary in those days for Doctors practised minor surgery themselves and luckily, Dad was on hand to take him to Dr Marshall at the bottom of Rycroft Glen. (Incidentally, that was the boundary between Totley, Derbyshire and Sheffield until 1934.

Like many footballers, Elijah suffered torn ligaments in the knee joint and spent much time at Edgar Allen's for treatment. After many such mishaps the Doctor warned him about the danger of continual playing, but it didn't stop him. Like our Mom, he could be stubborn at times.

Whether I would have been more interested in sport and football in particular, had I met a man who also was, is debatable and it was beyond the bounds of possibility that we would have spent good courting time at a football match, but I may be wrong. Our courting time was limited to Saturday evening and one evening during the week, usually Wednesday, during the Police School period, after which, times fluctuated according to shifts. On the afternoon shift we were relegated to one evening (Frank's day off), with the bonus of two days together every six weeks as the roster arrived at a weekend.

But you might say what did one do on courting nights? "Who are you walking out with?" someone would ask, or from friends, "Who are you going out with?" for that is exactly what we did. We all knew the footpaths which led to quiet nooks and corners and I would think that every inch of Gillfield Wood was familiar. Not that many secluded spots were used for devious purposes; most girls were scared stiff of the consequences if anything went wrong, although there were one or two with dubious reputations. There was one girl, not exactly a village girl, who lived at Green Oak. Every night around 6.00 p.m. she waited for the motorbike riders coming from Sheffield; the first one to agree to her price gained a pillion rider into Derbyshire, returning the girl in about an hour to await the next customer.

There was the young girl who, after a coach trip to Blackpool, returned drunk and was, in effect, raped by one of the half dozen village boys, also drunk. The poor girl was kept in the attic by her Mother for the whole nine months, taking her out for a short walk every night at midnight when the road was deserted. The neighbours had been told that she had gone away to work, but Ida and I saw her sitting in the attic window every evening until she left for a distant Nursing Home for the child to be born. Such was the disgrace which befell the parents as well as the girl.

Fortunately, there were many footpaths around Totley around the Bents and up Moss Road and in earlier years, I had walked that road with Jobie, over the moor, around the hillside with the wind in my hair on beautiful moonlight nights, down the path through

Blackamoor to the valley between Dore & Totley. Frank was not so fond of walking, said he did plenty of that during the day, so our paths took shorter routes around Penny Lane or through Gillfield Wood. But one night when it was pouring with rain, we had gone, for a change, down the footpath in Tym's field in Hall Lane where we had earlier sledged in the snow and across the fields into Mickley Lane. Up this lane and around the bend past Cherrytree Orphanage, soaked to the skin, we saw the barn in Colin Thompson's field. The gate was locked but we managed to climb over it and make a beeline to the open front. We went inside and there spent a quiet hour together away from the rain and crowds. It was in that barn, on that night, that my future husband first told me he loved me. Romance in the rain, or just the country smells of the barn?

There was one tree at Old Hay, just off the path leading to Mrs Dean's cottage, which had a convenient dent in the trunk, against which Frank would lean in comfort with his arms around me. On another wet night, rain ran down the trunk in a veritable river and later, when we arrived at the bus stop where the lights were bright, I saw the back of his Mac, which was bright green with moss and Protococcus from the tree trunk. There was little I could do about it, but fortunately it was a late bus with very few passengers and Mrs Brewitt, his landlady, asked no questions. She was used to the ways of policemen anyway!

After three months in the Police School, the recruits 'passed out' just before Christmas 1934, and from now on, our courting times had to fit in with the three-shift system of the Police roster. The roster worked backwards, i.e. nights, afternoons and mornings; consequently there was a quick changeover from nights to afternoons and another from afternoons to mornings, with a long changeover from mornings to nights, essential due to the impossibility of changing from nights to mornings. This arrangement gave the men, in effect, an extra day off that week.

Days off also worked backwards, i.e. Friday, Thursday, through Wednesday to Monday and a long weekend every six weeks. This was before the days of patrol cars when policemen patrolled the streets, making regular points or meetings with the Beat Sergeant to report, not only on the events of the day, or night, but to ensure that the Officer was still on the beat, and not absconding, or in danger. There were three policemen in Totley in the 1930s, all controlled by a Sergeant who lived in the Police Station in Grange Terrace. After a few years in one village, an officer might be moved to another village, it was said, so that they didn't become too familiar with the residents. However, Officer Paskin, the great champion of justice, who never failed to visit the parents of an offending child before, or instead of, reported him, seemed to be resident in Totley for a great number of years. Or perhaps I remember him better as being on the village beat; it was he who came to see my Father after the escapades of the boys.

The first few weeks of walking the streets and facing the public could be very nerve racking for a raw recruit, and many tales were told of embarrassing and hair-raising incidents, some of them particularly gory. Like the morning Frank was walking down Ecclesall Road, just passing a row of large houses. Suddenly he heard loud screams coming from the garage of the last house in the row and rushing up the drive, saw a young woman lying on the floor of the garage in a pool of blood. As part of their training, all police had to take an intensive course in First Aid and, as Frank told me on arriving home, "My bloody mind went round in circles trying to remember what the procedure was."

It appeared that the girl had been doing something whilst standing on the top of a ladder, when she slipped and fell on to a joiner's bench below. A screwdriver on the bench had been driven into her leg, severing the femoral artery and blood was pumping out on to the bench and running in a stream on the floor. Seeing how dangerous the situation was, Frank threw off his helmet, pushed the girl's clothes out of the way, and put both fists over the artery to stop the blood. Almost immediately, the girl's mother appeared at the door between the garage and the kitchen, took in the scene and started shouting "Rapist, rapist," get off my daughter you rapist." This wasn't an occasion for finesse, nor police diplomacy and Frank, angry at her assumption roared, "You silly woman, shut up and go and ring for an ambulance." But the woman was hysterical. Jumping on top of him trying to pull him off, she still shouted, "Rapist," until at last, she had the sense to understand the situation. The ambulance arrived, the girl was taken away and her mother showered profuse thanks on a sweaty, bloody police officer.

But not all incidents were as dramatic, or as dangerous. Frank was on night duty once, on a dark winter's night, when the frost was exceptionally keen. He was walking down Brocco Bank, near Hunters Bar, puffing away on his pipe and content with the world, when he heard a faint creaking noise. He was walking by the side of a high wall which held up the bank of St Stephens Church, the ground reaching the top of the wall in the Church yard. He went a few more steps and heard another creak. He looked around, but saw nothing unusual. There was another creak and another, louder this time. It was moonlight and very eerie, but still there was nothing to see. Suddenly there was a louder noise and something came crashing down behind him; there was a howling wind and a deafening bang. As if the very devil were after him, he abandoned his pipe, dropped his cape and took to his heels, not stopping until he reached Hunters Bar.

Of course, everything has to be reported, or that's what he thought at the time, so after taking a deep breath, he started back up the hill to see exactly what had happened. The explanation was simple and it wasn't anything he was going to report, for the culprit causing the crash was a tombstone which had stood near the wall in the graveyard. Evidently frost had cracked the base and it had gradually creaked its way out of balance until, taking the line of least resistance, it had fallen over the wall.

Something very similar happened to John Shaw, who eventually was Best Man at our wedding. John was on nights in a district where there were some small firms and much dereliction. John had been trying doors and windows for security and was approaching a strip of waste land on which stood a derelict warehouse with many broken windows. As he drew opposite the building, he heard a noise coming from within and walked towards it, at the same time bolding his torch in one hand, with the other on his truncheon. He crept closer, to a small side window with only fragments of glass left in the frame, from which the sound seemed to

262

come from. As he reached the window, he drew his truncheon, at the same time shining his torch through the aperture. John remembered very little of the next few seconds; something hit him hard in the chest, knocking him flying, helmet rolling along the waste ground. But, whatever, or whoever was the intruder, had to be followed, so John set off at the double, following the scuttling noise still audible amongst the ruins. He had retrieved his torch and, nearing the point where he thought the culprit was hiding, switched it on just as the scuttling recommenced, then he saw what it was. Nothing more than a great big ginger cat. Another incident for storytelling; not for the police notebook.

By the summer of 1935, the relationship between Frank and me had progressed to the point that it seemed decent and proper for Frank to take me to meet his family, and although I was only 19 years old, my Father offered no opposition. Frank's mother lived in Easington Colliery on the north east coast of Durham with his elder brother Walter. His sister Kitty/Catherine worked in gentleman's service in Bury but had returned home to meet me during our visit. I liked Kitty immediately, and was lively and full of fun and we became firm friends. Kitty was 14 months younger than Frank, the surviving twin of Thomas, who died a day or two after the birth. Margaret, an older sister of Aunt Em as my future Mother-in-law was known in the family, who lived with her children, Walter, May, Bertha and Arthur at Burnhope near Stanley in County Durham, came to visit her sister at the critical moment, when the house was in turmoil over the death of Thomas and Aunt Em was still in a state of shock.

Margaret decided to take the young Frank, a toddler of 14 months, home with her until the situation improved. For one reason and another never explained, Frank stayed at Burnhope until leaving school at the age of 14, when Margaret sent him back to his family. "You're 14 now," she said, "You'd better go back and work for your mother; she can do with the extra money." But, although Francis, her husband, was now dead and she could certainly have used the extra money, Aunty Em sent her son back to his Aunt with the sacrificial message, "Your Aunty Maggie's looked after you all these years,

263

you'd better go back and work for her, that's your home." So, he returned to Burnhope and found a job as a surface worker at Burnhope Colliery, being too tall for work down the pit.

The pit wasn't exactly kind to the Rundle family, so it was probably fortunate that Frank didn't qualify for an underground job. His Uncle Ted was killed at Shotton Colliery soon after the Second World War when, standing with the pulley-man as the line of tubs were being drawn to the surface, the great hawser broke, the loose end whipping round and wrapping itself round Ted's neck, decapitating him. Then there was Francis, Frank's father who, a few years after Frank's birth, was involved in an accident at Burnhope when his foot became trapped underneath one of the railway lines. According to Emily, and everybody else who knew him, the resultant loss of his leg was his own fault. The men helping to release his foot told him to lie still, but he ranted and raved, tugging at his leg so that no-one could get near to clear the debris, when a tub train could be heard coming down the line. He tugged harder and harder, until the tubs hit him and the leg was so badly injured that it had to be amputated.

Artificial limbs weren't the most sophisticated aids in the early 1920s, and Francis' wooden leg was no exception. It was painful to wear and when Aunt Em helped him to put it on, he wasn't averse to landing out with it and blaming her for all the pain. When something didn't quite suit him he regularly yanked it off and beat her with it. It was, perhaps, fortunate that Frank didn't spend his young life with him, for his temper was bad enough without tuition from his father, who died at an early age from pneumonia. Em said "He so hated wearing that leg, that he never got any exercise, there's no wonder he got pneumonia."

In 1935 Margaret died and Arthur and Bertha lived at Pavilion House, Burnhope Colliery, with Christopher, Bertha's son. Margaret's husband Ralph had been in the R.A.F.C. during the First World War and had returned to the post of ambulance man at the colliery in charge of Rescue & First Aid. Frank said he always remembered him dressed in a white coat. Pavilion House was situated actually in the colliery yard. It was a big black house of an unusual design, with a very large living room, quite dark, even on the brightest day and being surrounded by black coal, there was no garden to brighten the exterior.

The darkness of the house did not detract from the welcome I received on arrival at Pavilion House. "Away in Hinny, mak' theself at yem", greeted me as I stood on the threshold, striving to see in the dim light. I looked askance at Frank just behind me, and he interpreted for me. "He says, come in and make yourself at home," he explained. My eyes soon grew accustomed to the darkness, and I saw a man sitting on a buffet on the end of the fender and as I moved further in, he rose to shake hands. He was a short man, not like Frank, and I noticed, as Frank had warned me, that he was lame. As a veteran of the War after being taken prisoner, he had lain on the battlefield for two days and only with the expertise of the German Doctor, whose praise he often sang, was the wounded leg saved, albeit much shortened, for he now wore a heavily built-up boot.

Almost immediately Bertha appeared from the little back kitchen. She was even smaller than Arthur, the primmest, daintiest person I had ever met, a bit subdued over the years perhaps, owing to her having 'fallen' as people described the situation, but she was not cowed in any way, and was mighty proud of her son.

The visit was more in the way of meeting all the relatives and as well as those at the colliery, where Arthur was the pit pony keeper; there was Walter Scott, his brother who was the colliery joiner. He lived nearer the centre of the village with his wife Sarah and William/Bill and Myra, his son and daughter and Sarah's mother, who had lived with them all their married life and was a real 'tartar' of a mother-in-law. Sarah spent all her time crocheting tablecloths and storing them in drawers and boxes. It was hard work trying to persuade her to sell one, but she was generous enough to give us one for a wedding present.

Then there was Alf Lees, Aunt Em's brother and his snooty wife Lily, who lived at Beamish, and their three children Jack and Trevor, both married, and Jenny who worked away from home. It was Jack Lees, (Manager of Northern Goldsmiths at Newcastle), who obtained the piece of family history from cousin Frances at Glossop.

Frances was the daughter of Francis Lee to whom there is a brass plaque on the wall inside St John's Church, Newcastle upon Tyne. Francis Lee was the brother of Walter Scott Lee, father of Aunt Em, Alf, Margaret and Bertha. Aunt Bertha was the last relative I met. She and her husband Tom lived in a large house in Osbourne Road, Newcastle. Bertha was a devout cat lover who owned a huge spayed female cat who was in the habit of nipping into the oven at night after the fire had gone out, where she could find a nice warm bed. Tom usually arose first, lighting the fire and preparing breakfast and this happened one unfortunate morning, when he automatically closed the oven door before lighting the fire. About an hour later, both Tom and Bertha smelt something burning and on opening the oven door, they found the poor cat roasted to death. Poor Bertha never got over the shock. Tom and Bertha Hewitt had no children; they lived a truly 'Derby and Joan' lifestyle.

The rest of our holiday was spent around the village of Burnhope, a typical colliery village with rows of brick houses, where life revolved around the 'Club' (The Miner's Welfare Club), and the goings on at the pit. There was little for people to do in the evenings except to go up the club to drink, play cards or dominoes, both for money; it was one of the things one was expected to do, even as a visitor, but on the evenings I was taken there, I found it boring and a sheer waste of time. But then, I'm no drinker, not a domino player, nor yet a frequenter of any establishment where drinking is the main pastime. Consequently I was very much the odd one out, this 'posh' girl that Frankie Rundle had brought home (God forbid) and when they were told by Frankie that she was the daughter of a Colliery Manager, (which wasn't exactly what they thought), I found that I was somewhat of an exhibit and a fashion model with my big brimmed black hat and expensive (for me) black and green dress. But, in case you might think that I had suddenly come into a fortune, it was more as Frank said "Your flair for wearing clothes," a tribute more to my Father than me, for he threatened to put a brush steel through the armpits if the shoulders dared to droop only a fraction. He even forbade the boys to talk with hands in pockets; they should be swung as though marching, with head held high and the breath taken in deep draughts. Must be the reason why I still have a farmer's walk, through marching up the furrows with the feet at a 45 degree angle to prevent slipping.

There was one other place I had to visit and be introduced; a small pit village in County Durham, where Ted/Edward Rundle lived with his wife May (Armstrong) and their daughter Margaret/Peggy. Peggy, of course, was Frank's cousin; Ted was his uncle, which complicated things a bit, for now May was his cousin being the niece of his father. She was also now his Aunt, whilst Peggy was now his second cousin. In other words, both mother and daughter were his cousins.

Shotton was a typical pit village like Burnhope, where life revolved around the pit. Both villages had their own brass band which turned out on Sunday mornings and any occasion where music and marching were called for. And, of course, they had a Miner's Welfare Club which, thank goodness, I wasn't asked to attend as Ted was strictly teetotal and I'm sure the Club was, to him, like the old man in the caravan, a 'den of iniquity'.

On this my first visit, I learned that Peggy actually lived at the Vicarage with the Rev. Rainbow, his wife and Fred, their younger daughter before she married a farmer in County Durham. Mary, their elder daughter was, by this time, a Lecturer in English at Durham University, later having married a fellow Lecturer she made her name as Mary Stewart, the famous novelist.

Why the arrangement first came about is not clear. Peggy was no servant, rather an adopted third daughter, but both Ted and May were devout Church goers and their lives appeared to revolve around the Church, the Vicarage and particularly the Rainbows. Ted seemed to hold their authority was above his own and May was always subservient to their will, which may explain why they were prepared and happy to relinquish their daughter to the control of the dominant Rev. Rainbow and his equally dominant wife.

But, on our holiday in 1935, we had many opportunities to walk together up on the 'falls' as the high ground around the village was called. Not as high as our heather covered hills and green with grass, spotted with clumps of trees. Back at home again, life continued as before. Once in a while when duties permitted, we paid a visit to the Empire Theatre in Sheffield, Frank's favourite place of entertainment. It was a variety theatre where such famous names as Tessie O'Shea, George Formby, Frank Randle and Max Miller regularly featured on the programme. Mother Riley and Kitty O'Shea, Rob Wilton and Sandy Powell regularly appeared, especially in Pantomime.

Frank was very reluctant to give up these visits, "Not even to save to get married," he said, which was unfortunate for at Christmas 1935 we decided to get engaged and on his next weekend off paid a visit to Samuels, the Jewellers, to buy a ring. It wasn't an expensive one and there was a sale on with a third discount as an extra incentive. We left the shop with a little box containing a gold ring set with three diamonds on a cross-over pattern. There was a story at the time that the three diamonds set in such a pattern meant "I love you." Romantic, perhaps, though I rather think it was the affordable price that clinched the deal, a mere £8.10s.0d with the discount off.

Then there was the business of putting it on my finger, and Frank decided he should do the job properly. I was yet only 20 years old and courtesy demanded that the girl's father be asked for permission to become engaged, so there was no option. That night, 16th January, we returned home from making our purchase and Frank waited until my Father returned from the pub; the three boys having already returned, a little curious as to why he was still there. By the time Dad arrived, the last bus was within 15 minutes of leaving the terminus at the Cross Scythes, so there was no time for nerves, nor beating about the bush and Frank jumped in with both feet.

"I'd like to ask your permission to get engaged to Josephine," he said, coming straight to the point. Father looked at him, then at me, taken a bit off guard. "Oh," he began, "That's what you're waiting for, is it?" he said, not thinking of anything more original to say. "Yes, Mr Salt," Frank continued, "we'd like to get engaged tonight, if you'll let us." Another look from Father, who by now had collected his thoughts and then he looked at me. "Is that what you want lass?" he said, and when I nodded he continued, "Aye lad, of course you can, I've no objection to that, if that's what she wants."

There was an embarrassing silence as Frank took the little box from his pocket, and turning to me sitting on one of the buffets on the ends of the fender, with everyone leaning forward, he put the ring on my finger. Then with a quick embarrassed kiss, he said "Good night," went out of the door and made a speedy exit for the bus.

As part of the social programme of the Police, dances were held at the Niagara Sports Ground at Hillsborough and as Frank was in the dance band as well as the Silver Band, I always attended, usually sitting in a corner near the stage, where one or two unattended men would come and ask me to dance, and once or twice during the evening, Alf Longmore played a saxophone solo and Frank would leave the stage and dance with me.

Alf had been in an orchestra on board a cruise liner before he entered the Police Force a few years earlier. He was now a Detective Sergeant and a good friend of Franks. He knew exactly which tunes were the best and most romantic; as the lights went down all the courting couples and young married 'coppers' loved them.

Just after we got engaged, Frank said he would like to buy me a new dance dress and although I was rather dubious about what my Father would say, I agreed; the offer of something new was tempting and the necessity to save hard had not yet hit our consciences. There was a private gown shop at the bottom of the Moor called Lewis's who sold exclusive gowns, many made in their own workrooms. They were well known for quality and stylish creations and rather expensive but this was just before Christmas and the annual sales were on.

The occasion was a little embarrassing as I tried first one and then another gown, stepping out of the cubicle each time to see which one my fiancé liked best, a picture my Father probably visualised when he first heard of the purchase. One was a slinky model, too tight for easy dancing, others were either too elaborate or too old and sophisticated but one, Frank thought, was just right. It was a pink creation with a satin bodice, trimmed with net frills and large puffed sleeves with rows of frills all around from top to bottom. The crinoline type skirt was very full net over satin, with graded satin roses from waist to hem and little blue roses in the centre of each; a fairy tale dress. Around the bottom, which was exactly three yards, there was a five layer double frill of net, which, when Elijah danced with me, he said it "Got round his damned feet, he couldn't dance properly."

It was beautiful; a sensation the first time I wore it. One young 'bobby' saw me sitting in my usual corner, Russell was his name. "Are you real?" he said as he stood in front of me. I was somewhat embarrassed and just laughed, but muttered "Yes," "I thought if I spoke you'd pick up your wings and fly away", he laughed, then "May I have this dance please?" he asked, and as Frank looked on from the stage, we danced around the room in style. "He fancies you, you know," Frank said when we next danced. "He's serious an' all; says he'd like to take you out." I thought this was just a bit of kidding, but Russell was serious, as I found out very soon, when he said he was waiting for us to have a row so that he could jump in and take over. That didn't happen and Russell got a transfer to the north very soon after and eventually rose quite high in the hierarchy of the Police Force.

My Father was not pleased with my new dress. "Where did she get that dress?" he asked my Mother. When she told him, he was very cross. "He's no business to buy her clothes before they're married," he said. My Mother tried to smooth things over, but he kept grumbling. "It's not decent for a man to buy clothes for a girl until they're married," he persisted, "it's too familiar." But, he didn't stop me wearing it.

In July that year, we attended the wedding or our close friends Muriel Coates from Lane Head Road and Cliff Freckingham, from Sheffield. They say that one wedding leads to another and Muriel and Cliff's wedding certainly started us thinking seriously of our own. The trouble was money. Frank had none and what's more, he wouldn't save.

One day we were standing talking to Alf Longmore, who was engaged to a society girl whom he had met on one of the ships on which he had travelled. When he knew that Frank wasn't saving he said, "Good God man, get going, there's no way my girl's old man would let me marry his daughter if he thought I wasn't saving." Perhaps I should have told my Father, but I doubt

270

whether he would have been as concerned as Alf's prospective father-in-law. Furthermore, I was determined to get married, not for any romantic reason I fear, but in hindsight because I wanted to run my own home, to have a proper bedroom with a little privacy, not a bed behind a curtain in the corner of the best room.

Such thoughts were not foremost in my conscious mind at the time, I thought my expectations for marriage were normal, where sex, as it is erroneously called these days, was an expression of love, incidental but essential for the production of children, for I did want children, six daughters in fact. Comes of reading too much 'Little Women' I suppose.

The first thing to be decided upon was the date of the wedding. It was a simple thing for me to leave Photo Finishers on a week's notice, but Frank's annual leave was due in only a couple of weeks, too soon for arrangements to be made; it would have to be on a long weekend and the next one was due on 21st November, just over three months ahead. But, before that, one important matter was to obtain permission from the Chief Constable. He could put a 'spanner in the works' if he thought I was not a suitable woman to become the wife of one of his policemen. Some men were refused permission, for various reasons, in which case, the only solution was to make the girl pregnant, when with the addition of a reprimand, permission was grudgingly given.

An application was duly entered and two weeks later, a Chief Inspector and Helen, one of the two policewomen on the Sheffield Force, came to see my Father. Questions were searching and deep; about my Father, what was his job, how long had he had it and who was his employer? Where was he born, who was his father and what did he do and had any of the family been in prison? On and on went the questions until the Inspector was satisfied that my pedigree was satisfactory. Then the policewoman turned to me. How long had I been courting; had I been engaged before and if so, why had it been broken off? I was free to marry, she supposed, but did I know what was expected of a policeman's wife with questions about health, habits and living a blameless life. By the time she had finished, I felt well and truly flattened. If she had been trying to turn me off marriage, she couldn't have been more thorough. If it had been anyone but the police, I think my Father would have blown up; as it was, I think, at the end of the last interview, he had persuaded himself that it was an honour for his daughter to marry a policeman.

Permission was granted, with the best wishes of the Chief Constable and the date was firmly fixed for 21st November at Totley Church. There would be no honeymoon, a big disappointment for me, for that was, I thought, the most romantic part of the whole business, leaving on a train, friends to see us off and all the razzmatazz. As it turned out, it was a fortunate choice of date, we didn't have to make excuses for not going away, there wasn't time. The real reason was we couldn't afford it, not even a weekend.

The major consideration was, of course, a house. We had to have somewhere to live and after putting out a few feelers, Frank learned from a sergeant colleague who lived on Abbeydale Road, that a house was going to be re-let in the near future a few doors away from his home. The landlord, Mr Graham, a Jewish furniture dealer, would welcome a policeman as tenant, as their rent was secure. (15s.0d rent allowance was included in police pay and rent books had to be presented at West Bar Headquarters every quarter for inspection).

We were offered the house and although it was very dirty, we were told we could have it free from rent for a month before the wedding to clean and decorate. In the meantime there were many things to do and arrangements to be made. From the day we had decided to marry I had started collecting for my 'bottom drawer'. Lunchtimes at Photo Finishers were spent in embroidering cushion covers and tablecloths, pillow slips and the like and by November I had quite a useful 'linen drawer'.

During the 1930s, the motto of Woolworths' stores was 'Nothing sold over 6d' (2½p). Almost all household utensils such as colanders, pans, basins, jugs, cutlery and linen could be bought for 6d or less. Larger items like larger pans were sold for 6d per item; 6d the pan and 6d the lid. There was little that could not be bought at Woolworths. I really think that all newlyweds furnished their kitchens and cupboards with Woolworths' green or green and yellow cooking tools and utensils. Every week I paid a visit to the store and, for the sake of records and posterity, every item was entered in the little alphabetical book I kept in my 'bottom drawer'.

One of the girls ran a club through which, for 1s.0d a week, one could buy goods worth £1.0s.0d. A draw decided in what rotation members could receive their goods and suitable consideration was given to particular dates for those about to be married. I joined the club and on my allotted date, I chose a set of jugs with pictures of Old England on the side for 4s.11d (25p), one or two small patterned tablecloths at 2s.11d each (15p), a fruit set, (a large bowl with six small bowls), a set of three basins and a set of table mats, 2s.11d (15p). This last item was quite a luxury, for I had never sat down to a meal without a tablecloth and the only time I had seen table mats in use was on the dining table at Totley Hall. I was having ideas above my station so to speak, as my Mother often said to me "Totley Hall gave you grand ideas," not unkindly for after all, that's what she had predicted to my Father when persuading him to let me go, wasn't it?

My 'bottom drawer' was a large wooden Victorian ottoman which had belonged to our Great Great Aunt Julia Newbry. My Father had bought it, along with the suite of dining room furniture from her home in Cheltenham which was inherited at Uncle Arthur's sale after his death. My Mother had used it for the past seven years to store sheets and blankets but now, she said, it would make a good store for my 'bits and pieces', especially when Mrs Coates offered to store it in her attic until the wedding. I could go round there anytime to add new purchases; she was intrigued as the 101 items were carefully wrapped and packed in each week.

It wasn't too long before my Mother became infected with my enthusiasm and each time she went to Sheffield, she returned with some little gadget like a potato peeler, a tin opener, a cooking fork and watched me add them to the little record book so that she always knew what items were still needed. By November the ottoman was full, the lid had difficulty in closing and I had all the linen, pots and pans and cooking tools I was ever likely to need. Some are still in use in 1991, which says a lot for Woolworth's quality.

In early August, Frank spent his week's annual leave at Burnhope for the purpose of telling Arthur and Bertha of the pending wedding. Both were delighted, Arthur being very generous in his offer to buy us a dining room suite for a wedding present, giving Frank 15 guineas with which to purchase it (£15.75). By the time he returned, he had decided to buy the room suite on hire purchase and add the 15 guineas to his frugal savings for immediate expenses and with this addition, the exchequer now boasted £30.0s.0d

At the beginning of September, we read in the local newspaper that a furniture firm, Franklins, at the bottom of Ecclesall Road, Sheffield, were selling all their stock by auction and concentrating on the other side of their business, dyeing and cleaning. We decided to go to the auction as we needed carpets and many small items of furniture and by the time we had bought what we could afford, we had two carpet squares, one for the sitting room which was four yards square and cost £8.10s.0d; the other for the bedroom, 3½ yards square at a cost of £5.0s.0d. Two Queen Anne mahogany chairs were added at £2.10s.0d each and an oak blanket chest for £1.0s.0d. All were taken round to Mrs Coates' attic. "My, our Muriel had a lot of things, but she never had any chairs as grand as these," she said admiringly.

Another firm having a half-price sale was Walkers (under the clock) about half way up the Moor. A visit there reaped a box of silver fish knives and forks and six silver serviette rings, (my vision of grandeur at our dining table). At the same time we chose a Westminster chiming clock which was to be a present from Geoff, and eventually a prized possession to stand on our sideboard.

If only foresight could have warned us of things to come, we might have thought twice about our purchases for six weeks before the wedding, my Father told me the shattering news that he couldn't afford to pay for it. "If you want a wedding lass, you'll have to pay for it yourself," he said. I was dismayed, completely shattered by his words. All the guests had been invited, the tea room at the Cross Scythes had been booked and a meal for over 70 people ordered. As we weren't going away, a small band had been ordered for entertainment and dancing after tea and drinks were expected for many friends visiting for the evening. "I'll still buy you the three piece suite I promised," he said, "but it will have to be on hire purchase, I can't afford it otherwise."

This was a disaster, made worse only that day when Frank, on his way through the city, had stopped off at Auction Rooms and bought a canteen of cutlery and a Japanese tea set. "One's for your birthday," (my 21st was due three days before the wedding), "the other's for your wedding present," he said. I was cross, extremely cross. Both items were unnecessary; why should he spend like this when we were so short of money? I knew I should be grateful for the thought though. We had plenty of cutlery; bought through a girl at Photo Finishers whose uncle was a cutler and I didn't even like the tea set, it was a useless trinket when we needed so many things. There was another disappointment to come, but first, a crisis of another kind.

About a week later, during the middle of October, Frank was taken ill with a severe bout of bronchial asthma, a recurring complaint in autumn since the demise of the true asthma he suffered from as a child. His lodgings were very near to Photo Finishers off Abbeydale Road and I had visited once or twice during the week and in the evenings, but on the latest visit, Mrs Brewitt, his landlady, informed me that the Police Surgeon, Dr Forbes, wanted to see me and an appointment had been made for lunchtime two days hence. I had a quick lunch on the day in question and duly reported to Dr Forbes. What he had to say amazed me. Telling me to sit down, he shot the first question "You are the young lady who's going to marry this man?" he said. "Do you, my girl, know what you are letting yourself in for?" I was struck dumb for a full ten seconds and then started muttering, "Y-yes". He looked very grim and proceeded to give me a lecture. If I married him, and he fervently hoped I would not, I would be marrying a whole lot of trouble for myself. I listened aghast, I couldn't believe a Doctor could be so pompous as to say whom I should marry or not. But this was the Police Surgeon and perhaps he had some sort of authority to stop the wedding after all. Such were my thoughts, for the human brain is a mighty quick computer. I stammered, "I don't mind." "You should, young lady; you should change your mind whilst you still have time," he clipped. I looked at Frank, but I think he felt so ill that this all went over his head, although he had had a lecture from the Doctor before I arrived and I got no help from that quarter.

"You know, my dear girl," he persisted. "This man is going to have these attacks every October when the weather changes and you are going to have to nurse him." Again, I could think of nothing to say, except that I wouldn't mind and at last he realised there was nothing else to say to change my mind. "If you are determined to go through with this marriage," he growled, "then, my girl, no cats." That was his final word. I weakly informed him that I didn't like cats, which wasn't true, for we had always had a cat and but for his warning, we might someday have had one. "Very well," he said, as he got up to leave, "Let it be on your head, don't say I didn't warn you."

As in most firms when a girl left to be married, there was a collection at Photo Finishers for the purpose of buying a wedding present. Discreet questions were asked by those closest to me, as to what I would like and, after much thought, I said I would like a wall mirror. So far we didn't have one, couldn't afford one and naturally we would need one if we weren't to be running upstairs to the dressing table every time we left the house. The collection was made and the presentation arranged for the day before I was to leave. There had been much discussion, I was told later, about my request for a mirror. "We can't buy Salty a mirror," said one young woman who had always been rather scathing about my Father meeting me in his car every Friday night, never querying the reason. "She doesn't need a mirror," she said, "She'll have plenty of them. She'll do a lot of entertaining," she went on "She'll need things for entertaining." No matter what the others said, she persuaded them that with my lifestyle (whatever that was), I would like something fancy and that I had only asked for a mirror so that I wouldn't embarrass them. I had always known that they thought I was different from them and this woman had sometimes been very sarcastic. However, I put it down to the difference between town and country girls, a point often mentioned and although about half a dozen of them at some time or another had been to my cottage home, she evidently thought I

276

came from a posh home and had everything, which just goes to show how wrong impressions are formed through behaviour patterns. It is not always the one who pleads poverty who is the poorer, far from it and although prude is one of the sins, it does form a barrier to unwanted sympathy.

I knew nothing about the discussions before the presentation of my present and expected a really nice mirror from the money I knew to have been collected. Incidentally, the woman in question did not subscribe, saying I had more than her anyway! Miss Barton, the office Head was asked to do the presentation, then came the moment for the speech of thanks, which hadn't worried me. I had never shown any embarrassment or nervousness when I knew what I wanted to say. But, at the realisation that I wasn't going to receive the much wanted mirror, I was completely taken aback and for a moment, said nothing. No-one understood why Salty, of all people, could find nothing else to say but "Thank you very much." They expected a flowery speech, a perfect performance from this self-assured person, who was never lost for words and was never shy. What they didn't know was the great disappointment I felt; what did I want with a cocktail set? I wouldn't be able to afford the damned cocktails. And the little bon-bon dish to go with it was pretty, but would I ever use it?

Another embarrassing situation due to my Father's inability to pay for the wedding was the matter of the bridesmaid's dresses. It also brought another disappointment. It was the custom for the bride's father to pay for the bride's and the bridesmaid's dresses, all the flowers and wedding cars. Our financial situation would be sorely stretched to clothe all four bridesmaids already asked and the small attendant, a five year old from my Sunday school class. Ida, my friend and Kitty, Frank's sister, said at once that they would pay for their own; Rita's father was only too pleased to pay for hers, being very proud that she had been chosen from the class and Vina, a current friend of Elijah, who was included at the express wish of my Father. However, Marjorie, my closest friend from Photo finishers, who had expected my Father to pay for her dress, refused and said she couldn't afford it and was sceptical as to the reason why.

My Father had a soft spot for Vina, primarily because she had no mother. She kept house for her father and three or four brothers and any girl in that situation won my Father's sympathy. If you had two parents you needed nothing else. When Marjorie dropped out I wanted Ida to be my chief bridesmaid, but Father said "You should let Vina be your chief bridesmaid," and so in his eyes, she was, but I always considered it to be Ida.

For a month before the wedding our new home underwent a transformation. Mom papered both bedrooms and the lounge whilst I made my first effort at papering the walls in the living room and Geoff turned his hand at painting. In three weeks, the house was spanking clean and we could start to move our furniture in. Mr Graham was a hard-headed businessman, but he knocked a little off the price of the oddments we bought from him as we were to become his tenants, namely, another 3 x 3½ yard square carpet for the living room, stair carpet, lino for the kitchen and surrounds in all the other rooms and two leather easy chairs for the living room for which we were to pay 2s.6d per week for a year. We were absolutely broke, until Frank's pay day, the day before the wedding. I had left work the week before and my wages were spent on last minute items and food for our first week of married life.

A week before the wedding the fittings and curtains were removed from the room and my bed was taken into the back bedroom of our new home. During the following week, my bed was the horsehair sofa in the living room. It was large and as wide as a single bed, although rather harder than a full feather bed, or soft mattress I had been used to. But, as my Mom often said, "You could always sleep on a clothes line if that's all there was."

I awoke on my birthday on the 18th November to find a single parcel on the sofa beside me. Opening it I found a pair of bedroom slippers, a present from my Mother; the rest of the family had not remembered it was my 21st birthday, so there were no other presents, although later in the morning, one of our neighbours, Mrs Ramsall, called to give me a fancy flower jug. Dad, with a bit of prompting from my Mother, offered a casual "Many Happy Returns." It was Vina's birthday just after Christmas and my Father, obviously better off than in November, bought her a leather handbag and a powder compact to put inside. A few weeks later he asked my Mother, "What's wrong with our Dene, she's a bit off-hand." "Do you wonder," my Mother replied, "she's disappointed. You bought a handbag for Vina's birthday and, as if that wasn't enough, you bought a powder compact too, and you bought nothing for your own daughter's 21st birthday, no wonder she's off-hand." "I'm buying her a three piece suite, what more does she want?" he argued, "It's her 21st, my Mother repeated, you could have given her something, no wonder she's disappointed." This evidently was the reason for no other presents; I should have known better than to get married so close to a birthday it seemed. But, my Mother's voice must have fallen on fertile ground, for about a month later, my Father presented me with a 21st birthday present, a bible, on the fly-leaf of which he had written "Lean on me".

For a week before our wedding there was a thick fog which brought all traffic to a standstill. There were no buses, people had to walk if they wanted to get anywhere and even then, it was difficult to see more than a few yards in front and the air stank with smoke and putrid air and we wondered if there would really be a wedding after all. But, on Saturday morning, the sun shone brightly, the air was clear and warm such as we never expected in November. It was a day for dresses, not coats, and the entire world seemed ready to wish us luck and happiness. I washed my hair and set it as usual with pins and curlers and still had them in when my Mother asked me to fetch something from the Post Office shop. I was crossing the road to return when I met Mr Turner, the friend from bowling green days. He had always called me his 'little sweetheart' and a few weeks before our meeting he told my Father that he had a wedding present for me and wanted me to take my fiancé to his home on the Quadrant one evening to receive it. We had answered the invitation and received a box of beautiful fish knives and forks made in the new Staybright steel, an expensive present, for which we thanked him whilst accepting a drink to wish us health and happiness. "Now young man," he said in a serious voice, "You are going to look after Josephine aren't you?" "Why, yes," said Frank humbly but smiling at his fatherly tone. But Mr Turner was serious as he looked at him with a very straight face as he said, "Because if you don't young man, you'll have me to reckon with."

On this, my wedding day, he had invited me to have a drink with him in the Fleur de Lys. At first I declined, to be seen in curling pins by all and sundry was not exactly glamorous, but he persisted. "What do a few curlers matter?" he said, "You are still my little sweetheart, so come on, let me have a kiss and wish you all the happiness you deserve." To my great distress, that was the last I saw of Mr Turner, except for a glimpse over the heads of the crowd in the bar of the Cross Scythes that night, a sad result of poverty.

The wedding had been arranged for 2.30 p.m. and by 2.15 p.m. Elijah and Geoff were in Church ushering our guests to their seats. Jeff was in the vestry preparing for his first appointment as a server. It was the proudest moment in his life, he said, to be leading his sister up the aisle. Mom had left the house looking every inch the Mother of the Bride in her long dress of wine coloured lace and carrying a bouquet of pink carnations and fern. Aunt Em, also carrying a bouquet, as was the custom and Aunt Bertha had joined them all and the bridesmaids had just left in their full-skirted blue dresses with frills from waist to hem, the three adults carrying bouquets of pink chrysanthemums, blue carnations and fern. Ida had expressed a wish for bronze chrysanthemums, her favourite flower and I had half promised to have them but the florist who was to make the bouquets was a friend of Frank Thompson, an old Army colleague of Frank's.

Mary had just returned from her London training, where she had learned the new art of dyeing flowers with a special powder which was sprayed on to the flowers through a straw whilst holding them in a pillowcase, and she was anxious to try the method for herself. With a little push from Frank, I agreed to change my colour scheme, the final result as above. Rita, the five year old, carried a basket filled with similar flowers, with a huge blue bow on the handle. Rita was the daughter of Frank Evans, who kept a grocery shop in Hillfoot Road, now the private home of Rita and her husband.

I was dressed and ready and Dad waited in the living room for me to come downstairs. I wore a heavy satin dress embroidered on the bishop sleeves and yard-long train with gold cord and sequins. My veil was my own design, copied from the one Norma Shearer wore in the film 'Smiling Through' when she was tragically shot at the altar. The picture had been a sensation, many brides wanted something to remind them of the film and many girls were christened 'Mooneen' after the heroine, not always to their liking. The headdress was a cap of net, banded over the front with a plaited band of satin and sequins. A large frill stood high around the back, the whole creation framing the face and finished at either side with a large white camellia.

The veil was three yards long, with a large appliquéd white satin lover's knot on the corner which trailed on the floor. My bouquet was from Rosalinda roses, the best cream roses just raised in the 19th century and still producing well and as was the fashion, fern from neck to hem There was lily of the valley fastened here and there on the trails and in the centre of the bouquet, a huge bog of cream tulle, which, according to Mary, the florist, was the current fashion in London.

I came downstairs carefully, trying not to step on the yards of net and turned the corner at the bottom of the stairs, where my Father caught his first glimpse of his daughter in her last hour of freedom. He took one look at me and then turned immediately towards the cellar door, muttering something like "I shall have to go down the back." He had just moved through the door when I heard a shout and a noise which could only mean that he had fallen down the stone steps. As quickly as I could move, I went to the top of the steps, by which time he had disappeared into the cellar kitchen. I didn't hear the back door, neither opening nor shutting and a few minutes later he returned, looking a little sheepish, but no worse for the experience. "It's these new shoes," he said, "They're slippery on the stone steps." I didn't query his explanation, it seemed reasonable enough, but later, when my Mother told me the real reason, I was very sorry that he had to hide his emotion; how much nicer it would have been to know what he was really thinking. But then parents never showed their feelings in front of their children in those days, it wasn't considered decent. "It was the sight of her, dressed all in white, I just wanted to put my arms around her, I didn't want her to be upset." It must have been the tears in his eyes he said, that made him slip on the steps.

Jeff led us up the aisle to the hymn 'Lead us Heavenly Father Lead us', the church was overflowing with guests and villagers; about 30 waiting outside. I was very calm, probably revelling in the limelight, rather than any feeling of nervousness. There were no 'hitches', everything was going to plan, until we reached the church gates on our way to the reception.

It was the custom at Totley Church to tie the gates of the drive to prevent newlyweds leaving until they had emptied their pockets, or paid a fine of half-a-crown (2s.6d). Luckily Frank had a half crown and we were allowed to pass through. Fortunately he had a little left from his week's wages, minus the cost of last night's Stag Party drinks, so he could pay up without embarrassment. Also, a lucky break for a change; Mr Hutton, the Vicar, had not taken the 7s.6d (37½p) for the marriage licence. He said it was his thanks for my services as a Sunday school teacher, saying my husband could never, in future, complain about the cost of his wife! That 7s.6d was a welcome addition to the meagre amount we could muster for our food for the first week of our married life.

We held our wedding reception at the Cross Scythes Hotel, in the tea room at the top of the flight of stone steps to the left of the front door. A group of Frank's colleagues, including Alf Longmore and Sgt. Ginger Parsons, who was to be our close neighbour, greeted us on the circular steps to the front door. They had been to the church, but were not staying for the reception and had waited to form an unofficial guard of honour and, as they said, to issue condolences to both sides! The usual speeches were delivered, lightened by the words from Mr Hutton, the Vicar, who was speaking as an old friend of the bride. The Rev. R J Hutton had a peculiar throaty laugh which was exceedingly infectious but his earthy sense of humour was, to say the least, unexpected. He said he had never had the honour of handcuffing a policeman before, "But what's more," he said, "I've managed to put a bit of salt on his tail." The ulterior meaning wasn't lost on the guests; there was uproar, especially as his own laughter showed how much he had enjoyed the joke himself.

As we were not leaving for a honeymoon, we had booked a five piece band through Vina's brother, who was the drummer and an open invitation had gone out to all the people in the village who attend the dance which followed the tea. Almost every villager turned up, the Stubbs, the Turner's, the Marshall's from Hall Lane, the Drury's, the Trusswell's, the Wortley's, the Green's, the Taylor's from Summer Lane, the Smith's and the Johnsons from Lane Head, and most of the able from Totley Bents, including Ida's mother, brother and sisters. The room was crowded, some dancing, some drinking, some coming, others going, until Mr Scott said he would have to send for further supplies before the pub could open next morning.

About 10.30 p.m., we decided to make a discreet exit and I went quietly to my Mother and whispered that we were going to disappear. We had previously made arrangements with 'Chippy' Fox who had been driving my Father's Wolseley car all day, to drive us to our new home and we thought we had been very clever to have left without being seen. But we hadn't reckoned about Muriel and Cliff and hadn't gone far when we realised we were being followed. No-one had been allowed into our house for the past week, to prevent practical jokers causing a lot of work after so much cleaning and preparing. A chase started, down to Beauchief, on to Millhouses and along Abbeydale Road, our pursuers gaining every minute.

With only a few yards to spare, our car stopped, we jumped out, me grabbing the train of my dress and lifting it up around my waist, a mad dash down the jennel, fumbling for the key, tumbling breathless into the kitchen, the door slammed and locked just as the gate crashers arrived banging on the door with cries of "Let us in, let us in." But even our closest friends weren't welcome that night.

Next morning, we were expected at Lane Head for tea and to bring back some of the wedding presents, but on venturing outside it seemed very doubtful whether we would make it that far. For a week before our wedding, there had been thick fog when traffic had been stopped and all buses taken off the road. Our wedding day had been a glorious window in what was to be a dark dreary two weeks of almost total invisibility. The day had been warm and bright as early summer, with not a cloud in the sky, but now, the clouds had dropped again and travel was very uncertain. Nevertheless, a bus turned up and we arrived home safely, although now a little worried about our return and we were not wrong to worry for we had just finished tea when Muriel and Cliff came round to see us, and to tell us that the buses had been stopped again. They were leaving in about ten minutes, hoping to get through the fog before it became impossible and offered to take us to Abbeydale Road on their way to Broomhill. It was a nerve racking journey, but just possible at snail's pace, until we reached the crossroads at Beauchief. There were no cat's eyes in those days; I don't even remember white lines and the junction at Beauchief was as impenetrable as no-man's land; even the trams had been stopped in case of accidents on the lines. There was nothing for it but to walk in front of the car and guide the driver across the abyss, for that's what it felt like in the stinking blackness. Frank rummaged for his handkerchief and took position about a yard in front of the car and, in this way we not only reached the other side safely, but eventually our own door.

Two weeks later, on our weekly visit home, my Father handed to me the account for the wedding breakfast from Mr Scott, the proprietor of the Cross Scythes. I had already done my sums and was not surprised to see the amount of £8.8s.6d for 67 guests at 2s.6d (12½p) each and 1s.0d (5p) for the child bridesmaid. My Father had told me the night before the wedding that he would pay for the champagne.

We returned home that night a very worried couple, but as we could do nothing about it, like all unsolvable problems, it was 'put behind the clock' so to speak, in the hope that, like Mr Micawber, something would turn up. By the time of our last visit before Christmas, nothing had turned up and when my Father reminded me with "Mr Scott tells me you haven't paid his bill yet," I only answered "No." I knew his concern was primarily for his own reputation, for he did not query the reason for the non-payment. "I think you should pay it straight away," was his only contribution. Now the problem was really serious, we could see no way that we could pay at all, never mind straight away, a sum of £8.8s.6d no matter how we fiddled the accounts.

On his first pay day after our marriage, Frank had returned home with his pay-packet unopened. Tossing it down on the table he said, "You'd better have that love, you'll do it better than me." I opened the packet and took out £3.7s.0d which included 15s.0d rent allowance, a commitment almost sacred as the rent book had to be produced every quarter at Police H.Q. When this amount was deducted, along with the 7s.6d to pay Wigfalls for furniture and 2s.6d to Mr Graham for furniture; lighting and heating and bus fares for the weekly visit to Lane Head, the sum was depressingly depleted. In his willingness to help, Frank offered "If I have enough for my tram fare, and 2s.6d for 'tabs' (cigarettes), you can do what you like with the rest." (Tram fares from Abbeydale Road to the city centre were 1d. From the city centre on to whatever beat was on roster that day, was another 1d, with a similar amount to return. Consequently, fares for the six working days could be anything from 12d to 24d a week. At the end of all the deductions, my housekeeping purse boasted a meagre 25s.0d. Not a lot, but with care we could have managed but for this final blow, and a solution had to be found pretty quickly, but what?

There was no time to waste, so when Frank came up with the idea of the pawnshop, it seemed the only answer, but what on earth could we take and what had we that would raise enough to cover the bill? The wedding presents; we had nothing else, except the few things we had bought ourselves and the contents of my old ottoman, otherwise 'bottom drawer'. We decided. Frank fetched downstairs his old suitcase; it was very old and had travelled a lot during his army life, but it was strong enough to hold all the things we could muster. Two clocks, the canteen of cutlery, the Japanese tea set, the carving set from our Best Man John Shaw, the fish knives and serviette rings, dressing table set from Jeff, the cocktail set from Photo Finishers and the sherry set from Ginger Parsons, the biscuit barrel and serving dish from the Sunday school, and any other presents we could cram into the case. To pack them safely, and to raise a few more coppers, we used Frank's best grey suit.

We couldn't risk going to a local pawnshop, although there were two or three in the neighbourhood, but Frank knew there was one on a road in Hillsborough, the other end of the city and this is where we decided to go. We took a tram to the city, then another tram to Hillsborough, alighting a little way from the shop on the busy main road. We were standing on the corner of the road where we could see Turner's shop and the 'three balls' pawnbroker's sign. "I can't go near the shop," Frank said, "This is one of my beats; I go in there with lost and stolen lists every week and they'll recognise me. You'll have to take it from here," he said, "Can you manage it?" I struggled a bit with the weight, and he carried it a few more paces before saying, "I mustn't go any further, you'll be alright now."

I reached the door of the shop feeling very depressed and degraded. I'd heard from my Mother and Aunt Annie about the poor Sheffielders who took their Sunday clothes to the pawnshop every Monday, and fetched them back every Saturday, but I'd never thought it might happen to me. Yet here I was, and there was nothing else for it, but to go in. Opening the door gingerly and struggling to lift the heavy case over the threshold, I confronted a man wearing a large hessian apron who appeared from the back of the shop. "What can I do for you?" he asked, as he looked at me in rather a questioning way. I told him why I had come and what I wanted, after which he asked to see what I had in the case. He watched as I removed first one thing then another, putting them carefully on the counter as I did so, sometimes muttering a price under his breath. After examining the grey suit he said, "I can't give you much for the clothes, half a crown would be the limit (12½p). "I'll have to fetch it back this weekend," I told him, "It's my husband's best suit and he will want to wear it on Sunday." Suddenly, he put the things down and looking at me closely said, "Look love, how much do you want to raise?" I looked a little sheepish and answered "We have to pay the bill for the wedding, it's £8.8s.6d." "Then just wait whilst I take out the cards," he said very kindly, "And I'll explain what you must do."

Going to the back of the shop, he returned with a handful of small duplicate cards and having asked my name, made out one for each item, tearing off the duplicate for me to save. "You've not done this before have you love?" he said. "No," I answered, feeling very humbled. "Now look," he explained, as he handed me the cards,

286

"Keep these in a safe place and when you want to fetch something out of pledge, bring the card with you with the money. But," he added, "Remember we only keep things for a year and a day and then they are sold."

I learned later that this was according to law, but wasn't strictly adhered to, for the auctions of unredeemed pledges were held not only once a year and could be almost two years if one had just been held. Neither did I know that one could attend an auction and probably buy one's own items back for little more than the pledge price. I knew nothing of the legal side of the business as I left the shop, with a certain sigh of relief that at least one problem was solved, the major one remaining, how was I to find the money to get them all back? Frank was waiting anxiously on the corner, eager to hear that I had the money and that there had been no awkward questions.

On our next visit home, I gave my Father the money to settle the account, for which he was pleased, but in the next breath he had another criticism of me. "Mr Turner is very disappointed that you haven't sent him a piece of cake," he said, "You know he's always thought a lot about you, and he bought you that good set of cutlery." I said nothing as he went on, "You know lass, you can't ignore your friends." I still didn't answer, I was too upset for I had always liked Mr Turner, and I hated him to think I had let him down, but felt there was nothing I could do about it.

This will sound very strange to anyone reading it now, for times have certainly changed. People were proud, even the poorest would not readily admit to such a situation, except in absolute poverty, which meant there was no food at all, no coal for heating, or clothes to wear, or clothes on the bed. Many homes threw the hearthrug over the bed at night in the absence of bedclothes. The idea of owning a car, a television, a fridge, or their equivalent did not appear in the standard of living in pre-war days, nor did their absence constitute poverty as some seem to think these days. That same philosophy of pride, whether it is considered a sin or not, prevented me telling my Father that I couldn't afford the little boxes in which the newlyweds sent out their little morsels of cake. Of course, I could have bought just one, but that would have been an admission of defeat. There was always hope, or so I thought, that eventually I would be able to buy a dozen.

However, 'eventually' hadn't materialised by the time my Father spoke and one didn't get away with giving cake in little twists of tissue paper or serviettes, that was a sign of poverty, or ill-breeding and particularly after such a delay, would be all too obvious. If there is indeed an 'after life', there are three men whom I would like to meet again, if only to apologise for something over which I had little control, my Father, my Headmaster and Mr Turner.

One sad result of our trip to the pawnshop was the absence of the customary housewarming party which all newlyweds looked forward to, when the bride could show her hand at entertaining and the husband could show off his prowess as a host and the home he had provided. But, without the wedding presents which everyone expected to be in use or on show in privileged positions, no excuses could explain the absence of the whole lot. "I'll see you at the housewarming, Joan," our Best Man had said to my Mother when he said "Goodnight" after the wedding. "We'll look forward to seeing them in use at the housewarming", Julian Evens had said after the presentation from the Sunday school. "I'll come and give you a hand at your housewarming," Muriel had said when she thought it was the extra work I was 'duffing'. So, there never was a housewarming and many of our former friends never bothered with us again. That was our greater poverty.

Except for the short visit to Burnhope, I had never seen Frank at home and lodgings were unnatural surroundings to assess the capabilities, or otherwise, of the man I was to marry. I had been brought up in a family of men, and women, who were capable of, at least, a reasonable attempt at some practical jobs, consequently it was a disappointment to find that I had married a man incapable of knocking a nail in straight, nor willing to 'have a go'. "I shall never be able to do a job as well as your brothers," he said, "They'd only laugh at my efforts, so I'm not going to try." And he never did. I soon realised that my role would have to be not only housewife and all that it entailed, but exchequer, decision-maker, handyman, legal expert and negotiator in all the problems of setting up a new home. "You see to it love, you know best," was the usual remark.

At the end of the first month, disillusionment was almost complete. Alone all day, money worries uppermost in my mind and a husband whose sole requirements appeared to be a newspaper and an easy chair in which to snooze. "It's nice to snooze isn't it?" he said one evening, rising for a few moments before relapsing into another session. Not the most romantic way to woo a young wife towards a satisfactory love life, where woman was considered subservient to the male.

I was immature, my husband said, so bloody immature it was unbelievable in this day and age. I protested that I was mature but I had ideals, particularly about marriage, which he said "were bloody daft." Alright, perhaps I was immature in expecting more and naive in thinking that marriage could be the pleasant fulfilment of dreams. All I knew was that I was very miserable and worried and there wasn't a soul I could talk to, in whom I could confide, although I did find it necessary to explain my unhappiness to cousin May when she called one day and found me in a flood of tears. She was surprised to hear that life was not the bed of roses I had hoped for, but thought it would improve as we got to know each other better, although I had a strong feeling that it would not.

"I'll show you what life's really about," Frank said one night. "I'll take you down Harvest Lane and Allan Street on Sunday morning to see all the cellar grates pulled up and broken; to see all the broken windows after all the domestic rows the night before and all the 'French letters' strewn about the streets and alleys, then you'll see what life's all about. The following Sunday morning, he took me down Harvest Lane and Allan Street as he had promised. There were the broken windows and the cellar grates and the unkempt faces peering from behind dirty ragged curtains and the 'French letters', which never having seen before, would not have recognised had they not been pointed out. Seeing them strewn in the gutters, in the alleyways and in the entrances to the jennels, I was amazed; how, I thought, could men and women raise so much energy for such antics, and put it all down to the copious beer they must have consumed.

At Photo Finishers I had been fascinated and amazed to hear some of the stories the girls told me about their love-making, but had put much of it down to bravado, competition with each other and too many dirty postcards. Now, I wasn't so sure. These latest revelations didn't convince me that everybody was like that and I said so. "We were different; we weren't like that ... were we?" I said, hoping he would agree. But he didn't. "Everybody's like that underneath," he said, which made me more depressed than ever with the human race, surely somebody had higher expectations from marriage than these sordid activities. If this was all it was about, then my disillusionment was complete.

My education did not stop there. I had to grow used to hearing more stories about street life, how the other half lived, and how everybody lived if they were being honest. There was the story about the couple he had disturbed in a jennel one night when he shone his light on them, just as the climax was due. The girl had both legs spread-eagle on the low ledges down the sides of the house walls, whilst the man huffed and puffed in his crouched position in an effort to bring his love-making to a satisfactory conclusion. As the light fell on them, there was an agonised cry, "Let him finish officer," the girl shouted in a desperate plea for satisfaction. With the light still on them, it was too late to do otherwise.

There was the night he came home from the afternoon shift, still in a state of glee about the happenings of the evening. It was Saturday, his sergeant had met him at a report point and as he had a few minutes to spare before his next rendezvous, had suggested they do a little detour. "Let's go and see old Sarah, she'll be home from the pub by now," he said. Sarah was an old woman known to all police, not as a criminal, rather for her habits. They arrived at Sarah's terraced house where, as usual the curtains had been carelessly drawn, leaving a chink through which they could clearly see her sitting on a low three-legged stool, like a milking stool. The sergeant peered through the chink and Frank stood close to him until he could see also. He was a little taller than the sergeant and could see easily, whilst the sergeant decided to stand on an upturned bucket standing near the dustbin.

Sarah had obviously been drinking and a bit unsteady on her feet, but as the two men watched, she brought out a tea cloth and a wooden clothes peg which she proceeded to wrap in the cloth, the reason perfectly clear to the eager watchers. She sat on the stool, her legs wide open and with a look of ecstasy on her face, proceeded to masturbate herself. The sergeant got excited as the performance accelerated and moved his position to get a better view. Unfortunately, the bucket rocked, the sergeant over-balanced, the bucket tipped over and he fell off, landing with a mighty clatter against the dustbin. The lid went flying as his helmet bounced across the street, before both men collected their wits and set off running down the street as fast as their feet could carry them. What Sarah's reaction was neither I, nor they, would ever know.

Of course, I tried to keep my face straight; I was disturbed and sickened, it would turn me off sex even quicker than before. But, as when watching Elijah chasing the farting pony, my sense of humour got the better of me as I visualised such a ridiculous situation and it served to break the tension.

There were lighter moments, like all marriages, things can't be all bad and it wasn't long before I realised that my husband had other things, besides sex, in that head of his. He was an intelligent man, only held back by his family failing of being slow and wasting opportunities for progress, needing a little pushing at times. Soon after we were married, at the end of his two years' probation, he was eligible to sit for the sergeant's examination. 'Moriarty' was the standard textbook for Statute Law and Frank was an efficient policeman so this part of the syllabus was straight forward. As question-master, I became well acquainted over the following months with the intricacies of law and the 'jargon' used to express its various aspects. English was no problem, it was far superior to my own; at least it ensured easy reading for a harassed examiner. But arithmetic, that was something else and not Frank's strongest subject by any means. He refused all help, even though it had been my strongest at school, saying he knew enough to scrape through. Unfortunately, with a good pass in every subject but arithmetic, the whole exam had

291

to be taken again and any suggestion towards this met with a blank refusal.

I was furious with his attitude, stressing that you should never give up until things are absolutely hopeless. After many arguments, he agreed to try again, in the meantime he would take a short course at a Correspondence College and applied to Bennett's College, Sheffield, where my Father had taken an Extramural Course before taking the examination for a Mine's Manager's Certificate before Mom and Dad were married in 1913.

This time, the examination was easy, to Frank's and my satisfaction, at least it was one hurdle over and the experience of working together brought a different attitude to our marriage, for we became great friends. He talked about aspects of Law, and Court procedure without, of course, disclosing information from actual cases and with his scientific brain and my avid appetite for learning, we often sat up until the early hours of the morning after an afternoon shift, he talking, me listening and questioning about the atmosphere on Venus, the rings of Saturn, the red planet Mars, or the possibility of men landing on the moon. "You know Josephine," he once said, (I always got my full label at serious times like these), "Man will land on the moon one day, it's bound to happen," he was so confident, "not in my lifetime perhaps, but they will do it." I'm glad to know that he lived long enough to know that his prediction came true and much more.

The nearest I had ever come to science was when Mr Wood had told us one day when, for some reason he was talking about the atom and, like many scientists of that time, had said, "If anybody ever splits the atom, it will cause a chain reaction through all matter, and be the end of the world." Of course, we know now that it didn't, but its effects could still be devastating. Consequently, these conversations with my husband were a revelation. Now, I was much more tolerant of the scientific magazines he was always reading, whilst my favourites were Weston's, tales of cow-girls in Stetsons and chaps, riding on the wide open prairies. Such magazines could be bought for a few coppers in the market and exchanged for new ones at half price when finished with.

I think I must have lived a previous life in North America for I always had an intense interest in anything Wild West from cow-girls to the treatment of the native Indians, as well as the history of such mixtures of races and cultures. My interest surfaced on the day in 1925 when Louie and I discovered the old caravan moored in the corner of one of Art Kirby's fields, over the hill and two fields away from the one my Father used for his pigs and poultry.

We had been exploring and gathering bunches of moonpennies, cornflowers and buttercups for our Mums when we spied it there, sitting like something from another world. "I wonder who's it is," I said, "Do you think somebody lives there?" for we could see smoke rising from the little chimney. "Let's go and see," I said, starting to walk across the field. Louie wasn't so sure, but by the time I had reached the short flight of steps to the door, she had joined me. The door was slightly open and, as I gingerly moved up the stairs, I could see inside and an old man standing at a small tortoise stove. He was stirring something in a little black pan but by the time I ventured to tap on the door, he had seen us.

Obviously, he was surprised but when I asked if we could come inside and look around, he opened the door and welcomed us in. "Of course, little girls, come in, take a seat down there," he said pointing to a long bench at the side of the stove. "I've never seen inside a caravan before," I told him, "How long have you been here?" He had been there for a few months he said, since he had retired to England to end his days here. He was 84 years old, he said, and he didn't want to die in America. My ears pricked up at the name America, for remember, dear reader that this was still the era of the Indian, before the days of fast travel and America was a world away. "What was it like? I said, "Have you met any Indians, and what did you do there?" "And why did you go?" I asked; the questions were endless.

Louie was beginning to get nervous, but I put her mind at rest, "It's alright Louie, it's quite safe," I told her, for I knew instinctively that this man would do us no harm. I stretched out on the bench and settled down to listen whilst Louie moved over on to a similar one at the other side of the caravan; I think she felt safer a bit further away from our new acquaintance. The old man gave us each a cup of lemonade and settled himself down on a stool in front of the stove and told his story.

He was born in 1841 and, when he was 16, had left home and gone to America on a free-passage scheme to work on a farm in Ohio, the state which was, at that time, the frontier. He stayed for three years, but left, and came back to England when recruiting started for the War of the Union. By May 1861, he told us, the new regiments formed in Ohio were moving into Virginia and he had no wish to fight for another country.

When the war was over, and he was now 27 years old, he decided to go back as opportunities were better over there and he had chance to work his passage on a small cargo ship. Over the next 40 years, he had moved gradually further west with the migrating population, until he reached Utah. Here his story became really interesting, for it brought to mind the stories my Mother had told us of the 'Shakers', the 'Sankies' and the Mormons, one of whom had returned to her family at Lane Head and tried to recruit members.

The old man told us of the Mormons custom of polygamy, of all the abominable carryings-on in the community, "Such a den of iniquity," he said, "Salt Lake City is the most evil city in the World." Even Louie was intrigued by this and we urged him to tell us some of the 'goings-on', but he said they weren't for our innocent ears, telling us "Never, never, should we go to Salt Lake City; in pain of being thrown into the proverbial pit." Shaking his head, he repeated over and over again, "Such a den of iniquity, den of iniquity."

We decided not to say anything at home about our visit to the caravan, but a few days later my Father said unexpectedly "By the way, don't go near that caravan up in one of the top fields, there's an old man come to live there from somewhere abroad, and nobody knows anything about him." "Oh, he's a nice man," I chirped up, before I had time to think. Dad's roof nearly came off, even when I kept saying he would do us no harm. "I've told you, you don't go near him; don't let me have to tell you again."

From then on, my thirst for that raw west new no bounds, I revelled in the story of Greta the cow-girl on the plains of Nebraska in Schoolgirl's Own magazine and the young bride who had gone out there to be married to a cowboy and her fingers had frozen to the door sneck in the intense cold. I was never interested in cowboys, only the girls, their lifestyle and more than anything, the wonderful landscapes, the Rockies and Prairies and the Indians. My interest has never waned.

At the end of November 1936, a bombshell descended on the country when the Bishop of Bradford disclosed the news, which those in high places and the American newspapers had been talking about for some time, that the new King Edward VIII was having an affair with Mrs Simpson, an American divorcee. This was still the era of empire, of national pride and a feeling of awe and respect the general public had for the monarchy and the shock was intense. The dispute reached a climax when, on the evening of 12th December, the King made his famous abdication speech to the nation. Ears were glued to wireless sets all over the country and there were few dry eyes when they heard him say that he could not go on without the woman he loved.

I desperately wanted to listen on such a momentous occasion, but a wireless set had not been on our list of essential items and a thinking cap was necessary if I wasn't to be disappointed. The neighbours were still comparative strangers, but I did know that the Godwins next door had a wireless set, for I had heard it once or twice when the door was open. As the time for the broadcast drew near, hoping that they would be glued to the set and not hear me, I left our back door, past the high sash window of our dining room and the jennel/passage in between the two houses and stood listening under the dining room window of the Godwins. Every word came loud and clear whilst tears rolled down my cheeks for the poor King who, with all his wealth and status, couldn't marry the woman he loved. I felt a little better after that, the rich and mighty can't have everything, so why should I moan about my lot.

Early in the New Year, it was obvious that there was to be an addition to our family and the baby was due to arrive on the 2nd October 1937. Not that the news troubled us unduly, except that I knew how difficult it was going to be to provide clothes and other necessities for the birth, and after. I had been attending hospital for treatment for weak gland trouble and the gynaecologist had suggested that having a baby might strengthen the glands, so nothing had been done to prevent it. However, when I attended hospital for confirmation, he was amazed to find that I was indeed pregnant, against all probabilities, for the uterus was upside down. "I don't know how the little buggers found a way in," I said laughingly. After deftly messing around for a minute or two, he finally set the offending organ the right way up again and told me to get off home and hope for the best.

Like all expectant young mums, my first concern was the provision of all the items on the list issued by the hospital for the actual delivery and care of the infant for the first few weeks. I thought it was time to confide in my Mother why I was so worried and although she was shocked to hear about the pawnshop, as always she had a solution to at least some of the items. From the blanket closet chest she retrieved a single woollen blanket which, although worn a bit thin was still in sufficiently good condition to make four cot blankets after cutting carefully, hemming all round and blanket stitching with wool left over from knitting. A flannelette sheet was treated in the same way, whilst a cotton one made four cotton sheets with one end bound with satin from a discarded blouse and two pillow under-slips which were stuffed with kapok as feathers were considered unsuitable for infants. Two strips from the cotton sheet made binders 6" x 24" for binding the cord for the first week or two, as although such items could be bought for a few coppers, as Mom said "Every penny counts and sheeting will serve just as well as bought binding."

She gave me her old 'Wheeler & Wilson' sewing machine on which to make them, and a dozen napkins from yardage towelling, another dozen from an old sheet and three nightgowns made from Shantung bought from Atkinson's at 1s.11d a yard. Babies wore gowns both day and night for the first three months but Mom gave me the three cotton needlework day gowns which my three brothers and I had worn. They were very long, covering the baby's feet by about 6" making him easy and cuddly to hold, although they were brutes to iron every day. I was also given the Christening gown we had all worn and still being used by later members of the family. A large knitted shawl, a satin bonnet and a Christening veil completed my son's layette, with woollen vests and matinee coats to be knitted on lonely evenings. Soaps, talcum powder, zinc and boracic cream and powder, safety pins and all the other little sundries could be bought as funds allowed.

Everything went well for four and a half months; however, on the 9th May a threatened miscarriage almost put an end to the 'little chicko' as Frank used to call the babe. I blamed the hospital, for I had that day had a somewhat unnecessary very rough examination and I flatly refused to go to hospital again, not even to take the bed which was to be held in readiness as the gynaecologist thought there might be trouble. Instead, I decided to engage a midwife, one of those women who were allowed to undertake deliveries, provided a Doctor was on call, if necessary. Such midwives, who undertook almost all home deliveries, would also live in the home and nurse both mother and baby for up to a fortnight, (ten days was the normal time).

There were recriminations and the welfare of the babe was put firmly on my head, but finally the gynaecologist agreed, provided the midwife made sure that the Doctor was present at the actual birth. Actually, he wasn't; events moved too fast, but that explanation will come later.

The date of the suspected miscarriage is easy to remember, for I was still in bed when my Mother and Father called on their way to Spalding for the Flower Festival on the 12th May, the day of the Coronation of King George VI. I was to have gone to Lane Head to listen to the Coronation on the wireless and then to Spalding in the afternoon and I was looking forward to both events. I didn't take kindly to seeing that Auntie Julia and Uncle Walter were going instead. In a week I was back in the driving seat once more and taking charge of the daily chores. Whilst carrying a bucket of coal up the cellar steps my Mother put her head round the cellar door to see what was happening. She was visiting on her way from a shopping trip in town and had called to see how I was progressing. Seeing me struggling up the steps with a heavy bucket she nearly hit the roof.

"Frank, whatever are you playing at, letting her carry heavy buckets," she shouted, "You'll have her in bed again, if you're not careful." He looked up unconcerned, "She's alright," he said, "If she can't manage she'll say so," and with that he went back to his book.

A few days later, having heard of a home midwife who lived locally, I decided to pay her a visit to her home in Broadfield Road, about ten minutes' walk away. After explaining the reason for my visit, she agreed to attend the birth and to live with us for the customary ten days of confinement, telling me to contact her a month before the baby was due, unless I needed her before that date. As advised, I visited her at the beginning of September when after making sure I had no problems, she issued this advice. I must go immediately to the herbalist on Abbeydale Road, near the top of Broadfield Road and buy an ounce of dried raspberry leaves. A quarter of these should be put into a large jug and covered with boiling water, left to cool, and taken, an egg-cupful at a time, every morning for two weeks, when I should see her again. "Each brewing," she said, "should last for one week." At the end of the two weeks, I reported and told her I felt very well, on which she told me to repeat the brewing, but for the next week I must drink the concoction just aired and see her again at the end of that time. I did as she bid, drinking the next brew quite warm and seeing her one week before the baby was due.

"Now," she said, "for the next six days, I want you to drink the tea hot and on the last day, as hot as you can drink it, and you'll be alright." The seventh day was the 2nd October and I felt very normal, with no hint of an impending birth. My Mother called and we decided to have a trip into town, as a friend had given me some money to buy a present. We shopped at Atkinson's where I bought a cushion and, as it was a lovely day, my Mother suggested we walk back to Abbeydale Road. I said I could manage it and, after about an hour, we arrived home ready for a good tea. Mother stayed until the last bus, about 11.45 p.m. and after returning home from seeing her off, Frank returned, remarking "The little chicko's not going to come tonight, we may as well go to bed." (Frank had been a Guardsman in Khartoum where babies were called 'chikos' and ours had been a 'chicko' since conception.

We were just about to leave the living room when I felt a minute twinge. We considered for a moment as to whether it was something I had eaten and then decided to consult Mrs Turner. The walk round to Broadfield Road took little more than ten minutes so within the half hour she arrived on the doorstep. "I'm sorry Mrs Turner, I think it's just a false alarm," I said." "Nothing of the kind," she answered, "I'm stopping now I'm here; it's no false alarm," as she bustled about getting used to our home.

We all sat around drinking innumerable cups of tea, Mrs Turner making me walk about almost all the time whilst still drinking red hot raspberry leaf tea. Nothing happened; 2.00 a.m. came and as it was the night for putting the clocks back, so we had to sit through that hour again. Half an hour later, at 2.30 a.m., I felt the first real pang. "Go and 'phone Dr Marshall, tell him to come at once," instructed Mrs Turner, suddenly very business-like. Frank departed immediately, returning a few minutes later saying he had to ring again at 6.00 a.m. "Go back and tell him to come at once," she insisted and as he left, she ordered me to stop drinking the tea and to get upstairs to bed.

Everything was ready, including the wicker cot which Mrs Parsons (Ginger's wife) had given me and which now stood waiting at the side of the bed. Actually it was a cradle with a hood which Elijah had fixed to a wooden base to raise it to bedside level. I was delighted with it for the fashion, for those who could afford them, were the white wicker 'treasure cots' which were decorated with lace and satin and trimmed with lots of bows of ribbon. My baby's wasn't nearly so grand but it had been lovingly decorated with a white satin lining and a floor length frill of blue spotted white muslin. The same fabric covered the hood in lots of fine ruching and broad full frills trimmed the edges of cot and hood, with two huge blue ribbon bows finishing the front of both cot and hood. One of the items I had bought out of a club for my 'bottom drawer' was a small pseudo wicker linen box with a velvet top. I had repainted the box pale blue and recovered the lid with new blue satin and embroidered the word "BABY" across

299

the top. This now stood at the side of the cot, holding all the napkins, gowns and other accoutrements required for a new-born. Of course, it would have been nicer to have provided a real baby basket to hold creams, soaps, talc's and the little brush and comb set and blue soap dish I had extravagantly spent a few shillings on, but as funds didn't stretch to that luxury, I had lined a shallow wicker basket with blue ruched satin, whose folds nestled lovingly around all the items, where they kept clean and tidy by a well fitted lid.

There was no excuse for everything being blue, for I felt sure it was going to be a boy. All the old wives in the village had confirmed this because they said; I was carrying it at the back. The little bath sat on a convenient stool; with white towels ready to wrap the babe in after his first dunking and clean white cloths covered the dressing table beside the bed, ready for the Doctor to spread out his equipment. But, events had moved fast and there was no time, or need, for this. As he put his head round the door Mrs Turned said sharply, "Come on Doctor, there's no time for that, the head's here." And so it was; an hour and a half from the first contraction, my baby was born at 4.05 a.m. on the 3rd October 1937.

Sweeping my wee son up into her arms she made a quick departure from the bed, leaving me in the hands of the Doctor with his needle and thread, for no baby could be in such a rush to see the world without leaving a little damage on the way but seeing him take his first ablutions, held high in the hand of Mrs Turner in front of an open window whilst she squeezed water over him from a large sponge I cringed. No wonder he proved so hardy!

"Now, young lady, tell me what you've been doing," Dr Marshall said, as he sat on the bed when both mother and babe were comfortable tucked in. "Er, nothing," I began, expecting him to be critical of such old wives tales. "Come," her persisted, "Mr Davies expected trouble, and here you are breaking records, and I want to know why?" I told him all about the raspberry leaves, expecting a mild reprimand, or at least an amused grimace, but when I had finished, he said, to my surprise, "Don't think you did wrong, it's very interesting; in a few years' time raspberry leaves will be the standard treatment for difficult births, just you see." I'm not sure that they have become as universally used as that, but I have seen on the shelves of chemists, bottles of raspberry leaf tablets which cost about 20 times more and are ten times less effective than the actual leaves.

I soon realised that Dr Forbes had been right, Frank was susceptible to colds and bronchitis or rather bronchial asthma, particularly during the autumn and this October the emergency was early. Like all prospective mothers, I had been looking forward to the ten days of confinement for that little extra attention which was afforded to the new baby and mother. After nine months of toying with the chores and problems of the household, it was considered a well-earned luxury to lie in bed and be pampered, for a change. But, not with my luck! I was angry, very angry when, after only five days my husband had to spoil everything by having an attack and had taken to the bed in the back room which Elijah had made and Mom had given to me on leaving home. Such inconsideration; such selfishness; why must it be now, when it was my turn to be looked after?

My anger was real to the extent that within a few hours, the milk, which had flowed so readily that it had to be drawn off, now dried up completely. They said it was the shock and I will not deny that I was worried, but the worry was not as intense as the resentment I felt against life and the God who was responsible for all things. Dr Forbes was called. His attitude was rather, "I told you so," which didn't help. Mrs Turner went into the bedroom with him. "Are you his mother?" the Doctor asked. "No sir," she replied, "I'm the midwife, I'm looking after his wife and she's been confined." "Oh my God," the good Doctor muttered, "Don't let her know how bad he is." "Are you going to look after him?" he enquired of her. "Well, yes sir," she replied, "There's no-one else." "My God, this is a nice time for this to happen," he muttered again, as he prescribed medicine and treatment. "I'll see him again tomorrow," he said as he went out of the room and downstairs.

Mrs Turner had no need to tell me, I had heard everything and resentment filled me. There was my husband, who had done nothing in the nine months towards the little 'chicko' he had fathered and he was going to get all the attention and sympathy. Where was the justice?

At the end of the appointed time, Mrs Turner left us and I was on my own, with a convalescing husband and my small son. I soon realised I was 'master in the house' a role, eventually which suited me. Not for me the secrecy of hiding a new dress in the wardrobe, or a small purchase out of the housekeeping money in some secret place until I could reveal it to 'my Lord' as I had seen some of my friends doing; not for me was it necessary to wait for him to be in a good mood before asking for some small necessary item On me rested the decisions whether money matters, or later, the education of our son; where we should live, and where we should move.

Life wasn't easy; the interruptions in our son's routine had resulted in feeding problems, for although all brands of baby food were tried, he refused to gain even an ounce. When at three weeks old and the price of milk was depleting our budget, I decided to take him to the Clinic in Orchard Street where Ostermilk could be bought at subsidised prices. He was weighed and I was allowed to buy a tin of No: 2 food. When he still hadn't gained anything the following week, I asked for one of the No: 2's and the second week, under protest, No: 3. "All his energy is going in activity," Dr Marshall said, for he was never still, even when sleeping.

In desperation, when he was six weeks old, I said I wanted to try cow's milk, but there were loud protests, as cow's milk at that time wasn't guaranteed free from the T.B. bacillus unless from an accredited herd. Ours was, from the farm of Art Kirby, so with the warning that I was doing it without their approval, permission was granted. First it was diluted to quarter strength, then half strength and still the little 'chicko' didn't gain, so full strength followed. Mrs Tomlinson, next door but one, who had always taken an interest in him, suggested Bengers food. This was a weaning food usually given at around three months old. I made a trial bottle, having to cut a bigger hole in the teat and, miracle of miracles, in a week he had gained one ounce.

With relief, I went out and bought a teat with a large hole and every morning made a basinful of Bengers to last the day. This, with neat cow's milk, at the tender age of eight weeks old guaranteed a small steady gain for this racehorse thin little boy of ours. One sad memory of my first trip to Orchard Street was the loss of the 6d piece I had received from Mr Wood the day I left school. I kept it in the front compartment of my housekeeping purse, which I had put on the seat beside me whilst I undid Arthur's shawl and somebody stole it. The little money it contained mattered not half as much as the loss of my 6d, and one of the nurses paid my fare home.

My life now took on the true meaning of housewife; love-making was put on the middle burner where, in my opinion, it rightly belonged, whilst the welfare of my husband and son were firmly on the front one. We were still hard up, but just managed to keep our heads above water. All the pawned articles had been rescued out of pledge, except the canteen of cutlery, but no visitor was going to miss that, for it was my wedding and birthday present. As previously mentioned, had I known that there would be an auction, I might have made an effort to retrieve it, but in my ignorance, I didn't bother and this chapter of our financial life was conveniently closed. However, other obligations had taken its place with three faces to feed instead of two, and as each week wore on, I found that by Friday morning the cupboard; and my purse, was almost bare.

"If I've got 1d for my fare and 2d for a packet of 'tabs' I can manage," Frank said, so every Thursday night, the coppers came out and 3d was passed over. If after that I was left with 3d, all was well; I could go to Brewster's shop opposite and buy a buttered teacake for 2d and a 1d bun and I could manage until teatime when Frank returned with his wage packet. Then the Friday night ritual began. Throwing all caution to the wind and because we were both hungry after our meagre lunches, I paid a visit to the little greengrocery shop two doors away and bought lettuce, cucumber and tomatoes, no matter what they might cost, only two when the first English came in at 6s.0d a pound, a whole half pound when they were cheaper. A tin of salmon from the corner at 3s.6d and we were well set up for our weekly party. At least once a week we went to bed feeling full and very satisfied with life, tomorrow could take care of itself.

So 1938 progressed agreeably towards our son's first birthday, when as a complete surprise, for he wasn't in the habit of remembering birthdays, my Father turned up carrying a wireless set. It was a birthday present for Arthur. By the way we had called him Arthur Scott, because Frank wanted to call him Arthur after his cousin who had had a lot to do in bringing him up, but I disliked the name Arthur because it could be shortened to Art, like Art Kirby, and I detested the shortening; not the man. Scott was the middle name of all the first born Walter Scotts in the Lees greater family, (Aunt Em was Emily Lees) since about 1832 when old Joshua Lees named his son Walter Scott after the poet, who was a dear friend. A plate was given to that first Walter Scott and handed down to each in turn, and now hangs on my spare bedroom wall until claimed by the next. I agreed to our son being called Arthur provided he also received Scott as his middle name and for the first two years I always referred to him as Scott Rundle. The wheel turns, he is now, and prefers to be Art Rundle. What did I say in the first chapter? No matter what parents do towards the naming of their children, someone will come along and change them. Knowing my Father, the present to Arthur was a subtle way of buying us a wireless set for, of course, it was not a present for a one year old and we were very grateful, especially me.

October had come round again and I was very wary as to how Frank would cope with the changing weather. But this year, I was more prepared and when the crisis came at the end of October, I went to the cellar head and fetched out the jar of goose grease which Mom had given me. When I was stocking my pantry before our wedding, she subscribed two jars of jam and the jar of goose grease. "You might need this sometime for Frank's chest," she said, remembering how she had used to rub my Father's chest on many occasions when he had a tight chest. A career in the pits had taken its toll of my Father's chest, as it had on many other mine workers and, although he had never developed the dreaded silicosis, he did suffer from occasional bouts of what he called 'tightness'.

After supper that night, I brought out the jar of goose grease and requesting Frank to lift his vest, was about to dip my fingers into the jar, when I noticed a thin layer of mould covering the surface of the contents. "That's funny," I said, "I didn't think fat would go mouldy, it must be damp on the cellar head." After removing the mould and inspecting the jar for a moment, I plunged in two fingers and removed a generous portion of the healing concoction. On to the bared chest it was slapped, and the rubbing began. "My, it's cold," was the immediate reaction from Frank, but as the rubbing proceeded, his mood changed. "God," he shouted after a few vigorous rubs, "it pulls." "Nonsense," I said, "it's you who are 'nesh'"

And the rubbing continued, hard and vigorous, as Mom had instructed. "To raise the blood to the surface and lift the inflammation" Mom had said.

The skin was now nice and red, the blood was near the surface, I thought, feeling very pleased with my efforts. "It's no good," came a sudden cry from the patient, "It's too painful, I've had enough." "Oh you're being childish," I said, not having any sympathy. "Dad never moaned and he had a mat of hairs on his chest." (Frank's chest was as smooth as a baby's bottom, as the saying goes). Not to be outdone half way through the treatment, I said crisply, "Turn round and let me do your back." Rubbing proceeded as before, but before long it sponsored the same reaction. "It's no good, I've had enough, it pulls like hell," he moaned, obviously in some discomfort so for that night, the treatment was finished.

The next morning, I asked how he felt. "Oh, I'm a lot better, its good stuff that goose grease," he replied, "You can rub me again tonight." So, that night the jar came out again and the procedure followed the same as before. I had been rubbing for only a few minutes when he stopped me. "You know," he said, "I don't know how your father went on with his chest, but I can't stand it anymore, it's too bloody painful." "Oh it's you, you are 'nesh' you're not hard like Dad," I replied but I was a bit mystified. Why should it pull as Frank had said? I had noticed myself that it was particularly hard to rub in. I picked up the jar. "Why would fat go mouldy? Why was it hard to rub in and why should it pull as Frank had said? I looked at the jar again and then decided to taste it. Looking at him I tried hard not to giggle as I said, "Its condensed milk." His face was an enigma, it would be impossible to describe all the expressions of emotions fighting for supremacy as his gaze moved first from the jar then to my face.

"You did say you felt better, didn't you," I stressed firmly. "You can't say it didn't do you any good." He looked at me long and hard, then as we both subsided into laughter, he quipped with a shake of the head, "You silly bugger." If an explanation is called for, then here it is. When I realised, on the morning of our wedding, that we hadn't ordered any milk, my Mother had given to me a small tin of condensed milk to tide us over until Monday. Having opened it on that first Sunday morning, as I had been told to do on similar occasions, never to leave food in opened tins, I had emptied the left-over contents of the milk into a jam jar and put it on the pantry shelf with the other jars and forgotten all about it. This, of course, explained the mould!

The moral of this story, if indeed someone is looking for one, is 'Faith does heal', and I defy anyone who says it doesn't. My medical treatment didn't prevent the usual autumnal visit from Dr Forbes, as even a day off had to be upheld by a Doctor's report. As expected, he more or less said "I told you so," at the same time suggesting that a move to a house with a bathroom might be a good idea, where Frank could dunk himself in a hot bath whenever he returned home wet or cold. We weren't too enthusiastic about a move; we now had a very nice home to which all the family had contributed in some way or another and where an important time of our married life had been spent. But, we decided to consider the possibility.

Gossip among the officers on their daily tramps brought the news of a new estate of privately owned houses being built at Gleadless, a small outer suburb of Sheffield on top of the ridge skirting the south east boundary of the city. Their interest stemmed from the fact that the investors in the properties were anxious to let some of the houses to policemen, as the rents were secure. We decided to pay a visit to the site, as yet undeveloped, with rough dirt roads, and few facilities. My Father, in particular, grumbled every time he drove down Seagrave Road, "These potholes will ruin my springs," he moaned, "why you have to come to such a God-forsaken place, I just don't know."

Nevertheless, on 6th January 1939, we left our first house and migrated to Gleadless in one of the first blizzards of the year. Mom came early in the morning to take Arthur, now 15 months old, for the day, bringing him back in the evening just before dark. It was a bitterly cold day, getting worse as the night came on, but she kept him warm whilst waiting for the circular bus by getting him to run a few yards up Carterknowle Road, running back to her and being caught and swung round in her loving arms. Bundled up as he was in his home-made cloth coat and hat, with a thick wool scarf wrapped around his neck, crossed over his chest and fastened at the back with a huge blanket pin, he was 'as snug as a bug in a rug'. By the time he reached home, his hands and feet were as warm as toast.

The new house was smaller than our first; we had to sacrifice the kitchen for a bathroom, having now to settle for a 3ft x 4ft kitchenette, which held the sink and two shelves on one wall. There was a gas point, but room only for a single gas ring which stood permanently on the draining board. The lounge was slightly larger than the old one and showed our furniture to better advantage, as well as boasting a modern tiled fireplace, which was much easier to clean than the old black Yorkshire range.

A smaller living room meant that we would probably have to dispose of one of our leather easy chairs, which were so comfortable for relaxing after supper. We asked Dad if he could take one, but he was quite upset, "I'm not taking your furniture that you have struggled so hard to buy," he said, "No, you should keep it," so keep it we did. The room was full but when the fire was glowing in our bright new copper coloured Tripless range, which required only a quick wipe over with a wet cloth, we fully accepted the lack of space in the luxury of curling up in comfort.

There was plenty to do, even in a new house, for as the walls dried out; we were advised that decorating could proceed. Outside was a different proposition. It was a new site and our back garden had obviously been used for depositing heaps of lime and sand and contained much of the rubble from the actual excavation for the foundations and only a single thin wire fastened to low concrete posts served to separate one garden from its neighbour. The lime was a problem and I found the most useful way to dispose of it was to spread it across the whole garden, which was 60 yards long and as part of an old field, I guessed it could easily accommodate the extra calcium. The sand soon found its own use, or perhaps it would be more accurate to say that Arthur found a use for it; it soon became his favourite playground, which was the first place to look if something was missing, like the enamel plate from my weighing scales, or the little fire shovel which I used for removing the ashes from the grate every morning.

Our financial situation did not encourage us to speed up the operation, consequently by the end of that first summer; the garden was little improved from its original state. Life was pleasant, albeit our strained circumstances, which the expense of moving hadn't helped. There was sufficient to keep me busy, with little time to think about being poor. Jumpers and suits were knitted for our small but growing son, a new coat and hat was made on the old 'Wheeler & Wilson' which although an old treadle model was very acceptable for my sewing.

So, the months wore on until August when, with much scheming and planning, we arranged with Uncle Arthur and Aunt Bertha to have a holiday at Burnhope in County Durham and we booked seats on the long distance bus which ran from Coventry to Newcastle, calling at Sheffield at noon. The journey was pleasant, although taking about five hours on the old A1 before the appearance of motorways. A half hour call was made at Boroughbridge, where I passed a mouth-watering half hour touring the antique shops which abounded in the town, although I knew I hadn't a 'cat in hell's chance' of buying anything, but they say "It's nice to dream," don't they? Frank preferred to take Arthur for a walk by the river. He had travelled like a seasoned traveller standing on my knee with hands firmly holding the seat in front, taking everything in like a true geographer, only murmuring when there was a call of nature. Luckily, in those days, when coaches didn't boast built-in toilets, there were plenty in the villages we passed through and the drivers were very understanding. This time it was Arthur's time to be introduced and shown off. There were plenty of friends and

308

acquaintances to visit and Frank was proud to show off his small son, so there was, luckily, little need to spend our meagre pennies on travelling.

One day, however, we decided to visit that to visit the north east without a trip to the sea was just not right and Whitley Bay, a favourite place, was only a short distance away. So, on Friday 1st November 1939, the local bus took us to Stanley and on to Newcastle where we intended to catch a tram to Whitley Bay. (Yes, trams did run from Newcastle to the coast in 1939). We arrived in Newcastle, leaving the bus in Marlborough Square, where we could catch a tram. "Have you any money?" came a quick question from Frank. "Only a few coppers," I answered, "Why, haven't you enough for the fares?" not a little worried for I knew he had been to the Club with Arthur the night before. "I can manage the fares," he said, "but I don't think I shall have enough to buy a cup of tea." (We had brought sandwiches with us, thoughtfully prepared by Bertha, a kind gentle soul, who went about the house so quietly and timidly).

When Frank had bought my new dance dress and after all his objections were forgotten, my Father, hearing that I wanted a bracelet had bought one for me. It was a dainty thing with groups of cirio diamonds joined together as a chain. When Elijah saw it he said he would buy me a ring to match, if I would like one. I said I would and it was that ring that I now had on my finger, a prized possession and the only ring, except my engagement ring that I possessed until I was 25 years old.

What could we do? We could go to the coast and eat our sandwiches without tea. We could stay in Newcastle and eat our sandwiches in the bus station with a cup of tea from one of the bars. I looked across the street where there was a row of shops, over one of which was the sign of the 'three golden balls' and an idea sowed its seed in my mine. It would not be the first time we had had to resort to the pawnshop, but I had hoped that those days were over and gone forever. I looked down at my ring. "How much do you think I'll get for it?" I asked. "I haven't a clue," Frank said. "Do you think Arthur would get it back for me?" I said, "We'd have a year to do it." "I don't think so," he replied, "although I don't like the idea of his knowing how hard up we are." Such false male pride.

I entered the shop with the same demoralised feeling I had felt on that previous occasion, with almost the same reaction from the shopkeeper, when he knew why I needed the money. Transaction completed, I left the shop better off by 2s.6d (12½p), a bare finger, and a very sad heart. After a pleasant day, watching Arthur playing with his bucket and spade, which we had rashly bought on the promenade eating winkles bought from an old fisher wife who sat in front of her little cottage at Cullercoats, with the pins she had supplied and eaten all Bertha's sandwiches, we returned to Burnhope to find a minor crisis.

The local policeman, who had called once whilst we were away, appeared again soon after our return, to tell Frank that he was being recalled due to the severity of the situation with Germany. There was a train at midnight from Durham, and we had been booked on it. There was no room for argument, and after all, we would have left on the Saturday anyway. The journey was quicker than the bus and a police car was waiting at Sheffield to drive us to Gleadless. Frank reported early next morning, "The news isn't very cheerful," he said, but that was all. There was a certain amount of apprehensive expectancy in the air that Saturday morning, for we had been kept informed about the situation in the short news bulletin. The last horrible war had ended only 20 years before and many people remembered the agony of it, others had heard it from parents. Still, London and Munich seemed very remote from our village and so life went blissfully on, with little indication from the general public that anything unusual was about to happen.

Everybody had been issued with a gas mask which, we were told, to carry with us at all times and all houses had a mound in the garden which covered the Anderson shelters, to which we must run as soon as the sirens went. But these were only precautions, we all thought, there wouldn't really be a War, would there? By Sunday morning, the 3rd September, it was general knowledge that something was afoot when the news came that Mr Chamberlain would speak to the nation at 11.15 a.m. The rest is history.

Chapter 12

The next few months were spent in relative idleness and, for a time, the extra freedom time to do my own thing was a welcome change. The garden was still in the primitive state it was when we moved into the house and there was a huge hole where the Anderson shelter had been before we sold it to Harry Childs the scrap dealer, as most of our neighbours had done. The first job was to bring some semblance of tidiness to it before winter set in. Frank was no gardener, so the responsibility was mine, not an unwelcome task as I had always admired my Father's achievements and welcomed a chance to have a go.

The ground from front to back was on a gentle rise, with about 30 yards at the back meeting the back gardens of the house in Seagrave Crescent, opposite. The pocket handkerchief size garden we had at Abbeydale Road had offered no challenge; a four yard square lawn, which was cut out with shears, with a small border down one side of the path which led to the outside water closet. This one was going to be much more interesting. My priority was a screen to create a semblance of privacy from the inquisitive gaze of the residents of the house opposite.

Arthur often went fishing in the pond in Bradley's field at the bottom of Seagrave Avenue, once bringing home a large handful of pussy-willow branches for me. I stood them in a vase of water and in a week or two they brought forth the biggest and yellowest 'pussies' I had ever seen, obviously the male Goat-willow. In another week or two they had rooted in the vase and were so healthy we decided to plant one in the garden, which didn't yet exist. It was April 1944, so we chose the 21st to do our planting, the 18th birthday of the Princess Elizabeth, later to become Queen. It grew and flourished to become, in two or three years, a half-standard with a stem about 5ft high because all the buds had been rubbed off to keep it bare, and a head which, in spring produced a beautiful golden ball of 'pussies' more glorious than the most floriferous cherry tree. By 1945, it formed a welcome point of interest about half way down the garden near the fence dividing the houses, still only a single wire hanging from short concrete posts.

I decided that willow would be the quickest and cheapest hedge and as there was an abundance for the collecting, I armed myself with a pair of secateurs and raided Bradley's field, returning with about 20 straight sturdy stems about 6ft long. I had already dug out all the 'twitch' and weeds and excavated to a depth of about 18", so after wounding the base of the stems, it was not a long job to insert them about 18" apart, with some of the strongest trimmings pushed in between to create early foliage lower down. "They'll never grow," shouted the man opposite (a main reason for the hedge!) "You're not expecting them to grow?" said a neighbour. But they did, and after the first year, when the tops were lopped, they made an effective, though not dense screen.

I made up my mind to do away with the slope and create a terraced effect, partly to use the abundance of flat stones which appeared every time a spade was inserted, partly to divide a section for vegetables at the back of the garden.

A crazy paving path divided the lower section, both sides eventually becoming banks of herbaceous plants with pockets of annuals. The path led to two shallow steps, with a low pillar on either side and double retaining walls to the fences on either side, in which aubrietias and other rockery plants could be grown, whilst holding back the soil of the vegetable area. The whole operation found an outlet for the heaps of lime and sand, particularly convenient and useful for the vegetables, as the site had been a rough field before building began.

There were days, of course, when gardening wasn't possible and, as winter drew nearer, I turned my attention to another hobby, which had been put into cold storage during the war. Out came the embroidery silks and a cheval set which had been laid away since the war, and this occupied a few weeks. But the silk ran out and there were none in the shops; fabrics were rationed and time started to lay heavy on my hands.

Idleness is acceptable if one is incapable of doing anything, but idleness inflicted on a reluctant, reasonably intelligent being creates the worse form of boredom. It rests even more heavily if part of the trouble is poverty, the inability to purchase the components to do the job. Cookery was another hobby, but when inspiration comes and one ingredient is missing for that delicious pudding or cake you want to make, you can't afford it, or it is not in the market, enthusiasm wanes and dinner ends up the usual economic 'hotch-potch'. Or if fingers itch to try out those more intricate stitches to be found in Weldon's Embroidery book, you can't afford the coupons, or the silks and cottons to do them. That is self-destructive. But, where there is a brain, then it should be used to find a way out and thankfully, the opportunity to do just that came one day during a boring, hopeless, shop-window shopping expedition in the city when, rummaging aimlessly through a table full of remnants, I came across a piece of fabric 45" square which was marked 'no coupons'. I asked "Why?" and was told that it was dress fabric, but the piece was too small to be used for the purpose, so it could be sold without forfeiting coupons. For the same reason, it cost only a few coppers. I examined it for faults, but found none. It was fine, much finer than the finest of embroidery linens and would require the finest of fine embroidery. It would be a challenge and I decided to buy it, all the way home thinking excitedly how I would use it. For years I had nurtured the idea of doing drawn thread work, never having done the simplest hem stitching since the little round sampler at school. Now I decided to try.

Before the war, it was the practice of many newspapers to offer cookery and household books, as well as items like cameras, in exchange for coupons cut from the newspaper. The Daily Express was one of these and my Mother and I had copies of 'Economical Cookery', 'Elizabeth Craig's Cookery Book', the 'Complete Book of Cookery and Household Management', as well as Home Doctors and needlework books. We didn't take a newspaper, believing it to be a luxury we couldn't afford, so the coupons were saved by my Mother and one book which she obtained for me as a birthday present which I particularly liked was 'The Weldon's Complete Book of Needlework'. It was a mine of information, covering every aspect of needlework and embroidery stitches of such high quality that it offered a real challenge. One chapter contained photographs and diagrams of the most intricate stitches and patterns of old embroideries in the Victoria & Albert Museum, of woven patterns on drawn threads up to 2" wide, and it was these which whetted my appetite. First was the mastery of simple hem stitching on this fine fabric which I had, perhaps rashly, decided to use for the threads were as fine as the finest silk and when drawn, they left a framework of threads that only the most perfect eyesight could distinguish and count. Fortunately, my eyesight was good.

The hem stitching was finished and surveyed with satisfaction and the appetite was eager for more. After studying the pictures in 'Weldon's' I made a broader band in each corner, each with a different combination of designs. An even broader band followed, with even more intricate patterns. Enthusiasm was now travelling at a gallop and there followed, in each corner, a 2" square of drawn threads, each framework filled with a different design from the book. I was really progressing now and thoughts turned to the centre of the cloth.

There was one picture that had always intrigued me. It was a section of a cloth in the 'Museum' showing four or five different designs woven on to a border about 2" wide, a large butterfly filling each corner. Threads had to be drawn to a depth of 2" leaving a framework as challenging as a blank sheet of notepaper in a typewriter when inspiration fails. Even with my good eyesight, I needed a magnifying glass in order to count the threads used in the original, so that the pattern could be worked out on paper to ensure there were sufficient number of threads to complete it.

As time went by, Arthur grew as interested in the cloth as I was, and wanted to know exactly what I was going to do next. One day he said he would like to have a go at hem stitching. A small piece of linen was found on which I showed him how to turn down a hem and draw out a few threads and he 'had a go'. The completed piece of hem stitching is somewhere in the archives with the red and black soldier made in stem stitch on another piece of cloth. Memories of quieter days!

After nine months' work, the cloth was almost complete. All the borders and three butterflies were finished, only one butterfly to go. However, when starting one of these intricate corners, I had to keep going until it was complete, as the fine threads were very easy to miscount, with the danger of losing one altogether, to the detriment of the pattern and it was impossible to unpick and re-do.

One morning, Frank had gone on duty and would be home around 2.30 p.m.; Arthur was having breakfast when he said, "What are you going to do today Mom?" "I don't know," I answered, "I don't think it's a gardening day, do you?" He agreed looking thoughtful. "Mom, why don't you do that last butterfly?" I looked at him and considered the prospect. It was almost 8.30 a.m. he would be leaving in a few minutes for school, returning for dinner about 12.15 p.m. "Tell you what," he said, "You do your butterfly, and I'll get some dinner ready when I come home, how's that?" "O.K", I said, "I'll start as soon as you've gone.

At 12.15 p.m. he came running in through the back door. "How's it going Mom?" is it finished?" he said, running across to have a look. "Nearly," I told him, "I've just got one or two stitches to do." "You carry on," he was so enthusiastic, "I'll get some dinner, will beans on toast do?" he asked. I laughed, answering "Yes, beans on toast will do fine." He put the kettle on the gas ring and impaled two slices of bread on the toasting fork and sat down beside me watching as he waited for them browning. The last stitch was complete. "There," I said, "it's finished," as he piled beans on each slice of the toast. "How do you like it now?" I said, holding it up to show all the borders and squares in all their glory. "Mom, that's great," he said, examining every intricate design. I could see he really appreciated all the effort that had gone into it. "Mom," he said, as he ate his dinner, "When I get married, I want you to give me that cloth for a wedding present." I was surprised at his seriousness. "I won't want anything else," he said, "but that cloth is mine." And so it was, when we went to America just after his wedding, the first thing he said was "Have you brought my cloth?" and, of course, I had.

The end of the war brought changes for everyone. For six years, work and the war effort had been priority but with the return of demobilised men, many to their pre-war jobs, the women who had kept the jobs going found they had more leisure time in which to do their own thing. For both men and women, clubs and Institutions came to life again; Operatic and Dramatic Societies resumed activities, or were newly formed, holidays were in vogue again. For many, who had grown used to an organised life in the Services, the newly created Holiday Camps were their saviours. One of the newly formed Clubs in Sheffield was The Arts Club, which had a craft section, drama group, choral section and social meetings.

How Frank and I heard of the Arts Club I don't know, probably in an exchange of gossip between colleagues in a police box during a lunch break, or possibly through Emo, a neighbour of my Mother's when the family moved from Lane Head. No matter how we came to join, the result was a very interesting and rewarding three years until the club closed in 1948, when most people had settled into a peaceful life and other entertainments and evening schools had become re-established.

For Frank and I there was much to offer. We both joined the Drama Group and enjoyed performing in 'She too was young', when I was the drunken cook and Frank had rather a 'busman's holiday' as the policeman who guarded the door. As one of the chorus of Vestal Virgins in 'The Virgin Goddess', I found voice as an alto, a new approach for me, but there was no doubt that my ability to reach the high notes was abysmal. After deafening our neighbours with my dedicated daily practice, I was rewarded when Elsie Foster, our teacher and conductor, whispered to Frank, "She's good, she hits the right note every time." Frank, like his mother, who was in Easington Choir until the age of 80, had a good voice, singing baritone in all the choral concerts. But when Jenkins Gibson, our producer told me to be a bit more haughty as Lady Audley, I found it almost impossible, subsiding into giggles at every attempt; I was much happier in

316

character parts, sobbing my heart out at some catastrophe or as an old street character or washerwoman.

Frank was not a practical person by any stretch of the imagination, but when the Craft Teacher introduced the new plastic material which had evolved out of war necessity, he spent hours on cutting and polishing two candlesticks, one for my Mother and one for me, and a lovely card box complete with hearts, clubs, diamonds and spades, symbols of the contents, stuck on the lid.

In 1946, my Mother and Father accepted an invitation to spend a holiday at Burnhope, County Durham with Uncle Arthur and his sister May. Arthur was Frank's cousin, many years older, who had helped to bring him up when Margaret, Emily's sister offered to care for him when the twins Kitty and Thomas were born. Frank always looked upon him in a fatherly way rather than cousin and was very fond of him for his help. Arthur had been a groom in charge of the pit ponies at Burnhope Colliery before it closed, when my Father had found a job for him at Strawberry Lea, again with the ponies. He had been a Prisoner of War in 1914-18 after being wounded at Ypres. After lying on the battlefield for some days, he was rescued and sent to Belgium, by which time he was so infested with lice beneath the skin that he had been in grave danger of losing his leg. He told me that the German Doctors were wonderful, particularly one who, when the others wanted to amputate, had persuaded them to leave it in his care. Arthur said he worked tirelessly and eventually saved the leg, albeit was now 3" shorter than the other and required a built-up boot. In consequence, he had a slight limp. There was little more that he could do in the way of work and he was grateful to my Father for at least extending his working life by a few years.

I went to Burnhope with them, staying for the weekend and travelling back with Dad, leaving Mom to continue the holiday with Arthur (our son) for another week. During the weekend we all paid a visit to Whitley Bay and Cullercoats. The beach was still out of bounds, as the last of the barbed wire had not been removed and rationing was still in force. Dad bought winkles from a fisher wife sitting outside her cottage and we walked on the promenade picking them out of their shells with the pins she supplied. Rounding the corner to a row of shops opposite the Seaman's Mission, Dad decided it was time for a cup of tea at the café, but he was rather nonplussed to find there was no sugar and he couldn't drink unsweetened tea. There was a dish of jam on the table, so without a moment's hesitation, he dived in with a spoon and sweetened his tea with a spoonful of jam. Innovation is the child of war!

When Mother and Arthur returned, Arthur handed me a chocolate box which May had found for him containing about a dozen skeins of silk packed carefully in tissue paper. "I saw them in the shop Mom," he said, his face beaming, "And I knew you wanted some, so I bought them for you." They were actually mercerized silks and I doubted that the colours would be fast, but I was determined to use them, if only to please my thoughtful young son. The problem was what fabric to use. To spend coupons on good embroidery linen was not a good idea, for the colours would fade with much washing of a usable cloth, so I looked around for another source.

When war broke out, all windows had to be darkened, either by shutters or black curtains, which could be obtained without coupons. I settled for curtains and had made them from sanitised cotton, which many people bought and bleached it to make into tablecloths and pillowslips. Although cheaper fabric ended rather blotchy and even the best was a dubious cream colour, like many things free from coupons we could 'live with it'. By 1944, my curtains were rather worse for wear and I had replaced them with better quality fabric. When the war was over, it was still in good condition and had been washed and put away for some future use. (Nothing was thrown away during the war, it might be needed at a later date; the beginning of my 'pack-rat habit'). The curtains were rooted out and armed with a bottle of bleach, I set to work, bearing in mind that even the best fabric could disintegrate if it was too strong, or left in too long. I was delighted with the finished result; it was clean, without a single blotch and a very acceptable cream colour. I was eager to test the silks, but first, the design.

All women's magazines gave free transfers and offered special bargains for cloths, chevel sets, table mats and the like, and over the years, I had collected quite an assortment from my Mother, Mrs

Smith and friends who never used them. Amongst them I found just the thing for my purpose, a set intended for a cloth about the size I could manage from my fabric. The corner motive was a large basket of flowers, the set including smaller bouquets for the sides and many single flowers to scatter about the centre. There was just one thing. I had already decided that it would not be a cloth to use, but a souvenir of the war (if that doesn't sound too macabre). The cloth from the blackout and the silks reminding me of my gift and how precious they were in that time of scarcity.

Using a cup, I traced a scallop all around the edge of the cloth and embroidered button-hole stitch very closely so that the surplus could be trimmed away without danger of fraying. This took rather longer than I had anticipated, for the silks were fine and inclined to form knots; not as the usual embroidery silks. But, with determination and perseverance, the edge was finished and the really interesting work could begin.

Three corners were completed and most of the smaller motifs, but before the whole cloth could be finished, other things interrupted and it still remains unfinished, wrapped in a towel which helped to keep it clean. No doubt it will be finished one day take its place with the other souvenirs of war.

1947 brought the saddest day of my life and one which would change my whole life. The cottage at Lane Head had been sold just before the war, after it had been offered to my Father for £200.0s.0d; an offer he refused. Since then, there had been a continuing argument with the new landlady who wanted the house for one of her daughters. The essence of his refusal had been that there were no houses outside the village beyond ours and he refused all offers nearer the village. Pressure mounted in 1947 just as a house on Moorwood Lane, about two miles into Derbyshire, came on the market and he decided to buy it, moving on the 24th July.

Two weeks after moving in we all went to Blackpool for a week, a holiday booked a few weeks before. Dad drove us there, returning home and fetching us back the following Saturday. I remember how he grumbled about the weight in the car. "What the devil have you got in your cases?" he asked, "You must have enough

319

tinned stuff in to last a month," he said "The back end touches the ground after every bump and the springs will be ruined."

Mrs Green had died since our last visit, leaving the boarding house to Maggie, her niece, who had lived and worked for her from the start. Maggie was, as one might say, 'one slice short of a full loaf', not exactly a 'screw loose' but 'just slow on the uptake', which did not reflect in her work for she was an excellent Landlady. However, one day we did query her understanding when having bought a bunch of watercress, Mom asked if she would pick it for our tea. When we arrived at the time we saw a small glass dish half full of leaves, Maggie, who said she had never had to clean watercress before, had thrown away all the stalks.

Whilst we were sitting on the sands, or viewing the shop windows on Bond Street, Mom talked a lot about her plans for the new house. She was full of enthusiasm, looking at wallpapers and curtain materials, bathroom fitments, for she had never had a bathroom before and she beamed at the thought of having a real kitchen instead of a sink in the living room. But especially, Mom thought the new house would encourage Dad to spend more time at home; he had already talked of some of his plans for the garden and was not as ready to leave in the morning. She hoped that his infatuation with Auntie Florrie since Uncle Teddy died would gradually wane. However, Dad was particularly cheerful the following Saturday, wanting to know if we had enjoyed our holiday and talking about things in general. When we entered the living room at the 'Leylands', we realised why my Mother's face descended to her boots as she saw what he had been doing whilst we were away. He certainly had shown an interest, for he had painted the walls, over the paper, with a bright mustard coloured paint. His eyes twinkled as he watched for our reaction; I watched to see Mom's. She was taken aback, sorely disappointed and her silence must have told him how she felt, but poor Dad, in his enthusiasm couldn't understand why we weren't all brimming over with delight at his efforts.

A few years earlier, whilst Dad was still employed as Manager of the mines at Pickford Holland & Company, he had started a ganister mine of his own after surveying farm land at Wessington, about 30 miles away. It was open-cast; 10ft deep cuttings from which, after removing the top soil, to be replaced when work was finished, the clay was removed, followed by an inferior layer of coal, then the deep layer of ganister, the hardest rock which was used for lining steel smelters and brick kilns. On the morning of the 27th August, Mr Riley and the eight workers were waiting for the cutter from the Butterley Company to cut another strip after the last had been carted away and Dad was in no urgent demand. Riley said he always came about 11.00 a.m. after calling in the 'Three Horse Shoes' at Wessington for a few packets of Woodbine cigarettes. Dad believed in a man having a smoke if he wanted one, said he'd rather a man light up when he saw the gaffer coming, it showed he'd been working; rather than the one who discreetly put his out, for he'd been smoking instead of working! Sound philosophy I don't know, but Dad believed it and to this end he asked Riley every morning whether those who wanted to smoke had one, if they hadn't, he was to give them one. It says a lot for the men that, even those who had to count their coppers never abused the situation. Mom said later that Dad seemed very reluctant that morning to leave the house. He played with Jane, Jeff's two year old daughter, for about an hour and then said he'd better be off. It was just before 11.00 a.m. About midday the news came that he had been killed by a small piece of hard clay which had fallen from the top of the cutting, about 10ft hitting him in the nape of the neck, the seat of the medulla, centre of the nervous system. He gasped and was killed instantly.

I heard the news from Frank when he returned home about 2.30 p.m. Aunty Em, Kitty and the girls had been visiting for the day and were waiting to see Frank before leaving. It was obvious from his face that all was not well and when he asked me to step out into the hall, I knew. "Which one is it?" I asked. "It's your Father, he's been killed at work," he replied. I looked up and saw Arthur sitting on the top stair; he had heard. I dashed upstairs as he ran into his bedroom and lay sobbing on his bed. His Granddad had been his hero; had roasted chestnuts with him; had brought him a football signed by all the Chesterfield team when footballs could not be bought in the shops; had played with him and forced him to eat his dinner because it was good for him and he had tanned his bottom when, with Keith Reynolds, he had rolled the coping stones from the wall at the end of the garden down the steep bank on to Penny Lane and had made him carry every one up again. Such discipline demanded respect; the tender moments created love and now he was gone. I didn't know what to say to comfort my son; my sorrow was as great as his, but he was young, had not yet become hardened to the sad knocks in life and he had lost his greatest friend.

Early in May 1948 I received a letter from Miss Marshall of the Nurses Recruitment Service inviting me to return to nursing and offering me an appointment for interview during the following week. When Frank returned home I showed it to him, expecting a very negative response. Instead he said he would not object, even though he sensed that, once I returned, it would be difficult for him to stop me again. "You've never been happy staying at home", he said, "and I suppose we could use the extra money." There was a short discussion, but in the end he concluded, "You may as well keep the appointment."

When the day arrived, I donned my Brigade uniform and set out for the bus stop at the corner of Hollinsend Road. I had been standing there for a few minutes when Mrs Harrison, a village lady I had met in the local, whose daughter was a Land Army girl who worked at Seagraves, the local nurseries, stopped and spoke. "What are you doing in uniform?" she asked, obviously surprised. "I thought Frank didn't like you nursing." I explained, but could see that she was rather dubious about the whole idea and after a short conversation, she made a suggestion. "You like gardening don't you?" she said. "I know because I've seen what you've done in your own garden. They want someone to work with old Herbert in the pothouse at Seagraves, why don't you go up and see Joe Harrison (no relation) the Manager, I know you'd enjoy working there?"

She left me in deep thought. She was right, I would enjoy working in a nursery and I had been a bit apprehensive about the arguments which would be certain to occur after a time if I did go back to nursing. Making a quick decision, I left the bus stop and made my way up Hollinsend Road for about 50 yards to the nursery. The house stood at the top of the drive leading into the nurseries and after knocking at the door, I stood waiting expectantly. With only a short pause, the door opened and an elderly woman confronted me. "I understand," I began "that there is a vacancy in the pot-house. I could see her surprise, a bit mystified. "Mrs Harrison has just told me, Betty's mother," I explained, "I would like to see Mr Harrison if he is available." She asked me to step inside, at the same time telling me that he was having his after-dinner nap; "But it's time for him to start again so he won't mind," she added. "Joe, Joe," she called to the man I could see snoozing in an armchair by the fire. "Wake up Joe, there's a lady here to see you." He raised his head sleepily then, when he could see more clearly, he sat up with a start. "What's wrong, what's the matter?" he asked.

"How do you do Mr Harrison?" I began, "I understand you want someone to work in the pot-house with Herbert, I'd like to apply for the job." His expression was indescribable. For a long time he looked at me then, obviously as mystified as his wife, said "This is a plant nursery lass, not one for kids." Only then did I understand their expressions, for I had completely forgotten that I was still wearing nurse's uniform. I laughed and explained. "Does tha like gardening lass?" he asked. I assured him I did, "That's why Mrs Harrison thought I could do the job." "Tha'll find it different from nursing tha' knows," he said, obviously making sure before committing myself. "I know Mr Harrison, but I know I'll like it," I assured him. "It's hard work lass," he persisted, still dubious about setting me on. "I don't mind hard work Mr Harrison," I told him, "my Father says hard work never killed anyone." "Alright lass, when does tha' want to start?" he wanted to know. I told him "Anytime, as soon as you like." "Alright, tha's got job," he said, "tha' can start tomorrow morning at 8.30 a.m. till 3.30 p.m. wi' an hour off for dinner." I thanked him very much, said good afternoon to Mrs Harrison and left much happier about my situation.

Next morning I learned a bit more about the routine of timekeeping. Two of the local men Horace Coe and Arthur West took it in turns, weeks about, to come in early, in winter to stoke up the greenhouse boiler, in summer to open up the glasshouses and vents, going home for breakfast at 8.00 a.m., returning with everybody else at 8.30 a.m. Their day was a very full one as they came back later to close up and stoke the boilers for the night. My day was shorter as I had made arrangements in order to be at home when Arthur returned from school.

Until I joined Herbert, my gardening had been confined to outdoor work; I knew very little about pot plant growing, but he proved to be a very patient teacher and exceptionally generous in imparting his abundance of knowledge acquired over 60 years of service at Seagraves. Questions, questions, every job he gave me to do brought forth more questions and his explanations were honest, no silly remarks, or jokes, as men usually tease new juniors, so that I never feared, nor hesitated to ask. He said he enjoyed showing an interested worker, finding something to explain a dozen times a day. How to recognise a good loam for making compost; how to mix a compost for 'sykes' (cyclamen) and why a compost for geraniums had to be different. The technique of potting quickly, essential for costing cheaper lines, like primula malcoides, the earliest batch timed for Easter trade on the market stand by charlotte, Joe's sister. There were primula obconica, cineraria and calceolarias and celosias and salvias whose rows lit up the benches like fire. Then there was a lesson on the production of fuchsia cuttings which, said Herbert, were produced much quicker and better if the stock plants had had one good front. There were stock plants of geranium (zonal pelargoniums), Catherine Schmidt, Mrs Pollock, Marechal MacMahon, Happy Thought and my favourite Mrs Henry Cox and pelargonium domesticum in a variety of pinks and begonia rex, crotons and dracaenas, all needing top dressing to encourage more cuttings. I learned from Herbert how to recognise and treat with meths an attack of scale insect on hoya camosa and stephanotis, large old plants with their trailing stems fastened to wires running the length of the glasshouse. I was fascinated by the clusters of hoya flowers, each dripping its supply of nectar as sweet as honey and just as sticky.

By the end of June the immediate rush was over and Arthur West was calling out for help with the chrysanthemums. All the earlies had been planted on one of the plots on the 5 acre field by Arthur and Ray, a 19 year old youth from Sheffield. The lates had been potted and stood in terraced rows, a cane inserted into each pot and fastened to a cross wire to prevent damage by wind.

There were reflexes, incurves, Japs and rayonantes, singles and anemone centered, all requiring watering by hand until well settled in their pots after which, when necessary, they would withstand the stronger flow from the hosepipe. I was assigned to the chrysanthemums and Arthur West. Arthur had been at Seagraves since he was a lad and now in his mid-40s, there was little he didn't know about raising and propagating plants. Furthermore, he was very ready to air his knowledge, not boasting, but when he met someone interested, he talked. And I was interested and he talked. He talked all the time we were running around with 2 gallon cans of water; it was a hot July and the insatiable thirst of those plants was unbelievable.

August approached and the first dis-budding. How to rub off the buds with dexterous flicks of the thumbs from the secured bud to the bottom axel. Which were to be grown on first crown, which were better on the second and varieties which demanded particular treatment appropriate to their individual habit? And those huge Japs, only two to a plant, with huge 'bell-skirts' of petals, each petal enticed into shape with nimble fingers before putting on display on the show bench.

In the early days of Arthur's work at Seagraves, he, like some of the other men, had been a showman and he had not forgotten how to prepare a 'Mum' for the class of three incurves, three reflexes or perhaps a single Jap. His fingers were thick and gnarled with hard work, but were as gentle and nimble as an artist. "Some showmen use tweezers," he said, "but tha' knows Joss, they damage the petals if tha' not careful and thi' fingers never do," as I watched him deliver his lesson on the perfect way to groom a 'Mum'.

As the months wore on, there were the inevitable weeds in the pots and each weed left to grow "eats up all the food tha' puts in to plant." So, with a sharp penknife and flick with the point just below the crown, the offending culprit was brought out without disturbing the surface of the compost. I remember one morning whilst flicking out the smallest chickweed and Arthur was doing the same thing in the next row, chattering away as usual, me listening so as not to miss a thing, when along came Joe. "What's that for Joss?" I heard him say. "What Joe?" I answered, looking up. "What's tha' left that for?" he said pointing to the littlest of little weeds in a pot at the end of my row, "Breeding?"

Then there was one of the more unpleasant jobs. Not that I minded doing it, but after all the routine vigilance and spraying, to find that dreaded insect 'leaf-miner' had dared to encroach and leave his trailing white pattern on those lovely green leaves it spelt murder. Murder in this case meant gripping with thumb and finger over the little bulge clearly identifiable at the end of the trail and nipping like mad, until the little offending blighter inside the leaf was well and truly dead. Just as I had been instructed by Herbert when the trails could be seen on his beloved cinerarias, on them it could spell disaster, as disfigurement of one large leaf of a cineraria could render the plant unsaleable. On a glass houseful of closely packed chrysanthemums after moving in autumn it could be disastrous, if not cleared before the move.

Throughout the summer there were the earlies to bed, tie in place as growth progressed; cutting and packing blooms into wooden boxes as each variety was ready for market. The mid-seasons were planted in beds, later to be covered with sheeting and protected on the windward side with canvas screens, all buds set for flowering at the appropriate time. In September the lates lifted into the glasshouses where they would flower from November until Christmas. The lates planted outside were lifted and planted close together in the glasshouse borders and well watered in to prevent flagging, those in pots set close together, pot touching pot and shaded for a day or two until acclimatised. Attention could then be given to other pressing work.

It was the turn of the geraniums. First, a short spell with Herbert for those cuttings to be taken from specimen plants in pots, then into the small greenhouse, cleared of a cash crop; ready for autumn and winter work under cover, where a pile of outdoor plants had been deposited from which to take an abundant supply of cuttings for potting early in the New Year. This was the time for getting to know the other workers better. There was Betty, Mrs Harrison's daughter and Kitty, another Land Army girl, who had been working outside during summer, and Ray, and Fred, who cycled from Unstone every day and played the 'Stock Exchange'. "You should play with shares Joss," he said, "You are intelligent, and it's easy." "Easy it might be," I thought, if you had the 'where-with-all' to start. I just told him I wasn't interested and left it at that. Horace Coe didn't join us until nearer Christmas. He was a quiet, reserved man, and I had a suspicion that Arthur and Horace 'cramped each other's style', so to speak, and Horace could always find something more pressing to do.

One day there appeared bundles and bundles of wreath frames and a day or two later, the van brought a stack of bags of sphagnum roses. It was time to think of Christmas. Arthur again took charge, pointing to me to sit beside him to be shown how to moss a frame for a holly-wreath. By Christmas there were hundred to do, so speed was a crucial factor but more important, was the right quantity of moss used in each wreath and later correct cutting up of cypress so that the finished wreaths could be marketed at a competitive price. The finished mossed rings were hung on long broom handles suspended in large tanks of water, where they would keep in good condition for later finishing and in November 'greening' started.

A production line was set up in the little greenhouse and great bundles of cupressus were brought in from the market. A lesson now on how to cut 'green' so that there was no waste and there was enough weight in the finished wreath to ensure (or imply) that it was a good wreath. All the wood should be included up to the thickness of the man's finger, but in such a way that it could be disguised by fans of smaller pieces only the very thickest ends of branches were not included. Half the battle was won if there was a good 'cutter' on the beginning of the line, if pieces had to be picked up and put down again as unsuitable, it was a waste of time and led to frayed tempers. For, don't forget, like all such occupations, particularly where men are involved, there is bound to develop keen competition as to 'how many 'as tha' done, and nobody like to be always last on the rung.

Cupressus was tied on, a large piece put down first, then adding some of the small pieces, which might otherwise be wasted, overwrapping with twine, holding fast with the fingers of the left hand whilst a fresh supply is picked up with the right, all the time moving around the frame making sure the frill around the edge is even and not too floppy and the whole frame is neat, secure and a good weight. By December, stabbing began. Stabbing was simply adding the holly, with whatever else the designed wished to add. At Seagraves this was only five pieces of statice incana, no ribbons, no artificial flowers and this is how I have made them ever since.

As with 'greening', a production line was set up and again the cutters were important. Obviously, the best wreaths could be made with all tips of holly, but to use all the tips in one wreath would leave the rest with a mass of cut ends showing. So, the art of the 'stabber' was to mix the pieces, so that all the finished wreaths were as identical as possible. This was doubly important if they were being made to an order and a sample had been used for fixing the 'middleman's' price.

I had a go at all the techniques, from cutting the holly from the branch into tips of pieces of about two pairs of leaves until only the thick stems remained, or were too thick for the mounting wire. Empty flower boxes and lids were reared up along the whole bench, each one as it became filled with pieces, passed to the wirers or mounters. The next two workers attached a wire with a single leg to each good sized piece of holly, or two, and sometimes three if the pieces were small, thereby forming a neat small bunch. As they were finished, bundles were placed neatly in rows in the boxes with heads resting on the rim, the next row reared up in the same way, so that the 'stabbers' could see what size and type of piece to draw out next.

Whereas cutting up both cupressus and holly were important jobs; that of the 'stabber' were the most important for he/she built up the shape, depth and design of the finished wreath. It was a two handed job, one hand underneath, all fingers working, catching the wire as it was passed through the moss and stems of the cupressus, deftly turning it back with the fingers, whilst holding the wreath on the hand, then turning the wreath around slightly for the next piece. The right hand drew a piece of holly from the box without disturbing the rows, pushed the wire in between the stems, through the moss for the left hand to grab. There was no hesitation between each movement, each hand had its own work to do and from start to finish, if the cutter had done the job well, the rhythm of 'right hand pick up, thread through, left hand bend and return wire' was a continuous flow. Only five clusters of berry and five of statice were required to finish the wreath.

The trimmers of the berry clusters were deft with the tips of the scissors, snipping off the leaves from between the berries leaving one or two at the bottom of the 3" stem. A wire was attached to it as before, care being taken to leave it long enough for the cluster to stand above the base of holly. Statice was cut and formed into neat fans, mounted and added in the same way as the berry. Work outside had not come to a full stop during all this time up to the last two weeks. Horace and Fred continued with digging and preparing frames and plots, tidying the herbaceous plots now that all the bunching of cut flowers had come to an end and boxing stools of chrysanthemums and depositing them in frames, to be covered until after Christmas when they would be brought indoors for raising cuttings. Tomato houses were cleared and sprayed and the chrysanthemums were cut back and fed to produce swarms of good cuttings early in the New Year.

Boxes of hyacinth bulbs, which I had helped to plant in boxes of riddled loam, 24 to a box, had been brought into Herbert's lounge around 5th November to be grown on for a week or two before being transferred for the Christmas market. A small pteria major or pteria cretica fern had been planted in the centre of each pot, to grow on after the hyacinths had flowered. Daffodils for sale in pots had been planted at the same time and those for cut flowers had been planted in boxes, some flowers being sold for pre-Christmas and Christmas trade, the rest filling one of the 100ft houses cleared of 'Mums'.

329

Sweet peas had been sown in pots and left to grow in frames for early planting in another 100ft house and boxed of brompton stocks, sown in September and pricked out in October, kept them company, later to be planted with them as a cash crop. Planting took place soon after returning from the Christmas holiday, the stock planted, staggered at a foot apart in the borders, the sweet peas in two rows down the sides of the path and trained up strings to the ridge. It was a joy to be the first to open the doors of the house in the morning, to savour the perfume of both flowers which met one like a breath from a secret garden.

Arthur had taken the first of the chrysanthemum cuttings, the large Japs which required a long growing season and were always propagated in early December or early January. He now continued with the lates, next longest growing, whilst Fred and Ray planted the sweet pea house, the girls helped in all sorts of jobs, from 'sizzling' new pots, scrubbing and disinfecting old ones, to soaking the large bails of peat ready for mixing composts. 'Sizzling', by the way, for those unfamiliar with the term, was simply stacking piles of new clay pots, (polythene ones had not yet been invented), into tubs of clean water, when they made a whistling noise as the air was drawn out of the pot and water took its place. To use new pots of potting plants would have resulted in the pot drawing off water from the plant, obviously of great detriment to the plant.

Horace was in his element. He had been on duty over Christmas doing the fires and vents and had taken the opportunity to sow the first of the half hardy annuals. It was traditional in the nursery to sow lobelia, trailing lobelia and antirrhinums on Boxing Day, as they required a long growing time to reach pricking out stage. The trailing type was required for hanging baskets during March and April. He would now sow the first tomatoes for planting in March in the borders of the glasshouses (ring culture was just beginning but was not universal in the trade), and further sowings of antirrhinums, petunias, stocks, asters, nemesis, French marigolds, calendulas, tagetes, pansies, polyanthus and every other known bedding plant which had a ready sale, would be sown according to the length of their germinating time. Dahlias had been brought in and boxed and put under the staging of Herbert's house, trimmed and turned upside down to dry. Now they would be set upright in boxes of compost and watered to start them into growth to supply plenty of cuttings. The boxed chrysanthemum stools were brought into one of the houses for the same reason.

I started another spell with Herbert. The first thing after Christmas was to clean the whole house, not an easy task with all the stock plants taking up space on the benches. The benches were made of wood and covered with riddled ashes from the boilers, a cheap covering, a method of discouraging slugs and snails and, it got rid of the heaps of ashes which accumulated through the winter. It was on the benches that I first felt arthritic pains in my knees. It is said that we are all susceptible from the day we are born. If that is the general rule, then I suppose I was lucky to reach the age of 33 before I felt the first twinge. Nevertheless, it made me realise that one can't prevent age, no matter how one tries to disguise it.

Firstly all the ashes were scraped into heaps so that any weak or rotted boards could be repaired. This meant climbing on to the bench and, with a piece of wood, usually the side of a broken seed box, scraping out all the nicks and joins between the boards and the sills so that the disinfectant could reach all parts. The inside of the glass was washed down with disinfectant, at least as far as the arm would reach, above the benches being the most important areas. Then the hosepipe was turned on to give a good wash down and gallons of disinfectant were sprayed on to the heaps of ashes, cleaning them of leaves and other debris, before spreading again over the new sterilised bench.

Herbert was sowing seeds and taking cuttings and when all was clean and tidy, I joined him. Coleus stock plants had been watered to start them into growth and the first batch of cuttings had been taken by the end of January and seed had been sown to supply an abundance of new colours. One bench held newly potted fuchsias from cuttings taken in November and December; another was filled with small pelargoniums and zonal geraniums for indoor decoration. I was in time to help with potting the next lot of geraniums, fuchsias and the final potting of hydrangeas which would be grown on until

331

July, when they would be stood outside in frames, to be brought back in September or October for 'bringing on' for sale in the following spring. There were baby cyclamen to be put into their first pots from the seed boxes, where they had been pricked out from an August sowing, taking care, as Herbert said, to firm the compost well before planting the corm so that two thirds of it was above soil level, then by applying water only around the rim of the pot, none would enter the crown of the corm causing it to rot.

Then came the turn of the begonias, lots of them from the large leaf decorative ones like begonia rex, to Cloire de Lorraine, which when ready for market were ablaze with clusters of pink flowers. Herbert had prepared the leaf cutting from the rex plants, thinking large healthy leaves and 'nicking' the back of the ribs at about 1" intervals, then laying them on top of a moist compost in a large seed pan and placing them in a closed propagating frame set up on one of the benches. They were now ready to be potted into very small pots, size 80's later to be potted into 60's and 48's for sale, usually around Christmas. Batches of cuttings had also been taken, as well as seed sowing and some of these were ready for potting, as well as the calceolarias now ready for their final pots, by which time it was my turn to move on, to help Arthur with the chrysanthemum cuttings.

There were thousands of them, or so it seemed. After watering and being brought inside, the stock plants had been working overtime in producing cuttings, now the turn of the earlies and dozens of 60's pots stood on the benches each carrying five cuttings around the edge and a bench at the end of the house had been turned into a propagating bench, where cuttings were ranged in close rows, sprayed regularly and shaded for the first two or three days with sheets of newspaper (mist propagation had not yet arrived). For those who are not conversant with the sizing of pots and are beginning to wonder, it simply means how many clay pots can be accommodated on the trays for firing in the kilns. If it is 80, they are 80's, if it is 60, they are 60's, 48 they are 48's, the last being 5" diameter. Simple as that.

By the time all the cuttings were taken, it was time to move on again, this time for a session with Horace in his tomatoes and bedding plants. The tomatoes for planting in the glasshouses were potted and standing like rows of tiny oak trees. They would go into their final planting during March. Those for later sale as plants were pricked out into small 60's, (3") when the two seed leaves had fully opened and stood in rows on the benches until space ran out, when they were transferred to the floor of a large house until marketed.

My first sight of a bench full of newly potted tomatoes was fascinating and showed; Horace said that they had all 'taken' for in early morning the two leaves were standing upright like oars in a boat on 'Boat Race' day. As the daylight grew brighter, they lowered them stretching them out as if to welcome the day. "They put their hands together to pray at night," said Horace, "and give thanks at dawn." Pricking out bedding plants was a continuous task, from morning to night. First lobelia, pricked out in little clumps, taking a pinch between finger and thumb, making holes with the dibber, six along the end of the box, eight down the sides, roots carefully inserted and settled in with a gentle pressure from the dibber at one side. Arthur and one of the boys came in to help when the weather was too bad to work outside. "One press wi' thi' dibber, no patting," said Arthur. "Tha' knows Joss, most newcomers pat, like this," and he demonstrated, inserting a seedling then patting at the side, then the other side, making a real 'meal' of it. The demonstration went on for quite a few seconds, pat, pat, then a grimace, and pat, pat again, getting closer and closer to the bench for the final pats. "By the time they've finished, poor bloody plants had it, it's dead." All this was in fun of course, but the lesson was serious.

I went back to Herbert towards the end of April. Most of the bedding plants were outside in frames hardening off for marketing and the rooted cuttings of dahlias which I had helped Arthur to take from the tubers were potted and growing on in the bottom house and Arthur was sorting out chrysanths ready to start planting at the beginning of May. The routine with Herbert was similar to last year, after which I joined Arthur and later, Ray and Fred for potting the lates. This was done in a lean-to shed, the turf stack being close at hand and a good area which served as a 'wetting' ground for wetting the bales of most peat for indoor composts. This last potting was done in loam, not riddled, in 10" pots which were well crocked for good drainage. "Tha' needs a rammer," Arthur said, "Wait a minute, I'll make thi' one," and away he went to come back a few minutes later with a piece of wood, about 10" long and about as thick as my wrist, the ends smoothed and worn with much 'ramming'. He had made my first 'dibber' for pricking out from the handle of an old paint brush, but this was a spare one of his own, used for many years and has since been used for many years more by me.

After 'crocking' the pots were half filled with loam using a small 'copper-fire' shovel. A plant was lifted from the box of a dozen, where they had been planted from the propagating benches and loam was piled around the pot, firmed first with the fingers, to set the plant firmly in the centre, then the soil was rammed again very firmly all round with the rammers, more being added if necessary, to bring the surface up to a ½" below the rim, the space allowing for watering. A final ram, a good watering and the plant was ready to be carried to its place on the terraced ash-bed and when the row was complete, canes were inserted, ready for tying in when the plants were high enough. From then on, my work was the same routine as the previous year; except for odd moments when I was called to do something when no-one else was available.

One of these times was when a man from the village came to buy a score of sprout plants, sown in frames by Fred during April and by now ready for final planting and selling. I soon learned to recognise the difference between sprouts, cabbage and cauliflower plants and the art of pulling single ones out of the mass without disturbing the roots of the rest, but it was inevitable sometimes that a little 'runt' would come up no matter how one tried to be careful. This time Joe happened to be passing and he called me over. "Joss, when tha' serves brassicas, never put runts in, they'll only come back and tell thi' they've one short." I thought this very strange but clocked it in my memory for future use and found later that Joe was quite right. "There's nobody as queer as folk and they'll do ought to get sommat extra, if it's only a sprout plant," he said.

Another occasion when I was aware of Joe's philosophy was when I was assigned, with two of the men, to dig in between the rows of roses, after they had been pruned back hard in April in order to produce long-stemmed flowers for the market stall and for wreaths. I was digging with my back to the wind because I don't like wind in my face. Joe was on his inspection rounds when, seeing us digging, he shouted "Joss, tha's got thi' back to t 'wind, turn thi' arse round and get thi' face to it." I called back that I didn't like the wind in my face, but he insisted, "It's a lumbago wind, tha'll gi' thisen back ache if tha' dunt shift thi' arse round." I did as he bid, no point in inviting 'I told you so remarks' if they can be avoided.

One day I was asked to go up to the top of the five acre field to join a team who were to dig it over ready for planting. We were to do single digging, in a team of five, one starting the first row, the second digger starting when the first had gone about 6ft, the third starting when the second had gone about 6ft along the second row and so on, whereby five rows were turned over at the same time. "Thee go first Joss," Arthur said, and I did just that, until three rows had been started, then I realised why I had been told to go first. I have already said that there were no silly jokes, no teasing, no sending me to fetch a left-handed hammer, but here I knew, was the equivalent, as cries came first from one, then the other. "Come on Joss, get a move on;" "Go on Joss, that holdin' us up." "Put some petrol in thi' spade Joss." "No way," I shouted, "you buggers, you did that on purpose." They all laughed as I ran to the beginning and took the place of last man. "Now one of you can be first," I cried, "See who can keep up now." Of course this was all good natured and only one occasion when a woman had to prove she was as good as any man, many times working harder just to prove the point.

It took a war to make men accept women into their little world and Seagraves was not alone in its attitude to them. All the men were polite to me, particularly as I was a married woman; Betty and Kitty were teased rather more and I was told that when Betty first arrived early in the war as a Land Army girl, the reception was somewhat cold and derogatory about women who, the men thought, wouldn't be able to do the job. Another reason why women had not been

335

welcome was rather more personal. I was told, as soon as I arrived, that the toilet was up at the house, but as time went on, I used to see the men disappearing behind one of the glasshouses which backed on to a high hedge and none of them were seen going up to the house. I wondered what was behind there, knowing that behind the other houses were cold frames used as standing grounds for stock plants. One day I was so curious I asked Betty, "What's behind that glasshouse, I see the men going there, but nobody else?" "Oh, there," she replied, "That's where their closet is." I gaped, "I thought I hadn't seen any of them going up to the house," I said. "No," said Betty, "There's a big tub round there with a board over the top with a hole in it," I nodded, but at her next words I was again curious. "Wait till tomatoes are ripening and you'll see what happens to it, they don't know we know, but we've seen 'em."

Just as she said, when the tomatoes were swelling all three women, who had done all the watering with cans up to now, were told to keep out of the tomato houses; the men would do it from now on. Sometimes when we were not there to see, the contents of the closet were spread on the borders beneath the plants and the hosepipes were fitted for the copious watering they would receive to water it in. One day, passing by, I decided to have a peep in but the stench of the 'night soil' was more overpowering even than our old closets at home and I went no further. My Father used to say that the closet emptying put flavour into the celery and he was probably right, for later, when I was serving a woman with a pound of tomatoes she said, "I love Seagraves tomatoes, there's a lot more flavour in them than anybody else's."

Now, I must confess that, if the ultimate in education in my young days was the ability to speak French, then I also confess that the ultimate in garden craft at this time was the ability to bud roses. I had seen illustrations in books and had learned about the method in the Correspondence Course (which I will tell you about later) but I had never had the opportunity to try. However, this omission in my education was destined to be rectified. One day in July when working up in the top field, I was working very near to the rose beds where Arthur, Fred and Horace were budding briars we had

336

prepared the previous October, fastening them into bundles of 25 and heeling them in until January to callous over when they were lined out 1ft apart, to make a good root system ready for the present operation. "Does tha' want to have a go Joss?" Arthur asked. "Oh yes," I couldn't wait. "I've got my knife in my pocket," I told him. (It was a budding knife which I had been advised to get when I wanted my own for taking cuttings and I was glad now that it was going to serve another good purpose).

Deftly following Arthur's instructions, keeping the bud in my mouth to keep it moist until I had made the 'T' cut and then slipping it inside as I had seen him do, and then, pulling a length of raffia through my mouth to moisten it, carefully tied it in place and hoped it would take. Arthur was so pleased, he suggested I do one or two more, "That's a real budding budder," he said. "Now, come next spring, tha'll see how good tha' are, when they show if they've taken." Sadly, I wasn't there to see such a miracle, much would happen before then.

When I first started working at Seagraves, it didn't take me long to realise that I was really interested, more than just a job, and I decided to learn as much as I could, starting with a gardening magazine, in which there were advertisements for two or three Correspondence Schools, one of which taught for the General Certificate of the Royal Horticultural Society. I made up my mind to have a shot. Whatever job was current I believed in learning as much as possible about it. The examination was in March 1949 and I was allowed to take it at the Vicarage at Totley with the Vicar supervising. The results arrived in August; I had passed, and with quite good marks too, particularly the Botany paper. It was a new subject to me, and I enjoyed it immensely.

I said nothing about this at Seagraves, it was only for my own satisfaction anyway, but one day in October, when Frank and I had arranged to go to Sheffield on business and he was to meet me at 3.30 p.m. at the nurseries, he was waiting outside the office talking to Joe when I crossed the yard to wash my hands after lifting wallflowers for market. I waved as I passed, learning later what Joe had been talking about. "Aye, she's a good worker is Joss," Joe had said, as he saw me wave. "She's enjoying it," said Frank, "She's always liked gardening." After a pause, he asked Joe "Has she told you she's got the R.H.S. Certificate?" "No, she hasn't, when did she get that?" Joe wanted to know. "She took the exams in March," Frank told him, "She's been taking a Correspondence Course, and got the results in August."

In August 1948, Frank left the Police Force, along with about a dozen other officers. Since the return of the reservists there had been a lot of discontent due to the feeling that they were being overlooked in favour of the young men who were being turned out of the new Training College at Harrogate. The rot started almost as soon as the reservists resumed duties after their Army discharge in 1941, when they were each expected to take one of the College trained officers 'under their wing' so to speak and initiate them into the rigours of street work, a part of training, Frank said, that was not covered at the College. "All their training is theory," he said, "and that doesn't make a 'copper', they're still wet behind the ears." The real grievance was that some of the 'old stagers' had reached the stage where they would expect promotion to Sergeant and some of them were even on the short list, including Frank, but the new policy was to promote the newcomers over their heads and they resented it. Having missed the chance when they were recalled to the Army, they now looked like missing a second chance, in fact, as they saw it, the only chance and they were not prepared to take it.

Some went into security work, some became Private Detectives, others, including Frank, went into business, not altogether the right job for him, as I said to Peter, the Sergeant who was considering taking him as a partner. "He's not a business type," I told Peter, one day when he came to see me to talk about the venture. "He'll be alright, I know," he said, "I've worked with Frank for 14 years and we get on like a house on fire." "But, he's not cut out for business," I insisted, "He'll never stand the strain of business, let alone manage a shop on his own."

Before joining the Police Force, Peter had been in the wallpaper business and had contacts with Crown Wallpapers and other firms where he could obtain supplies. As with many things, wallpaper was extremely scarce after the war and still so in 1948, so Peter knew he was on firm ground and could sell everything he could manage to buy. He was to buy from the factories and be his own 'rep' for orders from large firms, whilst Frank was to manage the retail shop. Then, as the business grew, a second shop would follow, which I would manage. The scheme was foolproof, or so it seemed but first of all, it meant trying to someone to exchange houses, as this was all going to happen in Derby, the town of Peter's 'roots'.

They both left the Force in August, Peter selling his house and moving to Derby but until we could establish an exchange, Frank had to go into lodgings, returning on Saturdays until Monday mornings. My prediction proved correct, as Peter finally accepted. Frank had been an excellent soldier and an equally excellent policeman, but he had no knowledge of business, or how to deal with fickle and unscrupulous people, coupled with the fact that he had little stamina. What would be the smallest job for a fully healthy person was a drawn out agony to him and the last straw hit his back one day when Peter returned to find the advertising stickers still on the windows, half scraped off, when the goods had been sold and the new stickers were waiting. He was very cross when he was told that many attempts had been made to remove them, but Frank explained, "Its hard work, I can't do it all at once."

I understood when he returned home that weekend and said he wasn't returning to Derby. They had mutually decided that it would be best for him to leave and so here he was. I couldn't altogether blame him, my criticism was for Peter, who thought he knew the man better than his wife and couldn't distinguish between the work of a policeman and that of a retail shop. The greatest blow was that the entire gratuity he had received had been spent by Frank in the nine months of this unfortunate episode. In modern terms it will not seem a great amount, but £169 was a great deal of money when wages for a policeman were £6.15s.0d a week (£6.75p) including 15s.0d rent allowance.

Now, with no job and no trade, a great big thinking cap had to be donned to get us out of the situation. Dole money was a pittance and even with my contribution, the future looked bleak, but Frank had an idea. As a policeman he had been a member of the police band. As a young boy, suffering from asthma, the village Doctor had suggested he learned to play a wind instrument and the trombone had been chosen because the Burnhope band could always find trumpet players, but trombonists were thin on the ground. So, to strengthen his lungs, he became a trombone player and at the age of eight went to the Crystal Palace with the Burnhope band to play in the competitions there.

Now, he fell back on this talent, not as a policeman, but as a transport worker. The Sheffield Transport Department had a silver band almost as good as that of the police, but to be employed as a bandsman, he had to be shown on the payroll as a worker and having no trade to be so described he was employed as a bus cleaner, at a wage of £4.10s.0d a week.

By an ironic quirk of fate, after we had been trying for an exchange house for nine months and had we obtained one, things would have turned out differently, we now had an offer which I, not only felt but knew, we must accept. Our Landlord had bought our house, along with many others on the estate, as invested property. He now wanted to raise some cash and had told Mr Saxton the Agent who handled the rent collecting, to choose eight policemen who, he thought, deserved to buy their own houses at half the market price of £650.0s.0d, not an unusual arrangement as sitting tenants were, by an unwritten law, allowed to buy in this way. Mr Saxton called for the rent the following month and told us he had chosen us as one of the lucky ones. When he had gone a discussion began, although I considered there was no cause for discussion, it was a chance to make some money and there should be no question of refusing. Frank thought differently. "How the hell are we going to find the money to pay for it?" he said. "Like everybody else, with a mortgage," I replied. "But we shall have to find something for the legal charges, and we haven't got a penny." He said. "Mr Saxton says the local charges will be about £39.0s.0d, I'll ask my Mother to lend it to us," I told him and the following Friday I did so.

"We'll pay you back as soon as the transaction is over," I told her and with that, she agreed, but stressed that she must have it back

340

as soon as possible. The next time Mr Saxton called I told him we would buy the house and he set the whole wheels in motion. He was a Sheffield Estate Agent and this was a simple arrangement for him. The inside of the house had been kept in good decorative order, as the description always says, whether it has or not, but the outside had not been painted since it was built eleven years before so the first job was to get it done so that we could make a quick sale later. We managed to raise sufficient for the paint and a ladder was borrowed from one of the neighbours and painting began, not by me, this was a job Frank could do exceedingly well and in a day or two we had a red and cream house which looked bright and inviting.

The legal business didn't take long and in about two weeks' time we owned our first house. However, when the bill arrived for the legal charges, they weren't £39.0s.0d, they were £79.0s.0d. "Now what are we going to do?" said Frank, "Where are we going to get £40.0s.0d?" "That's easy," I replied, "I asked my Mother to lend us £39.0s.0d, you can ask your mother for £40.0s.0d." "I can't do that," he said. "Why not," I insisted, "She's got as much as my Mother; of course you can ask her." The next weekend he paid a visit to Huddersfield, where she lived with his sister Kitty, and came back with the £40.0s.0d. The legal charges were paid and we became the legal owners of our first house.

"Now what are we going to do?" Frank said, now really worried. "How are we going to pay the bloody mortgage?" "We'll get another house," I told him, to which he made the quick reply, "How, clever bugger, how?" "I'll go out and find one," I answered, not really knowing how the hell I could, but was determined to have a good try, if for no other reason than to save face. The first thing was to go to the newsagents to buy a paper advertising houses for sale and to find one in a price range we could afford, whilst leaving as large a sum as possible to set us up in some type of business, for Frank had an ambition to be a Security Officer and no experience towards becoming a Private Detective as some of his colleagues had done. I saw nothing for it but for us to buy a piece of land and start our own nursery, otherwise our new-found wealth would go on just keeping body and soul together, with the same poverty when it had all dissolved away.

I found an advertisement for a house in Albert Road, Meersbrook, at the asking price of £800.0s.0d. This looked promising so, as soon as I finished work and Arthur was fed and left to play, I set off to examine it. I had little idea where Meersbrook was, nor what kind of district to expect, but having found Albert Road, was anxious to see what the advertised house was like. Anxious was an understatement and well justified, for when I saw it; my heart plummeted right down to my boots. It was little more than an 'up and down' house, one room upstairs with probably a minute box room over an even more minute kitchen. It wasn't only that I would never wish to live in such a place, nor in such a street, but that I couldn't see the possibility of a quick sale later, necessary if plans went as I wished.

However, as I had come, I might as well see inside, but when an old man answered the door and I had a glimpse of the interior, I couldn't face it. "Oh, I'm sorry," I said, "I think I've got the wrong house," and left in a hurry. 'Now what?' as Frank would say. How could I go home and tell him I hadn't found a house. Almost in despair, I started walking, first to the end of the street, then blindly turning right into Lismore Road. I had gone only a few yards when, passing a pair of stone villas, I noticed a large piece of paper fastened to the front bay window. Curious, I crossed the road and saw that it was a requisition notice put there by the Council. After the war, when so many men were returning and houses scarce, they were allowed to requisition empty properties after one year, obviously so in this case. I went through the gate and took a look through the window. All the furniture was there, as if the house was inhabited but when I went down the path at the side and looked in through the back windows, there was an even bigger surprise. It was as if someone had just left the breakfast table and the butter pot and the marmalade pot, both minus their lids, the teapot and other crockery were all there. If this house had been empty for a year, I wanted to know why?

Nipping over a back fence, I knocked on the door of the adjoining house and the door was opened by a woman, a little older than me, a girl of about four years old by her side. An older woman, who proved to be the woman's mother; hovering in the background. "Excuse me," I began, "I'm interested in the house next door, can you tell me anything about it?" She was a pleasant woman and although hesitating for a fraction of a second, she confirmed that it had indeed been empty for over a year and was to be auctioned as the notice said in two weeks' time. I asked a few discreet questions and soon she loosened up a little, eventually inviting me inside. "You know," she said, "I'd like to have you for a neighbour, come in. Would you like a cup of tea?" I said I would, as she continued, "I'll tell you all about it." It was a saga. A spinster by the name of Miss Lees had lived there and owned the place, but after the Sheffield blitz she had panicked and fled to Leeds to stay with her brother until the war was over. But the war lasted for another five years and the house had been empty ever since. The Council were quite in order to auction it, unless it was sold privately, which would suit the spinster better as the Council would take a percentage, plus expenses.

"Would you like to see inside?" asked the neighbour. I said I would and she produced a key, left by the spinster, but with no instructions to take care of the house, such was the hurry to leave. The state of the house was appalling. The butter, and marmalade, the remains of a loaf, in fact the whole table was covered with mouse droppings. The cellar-head (the pantry) was just as bad. Cobwebs were hanging all over the ceilings and walls and dust was everywhere. "God, what a mess," I gasped, "Five years of muck," but strangely there was no sign of dampness, nor any musty smell, except that of the mice. I remarked on this. "Well, you see," said the neighbour, "They were built by Miss Lee's father, he was a builder, consequently they are sound and as well built as they could possibly be.

We went back to her house and during the rest of our conversation; she disclosed the vital information which led me to pursue the matter further. I had ventured to ask if she knew what price Miss Lee was expecting from a private sale. "I know," said the neighbour, "that she'll accept £1,000 for a quick sale to prevent requisitioning." I was more than interested, as she could see. "I'm sure you could get it for that, if you saw the solicitors," she finished. I left the house and made a beeline for the Solicitors office, not far away.

"I'm interested in a house in Lismore Road," I informed the man who answered the bell on the counter, "the one with the requisition notice in the window," I added. He looked a bit surprised and hesitantly told me what I already knew, that the owner was ready to sell before the auction if a suitable price could be agreed on. "Would you like a key to look inside?" he said, as if half expecting me to say no. I didn't tell him I had already seen it, and accepted the key which he offered. After going back up to the house and staying long enough to let him think I had viewed it both inside and outside, I returned to the office. Taking the key, he asked me what I thought about it and, not wanting to appear too eager, I nodded, pulled a wry face and said "It's a right mess isn't it?"

He grimaced and mumbled something about being not too bad. "It's terribly dirty," I said "and all that mouse dirt," I pulled a face, hoping I looked sufficiently put off. He seemed uncomfortable as I continued, "and there's a horrible smell about the place, is it damp?" "Oh no." he was ready and I suspected relieved to have something positive to say "That's certain, it's not damp, even in the cellars," which I knew because I had examined them minutely. "Would you like to make an offer?" he said very meekly, rubbing his hands like a Jew hoping to make a killing. I hesitated, not wanting to appear too eager for I wanted this house for the £1,000 or I'd know why? "Well," I began, then after another pause "As it's in such a bad condition, would the owner accept £800.0s.0d?" I knew this was too much to ask for such fine houses which only needed a good clean, but I felt I had to go down a bit, so that he could appear to be driving a bargain. "Just a minute," he said, more eagerly now, "I'll just go and ask my Partner," as he disappeared through the door into a back room, emerging in only a few seconds asking "You wouldn't like to make that £1,000 would you?" Considering for a moment I said, "Would the owner accept £1,000.0s.0d?" "I think so," came his reply. "Alright," I agreed, "I'll raise my offer to £1,000.0s.0d." He quickly disappeared into the back room again, very soon reappearing to ask

344

"Is that a firm offer?" When I said it was he said, "Alright, the owner will accept your offer." The next statement nearly put me out of my stride. "We shall require a deposit of £100.0s.0d," he said, "Can you do that, it's necessary to clinch the sale?" I didn't hesitate. "Oh yes, that will be alright, but I haven't got that much with me, I shall have to go back home to get it." "That's alright," he said as I left the office with heavily beating heart, and little idea how I was going to get £100 just like that. Then the Gods struck with an idea. Mr Saxton would be selling our house; I'll go and ask him.

"I need £100 Mr Saxton," I blurted out as he came through his office door and asked if he could help me. "What the devil do you need £100 for, you're not in trouble are you?" he looked worried. I unfolded the story of the house and why we had to sell the one we had only just bought, he cheered up and positively glowed as he realised which house I was talking about. "Is it the one at the bottom of Lismore Road?" he asked. I said it was. "The one that's up for requisitioning?" I nodded. "And how much did you say you'd paid for it?" I repeated £1,000.0s.0d. He put his hand into his pocket and whipped out a cheque book, not hesitating for a moment in writing out a cheque. "It's the best bloody house in the district," he cried excitedly, "if you can get that for £1,000.0s.0d, grab his bloody hand off," he added, as I made for the door, "you've obviously got an eye for property, go out and find another, I'll get you £1,500 for that one next week."

I didn't go out and find another, I knew Frank wouldn't settle for that and I wasn't ready to entice his wrath any further, at least not yet! We moved into the new house on 1st September 1949, having sold the old one for £1,350.0s.0d. It would have fetched £1,500 Mr Saxton told us but as property was levelling down a bit and so that the sale could be completed quickly, we settled for the lesser amount.

There followed six weeks of hard and mucky work, whilst I cleaned and decorated from top to bottom, attics to cellars, stripping walls, scrubbing floors, lime-washing and papering. The kitchen, however, I decided to turn over to a professional decorator. The walls were thick with grease, the ceiling black with dirt and I bawked at scrubbing all the gunge away before I could paint it. I gasped when the decorators moved in and started painting on top of it. "Aren't you going to scrub it off?" I asked. "Good God no," came the reply, "Don't worry Mrs, when we've done, it'll be underneath, nobody will know." I was disgusted to think of all the work I had put in, but I wasn't going to live in it and the new owners would never know, so I let it pass.

Whilst all this was going on, I was still working at Seagraves but it was pressing for us to find a piece of land suitable for a nursery before we spent too much of our money. Arthur had passed the 'eleven plus' examination, commencing at Nether Edge Grammar School the same week as our removal, so he left home each morning, returning in the evening and started having my lunch in one of the small houses on the nursery. A new Math's teacher commenced at Nether Edge School at the same time as Arthur; in the shape of Young Senc, Old Senc's only son. Old Senc was Senical Augustus Boule, the husband of Joe Harrison's sister. Young Senc had been given the same name, a family tradition. He was an extrovert as his father, as Arthur West used to say, "If you want to get on the right side of Old Senc, give 'im a packet 'o salted nuts, he'll be able to sup more pints."

Young Senc entered the classroom on the first morning in cap and gown and walking solemnly to the front of the class, stood there, first slowly removing his mortar board, then the gown, rolling it up into a ball and dropping both into the waste paper basket with a flourish. Then wiping off his hands as if to imply a job well done; he turned to the class, saying "OK lads, fair enough". Needless to say he was popular with the class after that and didn't mind a bit when he was given the nickname 'Fair Enough'.

Between leaving University and taking up his first teaching appointment, Senc helped on the nursery, doing one of his favourite jobs, he said, painting and re-glazing the greenhouses. We were working on one glasshouse during the autumn half term and he was joking about some of the funnier aspects of teaching. When he knew that my son was in his class, he stopped joking, unusual for Senc and very seriously said, "You know that lad of yours would be a genius if the little bugger would work." I was surprised, as all Arthur's reports from Gleadless had been excellent.

"That's the trouble," Senc said, "The little devil can do his homework so easily, he doesn't bother doing it at home, he does it up the bloody wall during Assembly, I've seen him." This was news to me, as I told Senc, "When I ask him if he has any homework, he always says he's done it." "Oh aye," Senc said, "he's always done it and bugger me, it's always right, that's why I say, if he'd work instead of smoking at the back of the closets, he'd be a bloody genius." When I challenged Arthur about this, he replied, "I don't know what you're worrying about, I always do it, and who wants a genius?"

Finding a piece of land suitable for a nursery which we could afford wasn't easy. Every advertisement of land for sale was followed up, taking us from one end of the city outskirts to Killamarsh at the other, where, what had seemed promising, proved to be a small bank covered with gorse and bracken. The prospect looked hopeless when one day whilst visiting my Mother on Moorwood Lane, we decided to ask Oswald Morgan, who owned the field next door, if he would sell it to us. He declined emphatically, saying his grandfather had walled it round when it had been granted to him during the 'enclosures' early in the 19th century. He put the idea into our heads though, that we might be able to buy the field on the other side of the Leyland's, at present being used by Tom Fearn, of Moorwood Hall Farm.

The field, we were told, belonged to Mr Crawshaw of Cherry Tree Cottage on Moorwood Lane (actually it belonged to the estate of his late brother George and his mother, although there was always a somewhat persistent mystery as to how it was originally obtained). It had been part of the estate of two sisters who inherited it from their parents of Storth House Farm, in the 19th century. The estate had included all the land around Moorwood Lane and the Peewit Hamlet, but as the old people told, the little girls were very young and Solicitors got their hands on it and it gradually 'fizzled' away leaving them with nothing. The field in question was the last in the saga which according to old Mr Slin, a retired farmer who had once farmed it, "There's a jinx on it lass, and tha'll never get rid of it, not down to the last corner." Jinx or no jinx, although it was far from being an ideal plot, and knee-high in docks and thistles, it was 3¾ acres which had grown good crops and would do so again, I hoped. We settled on the price of £150 in November 1949 and almost immediately obtained an overdraft, using it as security.

But a bare field was not going to provide us with an immediate living, even had it been ideal, so thinking caps were donned for ideas. The first, and the one we followed, was a green grocery round, in other words, 'street trading', for which we would need a licence. Unlike a hawker's licence which at that time only lasted one year, a 'street trader's licence lasted a lifetime. As I still have mine, I suppose if the going got tough I could "God help me", go on the streets again.

The next idea was also one which we followed. I intended to grow herbaceous plants for sale using the flowers for cut flower sales and possibly wreaths and other make-up work, so it was imperative that I learn how to do them. I had seen Joe make rose buttonholes many times, but I knew from looking in magazines and trade catalogues that there were more modern ways to do them. In early September, Frank and I visited an exhibition at Earls Court and there saw a trade stand of the Constance Spry Floristry School and I was very impressed by the work on show and determined to learn this method. However, the cost was high and I should have to live in London for a time.

We discussed the possibility next day when Frank said he would have a word with Chambers. Mr Chambers and his wife sold flowers from a barrow at the end of George Street in Sheffield. He had been a petty criminal but Frank had once helped him on to the 'straight and narrow' after he was bound over in Court and he had gone straight ever since. He told Frank there was a florist in the Norfolk market who had trained in London who, if I should mention his name, he felt sure would teach me.

As soon as possible, I went to the Market Hall, found the florist, and explained the purpose of my visit. I wasn't ready for her response, not being aware of the friction which existed between the florist in the Market Hall and the grasping of every opportunity to belittle each other. I had told her that I worked at Seagraves, but that

I did not, at the time, want them to know, as I needed to continue working there, at least for another two months. This was a mistake, and one I deeply regretted as appearing to be disloyal to Seagraves, in particular Joe. I had expected the discretion I would have practised myself. I was to learn the hard way that no such thing existed in the floristry trade. This was confirmed only too strongly as the years passed.

In my experience, I found it to be the 'cattiest' most insincere trade, probably worse than the fruit and vegetable trading and I have never had cause to change from this view. The woman I had come to ask for help, on a recommendation from a man who respected her, the Manageress of one of the best known floristry businesses in the market, turned out to be the most abusive women I had ever met, shouting at the top of her voice, "Who the hell do you think you are?" as I gaped, astounded. She raved on "You can't learn just like that, you'll have to do like all beginners, mossing for a year, and working your way up." "I can't do that," I protested, "I haven't got the time," but she interrupted, "You'll have to, you can't just jump in and do the job without spending three or four years training." By this time she had left the stand and was marching round the Market Hall shouting, "She wants to learn floristry, but Seagraves aren't good enough," soon stopping in front of the Seagraves stand and taunting Charlotte, "She doesn't like your sort of floristry, Seagraves isn't good enough for her and she wants me to teach her." By now, a crowd had gathered, some following her around, some standing near me relishing the excitement, whilst I was humiliated, angry, embarrassed and thoroughly disillusioned.

I was still furious when Frank returned home and asked how I had got on. "You might well ask," I said, "I'll show 'em; who do they think they are? No wonder kids get fed up, a whole year mossing; not on your Nellie." "What's all this about?" Frank said as soon as he could get a word in, and when I told him, he said he would see Mr Chapman again. "You've no need to bother," I chipped in, "I've decided what I'm going to do." "And what are you going to do?" he asked with an expression on his face which showed he was ready for another 'wild scheme'." "I'm going to Constance Spry's,"

I answered, my mind now fully made up. "I'll get myself trained and I'll come back and start my own school, then show 'em who does the best floristry. Any girl," I told him, "who wants to learn will be able to without spending a year mossing. If they can't learn quicker than that, they should give up." There was no holding me back now, I had the bit firmly between my teeth and nobody was going to stop me.

I wrote to the school at 146A Old Brompton Road (opposite Harrods) and made arrangements for my first series of lessons during the last week in November; the price was the princely sum of £7.10s.0d (the price of a good average weekly wage for a man at that time), travelling to London the day before I was to commence. I booked into the Y.W.C.A. in Russell Square. It was sparse and the food was not like home cooking, but it was clean and adequate for my modest requirements.

Reporting to the school the next morning, the first thing that struck me was the austerity of the place, just three or four attic rooms at the top of the building. Considering the high society girls who went there, I had expected luxury and when I saw the vases and flower containers, I was even more surprised. But the quality of the teaching was faultless, and the end product just as I had seen at Earls Court. I was assigned to Miss Burns, a woman of about 45 (at a guess), a senior teacher, who was to teach me the rudiments of wiring and taping and making up as many pieces of work as I could learn in the time.

The first was a corsage made of violets, each one wired so that it could be placed with its face lifted and turned so that a flowing rhythm was created from the first single one to the more closely placed group in the centre of interest, one or two being lifted to give height, with some recessed to give depth, in what I was told, was the focal point.

I had watched every movement, every placing and having helped to attach the support wires to the flowers and learn how to cover the wires with gutta-percha (a rubber type material sold on reels and imported from the Far East through countries like Germany but unobtainable after 1960), when Miss Burns said "Now let's see you have a go." I fell to the job eagerly. Her corsage was carefully

350

taken to pieces, so that I could use the same flowers. (I soon learned that economy was practised, not only in the replacement of broken containers, but in flowers also, not that this distracted from the value of the teaching, in fact it probably accounted for my own economy later).

I was confident and had remembered exactly how Miss Burns had held each flow or so that it could be placed in position without damage, lifting and recessing as I had seen her do and in next to no time, my first corsage was finished. Miss Burns was delighted, but very surprised. "Have you done any floristry before?" she asked. When I said I hadn't she remarked "You are either a good copier or a very quick learner." I couldn't see the difference, not having done any before, copying was the natural thing to do, after making two or three from different combinations of flowers; a rose and carnation petals, freesias and a rose and one I liked best, made from hyacinth petals, all to my own designs, she said we could leave that for now and go on to headdresses. By now, wiring and taping were taken for granted, except that we looked like getting through more than planned, she suggested we use strips of crepe paper instead of gutta-percha, which was expensive.

After an assortment of headdresses in various combinations of flowers and foliage, we went on to bouquets. But first there was a break for lunch when I could catch up with my notes. I had made drawings of everything whilst Miss Burns sorted out the materials for my next piece of work, but the scribble I had made needed deciphering and writing out more fully before I forgot which was which. So, down the four or five flights of stairs to Old Brompton Road and into a little café for refuelling, then up the stairs again eagerly to start the next session.

The first bouquet was made with whole flowers, fashion for feathering had not taken hold yet, and Mrs Spry did not like flowers taken to pieces Miss Burns said. It was made with the shaggy small chrysanthemums taken from a bundle of white spray. Not the type one sees these days; they were the last throw of a larger variety which had shed its large blooms, these being the remnants which were rescued by the nurserymen as a final attempt at solvency. To go with

351

these were about seven white roses, the smallest used in the trail graduating the rest through to the focal point and grading out again in the top half. The principle, I noticed, confirmed by Miss Burns, was exactly like the corsages, and incidentally all other flower work including arranging, with a one third-two third properties to ensure good balance and all the other principles, with a variety of foliage amongst the flowers to life, recess and enhance them in the focal point. "And," said Miss Burns, "it should balance on one finger and return to the correct position, even if the bride turns it upside down through nerves." As all the flowers were white, the stems were first wrapped with narrow strips of white crepe paper to cover the thin binding wire used to bind all the stems in place securely, then over-wrapped with white gutta-percha. This, I learned, was to prevent rust damaging expensive dresses, incurring high damage insurance payments.

"There are those people, you know," my teacher informed me, "who have no qualms in suing for damage of which they couldn't afford in the first place, even society brides." I never forgot this piece of valuable advice; it made me every more pernickety in my work rather than risk complaint, although some of the methods had to be modified for the floristry examinations which developed a few years later, not for the better, I fear.

Thus proceeded my first day's training, the last pieces taken back to my hotel, where I took them apart and made them up again for my teacher to check next day. I went to bed tired but very satisfied with myself that night. The next day was spent on funeral work. First that proverbial mossing. After the first demonstration I mossed my first wreath, wondering how the hell an employer could allow a young assistant to do the job every day, all day, with nothing else as an incentive. After checking for firmness, neatness and a good shape which would not detract from the smoothness of the flower base, Miss Burns passed it as excellent.

I was just finishing my second bouquet when a young girl of about 19 or 20 who, I was told later had returned from a Swiss Finishing School, came into the room. She had spent that past year at the flower school on the Diploma Course, and was taking the tests which would enable her to qualify and she was very nervous, for the examining was strict. Miss Burns apologised for the intrusion but, she said, there were so many students taking tests that the rooms had 'run out'. I said I didn't mind, in fact I was rather pleased as I could see the quality and standard of the work expected for the Diploma. Her first piece of work was a small cross, with a spray of flowers across the centre. She went out of the room whilst Miss Burns examined it. She could see I was interested, so she called me over to point out and explain the things which had been well done and more importantly, those which had not.

I have often wondered whether the young student was awarded her Diploma for if the other teachers were as critical as Miss Burns, I have some doubt. But it gave me a good idea of the things I must look for when I began teaching my young girls and I wallowed in every bit of information I could drag out of my teacher.

By the end of the second day and of my sixth lesson, I had a book full of notes and diagrams which were the text book for all the practising I intended doing towards becoming a good, no an excellent, florist and teacher. I had taken time off from Seagraves, the first and only time I 'swung the lead' and feigned illness and I wasn't looking forward to returning to hear from Joe, who by now would have heard of the episode in the Market Hall and I was bit apprehensive about my reception. Not unexpected, he called me into the office as soon as I arrived.

"Why didn't you ask me instead of going to them in the market?" he asked and I realised he was more hurt than angry. How could I tell him his floristry was old fashioned and I wanted to be more modern? I mumbled something about how I had been told by Mr Chapman to go there. He accepted this, but followed with the question, or was it a statement, "I understand you're going to start your own nursery." Again, I explained why, "My husband has no trade; we have to do something before the money is all gone, and a nursery is the only thing I can do with any hope of him earning more."

I was surprised how easily Joe understood, but wasn't ready for his next question. "Where are you going; have you bought a nursery, or just the land?" I explained the whole story to him, how we had travelled all over to find land and had managed to buy a piece near Owler Bar, he was so understanding, I almost wept. "Now look lass," he began, "up there you'll be about the same altitude as we are here," and I agreed. "You want to get yourself a little book and put some dates down, Herbert will help wi' the plants, and I can help you wi' the outside." I put my hand in the back pocket of my dungarees and pulled out my little diary, explaining that I had kept the dates to help in the exam I had taken, not for any ulterior motive. "Ne'er mind why," he said, "I might a' known tha'd already got one, at least tha's been interested in't job." After asking when we hoped to take over the land and start developing it and I explained that we were going to live with my Mother as soon as her lodger left, which would be anytime from the end of January, he surprised me again. "Now look lass, go up to t' frames and choose 'thissen' twelve boxes o' stools, tha'll be growing 'Mum' won't tha?" I said I would. "Now tha knows how to make 'thissen' a frame don't tha?" I said I would have a go; I could use a saw and a hammer and nails. "Dig 'thissen' some sods," he went on, "build a wall wi' sods and put an old window frame over 'em, thi' plants'll be warm enough under there and tha'll have a good batch o' cuttings in no time." I thanked him for his understanding, a wonderful man, who helped out on a number of occasions after that, with advice, and in practical ways too when I needed stephanotis or hoya for bouquets, or other flowers unobtainable.

This couldn't be said for all the others I had to work with. Gone were the days of asking questions, except to Herbert, who never changed, Horace and Fred remained polite but remote, but the boys were constantly sarcastic and firing the bullet put in their guns by Arthur. A simple question like "Where can I find something or other?" would invite an answer like "We thought tha'd know, tha'rt academic," consequently no more questions were asked of them.

One particular trying time was after a load of Kentish marl had been delivered. Like all nurseries after the war when only food was allowed to be grown in glasshouses, the soil had grown sour and was less suitable for making composts, it was hoped that the marl would fill the gap. Joe approached one day with the question,

"Does tha think tha could do us a few experiments on it?" and when I asked why he said he thought it looked 'rum stuff'. "Texture's wrong and it dunt look as if it'll grow owt." I agreed with that, it didn't look very 'alive' to me either. "See if tha can find out what to put in it, will tha?" I had mixed basic compost as generally used for tomatoes and added various combinations of fertilizers including trace elements, as well as testing for lime. Using newly 'sizzled' pots to obviate disease, I ended with a row of pots on a bench in Herbert's pot house, each carefully labelled with its contents.

I was working with Herbert at the time and it wasn't long before the young 'bullet firers' moved in. On their way up to the top field, on the way back at lunchtime and at the end of the day, instead of walking up the drive outside, they came through the glasshouse, not losing any opportunity to take a sideswipe at the experiments, standing and tittering as they gained encouragement from numbers. I soon learned that men and boys have very little courage of their convictions when alone but are gregarious and full of confidence when supported by their peers. Hence, from now on, instead of single ones appearing in a trickle, they waited and pounced as a bunch.

Herbert soon realised what was going on and as soon as he saw them grouping for the kill, he used to say, "Put your coat on Joss, the vultures are coming, you'd better get off before they arrive." And so he saved me much of the aggro and soon put a stop to the invasion.

As Christmas drew near, I wasn't looking forward to working in the confined space of a small greenhouse with Arthur and the boys and listening to their sarcastic remarks when I knew I would be leaving soon anyway. Instead, I decided to make holly wreaths at home. A trip to the market supplied frames and wires and another on to the moors to gather moss, cupressus begged from a friend and holly, some begged, some bought from the market, and I was in business. A notice was put in the front window, "Holly wreaths for sale," the kitchen table served as a workbench and by Christmas I had made my wages and a little to spare.

I left Seagraves at the end of January 1950. There was still much to do to the house in Lismore Road and we were to move to Moorwood Lane on 10th March, the day the new owners were to move in. From that date 'Francott-Dene Nurseries', a name created from an anagram of 'Fran' from Frank, 'Cott' from Arthur's middle name and my nickname 'Dene' would, with an average helping of luck, be in business. Since our purchase of the house at Lismore Road, many properties had been requisitioned and the demand for houses had eased off, along with prices. For a quick sale, it was necessary, said Mr Saxton, to accept a lower price than the one he had originally promised. "However," he said, "I'll tell you what I'll do, I'll sell the lease separately (it was freehold) and I'll get you £100 more for that." He was as good as his word and when all the transactions were over, we were richer by £450 less £100 loan less stamp duty, less legal charges, less the accounts of Solicitor and Estate Agent. By the time we moved to Moorwood Lane, we had paid a deposit on a Jowett/Bradford 5cwt van which happened to be bright yellow, a lucky omen, bearing in mind what Tom had taught me, deposit on a 36ft x 9ft glasshouse, and a few thousand second-hand bricks, complete with mortar and concrete, from the abundance available due to all the demolition work after the war. Our finances then depleted, it was essential that we started earning.

Frank had, by this time, left his job on transport, but before leaving, one of the other bandsmen had told him that a trombone player was needed at Attercliffe Palace, a variety theatre the other side of Sheffield. He decided to apply for the job and being successful, commenced there as soon as we moved. He managed to buy a second-hand trombone and although the wages were low, the extra money was very acceptable for a few weeks. Unfortunately, he found playing for variety was different from that required in a silver band and, by mutual consent, the theatre and Frank decided to part. We were back to 'stage one'.

Chapter 11

At 11.10 a.m. on Sunday 3rd September 1939, I sat at the table in our dining room looking out of the window, watching Arthur playing in the sand and rubble which was our garden. He seemed to have no cares in the world as he picked up and threw a ball and happily waved back when I waved to him through the window. My mind wandered a little, it was Aunt Em's birthday and just a month away from our son's second birthday. My thoughts were mixed as the announcer said "This is London and here is the Prime Minister." Still looking out of the window as Chamberlain issued his historic speech I wondered, just what will happen? What will it be like? How long will it last, and I felt a faint hint of apprehension? But the feeling of excitement was stronger. War was something new; something not experienced before and these feelings I had experienced many years before when looking at the old photographs of the hospital at Dore & Totley and I knew that now I would know at first-hand what it was like. What sweet innocence!

The trouble was, in no small measure, that many of those who returned from the first Great War in 1918 gradually forgot the horrors of war, only remembering the camaraderie, the gregarious nature of men in confined spaces like the trenches, their 'buddies' who survived such dangers and gradually the glamour of it all took over. They remembered the fun times, the jokes and the feeling of having been important for a short time and the stories they told at home and in pubs whetted the appetites of the young for some sort of excitement and duelling the fire were the war films which appeared regularly for decades afterwards, all dramatising the world of war.

This attitude of achievement has been prevalent in the 'Old Soldiers, Pilots and Navigators', and others whose moment of glory belonged to their war service in the second World War, to be told in anecdotes and humorous stories, mostly by those who have achieved little in life since. About an hour after Mr Chamberlain declared war, there was a mild, unbelieving lifting out of the complacency in the community when, for the first time, the air-raid-sirens were heard wailing out their message of danger over the whole of the Sheffield area. Surely, everybody thought, they haven't had time to send planes here so soon, consequently, there was a half-hearted response, and no-one was eager to run for the shelters. However, there was a great sense of relief when the 'All-clear' sounded only minutes later, after the false alarm.

My thoughts were immediately brought back to reality. That it was a false alarm didn't matter, it had the effect of bringing me right down to earth and the possibility of what might happen. The excitement subsided; the first tensions were over and life returned to its same humdrum pattern, continuing thus until the autumn of 1940. Geoff and Jeff had volunteered for the R.A.F. on the outbreak of war, whilst Frank an ex-Guardsman on reserve, for which he had received the sum of £4.15s.0d a quarter since April 1934, had been deferred for three months as a policeman. His period of deferment had come to an end on 1st December, the day before his sister Kitty married Russell Garfitt at Gleadless church.

The reception was held at our house, my first effort at making and icing a wedding cake. Geoff became an aircraft fitter, Jeff was a cook-butcher, soon being drafted abroad to Aden, Haifa and Cairo, a wartime career both exciting and interesting, yet with all the danger of foreign action. His story warrants a book of its own to tell all the stories along the route to becoming Head Chef at the Officer's Mess at Padgate. Elijah volunteered two or three times for the Navy but without success as he was in a reserved occupation at the brickyard where he was the pattern-maker until entering full time teaching in 1947.

Britain was in dire need of planes and ammunition and there was a shortage of iron and steel for manufacturing more. Gangs of workmen scouted the streets removing wrought iron gates and cutting down iron railings from the front gardens of houses. We were told that they would be replaced after the war, but they never were. Appeals were made for household scrap metal, cooking pans, trivets; anything that would smelt down, including the set of iron pans my Mother had used for all our cooking until the advent of aluminium and enamel.

Old woollen garments were given to knitting groups which sprang up almost overnight, for unravelling and re-knitting into socks, mittens and balaclavas for the forces, and home-knitters produced squares for sewing together for blankets, first for the home-front, later for the 'Aid to Russia' appeal after the relief of Stalingrad. Jumble sales were held regularly so that items which could be spared by one household were allowed to circulate to others who might use them. At first, the proceeds were given to the 'Aid to China' appeal, after Japan declared war on China in 1941, later the 'Aid to Russia' funds after the relief of Stalingrad. I often wondered what had happened to some of the things I remembered like the elaborately decorated clock and vases from the room mantelpiece until Mom told me they had gone the way of everything else during one of her 'giving moments'; some, I wish we still possessed today.

Every man and woman over the age of 18 was liable to 'call-up' into the Services, Munitions Factories, or the Land or the Nursing Services, and Civil Defence. The only concession was that married women would not be sent away from home, although they had to be employed in some kind of essential work at home, in whatever employment was available locally, including shops, farms and in some cases, making uniforms at home on machines supplied by the authorities. Recruitment of all persons could not, of course, take place all at once. Call-up or rather Registration, was in alphabetical order, which allowed valuable time for those at the end of the alphabet to make their own arrangements.

Edith joined the Land Army, spending most of her service at Herne Bay, Kent on threshing machines which travelled round the farms in the area. Nancy was in danger of being drafted into a munitions factory somewhere in England. The prospect was not welcomed by Elijah, who thought that marriage was the answer. As a matter of expediency and after some discussion with Mom and Dad, it was decided they should move in with them. They were married by special licence at Ashford Church on 14th March 1942, Jeff's 22nd birthday and Mom's 50th, after which Nancy worked at Laycock's, Millhouses on munitions work until her health demanded a change, when she left and worked at Tindall's shop at the top of Main Avenue. Geoff and Mary decided to get married in 1940, after which Mary moved to Weston-Super-Mare, where Geoff was stationed. They later moved to Ashbourne in Derbyshire, where Christian was born on 31st July 1943, after which Mary was relieved of responsibility for any kind of work.

Men in reserved occupations and some beyond 'call-up' age, formed the L.D.V., the Local Defence Volunteers, later to be called the Home Guard and Air-raid Wardens who patrolled the streets during air-raids telling people to "Put that light out," if a little chink showed between the curtains, or a light was suddenly turned on. The Local Defence Volunteers were a 'serious attempt' by the Government to defend the country in case of invasion when so many men were abroad. In the first few weeks, they patrolled the streets, lanes and moors against parachutists, potential spies and foreign intruders. They wore black arm-bands printed with the letter L.D.V. doing duties on a roster system, usually one night each week from bases set up in each district. Of course, no-one had a gun, but the cry went out "Defend your country with pitchforks and pickaxe handles," and that's exactly what they did.

I remember Dad and Maurice Johnson marching up and down the road in front of our houses, between Totley village and the brickyard, which were their boundaries, in step like true soldiers, with pickaxe handles over their shoulders just like the real thing. Dad's base was at Abbeydale Hall, whilst Elijah's was at Owler Bar, first in the St John Ambulance hut, but later migrating to a stone shed just below and belonging to the Peacock Hotel for he was in the Holmesfield Division. They paraded for drill and inspection every Sunday morning in front of the Horn's Inn at Holmesfield, using broom handles, pickaxe handles, or anything they could by the remotest imagination resemble the function of a gun in 'Presenting Arms' or 'Standing at Ease'. Parading and taking orders in what really was a ludicrous situation went against Elijah's natural inclination and, after the last of probably many absences, he was suspended, or rather expelled from the Division. But this was many months later when, it seemed their services were not so desperately needed after all. Before that time, for anyone who had seen the television series 'Dad's Army', the Home Guard was very accurately portrayed, according to cousin Tom.

It was an ironic turn of fate, when my Father first heard that Geoff and Mary were planning to get married, his immediate reaction was to think of Mary's mother who was a widow, the same sentiment which had prompted him with Vina a few years before. In both cases, it was the deprivation of one parent, as though to have two parents excluded all other needs. His financial circumstances had changed little since my wedding three and a half years prior, yet now he was not only prepared, but actually offering to pay for his son's.

Of course, as a great patriot, he was proud of his sons for "Doing their bit," a possible influence when he said to me and my Mother, "If the lass wants a wedding she shall have one." We understood this to mean that he would pay for the hire of the room and pay the village women to help to prepare the food. Whether his generosity went as far as paying for transport, I don't know and as his own car would be used, this would only entail the cost of one wedding car. The cake was made by a friend of Mary's, for which she paid.

My Father seemed to take it for granted that my Mother and I would do the baking and ordering the food required for about 65 guests, a job neither of us resented, in fact, we both enjoyed and welcomed the excuse for a good cooking session, making cakes, buns, scones and teacakes, all according to the coupons we could beg, borrow or steal for fat, sugar and dried fruit. Luckily, bread was not rationed until after the War was over, so there was no limit to the mountains of sandwiches prepared by Mrs Stubbs and Mrs Ward in the tea room at the Fleur de Lys.

Mary and I had had one or two sessions making and fitting her headdress and veil and by the morning of the 10th May, all baking finished, tables ready for setting next morning, only the finishing touches were required. Rationing during the War did occasionally

361

cause one or two headaches, although everyone soon learned to barter and exchange. Our next door neighbour Mrs Bower could never find enough sugar to make jam, and we never had enough tea, Frank's favourite brew, so every so often, an exchange was made, irrespective of cost, which was never an important factor. For those who had the cash at the right time, there was opportunity to buy items not readily available in the shops for manufacturers were busy making planes and ships and bullets and cooking utensils and other household goods were a luxury not readily come by. Not having been over-burdened with money the last four years, I was more than ready to buy the set of pans I was offered for 30s.0d one day by someone 'in the know'. When Christine was one year old, I had managed to buy a doll with a pot face and a rag body, and Mom carried it in her basket when travelling from Sheffield to Ashbourne for the birthday celebrations. On her return, she told me of all the women on the bus asking "Mrs, where did you get your doll?" for a doll with a pot face was such an unusual find. All this was remote from the black market in goods, particularly food, but it was a fact of life that, if you wanted something bad enough, and had the money to pay for it, somewhere there was somebody who could supply it, and friends and relations would always 'chip in' with a few food or clothes coupons for weddings and other occasions. One bonus on the food front was the supply of tinned foods from America and South Africa which were not rationed, except by the shopkeepers, who allocated them on the fair system of regular customers only.

I remember the very large line of apricots, pears and peaches and equally large tins of pork from South Africa which made delicious pies, as well as cutting for sandwiches. Then, from America came dried egg, almost as good as fresh for all cooking and making scrambled egg breakfasts; and spam. Spam was a joke when it first appeared on the shelves, but it soon became a favourite tinned meat, remaining popular to this day. The allocation of meat per person per week was adequate, though not generous. Each was allowed most of the value of 1s.2d, later only 1s.0d, part of which had to be taken in corned beef and excluding sausage, a rare commodity, again allocated by the butcher to regular customers, or his favourites! Colin Thompson was

362

very fair, even a little generous to us, but we grew thoroughly fed up with the shoulder of lamb left at Lane Head for us to collect every week, we began to wonder how many shoulders of lamb he had, for we seemed to get them all.

My shopping was done at Frank Tyson's shop in Hillfoot Road (Rita's father). Every Friday I collected my 2oz of cheese, 2oz of butter, 2oz of lard, 4oz sugar each, as well as any other tinned or fresh items he had saved for me. We always had sufficient, rather than abundance for the rationing system was very efficient and fair, not like the fixed Great War, when Mom told me about queuing for a little liver, or a quarter of tomatoes.

Back to Geoff and Mary's wedding day. This wasn't the wedding that almost never came off. It was arranged for the 11th May but on the 10th May. In May the news broke that the Low Countries had been invaded by the Germans. Geoff was expected home on the 10th May but by then all leave had been cancelled and Geoff's telegram arrived saying he was not coming home. Confused, resigned and according to my Mother my Father said, "I dread to think what our Dene'll say when she knows." I heard of the cancellation when I returned from the 'Fleur' after seeing the final touches to the tables. As predicted, my reaction was volatile, to say the least. Auntie Florrie was sitting on the sofa when, halfway through the trade, my Father muttered, "Tut tut, not in front of Auntie Florrie." Aunt Florrie had been Dad's girlfriend before she had married Uncle Teddy and regrettably, he still had a soft spot for her. So, I was even angrier that he wanted to protect her delicate ears and I saw no reason to temper my language just to present a good impression. I turned to him. "Why not," I ripped out, "She understands plain English doesn't she? And I'm bloody annoyed; it's unfair and rank bureaucracy." But time was getting on and all the guests had to be informed of the cancellation and it was decided that my Father and I should drive around to all those whom we knew were coming and hope that the grapevine would carry the news to all the others.

We arrived back around 10.30 p.m. to find that Jeff had arrived. He had been more fortunate. He was in the kitchen at Margate when the news broke that all leave was cancelled but going to the door of the delivery area, he saw a bread van just about to leave after unloading the day's supplies. He already had his leave pass so, without more ado, he hopped on to the van hoping that the news hadn't yet reached the gate. It obviously hadn't for he escaped and managed to catch a train without difficulty.

We had been home for only a few minutes, feeling very despondent, when there was a knock at the door. It was a second telegram. 'Leave granted, arrive 1.00 p.m., Geoffrey.' There was joy in the household once more. Another journey, this time with Jeff, all despondency gone with the wind, calling on all the same people, in jovial mood. "The wedding's on after all," was the cry, "See you all at Church." Back home, it was almost 2.00 a.m. but we were not tired, only deliriously unbelievably happy.

Except that my two brothers were away, life was pretty much as it had been before. The danger of War was brought nearer home when we heard that Jeff's Scout friends had been killed, two of them, brothers, Vin and Ken Webster, whose mother was a widow who never recovered from her loss. Later in the War, two girls, Mary Wilkins from Green Oak and Mary Green from Summer Lane were killed, the first whilst working on an 'Ack-Ack' Battery, the second when thrown from a lorry whilst being transported to another base. One sailor, whose parents lived in the flat beneath Elijah and Nancy, was lost at sea during a torpedo attack.

After the wedding, I resumed my quiet life at Gleadless, still counting the coppers and like all war wives, in limbo. All servicemen were paid 1s.0d a day but as the Police Authority made up the wages of reservists, the 7s.0d was deducted before paying out the balance to the wives every Friday at West Bar Police Station. Frank's wages at that time were £4.3s.0d, leaving me, after paying the rent, with over £3.0s.0d. 7s.0d was, of course, more than Frank or many more soldiers had at home, but army food although adequate, was not a luxury and they all tended to get hungry in the evenings and spent some of their precious coppers on suppers and Frank was no exception, he liked sausage and mash and could afford to buy that and keep himself in 'tabs' as he called cigarettes, until Thursday night when he was completely broke. So there started a routine. Every Monday morning,

I paid a visit to the Post Office and sent a postal order for half a crown (12½p) which he received every Thursday morning. The remainder was my housekeeping money, sufficient for the basic needs of an adult and child, but with little to spare for 'jam on the bread' so to speak.

In March 1940, I decided to do a bit of dressmaking to supplement our budget, as many dressmakers were on war work, or had been called up and the shops had many remnants of fabric which were easier on coupons and clothes cheap to make. But the old 'Wheeler & Wilson' was not always reliable enough for the quality of work expected by customers, so I decided to buy a new one from Singers and pay for it monthly over a period of a year. My Mother agreed that I should let her old one be taken in part-exchange, even though they would only allow the usual £1 discount. They said they had never seen another like it; it was older than their oldest Singer. I thought this warranted a little more, if only as an antique, but they thought different, whether because it was not one of their own, I didn't know or that they didn't have an antiques department. The fact remained that my Great Grandma's sewing machine went the same way as all the others, down the cellar steps to the scrap department.

About a month later, the Manager of the Singer shop called to see me with an offer to buy back my machine for £45.0s.0d, twice as much as I had paid for it. The reason he said, was that all industrial machines had been requisitioned by the Defence Department for making service uniforms, many for tailors and tailoresses working from home. He said that all their larger domestic machines suitable for the job had been sold, and mine was the last to leave the shop so could they buy it back? It was a tempting offer but, after the first possible consideration, I thought that if it was worth that much to Singers, it was worth the same to me, so I kept it.

I soon set to work making siren suits and dresses for children in Totley, dresses and skirts for women and underclothes of pure silk and sometimes from the remnants of a damaged barrage balloon. I particularly enjoyed the Whitsuntide dresses for Frank Taylor's daughters and an under-set for Mrs Perkinton who kept the Post Office and Top Shop. Mrs Perkinton was an exceptionally nice woman and very hardworking. Her silk material, which she said she had had for years and never dared to put the scissors into, was a joy to work with. When I delivered the finished undies set and she saw that I had added embroidery to the skirt, bodice and knickers, she was overwhelmed. "I could never have made anything so pretty," she said, "I'm glad I waited."

One dress which I spent a lot of time over, so that it fitted perfectly, was for Auntie Julia. She was very forthright in her remarks and wouldn't have hesitated had something not suited her. She was a particularly generous woman also, the one daughter who took after her mother, my Grandmother, whose generosity was known to all the residents in Dronfield Woodhouse. But, Auntie Julia tended to expect generosity in return, so even though she knew why I was doing dressmaking, to earn money, when I said her dress would be 3s.6d, to my dismay she said, "Tha't not going to charge thi Aunty are tha?" I opened my mouth to ask her, at least to pay for the cotton and buttons, but before I could get the words out she said, "Nay tha can't do that."

At the beginning of August 1940, Frank came home on a week's leave, the first for nine months, except for two days at Christmas. He was a Drill and Small Arms Instructor in the 1st Battalion Coldstream Guards, stationed at that time at Caterham in Surrey. Training had been intense during the whole nine months, turning out 'trained' squads every six weeks instead of the usual three months, a task particularly difficult because many of them were conscripts who didn't want to be there at all and were difficult to 'whip' into the shape of Guardsmen. Unfortunately, Frank like many other 'Barrack-ground Instructors' had difficulty in letting go, and he brought their superior, dominating attitude home with him; it brought to mind the advice my Mother-in-Law had given to me on a holiday with us in 1939. After telling me about Francis, her husband, and Francis his father, who she said had violent tempers. She added, "Luckily, our Frankie's married a strong woman, I don't think you'll put up with his." I said I certainly would not, especially if it became as violent as his father's. "I hope not, and I'm sure you won't," she said.

I had soon realised that it wasn't the temper I had to deal with, perhaps because he had felt no stress in our poverty, or as a father, for he did nothing for his son, never holding him, or nursing him, saying he might drop him. Nor did he play with him, not because he didn't love him, but because it took effort, and effort didn't come naturally to Frank, it was much easier to look and watch someone else. As Edith once said in her particularly forthright way, "Poor Frank, all he needs is a top floor flat and no window box."

Two days into his first leave he lay back in an easy chair very content. "It's great to be home and have you do things for me," he said suddenly. I was unable for once to find a quick reply, disappointed that he hadn't wanted to come home to do things for me. I learned over the years not to expect anything, if a job needed doing, if I or Arthur needed anything, I did it myself. Consequently the freedom from obligation, I believe, kept his temper on an even keel. But there was a deep imperceptible hole in our relationship. There was an absence of the bonding between husband and wife and father and son; who missed many of the intimacies which were absent as the years went by.

These few days produced no great ecstasy on my part; what I had looked forward to for nine months fell flat as the proverbial pancake and Frank returned to Caterham a week later with only a few temporary tears. However, we had decided that Arthur and I should spend a holiday in Caterham and with this in mind; he would arrange accommodation with one of his fellow Guardsmen in Coulsdon, the nearest town. All was arranged, and we set off on our holiday the first week in September.

The first part of the journey was uneventful and we arrived at St. Pancras station, right in the middle of an air-raid. Leaving the situation, a taxi driver rather reluctantly agreed to drive us to Waterloo to catch a train to Coulsdon. "You shouldn't be on the streets you know," he said but was very understanding and a source of information. He asked if I had been to London before and when I said I hadn't, he did a detour, not only to miss the most vulnerable areas, but to show me the sights. Air-raids or no air-raids my first sight of London was exciting as I recognised some of the buildings he pointed out to me.

"Look pigeon," I said to Arthur, "There's Buckingham Palace," as if he knew what Buckingham Palace meant. Then there was the Guildhall, the Houses of Parliament, Westminster Abbey and the Tower of London and then across Westminster Bridge where he pointed out the Embankment that I had heard so much about. The streets were empty; except for the tin-hatted Air-raid Wardens who stopped us twice telling us we had no business on the streets and to "get a move on". But there were no bombs, the train left almost immediately and we arrived at Coulsdon without incident. Alighting from the train, I saw Frank waiting at the top of the slope leading to the exit and I was excited, partly due to the unexpected sight of London, partly because I was on holiday.

Walking as quickly as possible, holding Arthur's hand and dragging my suitcase, I reached him in eager anticipation. Dropping the suitcase, I turned to him, expecting at least a big hug and a kiss after three weeks apart. His reaction was like cold water. "Not here," he said, "not when I'm in uniform." I was completely deflated; all feeling for a romantic welcome was dispelled immediately. "Why?" I asked, "What's wrong with kissing your wife?" "It's not allowed in uniform in public," he answered and that, so far as he was concerned, was that.

We walked to the bus stop, he having given Arthur a kiss when I lifted him to receive it, but he wasn't allowed to carry him, or my suitcase. I didn't understand and was a little annoyed when I had seen many uniformed soldiers with arms around their girlfriends and, even on this platform, was another one kissing his wife or girlfriend, with much abandon. My ardour was severely bruised. A room had been found for us in the home of a friend of Frank's, who in peacetime had been a mental nurse at the local Mental Hospital. Bob Wilkinson, also an Instructor and his wife Eva were a cheerful, friendly couple who had three sons aged six, nine and eleven years old. They were all three intelligent and well trained in air-raid procedure a routine I was to experience on the first night when, just before dark, the sirens sounded and planes came over on their way to bomb Kenley airfield, a few miles away.

With little prompting, the boys went to the air-raid shelter in the garden, Arthur and I following closely after, to spend our first night there until the all-clear went in the early hours of the morning. Coulsdon was on the route for bombers on the way to London and air-raids happened every day and the Wilkinson boys were so well drilled that one day, when Eva and I were out shopping in the main street, I realised how confident she was, and why people could go about their daily routines with little fear.

It was 12 noon when the sirens sounded and we could see a group of enemy fighters in the distance and rapidly coming our way. From experience the residents knew that bombers would not be far behind and that anyone on the route from the coast to London was not safe and they were quick to find shelter from the 'strafing' they knew would happen in a few minutes. "Quick," shouted Eva, "into." I set off running, following her and all the scurrying shoppers with the same idea, cramming Woolworth's through the doorway of the stores as the noise of the planes drew near. "The shelter," Eva shouted, "end of the store, double doors." I saw the double doors which led down the steps to the basement, reinforced and equipped with seats all round the walls, but for a moment I stood inside the door watching with amazement the drill carried out by the assistants.

One assistant stood at the end of each bench, holding a huge Gladstone bag open whilst another opened the till and tipped the contents into the bag and raced towards the shelter. At the same time, two assistants at the other end of the long benches caught hold of the corners of a rolled up white cloth ready on the end of each bench and ran down both sides pulling the cloth over the goods on the benches, a dust sheet against falling debris. The whole operation had been done with the speed of lightening and by the time I reached the door of the shelter, all the tills were empty, all the counters were covered and the assistants were only to strides behind the shoppers.

When we were settled, I said to Eva, "That drill would please even the keenest Guardsman," and she agreed, "They've done it often enough," she added. "Will the boys be alright?" I asked her. "Oh yes," they know exactly what to do, they're used to it, they'll be in the shelter," she answered. She was right. When the sirens sounded, they stood for a moment to see if there was going to be a 'dog fight' then grabbing Arthur, Keith led them to the shelter where, he said, they had watched from the doorway as the planes strafed the street, firing indiscriminately at anyone who might not have reached the shelter. We had seen one elderly woman lying on the ground as we emerged from the shelter, but were told later that she would survive.

'Dog fights' occurred every day, usually in the distance, where the German planes had been intercepted by Spitfire fighters. Cheers would follow a Messerschmitt being hit to go hurtling to the ground but there was silence if a Spitfire suffered the same fate, to be followed by cheers when the pilot could be seen bailing out, his parachute billowing behind him.

Both night and day raids were by now, regular daily events. The first nine nights were spent for the most part, in the shelters and during that time I had seen Frank only twice, for a very brief time during the day. All Guards had to remain on duty during raids, even when a sleeping out pass had been issued and there was nothing we could do about it. After the seventh night, Eva was beginning to show strain, not only on her behalf, but for me, possibly because she felt responsible for my entertaining as well as my safety, when there really was no need, for I knew she could do little.

"If this had happened to me," she said one morning, "I should be really upset." "How do you know I'm not?" I replied. She looked at me, a little resentfully I thought, saying "You're so bloody calm." Had I been at home I might have given way to anger, but this, I thought, wasn't the time or the place, I still had to live here, at least for a few days more and even though relationships were rather over-stretched, it was better than giving way to resentment and taking it out of her.

Relief was to come from an unexpected direction. On the ninth day a telegram arrived from my Mother, "Jeff on embarkation leave; come home." And I went to the nearest phone box to talk to Frank, when we decided I should leave the following morning. There was a train at 8.00 a.m. which would get me to London and eventually to Sheffield by early afternoon. Frank came down from the barracks for about an hour, when we said our goodbye's with a little regret, and some relief.

A telegram was sent to Mom telling her of our pending arrival at Sheffield and I set out next morning with my suitcase in one hand and Arthur hanging on to the other. An air-raid warning was still in operation from the early hours and before we had gone very far, an Air-raid Warden stopped us and tried to turn us back. "You've no business on the streets during a warning," he told me and when I explained why I must get to the station, he said he really should stop me. Finally, he let us go with the warning, "Let it be on your own head."

Coulsdon station was outside the town at the top of a long incline, about 100 yards long, with fields on each side, divided from the road by wooden fences. About halfway up the slope on one side, was an old barn with its back to the edge of the road, the only building in sight. It had taken about a quarter of an hour to reach the bottom of the slope and little legs were getting tired after our quick walk. We were about half way and about 20 yards from the barn when the drone of planes made me look into the distance, where I could see three of four German bombers approaching. After the experience of the last day or two, my imagination ran riot on the possibilities. "Come on duck," I said, pulling at my bairn's hand, trying to make him go faster. The planes drew nearer, my thoughts raced. What silly ridiculous unlikely thoughts can travel through the human computer mind in times of fear, and I was afraid, I was petrified. They can see us! They're coming for us! They're going to shoot us! Then the adrenalin surged from the kidneys setting all the organs of my body into action. The barn was 3 yards away. "Come on," I panted, pulling Arthur, his feet hardly touching the ground, "They're not going to get us; they're not going to get us." Pulling him down beside me, I crouched under the wall of the barn, holding him close. "Be quiet pigeon," I whispered, not thinking for one moment how anyone up there could what I was saying.

The planes were passing overhead, but caution had to be abandoned, for the train would leave without us if we waited too long, we must move. I picked up my suitcase and grabbed Arthur's hand, trying to run up the slope. It was hard going and I was growing tired when about 20 yards from the entrance to the station, the station master came running out towards us. Grabbing Arthur under one arm, my suitcase in the other hand, he raced the final few yards, me following. "Come on love," he said as we reached the train, "Get under the seat and you'll be safe."

With great relief I entered the carriage to find all the blinds pulled down, a precaution against shrapnel I was told, and all the passengers under the seats. It was the businessman's trip and when I had time to think, I grinned at the thought of stiff upper-lipped businessmen and frivolous typists travelling to work underneath the tables of the train. A murmur went round the regular travellers, as I saw one of them take a peep round one of the blinds. Venturing a peep myself, I saw flying above the train, a Spitfire escort. Somebody shouted "There's one at this side too." They escorted us all the way to London and when reaching Waterloo Station, they turned and flew back the way they had come, presumably from Kenley.

The 'all-clear' had still not sounded when we reached St Pancras and caught our train to Sheffield, but although the blinds were drawn for a few miles of our journey, it was uneventful and we arrived at Sheffield safely to be met by Dad and Jeff. Whilst we had been in Coulsdon I had noticed a small growth on Arthur's neck, a 'bovine cyst' Bob had said when he advised me to see a Doctor as soon as possible. Next morning I took Bob's advice and paid a visit to Dr Marshall, who confirmed that it was a bovine cyst, in other words, a tubercular bacillus had lodged in a gland. "One consolation," he said, "He'll never have pulmonary tuberculosis; this will make him immune."

The mystery was how did it happen? Two other children had been similarly affected and all had been drinking milk from an accredited herd of cattle, which were tested regularly and proved free from the bacillus. When at home, Arthur had drunk only pasteurised milk, where there was supposed to be no possibility of infection, yet here were three young children all suffering from a complaint that Government regulations were designed to prevent. The source of infection was never found.

Dr Marshall managed to obtain a quick appointment and the following Tuesday I took Arthur to the Infirmary for what, I was told, was a simple operation. These were the days when visiting children in hospital was not allowed, the theory being that they became upset and took days to settle down again. So, it was with a heavy heart that I left him in the care of the white aproned nurses. I had undressed him and put him to bed, a debatable pleasure when I remembered the look in his eyes as if to say, "What on earth are you doing, it's not bedtime yet." But it was the trusting look which upset me most when with the excuse that I was going to the toilet I said, "I won't be long, I'm coming back," when I knew very well that I wasn't. I was sure that he would never trust me again, and even though my Father did his best to comfort me as I wept all the way home.

After many 'phone calls and ten days later, I was told that I could bring him home. As on the previous occasion; my Father took me to the hospital, armed with a wooden toy engine and a large children's book. I thought that these would help to absorb some of the emotion after so long an absence. More tears were shed, this time of happiness, at the look of wonder in my little son's eyes as he looked deep into mine. He had no eyes for the book and only absently held the engine; it was clear that Mummy was the main attraction and my heart was glad once more. We sat side by side on the back seat of Dad's car, his hand in mine, eyes never leaving my face in the wonder that I had returned. A week later we celebrated his third birthday with extra exuberance and happiness.

Ever since our marriage, Frank and I had visited my old home at the weekend, whenever police duties allowed, and for the last nine months, Arthur and I had continued this practice. Food had been rationed for a few months and I had registered with Frank Evans at his shop in Hillfoot Road, Totley, where I could collect my rations without having to queue anywhere else. Frank's daughter, Rita, was my small attendant at our wedding, so I had a certain affinity to the family. Not that it made any difference to the amount of rationed foods, but it did mean that if there was any scarce item suddenly available, or an un-rationed luxury, I had a good chance of getting a fair share.

For the first three months after our return from Caterham, our Friday visits had become a pattern of life, with little, except the absence of the boys to remind us that there was a War on. But on the 12th December there was a rude awakening to the reality of what War could mean. It was about 6.30 p.m. Arthur had just had his bath and was sitting in an easy chair in the dining room munching a biscuit, when suddenly there was the wailing sound of sirens and a few seconds later the faint noise of airplanes, still far off. We had heard planes before, of course, for our own Lancaster bombers regularly flew over on the way to targets in Germany. But this noise was different, not the steady hum of the Lancaster's, but the throb of the Germans. News of the bombing of Coventry was still fresh in our minds and this was no time to cogitate as I had done on the first days of the War; this time it was for real.

Shelter was my first priority and the table was my first thought. The Anderson shelter in the garden had never been finished, it still had no door and the thin layer of soil over the top was not thick enough to take a bombardment. The table was up against the wall and the sideboard on the adjoining wall would provide some protection. One after the other, all the cushions were flung under the table to provide a bed if the raid went on for hours, with some piled up in front to prevent shrapnel or flying glass. Soon the sky was alight with incendiary bombs, as we both settled down in our 'little house' as Arthur called it. He was oblivious to the danger, just thinking we were playing a new game, especially when, during the quieter moments, I had dashed upstairs to fetch a pile of toys and books to keep him occupied.

We were certainly settled, hoping that the bombs we could hear were not too near. The house shook, but it was difficult in this first raid on Sheffield, to know how near we actually were to real danger. As usual, my thoughts wandered to another matter, including our visit to Lane Head, which I had always prepared for by washing my hair every Thursday evening. I decided to come out of our 'den' long enough to give it a quick lather in the kitchen sink, then dive underneath again to put in a few setting pins to create the waves which were not entirely natural. (Hair was Marcel waved with hot curling tongues or if you had a hint of natural wave, it was pressed into shape with the fingers, using a few clips and pins to hold the waves until the hair dries. Rollers were not invented until the early 1950s by Emily Gregory, a hairdresser of Sheffield, who was later a private student of mine before the teaching of Flower Arranging was allowed in Evening Schools.

The air-raid went on into the early hours of the morning, when weary but relieved; I carried Arthur to bed and dropped asleep as soon as my head touched the pillow. The next morning the dreadful truth was known; the devastation of the Moor, High Street and Fargate, and the cruel loss of life when the Marples pub took a direct hit. Fires burned all around on the hillsides at Gleadless, Moorwood Lane and Owler Bar and on the moors towards Chesterfield. The target had been the steelworks area at Attercliffe and Tinsley but the planes had missed their targets, shedding their loads on the shopping and residential areas. Sheffield was alight from London Road to the Wicker Arches. Some said later it was the decoy fires on Eastmoor which had confounded and misled the crews when it became known that on a large area of fields and moors off Coghall Lane near the high rocks at the top of Baslow Hill, hundreds of small fires had been lit months before and kept alight to simulate, from the air, a suburb of Sheffield to mislead the bomber crews into thinking they had reached their target when they were still some miles away. The whole area on Eastmoor and the surrounding moors was a hive of activity throughout the War years, as precaution against enemy parachutists and enemy Agents.

Cousin May and Laurie lived at Spitewinter Farm at the time and were regularly stopped by members of the Home Guard and Polish volunteers who were stationed up there. Once they had reached their own gate, when they were challenged and might have had difficulty in providing they were the owners of the Identity Cards they offered, when a light shining on the face of the interceptor, enabled May to recognise a young man she had known at Dronfield Grammar School many years before. The day after the raid, workers who could get through to their work did so by begging lifts or walking, provided their workshop was still standing and capable of work. Others stopped on the way to help removing debris, or helping wherever possible. Sheffield was in shock, but the fighting spirit of the English, particularly the Yorkshiremen, was uppermost and the Germans weren't going to stop them working if they could do anything about it.

It was perhaps this same defiance which made up my mind that no air-raid was going to interfere with my routine, and this Friday was no exception. As soon as breakfast was over, I packed a bag with our night clothes, dressed Arthur in his warm siren suit, locked the door, and set off to walk the five miles to Totley. The journey up to Gleadless Townend, past the Balloon Barrage to Norton, Bradway, down Prospect Road to Green Oak and up the final hill to Lane Head was a long journey for little legs, but possible if we took it gently. We were passing the Balloon Barrage when a car stopped and the driver asked where we were bound. I told him and, a little surprised, he offered us a lift to the Norton Hotel where he had to turn off down into Lowedges.

The rest from walking revived us and we set off through Bradway feeling that the journey was not so bad after all. We had set off about 8.30 a.m. and just before 2.00 p.m. my Mother, shaking a rug before stretching it on the wall for brushing, looked down the road to see, what she said were "Two weary wanderers on the last stretch." She was, as was my Father when he arrived home, surprised to see us, for they knew there were no buses. "How on earth did you get her?" Dad asked. "We walked," I told him, and seeing the look on his face, added "They're not going to stop me doing what I want, if they bomb forever." He tutted and laughingly said "Yer right there lass."

It was quiet the next day, Saturday, most people still discussing the devastation of the shopping area and expressing sympathy for those who had been killed or wounded, but going about their business quietly as those people who hadn't really been affected could do. Those down the valley of the Sheaf could not afford to be so calm and most knew that the Germans, having missed the target the first time, would not rest until they had had another go at the steelworks in the Don Valley.

It came about the same time as the previous raid, about 6.30 a.m. on Saturday 14th December. We were too far away to be in any danger, for the planes had come from a different direction and were not likely to make the same mistake of dropping their incendiaries on the moors twice. People at Lane Head stood outside watching as the fires burned and bombs thundered out. From this high vantage point, if it hadn't been such a tragedy for Sheffield, it would have been a wonderful firework display. This time the bombs did find the works and history booked record all the firms who suffered severe losses. We were remote enough to watch, but not to be affected by it.

When I was a little girl, I used to sit on the bed and watch while Mom turned out the clothes closet in the corner of her bedroom. It was used for storage, rather than clothes, which were kept in the wardrobe belonging to the room suite which had cost £6.0s.0d when they were married. One by one items saved for some reason or another came out of the closet on to the bed, including the Mandolin Mom bought for £2 when she was twelve, and learned to play 'Cavalleria Rusticana' after a few lessons in Dronfield, and a bundle of photographs, my favourites, which were taken during the First World War of the interior of the hospital set up in the Union Church Hall near Dore & Totley Station. Archie Thompson was a boy of ten when the hospital authorities asked for some boys from Totley Church School to be allowed to attend sessions at the Masonic Hall, opposite the station where the volunteer nurses could learn to bandage and treat casualties from the War front.

Most of the women in the photographs were familiar to me, like Mrs Thompson, wife of Colin the butcher of Totley Rise, Nellie Gill, sister of Choppy Jackson, who kept the Top Shop, and later kept it herself. There was Dr Thorne and Nurse Barron, who brought Elijah and me into the world and Jessie Crookes my favourite teacher. I devoured those pictures and wished that there would be another War so that I could be a Red Cross Nurse.

My Mother knew all this, she had heard it often enough, so that I wasn't surprised, in January 1941 on one of my Friday visits, she said "Do you know what's happening at the Union Church Hall at Totley

Brook tonight?" Obviously she was going to tell me. "There's a meeting of the St John Ambulance Brigade." At this I was really interested. "Would you like to go?" she asked, "You can leave Arthur here with me, he'll be alright." Would I like to go, of course I would she knew that and I eagerly set off to walk the mile or so to Totley Brook.

Listening to the Officer of the Brigade with avid eagerness, taking in as much as I could, I remembered some of the pictures in Dad's ambulance books which had always fascinated me and I think my brothers too. There were pictures of the inside of the body, the bones and the organs and the curly intricate patterns and lines of the brain, but most of all, there were the bright full colour life-size pictures of the rashes that accompanied Scarlet Fever, Measles, Chickenpox, Erysipelas and other diseases which were prevalent at the time.

The lecturer turned to the subject of wounds, the difference between simple and compound, progressing to more serious ones which needed special treatment and might be encountered during a war. He was in the middle of explaining how to deal with an abdominal wound, where the bowels were protruding when there was a loud bump as something hit the floor beside him. A man, sitting on the front row, who obviously had a vivid imagination, had fallen to the floor in a dead faint. We all leaned forward, whilst the lecturer gave a practical demonstration on treatment for a faint, made more incongruous because the patient was the biggest man in the room, about 6'3" tall and weighing 18 stone. He revived very quickly and went sheepishly home. At the end of the lecture, the officer explained the reason for the meeting. All the nurses who could be spared had been drafted into the Armed Services and there was severe shortage in the hospitals and Civil Defence. Recruits were urgently needed and, to this end, a six weeks intensive course in First Aid was to be held at Totley with a view to filling the vacancies and to provide helpers in future air-raids.

My Father had been trained during his first years in the pits, receiving the medallion and a few bars after yearly examinations. On a number of occasions he had led a rescue team, the first man to enter the pit after an accident. Consequently, he was more than usually interested in the meeting when he returned home that night. After hearing about the fainting man he wasn't surprised, "It's always the biggest who fall first," he said, "And strangely, it's usually the men. And what's going to happen now?" he enquired, "What was the meeting all about?" My Father was shrewd, he knew there would be some good reason and when I told him about the classes and the shortage of nurses he said, "I expect you're going to the classes; First Aid is a valuable thing to know." I agreed, as my Mother offered to look after Arthur each Friday evening for the next six weeks. I attended them all, enjoying every minute, even the examination at the end, which earned my first Certificate in First Aid.

My Father arrived back home on the last night, eyes twinkling as they always did after consuming a couple of glasses. (He never drank pints, said they were vulgar, preferring to take his pint in two halves, in glasses, and without handles). He was glad to know that I had passed the examination and so was I, not only with myself, but because I had pleased him, possibly because he was my most keen critic. "And what happens now?" he asked, "Are you going to volunteer?" I was surprised at his question. "How can I?" I answered. He knew what I meant, I had a child which prevented me from working, but he thought differently. He was a patriot, for 'King and country' and if the country needed you, then that should be first priority. And to this, if at no other time, daughters were expected to be as patriotic as sons.

"If you want to go and do your bit lass, you can," he said, "your brothers are all doing theirs, if you want to do yours, then you can bring Arthur here, we'll look after him until it's all over." I talked this over with my Mother, who after all would be the one most affected and she thought it was a good idea. Dad had never been over-generous with the housekeeping money and when Geoff and Jeff left home, some had been deducted in lieu of board. With Frank away, I was not too badly off at least, but still could use a little more for any bargains which came available. My wages were to be 31s.0d per week (£1.55) and we agreed she should have 15s.0d for Arthur's board and care, thus we were both able to take advantage of any luxuries or scare necessities when the chance came. With these arrangements, I applied for a job and was accepted to commence work and training at Pipworth Road First Aid Post, Prince of Wales Road, on 1st March 1941. But, before that date, something happened to change the whole picture.

Early in the morning of 24th February, I received a visit from a police constable who brought the news that Frank was to be 'demobbed' and I was to take his 'civvy' clothes to Pirbright Camp (he had moved there from Caterham). There was a train to London at midday, he said and a Green Line bus would take me from Purley, the nearest place to the camp. My feelings were mixed. Of course I was pleased that my husband was coming home, but what would happen to my job? However, 'orders are orders' as they say and so I quickly set about making arrangements for departure on the noon train.

Packing a shirt, suit, shoes and socks into a suitcase, with night clothes for myself and Arthur, we caught the next circular bus for Carterknowle Road and the bus to Totley, arriving there about 11.00 a.m. A quick explanation to my Mother and goodbye to Arthur, I made a dash and just caught the next bus back to the Midland Station in time to buy a ticket and board the train with only seconds to spare.

Across London, I was too preoccupied to remember very much, to Waterloo and a train to Purley, where I was relieved to see a bus stop just outside the station. The numbers on the bus meant nothing, but I had a tongue in my head as Dad often reminded me and a question to a fellow traveller, assured me that the next bus would take me directly to Pirbright Camp.

It was about 6.30 p.m. and quite dark when I alighted from the bus, to see only rows of huts and I had no idea where I should go. Fortunately, a Guardsman appeared round a corner and surprised asked what I was doing there; a woman in the Camp at that time of night! Explaining why I was looking for Sergeant Rundle he said, "Oh he's in hut number 2, come on I'll show you where it is." After a heavy knock on the door of hut number 2, it was opened by another Guardsman in shirt sleeves. "What is it?" he said brusquely. "Sergeant Rundle is he in?" asked my escort, "there's a lady here to see him." "Bloody hell, Rundle, what have you been up to?" shouted the door-opening Sergeant, "There's a lady here to see you." There was another shout from inside the hut, "A lady, who is it?" "It's your wife," shouted my escort as, pushing the door wider, Frank appeared. On seeing me he feared the worst, "What the hell are you doing here, what's wrong?" "Nothing's wrong," I told him, "Don't you know you're going to be demobbed?" He looked more mystified than ever, until I told him what had happened and handed him the suitcase full of clothes.

After the first shock, he donned his uniform and went round to see the Warrant Officer, or whoever organised such things and came back about half an hour later brandishing his discharge papers with a broad smile on his face and a permit to leave the following morning. The next urgency was to find somewhere for me to stay for the night. He knew one or two mates who lived locally and one of them said he thought he could put up a camp bed in the kitchen if I could manage on that. When I said I could, he quickly obtained permission to leave camp, to warn his wife of the lodger to come, later taking Frank and me there to settle me in. It appeared that Sheffield Police had acted a bit prematurely when they heard their reservists were to return. How long it would have taken for the Army to act is only a guess, for the other reservists dribbled home over the following weeks but when a wife turns up, they can act quickly!

Before the War, life for a policeman and his wife was somewhat restricted. There were rules which now seem ludicrous, like an officer being forbidden to walk on a street without wearing a hat, which had to be a trilby, for caps were forbidden. They were not allowed to drink in their local public house, not to fraternise with the public. This last rule applied also to the wives and included not running nor subscribing to a mail order or other club. Wives were not allowed to work outside the home, although one of our friends was Senior Buyer for a Sheffield store, but she took the precaution of being registered and working under her maiden name and caused a few eyebrows to be raised by some people who suspected they were living 'tally' or 'under the brush'.

It was, of course, unusual for any girl to work after marriage, for men were very jealous of their reputations as master and provider and, although there had always been those who did 'charring' and casual work through necessity, it was the thought that friends might think one was working through necessity that prevented proud young wives, with ever prouder husbands, from working after marriage.

The War changed all this. When all hands were needed for the war effort, and even wives could be directed into some kind of work, it was inevitable that the rule preventing policeman's wives working be rescinded. Consequently, although not actually directed into work, no restriction was put on those who wished to do so. Some types of work were more readily accepted by the police authorities and nursing was one most favoured. Many policemen had married nurses, who automatically went into hospitals and Civil Defence, so I knew there would be no opposition to my doing similar work. Frank and I talked it over and he agreed it would be a good idea for me to take the job already arranged and to work, at least until the War was over.

The St John Ambulance Brigade is the oldest organisation offering First Aid in times of accident and war brought a growing demand for trained First Aiders. With many of their members now on service in the Forces or industry, there was a great demand for new recruits and this was the real reason for the Totley meeting. I joined the Brigade when I applied for the job and was assigned to the Sharrow Division, whose Headquarters were at Psalter Lane, Sheffield; knowing that I would be expected to do voluntary work as well as my other work. More importantly, I had to attend one evening each week when not on duty, for three months, for lectures and practical training towards qualifying for the Medallion. After that, a yearly test must be passed to ensure continued competence; although the last rule was not enforced on those whose work was in some kind of nursing or First Aid work, and awarding a 'bar' each year as in my Father's day had been discontinued; consequently there was a little incentive for such members to volunteer for the tests.

On 1st March on reporting to First Aid Post, 13 Pipworth Road, I joined an existing team of six Brigade nurses and one Officer, and six Civil Defence workers, who between them manned the three shifts, mornings, afternoons and nights, one or two of the nurses on staggered duties to accommodate the demands for nursery and hospital work. Three men manned the outer doors, two of them over retirement age, one exempt from active service owing to severe short-sightedness, Their shifts overlapped during the day, leaving one only on night duty, who was backed up by four or five volunteers putting in valuable service after their normal work and about 20 female volunteers reported on a roster system so that plenty of helpers were available when most needed.

Much of the spare time of the afternoon shift was spent in training the volunteers, secretaries, shop assistants, typists, housewives and retired women, none of whom had experience in First Aid. A State Registered Nurse came on duty from 9.00 a.m. until 5.00 p.m. and the P.M.O (Post Medical Officer) came in two or three times a day and always at midnight, if an emergency had not brought him in before.

The post was on the edge of a council estate, where any unusual occurrence warranted a report to a Doctor or hospital. Whether official or not, I don't know, but it was the habit for them to come to the First Aid Post instead and as this was during the time that District Nurses and others in authority could perform minor surgery, including suturing small wounds, it became rather a busy treatment station at times. One of the treatment rooms was always ready during the day, with sterilising instruments and an autoclave of dressings and swabs. If the injury was serious, Dr Sayliss was contacted and whoever was on duty assisted him, and Nurse Warburton.

The Officer of the Brigade tended to act as Supervisor, whether official or not, but as mere members we 'toed the line' to a certain extent, only the Civil Defence workers completely independent. There was polite acceptance between myself and Miss Bond, a paragon of duty, whose straight laced interpretation of the rules went against my philosophy that rules could be bent so long as they were not blatantly broken and no-one injured.

There was a local tailor who made the dresses and aprons and outdoor uniforms, but I preferred to make my own indoor uniform, so having obtained the regulation grey linen and using a pair of new cotton sheets, I produced a uniform which fulfilled all the rules of the official pattern, 17" from the floor, a large front inset pocket which could have held two poached rabbits and sufficient room in the skirt to ensure free movement when lifting and bending. It was this last point that violated Miss Bond's prim sense of decency. The pattern had shown a gathered looking skirt I thought looked like a full-sailed galleon in a gale, and all the other nurses had adhered to the pattern. I had made a gored skirt to relieve some of the bulk around my waist. It was against the rules. It was too tight. It restricted free movement. It was pampering to fashion rather than duty. I defied all she said, showing that all her criticisms were not soundly based on any rule she could produce. So, the arguments fizzled out, leaving respect but little affection on both sides.

Every afternoon Miss Bond insisted on having a 'question time' from which she directed questions from the Brigade text book and as the curriculum included Home Nursing as well as First Aid. The sessions were intense. The Home Nursing section had not been included in the original six week training so I was a raw recruit on such questions. After about three days I thought I was doing very well to remember the unfamiliar words micturition and defecation and what they meant. However, on being asked to define one of them, I gave the wrong answer. Wrath and torment rained on my head like a ton of bricks for I had made the classic mistake of all new students, a mistake I resolved to rectify immediately rather than be caught out a second time and my enthusiasm for beating everybody at their own game took root that day and flourished through that text book which never left my hands whenever there was a moment to learn.

Dr Sayliss had trained at the Royal Hospital, probably the reason why the Brigade nurses were seconded there for a month at a time to work as auxiliary nurses as part of their training, taking on some of the more menial tasks to liberate the few Sisters and nurses left on duty. This was in the days when nurses had to do the cleaning on the wards and sometimes decorating, as well as routine nursing, which was much more time-consuming than these days of machines and 'throwaway' utensils. In the days of Matrons, those paragons of discipline, who almost put the fear of God into those bed makers who hadn't made perfect envelope corners on beds in which patients hardly dared to move a bit toe in fear of spoiling the meticulous regimentation when pictured from the door of the ward.

After learning the basic principles of bed making and those very important corners, there were some mundane tasks as giving out bedpans and bottles, tuition for such basic necessities of life and good nursing given by Marjorie Lake, who wore two stripes on her dress sleeve, showing she was a Corporal of the Brigade. She was younger than me and as both she and Miss Bond came from Darnall, they were close friends and Marjorie was just as keen as her Divisional Officer. Consequently, my first week's training was thorough, to my relief the first time I helped a regular nurse in hospital in the morning's bed making, when she was pleasantly surprised that I could already do 'envelope corners'.

My first session started the following Monday morning, when I reported to Sister Day in the Casualty Department. After explaining the routine, I was left to get on with the job of directing patients into cubicles and preparing them for examination, or lending a hand wherever help was needed. There was no other nurse in the Department for the first week, until another one from a different Division joined us the second week, so time passed very quickly. Each day was pretty much the same, the steelworks providing many of the casualties; fractures from falling weights on to inadequately shod feet; burns from flying molten metal trapped fingers and injuries from machines. Some patients came straight off the street, sprains, falls on broken pavements and from epilepsy or through jumping off moving tramcars. Some more serious accident victims were brought in from the steelworks either by city ambulance or the firm's private one. These would have been treated by the Work's Doctor or their industrial nurse and after First Aid treatment had been directed to the Casualty Department for further treatment and possible admission. But by far, the most recurrent casualties were welders and munitions workers with motes in their eyes (minute pieces of steel embedded in the eye). Removal was dangerous; it had to be done with the tip of a small scalpel and was always done by the Sister, or an available senior nurse.

Afternoon shifts were usually enlivened in the evening by drunks, many of them well known characters who were there hoping for a free bed for the night. Others were abusive and obstreperous, like those Frank had told me to keep away from if I saw them in the street. I forgot his advice one day on my way to work when I saw a man lying on the ground in Seagrave Crescent and was silly enough to bend down to ask if he was ill and could I help. The abuse which met my offer would have filled the text book of the devil, delivered amidst flailing arms and legs that caught me completely off-guard, sending me flying. Regaining my feet, I set of running vowing that I'd never ever go to the help of a recumbent man in the street again.

It was during the third week in Casualty that the most disturbing patient (as far as I was concerned) came for treatment. He was a very big man, holding his arm at a peculiar angle, and in obvious pain. I put him in a cubicle and in a minute or two Sister Day saw him referring him immediately to the young House Surgeon on duty. The patient had a large, many headed carbuncle under his left arm, which the House Surgeon decided should be lanced and was so bad that the patient had to be anaesthetized.

After preparing the patient and seeing him on to the operating couch, Sister Day beckoned me to stand on the other side. The Anaesthetist wheeled the nitrous oxide and oxygen cylinders to the head of the couch and nodded as he manipulated the knobs. Sister Day took hold of the left arm, raising it high and revealing the huge angry carbuncle. Telling me to hang on tightly to the other arm, she beckoned a porter to hold down both feet. What I didn't know was that the apparatus was not reliable, it might work, but it might not, yet in the absence of spare parts, or a better machine, it had to be used. At a nod again from the Anaesthetist, the Surgeon took up a scalpel and, holding the carbuncle steady, inserted it making two cuts in a cross over the centre of the offending growth. There was an almighty scream from the patient and an agonised cry, "I'm not under; I'm not under." "Hang on nurse," yelled Sister Day, "You buggers, you buggers," shouted the man, writhing in pain under our restraining hands. The Surgeon didn't waver; whilst the shouts and screams rang louder. "You buggers, I'll have you for this," he proceeded to clear the slough and pack the cavity with gauze. Sister put on a dressing and sent the man on his way. Nothing was said by her or the Surgeon, it was just one of the hazards of War and the machine would probably work better next time anyway.

After spending my first month at the hospital, the next four weeks was my initiating into night duty. I had never before had the experience of being out all night, but I remembered how Frank had spoken of the quiet streets, the silence when the smallest noise from a warehouse or shop set them on their enquiring stalks up an alley way or an open doorway. As I walked up Seagrave Road towards the bus on the first night, the eeriness brought back memories of my young days before the roads were filled with cars and people for in the darkened streets and threat of raids, no-one ventured out after dark unless absolutely necessary.

After the two air-raids in December 1940, there were no more in Sheffield until the 'doodlebugs' put in a temporary appearance in November 1944. But this was not known at the time, so it was imperative that all necessary preparations had to be complete before dark. This meant that the two treatment rooms, cleaned by the morning staff, had to be set out with clean covers on the couches, instruments sterilised and equipment like splints, bandages and stretchers checked and treatment trolleys set ready for use.

The night shift started at 10.00 p.m. and by midnight everything had to be ready and we could settle down to supper. Dr Sayliss visited about midnight and often had a snack with us, before giving a lecture on some form of treatment relevant to the War, such as the treatment of phosphorous burns (from phosphorous bombs), or the finer points of anatomy and physiology and emergency delivery of babies. But his favourite subject was psychology and he fervently believed that many organic complaints could be treated through understanding the patient, rather than the organ. "It is a great pity;" he used to say, "that psychology is not given more time and importance in the curriculum for Doctor training."

One night he had been talking about the common cold (coryza) and as an experiment, asked for volunteers to show that 'catching cold' could be prevented by Psychology. It was rather a form of 'self-hypnosis', for what he asked us to do was first of all to cast off our vests, "Throw them away, burn them," he said. Then "Don't shiver, if you are cold and want to shiver, learn to control it, steel yourself against shivering." This seemed strange to us for we had been told that shivering was a safeguard by the body to counteract the effects of cold. He disagreed. Four of us decided to volunteer for the experiment; casting off our vests that night; it was a bit more difficult to control the shivering, but with perseverance we all succeeded and all I can say in support of the theory is that none of us contracted a cold for the rest of our time at the First Aid Post and I didn't have a cold for 20 years afterwards. "Shivering," he said "caused the capillaries to contract, when the lymph in the cells retreated to the deeper cells. The contraction continued throughout the circulation, eventually causing congestion at the seat of the lymphatic system at the base of the neck. The victim was now in a ripe condition for the virus to hold and having done so, the obvious outlet for the congestion was the nose." Whether clinically right or wrong, I can only say "It worked."

Dr Sayliss was a Jew and I remember one night when we had invited him and Kathleen his receptionist and constant companion at night, to have supper with us. We had moved to the new building where facilities were better and we had a separate small room for sitting in and dining. We decided to pool our resources and have a dinner, but although vegetables and fruit for pies were no trouble, what could we do for meat? The ration was 1s.2d per person per week and bearing in mind that good beef was about 1s.6d per lb. there was little left from the Sunday joint after Monday's 'fry-up'. Furthermore, some had beef; two had lamb and one had pork. After some debating, I offered to make a fricassee disguising the different flavours with spices and seasoning as we had had at Totley Hall.

We all brought our offerings on Tuesday night and I set about scraping every bit of meat from the bones, boiling these to provide a tasty stock as a base for the fricassee. To this we added sufficient milk and an onion studded with cloves, which was boiled to extract the flavour of the onion. The chopped meat was added, the whole thickened and the fricassee was ready for serving. Someone else had taken charge of the vegetables, and others the fruit dessert and by the time the good Dr Sayliss arrived, all was ready. We sat down and were just finishing the first course when I had a sudden thought, "Dr Sayliss, I'm so sorry," I said. "Sorry Rundle, what for?" came his answer. "There's pork in the fricassee," I moaned. As I knew he was an orthodox Jew and didn't eat pork. He laughed and said, "Don't worry Rundle, I've enjoyed it immensely, in fact I'll have some more, if there's any left." Beggars can't be choosers, as they say, during the War.

Pooling resources was one of the better aspects of war time life. People were ready to admit shortages, either sugar, or tea, or the ingredients for the wedding cake. There was no artificial pride, nor trying to live up to the 'Joneses'; rationing brought everybody down to the same level. 2ozs butter, 4ozs sugar, 2ozs margarine and 1s.2d worth of meat, of which 2ozs had to be taken in corned beef, was not a lot for a working man or woman. A quarter of a pound of tea a month was little enough for those, like my husband, who liked his 'cuppa', but everybody found ways and means of managing, sometimes by pooling resources, which is that we did at the First Aid Post 13 one night when somebody said how much they liked chutney. But it took coupons for the sugar and dried fruit and even green tomatoes were not plentiful, as most growers kept them to ripen over winter, or made their own preserves. We decided to bring 1 oz of sugar each and whatever raising or sultanas we could muster. One husband was willing to sell some tomatoes, and someone else begged a few windfall applies from a neighbour. I had never made chutney before, but when everybody else said they hadn't a clue, I asked my Mother for her recipe and took on the job of making it. The end product was delicious; each of us getting two jars in return for our contributions.

We were a very mixed bunch, one Spiritualist, one Catholic, one Anglican, one Four-Square Gospel, who was always asking if you had been saved and two elderly C.D. workers who were sisters and went to Chapel. I, along with the other Brigade members declared for Church of England. Except for the Catholic Miss Bond, our Supervisor, we all entered into discussions about religion and friction. She was so encrusted in her faith that she usually added a dissenting note rather than anything constructive, but when the Doctor appeared during a discussion, he entered in with gusto, which being a Jew, added a further discussion.

Mrs Nicholson was the Spiritualist, a well-known Medium who in her spare time lectured all over the country. She had a daughter aged 19 who was in the final stages of cancer, for which there was no hope in those days. She also had a younger daughter called Mary, the baby of the family, about ten years old, or thereabouts. Mrs Nicholson always sat at the top of the table next to me and during some of our discussions had described what procedure we should take should she ever go into a trance without warning. One night, in the middle of supper, when we knew she was worried as her daughter was at a critical stage, she suddenly threw back her head and started gurgling very loudly, as if choking. Marjorie, sitting opposite me, made a dive for the stiff collar and as she struggled to release the button, I grabbed the buttons on her dress and undid them to the waist. We knew from previous séances that her Sprit Guide was a Red Indian (not unusual you might say) and now we heard him speaking in hurried sentences "Must go to Mary, Mary is calling me, Mary is in trouble."

This went on for about a minute, after which we saw that she was regaining consciousness. "What did I say?" she asked. When we told her, she jumped up and ran to the door. "I must go and see what Mary wants," she shouted, as she went out. Returning an hour later, she told us what he happened. Mary, who was also a psychic, had wakened to find an old lady in a red gown standing at the foot of the bed. She was frightened and had called for her mother, when the lady vanished. Mrs Nicholson had questioned her about the woman and from the description she knew that it was her own mother; the red gown was the dressing gown she had worn up to her death a few years prior. She interpreted the incident as a warning or message from her mother that her old daughter's time had come and this proved to be true. We were not surprised when she didn't report for duty the following night, for her daughter had died just after she had returned home.

In 1940 the Council, sponsored I imagine, by the Government, had established children's nurseries throughout the city in situations where mothers of young children who wished to work, could leave their children. One of these was situated in Prince of Wales Road in a Hall which I believe was attached to St Teresa's Church, about half a mile from Pipworth Road First Aid Post. In the absence of other trained workers, other than the person in charge, the local nursery was manned by Brigade nurses and my third month was spent there on a day shift from 10.00 a.m. to 6.00 p.m.

The nurseries opened from 6.30 a.m. to 6.30 p.m., when the last child was expected to have been collected. This allowed the mothers to work a full time morning or day shift, and still be with their children in the evening. The Manor Estate was a poor area of slum clearance houses and although a number of Councillors, including one of our Civil Defence workers and a few prosperous business people took advantage of the subsidised rents, most of the tenants were low working class. It was said that many kept the coal in the bath rather than use it for the usual ablutions and one man, who had a 'rag and bone' round, was said to jeep the donkey in the bathroom!

Women on the morning shift could bring their children at 6.30 a.m. and collect them soon after 3.00 p.m. when their shift finished. Others came in about 9.30 a.m. to be collected before the nursery closed at 6.30 p.m. Many of them took advantage of the facilities to the point of abusing the system. The first job was to give the children breakfast, for most of them came in sleepy eyed straight from bed. Some had head lice, some with cuts and bruises, others dressed in dirty play clothes with unwashed faces and tangled hair. Very few came in clean and tidy having already had breakfast. On admission, all clothes were removed, the children bathed and dressed for the day in nursery clothes. Their clothes were washed and ironed, sometimes repaired, ready for dressing before being collected by their parents. Sad to say, many returned next morning dirty and unkempt, clothes torn and half asleep.

I hated nursery work. Not the children, but the whole principle of the idea and the way it was abused by some parents. My indignation came to a head one evening when I should have been off duty at 6.00 p.m., but had volunteered to stay behind and wait for the mother of one child who hadn't yet turned up, though we knew she had been on the morning shift and the nurse in charge of the nursery was unwell. 6.30 p.m. passed and I was annoyed, even more so when at 6.55 p.m., the mother turned up, full of the joys of living, and quite oblivious to the anger she had caused. "Oh I've had a grand day today," she blurted out, as if there wasn't a thing to worry about. As she went on I was amazed at her cheek and furious at her damned selfish attitude. She said she had arrived home at 2.30 p.m. and as it was such a lovely day, had done all her washing and got it dry for ironing. I was livid, for I had to go home and start my housework and had missed an hour through her. This was the last straw in the demise of my nursery work.

A few days later when I changed to the afternoon shift, I saw Dr Sayliss. "Do I have to go to the nursery?" I asked. He was surprised, knowing I had a child of my own. "Why Rundle, what's wrong?" he asked, "Don't you like working there?" I told him what had happened and how I resented having to look after 'those kids'. "After all, I am paying my mother to look after my son, and I don't want to look after dirty, miserable kids of parents who get it free and can't play the game." "Alright Rundle," he said, "I understand, I'll tell you what to do. Ask Goodwin if she'll change with you, she's crazy about children and I'm sure she'll swap your nursery shift for her hospital." He added, "It's probably for the best anyway, hospital might be too hard on her leg." Mary was more than willing to exchange shifts; she was single and had no family ties, so time was of little importance and one of her legs was 6" shorter than the other and she wore a built up boot to compensate. An interesting case for she also had a stiff knee yet managed to run and dance and completely ignore her stiff leg. Her knee had been tubercular when she was a teenager and there was a strong possibility that he leg would be amputated. But Mary had other ideas.

Doctors stood around her bed discussing the possibility and alternative measures when Mary said, "Why can't you just cut out the knee and join my leg bones to my femur?" The Doctors said, first that it would be impossible, then that she wouldn't be able to walk with such a stiff leg. But Mary persuaded them to try rather than amputate and had lived with her short leg and stiff knew for over ten years, remaining the most cheerful, good-tempered girl and workmate one could imagine.

My next session at the Royal Hospital was on a women's ward. It was very quiet after my experience in Casualty, in the days of strict Matrons who visited the wards every morning just before the Doctor's round. If there was the least little crease in the counterpanes, or if the envelope corners were not absolutely square, there was a reprimand all round. The elderly nurse, who had retired and come back as a widow to help during the War, was surprised the first time we made beds together. "Where did you learn to make hospital beds?" she asked. When I told her it was standard practice in the Brigade in home nursing training, she was amazed, even more so when she saw me bandaging an ulcerated leg for, she said, I could do it better than she could. I had had plenty of practice, Miss Bond, and the Officer at Psalter Lane had seen to that, whilst most nurses (even these days), seem unable to put on a good firm bandage.

After two weeks in the women's ward, I was transferred to the male medical ward where they were short staffed and I found this quite different. Where I had found most of the women grateful for everything done for their comfort and sometimes thankful for a complete rest in bed, the men groaned and moaned and refused to eat their meals, generally feeling sorry for themselves. To make matters worse, those who were recovering showed such a juvenile school-boy sense of humour, often at the expense of the nurses that often found irritating.

I was doing the usual pre-dinner bottle round one day when one dirty old man refused to hand over his bottle. Sister was waiting to serve dinner, so I continued to the end of the ward and then went back to him. He still refused to give it up, by which time the rest of the patients were kidding him and making fun of the situation. In those days of strict discipline, fun of this kind involving a nurse was frowned upon and the nurse usually got the blame for allowing it so I became very cross that I should be the one in the centre. "Come on," I hissed at the man, "Don't be so damned daft; give me the bottle." "You get it," he said, lifting the bedclothes. There was uproar in the ward, as some of ambulant patients moved nearer to the action.

Something had to be done before Sister heard the commotion. I whipped back the clothes, showing his naked lower half; grabbed the bottle and surreptitiously emptied the contents over him, pulling back the clothes before the onlookers could see and left him to sit in his wet bed through dinner, then reported to Sister that one of the patients had wet himself, leaving it her to administer the reprimand.

One morning Sister asked if I had ever been in the Theatre. When I said I hadn't, she said, "Never mind, I want you to take this patient down to the Theatre, I'll tell you what to do. I was a bit apprehensive but excited at the prospects and the experience and it would be a change from dusting lockers and mopping floors. A porter was summoned and Sister said he would take charge of the trolley to the doors of the Theatre, when I would take over until the patient was safely in the care of the Theatre Sister. Handing me a file, which I was instructed to hand to Theatre Sister, "She will tell you what to do and you must stay there until your patient has had his 'op', then bring him back here." She added, "There's no need to be nervous nurse, just do as you are told, you'll be alright." As I took the file from her and followed the porter into the lift, I fervently hoped she was right. We reached the door of the Theatre and the porter left saying "He's all yours now love," as he pushed open the doors for me to push the trolley through. Across the room Sister saw me come in and I gave her the file. After checking it, she went about the business of preparing for the operation, as I stood waiting.

My patient had been lifted on to the table and the Anaesthetist was standing at his head about to drip the anaesthetic on to the mask over his face when I saw Sister looking at me. "Have you been in Theatre before nurse?" she asked. When I said I hadn't she picked up a 3" bandage from a side trolley and flung it towards me, unwrapping as it flew through the air. "Wrap that up for me will you nurse?" she said. I picked up the end, thinking what a funny thing to do, deliberately unwrapping it only to have it wrapped up again. Nevertheless, I took the end between fingers and thumb and was about to start winding when I realised the Surgeon was about to start. I was curious and had to step slightly to one side behind the anaesthetist to see the scalpel enter the skin and craned forward as the cut was made deeper and forceps were clipped into the lips of the wound and laid over the covering cloth. I was fascinated by every move, edging a little nearer without being in the way of the anaesthetist's arms. The operation was coming to an end when he called out, "He's going." There was pandemonium and I soon realised that my patient was in danger of becoming a corpse. "Adrenalin nurse," shouted the Surgeon and it was there almost before the words were out. The anaesthetist had stopped work and was frantically examining his patient; the Surgeon was banging on the patient's chest with Sister taking over whilst he turned his attention to the wound. "He's not responding Sister, more Adrenalin," he called, the place now in complete turmoil. Finally the anaesthetist said, "It's no good, he's gone."

The Theatre went quiet, the Surgeon suturing the wound, the anaesthetist putting away the equipment, nurse counting the dirty swabs as routine; it didn't matter now if there was one left inside the patient, but routine was routine. Suddenly, Sister called across the room, "Nurse, give me that bandage you were rolling, will you?" I had completely forgotten the bandage, it was still trailing on the floor, I had wound no more than half a yard. Looking in fear at Sister for what she would day, I began "I'm sorry Sister." "Don't worry nurse," she said, and smiled as she took it from me. "You'll make a good nurse." I returned to the ward very despondent, without even the man's file to give to Sister. She could see that I was upset but had little comfort to offer except, "It's one of those things nurse, we have to get used to it." The rest of my hospital service was very mediocre after that.

As part of their voluntary hours service many Brigade nurses did duty at picture houses sometimes singly, sometimes in pairs. It was easy for me to reach Woodseats on the circular bus and there were few nurses in that area, consequently, I put in my two hours duty once a week at the Chantry picture house on Chesterfield Road, Woodseats. It was an easy duty, with little to expect except an occasional faint, an epileptic attack or twice in my experience, an early warning of childbirth. Films like 'King Kong' and 'Dracula' brought forth a few hysterical patients, which were soon dealt with. Picture goers were not so 'hard boiled' or sceptic then and took some scenes as 'gospel'. There were always two houses each night at all cinemas and as I always did the early one, I could go two months out of three, when working mornings and nights.

Wharncliffe Hospital was a wartime hospital for soldiers back from the frontline. On my two four hour sessions there, I was assigned to the ward for shell shocked patients and I was shattered to see men with nothing visibly wrong, who did nothing but laugh all day or suffered uncontrollable crying that nobody could relieve. Big, otherwise healthy men, who had lost all control of their feelings; with little hope of ever being well again. No doubt I would have grown used to it, learned to shut my mind off from their distress, as Marjorie Lake and Clapham did, (she even learned to get in bed with them on the recuperation ward, but that's her story, not mine). But I soon found the journey taking up too much time, Wharncliffe was on the northern outskirts of Sheffield and there was somewhere closer I found.

Sharrow Head Nursing Home was a short half hour away on bus and tram and Sister Goss, owner of the home, had done her training at the Royal Hospital at the time that Dr Sayliss was a junior Doctor and they had remained friends. Due to the shortage of nurses, we were allowed to do our voluntary hours there as well as the hospital. Whether there was gratis payment to the Brigade, I have no knowledge but sister Goss was a very generous woman, a Soroptimist, so I'm sure she 'squared it with somebody'. We were glad of the experience, nowhere else could I have seen and done the type of nursing I had the opportunity to do there. One or two nurses from the First Aid Post had been there at various times, dropping out for a number of reasons, but once started, that was my major voluntary work for the rest of the War, supplemented with duties at Farm Grounds at the holiday fair, at the City Hall for the Wilfred Pickles 'Have a go Joe' appearance and the usual cinema duties. And, of course, there were the parades. Recruiting was always uppermost and parades were regularly organised for the purpose, when we were inspected by a Visiting Officer and marched through the streets of Sheffield with an 'eyes right' for whoever was taking the salute on the Town Hall steps.

One occasion I remember very well in 1949 was when we mustered at Wentworth House and were inspected by the Commissioner, Lady Louis Mountbatten. She had walked through the lines and was back on the steps of the house and we had been told to stand at ease, when a Sergeant came round the back of the rows to see if we were standing correctly. (The men always tried to air their knowledge on such matters). As he passed behind me he tapped my shoulder and told me I was standing too straight, "Get yourself at ease." I told him I was at ease, that I was naturally straight not like some of the men on parade who needed a brush steel through their arms. This was a strict breech of etiquette and I was lucky not to be put on a 'fizzer' had that not been too much trouble.

Rock Hills Headquarters had been chosen for the venue for the reception, the Brigade to entertain her to tea. A quick whip-round was made for the ingredients for baking and the Authority gave us a few coupons for butter, tea, sugar and eggs and we put on quite a good spread. Only the Council members and hierarchy of the Brigade were invited to take tea, some members of staff put on temporary waitress duties, when there was a debate as to who would approach milady herself to replenish her teacup. The finger of choice fell on me, as having had a little experience in such things, although as I pointed out, the mistress of the house usually carried out such a task, not the maid.

We could hardly put the teapot in front of the lady so when the time came, I armed myself with it and approached her from the right side and stood expectantly for a moment. She made no sign that she knew I was there so, after second or two, I bent forward and whispered, "More tea milady?" and was a little taken aback when, though sitting silently when I approached, turned to her neighbour and spoke more words in ten seconds than she had spoken all afternoon. I moved away, serving the other guests, completely disgusted with high society and thinking "Our Commissioner has little in common with the rank and file in spite of the uniform."

During 1942, the C.D. Authorities decided to hold a competition between the First Aid Posts, about 20 in all. I was asked to captain the team of four from First Aid Post 13, not because I was any better at First Aid than anyone else, in fact Marjorie Lake, who did her voluntary service in the city ambulances, was probably a better choice, but she was nervous of being in charge and lacked the decisive qualities of a leader. I was at my best in that position, in fact. Mrs Smith had recognised it when she said, "The trouble with your Dene is she always wants to be leader." I always preferred leading than following someone who dithered and was not decisive in an emergency.

It was a knock-out competition, taking about four rounds, all held at different posts, some better equipped than others, and it was soon evident that Dr Sayliss had done a good job training and disciplining his staff. The final was held in February 1943, when we won the trophy, the final analysis being on good diagnosis, as there were one or two tricky situations when the wrong treatment would have been fatal. There was to be a reception for presentation of the medals and First Aid Post 13 was chosen as the venue, not only because we had won, but it was the showcase for the Authorities being purpose-built station. Unfortunately, a week before the reception in March 1943, I awoke one morning in severe pain and after suffering all day before calling a Doctor, was rushed into hospital for an emergency operation at 10.30 p.m. The trouble was appendicitis, with the added complication of an abscess and insertion of a tube drain. It was this drain which prevented me from attending the reception when I asked the Surgeon for permission to go, even on a stretcher. (Patients were sometimes allowed out in the ambulance for weddings and other celebrations, but I thought they could let me go too, but a nurse would have to go with me and she couldn't be spared). Consequently I had to wait until next evening to hear all about the party and to receive my medal from Mrs Clapham, a colleague with whom I had become good friends. It was a great disappointment, after leading the team to victory, not to be present for the celebrations. There was one bonus, however, when I went home to Lane Head from hospital for the requisite three weeks convalescence. A bed was put in the room and, as Arthur was away from school on his second week of Measles, we spent much time together reading and playing games until the sad day I had to return home without him.

'D' Day, 6th June 1944 came as a surprise for people in the north, not so to many in the south, the amazing thing was that no-one talked about the build-up of tanks and lorries lining many of the roads; certainly there were decoys in Lincolnshire and other embarkation areas but the slogan 'Careless talk costs lives' had been taken seriously by everybody throughout the War, so not even a whisper leaked out to the Germans. Not a situation one would enjoy in these days of freedom of information and do-gooders, who claim a God-given right to interfere.

My brothers would appear to have a knack of choosing invasion days for their marriages, first Geoff, now Jeff. Jeff returned to England early in 1944, whilst Edith was still in the Land Army at Herne Bay. After meeting for a weekend, they decided to get married, probably in the local Registry Office. When Dad heard this, he would have none of it, saying they should come home and be married at Totley Church as Geoff had done. Edith had been brought up by her grandmother since her mother had remarried, so as with Mary, he said Edith should have a wedding if she wanted one. Whether they were really bothered is debatable but they agreed to be married at Totley as Dad suggested. Mom and I organised the wedding breakfast and I made the wedding cake, everybody joining the last wedding in the Salt family at the Fleur de Lys.

At the end of that week, Mother, Arthur and I travelled to Burnhope to attend the wedding of Peggy, (May's daughter) and Joe Scott, a young man from the village. The wedding was notable only for the fact that Peggy borrowed my wedding gown and headdress and Arthur fulfilled his first duties as an attendant and very well he did it too. There were many in the congregation and sightseers, who remarked on his gentlemanly attitude towards Valerie, the other attendant, as they negotiated the steps outside the Church and he lent his arm during the procession.

In November 1944, it was clear to the Government that the Civil Defence Service would be no longer needed. Doodlebugs, unmanned rocket bombs, were falling intermittently on London, with an occasional one in the province, but in most respects, the War at home was over. The Brigade nurses at First Aid Post 13 were invited by Miss

Marshall on behalf of the Hospital Authorities to transfer to the hospitals to take one year's theory of nursing and qualify as State Enrolled Nurses, a new status created to enable married women to become qualified hospital nurses. Before the War, nursed had to resign on marriage and even those who were courting or had boyfriends were not accepted gladly. It was the day of complete loyalty in the job, with no distractions and Matrons, who were not married, frowned on anything which might divert the mind from duty. The War altered the system, as the First World War had changed the picture from women who, having been the main stream of labour could not then be refused recognition and granting of the vote. Suffragettes had paved the way, but the War had the biggest influence on the change. Now the second War and service by married women could not be ignored and nursing was one profession where something concrete could be done to adjust the situation, first for those married women who had helped to keep the hospitals working and could not now be cast aside to revert to the old system. It was recognised that valuable practical experience had been gained and in some cases, much theory had been learned, as at First Aid Post 13. Creating State Enrolled Nurses was a way to keep them in hospitals, particularly until the return of trained nurses from War service.

For some time I had wanted to have Arthur back home. Since he had reached the age of five it had been increasingly difficult always to arrange days off so that he could come home every weekend. Although I would dearly have liked to take the opportunity to become one of the first State Enrolled Nurses, the State Hospital, now the Northern General was at the other end of the city and a time-consuming journey. It also involved another three-shift system. To take advantage of this new opportunity, which I knew I would enter into with all the commitment it deserved, there would be angry rows beyond the end of the War, for Frank was growing more resentful of my nursing and a ridiculous situation had developed because he was jealous of the time spent with patients.

I finally refused to give it up until the end of the War, but promised that I would do so immediately it ended and he accepted that, albeit with not very good grace. We knew that this might be only a few months, so the new vocation was out of the question. However, the situation did not exclude other similar work and an offer was not long coming.

When Sister Goss heard of the disbandment of the C.D. System, she immediately offered me a full-time job, for the first few weeks working alternate nights and days with Staff Nurse Harrington. Nurse Harrington was an Irish woman who had come over to England to take up an appointment at Sharrow Head after training in Ireland. She had a brusque manner and her discipline was equal to the strictest Matron and her quality of nursing was just as strict; treatment of the complaint took priority over any form of familiarity, or favour to the patient.

I decided to take up the offer, at a wage similar to that which I had been earning, but when Arthur returned home at Christmas at the end of the autumn term, I would revert to the day shift, working from 9.30 a.m. to 3.30 p.m., enabling me to leave and return within school hours. The four hours voluntary work was transferred to Saturday morning permanently; one change being that Arthur went with me when Frank was not at home. This was an added bonus, as now I would help in the Theatre every Saturday with two of the most eminent gynaecologists in the city, one of which, Mr Stacey, had a son the same age as Arthur, with whom he could pass the time whilst we were working.

I left First Aid Post 13 on the 14th November, 1944 commencing at Sharrow Head the following Monday. The first week on days helped me into the daily routine; the second week reporting for duty at 10.00 p.m. to be briefed by Staff Nurse Harrington on procedures for the four babies and their mothers and a patient in a small ward upstairs under observation before a possible operation the following Saturday. He was a very gentle Jewish man who was suffering from a severe rash covering the whole of the scrotum. He was actually embarrassed and wouldn't let anyone attend him but Staff Nurse. The rest were routine patients who, I was told, would sleep all night. The babies were bathed every morning and 'topped and tailed' before their first evening feed, some by mother, others wholly, or as a supplement, by bottle. After that, all were bottle-fed at 11.00 p.m. and through the night, as necessary. My duties, after checking all patients, commenced at 10.30 p.m. when each baby was lifted, nappy changed, returned to the cot with a bottle. When all were fed and watered, I could settle down to the dinner (commonly called breakfast) which Sister Goss had put out for me ready to be warmed over a pan of water.

I had just finished my meal and checked that all rooms were quiet, with the prospect of a quiet night ahead, when there was a far off droning sound which gradually grew louder. I had neither seen nor heard one, but I knew this to be a doodlebug, one of those dreaded pilotless rocket propelled bombs which, so long as the drone could be heard, it was safe, but when the noise stopped, it would fall and explode. I held my breath for only a few seconds as the sirens wailed out, then dashed upstairs to the attic to wake Staff Nurse as I had been told. She was already awake and out of bed and as I reached the ground floor, she was but two strides behind me. Screaming and shouting came from one of the downstairs rooms, as Harrington shouted, "Get the patients down to the cellars quick." The cellars had been reinforced as a shelter, but the stone steps were not easy to negotiate with patients in flowing nightclothes, nor for carrying babies each one deposited in its own cot up against the cellar wall. I dashed into the room where the hysterical woman was shouting "It's a doodlebug, it's a doodlebug." The poor woman had moved from London to get away from the doodlebugs and in her hysteria, imagined they had followed purposely to kill her. There was little to do, other than slapping her face, which might have brought an assault charge, to make her shut up. She was still screaming when Harrington dashed into the room hissing, "Get that bloody woman downstairs nurse, or we'll have them all hysterical." I stripped back the bedclothes, grabbed her by the arms and propelled her to the cellar steps, a move which must have used up some of her surplus energy for, with little difficulty, she safely negotiated the steps and was deposited on a bunk.

The droning noise had continued throughout the transfer, at one point immediately overhead, when I had silently prayed that the noise wouldn't stop. The bang came a few seconds before the last patient was transferred and the 'all clear' sounded soon after, when the whole lot had to be returned 'from whence it came', That night was the last time that Sheffield was under attack, a stray doodlebug which had gone in the wrong direction, falling in a backyard off Ecclesall Road, luckily with little damage.

At Christmas 1944, Arthur returned home and life gradually evolved pleasantly into a regular timetable. My duties at Sharrow Head were both pleasant and interesting, Sister Goss doing all the cooking and leaving the nursing to Staff nurses and myself, with occasional help from another Brigade Nurse who was putting in her voluntary hours, usually when we were very busy. Sister Goss delivered all babies, each one a fresh experience for me and the wonder that a midwife who had delivered hundreds of babies in her working lifer could be so affected every time. "You know nurse," she said once as I held the mother's hand and steadied her leg, "the creation of life is wonderful," as she eased out the baby's head, then the whole body and passed it to Harrington waiting with a large towel, its little lungs bursting out telling of its arrival.

Before my first experience of Theatre procedures whilst I was still a voluntary nurse, she had stressed the need for obeying the etiquette expected. "Nurse," she said, "whatever is said in the Theatre is never disclosed outside." I said I understood. "Mr Stacey in particular, is very concerned about his patients and very cross, even rude; sometimes his language can be crude, if things don't seem to be progressing normally." I was interested and looking forward to the experience. She continued, "He is so particular, he tends to work on his nerves, and he, himself, suffers from an ulcer and the tension is not good for that." She paused then said, "We've seen him rush straight for the bathroom after a particularly difficult operation and be violently sick." She could see I was more than a little interested by the time she came to the real reason for telling me this as she continued, "That's why we take no notice when he talks or tell jokes when things are going well, it's his way of relieving tension. When this happens nurse, don't give a sign, and above all, don't laugh at the jokes, they are only letting out nerves."

I was the 'dirty nurse' in the Theatre; I didn't wear sterilised clothing or gloves. When the autoclaves were filled ready for sterilisation, the cotton swabs were counted, and during the operation, the Surgeon tossed the soiled ones over his shoulder and I picked them up with the forceps, laid them in a row and counted them before the patient was stitched up. Nurse Harrington counted those still in the autoclave and, of course, the numbers had to agree, otherwise a frantic search and recount would go on until they tallied. I always stood behind the Surgeon so at those times when I couldn't help a face-slip, he didn't see me, but I caught Sister Goss' eye once in a while and saw the warning there.

Once, however, I couldn't keep the laughter out of my eyes. The patient, who had come in for a simple operation, a 'D & C' in laymen's terms, womb scraping, was in the lithotomy position (legs suspended in loops from a frame at the foot of the operating table). Mr Stacey sat on a low stool facing her bared lower regions, in his hand a cauterising gun, similar in shape to a toy gun, except that a 'V' shaped electric element protruded from the business end. He spent some time testing the element to see that it was heating correctly, turning round now and then, looking at me and smiling. Then he was ready to start. Laying down the gun, he turned and stared at me, and I could tell by the look that he was going to say something rude. I braced myself, but when he said, with a devilish grin, whilst holding two fingers in the air, then pointing them at the patient as if pretending to shoot "Look nurse, one finger socially, two fingers clinically," I nearly burst, trying to prevent myself laughing outright. I glanced at Sister Goss waiting to hand the instruments. Her face told me that she too was laughing inside, as she slowly shook her head. Nurse Harrington was waiting at the instrument table with her head turned, she had probably heard the joke before, for her face was poker-straight; ever the epitome of efficiency was Nurse Harrington.

The first time I did duty in the Theatre with Mr Stacey it was for the removal of an ovary. The scalpel had just penetrated the skin when he turned to me saying "Did you expect the blood to flow like milk and honey nurse?" and when I said "No Mr Stacey," he seemed surprised. "Have you been in a Theatre before then?" he asked, and when this time my answer was "Yes, Mr Stacey," he seemed a little disappointed and wanted to know where. I told him and that the patient had died during the operation. "And that didn't put you off?" he wanted to know and seemed quite pleased when I said it hadn't. From then he realised I was interested and often called me nearer whilst he explained some points about the anatomy, a diseased ovary, a fibroid uterus, or just the adhesions from a previous operation which were causing pain. If I hadn't yet arrived in the Theatre, Sister Goss said he would ask "Where's Josephine, where's my little pet nurse?" One day, however, I didn't know whether to be pleased or angry. It was whilst we were having coffee after the 'ops' were finished and I had to leave for a minute or two to see to one of the patients. We had been laughing at one of his jokes when Sister Goss had remarked on the glitter, as she called it, in my eyes when I laughed. In my absence he said, "You know, I don't know whether she's lovely to look at or ugly, but she's a fascinating little bugger." When Sister Goss told me this later, I said I didn't know whether to take it as an insult or a compliment," but she was in no doubt. "I'd rather be called fascinating than beautiful any day nurse, and I'd take that as a compliment." Some nurses called him a 'butcher' but as I told Sister Goss one way, "If I ever need an operation, I'd want it done by Mr Stacey, I'd willingly put my life in his hands."

I learned very little from Mr Glyn Davies, the other regular gynaecologist who used the Home. He was a handsome man, whom nurses adored; well dressed, refined and rather vain, but never showed any emotion, nor bending in his attitude. When the operation was over, he left immediately, stopping neither for conversation or coffee.

The operation on a beautiful 19 year old girl showed the really serious side of Mr Stacey. It was exploratory, for the cause of pains in abdomen, which were expected to be symptoms of fibroids or other trouble of the uterus. The abdomen was opened and immediately there was a cry of "My God, Oh my God," from the Surgeon. His face was ashen, as Sister Goss craned forward to see the cause. The anaesthetist bent closer, Nurse Harrington and I moved nearer to see what was wrong. It was a sorry sight. The whole of the poor girl's intestines was a mass of tubercular growths, knotted so that hardly an inch of healthy flesh could be seen. We were all silent with horror; only Mr Stacey's

"Oh my God," broke the silence. The wound was sutured and the patient carried to her room, never to regain consciousness. He was devastated, "Such a lovely girl," he cried, as he dashed to the bathroom in agony. One person who didn't like the Saturday morning operation sessions was Arthur. He was happy enough playing with John Stacey, but either on the way home or when we reached home he would say, "Oh, I hate the smell of anaesthetic. Oh, get away, you stink." You can't have everything or please everybody can you?

My change of work hours brought another bonus; we not only had Arthur at home, but also evenings together for hobbies and other household occupations which lack of time had prevented. One of the pleasanter ones came unexpectedly. Christmas 1944 showed a relaxing of some of the tensions previously felt as we knew the War was finally coming to an end. But supplies of some commodities were still sparse, some non-existent children's toys being amongst the rarer. Arthur came home school one day with his latest request for Father Christmas. "I want a cowboy's outfit," he said very firmly. (One of the favourite games for boys was still Cowboys and Indians). "I don't think Father Christmas will manage that," I told him, but he wasn't placated; every time Christmas was mentioned, the same request was repeated. Frank and I knew we had to do something about it and after discussing the possibilities, decided on a plan of attack; we would make one ourselves.

Work started in mid-November when Frank, paying a visit one afternoon whilst Arthur was at school to collect a bundle of straight willow stems. These were safely stored under the bed in our room until they were dry enough to strip the bark and make into arrows. The first problem was a supply of feathers, some for the arrows, some for the headdress I was to make from skiver leather and cardboard. (I had a good supply of skiver from the days, early in the War, when as part of my War effort, I made belts with interlocking leaves, or strips plaited into different designs and colour-blending to sell at the Post or amongst friends and acquaintances. Whilst on that subject, I also made corsages and buttonholes from dried 'beach-mast' and pinecones arranged with one or two leaves and made toffee for sale at the First Aid Post to volunteers who wouldn't tell tales as it was against the law to sell food made in a domestic kitchen and the authorities were always suspicious of those people who had rationed commodities to spare for such things).

Other people at the Post knitted squares for making up into blankets; others made kettle holders, purses or needle cases. It was surprising how the imagination can conjure up ideas for making money for worthy causes and 'Aid to China' and later, 'Aid to Russia' were two worthy causes at the time.

On a trip into Sheffield one day, I found a tobacconist who had a small supply of pipe cleaners, just enough for our needs. They were multi-coloured which gave just the right finish to the elaborate headdress I made, first by covering a strip of cardboard for Arthur's head, fastening it into a circle, then continuing the skiver for about 18" for the tail of the headdress. As it was glued together, a feather was inserted every 2" or 3" until the finished headgear was magnificent enough for the chiefest of Indian Chiefs. In the meantime, Frank worked on the arrows. The stems of willow, now dried firm, were stripped clean and one end sharpened to a point which was inserted into a piece of cork. The other end had four slits about 2" long, into which four feather pens were securely glued. Now, all that was needed was a quiver. This problem was solved with the aid of an empty Vim canister covered carefully with brown skiver and boasting a shoulder strap made with the same material. The finished Christmas gift was carefully and lovingly packed into a mysterious parcel and on Christmas Eve, laid on the bottom of the bed of an unsuspecting little boy-cum-Indian.

Next morning we awoke to loud cries coming from the bedroom next door, "He's brought it, he's brought it, Mom, Dad, he's brought it." Suddenly the bedroom door burst open and in rushed a very excited Arthur wielding a bundle of feathers and an arrow, bouncing on our bed he thrust the feathers into our faces and nearly shot us through with the arrow, as he continued to cry, "He's brought it. You see," he said, when he returned to earth, "You were wrong, he could get me one, look," as he rammed the feathers on to his head and ran downstairs.

407

The War in Europe continued for another six months; the one in Japan for nine months. Rationing continued, even bread was rationed by 1952, a result of the end of Lease-lend and the beginning of the Marshall Plan. But the fact that the allies were getting closer to Berlin, even though there were tragic periods like Arnhem, tensions eased and many were making plans for the post-war period. 8th May saw the first Armistice and celebrations on the 9th brought street parties, dancing in the streets, flags flying from windows and children running around with miniature union flags. V.J. Day followed on the 12th August with more celebrations, somewhat quieter than V.E. Day but for those whose husbands and sons were still out there, it was a greater relief, for the atrocities and torture was known even before the main stream of servicemen returned home. Cousin Jackie Salt, the pleasantest of Uncle Teddy's sons, was released and sent to South Africa for rehabilitation. He had been cruelly treated with others whilst building the dreaded Burma Road, suffering from tuberculosis through shortage of food, bad conditions and ill treatment. He died in South Africa, too ill to return to England. Cousin Arthur, his brother, equally as pleasant, although he didn't laugh as much as Jackie was a seaman on the 'Warspite'. He returned home and lived with us for a time whilst he worked as a Sheffield policeman, later marrying Anne from Huthwaite, who didn't like Sheffield, or a husband who worked on shifts. After a few months they moved to Huthwaite, Arthur became an insurance man. When he first came to see us he brought a bunch of bananas he had bought green on his travels, knowing that we had none in Britain since the outbreak of war. He ripened them in a box beneath his bunk. When Arthur (my son) first tasted he spat it out as 'horrible'; he had never tasted a banana before and I think he never wanted another.

I kept my word, and the day after V.J. Day I gave in my notice to Sister Goss. It was a sad day on both sides. "You are a good nurse," she said, "It's a pity to give it all up." However, I continued to put in the four hours voluntary duty on Saturday mornings until a new nurse could be taken on, so I was let down gently. Nurses were returning so by Christmas 1945, my nursing career was ended. However, I remained a member of the Brigade for another four years until 1949, during which time there had been many small competitions and tests to keep the interest of members and in 1948 I was asked to captain the team from Sheffield 'B' Division for the first female competition in Sheffield for the Sheffield & District Shield. As on the previous occasion, this was not because I was the most senior member, for our Divisional Officer and a Sergeant were also in the team, but neither felt sufficiently confident to lead the team. The competition was held in Edmund Road Drill Hall, a huge place where a simulated street accident had been set up by ambulance men from a non-competing Division. The scene, as we entered the Hall was almost too realistic.

A damaged van stood at the side of a road, a victim laid beside it. Opposite, and a little further on, was a badly damaged car which had turned over and three more victims were sprawled at various angles around the scene, two with obvious injuries, the other needing careful diagnosis. A group of people were standing around, as pedestrians usually do, getting in the way and being generally curious, and a group of ambulance men stood watching from a distance, possibly the most nerve racking aspect of the situation, for this was their particular domain and they could be as critical as the Judges, who stood discreetly to one side. My first job as Leader was to delegate duties, one nurse to control traffic, one to 'phone for an ambulance, the third to work with me whilst I examined the victims for bleeding, fractures, etc.

Whilst the pedestrians were carefully controlled by the traffic nurse and the other returned to report that the ambulance was on its way, treatment progressed smoothly, without undue worry. But the fourth victim was a problem. Nothing had been found to warrant immediate treatment and after another careful examination we drew a blank again, until, like a bolt of lightning, inspiration came and I bent to smell the victim's breath; yes, it smelled of sweet apples. One of the Judges had been hovering very close all this time; I looked up at him and said, "Do you happen to have two lumps of sugar in your pocket?" He put his hand in his pocket and drew out two lumps and as I was offering them to the victim's lips, he smiled and said, "All right nurse, you can leave it there." With relief, I stood up as he spoke again. "Actually, sugar is no longer the treatment, but the new book with the latest instructions isn't out yet, so you aren't expected to know." Since then, the instructions have been altered again and the treatment is again two lumps of sugar. That was only half of the competition for although the man practised only First Aid, the nurses did Home Nursing as well, so after a five minute break, we had to switch our minds to that subject.

I firmly believe that it was the ability to 'switch the mind' which won this contest for us, as well as the few points gained from the correct diagnosis of diabetes which the other team had not managed to do. As usual after a test, when we emerged from the First Aid test, a discussion began as to what we had done and what we should have done, but I, as leader; soon put a stop to it. "Look," I said, "We have just five minutes, get your minds off First Aid, that's over, start thinking about nursing, bandaging, bathing eyes, bed-baths, varicose veins." When we eventually were called into the Hall again, a 'bedroom' confronted us. One patient lay in bed; another was sitting in a chair holding a bandaged arm which required a new dressing. A third, a young child who had fallen down on the way home from school, suffered a grazed knee and a bump on the head. We were more than ready, first to change the sheets on the bed with the patient 'in situ', whilst others in the team dealt with the other cases, even though we all recognised that the Judge was none other than the very strict Matron of the Royal Hospital.

In 1949, we were competitors for the 'Perrot Shield', a national competition for nurses, which also incorporated the 'Ashbury Cup' for the nurse gaining the most points in the competition. I remember very little about it, for by this time my mind was firmly on other matters. However, I found a marking sheet amongst other things in my archives and it shows that I achieved a total of 72, obviously not as many as the winner. My membership ended a few weeks later when other duties were pressing.

Chapter 13

When we had arranged to buy the land on Moorwood Lane, it was on condition that we were allowed by the Planning Authorities to develop a nursery and an application had been made with plans drafted by Elijah. We had been advised by Mr Worrall, the Planning Officer at Chesterfield, to include everything we thought we would ever need to save putting in subsequent plans at a later date. So, although there was only a remote possibility that we would ever be able to afford them, we had included three 100ft glasshouses, as well as smaller service buildings and a high water tower with a huge tank. I visualised that this would be necessary as, being the end of the pipeline, plus the high altitude, the pressure was very low and hosepipes demanded a high pressure to work with any efficiency. Also, the Agricultural Board offered a grant towards the first laying on of water, the only grant for horticulture, except for a grant for lime. But the grant for water covered only the cost to one point, in our case, the tower, from where all future pipes could radiate as necessary.

One mistake was made, when Mr Worrall asked if we were going to apply for a house. We said "No', we couldn't afford one and couldn't see our affording one in the near future." He said he thought we should include the plans for one, "After all, you don't have to build it straight away," he said. But that was so far in the future that we both thought the idea rather pointless. "Well," he persisted, "why not ask for a caravan?" "We don't need a caravan," we said. "No, but you might," he said, "and you could change the plans to a house when you could afford it." Poor Mr Worrall did his best to make us see sense, and we still said we wouldn't bother. In 1974-6 when I did put in an application, it was turned down flat; even the High Court would not grant permission. Which just proves what I have always held as a sound philosophy; 'grasp the opportunity whenever life offers it; it might not come round again'.

By the time we moved in, the plans were passed, but first a new drive and access had to be made, for the existing gate was on a dangerous bend and as the Planning Department hoped (with a capital H), to widen the lane sometime in the future, the entrance gate had to be set 10ft back for the new 30ft road. It has, like a lot of plans, never happened; it is still a little country lane.

I had never used a pick before, but now it was essential to make inroads into the ground to build a sound foundation for the access road. Somewhere in that foundation is a blue aquamarine which was lost from a ring I was daft enough to be wearing one day, a very precious ring which I had had made from the tiepin which my Father was presented with when he helped to win the Yorkshire Shield with the Bowling Club. A frantic search for two or three days never revealed the precious stone.

For about three months after Dad died, Elijah had slept at the Leyland's every night to keep Mom company on the lonely remote lane, against all her protestations that he should be at home with his wife and that she would be alright. However, as winter neared, she was persuaded to take in lodgers, as the house was large enough for them to live comfortably in a section of the house. After advertising, the Stevens family, Rex, Sybil and one year old David, moved in and over the next two years cemented a close friendship which lasts in the family to this day, Mom acting as Godmother to David at his christening at Holmesfield Church.

Rex had been a Captain in the Royal Engineers, Sybil a member of U.N.R.A. an organisation which worked on behalf of refugees. Rex had been demobbed and had taken a job in Sheffield, but by January 1950 had decided to move on (by promotion I believe) and expected to have left the Leyland's by the 10th March 1950. There was a delay and the move was postponed until May. Unfortunately, ours, scheduled for 10th March could not be postponed as it was also the date for the new owners to move in. Consequently, the house was overcrowded for a while, causing a few problems with sleeping arrangements.

We had been at the Leyland's for five weeks, during which time I realised that my Mother had not lost the habit of staying up until the late hours, in fact she loved to take the big white Alsatian dog for his nightly walk up the Peewit, a little hamlet about half a mile away, at midnight. Unfortunately, the delay necessitated me sleeping with my Mother and Frank sleeping on a camp bed in Arthur's room; arrangements not exactly conducive to a happy marriage. Consequently, during the five weeks Frank and I had little time to talk in the evening on his return from Attercliffe, and no privacy at all, a situation made worse because Frank, as a previous boyfriend had remarked, thought I took much notice of my Mother to the 'exclusion even of your husband'.

One of the most essential things before we could really start trading was that one of us had to learn to drive and, as I was too busy decorating and assuming that Frank would do the errand running whilst I was trying to work the land, he was the first to learn. I was half way through a six week course of driving with the British School of Motoring; my tutor was Dick Croxton, a lively extrovert, a man with whom I got on 'like a house on fire'. Unfortunately, wanting to compare notes on how Frank had been taught by another man, I suppose I mentioned Dick Croxton rather a lot and this day was the one when I realised how much Frank resented it. We had returned home from the 'greengrocery round' of which more later, when Frank said "Come on, we'll have a run round and you can have a bit of practice." He had passed the test on his sixth lesson and I wanted to use my sixth for the test in two weeks' time. We had just returned to the gate of the Leyland's and gone over a few points in the Highway Code when he said, "Next time I'll show you how to 'double-de-clutch'. For explanation, our new van had a crash gearbox which meant that the driver had to depress the clutch twice to keep up the 'revs' when changing to a lower gear and I had practised this on some of the hills around Sheffield, when Dick Croxton, my tutor heard that I would have to do it in the van. He also taught me to 'ride-the-clutch' a thing, he said, "I shouldn't really do as it wore out the gears, but saved a lot of changing gear when following trams up the Moor when they stopped every few yards." Whether good policy or not, for I knew I was dealing with a man who was sometimes on a short fuse, I told Frank I already knew and that Dick Croxton had taught me. He turned in his seat, and with a sudden swipe across my face, followed by two or three more, knocking my head from side to side, shouted "I'm bloody fed up with hearing about Dick Croxton, it's Dick Croxton this and Dick Croxton that, you don't give a damn for your husband." A tirade followed. He said I encouraged my Mother to stay up late so that I didn't have to be alone with him; I didn't want to make love, so I planned it so that I didn't have to. And much more, I was amazed; he had often told me I wasn't natural; always got my mind on something else rather than lovemaking, and I suppose I had been so engrossed in our new venture that nothing else had crossed my mind. After all, my philosophy was that life with the 'shekels' to pay the bills and put food on the table was far superior to 'love on the dole' and love had, by now, flown at least halfway through the window anyway, through poverty and I had no intentions of giving it a push right through. But, I was angry.

From the moment his mother had told me of his father and grandfather's tempers, with the warning not to put up with Frankie's he knew how I felt about violence. "The first time you hit me will be the last," I had told him and although I understood and sympathised with the reason for today's lapse, I reminded him of what I had said then. Getting out of the van I said "That's it, that's the first time; if there ever is a next time, it'll be the end of you and me." I walked up to the house where Elijah and Nancy were having a cup of tea. Elijah asked what the matter was when he saw the marks on my face. "Oh, he's only hit me," I said. Elijah turned as Frank came through the door. "Nay Frank, there's no cause to do that." "I know," Frank said, "I'm sorry, I don't know what came over me." The episode was soon forgotten, or at least 'put on ice' but the savour lasted, to raise its head again years later.

When we had first thought of building up a greengrocery round, we decided to follow Tom Bradley's system of putting introductory leaflets through the doors on all the roads we hoped to cover. With this in mind, we had a few hundred leaflets printed and distributed some of them a week before our first call. That was two weeks after we had moved, as every day without trading meant that we were dipping into our capital. On the first day I made up two display baskets showing a sample of all the items we had to offer and assured all housewives that the quality of the produce they ordered from us would be of the exact same as that in the basket. Orders were taken at the door, so that no housewife needed to come out to the van. (Middle class people at that time would not trade in the road, but they were prepared to spend more if they had confidence in the trader).The ordered goods were weighed and bagged in the van and delivered back to the house for payment. The scheme worked well and before long, we found the little 5cwt van was far too small, so we exchanged it for a 10cwt Bedford van which had been adapted for a Jewish man called Cohen to use for hanging gowns when trading in the market. The body was high and enabled us to stand inside, a big improvement in inclement weather and with shelves and compartments fitted down each side, it really was a travelling shop.

At first we both went to the market to buy fruit and vegetables and sometimes a box of flowers to encourage the idea of buying flowers from us, ready for when we had our own. Soon, with one round firmly established, I could spend more time on the field (you couldn't call it a nursery yet) for there was much to do. The sod frame had been dismantled to make way for the drive and if any plants were to be raised this spring, it was essential to build another. There were still plenty of second-hand bricks about from all the demolition after the war and, for £3 I had bought the first 3,000 complete with mortar and concrete still attached. Sitting on an orange box in the middle of the field, with bricks all around me, I chipped away with a hammer cleaning them of their attachments, ready for my first bricklaying.

Then, one day, by a stroke of luck, Elijah said he had seen an advert for a 12ft x 8ft greenhouse for sale somewhere in Derbyshire; the price a modest £8.0s.0d. He said that if I could use it, he and Geoff would go and examine it and if it was in good condition, they would dismantle it and re-erect it on a base made from the second-hand bricks. I thought it would be a very good idea; it would serve at once for raising chrysanthemum cuttings and some half hardy annuals which would survive without heat and mature in time for planting in May. Frank was no handyman, but he was strong and taller than either of my brothers, so he made a good labourer provided he could go at his own pace. All three men went to see and 'vet' the greenhouse, Elijah and Geoff, both craftsmen, pronounced it worth the asking price so, there and then, it was dismantled and re-erected on the flattest most sheltered piece of land in time for sowing seeds of nemesia, stocks, asters, tagetes and French marigolds. By the time they were ready for hardening off, I hoped to have a frame ready for them.

It wasn't long before we took delivery of the new glasshouse, just in time for planting with tomatoes, bought in this year, home produced next year. The foundation was built by Dan Reynolds, Jobie's brother, who was a bricklayer by trade and, as soon as the glasshouse was erected, a frame was built down the side using the foundation brickwork as the back wall. My first bricklaying was, to say the least, not professional, but it was level and the proportion of cement to sand in the mortar ensured it would not readily fall down. I had already made two steps from the nursery to the back door of the Leyland's with the verdict from the lads that they would last forever. Another, deeper frame followed, this time down the side of the small greenhouse, where the lie of the land, in a gentle slope, provided a difference in depth for larger plants.

In June 1950, I paid another visit to the Constance Spry School, this time for a course of lessons on Flower Arranging. I had successfully completed my first two weddings, working all night in the small shed near the gate which we had bought to use as an office (second hand of course). From these had come two more orders, one for Christmas Eve, the other early in the New Year. After the austerity of war, housewives looked for other things to do, more leisurely activities to fill the spare time they had, now that war work was not so pressing. Most women had by now heard of Julia Clements who had created an interest in flower arranging since a visit she had made to the U.S.A. But flowers were still scarce and expensive, for growers had not been allowed to use glasshouse space for growing flowers during the hostilities; food was more urgent and supplies were still not sufficient to fill the demand. Julia, later a firm friend, whom I met on many occasions both as a flower arranger, as President of London and Overseas Area of NAFAS, my own club, and at Ikebana and floristry meetings and exhibitions had devised a method based on geometric lines which would use few flowers and enable inexperienced housewives to complete an acceptable arrangement after only a few lessons. This created an interest in flower arranging, first in the Home Counties, spreading gradually until by 1950 in Young Wives groups, Women's Institutes and Townswomen's Guilds, and by 1953 to places like Creswell, Epworth and Worksop and soon to Chesterfield. The Chairman of the Greenhill Townswomen's Guild, who was one of our very good customers on Bradway Road, asked if I would give a demonstration to the members, many of whom had shown an interest and wanted to know what it was all about. I had made excuses to all demands until now, mainly because I was too busy, but now I realised it would be a good policy to be involved and might provide a very welcome income, albeit not a fortune, nor regular but every penny would help. However, I realised that no matter how well I could arrange flowers and my Mother said I had been doing that since I brought in my first handful of daisies and arranged them in an eggcup, I knew that I would feel more confident with a little professional tuition and to say I had learned at the Constance Spry School would carry a lot of weight (everybody is influenced by that 'little bit of paper', hypothetical or otherwise!).

As on the previous occasion, I booked in at the Y.M.C.A., and next morning reported to the school. This time my teacher was the Senior Teacher of Flower Arranging, Mrs Best. She was a lovely woman, younger than Miss Burns, very friendly and outgoing. We got on extremely well. During the time I was there the Evening News competitions were being held, I think at Earls Court, and she was entering an arrangement in one of the classes. On the second day, when I was finishing a task she had set, she put the finishing touches to a lovely large arrangement in what, she said, were Mrs Spry's 'clashing reds'. It was this arrangement that first taught me the rudiments of adding highlights, for mixed reds can be very flat without something to lift them, much as one would add white, cream or palest green or salmon pink to a painting which looks flat and lifeless. We discussed the technique to some length, during which she could see I was interested in the finer points, not just filling an outline with as many flowers as could be crammed in. This was also my introduction to the subtle use of foliage as a foil and 'shock absorber' for colours one would not otherwise consider using together.

The first arrangement I learned to do was a large pedestal arrangement using great heads of rhododendron and Sarah Bernhardt peonies, long sprays of blossom and the most beautiful and varied foliage one could wish for. As before, the arrangement was completed, taken to pieces and put together again and, as Miss Burns had done Mrs Best said I was a good copier and learned quickly. No matter whatever the reason, I progressed from the pedestal to a table arrangement; one for a windowsill, another for a mantelpiece, each using every different style and shape of container in the school bread-tins, broken vases, bowls of all sizes, learning how to squeeze and cut wire netting to fit each one and how to use the netting to help drape long stems over the side of the rim of the container, for there was no 'oasis' or other foam to make this easier. Even stiff gladiolus stems were coaxed and manipulated into gentle curves with the use of finger and thumb, to be firmly held in place by the cut of the wire. We ended the second day together at the show, after her invitation to keep her company. She didn't win, as I thought she ought to have done, but she didn't mind and was happy to explain the finer points of some of the other entries.

I returned home, full of enthusiasm for my first demonstration on the 9th July 1950. Practice was the essence of success and I set about practising with fervour but I didn't have the materials as I had learned with and funds didn't allow for spending on more than a small amount of flowers, so my thinking cap was donned once more and I came up with the idea that I should only practise one part of an arrangement at any one time, using as much foliage as I could muster from the field. I knew my flowers, thanks to my Father's enthusiasm for growing them. He had made huge sheaves containing the best from his allotment every Friday night during the summer, telling me to take them to one of my friends at Photo Finishers.

I had had friendly competitions with Arthur West to see who could put flowers into a sheaf and each week the number went up as we vied with each other for supremacy. When the annuals like cosmos, larkspur, godetia, bergamot and salpiglossis were in flower, I remember reaching the grand total of 45 different varieties, so I knew the shapes, colours and uses of an abundance of both flowers and foliage; the task now was to use my imagination in putting them together. When using two or three dock leaves I could visualise dracaena, when using moon pennies (wild marguerites), they were pyrethrums, dock flowers were used for spikes; branches of catkins were the finest blossom. With patterns in my head, I could visualise the end product as sure as if it were really made with exotic materials from the finest gardens.

As time went on and I could product my own flowers and foliage, I still followed the same pattern of practice. One night, after everybody had gone to bed I decided to practise ways of creating focal points. I had plenty of different shapes, both foliage and flowers and the practice went on until 3.00 a.m. I was too tired to take the huge arrangement to pieces (the outline made with branches so as to have a scale to work to), so I put it on the sideboard out of the way for dismantling later. My Mother came down as I was making tea, "Good God, what's that?" she cried, as she caught sight of it, "Have you got a job on?" I explained, telling her why it wasn't dismantled last night. She grimaced saying, "I know practice is important, but so is bed!"

My first demonstration was at Greenhill Village Hall, at the invitation of the Greenhill Townswomen's Guild. The hall was almost full by the time I arrived and when I was ready to start, was full with all the space at the back taken by those standing. Of course, this wasn't because I was demonstrating, but rather from curiosity to see that this flower arranging was all about, as it had never been seen in the area before. Mrs Best had explained Mrs Spry's method of demonstrating from behind so that viewers could see what was going on, and I decided to do the same. I knew that one or two demonstrators in London had tried this, doing their practising in front of a mirror, but had abandoned the method. I didn't like the idea of mirrors, preferring to carry the picture in my head, knowing that the outline was three dimensional and the front extended out as far as the sides with the focal point flowers slightly off centre to allow for large leaves to be incorporated, recessing and lifting to give a 3D effect.

The demonstration went well, especially at the end. Modern flower arrangements were made on pin holders as used for Japanese Ikebana and I had bought one in London from a Japanese shop and this, I thought, was the time to use it. Mrs Spry didn't approve of the new type of flower arranging, Ikebana (Japanese flower arranging), but many women in London and as far as Nottingham by this time were happy to learn because it used fewer flowers than traditionally, particularly the Spry mass arrangements. Although I had bought the pin holder, I hadn't used it and perhaps I was rather presumptive in thinking it was easy, a simple technique; just push the stem of the flower firmly into the pins and ease it into the position required. I had seen a number of these sparse designs at the show in London, in fact, one made with only five tulips and foliage had won first prize in a class for a modern arrangement. The challenge was to use it first for demonstrating.

There were only a few minutes left in the 1½ hour demonstration, so taking a shallow dish and firmly fixing the pin holder in position, I quickly impaled five iris, turning them this way and that and adding foliage for a 3D effect, finishing with a few pebbles to cover the holder. Just as I was finishing, Frank walked in to take me home, standing at the back until I had finished. He said, having heard the remarks from those around, it was my piece de resistance. It had taken no more than three minutes to complete and, I think was the reason for many of the audience wishing to learn, for they all had bits and pieces in their gardens which could be used without the abundance of flowers needed for mass arrangements. But, I had learned at Spry's and I remained a Spry fan, working on the principals of art, using materials in a natural way, as they want to go, rather than forcing them into rigid geometrical lines.

About this time, I saw Mrs Spry demonstrate at Buxton and was completely 'hooked' by her method of arranging from behind; as an onlooker I could appreciate how much more interesting and

420

informative it was to see exactly how each flower and piece of foliage was placed and the feeling of motion as a branch of blossom flowed forward from side front towards the viewer. I determined to follow this method no matter how long I had to practise. It needed practice, but I found that if I kept the design in my head and visualised what effect each piece would look like from the front, the result would be satisfactory. I was very thankful I had persevered in later years when demonstrating on television, when time was too limited to allow for frequent turning.

That first summer progressed quite well, the hardest job trying to rid the land of all the docks and thistles and the deepest couch/twitch grass one feared to encounter. One answer was to buy a cultivator with tines which would drag out the offending roots, leaving them to dry and then raking them off. But a cultivator was out of the question; we already had the van and glasshouse on hire purchase and still dipping into our dwindling capital to supplement the income from the round. There was no room for more hire purchase. So, like it or not, there was only hard work and perseverance to make sure there was sufficient ground ready in time for planting chrysanthemums, stocks, asters and other half-hardy annuals suitable for cut flowers and wreaths, which would, by September, be a welcome addition to our budget. Frank had managed to dig over the borders in the glasshouse after the twitch had been removed; he could take his time so long as they were ready for the tomatoes by the middle of May.

In August, the question of heating had to be considered, a real headache, for coke fired boilers and heating pipes were expensive. But without heating I would be very limited in crops to grow through winter and spring. Then, by a stroke of luck, we heard that a nurseryman at Brimington was clearing out his coke burning system and installing electricity. Frank and Elijah went to see them when the nurseryman offered us the Lancashire boiler and all the pipes for a small price which we could afford. They worked together to install them down the sides of both houses, crossing the 12ft space between them where the pipes had to be lagged against frost damage. This was a particular hazard at the high altitude and exposed position, as we found one night when one of the joints leaked and had to be repaired near midnight in 12 degrees of frost. Frank and I worked for about an hour, removing the lagging, re-sealing the pipe and replacing the lagging, our fingers very nearly frost bitten, made worse by a blizzard blowing at the time, with a wind-chill almost more than we could stand.

The job finished, Frank went inside whilst I checked both houses and made sure the pipes were filled with water again. When eventually I set off for the house, the blizzard was worse and a deep drift had built up filling the entrance to the back door, so I decided to crawl through a space in the bottom of the hedge. This was almost my undoing for, as soon as I reached ground level, the vicious wind was whipping through the gap, drawing the breath from my lungs. I thought my time had come and almost panicked, as I tried to draw breath and found it almost impossible. Pressing down even lower to the ground, where I hoped the wind would blow over me, I slowly backed out, my freezing limbs almost refusing to move. Gradually, I inched back and eventually managed to stand, slowly making my way to the drift.

By September, it was time to think of Christmas wreaths and all there was to do before we could start. First was a supply of moss and this we knew could be gathered on the moors, where it grew in the stagnant streams at the bottom of the gulleys as drainage from the hills. One Sunday morning, towards the end of September, we donned warm clothing, for we knew it could be biting cold, possibly with a touch of early frost, and knee-high gumboots protected our feet as we waded in the water. Within a few moments we were high up on Stanage Moors and down the slope into a beautiful secluded valley and soon we found easy pickings of sphagnum moss almost half a yard long as we pulled it from the deep water. We soon had enough to fill half a dozen sacks. A later trip in November when the first supply was used up, was not so easy. After early frosts, it was brittle and easily broken and we had to resort to using rakes to retrieve the shorter stems from the banks.

I had already made arrangements with a wholesaler in Sheffield Market to take all the wreaths we could make, the price to be fixed when he saw our first sample. "2,000," he said, "I'll take 'em all if they're good 'uns." I knew this number was out of the question, at least until I had trained Arthur and Frank, but it was a target which encouraged us to work hard. Cupressus could be bought in bundles from the market and Mr Shepley allowed us to gather holly in Holmesfield Park at the price of £15 a day, the same as the market traders paid, only they sent half a dozen men and went away with a lorry load, whereas we were only three, later only two. However, as a concession later, because I arranged the altar flowers each month for Mrs Shepley when it was her turn on the roster, we were allowed to pick holly for a week free. A sample wreath had been taken to the wholesalers and a price fixed; all that remained was to make as many as possible, and the money received from them would tide us over the three months until the bedding plants and other seasonal crops like daffodils and tulips from boxes in the glasshouse and brassicas from the frame were ready for sale. By the time we had finished and delivered the last wreath, I was very pleased with our effort. Arthur had proved a quick learner and a fast worker and Frank had managed to get his fingers round the clusters of holly, albeit rather more slowly.

1951 made steady progress in the glasshouses and stock was built up in dahlias, chrysanthemums and plants from seed such as polyanthus, which were a lucrative trade for Mother's Day trade as cheap bunches for Sunday school children to take home to mother. Mary was a good customer in this respect, taking a good supply of bunches to Millhouses Methodist Church at 2d a bunch.

The ground was stony and full of twitch grass in the new areas required for planting new perennials and extra plants of chrysanthemums and dahlias as well as peas and broad beans I hoped to produce as cash crops. Sheer determination and a refusal to be beaten, kept me working, particularly as I knew there were those who though I was crackers, 'playing at it' and that I'd never succeed.

The two weddings already undertaken had brought orders for another two and I had given three more demonstrations, one to a Young Wives group, the other two to groups of ladies who were members of the 'Ladies Circle' and 'Inner Wheel' and much interest was shown by other ladies with time on their hands, who wished to learn both flower arranging and floristry. All these brought welcome additions to our budget but the nursery was still considered my priority, where our future lay and so, hard work or not, it had to survive.

It was again September, tomatoes would soon be cleared, for we could sell all the green ones as well as those that ripened, for food was still scarce or rationed and many people made chutneys and pickles, including ourselves. The late chrysanthemums, grown outside from plants bought in, were ready for lifting inside the borders and soon the stools of the earlies would be boxed when they had been relieved of their last few sprays of useful flowers. We had built up another greengrocery round in Dore Village, Causeway Head Road, Heather Lea Avenue and the Meadway, which we both worked on Tuesdays and Fridays and the original round in Bradway and Twentywell Lane had been upgraded to two days a week, Wednesdays and Saturdays, when we had added Holmesfield by request for some people on the Council estate.

However, Frank wasn't happy. Most of the summer he had gone to the market alone, unless I had need of seeing one of the wholesalers and sometimes, when extra work was called for, he went on the midweek rounds alone. It was possibly the loneliness which helped to 'get him down', I don't know, but he was always happier working with someone else. We were both spread a bit think with all the jobs piling up at once and the strain was showing. To add to the situation, we had decided to add another outlet for the produce surplus to the rounds when we had chance to rent a small wooden shed in the centre of Totley Village. It was the old chip shop owned by Fred Unwin who lived in the bottom house in the 'Hillcrest' row, about 20 yards up Baslow Road. He was a tight businessman, but he agreed that if we repaired it, we could use it for a small rent. At first the shop was open only during the afternoons, which enabled me to work all morning and evening on the land; hard going and long hours, but after being granted a licence to sell cigarettes and tobacco and adding sweets to the list, the little shop soon proved worth the trouble.

I remember one particularly long day when I was working close to the hedge at the far side of the field. It was 10.30 p.m. on a beautiful moonlit night, when I was weeding the strawberry beds and Geoff appeared on his way to see Mom. "What are you doing?" he asked, I thought a bit sarcastically. I was always rather wary of remarks from the men folk, not only from my brothers but from some of the men from the village who called to buy brassicas or bedding plants who either wanted to become partners because they 'would like a hard working woman like you', or they thought I was 'crackers', that I'd never make it, but were only too willing to buy my plants. I listened to them all, none of them knowing why I struggled on, that if I didn't we might, by now be begging. How different it might have been had I had chance to be trained at a Horticultural College, like the young men in the village or if, like him, we had capital to make planning easier. I was tired and when Geoff went on "Is it worth it, surely you can't see what you're doing?" I answered cryptically with as much humour as my tired wits could muster, "I can see alright, I can still tell t 'other from t 'witch'. The latter, if you haven't already grasped it was Twitch/Couch grass."

As Christmas came round again, mossing started, followed by greening, finishing with holly and statice incana. A sample had been taken to market and the price fixed at 2s.6d (half a crown - (12½p). I had had to barter very hard the previous year for that amount, 6d more than the going rate because I knew they were worth the extra. When the first cheque had arrived at the end of the first week and finding it less than expected, I complained and refused to unload the next batch until the deficit was made up. There was an argument, but I persisted, "After all," I told Tom the wholesaler, "You don't even have to handle the damned things, your customers load them straight off my van into theirs." He hadn't argued any further, and paid the difference. But, this year he knew better than to try. We had managed to make 665 wreathes and with the £25 due for chrysanthemums I expected to receive almost £200 which, with the profit from a Boxing Day wedding would replenish our 'coffers' and ensure a good supply of seeds for spring sowing and keep us in relative comfort until the bedding plant season. Who knows, I thought, by early summer I might even obtain that sorely need cultivator.

425

The shock was indescribable when the wholesaler told me that the greater part of the money would be kept in payment for goods obtained by Frank and not paid for. I asked why he had let him have them without paying when the rule was that if you had a credit arrangement with a wholesaler, it was on the understanding that it would be paid the following week. He said he knew that, as the wreaths came in, the revenue from them would be sufficient to clear the backlog, so he hadn't interfered. I was shattered, but there was more to come. Another three wholesalers were owed money which I could not comprehend as having any relationship with the proceeds of the rounds and the shop. I went back to where the van was parked, too bewildered to cry. When Frank returned and the goods he had bought were loaded, he showed no surprise at my quietness, saying he was sorry, but he just didn't like the job. "I'm sick to death of going up people's drives only to be asked for 2lbs of potatoes," he said. "But," I answered, "If you sell them potatoes today, next time they may want cabbage, or tomatoes, and eventually they'll buy everything from us."

"Maybe," he said, "but I've had enough, I'm fed up with the whole damned job." "In that case, get out," I told him, "get another job and leave me to it." "You'll not be able to do it on your own," he said. "You leave it to me," I shouted, "I'll do a damned sight better than you seem to have done." "What will you do?" he asked, "will you go bankrupt, you can't do anything else as I see it?" He couldn't have said anything that would have spurred me on more. "Of course I'll not go bankrupt, I'm going to carry on, I've started the job and I'll finish it in my own way." "Suit yourself," he said, "bloody confident as usual." He knew how unsure I was, but the devil was still driving and the thinking cap was wearing a bit thin. However, as long as there was a thread left I could 'don' it and use the little grey matter I had been endowed with.

My Mother was not a bit surprised. "Have you seen the compost heap in the back?" she asked. "No, why?" I answered, wondering what other surprises were in store. I've seen him tipping boxes of tomatoes and lettuce after every round," she told me, "Let alone all the other stuff he hadn't sold." "Why didn't you tell me?" I asked. "Well I thought you must know, and it wasn't any of my business," she answered. "Poor Frank, he's not cut out for this sort of job," she said. "I know," I agreed, "I've told him to get another job, but that's easier said than done." "There's one at the brickyard," she said, "They want a mate for one of the drivers." The brickyard was at the end of Moorwood Lane, only ten minutes' walk away, and ideal, as the work would be light enough for Frank to cope with. When I told him he was surprised. "You wouldn't want me to work there would you, when your father was one of the Managers?" "You can work anywhere, so long as you get out of this business," I told him. "It doesn't matter two hoots that my Father was a Manager, he's not there now; you want a job and you'll never get one nearer home," I said.

He made an appointment and got the job, at the rate of £7.5s.0d more than he had received from the Police Force four years before, but enough to keep body and soul together, leaving me to clear all the debts, altogether just over £300.0s.0d.

There were legal arrangements to be made, and to this end, Frank paid a visit to our Solicitors and arranged for his name to be removed from the nursery agreement; I had already written to the Registrar of Business Names for the same purpose. "It's straight forward," said the Solicitor, "there's no need to get the Deeds from the Bank, it's automatic," he said. How wrong he was. The first thing I had to do was to see the wholesalers to whom we owed money, not a pleasant task and a bit degrading to my pride. My message to all four wholesalers was "Give me time, let me still trade with you and I'll pay off as much as I can afford each week until the debt is cleared." All four agreed. The only surprise, they said, was that I didn't know. They had let the debts shift on because they knew we were trying hard and trusted my husband to pay them when we could, but they all agreed he wasn't a businessman and would be better out of it. One of them, who now lives at the Peewit said "He's a nice chap lass, but he's not cut out for this game."

When my Father first knew I was going to marry Frank, he said to my Mother, "It's to be hoped that he never leaves the Police Force, 'cos I'm afraid he'll never be able to put in a hard day's work;

I'm afraid he'll never make old bones." That really was the trouble, no matter how hard he may have tried, he just found the workload and the hassle too much for his constitution. I had seen it when I warned Peter, I had known when we started the business and perhaps had expected too much. As my Mother had often said over the years, if I had criticised someone's stamina or enthusiasm, "Everybody's not like you, everybody's not as strong and determined as you are and it takes all types to make a world."

After my Father died in 1947, all three boys and my Mother decided that his business, the ganister mine at Wessington, should continue. I would have agreed also had I been asked, but being a woman, my opinion didn't account for much and I was never asked. The question was who should run it? Both Elijah and Geoff were now teaching and although Elijah offered to leave that for the sake of the business, Mom said, "No, your Father wouldn't want either of you to give it up after all your studying." Jeff, a butcher, was studying to be an Inspector of meat, but he offered to give up the idea and take over. After some discussion, this was agreed and for a time, the family lived with Mother at the Leyland's until the ganister ran out about a year later. My Father, in ganister for most of his working life, would have known where to find the next supply, but Jeff hadn't the knowledge and experience to do the same. During the time he ran the mine the boys and my mother had decided to buy a lorry and do the carting instead of using an outside contractor. The first lorry hadn't proved a great success. Bought from a local garage, run by a local man, it turned out to be a 'Friday car', as indicating that it was a dud. This caused much expense. A second one joined it and, for the past two years, Jeff, who had moved to Congleton where the work was, had run them as a haulage business. He was paid a wage of £8 per week and Mother drew £3 a week to supplement her pension.

When we moved into the Leyland's we had agreed to pay my Mother the same rent as the Stevens, but there was one difference. They had had the use of much of the front garden for growing vegetables, almost the size of an allotment and had I had the same privilege it would have seen us through the first months until some ground could be prepared on the nursery, at least to provide vegetables for the house. Taking this more or less for granted, I was sowing carrot seed one day when my Mother appeared and asked what I was doing and when I told her, she said "You'd better leave more space; Geoff or 'Liga' might want to put something in." I stopped what I was doing and never attempted to use it again and no-one else did either, it just grew an abundance of weeds.

I think initially my Mother resented us moving in, she liked her own company and although she was much better off financially, it was no substitute for being alone. But, I reasoned, she had been happy with the company of the Stevens, or so I thought, but I always knew that she was always wary about what the boys might think. Had it been one of them instead of me, her attitude would have been different, for she never showed any resentment when Jeff lived there. It may have been that she could show her true feelings with me without pretending, I don't know. All I do know is that, as many of the villagers had said, "They are your mother's blue-eyed boys, and you are your father's girl." Some people said she was jealous because my Father took me out and left her at home, again I don't know. But I have often wondered why I was always trying to please her; was it because I was never sure what she thought about me, and I just wanted to be loved? I don't know.

Just after Christmas 1952, Jeff told Mom that he wanted the business; he didn't see why he should run it for the rest of the family, I suspect with Edith's backing. My Mother resisted; it had been Dad's business and she was reluctant to part with it. Jeff said he was about to make another contract for carrying sand and had an offer of help in buying a lorry of his own, which he would do and take on the contract himself if she didn't agree, leaving the business with two lorries and no work.

My Mother spoke to Elijah about it and as there seemed little to do to prevent it, she agreed to let Jeff have the business; lorries and all, free gratis. The same day, Jeff came to see me in the nursery. I hadn't been privy to the discussion, I never was; I was a girl; I even had to 'gate-crash' the meeting with the Solicitor after my Father's funeral, when neither Frank nor I had been asked to attend. When my Mother asked why I had come into the room, I answered that, as

429

I was my Father's daughter, I should attend as well as his sons. "We can look after your interests," Elijah said, but I told him I would rather look after my son. The Solicitor was surprised, said he didn't know my Father had a daughter and, of course, I should stay, as he invited me to sit down.

Jeff had come to ask if I would keep my Mother from now on; "It won't be easy at the start," he said, "I shall need more money; I shan't be able to pay her the £3 from the business anymore." I told him it was hard for me too, as I had just started on my own and had debts to pay. "Well, if you ever need any help, I'll see what I can do," he said and I knew it was a 'fait accompli'. From that day, instead of a rent of 30s.0d as Stevens had paid for lodgings and the use of the garden, we paid an extra 6s.11d for the whole of the mortgage, part of which had been added when Jeff at the end of the first year had run into debt and Mom had borrowed £200 from the Building Society to help him out.

Up to now, we had contributed to the lighting, cooking and heating bills, but the new situation demanded that we pay the whole, including all the food and household expenses. Mother's pension was 10s.0d per week which, we said; she could keep for her help and cooking; it was little enough to keep herself in clothes and other personal accessories. I already paid a woman from the village to come two mornings a week to do the housework, and this continued. For the next two years, I pulled out all the stops and used all the sales technique I could muster. Mrs Finlay, who had worked in the house up to now, agreed to work in the shop in the mornings and Mrs Wortley, another village woman, took on the cleaning.

Fortunately, for the past two years, orders for weddings had trickled in quite regularly bringing in a welcome addition to our budget. I grew used to working all night in the shed/office near the entrance gate, though some people thought I was taking a risk. But danger did not seem important at that time and I didn't suffer from nerves.

It was after delivery of a wedding order to Thornhill near Bamford that I decided to pay a call on an old friend of my Mother and Father, who lived at Hathersage. The daughter of Mrs

Underwood had died about four years previously during childbirth and her 70 year old mother had brought up the little girl and her five year old sister, with the help of her son Roland/Roly. I had known Roly since I was about twelve years old during my holidays with the Elliott's, and in my later teenage years had visited the Underwood's with my Father many times when they lived in a cottage next to the 'Scotsman's Pack' public house. Mr Underwood has been a professional gardener and with my Father's enthusiasm for the subject there was always something to talk about and questions to ask or sometimes Dad would buy plants which took his fancy.

Roly had grown up gardening and was equally enthusiastic; consequently it wasn't strange to find him interested in my occupation whilst exchanging news of the years since Dad's death. Before I left, he had offered to come and 'give me a hand', and the following Sunday was chosen for the family to visit for the day, allowing the Moms to reminisce to their heart's content.

We can all be wise in hindsight and it possibly was not the wisest thing to do when I had a husband whose help was minimal. But, we can't put the clock back and even foresight would not have allowed me to miss the opportunity of help, particularly from one who knew what to do and had the strength and inclination to do it. From the first visit, it became a regular Sunday ritual for either Roly alone, or the whole family, to come after lunch, staying as long as there was work to be done. The two girls loved the freedom of playing in the large garden or in the nursery, for they had no garden at home and the freedom of our fields and open spaces was near paradise.

But the arrangement was too good to last. At first Frank was only too pleased for Roly and his help and never failed to thank him profusely for doing what, after all, he should have been doing instead of sitting dozing in a chair beside the fire. Mrs Underwood was now 75 years old and it was perfectly obvious that five and nine year old girls were a source of great distress to her when she could not do the things for them which she thought she should do. One of these was bath night, washing hair and other little toiletries a mother would do, and it wasn't long before I took on the job, not only for them, but for her too. Every Saturday night I went to Hathersage and turned myself into 'bath lady' cum hairdresser, cum confidant and councillor and substitute mother to two little girls. Oh yes, they had a father, who lived with them, but he spent all his time with his friends away from home, never interfering, never helping in the upbringing of his daughters; in essence, he just wasn't there!

I must point out here that all this was with the tacit and unstinting approval of my Mother. If, at any time, I was reluctant to pay the usual visit, either because I was tired, or I thought it more judicious not to go, she would listen then insist that I should go, either because I deserved a night off, or for the sake of the girls. I knew the situation was delicate and I also knew that both families, in my teenage years, had had designs on a more serious relationship between Roly and me, but I don't think this influenced her actions now, although she knew, without being told, that there was something missing in my marriage, not in any way sexual, rather in fun and light-hearted bantering and repartee and Saturday night was a time for rectifying the deficiency.

In July 1953, Roly brought a message from the Hathersage Horticultural Society. They were inviting me to put on a trade stand at their annual show in August. The judges, as in previous years, were to be the three broadcasters from the Radio programme 'Gardener's Question Time', Alan Gemmel, Fred Loads and Bill Sowerbutts. Roly explained the reason for the invitation. The same rose grower had been awarded the large gold medal and best Trade Show Award for many years, even though, for the last two or three, the standard of the display had been very low and other exhibitors were growing very discontented. "The trouble is," said Roly, "he always invites them to lunch at 'The Scotsman's' and people are beginning to think its fixed, they want somebody to beat him and your show could do it." I was flattered by their confidence. I had been awarded a large gold medal at the Sheffield Chrysanthemum Show and the Sheffield Show in 1952 and intended exhibiting again in 1953, but beating a man of so many years' experience was different. However, I went to see the Chairman of the Committee and said I would have a go.

The display was hard work and shows are costly; there is no real evidence of resulting business, sometimes for months, but my

432

display included bouquets and other wedding work so perhaps a new venue could reap results. The display was finished, the last finishing touches complete and I was well satisfied with the result. When the judges came round I could see they were impressed and not a little surprised to see a totally different exhibit. We stood back as they debated, perused, cogitated and deliberated, until after almost half an hour, they moved away to examine once again the stand of the rose grower.

We watched, amazed as they stood talking, not only between themselves, but also to the exhibitor himself. It was all too obvious they were in a dilemma, not sure which stand should receive the award. Then, as they came towards me, I knew the worse when Fred Loads spoke. "We've decided to give the award to the rose stand. I'm very sorry, you have a beautiful display, but really Mrs Rundle, you can't expect to beat an exhibitor of such longstanding can you?" I was astounded, not because I hadn't won the top award, but for the reason. I was disgusted and the three men knew it. "He's been exhibiting here for years," Bill Sowerbutts said, "and, after all, this is your first time." Two or three members of the committee came to see me, but there was nothing they could do. "You should have got it," said one. "Yours is a damned sight better than his," said another, whilst they all thanked me for the effort and "At least", said one, "he'll perhaps pull his socks up for the future, he's had a bloody shock today," as he nodded towards the half dead, badly arranged bowls of roses.

The following Sunday, we had just finished stacking away the show fitments in a shed at the top of the orchard and were talking in the office/shed, Roly consoling me by telling me I'd done my best, when we saw Frank walking down the garden of the Leyland's near to the hedge dividing the two properties. There was an opening in the hedge just in front of the shed door and we watched as he stooped and came through and into the shed doorway. But we weren't ready for his tirade of abuse, accusing Roly of groping in my blouse, which was ridiculous considering I was wearing Land Army dungarees with a bib up to the neck. A hearty row followed, during which he told Roly to get out and me, he would see later. "Oh no," I said, "You'll see me now, and I'll tell you this, if you insist he goes, then you can get up off your arse and do what he does - work!" But Roly said he wasn't here to cause rows and he would go immediately. So, once again I was on my own, except for the help I get from Arthur, although still at school, had made seed boxes, pedestals for church arrangements and shows, troughs and boxes for display work and a whole row of frame lights, as well as valuable help on the land and at Christmas.

Two days later, I was confronted by a somewhat contrite husband, trying to make amends, giving me his reasons for the sordid outburst and wishing to make amends. Basically, his theory was that no woman could refrain from having sex for so long and if I wasn't getting it from him, I must be getting it somewhere else. My reasoning that there were other important things to do besides sex cut no ice, nor the fact that my energies were being used in work and the necessity to pay bills, an opinion justified, I thought by the difference in our lifestyles for whereas I rose at 5.00 a.m. for market and continued on the greengrocery round and nursery until late in the evening, he sat in the seat of a lorry from 8.00 a.m. until 5.00 p.m., then his day was finished. But, like all men, where sex is concerned, he voiced his own solution and passed the 'buck' to me. This is a delicate subject to write about, but I feel it is important to understand the way of events and I'll be as discreet as possible in my explanation.

In 1938 when it seemed that was war inevitable, Frank voiced the thought that it would not be a good idea for us to have more children, although I must say, there had never been any suggestion that we would. I agreed and before long flatly refused to have anymore as I thought he didn't pull his weight with our first, neither fair to the baby, or to me. To this end and so that the control of such matters was as much in my hands as his, I refused to risk any form of contraception, preferring to trust to my own judgment and my husband's dexterity in preventing another pregnancy. Frank knew I had never got a ha'peth of enjoyment out of our lovemaking, referring to this as the reason for my lack of enthusiasm. "If you'd just try something, you'd enjoy it," he said. I had my doubts at this stage, but anything is worth trying for peace and quietness I thought, so I agreed. On his next visit to Sheffield he returned with a packet which

434

he said was the best he could get, and foolproof. But there is nothing foolproof in this world, as I found out a month later.

In July I thought I could now afford something new to wear; being tired of making do and feeling dowdy at demonstrations and other occasions when I should be smart. The last item I had bought was a calf length coat in 1948 when the 'New Look' fashion came to Britain, after the short skirts of wartime and now was the time to buy two new suits, both very chic and confidence-building. Now, I felt very let down for, when I tried to struggle into the skirt of one of them, I had put on weight and it didn't fit; I knew I was pregnant. Of course I blamed Frank, he had done it on purpose, he was bloody careless and that was the end of my love life, forever, I'd never trust a man again.

He was contrite, apologetic; he hadn't done it on purpose; he would examine the 'French letter' (that's what they were called in those days). On inspection there was a hole in it and he was angry; was going to sue the firm, it had cost half a week's wages and should have been reliable. Hearing this, I calmed down, but the problem remained; what was I going to do? I still had debts; I was earning good money, sometimes £25 a week on the rounds, more than three times my husband's wage and I was loathe to give everything up before I had established a decent lifestyle.

The answer, as I saw it, was to say nothing, tell nobody, not even my Mother and that hurt more than anything. I would tell no-one, except one person. One of my customers was the wife of a chemist, who made 'pin money' out of dressmaking. She had made two summer dresses for me, by which time we had become great friends. I told her about my problem; the result, a confidential talk to her husband and a bottle of tablets for me. They didn't work, or the next or the next half a dozen different concoctions, until finally, after five months, I realised this baby wanted to be born. "I'm not surprised," said Dr Marshall, when I went to see him and told him what I had taken. "Nothing will shift it, you've got an inside like a horse and it'll hang on to the end." I said, "How was it I nearly had a miscarriage then?" "Oh that, that was just gland trouble; but we had to be careful, this is different, you'll carry this one you'll see."

I broke the news to my Mother two days later. "I wondered when you'd tell me," she said, "You can't keep anything from mothers can you?" When I told her what I had done, and why, her philosophical answer was typical. "I don't know what you're worrying for, it'll all come right in the end." "But," I said, exasperated at her calmness, "what am I going to do about the nursery and the rounds?" "You'll find a way," she answered with a strange conviction and faith, either in her understanding of me or her unbounding faith that all things come right in the end. I wasn't persuaded, "You know I didn't want any more children, and you know why," I reminded her. "Aye," she said mysteriously, like Mother Shipton voicing one of her prophecies, "but this one's coming for a reason, you'll be glad one day, just you see." I didn't say any more, but from that moment, all seemed to be in order and natural and I began to make plans and to be happy about the coming event.

Then came another embarrassing moment when the news was broken to Arthur, now 16 years old, well established as the only child and plunged into this embarrassing situation in front of his friends. One saving grace was the comforting fact that the mother of Bill Smith, one of a group of school friends who visited us occasionally, had also just given birth to a baby girl. Nevertheless, Arthur was hurt. "What were you playing at, at your age? Why didn't you think about me? What's going to happen to the nursery now?" "The nursery will carry on," I told him. "Yes," he said, "but I always thought it would be mine, and now there will be somebody else." "You don't need to worry about that," I told him, "You are the one who helps me and you will be the one to get the bursary if and when you want it." This seemed to satisfy him, however, there was just one more question to settle, the name of the new-born when it arrived. "I want you to do one thing for me, let me choose the name," he said. I said "OK, that's fine." "If it's a girl I want to call her Yvonne Marie," he said. He told me later that he first chose Theresa (a name I don't remember hearing). I did ask why he chose the two names, to which he answered, "I like them."

Later, talking to Frank and my Mother about what Arthur had said and whether Frank had any alternatives, my Mother piped up

"Call her Lucy." "Why Lucy?" I asked. "Well, it's as good as any," she answered quizzically. I knew that her best friend at school had been called Lucy and Mom's favourite current song was 'Put your shoes on Lucy', so I assumed these were two of her reasons and I also assumed that, although her answers were rather flippant, she would like to have some influence over the name. I knew that I was going to rely on her to some extent if I was to carry on working and this was sufficient reason for me letting her have her wish. But Lucy, I thought, was rather ordinary, mundane, in between Yvonne and Marie, so I changed it to Lucille, making her (forgive me England) very French indeed; after all, my name is French, so why not hers.

There was much to do before a name was required, there were still over three months to wait, if everything went according to plan, but before settling down to business once more, I decided to pay Sister Goss a visit and book into Sharrow Head for the birth. It was six years since my last duty there and she was very surprised at the reason for the visit. But, I was welcomed with open arms and a vehement "Yes" to my request to have the baby there. That settled, the next two months passed without events. Then, it was inevitable that life would have to follow a different pattern but where to go from here? The rounds had done well, all debts had been paid off, except for £16 which would be cleared during the next month, then it was back to square one.

One Sunday Jeff and Edith came and during the conversation, Jeff asked what I was going to do about the greengrocery rounds. "Nothing," I told him, "who would want a round anyway?" He suggested I put an advert in the paper. "I'll pay for it if you can't," he said. This offer I neither needed nor would take, but I did put an advert in the Sheffield Telegraph and received one reply. It came from a man well known in the Sheffield market, not for hard work, rather from spending a lot of his time there and occasionally doing odd jobs for some of the wholesalers.

Bob Simmonite was a small man, who always wore a bowler hat and a tatty raincoat. After making arrangements with him, we met early the following Thursday morning in South Street, Sheffield where I always parked whilst buying fruit and vegetables for the round. After a somewhat lopsided conversation, for he wasn't a man of words, we agreed that he should pay me £60 for the whole round, excluding the van; he would supply his own conveyance after the takeover. An amicable arrangement was made, whereby he could pay me in instalments, the whole to be paid before or on the take-over day and during the ensuing two weeks, I should manage the rounds to enable him to know them and become known and he should manage the last two weeks, doing his own buying, sorting and pricing, whilst I would help by serving and weighing in the van, leaving him to make house contact with the customers.

It was evident from the first day that Bob Simmonite did not like doing more than was strictly necessary in the way of work. "Do you have to go up every drive?" he asked when we reached Bradway Drive. "Don't any of the women come out to the van?" "Of course not," I told him; "My customers are not that sort of people." "Why?" he wanted to know, and "Don't you ever stand and shout?" "Of course I don't," I assured him, "I'm not a person like that." He couldn't understand why the customers I served would not readily buy from a street trader who just stood in the road shouting "taters', ripe tomatas' lovely apples" expecting them in their pinnies, to do their own fetching and carrying. For the first two weeks I was the one doing the fetching and carrying as arranged, even though I was in the last month of pregnancy. He was more than content to sit on the step of the van waiting for the next order and then watch me as I weighed out those items I couldn't trust him with. The last two weeks I let him do the running, amid much huffing and puffing and grumbling about his legs aching "With all this running about," he said. It was obvious from the moment of loading in the market that he was going to try to get out of the heavy work. He couldn't handle the cwt. sacks of potatoes or the heavy boxes of oranges and bananas and expected the delivery lads to do it all without offering the smallest tip.

I might say here that orange boxes were awkward things to negotiate. They were made of wood, about 2'6" long with a wooden partition forming two compartments each about 15" square which held any number between 100 and 500 oranges according to their grade and place of origin. The boxes were very heavy and held together by 'orange rope' (plaited fibre) which we used to beg as children to make skipping ropes. Apples came in bushel boxes made of thick wood and returnable. They were heavy, especially when full of fruit and cumbersome in the necessity for twice handling. Bananas were marketed in even heavier boxes, also returnable. They were about 3' long x 12" square, with a lid to keep the fruit cool in summer and free from frost in winter. But potatoes were the most awkward and heaviest. Marketed in 1cwt sacks, some to be emptied into the compartments built into the sides of the van, others for refilling, stored under the shelves, to be pulled out when needed; they were the mainstay of the rounds, but very exhausting to handle.

The money for the business was paid in very small amounts, £5 here, £5 there and, by the last day, the amount still owing was £17.10s.0d. My baby was only two weeks away so there was no time to bargain further, it had to be settled today. No mention was made about payment when I met Bob Simmonite in South Street; he just gave a quick nod, "Morning," he said and then went on his way to do his buying. A minute or two later, Fred, a porter, arrived with two bags of potatoes and was surprised when I said "Just put them down there will you Fred?" pointing to the pavement. "I'll put them on for you," he said. "No, it's alright, just leave them there," I told him, "It'll be alright, thank you." He went away still unsure as he turned the corner and looked back. Another porter came with apples, oranges and a load of other fruit, a third one bringing supplies of vegetables and a couple of boxes of flowers. With them came Fred, still wondering what was happening and as the other two set down their loads on the pavement, he said "Is everything alright Mrs Rundle?" "Yes, thank you Fred," I said, "Don't worry, everything's under control." He looked a bit dubious, "Look," he said, "We're going to have a cup of tea; we'll be in the café if you want us." The café was a little further up South Street, where the porters always went for snack meals and cups of tea.

A moment later, Mr Simmonite came round the corner carrying a box of bananas on his shoulder. A few more steps and he reached the van. "What's this, why have they left things there?" he said. "Because I told them to," I said. "Why?" he said, he really was naïve; he didn't even guess. "Why didn't they load them?" he asked, not a little peeved. "Because there is some business to complete before they are loaded," I told him, "A small matter of £16.10s.0d." "But," he began. "No buts Mr Simmonite, my money or no loading." He prevaricated, muttered something, then he saw the porters coming down the street. "Can't we just get them on, and then talk?" he was now somewhat embarrassed. "No," I said, "Give me my money and then we can load." The lads were now very close, "Everything alright Mrs Rundle?" Fred asked as he paused beside the van. "Yes, thank you Fred," I assured him. "If you're sure," he said hesitating, then walking away to stand on the corner looking back until we eventually drove away. "Look, can't we talk about this inside?" said the now subdued Mr Simmonite. I agreed, walking away to sit in the driver's seat whilst he sat beside me. "Now," I told him, "hand over my money and let's get off." He still hummed and harred, eventually asking how much it was. "Come on," I said, "You know damned well how much it is." He put his hand in his pocket and drew out two notes, which I immediately took from him, holding my hand out for more. He hesitated then drew out two more. I took these and a £1 note to follow. "Come on Mr Simmonite," I said, "If we don't get on you'll never sell this load." "Can't we set off," he said, "I'll settle when we've finished." "You'll settle it now," I said holding out my hand, "I want £4.10s.0d please." He pulled out a few more notes and counted out £4.10s.0d tentatively handing them to me saying, "My you're an 'ard woman." "Come on, let's get loaded," was my only response, trying to stop myself laughing as I jumped down and grabbed a crate of cauliflowers.

The next two weeks were exceptionally busy and even without the rounds it was difficult to find time for all the preparations necessary before 17th May, the date the babe was expected. The bedding season was in full swing so boxes of bedding plants could be delivered and those retained for home sales could be kept in frames and dealt with in the evenings by Frank and Arthur for, although not fully reconciled to the situation, he showed little more than an occasional grunt and in times of necessity, was a great help. The glasshouse had been planted with tomatoes, only requiring watering, ventilating and if the weather turned particularly cold, the boiler stoking. The latter was no hardship for Frank, for he often took on the job of raking out the boiler and reloading. Chrysanthemums and dahlias could wait for planting until I returned. Now all that was required was that I should give birth to the girl I had been hoping for.

I wasn't disappointed, for at 2.30 a.m. in the morning of the 18th May, I received the first sign that things were happening. "We'd better get moving," I said to Frank, "You'd better ring Sister Goss." In half an hour, I was safely in bed in a downstairs room set aside for me and events moved fast. "I'm sorry nurse," said Sister suddenly, "It's a breech and you'll have to work hard." This was very unexpected as Sister had examined me only an hour earlier when all was well, but for some reason, the baby had turned suddenly and would now be born feet first.

I wasn't worried, having every confidence in both Sister Goss and Nurse Harrington and, after a few minutes of intense concentration and much pushing and grunting on my part, at 6.20 a.m. our daughter entered our lives. She was beautiful. Like all breech babies her head was perfectly formed and her cheeks were, as Sister said, "Like two rosy apples." She had, Nurse Harrington said later, a small birthmark on the nape of her neck, "But that won't matter, her hair will cover it," she said.

I returned home after ten days, the usual time for confinements then, and in two months' time Arthur left Nether Edge Grammar school to commence his career as a nurseryman. This wasn't entirely a success. Arthur was an intelligent young man with great potential and the nursery was too small for his unbounding energy and enthusiasm, which would have been more suited to 100 acres and Ferguson tractor to satisfy his ambitions at the end of each day. Nevertheless, he worked hard and conscientiously, doing all the jobs I asked without complaint or question, and I was particularly thankful for his help at this time when I needed it most. However, it was evident as the weeks went by and his frustration started to show, that he had to make a move, but where? He was loathe to leave what he had grown up expecting to inherit and felt that he was, in some way,

441

letting the side down and it took all the diplomacy his Father and I could muster, to persuade him it would be in his best interests.

By another quirk of fate, Frank returned from work one night and broke the news that there was a vacancy for a Laboratory Technician at the brickyard and Jim Mercer had spoken about the possibility of Arthur taking on the job. "'He's an intelligent lad you know; and I know Mr Salt would have been glad to see him here. He was mighty proud of his grandson and had great hopes for him." "I'll talk to Josephine about it," Frank promised, "And I'll let you know." He did talk to me about it and my immediate response was "He's going." Amid objections from Arthur, "I'm not going, I don't want to work in a laboratory; I don't want to work inside, I want an outside job." However, an appointment was made and he kept it. To our astonishment, when he returned and said he hadn't got the job, we couldn't believe it. Frank spoke to Jim but was surprised when he said "I offered him the job, but he refused it, said he wanted to go in the Merchant Navy." I was even more surprised and not a little annoyed. "You don't even know whether you could get into the Merchant Navy and why bring it up now, you've never hinted that that's what you wanted." His reply did nothing to convince us that this was but a ploy and I, with Frank's support, insisted he must attend a second interview and this time he would take the job which, with little more objections, he did. One of the conditions was that he attend College one day each week towards H.N.C in either metallurgy or glass technology; and he chose the latter, although with somewhat mixed feelings. He was a 'science' man with chemistry, physics and maths amongst his qualifications and another scientific subject offered few problems. He worked hard and conscientiously to the great satisfaction of Jim Mercer and the rest of the department. But he wasn't completely happy, and when, nine months later I returned from hospital after an operation arising from the old gland weakness, and a prolapse, which necessitated only light work for three months, he took the opportunity to return to the land.

"You need me now, Mother," he said one morning. "I'll do the heavy work; you can concentrate on the lighter stuff." I could see some sense in what he said, but I wasn't happy about such a retrograde step. We were back where we were before and I was worried for his future. Thinking hard and long about the alternatives, I said one evening, "I don't want you to waste time, if I say yes, will you stay on at College and study towards something else if it doesn't work out?" "Mother, I've already made up my mind," he shot at me "I'm going to study for University. I'll write to one or two and see if I can study Geography and I believe Durham is the best, so I hope to get in there. Now," he finished, "Do I come back, or is there anything else?" There was nothing else, and he gave in his notice the following morning, much to the sorrow of Jim Mercer.

Durham University was Arthur's goal, but the one subject necessary for entry was Botany, a subject he could not stand. "I'm not interested in plants and how they work," he said. "I want to be a geographer and travel, not a botanist with a little magnifying glass." But if botany was essential, then botany it must be, but how? Botany was not taught in 1955 as a separate subject, biology was the fashion and that's what the Colleges offered. Until Miss Rodgers, the Biology Teacher at Chesterfield College of Technology offered a solution. "If you would like to sit in on my lessons in a corner at the back of the class," she said, "I'll sort you some books out, and let you have a microscope and you can do your own studying. If you do come up against any difficulties, just ask, I'll try to help."

The rest of the year and the first half of 1956 passed pleasantly; I made no mention of the times I saw him leave the top field and make his way to his bedroom with a sample of moss or other weed he had found to examine under the microscope Miss Rodgers had lent for use during the College breaks, nor when he returned from drilling enough carrot seed in a 50ft row which would have filled half an acre. "That's done," he said, when he had been away only a few minutes, "What do you want me to do now?" I had grimaced and held back a smile, "You've not finished by now, have you?" I had asked. "Sure I have," he replied, "a little job like that doesn't take long." I had held back from saying anything else, but a few weeks later I told him, "You'd better go up the field and thin out those carrots they should be ready by now." I knew the row was about 3" wide and looked more like cress than carrots and wasn't a bit surprised when he returned saying, "I can't thin the damned things without pulling them all up, and they're not ready anyway, they're only like threads." I knew I needn't say anything, he'd learned a lesson in thin sowing.

When the exam results came out that year, he was the proud owner of, not only an 'A' level in Botany but a distinction in the bargain. What's more, he now said he liked botany and was looking forward to studying more. Next year he added the necessary 'A' levels in English, Maths and Science and was well qualified for Durham, if there was a vacancy. There was one vacancy and two applicants. On the train north, Arthur met the other hopeful geographer, by the name of Rawlings. He was a pupil of King Edwards Grammar School, the most exclusive in Sheffield. He had 12 'A' levels and at this news Arthur's spirits sank and were deep in the depths of gloom when he arrived home that evening. "I've no chance," he said despondently, "With 12 'A' levels, I'll never even be considered." "Don't be too sure," I consoled him, "What questions did they ask?" "I was in the room only five minutes," he answered, "Questions that meant nothing, like name, address, qualifications, which school?" "Nothing else," I asked. "A bloody silly question," he said, "What did I do on the way up to Durham?" I gasped, "That wasn't a silly question, it was the leading question," I told him. "What did you answer?" I asked. "Oh, I said something like there's nothing but bloody pit heaps in Durham, I don't know whether I want to come here after all." "Well, we'll see," I told him, "You might be surprised."

There wasn't long to wait, in a little over two weeks, the news came, "You have been accepted; report on the 3rd October"; Arthur's 20th birthday. My assumption that there had been a leading question proved correct, for just before he left in 1961, Professor Fisher told him, "You remember I asked you what you had done on the way up and you'd given that sarcastic answer? Well do you know what Rawlings said? He said he had read a book." He had so many qualifications he could have gone into Maths, English, French or any other Faculty, I wanted a geographer and no geographer just reads a book."

Many things had happened during the past two years as well as Arthur's career opportunities. We had been asked in 1955 if we could take on a half-day's work to tidy the gardens of Miss Savory in Cordwell Valley, where she lived with her mother; wife of a past Licensee of the Horns Inn. She was a cantankerous old girl, as we found out soon after taking on the job. The garden was knee high in grass and weeds from years of neglect and we had carte blanche to do whatever was necessary. But Mrs Savoury had other ideas; as soon as we started work on a patch of nettles or other obnoxious weeds, she emerged from the house waving her stick shouting abuse like "Get out of my garden, get out before I put the police on you," or "Leave my garden alone, you've no right to come here." Obviously she was not altogether in control of her senses and Miss Savoury told us to take no notice. Such were the conditions of service, one telling us what to do, the other trying to stop us but the back gets broader and the skin more like a duck's back, so we stuck it out until Arthur left for University. The money was good anyway.

Another contract for garden maintenance was offered almost at the same time, at Eweford House, the home of Dick Black the Timber Merchant. I had often gone to the timber yard for off-cuts of wood for use as bases for flower arranging and after a time, I wandered around the yard freely looking for likely pieces. The foreman of the yard soon learned what to look for; a slice from an ash tree which would hold its bark and polish well; a slice cut from the burr of an elm which, not only polished well, but had a close patterned flower to enhance the arrangement, a roughly shaped piece fit only as waste, but just the thing to make an unusual base and he would put them asked until my next visit. I often spoke to Dick Black, always interested in this new-fangled hobby of women and before long the question of gardening was voiced and a request to take on his garden, very different from Miss Savoury's and a pleasure to work in, as was the next one belonging to Ryder and Mrs Briggs at Cordwell house. Here we built a deep sunken garden with water from the brook flowing down the huge pieces of stone holding back the sides into a pond below, the rocks inter-planted with wide variety of primulas and rockery plants. We were quite proud of our efforts and won the job of maintenance from it. Not only that, but on each workday, we were invited to a scrumptious lunch, usually a casserole of beef or a pot roast of brisket served with all the usual vegetables as well as generous cups of tea and coffee; a biscuit or piece of cake thrown in.

Then there was the rockery built in the front garden of the Coopers and the lawn excavated and laid for Miss Lockwood, both on Main Road, Holmesfield and many other grubbing out or planting jobs, all lucrative means of keeping 'the wolf from the door'. I might add that, for all his help, Arthur refused to take any wages. When he had asked to return to the nursery he had already been helping Elijah in the evening to supplement his spending money and he continued to do this, buying the necessary text books himself rather than burden me with the expense. "You'll have to feed me Mother, that'll do," he said. So, for two years, I enjoyed the luxury of free labour and the garden maintenance was an acceptable outlet for his energy and welcome 'grist to the mill' for me.

Now just let me back-track a little and explain the position. When repatriation of prisoners of war was complete and there was no longer any need for the P.O.W. camp at Lodge Moor, the huge nissen huts were sold off cheaply. Elijah had long wished, like Dad, to grow mushrooms, but on a larger scale than the little shed at the side of the house at Lane Head and the nissen huts were ideal for the job. But where would we put them? One day, voicing his ambitions to Frank, Elijah asked if he could erect one on the nursery land somewhere near the old entrance, which would be handy for delivery of manure. Although as Frank said, it was now my nursery and up to me whether I allowed it or not, he had already said "Yes," leaving me little room for negotiating. The first hut was erected early in 1952 and another followed soon after. The same year Elijah's second child Jennie was born and life was proving a little difficult in the top floor flat they occupied in one of the Hillcrest row of houses opposite the memorial. Again, he approached Frank about the possibility of buying a piece of land on which he could build a house and again, the decision was partly taken out of my hands, leaving me to negotiate a price and to this end, I sought the help of a Sheffield Estate Agent, Eadon, Lockwood & Riddle. The land in question was one-third of an acre which, on current prices, said the valuer, was £70.0.0d, a veritable fortune to me, the prospects of which were a salve to my feelings at the loss of a piece of my land. I was a little nonplussed when, after telling Elijah the price, he offered only £50 and that, provided he obtain permission to build.

I had been wrong in assuming that, if a buyer wanted a product, he would at least agree to pay the current market rate. It proved rather the other side of the coin; when you know the vendor is hard up, you know he will settle for a lower sum. For as much as I could have used the other £20.0s.0d, I was thankful for the £50.0s.0d, less the charge of £10 for the valuation, a poor deal, which left not a little resentment in me and one which, many years later, proved to be a very costly one when I applied for permission to build my own house.

By 1954 permission was granted to Elijah to build his house for, as an established mushroom grower, he was considered to be an agricultural worker when, in fact, he was a handicraft teacher.

For the next three years, both Frank and Arthur, and occasionally myself, had helped with mushroom picking when the beds were in full crop, and during 1955/57 Arthur had helped with the muck-turning and picking every night. (Mushroom growing in those days involved a lot of work turning and stacking manure five times before carting into the sheds and filling the beds, which, after a few days of settling to the right temperature, could be planted with spawn, kept damp and sprayed with insecticide to keep down the mites and in the following three months produced three 'flushes' of pure white mushrooms).

By 1953, the new craze for flower arranging had crept further north and there were now many small flower clubs in Nottinghamshire, Lincolnshire and Derbyshire, all requesting demonstrations and lessons for those who were more ambitious towards exhibiting and competing at Flower Shows. I travelled to places like Cresswell, Worksop, Epworth, Misterton, to Bradford and Wakefield and locally to Ecclesall, Sheffield and Chesterfield in rooms over shops, in back rooms, in Church Halls or schools, to single men and women in their homes or to small groups of friends and inevitably, this led to the question of starting a Flower Club in Sheffield.

One very enthusiastic group at Ecclesall asked if I would start a club and give a course of lessons to start them off. I told them I was too busy to do all the organising but if they could form a committee, I would support them and give a group lesson once a month free until they were established. Nothing came of the idea; enthusiasm wanes easily when there is work involved. But, there was one enthusiast in Sheffield, one who had been working free gratis for years as a member of the Sheffield Horticultural Society in trying to raise the standard of flower arranging in the local Horticultural shows. To this end, she organised an 'Academy' once a year for enthusiasts to exhibit their arrangements, awarding coloured ribbons to the standard reached. In 1956 she had heard that I had started teaching at Woodseats Evening School and when I met her at the Horticultural Show that year, she asked if I would judge the arrangements at the 'Academy' and award the 'ribbons', a task she had done herself up to now, but as she said, "An independent judge and a teacher too, would add more status to the whole show."

From this beginning, I found myself the following year judging the arrangements at the Horticultural Show and for the next few years saw the standard raised and the whole idea of flower arranging change, even amongst the men. It was, of course, a source of sarcasm, or at best amusement, like the time I was asked to give a demonstration to the members of the Chrysanthemum Society after the show in the Edmund Road Drill Hall. The demonstration was held in a pub, where they always met after the show and the beer flowed, with spirits high. At the end, during question time, a voice chimed from the back of the bar lounge, "What would tha' do wi' these?" as he held up three huge Japs which he had exhibited in the appropriate class. He obviously thought I would be caught out; not so. Ever having to retaliate to the whiles of men, I took the three Japs saying "Yes, of course I'll show you how to arrange them." Selecting a heavy shallow dish and the biggest pin holder I had brought with me, I anchored it with another large one turned over on its pins behind. Picking up the first flower, I looked at it for a second, then took my scissors and snipped off the stem just above the bottom two leaves, leaving it short enough to balance, yet long enough to add the other two. The room was silent up to now, but when I took my scissors and cut the second one about one-third up the stem, there was a gasp.

Carefully placing this one, as the first, firmly on the pin holder, but orientated slightly to the left to create visual movement from the first one turning right, I picked up the third. I could feel the tension and the man at the back looked as if he would have apoplexy, as I took the scissors and looking hard at him, put them through the stem about 6" from the bloom, to the accompaniment of his loud cry of agony "My lovely Japs, what's tha' done to 'em." Without hurry, I picked up the severed stems and trimmed them neatly, each above the topmost leaf and amid murmurs and grunts, impaled each on the pin holder, at the side, at the back and flowing forward from the front creating a 'fan-like' 3D silhouette, finally covering the pin holder with a handful of large pebbles to create visual weight and balance. Then I looked at the poor man and asked if he had any questions. He floundered; mumbled something about his Japs and looked a peculiar shade of puce, whether really for his Japs or because he had failed to catch me out, wasn't clear but another question from me tended to calm the situation. "What did you grow the Japs for?" I asked him, "The flowers or the stems?" "The flowers," he mumbled. "Well, here you have the flowers," I said, "and you also have the stems, what's more, you also have what you asked for; an arrangement, agreed?" He agreed, be it very grudgingly.

Although by now there was a growing demand for learning the art of flower arranging the Education Authorities did not recognise it as an educational subject, to be taught in its own right. However, they did concede that one or two lessons could be included in the syllabus by teachers of gardening. When I began teaching at Woodseats Evening School in 1955 it was as a teacher of gardening and my syllabus, presented to the Headmaster (in triplicate) gave a detailed account of subjects to be taught. But, he was well aware that my students' first interest was flower arranging and readily accepted it and my schemes of work which showed how to grow flowers, foliage, shrubs and bulbs for use in flower arrangements and how I taught was left to me. He often popped in to listen and to see the results and one evening, two years later, he was overheard telling a

449

visiting Inspector "Mrs Rundle is the only teacher I know who teaches flower arranging educationally."

One rule which did work to my disadvantage was that which allowed all teachers of gardening to take an evening off from actual teaching and invite a visiting teacher to take the class. These 'special lectures' were allowed once every session and had to be used in the past to allow specialists in growing, perhaps unusual plants, to pass on their knowledge whilst the teacher 'sat in' and listened. All the teachers, except me, were men and only one, Mr Marsden, had shown real interest in flower arranging, but they all saw the 'way of the wind' and applied the system to their own benefit. I being the only teacher of the subject became their visiting lecturer, talking to classes at Hunters Bar, Sharrow Lane and to Mr Nelson's class at Weston Road. As I already taught every evening it was necessary for me to hand over to my best student, who supervised in my absence and was paid accordingly; myself forfeiting payment at Woodseats for that earned at the other schools. My students were not interested in general gardening as taught by the man and would not have attended, I fear, if one had visited. Consequently, I never enjoyed an evening off with pay. But it had its advantages, as it served to advertise flower arranging and put me on their map so to speak and it had some interesting moments.

Although the classes were composed almost wholly by men, all serious gardeners, they were intrigued, asking questions on all aspects. I recall one night when I had been demonstrating how to use household objects to save expenses (one criticism of flower arranging was the expense. "It's not for us poor people," was a common cry). I was using a candlestick and a small sugar basin fastened on with Sellotape (candle-cups had not been invented then) and had started to demonstrate a 'Hogarth curve' and started the outline, explaining that Hogarth's 'line of beauty' and illustrating how to obtain greater depth (3D) by imagining one was working within a sphere cut in two, one half above the other and arranging the stems as through a glass paperweight. I had just finished this explanation when a voice piped up from a little man at the back, "Will you explain all that again Miss?" I did so, pausing now and then to ask if he and the class

450

understood and having finished; I looked at the man, who still looked in somewhat of a trance. His next remark told me that he had indeed understood, for when he did find words they were, "Why lass, that's trigonometry!" Before long I was judging at the Sheffield Show, the Chrysanthemum Show and some of the classes of the Sheffield Cactus Society Show, as well as the small shows held by the new Flower Clubs at Chesterfield, Cresswell and other parts of Derbyshire, Lincolnshire and Yorkshire.

During those early years in the 1950s I sometimes caught the sleeper train to London with Nancy, she to spend the day with Cath, her sister at Clarence House, me to visit a Floristry Show, Lecture or Meeting of The National Floral Arrangement Society, reporting back at Clarence House or later at Kensington Palace, for tea before returning home. I had joined the National Flower arrangement Society in 1949 when Frank and I had visited their stand at Earls Court and in 1956 had taken the Judge's test along with about half a dozen other members, two of which became Chairmen, one a well-known author and exhibitor. In 1957 the Society was approached by N.A.F.A.S regarding a proposed affiliation. There were endless meetings and negotiations and much opposition from members who were jealous (if that's the right word) of their status as the first Flower arrangement Society and a little cynical about the reason for the change (that N.A.F.A.S was becoming confused with N.F.A.S). Many thought that, as the 'National' was established first, it should retain its name, but the weight of the affiliating clubs and larger membership held greater weight and on 26th September 1960, the National floral Arrangement Society ceased to exist. Instead, two separate areas of N.A.F.A.S. were formed, 'The Home Counties' to which members living within their boundaries automatically became members and 'London and Overseas' which included all overseas Clubs and individual members who lived outside the boundaries of the Home Counties. I became an individual member of London and Overseas and have remained so ever since, automatically becoming an Area Judge, Teacher and Demonstrator of that list. Had I wished to become a National Demonstrator and Judge, N.A.F.A.S. ruled I must become a member of my own local area and take the tests in that area, even to the point of taking the area test again. This I thought was grossly unfair and said so, particularly as only individual members were so penalised. My nearest area was Nottingham; for which there was a long waiting list for membership and although one would expect a reasonable consideration under such circumstances, such was the hierarchy at the time that they did not look kindly on a Judge/Demonstrator from another area usurping their 'patch'.

From 1956, the insatiable appetite for flower arranging had hit Sheffield and in that year the Sheffield Society of Floral Art was born as a natural progression by Academy Exhibitors and members of the Horticultural Society and in 1957, at the end of a 13 week course of lessons to members of the 'Ladies Club' in their meeting room in Queen Street, they arranged an open meeting in St. John's Church Hall, Abbeydale which led to the inauguration of the Sheffield floral Art Club. Sadly there was much animosity between the two clubs and I found myself 'on the horns' between the two, having students in both groups. The most diplomatic way out was not to become a member of either, preferring the independence of being Patron, a position fulfilled each Christmas by being invited to the Christmas Dinner as Guest of Honour, giving the 'toast' to the Society/Club. The last time I attended the Society Dinner in 1964 before leaving the district, my speech contained a mild rebuke in the hope that the two clubs would become reconciled and work together. The message went home and the following year they held a combined exhibition which was a great success and I thought the hatchet was buried, but good intentions did not last and by the following year they had reverted to form.

In 1956, I decided to add Ikebana (Japanese flower arranging) to my list of qualifications after attending an exhibition in London which had been advertised in the N.A.F.A.S. magazine. I was drawn to Ikebana on learning about the philosophy and symbolism involved both in the training and subsequent practice. One of the dos kado (the ways of life) I was intrigued by the disciplines involved, a greater challenge than western flower arranging. Mrs Stella Coe had returned to England after living in Japan for a number of years and as a Senior Teacher of the 'Sogetsu School' was forming a 'branch' of the school in London. I attended the meeting and exhibitions in 1957 which made such an impression on me that I arranged to take lessons. Mrs Coe said she was too busy to give private lessons but put me in touch with Mrs Thelma de Mel, wife of a Singhalese Diplomat and it was Thelma who, over the next ten years, guided me through the four Diplomas on the way to becoming a teacher in 1968. This meant journeys to London on the sleeper with great bundles of branches for the necessary practice and a box of flowers, some from the market, some home-grown.

The first time I went I travelled by car and drove to Convent Garden the following morning to buy foliage and flowers, but this proved costly, both on time and money and I wasn't too pleased when a policeman stopped me at the lights at Trafalgar Square/Shaftsbury Avenue and questioned me about a licence to carry goods. It was very difficult to persuade the unbelieving, suspicious young recruit that they were all for my own use and not for resale. After that, I decided to use the railway.

Training was slow and tedious to the occidental mind and in those days, teachers followed the Grand Master's order, making sure that the requisite hours of practice had been put in before a Diploma could be awarded. In the book of instruction there was even a note from him to the effect that, if a student asked "How am I getting on?" or "How long before I receive my Diploma?" it showed that the student was impatient and was not learning the true lessons of Ikebana and should be dismissed. My teacher was an oriental; inscrutable and like all the teachers of Ikebana at that time, eager to make more money so the rule was obeyed and the lesson stretched to the full year laid down before the test and award of the Diploma.

My lessons, once a month, lasted four years. If I could pay my fare and had half a crown in my pocket in case of emergency, I could manage. Thelma always made, what she called 'pot luck' stew with everything thrown in, or one of her curries made from her own mixture of spices, so I knew I wouldn't go entirely hungry. I found the whole philosophy of Ikebana fascinating and still do, with all its symbolism and meaning. But I am a little sad that, over the years, it has become commercial in its approach; more an art than a philosophy. My trips to London ended in 1960; for what happened after I'll explain later; I must remain for a while with 1957.

There was no doubt that when Arthur left for University, there would have to be a certain amount of change in the routine of the nursery. I would, once again, be on my own, except for the occasional help from Frank in the way of weeding and stoking. The most immediate problem was cash flow, for although demonstrations and private teaching brought a certain amount of ready cash; something had to be found to replace the regular income we had enjoyed from garden maintenance and construction. I didn't shy away from hard work, but there were occasions when two pairs of hands were necessary, therefore, that part of the programme had to end.

Frank and I had already spent three Sundays gathering moss on Stanage Moors so there would be no delay in the wreath programme, as Arthur would be home for Christmas in time to help with the bulk of work and market deliveries. Payment for them, along with the cheque for Evening School in December, would stretch through the following months and pay for the spring seed order, supplemented by sales of alpines and herbaceous plants when the weather was open.

Alpine and rockery plants had always proved a lucrative addition to our cash crops; they thrived in our climate and altitude of 1,000ft and were found by customers to be particularly hardy under their more amiable conditions. They had been a source of amusement and exasperation sometimes, like the time we had a plunge bed full of aubrietias in a combination of colours which could have put the rainbow to shame. One of our neighbours, a well-to-do man, whom I knew, but had never actually spoken to, saw the huge patch of colour from the road to his house high up on the ridge overlooking the nursery and had called to buy plants. He showed more than the usual interest and showed that he was no ignoramus when it came to growing them, but when I had finished packing and was handing him his change, he made the suggestion that sent my estimation of him down by about three rungs. "You know," he said, "you should have a man to do the heavy work." I hesitated for only a second, after all he was a valued customer who might call again, but I would feel caution rapidly being thrown to the wind. "Why?" I blurted a little sharply. "Well," he hesitated, "a hardworking woman like you, with a man, you'd make a fortune." Oh no, I thought, not another. This was the third man, including the milkman, to make this suggestion in the past year and they all seemed to have the same idea. "Look", he said, seeing me hesitating, "I can afford to put some money into the business and I'd like to be part of it." He probably saw the disgust on my face as I asked, "Are you seriously making an offer?" and he nodded "Yes." I knew I was really going to burn my boats, but I was growing a little fed up with these men who hadn't the gumption to start on their own yet, as soon as they saw a 'hard working woman' they wanted to cash in. I was furious. "Mr (...) I said, you want a nursery because you see a woman doing the work, well, if you really want a nursery, go buy a field. I don't want a partner, I don't need a partner and I don't want another liability, I could probably work you into the ground the first day anyway."

A pleasanter situation was on the day when Frank and I were surveying the same plunge bed, this time filled with about 400 leontopodium alpinum in full flower and ready for sale. When I had seen the name Edelweiss as I was making out the seed list in spring, I had gone all dewy eyed thinking about the Alps; the snow covered peaks and long skirted Victorian ladies climbing the easy path to the summit of the Matterhorn, and in a weak moment had ordered a packet of seeds; resigned to the fact that this was the only way I would ever see the romantic flowers myself. The packet, of course, was a grower's packet, not the little 2d ones sold to amateurs who produced, if lucky, 20 or 30 plants. They germinated like cress and every single one was pricked out and lovingly potted, and set out in their rows like a regiment of soldiers with starry grey velvet faces looking up wistfully in the hope that someone would pluck them as eagerly as their cousins on the snow-capped foreign mountains.

"What are you going to do with 'em now?" Frank asked. "Sell 'em," I said, more confidently than I felt. "Clever bugger, as usual," came his retort, "How the hell are you going to sell that lot?" I didn't hesitate, "I'll sell 'em," I repeated. "I'll advertise 'em," I said, as he walked away with the air of someone who has heard it all before.

But, the idea remained. For the past year I had retained a small box advert in the Sheffield Telegraph gardening section every Saturday morning and every Tuesday morning the office girl rang to see if there was to be any change, either in content or format. By the following Tuesday morning I had made up my mind and at the due time said "Yes, I would like to change the format, just for one week." When I explained, she laughed. "Are you sure Mrs Rundle? Are you sure this is what you want?" I told her it was. "Well, at least it's different," she muttered. "I'll see to it." The newspaper arrived on Saturday morning and after checking it, I tossed it over to Frank. He looked at it, then at me, unbelievingly then, tossing it back, he tittered with a little shake of the head, "You are a silly bugger sometimes." The advert read:

WHY RISK TOUR NECK IN THE ALPS
WHEN YOU CAN BUY THE
EDELWEISS
AT
FRANCOTT DENE NURSERIES
OWLER BAR
SHEFFIELD
Price: 1/- each or 3 for 2/6d

The day after, Sunday, was the only day in the history of nursery when a coach was parked outside the gate. On a tour around Derbyshire, the club who were on a day's outing, had stopped in the area for refreshments and one of the members had bought a Sheffield Telegraph. Seeing the advert some bright woman had asked the bus driver to make a little detour so that she could see the Edelweiss and he had agreed. The sales we made that day, plus the few inquisitive villagers and strangers cleared the plunge bed of all but few small ones with less 'starry eyes' than the rest.

By 1958, it was obvious that the small office shed was not entirely suitable for the work involved in weddings and funerals and my mother was very nervous about my working so near the lane entrance through the night. I had occasionally cleared a bench in the

456

glasshouse for extra space for wreath making, but this was not always convenient, especially in spring and summer. On a very rare day out in August of that year, Frank and I spent a day at Bakewell Show, soaking up all the new ideas and equipment available for those with a large enough bank balance. Such luxuries were not for us; our needs were of a more down-to-earth character, like a shed which could be converted into a workroom-cum-classroom-cum-storage room. It also had to be a building which we could erect immediately without planning permission and, above all, something I could afford, albeit on hire purchase. After much discussion about the type of building we could erect on agricultural land without enticing embarrassing questions from the Planning Department and inquisitive neighbours and passers-by, the decision settled on a deep litter house 36ft x 20ft with continuous windows down each side.

These would cast light on all the bench space expected to be fitted down the long walls rather than risk 'blind spots' in between single framed windows. They also detracted from the fact that the building was being used for other than agricultural purposes; the answer to a question often asked, "Why don't you hang curtains at the windows?" Inside, however, it was cosy and comfortable with a 'Curiour' (Parkray type) fire at the far end and red carpet on the floor. Arthur was home from University on summer vacation and he cheerfully fitted benches down both sides with cupboards beneath for storing bowls, cases and other miscellaneous items as only flower people dream of; like the driftwood gathered in smeakley streams. Which hadn't drifted anywhere, but was the right shape for a future arrangement or lesson; like the huge dragon-like real driftwood seen on the beach at Llanddwyn Island on Anglesey and dragged on to the mainland, up the beach and sand hills to the park and hauled into the van to be used at some future date for display. There never was such a mélange, such a heterogeneous mixture in the most affluent pack-rat's palace.

On a bargain-seeking tour of the second-hand shops on Abbeydale Road, I found half a dozen large tables and a dozen stools which had been replaced by new furnishings at a local school and from the same source retrieved a blackboard and easel which required

457

only a new coating of 'lampblack' to raise it to usable standard. The final touch was to register the new business, the real reason for all the hard work of the past years, apart from earning a living, which entailed writing to the Registrar of Business Names, a necessity in those days if one wished to trade in anything other than one's own name. 'The Francott Dene School of Floristry' under the umbrella of 'The Francott Dene Nurseries' was the first Flower School outside London. Its aims to teach anyone who wished to learn high class, high craft floristry with its ancillary subject of flower arranging. Florists up to now, had a poor reputation for flower arranging, particularly noticeable now that there were so many amateurs creating well-designed arrangements in competitions and exhibitions. Of course, as I often pointed out to students, florists are working to someone else's budget; they cannot afford that extra rose or piece of exotic foliage, nor can they afford to spend all night on that pedestal arrangement as an amateur exhibitor often does. Time, as well as materials, cost money and if the customer will not pay more, something's got to give. "But, I said," never let yourself be blamed for poor workmanship," other ways of economy must be found and the first was learning to design; I mean really design, letting the materials dictate the pattern so that the effect was natural and rhythmic, not stiff and static as the flat fronted, close packed globes and triangles of the usual street or market florist ... or, I am sad to say, none of the amateurs who were self-taught from pictures in books now appearing on the bookshelves. All students, florists and flower arrangers alike, were taught on the same principles of design. The end product was exposed to be of the same high standard from both groups.

It was now nine years since we had bought the field and the road had been far from easy; there had been too many unexpected boulders to shift, too many bridges to build over hidden streams, and many, many moments of near despair. Like the afternoon when I saw the wife of a schoolboy I had known, a dim snotty-nosed dirty specimen of a boy, who on leaving school had gone into property repairing and odd-jobbing. She was driving her husband's Daimler car; 'a stuck-up madam' said the villagers, 'too big for her boots'. As she passed the gate my thoughts wondered. "Why is it?" I said to my Mother when I went in for a cup of tea, "Why is it that she can drive a bloody great Daimler, and I'm scratting here like this?" Mom looked at me for a second then, "Aye lass, you don't know what goes on when their doors close at night." It made me think. Two weeks later, when the news broke that they had gone bankrupt; the house had to be sold, the car must go; they had lost everything, I wondered at the wisdom of my Mother.

There was the time in 1952, a few weeks after I had taken over the nursery. I owed a bill for Income Tax which I hadn't a hope in hell of paying. It wasn't the first time I had been faced with the same situation, and it was lucky that all creditors didn't pounce at once. I had learned early just how long it took to clear a cheque and how many days I could stall before making out a cheque myself; money was always passing through the air from debtor to creditor and vice versa and never seeming to settle long enough on either to cause undue trouble. But this was different; this was official and, said the letter from the Court, if the sum of £50 was not in Court by Monday morning, the case would be heard at 10.30 a.m. and I would be a debtor.

I knew well enough from the days of Frank's Court appearances that if I could pay some of the debt it would stop the hearing. But, I had nothing with which to pay. On Friday morning Mom called me in for the usual cup of tea, when she noticed that I looked miserable, (her word, not mine). She already knew why and her "Aye lass, something'll turn up," didn't surprise me; she was even more optimistic than Mrs Micawber, always predicting that 'something would turn up." "Nothing can turn up," I said. "Doesn't anybody owe you anything?" she asked. "No, nobody, not this time, there's nothing to turn up," I repeated in despair. "Aye lass, cheer up," she chirped, "I tell you something will turn up, just you see." I was in no mood for such optimism and went out in sad contemplation.

The next day, Saturday, my mood was digging into deeper depths. I hadn't slept and was so worried I felt physically sick. I couldn't settle to work and after opening the glasshouses, I went inside again and stood in front of the fire holding up my skirts to feel the friendly warmth. "Are you sure nobody owes you anything?" Mom asked, more or less to make conversation I thought. "No," I replied wearily, "I've told you, nobody owes me anything." "Drink your tea," she piped, almost too cheerily, "Postman will be here soon." "Some good that'll do," I quipped. "Aye, you don't know; I tell you something'll turn up, just you see." And, so far as Mom was concerned, she believed it.

I stood there holding my skirts for a little longer, and was about to turn for the door when a car could be heard coming up the drive and in another moment a voice called out "Good morning Mrs Salt," as a letter came flying through the door into the kitchen. Slowly I moved towards it half expecting another bill. It was addressed to the nursery, so curious I carefully opened it, taking out the letter enclosed, and a cheque for £18.10s.0d. I gaped, turned it over, gaped again, until it finally got through to my befuddled wits that it really was a cheque, for me. I had £18.10s.0d, I could pay something into the Court and stop the hearing; I wouldn't be a debtor after all. My relief was hysterical; falling on to my knees, head in hands on the edge of the table, in fits of hysterical sobbing, I shouted "Oh, thank you God, thank you God, Oh God, thank you God," over and over again and completely out of control.

"What on earth's the matter?" Mom said, as she came and put her arm on my shoulder. I couldn't answer, until all the tension had subsided, then, still sobbing I held out the cheque, "This came," I whispered. "Come, come lass," she said, as she lifted me on to my feet, "I told you something would turn up," as if it were the most natural thing in the world. I had been right when I said "Nobody owes me anything." Nobody did, unless you consider that a Government Department who hands out grants for various commodities really owe it, for this was a cheque from a Government Department. When we moved on to the nursery in 1950, we had been advised to apply for a subsidy on lime after the Agricultural Department had analysed a sample of soil and found it deficient. At the same time, we could apply for a grant to have water laid on to one point with a meter at the gate. We were at the end of the supply line and due to the altitude; the pressure was low and certainly not sufficient for the expected use of watering hoses. To help the pressure, I had obtained planning permission for a high water tower at the top of the field holding sufficient weight of water to create the necessary pressure for the glasshouse and any new ones we might erect later. The wheels of Government grind mighty slowly and by the time I took over the nursery itself, I knew the tower was unnecessary, so had put in another application for the 'point of outlet' to be actually in the glasshouses. Since then I hadn't given it another thought, until now. This was the cheque received today, £18.10s.0d towards the installation of water on Francott Dene Nurseries, two and a half years after the first application.

Undercapitalisation; that's the word Arthur used when describing our cash flow problem. It had been the problem all along; balancing the swings against the roundabouts, robbing Peter to pay Paul, playing 'put and take' like a game. All small businesses suffer from the same malaise; laying out money for materials, doing the job, then waiting until the following month, or the next, for settlement of the account. And the irony of the situation usually is that the busier you are, the more the business prospers, the more money is laid out. Consequently, all you are worth is on paper, never in your pocket or in your own bank. This was the problem in 1957 when Arthur went to Durham University. Some students were lucky and received a full grant, others, sons and daughters of salary earning parents were means-tested on their income after all essential outgoings were considered, but for business parents, those accursed account books were assessed, not the few copper they might be lucky enough to have in the pocket.

When Arthur left the brickyard and said he was going to University, I didn't consider twice. When Elijah voiced the thoughts of the rest of the family, except I believe, my Mother, he said, "How are you going to send him to University? You can't afford that sort of money," a little sarcastically I thought. I replied simply, "He's going. If he passes for University, then he's going, I'll find a way." "You're daft," said Elijah, 'high and mighty, he's not a University type." "Well, he's going anyway," I insisted, "And he'll show you."

In general terms, of course, he was right. No-one from our family had been to University; we were a working family and I mean really working, not just class distinction. We had been brought up, a bit like Puritans one might say, to make a virtue out of work and to glory in a job well done. But that, I thought, could easily be changed if the will was there and, if I could speed things on their way, my son would change the system.

However, it was hard and even harder on him. "I've got a hole in my shoe; send me some money to have it repaired." "I've put another patch on my trousers, and trying to cover it with my hand, can you afford another pair?" "I need a dinner dress or I can't get up and speak in a meeting." "Mom, I'm taking a girl to a dance, send me a pound for drinks please. "What a good job for Arthur that he was popular with the girls (boys too I believe); he joined in everything, became President of the S.R.C. and, according to one friend, if he walked into the common room and called "Who'll buy me a coffee?" there was always one more than willing.

The first time he brought his current girlfriend home for the Easter vacation, I almost panicked. When I got the letter, the house was in a mess; no decorating had been done since Dad had painted the living room in 1947, and I had no money for paint or paper. The most pressing was the hall, landing and stairs; little hands had crawled up the wall on the way to the bathroom and the large window had cast bright light on the opposite wall fading the paper to the palest tint of its original colour. I talked to Mom about the best course of action and made a quick decision. Rummaging in the old ottoman I found two rolls of paper left from my decorating days at Lismore Road and estimated that they would be sufficient to cover the long wall opposite the window and the bit over the well. But I drew a blank on the wall under the window. So, the plan of action was to strip the faded paper from the long wall, still in good condition, except for the colour, and use it to paper the wall under and around the window. I figured that, in the shade, it would not be quite as conspicuous as it had been with the light shining direct. The problem was, to remove the long lengths of paper without tearing, or leaving half the backing on the wall. I had no alum, which would have helped; the answer was lots of water and patience.

With my biggest whitewash-cum-paste brush and buckets of warm water I set to work on a ladder borrowed from Elijah which I'd wedged against one step and the wall over the well. Precariously, with bucket hanging from a rung of the ladder, I slapped water up to the ceiling, as far as I could reach from side to side, and down to the steps, until the whole wall, and I, were completely drenched. On the opposite wall, I set to with scraper and water, until every scrap of paper was removed, then on terra firma once more, I made a huge bowl of flour paste and left it to 'cure' whilst I had a cup of tea.

The next part of the operation was a classic exercise in precision. Perched on the top rung of the ladder, at an angle of 45 degrees from stairs and wall, I very carefully eased the first strip of paper until it hung from my fingers down the wall. A careful turn whilst passing the strip underneath the ladder, to be carefully caught again at the other side, then gingerly lifting it to the ceiling and pressing it to the wall, which I had previously plastered thickly with flour paste so that there was no danger of the soaked paper not sticking, and the first strip was in place.

Carefully descending the ladder and leaning forward almost on my tummy, I smoothed down the paper with Mom's papering brush with its soft bristles that wouldn't tear the fragile covering. I grinned; success; if I could stand the strain and provided all the strips came off as easily as the first, I was on a winning streak. Slopping a bit more paste on for the next strip, I proceeded as before and everything went well; provided my nerves didn't give way, we would soon have a newly papered wall. Nothing did go wrong and the faded paper seemed to have gained a little colour now that it was in the shade. The next phase was relatively simple, although tiring for already tired arms, but success breeds success and in two hours; we had a newly papered staircase which would pass the muster of the most critical judge, albeit that one wall glowed with new paper whilst the other sank its embarrassment in the shade of the one opposite.

Since the first wedding in 1950, the number of orders had grown steadily each year, mainly through recommendation, but also as a result of the large gold metal awards at Endcliffe Park and Edmund Road Drill Hall shows. Both Arthur and Frank helped with the erection of the stand and Arthur made all the fittings, pedestals and tables on which the exhibits were displayed. The centrepiece of the stand had remained the most throughout, except that the nameplate above now read 'Francott School of Floristry' instead of 'Nurseries'. There were three lighted alcoves for which we carried a twelve volt car battery, or a transformer to convert the mains electricity to the lower voltage. The display had also changed over the years from purely nursery plants to bouquets and other wedding work using unusual foliage with garden flowers to create modern designs. After Arthur left for University, Frank continued to help; in fact he rather enjoyed the novelty and experience, especially when we went to Harrogate Spring Show for the first time in 1958.

This was a new venture for me, but I decided to stick to the basic routine we had followed in Sheffield, with a very satisfying gold medal award. The show, of course, had a large flower arranging section to where Frank disappeared whilst I finished off by draping satin and tulles to complement the work and enhance the whole stand. He was fascinated by some of the arrangers, particularly the three youths who always worked on their exhibits together, pointing and gesticulating as they moved a flower or piece of foliage; standing back in posing posture as they discussed whether this was alright or that better. He sat on the edge of a nearby table thoroughly enjoying himself and grinning from ear to ear when I caught up with him. One class, which didn't seem to attract many exhibitors, was the professional florists' class for bouquets. The work was mediocre with only about half a dozen exhibits, but I was told the class was to be upgraded the following year when the class would be a set piece exhibiting a pedestal arrangement, a table arrangement, a bouquet and a corsage, all for the same wedding to be staged in an alcove 6ft wide x 3ft deep. I decided to enter; although I knew that time would be the critical factor if I were to enter a trade show as well as the Floristry class.

When the time came in May 1959, we set off early and all went well; the trade stand was completed leaving me with plenty of time to stage the four pieces of work I had made the previous day, leaving finishing touches to the large arrangement when in position. I had brought lengths of tulle and satin for drapes and satin to ruche meticulously over the base, an operation which devoured a considerable amount of time, so that I was thankful we had had the foresight to leave early.

We left for home, returning the following day to spray all the exhibits and make any adjustments to the trade stand as necessary. I was delighted and at the same time, a little disappointed to find that I had been awarded the 'runner up' prize in the professional class, but delighted to see the card on the trade stand; I had been awarded a large gold medal and 'The Mrs Davidson Cup' for the 'Most Artistic Trade Stand'. With this boost to my confidence, I took particular care with all the make-up work, determined next year to be the first in both. As I have mentioned previously, "Just when you think you can make both ends meet, somebody moves the ends." It's also a fact that, "Just when you think you have it in the bag, the bottom drops out." This time the culprit was fog and I mean fog; thick 'pea-souper' fog.

We struck it on the outskirts of Leeds, near the river, which obviously was the cause. Traffic was almost at a standstill, the delay nerve racking and tense; by the time we reached Harrogate, we were two hours later than expected and time is something one can't buy. No matter how quickly we worked, those minutes lost never caught up and by the time the Stewards called 'time' next morning, I was frantically ruching and planting, yet knowing that, if I were the judge, I would certainly 'dock' a few points, which he did.

The system of judging the professional class was that the winner one year stepped down and judged next years. The winner in 1959 was George Smith, one of the flower arrangers who worked at Farrah's florists of Halifax and he was now the judge. He stopped me in the flower arranging section. "You know," he said, "you would have been first if you'd done your drapes like last year." I wasn't surprised; I knew he was right about the ruching. "Last year," he said, "your ruching was the most perfect I've ever seen, every little pleat was so carefully done, but this year ... "I told him what had happened and he was sympathetic. "If it's any consolation, I loved your bouquet and that pedestal arrangement was just terrific, but there were so many points allocated for drapes and finish that Derek just beat you to it." So, once again, I was runner up.

In 1951, an advertisement in 'The Fruit Trades Journal', a weekly publication, informed readers that a group of florists throughout the country wished to form a Society of Floristry, its aim to promote and encourage the art of floristry and to promote and conduct examinations and competitions. The advertisement suggested that anyone interested in joining, or taking the examinations should contact the advertisers. I considered for some weeks; what kind of work was expected; would the methods I had learned be accepted; how much practice would I need? I was dubious, remembering my experience with the florists in Sheffield and decided to wait until I could find out more. Getting the nursery on its feet was a more pressing problem and the idea was put on the back burner for the time being. However, on one of our trips to London, I decided to visit the shops of two of the Founder Members of the new Society to see for myself the kind of work they turned out. There were no Exhibitions or demonstrations so far north at that time and this was the only way of knowing what type of work was practised by those who were to set the standard for the whole trade.

To say I was surprised is an understatement; I was appalled and disappointed. Of course, I knew this was not exhibition floristry, but I had expected it to be closer to examination floristry, or why have examinations? This was not even good commercial floristry as I had been taught and now practised. And, I reasoned, if the aim was to raise the standard of floristry; why should that, made for customers, be so inferior. Naïve, you might think, but I resolved there and then that every bouquet, every wreath, every arrangement I turned out, would be to the same high standard as those for exhibition or examination and to help me achieve such high ideals, on every opportunity I visited the shops of the Court Florists, 'Moyses Stevens' at Victoria and Berkeley Square, then a quick trip up Hill Street to the Constance Spry shop in South Audley Street. The style of work was totally different at each shop, but both were so perfect I would stand outside the window, examining every flower, every aspect of design;

straining to see how the back was finished; how colours had been blended; how each design had been finished with ribbons or other embellishment; the latter never in the 'Spry' arrangements; Mrs Spry did not believe in ribbon adornments.

On one occasion, I was conscious of the gaze of the assistants as I craned to see the smallest detail, but this didn't deter me, "They don't know who I am," I thought, "probably someone going round the bend, so why worry?" But there was one occasion when I couldn't resist going inside. I had espied, on the back wall of Moyses Stevens in Berkeley Square, a large display case full of artificial bouquets, headdresses and bridesmaid novelties and a closer look was imperative to my satisfaction at a day's work well done. Still somewhat embarrassed I paused in the doorway to look at a selection of figurines and other porcelain ornaments in a display case which filled the left hand wall, especially a cheeky little wren, his tail cocked up in defiance of the whole world. Then, feeling just as defiant, I walked boldly through the door as Daniel into the lion's den and after a few steps, paused beside a huge arrangement standing on a polished table admiring it from every angle and making a mental image of its contents. Moving on to another table, then a third, I found myself on the inside of the window I had viewed from outside and a front seat view of the back of the arrangements. Pleased with my progress so far and growing ever more nervous of the assistant who had been at my elbow all the way, I eventually arrived at the show case containing the bouquets.

Could I pass for a mum contemplating her daughter's wedding? I mused; if challenged, would I pass as a prospective bride? In for a pound, so to speak, I continued to examine the goods on show, but I soon realised that it wasn't going to be easy to get out of this place; it was obvious that, having viewed the goods, I was expected to buy. As I turned to cross the floor towards the door, the assistant moved closer ready for the 'kill'. I turned suddenly and confronted her head on. "There's a little wren in the display case in the doorway, how much is it?" I asked politely. She was surprised and a little nonplussed, "Er," she started, then quickly composing herself, "I'll just look Madam," as she retrieved the key from a peg on the wall.

She returned from the door bearing the wren, "It's £1.10s.0d IMadam," she said. Without hesitation, although I knew this was almost every penny I had in my purse, I smiled as I said "He's beautiful isn't he? I'll have it." A surprised assistant wrapped up the little bird and packed him carefully in a box. "Will you put a little bow on it please?" I asked and smiled as she did so, hoping that by this time she had come to the conclusion that I had been looking for a present. Not that it mattered, for now I could get out of this exclusive shop with at least a little dignity.

By 1959, I decided to have a shot at the Diploma of The Society of Floristry which, at this time, one was allowed to do without taking the Preliminary and Senior examinations and the written part could be taken locally under an independent supervisor. The next examination was to be held in London in March, 1960 when I was a bit nonplussed to hear one of the other candidates, who told us she had taken it twice before, that all the set questions had to be finished; this on the assumption that, if the van was waiting to deliver a wreath or wedding order, it was no good saying it wasn't finished. To make matters worse, she told us, "You have to reach 93 per cent in the marking. I was not the only one who almost panicked.

The tests were partly practical, partly oral and partly through questioning on the uses of different gauge wires. The last I found easy, although I didn't have the advantage of doing make-up work every day and was more than well pleased to find, on being questioned about 'colour' that my knowledge of the subject was far more detailed than the three examiners, "Yes, that will do," said one, "you are getting very technical."

The practical tests lasted for three hours in the morning, less time out for the above tests, with a break for lunch at 1.00 p.m. before another three hours in the afternoon. It was during this break that I heard two of the candidates, both having learned at the Constance Spry School, discussing their methods of cutting down time. They both had been told by colleagues that it was almost impossible to finish in time, particularly in wedding work, if such meticulous methods were used. "Something has to be cut out," one of them said. I listened as the other said "I've practised missing out the wiring when

468

assembling my bouquets and I find them, secure enough, so that's what I shall do." This worried me not a little, and I thought what a pity that such wonderful work had to be sacrificed to pass an examination which was supposed to be raising the standard of work. Anyway, I hadn't practised such omissions and could only do the work I was used to, consequently, I wasn't in the least surprised when the Invigilator called 'time' and I hadn't finished my last piece of work, an arranged basket for presentation. I stopped work and was clearing my bench when Mr Fowler, Treasurer of the Society and helping in carrying the finished work to the examiners room stayed at my table. "Have you started your basket," he asked me. "No," I answered, a bit annoyed and very disappointed,. "Have you chosen your flowers?" he asked. "No," I said again. "Look," he persisted, "Just choose a few flowers, you'll at least get a few marks for 'choice of colour', just stick one or two in to show you've fixed the wire securely." I refused. "It's no good, I can't finish anyway."

Had I known the two candidates were not quite right, the final points were more important than finishing, I could so easily have grabbed the few necessary for a pass. As it was, I failed, and it was no consolation to see in the June edition of the Society's magazine, a photograph of the headdress I had made, with a caption pointing out the exquisite work. I made sure that shortage of time would not fail again and much as it 'went against the grain' to alter my own work methods, I did so and the following March was successful.

By 1959 both Frank and I felt in need of a holiday. It was eleven years since our last, without even a day off. My brain and bones cried out for a rest. In 1955, whilst I still had the large van, I had suggested to Frank that a mattress would convert it into a mobile sleeper, but he would have none of it. "If I can't have a holiday in a hotel, I'm not going," he said. After all my persuading and quoting, with tongue in cheek, he was adamant, "No hotel; no holiday." The chance of a cheap holiday had passed for early in 1956, I had to let the old van go for scrap. It was 20 years old, its cable brakes always freezing up in cold weather or, a dangerous situation on market mornings down the brickyard hill and negotiating the Totley Rise bend. I often said a prayer on the stretch before the lights at Beauchief, changing gear rapidly down for the last few yards, hoping to arrive as they changed to green.

The final warning came when Arthur and I were returning from market about 7.30 a.m. we were negotiating the island and passing the police box on the corner of Granville Road hoping we could pass by safely without being stopped, for we knew the brakes were suspect, the horn and windscreen wipers didn't work and the rear window was minus its glass. We were just beginning to breathe freely when the door of the police box opened and the driver emerged just in time to see the back of our decrepit can. He jumped into his car and the sirens blared out as he followed us on Queens Road. The slow walk back to the van bode ill and my heart sank as he leaned his arms on the windowsill and bent forward to ask the first probing question. "Your van?" "Yes," I replied humbly. A pause then; "Licence," which I quickly produced. Still suspicious, he lingered, still casting eyes over the inside of the van. "Do your brakes work?" the question was shot like a bolt. "Perfectly," I replied without turning a hair, "They've just been re-lined." "Can you see through that mirror?" he said pointing to the inside mirror. Then he said "Get out, let me look." I obediently did as he bade. He fiddled with the windscreen wipers, turning them this way and that and my heart jumped in case he should switch them on. He sat silent for what seemed an eternity then, suddenly his hand shot out to open the door and, as his second leg hit thee step, be brought his other hand down hard on the horn in the centre of the wheel. I jumped in amazement as it blared out, catching Arthur's incredulous, astonished look; we just didn't believe our luck.

Soon after this episode I was driving down the steep road from Holymoorside to Baslow after delivering a wedding order when I realised that the second gear didn't work. To make matters worse, the brakes were weak and didn't respond as they should and I was not a little worried in case I couldn't stop at the junction at the bottom. "What are you going to do Mummy?" Yvonne said when I swore because I couldn't get into first gear. "I don't know pet," I answered, then "Hold tight, let's hope there's no traffic coming round the island." With this I said, "Hang on pet, hold tight on to your seat," and tightened my grip on the wheel hoping for the best and praying hard. We were lucky, the road was clear, but I couldn't risk going straight round the island, we were going too fast and might turn over, there was only one solution, to go straight on into Baslow, a flat road for half a mile.

We were about 50 yards past the gates of Chatsworth before we finally came to a halt. The journey home was tedious and slow travelling in first gear up Baslow Hill and over the Moors to Owler Bar. This was the moment when I realised that the time had come, the old van must go.

There wasn't a chance that we could afford a holiday according to Frank's criteria; it seemed another year would pass without one when we had a visit from a neighbour whose sister-in-law lived on a farm on the Isle of Anglesey. She took in visitors; friends of the family and our friend told us, would welcome us and more importantly, would charge very little. This was a compromise, it wasn't a five star hotel, but I managed to persuade Frank and during the long vacation when Arthur was at home to take care of things, we spent a wonderful week exploring the island, picnicking on the beaches and seeing the sites of North Wales. Things were going well in 1960, when Arthur was once again at home on what we expected would be his last summer at home; his final examinations would be taken in 1961 after which we assumed he would follow his own career. So we decided to visit Anglesey again. It was just as beautiful; we enjoyed it just as much, but on our return our relationship began to deteriorate, leading to a period which I know will be very difficult for me to describe. I shall try to see the problem from both sides, although the personal hurt and sadness inflicted by those who were very ignorant of the circumstances and made no attempt to understand, still leaves a very sore wound which is in danger of re-opening, bringing resentment, anger and a hint of bitterness, which I have tried hard to bury and forget. So, please understand if I give only the facts which are necessary to understand how life progressed during the next 30 years and suffice it say that some things need not have happened.

Chapter 14

The trouble, if that is the right word, crept insidiously nearer, undetected by me, although my Mother, in her wisdom had seen the signs and wondered how long before I became aware. It probably started as far back as 1955 when Arthur came to work on the nursery full time. Partly due to my operation, partly to the situation needed by his 15 month old sister, I began to rely more and more on his help. I was oblivious to the fact that Frank felt left out, only that he was sometimes moody and bad tempered. My priorities were work and survival, with sexual relationships at the bottom of my list, whilst Frank's measurement of happiness was the success of one's sex life. He didn't understand when I reminded him that he had brought us to this situation through leaving the Police Force and only hard work would get us out of it. Oh yes; it was pointed out to me that I was wrong by Auntie Julia. "Nay, tha can't do that," she said one day when I said I had no time or inclination for sex; "it's thi' job, tha't married to him and it's up to thee to keep thi' husband healthy." This age old attitude hit a cord in my belief that men in general treated women as chattels, to be used, that marriage provided legal sex on demand from their husbands and it succeeded in strengthening my own attitude. I refused to be used when so little seemed to be returned by way of affection and practical help. Of course, we both knew that the operation had not helped; sexual satisfaction is well nigh impossible when the pain of it is too great; it was easier to avoid it, particularly with so little encouragement.

This unfortunate state of affairs had continued until October 1957 when Arthur left for Durham. Frank became less moody and began to take more interest in the nursery and his help at the shows was very welcome. Life was much more pleasant, except when I was

473

invited to help with judging necessitating a close association with other, mostly male judges. Quiet remarks were made and sullen faces were common when I was photographed or seen in the company of any of them, all of which I shrugged off as silly and unnecessary, and the event passed. But, vacation brought back the old withdrawn, moody attitude, each one more obvious, although I still didn't associate the outbursts with Arthur until during the long vacation of 1960 when Arthur had been left in charge of the nursery during our holiday.

A week after our return, a situation arose which seemed to be just a silly childish tantrum, but later evoked an issue from my mother, "He's jealous of Arthur," she said. I laughed. I didn't believe her. "Jealous of his own son, no way!" was my response. But it was obvious that something had upset him seriously for he told Arthur he had had enough, he was going to throw himself in the river. Although unknown to me at the time, Arthur talked to him for half an hour, eventually extracting a promise that he wouldn't do anything so daft, that there was no need for it and life would be much pleasanter if he took more interest in the place and quit worrying. Nothing more was said at the time and life went on much as before when Arthur went back to Durham. Work on the nursery went on comparatively smoothly; Frank helped with mossing wreath frames, wiring cupressus and other jobs he could manage during the weekends provided they were not too strenuous for his chest, until two weeks before Christmas when Arthur returned once more and set into wreath work with fervour.

All went well for the first week, gathering holly from the Holmesfield Park (by permission from Jack Shepley for sum of £15 a day), cutting, wiring and stabbing and the first deliveries made to the wholesaler in Sheffield Market; it seemed that everything would go smoothly, all working together, for once. But, that proved too optimistic after an offer of free help from the Secretary of the Chrysanthemum Society who had paid a visit for some Society business and seeing we were rather 'pushed' added an extra pair of hands. His help proved invaluable, his experience in wiring stems quickly adding to the piles of holly for stabbing and his very welcome sense of humour created such a lively atmosphere that one couldn't have forecast anything spoiling it. How wrong and how stupid not to have seen the signs.

Around 11.00 p.m. Frank got up quickly and said, "I'm going, I've had enough," and leaving we thought, to go to bed as he had to get up for work the next morning. The Secretary left about midnight and Arthur and I carried on until we had finished enough wreaths for a load to be delivered around 5.30 a.m. ready for the marking opening at 6.00 a.m. We finished around 3.30 a.m. and after loading the last wreath I told Arthur to get off to bed as he was doing the delivery. I went down to stoke up the greenhouse boiler and check that all was well before I too went inside. I was tired; all I wanted to do was to rest my weary body. But Frank, whom I thought was asleep, had other ideas, turning on me so strongly I just lost my temper and told him to leave me alone. What followed is indescribable, accusations about other men, if I didn't want him I must be having someone else, no-one could go without sex, it wasn't natural. What's more I never laughed and joked with him, I never looked at him as I did other men. He was now beyond sensible reasoning as he rushed around the bed towards the door only stopping to grab my nightdress and rip it from top to bottom. As he disappeared downstairs, Arthur came rushing out of his room. "What's happening, are you alright?" he said. "Yes," I answered, as I cuddled Yvonne who was now awake and wondering what was happening. We stood there for only a moment until Arthur said, "Go back to bed; I am," and as he turned to go he muttered "Let him go, I've had enough, he promised me he'd change, now he's had it, he's no longer my Father."

When I got up the next morning, I found Frank had left the house, and I was glad of the respite. But about 4.00 p.m. there was a 'phone call; it was Frank. A garbled message came down the line, as if the speaker were drunk, but after trying to get some sense out of him, he informed me that he had taken a bottle of aspirins, "Well, not the whole bottle, about 90," he said. After listening to his pleading "Come and get me, come and get me," I went into the shed where Arthur was wreathing and told him. "It's your Father, he's in the callbox at the Horns, (the pub in Holmesfield); he says he's taken

475

nearly a bottle of aspirins." "Tell him to take the rest," he replied, "it's nothing to do with me." "Go and get him Arthur," I said. "Why should I?" he answered, "Let him stew." "Arthur," I pleaded, "We can't let him peg out in the call box," "Why not?" he hissed. But, after a little more pleading, he reluctantly went to fetch him.

I was back in the shed when they arrived back and Arthur asked, "What do I do with him now?" "What state is he in?" I asked. "Bloody confused," he answered. "Make him sick," I said, "give him a pint of hot water with a tablespoonful of salt in it," and as he left the shed, "and see he drinks every drop." He returned about 15 minutes later. "He's drunk it, but he's not been sick, what do I do now?" he said, resigned to the task. "Give him another pint and put in a tablespoonful of mustard," I told him, "that should do the trick." He returned 10 minutes later saying "That's worked, he'll survive; he's gone to bed." Arthur and I continued working, retiring again very late. Frank was still asleep when I got into bed but I had already made up my mind that I was going to see a Solicitor in the morning and at breakfast time I told Frank of my decision. "I'm not surprised," he said quietly, "You know what he'll say don't you?" I didn't reply; as soon as Yvonne left for school, I put on my coat and left.

Mr Carr was the husband of a past student and, although I hadn't already met him, it took a little of the strain out of our first meeting. It probably had something to do with his attitude towards the way he dealt with my problem. As soon as I mentioned the word separation he refused to consider that possibility. "You want a divorce, not a separation," was his immediate advice. "No," I was adamant, "I don't want a divorce; I won't even consider it," I told him, "I just want a separation." "My dear Josephine," he insisted, "if you get a separation you'll have a hell of a job getting a divorce when you do want it." "But," I insisted, "I shan't want a divorce, ever." "That's what you say now, but you'll want to re-marry some day and then things will be very difficult," he said, "You are an attractive woman you know, and I'm sure you'll have many offers." I was growing quite exasperated. "Look Mr Carr, I have no intention of ever getting married again, I don't want another husband, I just want to be left in peace." In a last effort to change my mind, he sent for two of the other partners in the practice and when they arrived, without any explanation, he told them, "Tell Mrs Rundle she needs a divorce, not a separation." Two clerks had followed the Solicitors into the room and now joined in to agree with Mr Carr. I could see there was no way they were going to listen to me, "Oh, have it your own way," I said, "but I tell you, it's not what I want, I don't believe in divorce and I shall never get married again." (Contrary to all the directions about reconciliation, there seems to be very little effort on the part of Solicitors, perhaps separations don't earn as much as divorces, they certainly don't take so long if mine is an example.)

By the time I left, arrangements had been made to send a letter to Frank informing him of a pending divorce and that he should leave the house by 7th January, 1961. This date was two weeks hence. "We can't tell him to go before Christmas can we?" Mr Carr said, and I agreed. When I returned home, Frank asked me what had happened and when I told him that Mr Carr had advised me to have a divorce, he said, in a resigned voice, "I knew he would."

Work went on in as near a normal a way as possible for the last week before Christmas; Frank did his best to be pleasant, to the point that one morning, when he was particularly trying to please, Arthur was prompted to say, "Mom, have a row with my Father, I can't stand this unnatural smarminess." Poor Frank, it seemed he couldn't win. Christmas Day came and went and on Boxing Day Frank was moved to thank me for letting him stay over Christmas, saying that he had enjoyed it very much. The following day passed uneventfully and I went to bed leaving him reading a magazine. Next morning, I wasn't ready for his accusations, no temper, no strings of abuse, just a quiet gloating, "I've caught you out" tone of voice and the policeman in him brooking no excuses. It appeared that, last night after I had retired, he had knocked my handbag off the settee and the contents had spilled out on the floor. As he picked them up, a small box opened and out fell a small powder compact and a note saying 'Happy Christmas, thanks for everything,' and it was signed Derek. Of course, Frank's mind immediately translated 'everything' into something sexual, refusing to accept any explanation in his eagerness to turn the tables and nothing I could say had a hope of being believed.

The compact had been given to me three weeks before Christmas by the foreman of the timber yard when I had called to pick up some wood bases for my night school class. He was an unhappy man, the age-old story of wife and daughter ganging up on him. Divorce had never occurred to him, partly because, as he explained, marriage was his commitment, partly because his one dread in life was that he would lead a lonely old age. Workmen, he said would only make fun of him if they knew, so he had never voiced his feelings to anybody, until I turned up. There was a little coincidence brought to light very early in our first meeting when I realised that we did the garden maintenance in his boss's garden at Millthorpe. His boss and he had gone to Dronfield Grammar School together and had been friends ever since and it so happened that he was the same age as me, which made me realise that, had I been allowed to take up the scholarship, I would have started on the same day. It only takes a little thing to break the ice and start a conversation and over the few months since that first visit, I had listened to his stories of strife at home and sympathised with his predicament. One day I said, probably not very wisely, "You'll never be lonely, you don't know what the future has in store and old age is a long way off." I was surprised when he gave me the Christmas present and at first refused to take it, but I accepted it after his rather sorrowful, "I've nobody else to give one to and I'm grateful to you for listening." I put the present in my handbag and forgot all about it; in fact until Frank gave me the note, I hadn't even read it. It altered nothing, except that Frank decided to leave that night instead of waiting until 7th January.

Telephones worked hard at the brickyard until Mr Mercer, the Manager an old friend of my Father, made arrangements for Frank to work at Pickford & Holland's works at Blaenavon, Wales and he left about 11.30 p.m. The last strange act in this saga was when he said he hadn't any money and could I lend him some for his train fair? I had £10 which I handed over without argument and when he said "As soon as I get settled, I'll send it back," I told him not to bother. "How much do you want for maintenance?" he asked. "I don't want anything," I told him, "but you can send something for Yvonne."

478

"How much will that be," he asked again, "£2.10s.0d is the current legal amount I think," I answered, and with that he left.

The following Friday, the first crunch came, I hadn't any money for groceries, that £10 was supposed to have lasted until the following week when a cheque would arrive for night school salary. I usually did the shopping on Fridays; this week looked pretty thin, then I remembered what Jeff had said eight years before. "If you ever need anything, I'll see what I can do to help." Thankfully I managed to be independent up until now, but this was the time to lower my pride and ask for his help. His reply to my request for the loan of £5 for a week until my cheque came was like a kick in the teeth. "Frank's gone. Do you know what you should do,? Follow him." I couldn't believe it. "No," he added, "I can't afford £5.0s.0d," and he rang off. For the first time, and only time, I fetched the groceries from the little shop on the Common and asked Margaret for credit, feeling very, very let down. I was even angrier years later, after Jeff himself was divorced, when Edith, his ex-wife recalled the event by way of letting me know what a 'heel' he was. "He came away from the phone laughing," she told me, "Lend her £5.0s.0d? No fear," he had said, "Let her stew. I wondered how long it would be before she had to come off her high horse." I couldn't believe this and I suspected that Edith was enjoying it when she added, "He said you're always so bloody competent, you'd find a way." Thankfully I did.

I was surprised the day after Frank left to get a 'phone call from Derek, could I go down to see him and he murmured something about a 'phone call from Frank. Derek was disgusted that a man could talk, as he did, about his wife and he rang off. He apologised for getting me into such a situation but I assured him it wasn't his entire fault. I should have shown him the damned compact, but work had pushed it to the back of my mind. "Look," he said, "this has put you in an awkward situation and if there's anything I can to do help, let me know."

There was a strange peaceful atmosphere about the house for the following few weeks. Discussing the situation with my Mother one night she said, "If you hadn't have told him to go, I would, it was like living on the edge of a volcano; I was fed up with his bad-tempered moods." Of course I knew she wouldn't, but it did let me know how she felt. The following week I received a letter from Frank and a cheque for £2. I knew the reason for this. He had obtained lodgings with a very nice old couple called Thomas who, he said, treated him like their son. I knew that would suit him; he liked someone to make a fuss of him. However, the tone of the letter showed he hoped it would be only a temporary parting, a flash in the pan; I had made a point and he had learned his lesson. A letter arrived every week in the same vein for the following month during which none of the family knew the reason for his absence.

They had missed him and Mother had hinted, but nothing was said to me. But now Geoff was more forthright in his accusations, "You should have thought about the rest of the family," he told me, "we have our reputation to think about," "I don't suppose it will make a scrap of difference to you," I told him, "my business has never bothered you before, I don't see why you should bother now." It was obvious that I should not expect any support or sympathy from my brothers, if everybody had left us alone there would probably never have been a divorce. Such was the antagonism and interference that any reconciliation was impossible from that moment onwards.

One of Frank's pals from the brickyard had obtained his address and every evening the brickyard lorry drove slowly past the nursery on its way back to Barlow, and whatever I happened to be doing at the time was included in a letter to Frank the next day. Everyone who happened to come to the nursery was observed by someone, sometimes noting them as customers, sometimes with a more sinister motive.

At Whitsuntide, Derek offered to do some work for me for which I had bought the timber from his yard. He was seen working and a few days later Frank received the information that he was here supposedly helping me. How do I know? The letter was one of half a dozen sent to Mr Carr by Frank's Solicitor as proof of my illicit relationship and Mr Carr gave two of them to me to show how I was being monitored, or to be more specific, spied on.

During the next six years, until our divorce, no-one except Ida asked me what had happened, nor bothered how I was coping, and no-one was at all interested in Yvonne's or my Mother's welfare. Before leaving, Frank had said that he would not contest the divorce; it would go through quicker anyway if it was not defended. He said he would sign over his half of the land if I obtained the Deeds from the Bank. The nursery had already been turned over to me in 1952 when Frank left the business, but at the time, our Bank Manager thought it unnecessary to go to the trouble of getting the Deeds from the Bank vaults at Leeds, implying that the change of ownership would be automatic with the turnover of the business. The Deeds arrived about a month after Frank left, and with them came a shock for me for I found that my initial had been left off by the Solicitor, unnoticed by Frank when he had signed them on completion of the purchase. I had queried at the time why it wasn't necessary for me to sign and he just said that Irons, the Solicitor, said it wasn't necessary. This put a different picture on things. Frank had hinted in his letters that the parting was only temporary, now he was more open about wanting to return, holding the Deeds over my head as a bribe.

He told Elijah that I would never risk losing the nursery, "If I hold out long enough, I know she'll have me back just for the land," Frank said. How wrong he was. The wrangling went on for five years. When he realised that I would not fall for the bribe and Arthur would no longer own him as his Father, he wouldn't hand over the Deeds as "She'll only give it to him," he said. The argument went on for five years, during which every man I spoke to or had any business with, was added to the list of those with home I had committed adultery. Each was investigated; each name was removed, until both his Solicitor and mine thought that Frank was going 'round the bend'.

The trouble was the terms of the divorce petition, cruelty. He had an exemplary record from the Army and an exemplary character from the Police, and no woman was going to take that away from him. The divorce could not be completed until the property claim was settled. After five years, everybody was fed up with the delay, although I suspect that the Solicitors had done very well financially out of it, but the case finally came to Court early in 1965. Both parties met in a corridor the Barristers passing from a huddled conference back to their respective clients, each time putting a new proposition in an effort to obtain an agreement. But there was no agreement; Frank would not agree to cruelty and I would not agree to adultery. I had even offered to get a Doctor's certificate to show I could not have done so, but they had not listened. They wouldn't believe, as Frank wouldn't that anyone could manage without sex. Had they listened, the divorce would have gone through within the first few months.

Three months later, there was another Hearing, another meeting in the corridor, another deadlock. But the Recorder said the action must be settled that day. Frank still refused to sign over the land to me, for the reason already given and the Barristers passed to and fro for two hours in an effort to find a solution. Eventually, Frank agreed to give the land to Yvonne, now 13, provided two Trustees could be found to manage it until she was 21 years old. After some discussion, and a few 'phone calls, it was decided that, provided they agreed, Elijah should be one Trustee for Frank and Cousin Tom the other, for me. The way was now open for the divorce the following February. There were the usual huddled meetings in the corridor, Mr Lloyd, my Barrister offering various solutions put forward by the two Barristers, each one turned down by one or the other. Finally, Mr Lloyd came up with a compromise; that I should allow a divorce for desertion, by me. Frank would get the divorce and I would be the respondent. At first, I flatly refused. "Why should I be proved the guilty party when all along Frank had accepted the blame?" I said. "Because," said the Barrister, "you turned him out and when he asked to come back you refused, so you have no grounds against desertion. And," he continued, "more importantly, in that Courtroom are reporters from all the local newspapers; you are a well-known businesswoman, you have two grown up children, one of them with a job that would give them a 'beano'. Is it fair to them to risk such a scandal?" I listened to all the arguments, but I resented the fact that, after all this time, I should have the stigma of being divorced. "Why can't I divorce him?" I asked. "For the very good reason that he has letters proving that he was prepared to come home and start again, partly because you turned him out and the Solicitor's letter proves it," Mr Lloyd explained. So I agreed, for those reasons given, to be divorced for desertion. But I was angry, so angry, when I heard Frank

482

give his evidence. "You won't have to give evidence," Mr Lloyd said, "but your husband will, and whatever you do, don't give any indication as to whether what he says is true or not. Just stay quiet and it will all be over in about ten minutes."

We entered the Courtroom and the first person I saw was Derek, whom I hadn't seen for two years. "Why is he here?" I asked. "You see that man behind him? That's his wife's Solicitor," was the answer, "he's here to get evidence for her divorce." "Well he's barking up the wrong tree anyway," I said, "he'll not get that here today." It took only a couple of minutes for the preliminaries from both Barristers and then Frank entered the witness box and said the oath. Then the questioning began; when we had parted; how we had parted; then the question why? What had happened to break up the marriage? I wasn't ready for his answer, and was amazed after all the names on the petition with whom I was accused of adultery and now he stood there quite openly, under oath, saying "She refused me a marital relationship". "Why did she do that?" asked his Council. "Because she had had an operation and it was too painful," was the answer. I watched amazed as Mr Justice Payne looked down at the petition, turning the page, and going down the list with his finger, and I would have dearly loved to know his thoughts when he looked up, turned to Frank and asked, "You are saying that your wife couldn't have marital relations because it was too painful?" "Yes your Honour," was Frank's reply. "And that's why your marriage broke up?" asked Council. Again the answer was "Yes." The Q.C. looked hard at him and was quiet for a minute and then he called Mr Lloyd to his throne.

After speaking for a second or two, Mr Lloyd came to me and asked, "The Judge wants to know how much maintenance you want." I said I wanted nothing, but I wanted some for Yvonne. He returned to the Judge, who, having been told, looked at me and said, "Ask her again, she must want something. Again, I said I wanted nothing for myself, only for Yvonne. "How much does she want for child maintenance?" was the next question from the Judge, £5 a week," was my answer, knowing that this was far too much, considering I had been receiving only £2.5s.0d a week. Mr Lloyd knew this too, for he immediately said, "You'll not get that, I'm sure he can't afford £5 out

483

of his wage." "Well try it," I told him, "see what he has to say." Of course, he was right. The next question from Mr Justice Payne was, "Ask her if she will accept £3 a week," and of course I said I would; no use arguing when you know there's no point. At least it was 15s.0d more than I received at present, but I did wonder what would happen to that 5s.0d a week which was supposed to have been put in a banking account for Yvonne.

This last remark probably requires an explanation. This is how it happened. I have already explained that before he left for Wales, Frank asked how much I wanted for maintenance and we had agreed on £2.10s.0d a week. This was received by post as arranged, but on the 5th week the cheque was for £2.5s.0d and the letter explained that in future this would be the amount he would send, whilst the remaining 5s.0d would be put into a bank account for Yvonne for some future date. I didn't believe a word of this and knowing Frank's promises and intentions of the past, forecast that there would never be a bank account. But I didn't argue about it, it didn't seem worth the effort. Now events had caught up with him and the Court had set the price. To that there was no argument. Give credit where credit is due; when Yvonne reached the age of 16 and maintenance could have ceased, she remained in education and in recognition of this, Frank kept up the payments until the age of 18.

Now we come to the most bizarre event in the whole of this ridiculous situation. The Judge left the Court, followed by Counsel and the rest of the Officers of the Court, whilst Frank made his way towards the back of the court to where Mom and I were standing waiting to leave. I had turned on standing up and now had the satisfaction of seeing all the disappointed reporters leaving empty handed. I was speaking to Derek and asking him how he was faring and got the impression that he would like to talk longer, but unexpectedly Frank came towards me and with a glance at Derek, even a hint of a satisfied smile asked, "So what's to happen now?" "Well, we are going for a cup of tea," I said, indicating Mom and I, but not excluding Derek entirely. "I didn't mean now," Frank said, "I mean you and me?" "I don't know what you mean," I said, somewhat confused. I considered the matter of 'us' was at an end, except for the compulsory six weeks waiting for the Decree Nisi, and said so. "What about trying again?" was Frank's surprising question. Confused, I asked what he meant. "Well, what about getting married again?" he said, and I could see he really meant it. "You must be kidding," was all I could muster. "I'm not; what about it? I don't want to live in digs all my life." I was astounded and angry. This is typical; all he's bothered about is his own comfort. It also confirmed what I had always thought; this whole business had been only a means to save his reputation.

The reason on the original petition had been on the grounds of cruelty, always resented by Frank on account of his exemplary character from both the Army and the Police. Had it been on any other grounds, I'm sure the divorce would have gone through undefended, if it happened at all. I told him now that there was no hope, nor intention that I would ever marry again. "I have my life," I said, "and you have yours, there is nothing for us anymore." He accepted this without the least emotion, simply saying "Let's go and have that cup of tea."

We headed for the 'Wig & Pen' Tavern in Campo Lane; Frank walked up with Mother and I with Mr Lloyd (my Counsel). He expressed what to me was a disgusting amount of pleasure at the way the case had gone. No hitches, no arguments in Court, and altogether a satisfactory solution. But I turned on him in disgust. Had he, and all the rest of the grabbing chauvinistic self-opinionated crowd of legal conspirators listened to me, and allowed me to have that medical examination, there would have been no case for me to answer, no long list of names of innocent men, no wasted six years whilst legal minds revelled in their growing bank accounts. Of course, all this rolled off his back like water from a duck. He shrugged and repeated "It was a satisfactory end; at least you should be pleased there will be no newspaper reports." The whole 'set-up' confirmed my opinion of men, legal or otherwise. They are controlled by their obsession with sex and cannot understand that there are those whose world does not revolve around it. It clouds their judgment and deprives them of common sense. No woman can manage with them, and any who say otherwise are sarcastically disbelieved.

485

As for me, what had, up to now, been tolerance, was gradually developing into disgust. I doubt if it has ever changed except for one or two individuals. But many things happened between 1960 and 1965 and I must go back to January 1960 when Arthur returned to Durham for his last term.

This was the worse time of year on a nursery to be short of money; seed and fertiliser bills must be paid, and petrol found for marketing bedding plants, deliveries of herbaceous plants and general running of the business until the first cheques came in towards the end of May. The cheque from night school in January and after Easter would help, but I knew I would not be able to send Arthur the odd pound now and again, as before. This was his last term before his finals in June and I knew I couldn't let worry over money (any more than at present) cloud his thoughts at such a crucial time. With little hesitation, I wrote to Jack Longland, Director of Education in Derbyshire and threw myself on his mercy. I knew he had a lot of interest in Arthur's progress and subject as he had been a mountaineer and explorer before coming to Derbyshire. I wasn't disappointed. By return of post he promised an extra £38 which would be sent to Arthur without delay. This sum may appear to be a mere pittance on today's values, but as an extra to his very small grant, it was most acceptable.

At the beginning of May, I was offered the biggest challenge so far in my floristry career. In his last year, Arthur had been elected President of the S.R.C. (Student Representative Council), and as President, could choose the theme for the decorations for the June Ball. They already had designs of fish, dinosaurs and other spectacular extravagances but never a theme on flowers. I received a letter from Arthur setting out his ideas and inviting me to do all the necessaries if I was interested. Of course I was, and in order to view the Great Hall of the Castle and Hatfield Hall, which would be used for dancing and to measure both for the quantity of flowers, foliage and sundries.

After all the viewing was completed we decided that the two venues should be different; the Great Hall with an 'old world' profusion of mixed colours, with garlands hanging from the roof to create a lower suspended ceiling effect, whilst Hadfield Hall, much more modern, should have pedestals and other more modern set-pieces. I had travelled to Durham by train as I knew that construction of the new A1 Motorway was causing some delay and I could travel back the same day without any undue strain.

On the return journey, the train stopped at Darlington, and two women joined it; obviously mother and daughter. They had attended the wedding of another daughter (gleaned from their conversation) and spent some time discussing the bride, the guests and the flowers, some of which I had seen through the polythene bag which the young woman had placed on the table. I was intrigued as I listened, for the bridesmaid, for she it was, lovingly lifted the bag and gazed at it, all the time exclaiming "How lovely, beautiful, such lovely roses," and so on until the temptation was too great and my curiosity growing. She finally undid the bag and drew out the bouquet she had carried that afternoon. I was mesmerised, I couldn't believe it. She fingered the wires, devoid of any covering tape and opened them out to reveal nine roses, each at the end of a wire and backed by three, now withered, rose leaves. After lovingly stroking them with a delicate finger, and smelling their delicious perfume, all the time expressing her delight in their beauty, she re-folded the bouquet, three rows of three roses and carefully threaded it back into the polythene envelope. I wondered, why do I go to so much trouble when the customer only sees the flowers? Here was a bouquet which could be posted and the bride would be just as satisfied, or would she?

June arrived, the date for travelling to Durham for the Ball. I decided to take Glennis with me (the student I mentioned in a former chapter), and she was returning home by train the next day, whilst I was to stay at the Ball. Hatfield Hall was no problem; predominantly modern pedestals, with other pseudo-Japanese arrangements at vantage points; it was quickly done in the morning, having spent the rest of the previous day sorting out and conditioning the flowers, foliage and preparing containers. However, the Great Hall in the Castle was somewhat of a challenge. The great vaulted ceiling rose so high the rafters disappeared into inky darkness and the high windows needed ladders to reach their sills. The answer was, to simulate a false ceiling with flowers, hanging wreaths and witch-balls made with bright reds, yellows and apricots, with loops and trails of ribbons

487

which would move and sway in the air above the dancers. The windowsills held waterfall arrangements with long trails of ivy and ferns mixed with clusters of gypsophila to simulate spray, whilst to bring the whole picture down to eye level, two 12ft high arrangements rose from ground level at either side of the stage on platforms made from boxes and planks rummaged out from 'who knows where' by the willing students who volunteered to help.

The students were wonderful. They appeared from nowhere as soon as they saw us preparing the wreaths and witch-balls and couldn't wait to get their hands in and have a go. They were the first to realise what a difficult task it would be to hang them, until two of them had the bright idea of letting ropes down from outside, through the joins in the ridge tiles, allowing us to fasten 6ft lengths of ribbon to the ends, which were then attached to the looped ribbons of the decorations. There was no shortage of volunteers; everybody was more than willing to help and vied with other for the chance to climb on to the roof of Durham Castle.

We waited in suspense until the first rope appeared, and the first wreath was hauled into position, then it was only a matter of time before all the wreaths, witch-balls, windowsills (reached on ladders and high steps rustled up from somewhere), and huge set pieces were in place and the only job left was the clearing away of all the rubbish. The female students hadn't been left out of all the excitement. They had seen me making a corsage to wear at the Ball, and all had a go at making their own. (It's a pity such a fashion has died, what does a beau give to his lady companion these days I wonder? Alas for romance!) There were still a few flowers left and Glennis had a lot of fun teaching them how to make a garland. When it was finished, they said it was their contribution s they fastened it to the wall between two windows.

Graduation Day was the next reason for a journey to Durham. It was such a proud day for me and I wouldn't have missed it for the world. The fact that I couldn't afford a new outfit wasn't going to stop me, so out came the pure silk dress I had bought in 1953, which fortunately fitted perfectly. But what could I do about a hat? I couldn't afford one, but couldn't go without. Ingenuity is the answer to some problems, and this time it served me well. Somewhere I had an old hat which I could use as a mould, and it took only a few minutes to cut away the brim and cover the cut end with white ribbon. The problem was. How to cover the top? The current fashion was for flowers, ruched ribbon and net, but with time short, I had to wait and hope that the shops in Durham City would solve the problem for me. This was more difficult than I had expected; there were few shops in Durham who catered for amateur milliners. However, after combing Silver Street and all the other possibilities, we finally found a shop in the Main Street who supplied limited choices of hat net. I settled on white, the original colour of the hat, and half a yard of white ribbon for decoration and sat in my hotel bedroom until 2.00 a.m. ruching the net, making ribbon bows and roulettes and by 11.00 a.m. the following morning, took my seat in the Great Hall of the Castle and proudly watched Arthur accept his scroll and with a broad smile, walk back down the aisle to re-join the other graduates. The hat, by the way, is somewhere in the boxes of cast-offs in the loft.

The rest of the summer passed as all the other summers had done, except that they were a little more peaceful. But, like many other graduates, he wanted a job and as a glaciologist, his kind of jobs were few and far between. My suggestion that he spend another year at University and take a 'Dip. Ed.' was turned down flat. "If I had to teach geography," he said, "I'd want a helicopter to photograph the world, 'cos that's the best way to learn geography." "What about botany?" I asked. "No Mother," he said emphatically, "the kids deserve better than that. I couldn't get down to their level any more, and that wouldn't be fair." A year before, Hal Lister, his Glaciology Tutor, had led an expedition to Easter Island and Arthur would dearly have liked to go with him, but Prof. Fisher, Geography Faculty Don said "No," on the assumption that if he went now, and tasted the life out there, he wouldn't want to come back. Wise man! Now, he was itching to go and growing more anxious daily; there weren't many jobs on offer for a budding glaciologist.

As a criticism of the British I must add that, when Arthur started his study at Durham, he wrote to the Falkland Island Dependencies to enquire about the possibility of joining an expedition when he qualified. They had answered his letter, suggesting that, as soon as he graduated, he should let them know, when he would be favourably considered. Well, he had written but with typical 'muddling' they never replied. This was at a time when there was much criticism about 'the brain drain', when hundreds of trained students and University Graduates were leaving Britain for America. There was little wonder!

Sometime towards the end of July (I think I am right about the date), Arthur received a 'phone call from Hal, telling him that the Americans were looking for someone to join them on an expedition to Antarctica and he thought Arthur would get the job if he applied. This was the answer to a dream; just what he wanted and he kept his fingers crossed until he received a reply. Yes was the answer, provided he could pass all the rigorous medical examinations and could be on American soil by 4th September, the job was his. By this time it was well into August; there was little time, for the medicals were really intensive, so meticulous that one expert would examine teeth; another eyes, yet another the heart, the lungs, the limbs, until every part of the body was deemed perfect.

The trouble was that these experts were distributed all over the country, one in London, one in Manchester, another in the Midlands, none of them were local and by the time one had sent his report, time was running out if he were to fulfil the criteria of being in America by the 4th September. There was a heart-rending wait after the report went to the American office in Manchester; nerves were frayed and tempers on a short fuse. Days went by; the waiting was unbearable, for he didn't even know whether he had been accepted. I suggested he 'phone, but for two or three days he refused. "They must know by now, so why don't they let us know?" he said. With five days to spare, he did ring, to hear a woman's voice cheerfully declaring, "Why laddie, of course you've got the job, what are you worrying about?" One thing that had been worrying both of us was would the operation on his knee and chipping of the condyles of both knees be considered too serious for the rigorous work in the Antarctica? But she assured Arthur that there was no need to worry, there were a lot more serious things than knees, and he hadn't got them.

Now things moved fast. It had cost quite a princely sum in rail fares and accommodation for the past month, and funds were running out. The first thing was to book a seat as quickly as possible to the U.S.A. on the 4th September and fortunately I could raise that amount. But Arthur had to live in either New York or Washington for a week before reporting for the briefing session and that wasn't going to be cheap. Luckily, I had a good friend in Ida, who had been one of the bridesmaids at our wedding. We had been close friends since I was 18 years old; had been on holidays together and done all the things that close friends do. Now I was about to ask her to lend me £20.0s.0d, the very minimum that Arthur could manage on for the week. I didn't like the idea of borrowing from such a close friend, it seemed to me like abusing a privilege, but Ida understood immediately, only making one proviso; that I repay the loan in a fortnight. So, we were now set for that memorable day when we set out for the journey to Ringway Airport and the 707 which would wing him away from England 12,000 miles to the Antarctica.

The journey over the Pennines to Stockport was with mixed feelings for both of us. For Arthur it was a journey into the unknown. This was where he would prove himself, how he would cope with all the discomforts of the life on ice; and it was where he would put all that he had learned at University into practice. For me it was a mixture of pride that he had achieved all he had hoped for, mingled with great sadness that he would no longer be with me, not only for his practical help, but for his understanding and support that had helped me through the last year. We actually turned back at Stockport, returning in silence to the Leyland's. Something was worrying him and it wasn't clear what, until over a cup of tea he said he wasn't happy about leaving me behind in such a precarious position. He wasn't sure how the family would treat me, for he had little faith in any of them, even Elijah who, until recent events had been respected and thought of with affection denied to Frank, his father.

After about an hour of reassuring him; we set out again; this time rather more urgently, having lost so much time already. We arrived safely with time to spare and eventually the time arrived when we had to say goodbye. Neither of us could guess what lay ahead; in

1961 the Antarctic was a very dangerous place, only four years after the first crossing by Fuchs in 1957, the 'International Geophysical Year'. I stood there until he disappeared through the gate, then made my way outside to the rough grass area, where other friends and relatives were collecting to wave goodbye to their loved ones. By this time, tears were pouring down my cheeks; my feelings were at rock bottom.

When eventually I saw the familiar figure walking along the tarmac and up the gangway, I could hardly see through the tears, now uncontrollable. This young son, on a journey to the other side of the world, would I ever see him again? All I could see now was his Abercrombie overcoat, his pride and joy, and the long wave from the doorway of the aircraft, before he disappeared. I stood there until the aircraft left, watching it rise and level out, until it finally disappeared in the clouds. I wept all the way home and almost every waking moment for the following week, lonely and distraught, as I had never thought possible.

It took some time to settle down to a routine of work, lightened by the first card from Arthur in Washington, with news that he was enjoying the experience of a different country, of the squirrels in the squares and the lovely warm weather. A later letter from Skyline Lodge in Virginia overlooking the Shenandoah River showed how happy and excited he was and during the briefing sessions, how confident he was that all would be well and he was looking forward to the whole experience. Later cards arrived from Hawaii, from Fiji and from New Zealand, Headquarters of the National Science Foundation, of which he was now a part.

All these helped to temper the lone feelings and work had to go on. Ida received back the loan in the promised two weeks, but money was tight. I could get on with mossing wreath-frames in between other jobs, as we had gone early on to the moors and gathered half a dozen bags of moss before Arthur had left and there were still plants to lift for customer's early planting. The trouble was cash flow, money for living, for groceries and petrol and all the other items that had a habit of creeping up behind me. Like the motto hanging over my bed, not rude, just practical. 'Just when you think both ends meet, somebody moves the ends'. Somebody always seemed to be moving my ends! Indeed something which would bring a regular even small amount in between the night school cheques and the only possible solution I could see was a shop, I could buy supplies from the wholesale market to supplement my own and possibly win more orders for weddings and funerals, for although these had been steadily growing, I knew I could cope with many more. The more I thought about it, the more it seemed a good idea; Glennis could manage in the shop since she had passed her senior examination in June and if I did the marketing and deliveries in the morning, I could still work on the land as usual.

Since Arthur had returned from Durham, Derek had come at the weekends to help with odd jobs; not being a gardener nor yet a cabinet-maker, he was a dab hand at stoking boilers, shifting and riddling soil; or any other maintenance job I threw his way. And he got on well with Mom; she liked him and his sense of humour was a refreshing change. Arthur and he had worked together and he had promised him that he would keep an eye on us all whilst he was away. He was a very practical man, facing up to all events with a down-to-earth, feet on the ground attitude, which suited my way of thinking. He knew the situation over money and in November came with the news that there was an empty shop in Hereford Street in Sheffield for rent and no 'key money' involved.

Now that the crunch had come, I became a bit dubious. It was very near Christmas, when I knew I couldn't give full attention to fittings and fixtures needed before opening. But, I agreed that Christmas was also a good time to open a flower shop and Glennis was also enthusiastic. I decided to view the property and find out about the rent and conditions in the lease.

The shop was presently leased to a Jewish shopkeeper who had a jewellery shop on the opposite side of the street at the Moor end. He actually leased all the shops on one side of the street and some on the other, letting them on 'sub-leases' to the actual shopkeepers. The rent was reasonable, considering that Hereford Street had always been known as a good trading area and it was only a small shop, it would not cost much for fittings. I was glad of Derek's enthusiasm and when he offered to do all the fittings, obtaining the timber and other materials from his firm, I decided to take it, fixing a date two weeks before Christmas for the 'grand opening'.

By the time the shop was ready for opening I was very pleased with the result of Derek's work, although some fittings had produced conflicts of opinion as to what was and what wasn't possible. It proved larger than at first thought; there was quite a large back room with a stone flag floor, a tap and a drain which, with the large workbench bought for a pittance from a junk shop on Abbeydale Road, made an adequate flower store for unpacking flower boxes and conditioning and a large paved yard and drain proved invaluable for dealing with all the rubbish left from make-up work and a standing ground for spare flowers and foliage at busy times. The front shop was large enough to take a screen with an archway leading to an area of 9ft x 14ft to be used as a work room for wedding work (the back room was used for all funeral work, sheaves and arrangements, which were far more 'messy' than bouquets and corsages). All in all, it proved a very easy shop to work in, with plenty of shelf space for vases and containers, both for work and for sale, and the huge polished dresser with carved dog's heads at the ends, which stood at the back of the shop area, was great for storage, with its deep drawers and the mirror back was useful when assessing bouquets and wreathes, because the reflection shows up any defects in balance and an overall distribution of colour, better than a closer direct look.

Everything went well for the first two weeks and we had an excellent Christmas, although it did mean that I made many more trips than originally intended. The first day of buying I had only £30 to spend knowing that we had to sell everything, not only to get back the £30 but for extra money to improve sales and build up stock and sundries towards a prosperous shop appearance.

One piece of advice was given to me during the first week by Mrs Ashton, who owned the china shop opposite. In line with other florist and food shops who had blinds to protect their goods during sunny weather, I had opted for one with red and white stripes. Mrs Ashton came across on the first sunny day to warn me of the danger of red and white in that particular street. The trouble is, she warned

494

me was that Hereford Street is the direct route from the tram stop on the Moor to Bramall Lane Football Ground and, "If United lose the match," she warned, "They'll have your blind down before you know what's hit you." I took her advice and immediately rang the firm and changed the blind to blue and white. We soon found that, if United won, the fans were so elated that they would buy bunches of flowers for the wives, fruit for the children and those who were too inebriated to know what they were buying would empty their pockets for anything the assistant put into their hands. Consequently, as soon as the news of a win came on the grapevine, all the spare flowers were dumped into metal containers and put outside the window and in the doorway, ready to be grabbed by eager buyers. It was even possible to stand at the door, (inside, of course, as outside would be considered street trading, which, without a licence, was against the law). Holding a vase for a drunken fan to grab as a present for the wife, paying whatever was asked without question.

When I decided to take the shop in November, none of the research had indicated that change was in progress, nor intended, yet two weeks before we opened, the street was made into a 'one-way system' and a traffic island was installed at the Eyre Street end. The effect of this was hidden during the Christmas period, but immediately after, it was obvious that it was making a difference. What had been a very busy street for traffic from the Moor to Bramall Lane, St Mary's Road and Queens Road, was now almost devoid of through traffic. This made a lot of difference to trade and there was much grumbling from the existing tenants. I had no way of measuring, but I did find that trade was not as good as other past tenants and shoppers had led me to believe. However, although slow, as trade usually is just after Christmas, we did manage to hold our heads above water and soon became known for our make-up work, especially funeral sheaves since the first one was made for a member of the St Mary's Old Folks Club and bouquets for the 'buffer lasses' from a local knife manufacturer. The 'buffer lasses' came during their dinner time break, dressed in their brown paper aprons and caps and wearing leggings also made of brown paper. It was an exceedingly dirty job and they were considered by many people as being the lowest of the low workers but they were an honest bunch with a raucous sense of humour who brooked no nonsense when it came to striking a bargain. And, underneath all the dirt, they were women, would-be brides, with all the sentiments of the fashionable secretary or business magnate.

I remember the first time they came, about eight of them, to help one of their colleagues to choose her bouquets and were willing to try this new shop which, said one, they had heard didn't charge the earth for half a dozen roses. Glennis was in a stupor so as I happened to be there after delivering a funeral order, I took charge, handing the bride-to-be the book of designs and prices for her to make a choice. Her friends clustered round and some discussion took place and I could tell that money, or lack of it, was going to be the deciding factor. So, on the principle that if you don't take the order, someone down the street will, I stepped in. "Can't you find any you like?" I asked. The poor girl looked a bit embarrassed. "I like some of 'em, but I can't afford them that I like," she answered. "What kind of flowers would you like?" I asked, and when she looked uncertain I said, "Do you like roses, carnations or a mixture?" She hesitated then said, "Roses and some of that," pointing to stephanotis in one of the photographs. "Do you have a budget to work to?" I asked, "Most brides do," as she looked rather mystified I continued, "You know what I mean, so much for your dress and so much for the reception and what's left over for flowers." She nodded, and I knew I had the order. "Look," I said, "Will you leave it to me, tell me what you can afford, and I'll see that you have the bouquet you want." She was surprised, but I assured her, "Just tell me the flowers you like and then leave it to me." I knew that I could make a bouquet using flowers sensibly and artistically with a minimum of flowers, which would beat any 'cram-jammed' flat, uninteresting, ill-designed atrocities which were turned out by other florists and for a much lower price. The bride was delighted. From that wedding we won the orders from all the 'buffer-girls', who always asked for "One of your bouquets for £5.0s.0d" or whatever price they could afford.

Everything went well until the 16th February 1962. That was the night the hurricane struck. It was about 5.00 a.m. when I was awakened by an almighty crash in the nursery and the noise of wind in the eaves was overbearing. I jumped out of bed, just in time to see the last of the large glasshouses collapse into a heap of contorted metal and broken glass. I rushed into Mother's room and looked through her window wailing "All I've worked for twelve years, gone in a bloody gale." It was more than a gale; it was chaos all down the valley. Trees were uprooted in Gillfield Wood; the bridge at the bottom of Mickley Lane was flattened and the Chemical Yard flooded. Right down the valley of the Sheaf there was destruction. Nothing in the way of the mighty gusts escaped untouched. The large heavy roof of one of Elijah's biggest sheds was lifted and slewed round to an incongruous angle and everywhere there was devastation. I was numb, so angry that fate could deal such a blow just when things were looking brighter, so disgusted that I didn't even try to rescue anything out of the debris. All the boxes of newly pricked-out lobelia and antirrhinums, lettuce and early tomatoes; all the freshly potted primula japonicas intended for Mothering Sunday and Easter trade, all early sown seeds of bedding plants and bowls of late-flowering bulbs, were mixed up with stock plants of chrysanthemums brought in for early cuttings, rooted cuttings and stock plants of geraniums and boxes of dahlia tubers.

For three months the site was left untouched, nothing was rescued; what was the good when there was nowhere to put the rescued? Had I any insurance? No, no insurance firm would insure horticultural buildings, particularly glasshouses for damage through storm and tempest. I could have obtained insurance for flood but when would I claim? I was hardly like to suffer floods at the top of a hill 950ft above sea level. After three months, Elijah asked whether I was going to build another glasshouse, smaller, out of the pieces which might be rescued. I said no, I should concentrate on the shop and hope that I could make a living out of that. So, it was arranged that he would rescue whatever he could use to make a small house for his own use, and it still stands as the only memorial to its poor ancestor.

It was now more important than ever that the shop must earn a living for us all; except for sales from herbaceous plants, there was little income from the nursery. What wedding and funeral orders might have been taken, these were now automatically 'phoned through to the shop and delivered from there. If, as Dad used to say, "Let your disadvantages turn to advantages," was true, then this was the time to try out his philosophy. The large teaching shed was still standing and floristry lessons were still held there. Now, after some months of pressing by flower arranging students to start a class in floristry, I decided this was the right moment to try it out. I had always been against the idea of teaching housewives; it was against all the principles of the Society of Floristry, who were anxious to stop poor back-street make-up at the expense of those who paid rent and overheads in their shops. But, survival was the game for me now and at least these women were prepared to learn how to do the job properly. Six students signed on at once and paid for the first term in advance; this provided a very welcome income to take us through the summer months and over the quiet holiday season.

Early in March, I made an application to Interflora, the Relay florists, for membership, thinking that the extra trade it would encourage would enable us to keep a bigger stock of goods and help to fill my time now that I spent less time on gardening. The fee was £10 which was non-returnable, but I felt that the expense was justified. Again, I was wrong. I had reckoned without the antagonism of the other florists in the same delivery area. They belonged to the same family, children of a longstanding family of florists, who resented someone trading in competition. Had I been any untrained person simply opening the usual type of flower selling business I am sure nothing would have been said, but it so happened that I had ordered a 'Pearl & Dean' advert on the screen of the cinema in Ecclesall Road near to the home of one of the wholesalers in the market. My name covered the huge screen, with the letters after it 'S.F.Dip' which, of course, was the Diploma of the Society of Floristry for which no other florist in Sheffield or in the surrounding area had qualified. On my next trip to the market, I found myself in a similar position to that encountered in the Seagraves nurseries; sarcastic remarks; rude comments and very unpleasant treatment when buying flowers. Of course my requirements were small compared with those of the large well-established florists and didn't command the same respect and one of the chief culprits, as well as those of the family firm, was the son of the wholesalers whom I had given as a reference for my application for Interflora membership.

He had just entered the business from either College or University and had all the arrogance and rudeness that seems to accompany some graduates who have not had to work their passage. His father was a kind man and I had confidence in his honest reference. However, whether from pressure of others; or because I was only small fry and not worth encouraging; my application was turned down. No reason was given; even the 'field man' had seemed impressed with the work he had seen on his visit, so I had no idea why until one day about three months later. I was attending a Council Meeting of the S.O.F. when Mrs Tasker, the Secretary congratulated me on becoming a member of Interflora; she was also Secretary of Interflora and had been at the meeting when my name was put forward. She told me, my application had been accepted. I said she was wrong, my application had been turned down, but she was adamant. "I know you were accepted," she said, "do you want me to look into it?" I was pretty disgusted by now and emphatically said, "No." I had decided to apply to Teleflower instead. Teleflower had members from nurseries as well as shops and this proved an advantage. There was no fee, and both the nursery and shop were accepted for membership.

I had written to Arthur and told him about the damage from the hurricane so he was prepared, but still shocked at the extent of the damage when he returned in the summer of 1962. Assessing the problem, he decided to rebuild the section of greenhouses which had been between the large glasshouse and the small propagating house; with this I could, at least, raise a few bedding plants for sale in the shop and a few tomatoes for the house. He didn't agree with the shop; I should have waited until he returned home, then I could have found one in a better position. I said that was a good position before the street was made 'one-way' but it was no excuse. It's always easy to see by hindsight.

In October 1992, Arthur left for America and in November returned to the Antarctic, this time to lead his own expedition. On his return the previous March the National Science Foundation had sent him to Greenland with a new recruit straight from University to train for this expedition. I remember him telling me of his lack of stamina and experience of hard work, flabby muscles and all. He told how they had pulled a heavily laden sledge, both of them on skis, with long traces in a 'V' shape in case one of them fell down a crevasse, when the other could haul him up to the surface again. He explained how he had let his trace go slack when the lad was flagging so that he would have to work harder to move the sledge. I thought this was cruel and said so, but he grimaced saying, "Mom, if I fall down a crevasse I must know that he is strong enough to pull me out, just as he relies on me," and there was a glint in his eye when he added "and a man's not a light weight to pull out of a 100ft crevasse." At that moment I thought "How like your Grandad you are, he could be ruthless when he had to be."

For the next few years there was steady progress and we managed to keep our heads above water; and the floristry classes and night school income kept the wolves from the door. Arthur returned home in the summer of 1963 for a short visit and he wasn't very happy about our hand-to-mouth existence as he called it. He had been successful in his own career and returned financially secure and expected to see me also free from monetary worries. Before he set off again for the Antarctica he made arrangements with his bank at Durham to loan me £50 in any one month in case of emergency. This proved a Godsend but when my Bank Manager began to abuse it, seeing an opportunity to receive money into his own Bank if I got to the last few pounds in my account, I put a stop to it and continued to plod on in a quiet way.

One set back, however, was when I grew suspicious of Glennis' honesty. I had wondered sometimes when she was working on the nursery, when small things were disappearing from the house in which she was accepted as one of the family. Now I found money missing from the till and on two occasions from the bank bag after cashing up the day's takings ready for paying in. A trap was set, but Glennis didn't up for work the next morning; she probably had guessed that I had become suspicions. About a fortnight later, I received a 'phone call from a florist in Attercliffe, whose first question was, "Did you have a girl called Glennis working for you?" Of course, I said I had, but when she asked why she had left, I wavered, saying it was a matter between her and me. The woman was angry, accusing me of covering up an offence. "I should have prosecuted the thief, (her words); it wasn't fair to other employers." Obviously, Glennis thought she had got away with it once and had tried again, and her new employer intended to prosecute. I refused her request to give evidence, explaining that, without concrete evidence, it was futile and would be thrown out of Court, whilst advising her to make sure she had evidence before taking it any further. I heard nothing more, so I assume she did nothing. It is very difficult to prove guilt without absolute incriminating evidence and can be very costly. It had already been costly for me, just when I could ill afford it.

It will be obvious to the reader that my time was becoming rather too thinly spread and so an arrangement was made with Derek whereby I could spend more time away from the shop, He had changed his job early in 1962 to a timber firm based in Hull, but who had no offices in Sheffield. His wife was uncooperative which prohibited him from working from home, hence the necessity to find another office. We came up with an answer which suited us both very well. I would still do the marketing on Tuesdays and Thursdays and any time in-between if extra trade should make it necessary and then, if there were no early deliveries, I would be free to work on the nursery until 5.30 p.m. when the shop closed. Carol, another student, would take charge in the shop, except at very busy times and take telephone messages for Derek. He would pick these up at 4.30 p.m., after which he would do any deliveries which had accumulated during the day. This arrangement went very well and suited us both, leaving me with much more time to do my own work.

The family knew nothing of these arrangements, except, of course, my Mother and soon it was to lead to more mischief and interference, particularly due to our arrangements on Saturday night. On most Saturdays, there was a football match at Bramall Lane with a consequent increase in foot traffic from there to the Moor and additional trade in the shop. As Mrs Ashton had predicted, if United won, the local pubs did a good trade and by the time the inebriated fans reached Hereford Street, they were ripe for slaughter. We soon learned to stay open until around 8.30 p.m., even though it was strictly illegal. To get over this obstacle, in case by some unlucky fluke a policeman should stroll down the street, I let Carol go home at 5.30 p.m. as usual (compulsory closing day at that time was Thursday), whilst as the owner, my shop hours were overlooked and in any case, we were always tidying up and putting the shop to bed for the weekend. (A long job when the window had to be dressed with a weekend display for advert, all the interior left tidy and the floor mopped in case any weekend viewer proved over curious.)

After all the extra work and the fact that we hadn't eaten since a small snack at lunchtime when I fetched Yvonne to the shop for the afternoon, we were all tired and ravenous. There was a good Chinese Restaurant on the way home and that's where we relaxed and wound down for an hour before the rest of the journey down London Road, along Heeley Bottom, Chesterfield Road eventually arriving at the Horns Inn at Holmesfield about 9.45 p.m., weary but well satisfied after a good day and ready for a good drink whilst Nancy (Mrs Barton) unpacked her week's greengroceries and flowers and paid the bill. Derek stayed just long enough to say 'hello' to Mom and enjoy a cup of tea before he left for home around 11.00 p.m.

One of the letters sent to my Solicitor (mentioned previously) told me how our innocent Saturday was being interpreted: 'it was just an excuse to say we were at the shop until 8.30 p.m.; we were out together somewhere enjoying ourselves; I left Mother to look after Yvonne whilst I went off gallivanting; the shop was just an excuse to get away.' Of course, Frank believed it, although my Mother knew nothing of the gossip until I told her when I received the letters.

There was the occasion when I was asked to make a life-size tribute for a member of the Tigers Motor Cycle Club who had been killed during a race. Their logo showed a rider in full 'gear' riding towards the viewer with leg outstretched whilst rounding a curve and this was the design they wanted, life-size! This was the biggest challenge I had had in make-up so far and to add to the exercise, this was noon on Saturday and the tribute was wanted for 10.00 a.m. on Monday morning. Not a problem during the week, but this was

Saturday morning when the Sheffield market closed at 12.30 p.m., which meant that flowers were the first priority and a dash to the wholesaler was the first move.

For the frame, I needed a 36" wreath frame, for which I dyed a quantity of reindeer moss already in stock which was also used for the 'Ace of Clubs' logo on the front of the suit. A 5ft frame was used for the body, with a wreath frame attached on which to build the head. Two small crescent frames were supports for the arms and a large crescent frame acted very well for the outstretched leg. White and red carnation petals were suitable for the helmet, bandana and wheel hub, but what about the suit, the colour gunmetal and so large as to a huge amount of flowers? Where could I dye so many? Where could I even obtain so many at 12 noon on Saturday? This is just such an occasion that keeps your faith alive when all seems to be lost.

The wholesaler had packed away, or sold everything before drawing the shutters on the stand, except he suddenly remembered that he had stacked away in a corner ten boxes of asters that nobody wanted. They had no name, only a number as they were the result of a breeder's experiment that hadn't proved as successful as he had hoped. I went across to the corner after him and watched as he opened the first box and there was the answer to my prayers; the foulest coloured asters, a dingy dark blue colour that no-one except in the direst of emergencies would even look at twice. "Just right," I shouted, "how much?" "Oh, give us ten bob (50p) he answered, "he'll be satisfied wi' that." Relieved, even elated at the bargain, I loaded the treasures and moved very fast homewards.

It took me all the rest of Saturday to make the frame with an assortment of frames, wire netting and wire fixings; working into the night to add a whole bag of moss to build out the frame to a life-life figure. Sunday was spent in adding the flowers until very late when it was finished. But how could it be transported to Liverpool for the funeral? This was where Derek came in once more. "If I take the door off the shed they could carry it on that," he offered. It was done, and when the van arrived to take it, that's how it travelled to Liverpool where, we were told next day when the door was returned, it was fastened to the radiator of the hearse and looked like a real 'outrider'.

For the next two years there was steady progress and we managed to keep our heads above water; the floristry school classes and the night school income kept the wolves from the door. When Arthur returned home in the summer of 1962 he wasn't very happy about our hand-to-mouth existence as he called it; his concern being due to what he considered unfair treatment to me by the rest of the family and he believed that I had no home security. He trusted none of my brothers and believed that my Mother was being influenced by Elijah in particular. He had been successful in his career and returned financially secure and wished the same for me and Yvonne. I believe at this time that he expected eventually to return to England and a home for us altogether. One morning he approached my Mother with a view to buying The Leyland's as a future home for us all, including her. She said he must ask Elijah. (The old-fashioned idea was that the eldest son made all the decisions and Mum still believed it). Elijah was abusive, called Arthur a little upstart and to b…r off. Naturally, Arthur was hurt, not that the offer had been refused, but the manner it had been done and from then on the man who had been closer to him than his Father was not spoken to or referred to for over 20 years. However, it made him more than ever determined to provide a home for Yvonne and me and to this effect told me to buy a house in his name somewhere in Derbyshire where I could create a residential school of floristry and big enough for all of us and our friends.

It soon became obvious to me that I had to choose between my son and my Mother, as Arthur made it clear that he would not be returning to the Leyland's in future so a trip into Derbyshire seemed to be the next move, and the nearest Estate Agent was Philip Roose at Bakewell but before going there I decided to view a farm and buildings advertised in a Sheffield Estate Agent's window at Brighouse in Yorkshire where Kitty, Frank's sister lived. It wasn't Derbyshire as Arthur had stipulated, nevertheless I thought it deserved a visit, it didn't, at least not for my requirements.

Situated at the top of a mile long dirt track road passing under an old railway bridge, which would have been a poor enticement for students and much too costly to resurface, it was soon evident that this was going to be a futile journey. The farmhouse was large, but

504

old and dark and although the farm buildings were large and in good condition and would have been very useful, this was not a suitable position for a school and the price was too high anyway. Philip Roose an Estate Agent at Bakewell appeared to be the best chance of finding somewhere in North Derbyshire so back to Bakewell to see what we had to offer. There was very little, at least the size I was looking for and the price to go with it, however, there was a property in Youlgreave about a mile up the hill from Pickory Corner that had been empty for two years. I said I would have a look. It was a three-storey high bay-windowed Georgian house built in 1734 and had been the home of a Doctor for many years, followed by his daughter until she married a man who had returned from Nigeria after spending 27 years as the foreman of a gang building a new railway system from the coast up to the northern boundary, His stories about life there and the 'whites" relationships with the 'blacks' wasn't always pleasant listening. The newly married couple had lived in the house until they moved into the modernised Mews at the end of the drive at the side of the house and put the house up for sale. A large unkempt garden and an old disused outside toilet were the sum total of the property. But, the inside was unique.

The front door opened into a long passage between two large reception rooms, ending up two steps to a small room that had probably been a kitchen, and on the left a door into the old Still room with a stone flagged floor and stone benches along two walls. Two doors, one from the small room, another from the Still room led into an 'off-shot' 15ft square kitchen built from Derbyshire stone chippings; obviously a later addition, for the house was built entirely of large blocks of sandstone, with mullion windows except for the two large bays. A three storied house, it had six bedrooms, two large ones on the first floor with windows looking out on the main street of the village and both retaining the wide original floorboards with the usual gaps between them through which any 'goings-on' could be seen on the floor below. Between these two rooms and accessible from both through connecting doors, was the original powder room about 4ft x 2ft 6" originally used by gentlemen for powdering their wigs. The room also had a small window looking out on to the main street. A smaller room about 12ft square that was the only sign of modernisation contained a large bath, an old fashioned wash basin and a small homemade unit under the cistern.

At the back of the house on the first floor was another room about 12ft square, a dark musty room with only a very small mullion window that gave the impression of never having been used for the lifetime of the house. On the second floor were another two large rooms and a smaller one approximately 8ft x 12ft all quite regular with no obvious signs of their history. But the part of the house that gave me cause for concern was the staircase which rose from the end of the entrance passage by four steps turning the corner with two triangular steps, to another short flight to the first floor where, to the left through an archway and short passage was the entrance to the bathroom. I could see that the house had potential, but much work was needed to make the house habitable, especially for students who would be paying, not only for tuition, but for a temporary home and home comforts. But it was structurally sound; the wide windowsills illustrated the huge blocks of sandstone from which it had been built; the roof looked sound when I viewed it from across the road and in a house 230 years old there was no musty smell or signs of damp, although obviously much work and expense were necessary to make it habitable and respectable to bear the name of 'school'. The asking price was £2,000 not bad I thought, so back to Mr Roose and an offer to buy. The offer was accepted and the real worries began.

To be a school it had to have students, so the first thing was to put an advert in the 'Society of Floristry' magazine and hope that someone out there wanted to learn. By the time the purchase was finalised there were two firm bookings and I felt more confident that this was going to work. The cost per student was £108 per term which would cover the cost of flowers and other materials, plus tuition and board and lodging and there were plenty of sundries, vases, frames, wires, pin holders etc. from the existing school at least for the first year. To add to this, having cancelled all future demonstrations and transferring to Sheffield and other night school classes to previous students I signed on for my first evening class at Bakewell which would ensure that we kept 'the wolf from the door'. It was by now the middle of July; I had just over six weeks to make this house I had committed Arthur to buy into a respectable and acceptable home, not only for my family, but for someone else's daughters too.

There was no time to waste. To assess the immediate areas where I needed to start, I left the shop leaving Carol (another student) in charge and headed for Youlgreave where, after doing a tour of the whole house and examining the woodworm-riddled staircase, I suddenly wondered what I had let myself in for and sat on the stairs and wept.

Back at the nursery there was another matter to occupy my time and thoughts. Yvonne was now ten years old and due to be taking the eleven plus examination the following March. Lady Manners Grammar School at Bakewell three miles away had facilities for boarders and I thought this would be beneficial to her, particularly in the evenings when I was away teaching or otherwise engaged in school business. To qualify for a place there she had to pass the eleven plus examination. However, I had heard, through a friend, that there was not to be an eleven plus at Holmesfield Primary School anymore because it was going to be part of the comprehensive system.

Somewhat perturbed, I paid a visit to the school and confronted Mr George the Headmaster, who denied it, said he knew nothing about it. I didn't believe him and told him that I had it on good authority that no eleven plus would be held at Holmesfield this year. This arrogant man then said, "I don't why you are so bothered. Yvonne would never pass anyway, so there's nothing lost." I was furious, "Then it's your fault," I said, "Mrs Willey (the previous Headmistress) told me to start saving as I had another university student on my hands, so if she doesn't pass, then you are to blame."

It was only four weeks to the start of a new academic year, so I had to move fast. A quick call to the Headmistress of Totley Brook School and an explanation as to why it was important for my daughter to take the examination and Yvonne was booked in for the next year. I knew it would not be easy for her, but not at the time how difficult. Mrs Newman, her new teacher rang me after the first day to tell me that Yvonne didn't know arithmetic tables, obviously because the Head teacher at Holmesfield knew that they weren't necessary in the comprehensive system. "I have a suggestion," she said, "it's important that Yvonne knows them before the exam, so if you agree, I'll give her an extra lesson every lunchtime. I know it will be hard for her, but I'm sure she's capable of doing it." So it was that, when Mrs Newman received the results of the exam the following May, before they were made public, she rang me in tears of happiness and satisfaction to tell me "Yvonne has passed."

On the 20th May 1965 at the interview at Matlock, she was accepted as a pupil at 'Lady Manners' and started as a boarder there the following September. For the last term of 1964 she attended Totley Brook senior school, 'Norwood High School' Norwood Road, Sheffield and told me many years later how she hated it, but then, unlike children of today, they did what was expected of them, especially when they knew it was for their own good.

This problem solved, work began at Auburn House. Most important was accommodation for the two students, a bedroom and a sitting room where they could study and relax and the two first floor rooms were just the thing, particularly with the connecting door through the powder room which allowed some privacy. Cleaning, papering and painting proved no problem, nor was one of the large reception rooms to convert to the classroom. With a good clean, fresh paint and new curtains it was quite a pleasant workroom. Next was the small room that was to be the dining room for the students, and for me to relax on my own from Friday evening when the students went home, to Sunday evening when they returned.

A bedroom for me and one for Yvonne when she came home were no problem, as she chose the small one on the second floor, I settled on one of the larger ones and cleaned and decorated them accordingly. The other large one would suffice for Arthur when he returned from Antarctica, but the main problem was the bathroom and the stairs. I wasn't confident that they were safe. However, I decided to take a risk and leave it to Arthur when he visited in October before returning to Antarctica in November. The bathroom called for a little joinery. First to box in the bath, for which I used lengths of cladding and with a coat of varnish, looked pretty good. A cupboard in the same material made a good disguise for the cistern, another one underneath sufficed as a 'hidey-hole' for cleaning materials and utensils. When the floor was covered with linoleum, a touch of paint on the small window, made a very respectable bathroom that would suffice for the time being.

However, all these rooms needed furnishing and I had little money to throw around. What does a person do in such circumstances but find a good second-hand shop or better still an auctioneer. Frank Lyte's, St James Street, Sheffield was the answer. A quick look in the Sheffield Telegraph for auction dates and I was there for the viewing and later sale. Two single beds were the first purchased, one a hand-made mahogany made by John Walsh of Sheffield, the other a Queen Anne style in walnut veneer. A huge wardrobe in solid mahogany with lots of hanging space and an equally large drawer below was 'just the ticket' and, on settling the account, because I had bought the wardrobe, the auctioneer freely added the beautiful Queen Anne dressing table to go with it. The small suite I already had sufficed for the students' sitting room and the large three piece suite, with the piano and other bits, furnished the other large room downstairs that was to be used as our sitting room. I was lucky to have an antique mahogany folding side-table knocked down to my bid of £8.10s.0d a bargain as it is now worth a great deal more than that, and was just the right size for the small room that was to be the student's dining room.

Last to be considered was the kitchen. A stone floor, a huge white sink in one corner under a small window looking out on to a flagged yard, from which rose a short flight of steps to the garden and a second, bigger window looking out on to the garden, were the sum total of the kitchen. I had already ordered an Aga cooker as the best way to supply heat as well as a good cooking facility and a large electric cooker to serve as a back-up. Whilst waiting for delivery and fixing, I set about papering the walls with a bright washable paper covered with fruit and vegetables in reds and greens to give the place a warm cheerful appearance, then the final thing to make the place habitable were carpets. One important thing I had done in the weeks that I had been working in Youlgreave, was the question of a cook, for I knew I couldn't teach and cook at the same time, and the best

509

way to find out if there happened to be anyone in the village who might fit the bill was to approach 'the gossip of the village'. I had heard on the grapevine that the lady at the electrical shop on the main road opposite Auburn House was such a person and, sure enough, she pointed me in the direction of the village policeman's wife Elsie, who had been a cook in the Army during the war. I quickly found the policeman's house and half an hour later had engaged a super cook for £3 a week who very soon became a sincere friend and a source of information.

She told me of a woman at Winster, a village a couple of miles away who bought 'end of rolls' of lino and carpets and sold them by the yard at very cheap prices. This was good news, so I decided to make her a visit and was not disappointed. I soon chose carpets for all the rooms and stairs, and lino for the kitchen, bathroom and the long front passage and felt a great deal happier as I drove home that night. Everything was delivered the next day, and in two days, with Derek's help, all the floors were covered and the house ready for habitation. On the 4th September 1964, for better or worse, Yvonne and I became the new inhabitants of Auburn House, Youlgreave; the new 'Francott Dene School of Floristry'.

It was soon very clear that life at Auburn House was not going to be a bed of roses, at least for me, for the first few months there was still much work to do if this was to be truly called 'home'. The small dark bedroom was draughty due to the broken window and the dark still-room needed attention if it were to be useful, but what form that attention should be, I hadn't yet decided. Luckily it wasn't necessary to pass through it as there was the passage door in the kitchen so, for the moment; I did as my Father taught me. "If you have a problem and can't do anything about it, put it behind the clock until you can," and for the time being, behind the clock it went. I never did do anything about that still-room, the stone bench was handy for keeping food and milk cool and it became a convenient place of storage for anything Elsie decided to confine to it, so at least, it had its uses.

Two weeks after moving in, the two students Anne and Barbara arrived at what was to become their home for the next nine months, and were very happy with their two rooms and the quaint powder

510

room between, which now boasted a small dressing table and stool and was quite private. We soon settled into a routine; Yvonne caught an early bus every morning and soon settled in at her new school and the arrangements at the shop met few problems.

On the 3rd October, his birthday, Arthur arrived for two weeks before returning to Antarctica and he wasn't impressed by the house; thought I should have looked further afield before settling for such a dilapidated building. But, what was done was done, and next morning he quickly sought Mr Oldfield, property repairer who lived in the village and made arrangements for repairs and alterations as deemed necessary. The most important were the windows to eliminate the draughts and he made it clear that the mullions and all other repairs were to be in keeping with the Georgian period of 1734.

This became interesting when the front bay window and the sills were being dismantled for repair. The sills were found to be fitted with hinges and when lifted, they revealed the original shutters, still in good condition, with their ropes still intact. The pulleys were still in situ though very stiff through lack of use, and with a good oiling and manipulation within an hour they were working smoothly. With the frames repaired and refitted, we had beautiful authentic 18th century widows with fully working shutters. The next most serious item was the staircase. Mr Oldfield examined it carefully and decided that the woodworm damage was old and there was no more danger, but as a precaution, every inch was soaked in woodworm killer, the carpet re-laid and the problem was solved.

At the end of his two weeks stay, the whole house had been vetted, repairs and refurbished with new bathroom and kitchen fittings and a few additions here and there. We loved its quaintness and I personally was proud and happy to be part of its history and it could at last be called 'home'.

However, life is never free from problems for long and one that had been pending for a few weeks was now in need of attention. During the summer of 1964, the traders in Hereford Street heard rumours that half the street was to be demolished to make way for development at the bottom of the Moor, and in September the shops at the Eyre Street end received their compulsory purchase notice. This was rather a set-back, but fortunately a larger shop nearer the Moor end of the street was empty and owned by the same landlord who offered it to me for a very reasonable rent. There was only a five year lease left, but an immediate living was my priority at the time. The shop and the window were three times the size of the existing one and both had great potential, also the position nearer the busy Moor shopping area was much better for passing trade. But I was rather dubious, having been let down once by the Authorities; I wanted to be sure that there were to be no more developments before I went to the trouble and expense of moving.

The landlord assured me that the Moor end was not going to be developed and I believed him; after all his shop was also involved, as were the hairdresser, the china shop, the butcher and the furniture shop. Nevertheless, Derek suggested that he could see his friend in the Town Clerk's office for more information and he was reassured that there were no arrangements for development at that end of the street and the leases would be renewed when they ran out in five years' time. There seemed nothing to worry about. Once more, he obtained the materials at cost and did all the fittings, peg-board on the walls, shelves, a partition dividing off the area for working and all the extra fittings ready for moving in two weeks before Christmas 1964, It was a good Christmas; trade was brisk and the new shop greatly admired. The following week was promising and we all looked forward to a very healthy business in 1965.

On New Year's Eve, the bomb dropped when a letter from the Town Hall informed me that a compulsory purchase order would be issued on the property sometime in the future for the purpose of redevelopment. I was angry, but a call to the Town Clerk's office only confirmed the news, with only one grain of consolation, that it would probably be some time before the compulsory order would be issued. The difficulty was that once it was issued, there was no hope of further sub-letting and there would be very little compensation for so short a lease. In my anger and disappointment, it took little time to make a decision, the grey matter works quickly when the need arises and mine went into overdrive.

By lunchtime I had decided to close the shop and advertise it for sub-letting, my reason being that there was no sense in building up a business if there were to be no payment for 'goodwill' at the end, and once a compulsory purchase order was issued, a business was worthless and sale forbidden. Also, any monetary compensation for the building was, of course, paid to the owner of that building, which in this case was the Church Authority who let it to the jeweller.

Consequently, I didn't intend to wait until the compulsory purchase order was issued. A quick ring around the florists I had taught secured jobs for the two assistants to commence on the 2nd January, and at closing time we started the removal of the peg-board and other fittings and the new plugs and electric fittings that we had installed. By 10.00 p.m. the shop was once more a mere shell and the shed on the nursery was stacked to the door with timber and shop furniture. Derek was not happy about the move for he had lost his office and telephonist and seen all the hard work during the last month disappear at a stroke. He wasn't convinced that the shop wasn't worth hanging on to as a source of income, even without 'goodwill', but I was sure and decided that my future lay in the school at Youlgreave, which, as things turned, was a wise decision, although it proved the beginning of the end of my friendship with Derek as Youlgreave was too far from Sheffield to visit. And after one occasion, I saw him no more until the day of his divorce in 1966. On the following day I put an advertisement in the Sheffield Telegraph for a new tenant and received one reply. Fortunately, it was from an Estate Agent who, when I told him about the compulsory purchase order, said it mattered not as his clients would follow him when he had to move on.

So, for the next five years, during which the 'order' had still not been issued, I drew the rent from him with the addition of a few pounds over for myself; not at all a bad move, for I now had time for my own work that started with an extra night school teaching job at Bakewell in the New Year.

Chapter 15

The first term of 1965 progressed remarkably smoothly, and I was thankful for the freedom from worrying about the shop and the travelling it entailed. We had all settled into a routine that suited the students, myself and Elsie, who called at the butcher's shop on her way through the village each morning and collected anything else we might need to see us through the day and, although her original brief had been to cook lunch, she soon developed the habit of making buns or biscuits for tea, setting the table, and making sure that all was ready to serve when teaching for the day was over. One bonus, not foreseen, was that Andy, the village policeman, patrolled the main street and all the roads around the village in the evenings and when on night-duty. When Elsie arrived every morning she could tell me where the students were the night before, who they were with, and what they were doing, and it was a great relief for me, as I am sure it would have been for their parents, to know that there was no need to worry about their safety, or well-being. Not that I had any doubts; they were both exceptionally nice girls whom I never had to worry about, and was delighted, a few years later to hear that Anne was to marry a Youlgreave boy whom she had met whilst a student at Auburn House.

During a conversation two weeks into the term, Elsie remarked that I had no washing machine and, guessing that I did it by hand at the weekend when Anne and Barbara had gone home, she suggested that I buy a second-hand one. "If you like", she said, "We'll get one from the Auction at Buxton on Saturday, they always have some in and it won't cost much", and she continued "Andy'll fix it up for you". The following Sunday morning they arrived with my washing machine, which had cost the princely sum of £4, and by lunch-time when Andy had fixed it, and the first load was in, it was music to my ears. Needless to say, the washing became another of Elsie's jobs when she volunteered to do it. "No problem," she said, "I can just as well see to that while I'm peeling spuds and you can get on with something else at the weekend."

That something was fitting out the kitchen to provide some working areas and cupboards for storage. Luckily I could use a saw and follow instructions; the problem, if that's what it was going to be, was finding the cash to pay for necessary materials.

Ready-made units were expensive and it was a large kitchen, however, considering what was available at the time, I remembered that I had seen some ready-made cupboards made by 'Liden' in solid wood that only required painting and, considering that these would be more durable than the usual complete units made from chipboard with ply-wood doors I settled for them, and decided to cover them with yellow Formica, the fashionable material at the time, in yellow to match the black and yellow Aga.

Every weekend when the students had left for home, from now until Easter, was spent in sand-papering and painting, cutting and gluing Formica, and, the most difficult part of the exercise, getting everything to fit! The limestone-chip building did not lend itself to straight walls, and there was a gap of an inch at one end, to almost three inches at the other end, at the back of the Aga cooker that continued into the corner to a narrow window about 10" wide in the two-foot deep wall. To complicate matters further the sink was also near the corner on the adjourning wall, allowing only limited space for manoeuvre. There was only one solution; to build a shelf and fill the gap at the back, then make a small drawer with a space for trays beneath to fit into the corner. This was the plan, and although there were moments during the next few weeks as to whether I could do an acceptable job, by Easter the whole kitchen was equipped with yellow units trimmed with black edgings, and the old sink boasted its own cupboard. The cute shelf, with one or two 'knick-knacks' here and there, gave the kitchen a warm homely atmosphere, and now, we had plenty of storage space. The next most pressing job was on the first landing. The plain archway framing the area that led to the bathroom and toilet was crude, and I guessed that with a good coat of plaster in a suitable colour, stippled as was the fashion at the time, it could be re-shaped and probably result in a much more impressive feature as one turned left at the top of the stairs Also it would be cheaper and easier than paper. It wasn't easier, it was much harder, and it took a great deal longer; nor was it cheaper, but the result was even better than I had hoped, for the final coat of magnolia paint that covered the plaster, reflected the light and brightened-up the whole landing.

I looked forward to the weekends, with freedom to think and work out a programme for the following week, and a huge pan of home-made soup to welcome the girls home again on Sunday night made for very enjoyable weekends.

And so we came to the end of the second term, the next one would see the result of all the hard work, by all of us and, I hoped, bring excellent results from the Society of Floristry exams in June. I had gambled on the assumption that residential students would be more dedicated and study harder than the usual day-release shop assistants so had planned for them to by-pass the preliminary examination and go straight for the Senior, which normally would have taken two years. Now we had come to the beginning of the Easter holiday. The girls had left for home on Thursday, and yesterday, Good Friday, I had fetched my Mother to give her a 'change-of-walls' for a week It was Saturday night; we had no bread, and I had only the princely sum of sixpence. "Would you like porridge for tea?" I asked Mum and Yvonne, " 'cos we ain't got any bread." Yvonne just grunted, probably hoping that by the tone of my voice it was just a joke, Mum was more used to such situations and took it more seriously. "No I wouldn't" she said, and once more came to the rescue. Looking in her purse to see how much was left from the pension she had drawn on Tuesday she turned to Yvonne and said "Here's a shilling love, go and get us a loaf and bring me a Derbyshire Times, let's see what's happening this week". Luckily the village shop didn't close until nine o'clock, and there was always some bread left over to be dunked and re-baked, or sold cheaply the day after. So, at

517

least we had a meal that night, and who knows what can happen if you keep your fingers crossed?

Sunday dawned and we got through the day with the remains of the loaf, and a good Easter dinner, but what would Monday bring? Day dawned, cold, but bright, with pale sunshine, which promised a pleasant day to come, but there was still the niggling thought as to how we were to get through the week with no money. Beyond that there would be no problem; my cheque from the Bakewell Night-school class would arrive on Saturday and the students would return on Sunday night each with a cheque for £108 for the next term, but what now? "I'm sorry love, I haven't any more" said Mum, followed by her usual question for such a situation "Doesn't anybody owe you anything?" "No, I answered, nobody does owe me anything". "Never mind", she said "something will turn up." I had grown used to Mum's philosophy in life, like Mr Micawber she always believed that something would turn up, and the mystery was that, up until now, it always had. This time I couldn't see what could possibly turn up.

Yvonne returned with the loaf and the Derbyshire Times, and Mum spent an hour going through all the news and gossip, births and deaths, reading out loud some little snippets I might be interested in. We had had a conversation-cum-discussion as to what I would do after the end of June. So far two new students had booked for next year, and there were two more whose parents were considering whether they could afford the fees. I was not worried about the coming year; we had managed with two students this year, and could do so again if necessary. If the other two did arrive then, by adding another bed in the room used by Arthur, we would reach our limit of accommodation and the extra work involved. As it turned out that would have been no problem for Arthur didn't come home for another two years, having over-wintered for two years 'back to back' in Antarctica; to date the only American to have done so, and at the same time was awarded the Antarctic Medal. This may also be the time that 'Rundle Peaks' was named after him, but I am not sure whether that was 1965, or earlier. However, reminiscing never solves problems, and the one now still pressing was, 'What are we going to live on this week, and the ten weeks from June to September?'

518

"There's something here that you might be interested in". Mum was still reading her paper, but, catching a glimpse of somebody coming down the steps to the back door, she paused; "You've got a visitor", she said, "It's a man". I looked out of the window and sure enough we had a visitor, the man who lived in the Mews house, Mr Bates. What could he want? I wondered as I opened the door. "I'm sorry Mrs Rundle" he gasped, as he held out a ten-shilling note "I clean forgot all about it". I stood amazed, not believing what I saw. "But," I stuttered. "I know I should have brought it before" he said, and then explained "it's for those flowers you sent for me by Interflora six weeks ago, I really am sorry." He turned and made his way back up the steps, and I stood there for a moment looking down at that precious, beautiful, piece of paper in my hand. Closing the door, I went into the sitting-room and held out my hand in front of Mum, "It was Mr Bates" I said, "He's brought this, says he owes it for flowers." She just looked at it then, quietly, said "I told you something would turn up," and then went back to her paper

There was silence for a few minutes, then, "It's here look, here's a job you could do" as she pointed to an advert in the 'Positions Vacant' column. Casually I glanced at the short notice, 'Wanted, Craft Instructor to teach Physically Disabled People. Successful applicant will work with Occupational Therapist. Salary £760.00 per annum. Application forms to be returned by April 30th'. "Why would you think that would suit me?" I asked. "Well, you can do basket work, and weaving, and you know how to make stools," she said knowingly, for of course, she had spent many short visits in homes for disabled people, and had seen all the usual crafts taught for rehabilitation.

"But I don't want a job," I said, "I only need something for two months." "I know" she replied, "but you could do it for two months, and then give your notice in." "That wouldn't be very fair though," was my answer to that, but she insisted. "Send for an application form and see what it's all about," then as an afterthought, "At least you'll know all about it." Result: next morning, Easter Monday, knowing that the village shop would be open until lunch-time, Yvonne and I went on a 'Spending spree' buying all the goodies we could get for our ten shillings, and I posted my letter requesting an Application form for 'Craft-Instructor' for the Derbyshire Welfare Dept. and immediately dismissed the thought.

The following Saturday the Application form arrived and I duly filled it in to satisfy Mum. I had only three days to reply before the application date, and a few days later received the notice to attend an interview on the 19th May. Mum was delighted.

I had never had to attend an interview in my life, so this was something new for me. At the ripe old age of forty-nine-and-a-half one doesn't expect such things to happen but, as I often said to Yvonne when something unexpected happened, "Put it down to experience".

I arrived at County Offices, Matlock on the 19th May at the appointed time to find that there were five more applicants, all of them much younger than me, in ages ranging from 22 to the oldest, a Vicar's wife age 41, I knew that I had little hope of getting the job, but at that stage it didn't worry me; this, after all, was just an exercise to please Mum. Two of the applicants were called into the interviewing room before me and, after about 5 minutes, each disappeared down the corridor without a word. My turn was next.

Not knowing what to expect I was surprised to see about twenty people sitting around a huge polished table, in the centre of which was an empty chair facing me. With a wave of the hand the woman opposite who, I learned later, was the Chairman of the County Council, invited me to sit down. I did as was bid and the questions began; the usual ones at interviews as I became used to during the following years; "Why did you apply for this job?" "What experience have you had?" "Where did you hear about the job?"

I felt that these questions were just to give all members of the Committee a chance to speak, but not really relevant or important. Except for one, which may have been the leading question (there's always one), but a later one proved not so. The question came from Miss Smith Head of the Dept. for Physically Disabled People. "Mrs Rundle, if you were asked to visit a bed-ridden man, who all his working life had been a gardener at one of the large houses in the area, and he wouldn't do any craftwork no matter what was offered, what would you do?" With tongue in cheek and as a 'spur of the moment' idea, I blurted out, "Take a large sheet of polythene to cover the bed, a bag of compost, a shallow bowl and a few rock plants, and tell him to make a miniature garden for his wife." There were a few straight faces, but one or two did manage a 'Slip of the face' as they looked at each other, and I thought I'd 'muffed' it. But then came the real leading question, from the Chairman, who hadn't asked one before, only inviting the others to speak "Mrs Rundle," she said respectfully, as all the others had done, "forgive me for saying this, but you are a rather more mature person than we expected." I didn't flinch, after all she was only telling me what I already knew. She continued, "If you were to get this Post you would be working with an Occupational Therapist who has just left University and is only twenty-four years old, how would you feel about that?" I answered without any qualms, "If she has just left University I'm sure she will have a lot to teach me, but, in the years of my working life I have gained a lot of experience of many things, so I'm sure there will be something I can offer her."

After being asked to stay behind, a polite nod and "Thank you" from the Chairman and murmurs from the rest, of the Committee, I left the room and waited whilst the other three were very quickly interviewed and dismissed, except the Vicar's wife, the next oldest applicant who was told that they would let her know. I was called back into the interviewing room and without any more formalities was offered the job. "When can you start?" asked the Chairman. "July 1st," I answered, "if that is satisfactory". It was and I duly reported to Miss Smith, Head of the Dept. for Disabled People, at Bank Road, Matlock, on July 1st 1965, at a salary of £706 a year, and started one of the most rewarding, happiest, and satisfying jobs I have ever done.

Returning home there were things to be done, and 'Ends to tie up' before July 1st, not forgetting that tomorrow, the 20th May, was the interview with Jack Longland, Chairman, and the Education Committee, for Yvonne's entry into Lady Manners Grammar School at Bakewell. Things had changed since my application as I would be at home in the evenings and there would be no students to cause concern. I put these points to the meeting immediately, and told them about my new job, which I knew by now that I would not give up in

521

September, and pointed out that it wasn't so important now that Yvonne should be a Boarder. After congratulating me on my appointment, Mr Longland, who knew of me through dealing with Arthur's University Grant, although he gave no indication that he remembered, said 'That's alright Mrs Rundle, we still think Yvonne deserves a place at Lady Manners, and I'm sure she will be very happy there. Congratulations, Yvonne, on passing the 11 Plus exam."

Letters were sent immediately to the two students who had already booked in, and to those still considering, telling them that due to unforeseen circumstances the full-time course had been cancelled. The weekly class of flower-arrangers, who had joined the two resident students one day a week, were told that their class would finish at the end of June. However, two of them who were taking the Floristry Preliminary Examination in June decided to go on to the Senior, and to have their lessons on Saturday mornings in their own homes in Sheffield, so I knew I was going to have a very busy year ahead.

On the nearest Saturday to June 24th each year, the annual Youlgreave Festival and Well-Dressings, one of the oldest in Derbyshire, took place during the students' last week. There were five Wells, each with its own team of workers and designer. Two weeks before the date the boards that held the flower designs were sunk in the river in Bradford Dale, down the hill from the village, and were left to soak, so that the clay, when applied to the boards, would not dry out whilst on display. Originally the clay was retrieved from the river, but now it was bought ready for use to eliminate the work and effort required in cleaning and working the river clay into the smooth texture required.

A week before the Festival the boards were retrieved and taken to the respective buildings where the teams would work, first adding the clay to the whole board, then adding the flowers as the designer had planned. Extreme secrecy was imposed whilst the flowers were added to make the intricate designs, for there was great competition between the teams, and much interest on Saturday morning when the finished boards were erected. The work-sheds were strictly 'Out of Bounds' to anyone not involved in the work but, by quiet negotiations with one of the leaders whom I knew very well, Anne and Barbara were allowed to stay up all night and observe the methods of placing flowers and other things in design, and even to 'have a go' themselves. However there were rules. They could stay until 6.00 a.m. and see the finished boards erected, then return, go to bed until lunch-time, and at 2.00 p.m. join the procession around the wells and the Services of 'Blessing the Wells' held at each of the five wells. It was voted a wonderful experience by both girls, and much appreciated for the chance to see something unique to Derbyshire.

The Floristry Examinations were now over, and as hoped, the two students later heard that they had passed with distinction, and had received from me the only two Certificates ever awarded from 'The Francott Dene School of Floristry', which were given only after they had passed the Society Examination for the precise reason of preserving the value of the Certificate, and the integrity of the school. (There were many in the Society of Floristry who would have devalued it and my school, but for this proviso!)

On July 1st I duly reported to County Offices and met Miss Smith, who took me to the Welfare Office on High Street, Matlock, where I had been allocated an office 'Back to Back' with Miss Taylor, Teacher of the Blind, who lived at Tansley, who, over the following months would become a very close colleague. Here Miss Smith quickly explained what my duties were, and told me a little about the people in the various classes. About half an hour later Anne Newbury, the Occupational Therapist with whom I would work, walked into the office, and I knew within the first few minutes that we would be able to work together.

After another ten minutes with Miss Smith we left County Offices for my first visit to a 15-year-old spastic girl, and a boy the same age suffering from Hydrocephalus, both living in my own village of Youlgreave, but whom I had not met, nor known about before. I soon learned what my role would be. Until now the Occupational Therapist had made all the visits, assessing for particular disabled conditions for Aids, (anything that would help to make the daily tasks of life easier, not anything to do with the now well-known 'AIDS'), and also to decide and supervise whatever type of craft-work would help the disabled person, whatever that disablement might be, to rehabilitate back to good health, possibly returning to full employment, or just to make life easier; more enjoyable; make them feel just a little important or, at least, to try to prevent them getting worse. From now on, the system would change and although we both would do the first visit, after discussing and deciding together what craft would be best, I would be on my own.

We decided that the boy, who was severely disabled, would probably manage to make a waste-paper basket, as its larger size would be easier to manoeuvre than a tray. The spastic girl was different, for she was an intelligent girl with a strong sense of humour, her only disabilities being in the movement of her limbs and hands, and her ability to speak. Helped by her Mother, who understood her signs and sounds, which I soon learned to interpret for myself, she let us know that she would like to make a tray. I had loaded my car with a selection of articles; trays, bases, stool-frames etc. and an assortment of cane; willow; beads; wool, and anything else I had been advised might be useful. From these I chose a simple tea-tray with suitable cane, and so my first lesson in cane-work began. I couldn't have chosen a better patient, client, person, call her what you will, to make me realise that this was going to be the most enjoyable, satisfying, job I would ever do. We had gone through the preliminaries of soaking the cane, putting in the stakes, and began the art of weaving. I showed how to bend the cane in front of and behind a stake, and she had a go.

The philosophy of 'Try and try again' was not the prerogative of Bruce's spider; this time it was the great effort and determination of a young girl, who was not going to be beaten by a few jerky movements. With all fingers tensely splayed fan-wise and protruding tongue showing the effort involved, the weaving cane was carefully manoeuvred in front of a stake then, time after time, just as it was about to pass behind the next, it sprang out of her fingers amidst roars of laughter, until, with intense concentration and a whoop of joy, the cane finally made it and remained in place, and all done with no sense of frustration, impatience, or irritation shown by a more able person. It took weeks to finish that first tray, but her attitude never flinched.

Her pride after the first one was finished a few weeks later and given as a present to her Mum, was her, and her devoted Mother's reward.

Part of my job was to hold weekly afternoon classes for Disabled people; at Matlock; Wirksworth and Buxton, and I soon found that there was much room for improvement, not only in the type of work they were doing, but that half of them were doing nothing at all, especially the men. It was just a half-day out for most of them, to play dominoes or cards or just to sit doing nothing except watch the women working. All the women were doing something, and as usual at women's meetings, it was knitting and embroidery. Watching them and listening to their chatter I soon realised that they were bored, or resigned might be a kinder word, and would welcome a change.

As part of my 'Getting to know them' policy I sat with them, taking an interest in their work, at the same time gaining an insight as to what they would like to do. From this it was clear that what they would most like to do, apart from doing something new, was to go on a holiday. Remember, this was 1965 when people did not automatically go on holiday; a day at the seaside was all that most could hope for, if they were lucky. This is why I found myself driving over the Pennines to Glossop one morning before the Buxton class, where I knew there was a toy factory, where they made every toy one could think of, and I was sure that I would find something that Disabled people could manage. I introduced myself and asked if I could see the Personnel Manager who I thought would be more sympathetic than the Manager himself. It was a good guess for he was most understanding, and after some discussion as to what disabled people might do, and how much they could expect to receive for their labours, I came away with five huge boxes; four of them containing counters in different colours, the fifth one with large counters and packets of small squares of tissue paper. Yes, you guessed it, 'Tiddley-winks'

I hurried back to the Buxton class, who were all eager to see what was in the boxes, and within half-an-hour we had put the tables together with chairs on both sides, and had a production line where everybody had a job to do, men as well as women. When I told them that they were going to be paid, and the money would be used to take them on holiday to Skegness next year, most of them couldn't wait to start. All the men were enthusiastic, as they never did anything anyway, but one or two of the women wanted to continue with their knitting and sewing, but they had to join in sometimes in order to go on the holiday, and this proved not a problem.

Working in twos, partly so that everybody had a job, but also because, by the laws of nature, they 'Policed' each other; I knew that if a mistake were made, the other would be quick to notice, as I couldn't have my eyes on all at once. I had also asked them all to bring a mug, and, having cajoled Miss Smith into allowing me to buy an electric kettle, a welcome 'cup o' tea' break was enjoyed by all. It was a very rewarding sight to see everybody happily working. The boxes were placed down the centre of the table with the tissue-paper squares at one end and an empty box at the other. The first pair of packers on each side put four red counters into a tissue paper square and passed it to the next pair who added four yellow ones and so on, to the last pair who had the box of large counters and added one of each colour. At the end of the line was the checker, whose job was to check that each packet had the correct number of counters before giving the paper a firm twist and putting it in to the box at the end of the table. My Psychology told me that this had to be a man in order to make them feel important and to keep working, and this was the most important part of the exercise if there were to be no complaints from the firm (and the women didn't mind).

For their labours they would be paid one penny per twist, which I would collect each month when I fetched further supplies. which varied according to whether the game was Ludo, Snakes and Ladders, or other board game, when a Dice was substituted for the large counter. This doesn't sound a lot but, by the end of May 1966 they had earned enough to pay for a coach and a week's holiday for the Buxton class, and some of the Matlock class, at the 'Disabled People's Holiday Camp' at Skegness. A bonus for me was permission from the Welfare Officer to take my Mother as well, because she was disabled and also lived in Derbyshire. Altogether a good time was had by all.

I have found throughout my life that folk are all pretty much the same, yet there is a subtle difference in both attitude and behaviour as one moves into a different district. It could be the difference in hereditary occupations, as farming communities and those of lead-miners, coal-miners, quarrymen and stone-masons, all have their own attitude to life and particular type of humour. I found this as time went on in the class at Wirksworth, a large village a few miles south-west of Matlock, and only a mile-and-a-half from the old Arkwright cotton-mill at Cromford. Here was a group of quiet, homely, very friendly men and women who might have been at an 'Over-sixties' meeting rather than a class for the disabled. It was relaxing and pleasant as with a group of old friends, so that when eventually I left I was very touched to receive from one quiet lady a gift of a purse with her letter of thanks for (in her words) "Those lovely smiles you gave me". The purse was never used and is still in a drawer with its very moving note.

However, things are never 100% satisfactory, that's too much to ask, and there was one fly in the ointment that I felt needed 'Nipping in the bud'. One of the men kept skipping the work; he sometimes arrived late and blamed it on his 'Emphysema', which causes difficulty in breathing. I had sometimes seen him arriving by taxi, and on occasions he had left early saying the taxi was coming early, when in fact it was rather more to enable him to get out of the work of clearing-up and leaving the room tidy.

One day I arrived at Wirksworth early. It was market day and I needed two cups to replace two broken ones from a service I had bought on a previous occasion. I made my purchase and started to walk towards the Hall where the class was held and not gone far when I saw a figure walking rather briskly up a road of fairly steep gradient and was somewhat surprised to see that it was Earnest the sufferer from Emphysema. Now the Emphysema that I knew would not be compatible with a brisk walk up a steep road, so when he arrived, by taxi, I broached the subject. "Have you come by taxi, Ernest?", answer "Yes"; "That must be expensive", answer "No, the Social Services provide it"; "Do the Social Services provide a taxi to take you home?" "Oh aye" he answered with a sense of importance. The whole class was now interested, as they were well aware of Earnest's habits, and would be glad to see them challenged. "Earnest" I said, "did I not see you today walking home up the hill from the market?" Earnest stared for a moment then started to say "I don't know", but wavered in the gaze of the class and admitted that it was. "Don't you think you are being a bit dishonest Earnest?" I asked and as he didn't answer I continued, "You either stop it, and cancel the taxi or I shall contact the Social Services myself". He never came by taxi again, but did continue to come every week, proving that he could manage the hill after all

The class at Matlock was the most interesting, and the one that stretched my imagination most. They were lively, enthusiastic, and most of them were ripe material for stretching their abilities and doing something different. I soon realised that Tom Lilly, a senior employee of the Derwent Water Board before he became disabled, was intelligent and enthusiastic. He had been making Seagrass stools for a few years, which found a regular market on the Welfare Stalls held at Bakewell and Ashopton Shows, and the occasional Welfare Craft shops that were rented for a week, or perhaps two, where a shop was temporarily vacant, and goods were sold from all the Welfare departments, including the blind. I said to Tom one day, "Tom you've been doing stools like this for some time now. Would you like to do a different pattern?" "I only know this one," he replied. Here was an opening. Finding a pencil and paper I explained how he could make a chevron pattern by counting the Warp strings and vary the number of Weft strings in a different colour on each line. It was up to him how to work it out so that he could fit in complete rows of patterns. He was highly delighted and enthusiastic, and when the first one was finished and taken up to County Headquarters for sale, the surprised and complimentary remarks from the office staff delighted him even more. From then on there was no stopping him. In three months' time he progressed to Florentine pattern as in embroidery, and from footstools to full-sized fire-stools using two or three colours, and he was a very happy and contented man.

The women at Matlock were also enthusiastic and willing to do something different, and this took me on another journey, with my Superior, Miss Smith's permission, to take another trip over the Pennines, this time to Congleton. My brother Jeff lived at Congleton at the time, and when visiting I had heard of a firm called 'Conroys' who made nylon underclothes and other goods made from different types of nylon fabric. I knew that one of my ladies could use a sewing machine, and she had said that she would like to make for herself some underskirts, so I was delighted when the Personnel Manager returned to the room where I had been waiting, carrying two huge bags of nylon fabrics of varying widths, weights, and colours, a third filled with nylon rolled edging, a waste product from the fabrics they had made up into underskirts, panties, and other items of ladies' wear. The biggest surprise was a huge bag of lace, some still in their cardboard and cellophane packs, in widths from 1" to a full 9" in the most beautiful patterns I had ever seen. I knew we were going to have a lovely time back in Matlock.

It took little time for the seamstress to choose a few pieces for her underwear and soon the little old hand-operated sewing machine we had acquired was turning out a few pieces for the other ladies in the class for a few coppers to add to our holiday fund. The nylon rolled edging was rather a challenge but I soon found a use for it, not only in class, but also on domiciliary visits to both men and women as a change from the usual cane-work. Bathmats was the answer, weaving the craft. All we needed were one or two simple frames on which to weave the patterns, for the small weaving frames available usually for home visits for making scarves, shopping-bags, and other small items were not suitable for bathmats.

Begging was the answer. Old picture frames that could be taken apart and re-fixed to a size suitable for a mat that could be used either in or out of the bath, and the cost would be just two or three tubes of strong glue and, as a bonus, a job for the men! Out went the appeal for attics and sheds to be searched and soon we had a supply of old frames that, with a bit sawn off here and there, and sizes deftly matched, a set of sturdy weaving frames were produced on which to make bathmats in every pattern from checks and squares to chevrons and diamonds in colours to suit every Formica-fitted bathroom in Matlock They also came in useful for Home visits for those who welcomed a change from cane work, dishcloths and stools, and were the more important part of my job, as many of them were housebound, and in need of therapy to help them to return to work.

One man who lived at Calver had worked as a Machine-technician at Calver Cotton Mill where his wife had also worked as a Weaver before a stroke put an end to their working lives. Tom not only needed the therapy of work, but £1.10s (£1.50) a week he was allowed to earn in addition to the disability pension was an incentive to work every hour of every day in order to get back to work. Tom and his wife made rugs; Dora designed them and taught Tom how to produce the designs, and they were beautiful, but not sufficient reward for the time and amount of work involved. So Tom was loaned a frame for bathmats, and whilst he wove his rugs and an occasional bathmat, Dora also wove bathmats that were collected each Friday, thus helping the weekly budget.

Another man whom I visited at Baslow who had also worked for the Derwent Water Board, was also recuperating after a Stroke. He was very irritable and impatient in his attempt to return to work and although he had undergone speech therapy whilst in hospital, he was still very frustrated and difficult to understand. He was so determined to return to work that he could earn the allowance of £1.50d a week in one day, and spent the rest of the week fuming and 'Getting up the back' of his wife, which wasn't very good for her health either. The restriction on the amount a patient was allowed to earn whilst on disabled person's pension was a big handicap for those men and women who were anxious to return to work, for the work itself was the rehabilitation and to restrict it was, in my reckoning, defeating the object. As I saw it there was a solution, although it meant 'Breaking the rules' a little.

There was the man at Buxton who had half his lung removed through smoking and was in great pain through post-operative adhesions. He flatly refused to do any craft work at all and sat in his chair all day just grumbling and driving his wife 'Up the wall'. At least up to now. His wife was wonderful, spoke her mind, a strong sense of humour, left him to grumble and got on with making delicious apple pies. She was in the middle of doing this when I first called, and hearing her shout "Come in", I entered. My patient was sitting beside the fire as he grunted "Good morning", whilst his wife was in the kitchen just lifting out the first pie. On hearing her invitation to "Sit down and I'll bring you a slice", I did so, but when she entered the room I knew by her surprised expression that she was expecting Anne. I introduced myself, and gratefully accepted the apple-pie she handed to me with the explanation, "Mrs Newbury liked apple pie, so I always make one when she's coming". After that first visit I followed a ritual of knocking, opening the door, and shouting, "Apple-pie", and although being rather disappointed that I hadn't persuaded my patient to do some craftwork, I was gratified later when his wife said he was better tempered and even more talkative than he used to be. So, I suppose, if you can't win one way there's always another! That was my introduction to the Starkey family, with whom I kept in touch for many years until I presumed that death had put an end to the correspondence.

Another patient who I visited at Buxton was a tall elegant lady who had been a well-known Concert Pianist, whose disabled condition dictated that she had to use a stick to walk around the house. It did not detract in any way from her rather superior manner, although that was easy to ignore during her highly intelligent and friendly conversation. She was very proud, and conscious that her status in society was somewhat lower than had been enjoyed previously, and this was sometimes expressed with a hint of bitterness, as on one occasion when I happened to visit a few minutes before she was expecting the 'Meals-on-Wheels' lady. She was about to switch on the oven to keep the meal warm when, with a flourish, she opened the oven door and in a strained voice said "Look how clean it is, that's all it gets used for, warming meals, I can't cook any more, I can't afford to anyway".

Yet she refused to do any craftwork in order to earn a little more money, nor join the Buxton class, and I got the impression that she considered it the loss of her dignity; the last straw. If that sounds too unkind, it may have been apprehension, or even fear of becoming involved with a type of people of whom she had no previous experience. Whatever the reason, she was glad of a monthly visit,

531

when I listened and learned about those days on the concert platform and all the Celebrities she had met on the way, with sometimes a little insight into this proud, lonely woman's life. My reward, if I can claim it, when finally I left this job, was her plea to keep in touch, which I did, through letters, and an occasional visit when time allowed, for a long chat over a 'Cup of tea'.

An opportunity to visit Tideswell was always a pleasure, but to say that about the man whom I visited there once a month would be stretching credibility rather too far. Advent was a retired Wood-carver and I was admitted to the house by his wife, another long-suffering, cheerful, down-to-earth woman, who, with a wave of a hand pointed me to a door with the words, "He's in there as usual, go in lass". I entered and was a little surprised to see that it was a bedroom, not any sort of bedroom, but one the likes of which I had never seen before, nor seen since. Everything was carved. The bed-head rose almost to the ceiling and every inch was covered with life-like animals, flowers and birds. The stool that Advent invited me to sit on was also carved; top, legs, and staves, and on the opposite side of the room was a huge carved mantelpiece that reached from floor to ceiling and was so wide that it almost filled the whole wall. Like the bed, every inch was carved with birds, squirrels, mice, and flowers so many that more than one visit was needed to take them all in.

But Advent didn't want to talk about them, he didn't really want to talk about anything. A huge shed in the lane at the side of the house, still full of his tools and workbenches, had been his workshop but he wasn't interested. He made it clear that he was no longer interested in carving and didn't want to talk about it. That part of his life was over. I continued to visit Advent, as he was on my visiting list and I was supposed to keep in touch, but with little hope that he might change his mind. On my way out one day over a cup of tea with his wife she said, "He does look forward to you coming, you know, but you'll never get him to do owt, he's made his mind up and even I can't change that." She paused, then added "You know he can get about as well as any man, but his working life is over and he just wants to stop in bed all day, so I let him."

The visits continued and once a month I sat on the beautiful carved stool beside his bed and went through the routine of small talk and hesitant suggestions that he might like to do some craft work, always with the same response, but he was mellowing. Once I even ventured to ask if he would like to make a miniature garden, but the look I received taught me not to mention that one again, However, underneath his extremely hard, grumpy, non-cooperative exterior, I sensed a kind man who, after such an active life was simply fed up and sad that he wasn't able to do the job any more, and too old and set in his ways to try something new. As a final stroke one day when he had been more talkative than usual, with tongue in cheek I shot a question at him, "Advent, would you like to knit dishcloths?" His steely eyes flashed as he looked me straight in the eye and I thought "At last, he's going to jump out of bed", but he 'stayed put' and behold we both laughed. He really was a wonderful man and I soon took his wife's attitude, 'That's how he wants it, so I let him'.

I now realised that I had three people who didn't want to work, and at least two who, for very good reasons, needed more, so on my next visit to Baslow I offered the Water Board man more trays. These were the items that he did well and enjoyed doing most. I reminded him that he was allowed to earn only £1.10s. a week, that I would collect and pay him as usual on Friday morning, but would book the extra trays to one of the men who did nothing. My reasoning, as with Tom's bathmats, was that no-one was getting hurt and they were both going back to work in quick time when their disablement pay would end. Bending the rules? Probably, but as no one would be any worse off, I didn't feel too guilty. In three months' time two very happy men returned to work.

I was born a Derbyshire 'Tup', and throughout my life I had driven, or been driven around the whole of the north east of the County, yet during the next few weeks my job took me to places known and travelled through, but not really visited. An occasional visit to a lady at Windmill near Great Hucklow, to collect the garments she had knitted and to leave her fresh supplies of wool; where my cousin had a farm and supplied a welcome cup of tea and a chat when time allowed. Through Moneyash with its single petrol pump, where petrol was served in a huge galvanized jug by the owner, then on to Flagg near the 'Bull i' the Thorn' Pub, on the way to Buxton, where I called sometimes to enquire about a patient there and met her daughter who hated her name 'Mooneen', given to her by her Mother after the heroine in 'Smilin through', the weepy film of the Thirties in which Norma Shearer was shot at the altar. Her wedding veil was copied, not only by me, but many other brides of that era. Then over the hills to Peak Forest, or along the valley through Matlock to Cromford to see a lady who crocheted beautiful doylies, and Via Gellia, where the air was full of the scent of Lily-of-the-valley that carpeted the woods along the roadside.

In three months my knowledge of Derbyshire geography was raised at least two notches. However, the most thought provoking person was a young lady about 20 years old who, even now, makes me wonder. When Anne was about 18 years old she developed epilepsy and immediately became a recluse who would not venture outdoors, nor see visitors; even her previous friends could not entice her to go anywhere or do anything. However, as she lived in Matlock and was on my list I decided one day to pay her a visit.

Her Mother answered the door and after introducing myself, asked if I could see Anne. As I expected she explained that Anne would not usually see anybody, but when I pointed out that this was just an introductory visit as I was the new Craft Instructor, she said she would ask her to see me. I was introduced to a very pleasant girl, not really the recluse that I had expected. After introducing myself and speaking with her for about 20 minutes, my first interview ended with an agreement that she would try weaving, and I found myself a few days later at the door again carrying a supply of different coloured wool, and a small weaving frame on which she could make a scarf. I wasn't surprised that the scarf never grew more than two rows a month, but my visits were a chance to see more of her and gradually to hear her become more talkative, yet she still refused to go out.

Due to holidays of Blind and Mentally Handicapped Instructors at Tansley and Chesterfield, when I took over their classes, it was three months before I saw Anne again, although I had kept in touch by telephone in case supplies were needed. Therefore I wasn't really surprised when her Mother rang and asked if I would call as Anne wanted to see me. This really is an improvement, I thought, but I wasn't ready for the story about to unfold. The girl I now met was a different person from the one I had last seen, and was anxious to tell me all about it. What follows will sound as unbelievable as it did to me, but it happened and I have no explanation.

Two weeks previously a friend whom Anne hadn't heard from for months rang to tell her that on the following Monday there was to be a Healing Service at the Episcopal Church that they used to attend, and would she go with her? Without any hesitation, she had said "Yes". The friend had called for her and they went to the service together. However, Anne wasn't confident enough to sit in the congregation and had remained at the back of the Church so as not to be noticed and the service proceeded in the usual way until the actual healing part of it began.

Anne listened and watched as various people left their seats and went to the front to receive the 'Laying on of hands' as part of the healing process, but she did not, nor did she even think of doing so herself. The last person returned to her seat, and the Congregation expected the usual 'Blessing', but the Minister hesitated as if waiting for something, and after looking around the congregation he spoke. "There is a lady at the back who wishes to come forward", but nobody moved. He spoke again, "Will the lady at the back come forward, do not be afraid."

Anne explained how she felt, first not really thinking that he was speaking to her, then when he spoke again something happened and she was compelled to get up from her seat and walk to the front, and she wasn't afraid, in fact she felt as if in a dream. After the 'Laying on of hands' and returning to her seat she and her friend returned home. I listened to all this in silence until, with tears running down her cheeks and eyes shining she said, "Mrs Rundle, I don't know what's happened and I don't understand it at all, but I haven't had an epileptic fit since. I'm cured". Her Mother had been listening, and though she had already heard the story many times in the past week, her face told it all. I still wonder!

In September 1965 Yvonne started another phase in her life when she left for the Boarding House of Lady Manners Grammar School in Bakewell. She soon settled in with the other boys and girls who, although from different home backgrounds, had all qualified for entry to a State Boarding School. During the first few months she appeared to be enjoying the experience, but as time went on there were times, I think, when she wasn't happy. The Boarders were a mixed bunch in the charge of Mr and Mrs Hogg, an understanding couple whose job I'm sure was not without its problems. By a happy coincidence in 1966 she was one of a group of pupils from Lady Manners Boarding House who were Confirmed at Bakewell Parish Church, where Arthur had been confirmed in 1949.

It was very quiet now at the weekends, although I went back to Holmesfield on Friday evenings to stay for one or two nights with Mum. At first, Saturday morning was taken up in teaching two Floristry students at their own homes who were hoping to take the Senior examinations in June 1966, and the last two flower arrangers from the last class at the school who were hoping to become demonstrators. The afternoons were used for shopping and odd jobs, Sundays for hair washing and other toiletries, and whatever other odd jobs needed to be done. It was on one of these occasions that I had taken Mum to 'Leadbeater and Peters' the Opticians, because her eyesight was fast deteriorating and I heard the sad news that nothing could be done to improve it. I shall never forget her panic-stricken face and agonised cry when she walked out of the examination room with the optician, "Josephine they say they can't do anything for me". The Optician, a kind man explained, "I'm so sorry it's the back of the eyes that have deteriorated and are too far gone to do anything." This was her most cruel blow, for reading had been a lifetime hobby since childhood, and reading newspapers was a favourite pastime, and source of all the things that were happening outside. When they became difficult to read she just looked at the headlines, and cut out any article that might be interesting, saving them until someone came along who would read them for her. It is a sad thought that there are still at least three boxes of cuttings here that obviously have never been read.

One Friday towards the end of September whilst I was delivering finished craftwork to the store, Miss Smith called me into her office. "Have you ever thought of qualifying as an Occupational Therapy Craft Instructor?" I said I didn't know there was such a thing. "Oh yes," she said, "and I think you should take the examination, but there are certain crafts that are accepted as qualifications and Floristry isn't one of them. Have you any in weaving, basket-work, or any other crafts?" I said I hadn't. "What about dressmaking, you are teaching that now, aren't you?" "Yes," I replied, "and I could get a qualification in that." "Just like that?" she questioned, waving a finger. "Yes, I've done dressmaking nearly all my life, no problem," I answered. "Right,"she said, "I'll put your name down straight away; you just get that Certificate." It took only a quick 'phone call to Sheffield Technical College to speak to a very surprised Senior Mistress of the Craft Department, to ask if I could join the City & Guilds Course in Dressmaking. She remembered that I had taken the City & Guilds Craft-Teacher's Course a few years previously as a Floristry Teacher and was intrigued by the change of craft, but happy to have me in the class, even though I was two weeks late in joining.

Christmas came and went, and in February 1966 came the hearing of our divorce case, and on the 14th May I received the Decree Nisi, when once again I was a 'Single woman'. Not that it made much difference because I had no intentions of marrying again, although I admit, with a certain amount of irony, that there were chances, three in fact in the following three months. One man, a Florist from Chesterfield and husband of a previous student who had died two years ago, stopped me in Sheffield market at 6 o'clock one morning and proposed. When I said I wasn't interested he handed me his bank book saying, "There's twelve thousand pounds in here, you can have it all if you'll marry me". I wasn't even flattered, just irritated that any man should think that I wanted, or needed, another husband.

Early in 1966 I received a letter from Robinson's Cardboard Box Makers of Chesterfield with whom I still had a contract for all the floral decorations for Social events, Presentations and other functions, to inform me that the new extensions to the Factory would soon be completed and requesting me to do the floral decorations for the official opening in July by The Princess Margaret. My briefing was to decorate two reception rooms, an Ante room for the use of The Princess and her Lady-in-waiting, 12 tables to seat about 100 guests, and a bouquet to be presented to The Princess by a blind girl who worked in the factory. This would be a challenge for I had never made a bouquet for a Royal Lady, although I knew that members of the Royal Family did not waste anything and flowers given to them, including bouquets, were very carefully taken apart and the flowers used for decorating the Palace. In modern floristry at that time, (although styles have altered somewhat since), some flowers like carnations and roses were taken apart, the petals being re-assembled and wired into small clusters before being carefully wrapped with Gutta Percha in order to accomplish a chosen design. In the process of being taken apart many flowers were of no further use, and others were very difficult to unwire. Consequently, bouquets for Royal occasions were designed for easy dissembling by using only whole flowers that were fastened together using only Gutta Percha, which was easy to remove (a rubber substitute is now used since the source of the natural Gutta Percha came to an end).

Most professions including Teaching and Crafts allow time out to take refresher courses, or to do other work in their own craft, in order to keep up with current trends. Therefore, when I mentioned the letter to my Supervisor, Miss Smith, I was not surprised when she said, "But of course you can do it. It's part of your craft and you are allowed time out to do that". So it was that I found myself at six o'clock one morning in the bustle of Sheffield Wholesale Market buying flowers, foliage and all the other accessories I would need for a job that, although it meant a lot of hard work, was what I enjoyed doing, and it meant a little more 'Grist to the Mill' (Money in the Bank), as we say in Derbyshire! All went well, although the work took much longer without the help of an assistant to help with flower-conditioning, preparing containers and other essential jobs. However, the result was very rewarding, particularly when I was invited as a guest (primarily to attend and instruct the blind girl) and to be presented to The Princess myself.

538

One morning over a cup of coffee and weekly discussion about visits and aids at the cafe in Bakewell, Anne dropped a bombshell with the news that she was expecting a baby and would be leaving in about two months' time. This was wonderful news for her, but for me it was going to be the end of a wonderful work partnership and also as a friend. As a temporary measure the Occupational Therapist at Chesterfield would visit once a week until a new one could be appointed. Happily, Mrs Baskerville, nearer my age, was easy to get on with for we had much in common, including a recent divorce, and we continued to work as I had done with Anne. Three weeks later Heather, from Harlow, Middlesex, who had just returned to England after spending a 'Year out' doing voluntary work in Dar-es-Salaam, Tanganyika (now Tanzania) joined the team and the old routine continued much as before.

Miss Smith called me one morning to discuss a problem at Chesterfield, not with Physically disabled, but with Mentally disabled young people. At present there was no Instructor so the boys were accommodated in the Woodwork Dept. but it was very limited, and the Welfare Officer was looking for something that would be suitable for all the group, both male and female. "I would like you to go to Chesterfield" she said, "and see what you can do". This, I thought was out of my depth, for I had had little to do with Mentally-disabled persons, except when I had taken a class twice for the less disabled when 'Standing in' for their Instructor who was away on a Refresher Course for two weeks, as I had done once for Miss Taylor, Teacher of the Blind, with whom I shared 'Back to back', but they already knew what to do and only required supervision.

This class would be very different and could only be assessed by paying a visit to the woodwork teacher to see the boys working, where I soon realised that, perhaps the usual crafts were not suitable. I decided to have a word with the Personnel Manager at Robinsons, in the hope that he could suggest something that might be suitable, as I had done at Buxton. He was very understanding saying "Leave it with me, I'll see what I can do".

A few days later I found myself in his office discussing suitable 'Outwork', which if satisfactory would earn a little for a holiday, or

539

a day out, and the firm would supply all the equipment necessary to set-up the project. This was good news and on receiving the 'Go-ahead' from Miss Smith, who made arrangements for a suitable room, and those who would attend, the new project was under way!

It was simple, at least in theory. A quantity of cardboard 'Flats' were delivered, each to be folded and formed neatly and securely into boxes, and for each box a penny would be earned. A production line was formed to give a small task to everyone. Each fold was done by a single person and they soon learned which fold to do first, second, third, and last, until the boxes were complete, clean, without creases, and satisfactory.

The exercise was a success and after the first delivery was assessed by the firm's Quality Control the job was extended to include wrapping the boxes in brown paper ready for delivery direct to the firm's despatch department. Sheets of brown paper were delivered with the next consignment of boxes, along with a glue-pot, slabs of glue, glue-brushes and a small gas-ring. The task was to wrap the boxes in the paper and glue the folds at the ends securely, but the folds required were not those familiar to most people, i.e. top first, both sides, bottom last, but, both sides first, followed by tops, bottoms last.

Whilst considering the safety factor, I was concerned about the glue-pot, for I knew that I couldn't have my eyes on all of them all the time. However, I did know that although mentally disabled persons might be slow to learn, when once they had learned and been given a job to do, they would do it well, and 'Raise hell and high water' if anyone interfered or did it wrong. It was with this in mind that I decided to create two production lines, hoping that the experience they already had in doing one fold on the boxes some of them would be capable of doing two, releasing the rest of the class for the new task. The boy who seemed to be the most capable was put in charge of the glue-pot, on strict instructions that he was in sole charge and had not to let anyone else use it. His job as last in the line was to paste the glue onto the tip of the last fold of paper on both ends of the boxes, with an assistant to hold the boxes steady until the job was complete. The rest of the class were allocated one task each, to make one fold, then pass the box on to the next person until both ends were correctly folded and passed to the 'Glue Man' to finish. It worked, given one task to do each person was very careful to do his/her own task perfectly, and 'Woe betide' anyone who made a mistake! They were their own 'Quality Inspectors'.

The Society of Floristry was founded in 1951 by a group of florists in order to improve the standard of work and to end the practice of working from home by housewives and others with no training. This was thought necessary when some of their work was shoddy, badly designed, and in some cases fell apart whilst being carried by the bride or recipient of a presentation bouquet; a situation that was bringing the profession into disrepute. A Diploma Examination was created by the newly formed Society through which existing florists could become members of the Society, and first and second year examinations for floristry assistants/trainees, which would lead to the Diploma after two more years' experience

As an existing florist I qualified for the Diploma, but knew that I lacked the 'shop-floor-training' from where many of the written questions would be drawn. Consequently I delayed my application until March 1959 after successfully exhibiting in the Professional Floristry Class at Harrogate Spring Show in 1957 and 1958. On the first occasion I had gained second place in the Floristry Stand Class, which comprised of a Bride's bouquet, a Corsage for the Mother of the Bride, a table arrangement, and an arrangement in a pedestal vase for a side table at the reception, all to be displayed on a 6ft by 3ft table suitably draped for display. At the same show I had won a Gold medal for the 'Francott-Dene-Nurseries' Stand in the Horticultural Trade Classes competing with 'Parks and Gardens' and 'Horticultural Nurseries' from many northern cities.

At the 1958 Show I was awarded the 'Mrs Davidson's Cup' for the most artistic Trade Stand, and again second prize for the Professional Floristry Stand ("Which," said the examiner ,"would have been first if the draping had been as perfect as the year before, because the standard of the floristry is exceptional"). I must admit that this was a huge disappointment because the other contestants were high-ranking, well-known and respected Florists and

Demonstrators, and first prize in such a prestigious competition would have been a great boost to my confidence as well as good for business. I knew that had we not hit a thick fog at Leeds on our way to Harrogate causing a delay of over an hour, there would have been time to do a better job on the draping. However, as I was to find on many occasions in the future, 'Such is life', and at least I now had confidence in my work to enter for the Diploma in 1959, a six-hour examination, from 9.00 a.m. to noon, and 1.00 p.m. to 4.00 p.m.

As things turned out I need not have worried, for my work was above the standard of the other florists except for one other young woman who had also learned at the Constance Spry School and had later worked at their shop in South Audley Street, London. This was the second time she had taken the examination for, like myself, she had not had time to finish the work. I had reached the point of having chosen the flowers and prepared the container for the last item when time was called, and I was exceedingly exasperated when the helper came to collect it and, seeing that it was not finished had left the room to report to the examiners.

The Invigilator, a very senior member of the Society Council, was called and after a few minutes came to see me, "Look", he said, "You've chosen the flowers and foliage for the arrangement and prepared your container just put the flowers in the basket quickly." I was tired and angry and refused. "Don't bother arranging them, just put them in the basket," he repeated, almost begging me to do what he asked, but by this time I was so exasperated, disappointed and angry that I refused and thereby failed the exam.

Ironically, I wouldn't have failed had I known, as I did when I became an examiner myself, that the marks for the choice of Flowers and Foliage and preparation of the container would have given me the necessary marks to pass, but we can all learn by 'Hindsight'. Whilst preparing to leave the hall the Constance Spry trained young woman spoke to me. "I hear you were trained at 'Sprys' so was I, you didn't finish did you?" "No" I snapped. "Neither did I first time round," she said, "I suspect you ran out of time like I did, because there just isn't time to do all the taping that we do." I said I thought the whole idea was to improve floristry, after which she enlightened me. "They've learned by 'Sitting next to Nelly', from Mothers and Grandmothers, their standards are 'Shop floor standards, money in the till, just enough to satisfy customers'."

She knew that I was frustrated and not a little disgusted, but insisted, "Do like me, miss some things out, just for the examination, cut corners a bit, and you'll pass next time". I followed her advice, took the exam in 1960 and received the Diploma with very mixed feelings, particularly after the Society magazine in June 1959 showed a photograph of the headdress I had made at the examination with the caption 'An example of the excellent work by an entrant to the examination in March'.

Nothing comes without responsibilities, as I was soon to find out. With the Diploma I now became an examiner travelling to Colleges in Leeds, Bristol, Wythenshawe, Glasgow, Whitehaven, wherever Day-release classes were held and examinations organised. All this was done on a voluntary basis that had to fit in with the 'Paid' job, and sometimes, if one were an employee rather than an Employer, it could be a problem. Once more I found a sympathetic ear from Miss Smith when, in June 1966, I was asked to go to 'Southeast Northumberland Technical College' as Chief Examiner, with the responsibility to correlate both the first and second year exam results and complete the computer sheets (rather crude at that time), ready for the Examination Committee in London to assess, adjudicate, produce and send out the results to the candidates. Three more Members would be there, Peter Miller from Ilkley, Alan Milner from Lytham St. Annes, and Elizabeth (Betty) Buchanan from Glasgow, who has remained a very dear friend throughout the years.

When I arrived at the College two of the other examiners had already arrived and had heard that the Floristry teacher was leaving. She worked for a Florist in Newcastle and did not like teaching, consequently the Principal was trying to find another teacher, preferably a full-time one, and had given the two examiners a list of Salary grades. Betty handed it to me as soon as I arrived with the words, "Here, you have it, you are the teacher, we are just florists and not interested".

The last examiner had now arrived and he dismissed the idea, agreeing with Betty, and handing it back to me saying, "You're the teacher, it's not for me", so I pocketed the salary list and we set about the business we had come for. After inspecting the examination rooms and agreeing that everything was ready for the first session at 10.00 a.m. next day, we all retired to the Hotel in Newcastle where we had been booked in for the night.

It was an early start for we had to find a suitable 'Accessory' for the Seniors to incorporate into an arrangement to be sent to a customer as a birthday gift, the cost of which would be passed on to the Society Treasurer. Nothing suitable could be found in Newcastle Wholesale Market so, hurriedly, we dashed to Woolworths toy counter and there found two suitable items that would stretch the imagination of the examination candidates, both in their choice, and the way the accessory was incorporated into the arrangement. I had written the examination questions myself and, although they had all been passed by the Moderating Committee, I did have some reservations as to why I had designed this test, when we could have been enjoying a comfortable breakfast in the Hotel!

I had been back at work for a few days before I remembered the paper that Betty had handed to me and on reading it immediately found it interesting, particularly the salary offered, which was twice as much as my present one. However, I didn't take it too seriously already having a job that I enjoyed, but a few days later in conversation with Elijah about teaching, salaries, and behaviour of pupils, I handed the paper to him to confirm the difference between salaries of State school education and that of Colleges. "Are you going to apply for the job?" was his first question. "I hadn't thought of doing," was my instant reaction, "I've worked for 15 years to build up my business so I can't give that up." "Why not?" he said, "You've proved what you set out to do, to start a school where youngsters can be trained without doing menial jobs for a year, and you've established a different way altogether how training should be done, so why not take it further and into colleges where more kids can be trained free? I still wasn't sure, but said I would send for an application form.

It arrived a few days later with all the details of the Post and qualifications necessary. I filled in the form, an interview was arranged, and a week later I sat in the office with the Principal, Mr Garside, drinking tea and discussing qualifications, past and present employment, teaching experience, and other relevant items; but still I wasn't sure and I said I would think about it and let him know. Next day Elijah was astounded when I described the interview and my indecision. "I don't know what you are thinking about," he said, "You are offered a job here doing exactly what you've been doing for 15 years, doing your own interviewing, your own marketing and buying, the whole top floor of the college to teach in exactly the way you've always done, and an extra £250 a year responsibility allowance, what else do you want?"

I didn't answer, still feeling that I was letting myself down after so many years of building myself up. After considering all the reasons why I should take the job, I decided to contact the Principal to arrange another interview, and once again found myself in his office drinking tea and discussing once again what was on offer, and why I should accept the job. There was stalemate for a few moments then, without knowing why, because I knew nothing about Lecturer-grades, I asked if there was any possibility of my getting a 'B' Grade, although I didn't realise until later that this would mean a salary of another £1,000 a year. Immediately Mr Garside shot the question "Why, would you come if we offered a 'B' Grade?" as his hand went straight to the phone to ring the Director of Education in Newcastle. I listened as he explained that he had Mrs Rundle here in his office and, "Can the Establishment stand another 'B' Grade?" Putting down the 'phone after a few moments he said, "Yes, the college could stand another 'B' Grade, would I now say "Yes'?" I still hesitated and said I would think about it and let him know, however, I would have to give a month's notice to my present employers. This was not a surprise, but as it was now the last week in August it meant that there would be no intake of full-time students this year.

Once again Elijah was critical. "I don't understand you at all," he said, " a job just like the one you are doing, at more than twice the salary, somebody else doing the worrying, and a pension when you retire, what else do you want?" I was finally won over, but sad to be leaving a job, though originally only intended to be temporary, had earned me many friends and was the most rewarding I could ever hope for. However, now as a single parent it was up to me to earn as much as I possibly could, and Elijah was right that I should move on. Always ready for the challenge of a change, once my mind was made up I reported to Miss Smith and handed her my notice on October 1st, and was somewhat surprised at her reaction.

"I'm glad you've decided to take it," she said, "You're wasted here, you are a teacher, you've encouraged disabled people to do things they never thought possible, and given them confidence to try. You should be a teacher, but I shall be very sorry to see you go." Two weeks before I was due to leave, Miss Smith received notice that an Occupational Therapy Assessor would arrive in a week's time for my interview, and to accompany me on my Home visits; after which, if successful, I would be an Occupational Therapy Technical Instructor. Needless to say this appointment was cancelled.

The day before I left, Miss Smith invited me and all the other 'O.T.s' with whom I had worked, and the Welfare Staff from County Offices, to a farewell lunch at a nearby Hotel in Matlock to thank me for the work I had done, and to wish me luck in my new job. As we walked down the steps of the Hotel on our way out she drew me to one side, "You should know, there's never before been a reference as good as yours from the Welfare Office, it was amazing." Unfortunately, I never got to see it!

I left my office the day after with mixed feelings, sadness at leaving, excitement for a new venture, but with many friends who promised to keep in touch. I intended to travel between Youlgreave and North Shields each week until I could find a suitable house, and in the meantime had arranged to stay with my ex-husband's relatives at Burnhope, County Durham, and commute daily between there and College. A week later on 7th November 1966 at 8.30 a.m. I reported to Mrs Anderson, Head of the Crafts Dept. at South East Northumberland Technical College ready to start my new job.

Chapter 16

On Sunday 6th November 1966 I left Auburn House, Youlgreave, with very mixed feelings of excitement at the prospects of a new challenge and sadness at leaving so many friends behind in this village, and in those I had visited during the past two years. I faced the biggest change in my life so far, not only for the first time working in the closed atmosphere of an Establishment, the routine of which I knew nothing; but in closer relationships with colleagues than I had previously had to contend, and the new life I had to create 200 miles away in the North of England. I knew from previous visits that I had enjoyed, when visiting Frank's relatives, that their customs, characters, and language were very different from those in my native Derbyshire, and it was to one of those relatives, May Armstrong my husband's cousin, in Burnhope, County Durham, with whom I was going to stay, that my present journey was taking me.

My arrival at South-east Northumberland Technical College was unannounced and my first meeting with Mrs Anderson, Head of the Crafts Department, was short. Reporting to her office she welcomed me into the College and after a few preliminaries, explained that my actual teaching time as a 'B' Grade Lecturer was 20 hours a week, the remaining 10 hours of the 30-hour working week being allowed for marking and preparation of lessons. I was then introduced to Mrs Doreen Clarke, the Senior Lecturer of Hairdressing, into whose hands was passed the responsibility of showing me around the College and explaining how things worked. At lunchtime in the Staff-room Doreen introduced me to the other Lecturers and Heads of Departments, and later gave me my first lesson on the use of a 'Xerox-Copier', a machine that was to save me a lot of time in future in producing 'Handouts' to supplement both practical and theory lessons, particularly for day-release and evening students.

In the absence of a 'Full-time Course' due to my mid-term arrival at college, and the first weekly 'Day-release Course' not scheduled until next day, Mrs Anderson had negotiated with the local Flower-shop Owners, whose qualifications had already been accepted by 'The Society of Floristry', to attend a two-hour Evening Course each Monday evening in preparation for the Diploma Examination in 1967, an arrangement in which Doreen had helped through her daughter, June, who worked for one of them, and had passed the Senior Examination in June. Later I was to find that this was a valuable introduction to the Owners with whom I had to negotiate in future, not only to allow their assistants to attend Day-release Classes (not always easy), but to find the most suitable shops where students could be seconded for 'Shop-floor' work experience.

The first of the 'Owners and Managers' classes was scheduled for that evening from 7.00 p.m. to 9.00 p.m., a group I faced with some trepidation as I knew from past experience that some of them would be set in their ways and not easy to convert to modern methods. However, finding myself once more in front of a group of adults took me back to Night-School Flower-arranging classes in Sheffield and Bakewell; I soon felt at home with them and my new surroundings, especially as all of them were at least familiar with, and used to handling different flowers and foliage.

There were, however, many aspects of modern floristry that were new to them and, as I was to find out as the weeks went by, that some of them wondered why they were necessary. The most difficult for them to understand was 'Colour', what it is, how it is produced, why we don't all see it in the same way, and most important, how to use it, for they had been dealing with coloured flowers all their working lives and didn't see the point. The solution to some of their questions, as I was to find out in the student classes, was to use the drawings and charts that I had made for the Flower Arranging Classes as visual aids; the structure of the eye showing the 'Rods and Cones', a 'colour-wheel', and a card with a red cross on a white ground by which they could test for colour-blindness, and to convince them that colour is how their own eyes interpret it from the pigment in all things. Through the colour-wheel they learned how to analyse colours in flowers and foliage, and which combinations would be more likely to please the customer or recipient. Flowers and foliage are never only one colour. A pink rose is not just pink, and the most interesting colour combinations are made by analysis and the effect that can be produced by different combinations; for, unlike the artist, the florist cannot mix paint on a palette but has to work with Nature's colours and choose combinations that please the eye, or are suitable for the occasion.

This last chapter, covering the next fourteen years of my working life, is in danger of becoming a book in its own right, so, only the more interesting events will be included or those which I think will describe my life in a College and after. I was soon to find that full-time Courses in State Colleges were open to all citizens of school-leaving age, which in 1966 was 15yrs, to the age when the Course could be completed before retirement pension age. Consequently any person between 15yrs and 56yrs for women, 62yrs for men, could join any Course of three years duration, provided they had the necessary educational qualifications. To accommodate those without the necessary 'O' Levels for their chosen subject there had to be one Course without 'O' Levels to offer to the applicant and at S.E.N.T.E.C that Course was Floristry.

Consequently, I had to take students not only of all ages between school leaving to retirement age, but also of varying degrees of intelligence and capability. This is where my experience with the disabled persons proved helpful, for I found myself on two occasions, one with a female student classified as S.E.N. (having special educational needs), followed a year or two later by a fifteen-year old delightful, well-mannered girl, daughter of a very well-known local Official in the Education Office in Newcastle, who, on reaching the age of 16, would no longer be the responsibility of the Welfare Dept., but The Education Authority, and he was worried as to how she would be treated, especially by those, young and old, with whom she would come in contact.

Her Father had sought the help of her Doctor as to the best course to take, and he had advised him to "Send her to the top floor of S.E.N.T.E.C. for a year with Mrs Rundle, she won't be able to learn much, but she will learn how to get on with other people and behave in public."

When Mr Garside had visited me a few weeks before and told me about this girl, I was a bit apprehensive, and concerned that my classrooms might be used as a Rehabilitation-Centre, but he assured me that this was not the case. Her Father, he said, was a great friend and Colleague who was at his wits end to do what was best for his daughter, as he thought she might be gullible and easily led into trouble. He said he agreed with the Doctor: a few months with ordinary people in an atmosphere that would not be daunting to her, and joining in with the activities of 'Normal' people could have untold benefits. But the decision was mine; if I thought that she would be a disruptive element in the class he would understand. Of course I said I would take her, and never regretted doing so. The other students became very fond of her, and she tried her best in all lessons. No stress was put on her, neither in theory nor during practical work, and one or two very simple questions designed for her for homework sufficed to make her feel part of the class. Her enthusiasm and obvious love of flowers helped her to attempt most of the practical work to the point that, towards the end of the year, she made a great effort, with a little help, to make a corsage for her Mum to wear that night at an Anniversary dinner; a gift I was told later, that was the most precious her Mother had ever had.

I was surprised and somewhat pleased to hear that another class had been booked before I arrived, after a request from a woman who lived in Whitley Bay, whose daughter had been a student in my advanced flower-arranging class at Youlgreave. On hearing from her daughter that I was going to teach at S.E.N.T.C. she approached Mr Garside with a request to start an advanced class for a number of ladies who had been learning with a local flower-club. Of course the Principal was delighted, and thus I found myself on Thursday evenings 7.00 p.m. to 9.00 p.m. with a ready-made class of 31 enthusiastic ladies all 'chomping at the bit' and eager to learn. What more could a teacher want? Three years later sixteen students from this class formed a three-year advanced class towards creating a Northumberland Teacher's Certificate to qualify for part-time teaching in the County night-schools, and was the forerunner to the 'City and Guild's Creative Studies Course' a universal qualification for part-time teaching Flower-arranging in Colleges.

I was very fortunate during that first year to have such an understanding Head of Dept. as, having little homework to mark, and after completing 'Schemes of work' and 'Lesson plans' and submitting them in triplicate to the Principal according to the rule, and having fun designing and producing 'Handouts' to help with the necessary theory for the current courses, I had time to take advantage of Mrs Anderson's suggestion that I should go out and use the time to find a house so that I wouldn't "go running back to Derbyshire", her words not mine! This is when life really began, when I felt that I could really become a north-country lass, when Doreen had permission from Mrs Anderson to take 'Prep-time' out and go with me searching for a house. Of course, this is where I had Arthur to thank, for I had been able to save very little during the months I had been with Derbyshire Welfare, and the necessary deposit for even a small house was not within my range. He had the solution, perhaps with a bit of persuasion from me, for I had put a lot of work into Auburn House and both knew that it had enhanced the selling price. So he arranged that half the profit was to be paid into my bank account to pay the deposit, with a little left over for living until my salary made me independent.

So began our search, with many a laugh on the way, as when we followed an advertisement for a large three-story villa in Rowland's Gill that looked very promising until we arrived at the toilet that was unlike anything that we had seen before. On first sight we laughed, and kept on laughing at the throne before us; three round steps up to a dais, surmounted by a white throne suitable for a Queen. It was examined, looked at from all angles, sat upon and peered into, only to be told by the vender a few minutes later that the owner had hung himself in the Hall. At the end of six months I knew Northumberland almost as well as Derbyshire. Berwick, Bambrough, and the kipper curing sheds at Seahouses, Lindisfarne and the Farne Islands bird sanctuaries, and learned about Grace Darling the heroine of the Longstone lifeboat rescue. All this on the day that we had viewed the old School House at Felton as a possible new home, one that was seriously considered until I learned of the heavy snows in winter when it would be almost impossible to reach the College, never mind the market. Not so conscientious was a male teacher who, on hearing why I had turned it down said, "You should live where you like, I live at Amble (on the north Northumberland coast), and if I can't get in I just ring-in and tell 'em so".

After six months searching, and considering the possibility of not getting to College in winter, I settled on a large pseudo-Tudor house in Monkseaton; offered the price asked and returned to Youlgreave for the summer holiday, during which time the necessary Searches, Mortgage and other tedious arrangements should be completed. Returning to College at the beginning of September and contacting the Halifax Building Society I was angry when they argued and made all kinds of excuses like "There is no garage to the house", to which I responded "I know, but I don't use a garage anyway". I soon realised that all the prevaricating was because I was a woman, and even in the Sixties women were not thought suitable to buy houses without a man's support. However, with a show of determination and what some have called a 'Fiesty' bit of behaviour that was often necessary on such occasions, I was allowed to buy No. 15 Queen's Road, Whitley Bay, Northumberland; my own first house, that was to be my home for the next 21 years.

It took only a few weeks for me to realise that Colleges are business houses as well as for the purpose of Education when Mrs Anderson informed me that she had arranged for Tyne Tees Television to pay a visit to the Floristry Dept. during a teaching session with a view to enticing more school-leavers into the Full-time Courses whereby her Department would be up-graded, and her salary enhanced. On the date arranged a whole crew turned up in the middle of a practical lesson, bringing with them microphones, cameras flood-lights and all the tackle necessary for the 'Shoot', which was about the finer points of the making of a funeral wreath. I assumed that it would be straightforward and business-wise with me at the blackboard, pointing out to the students the finer points of design and workmanship. Everything was ready and I began to speak, the cameras began to roll, when suddenly the man in charge asked what I thought was a silly question, particularly at that point. "Is that how the Americans do it?" I stopped and stared at him, angry at the interruption, and more angry that he should bring America into it. "What on earth has America to do with it?" I burst out, "This is England, or perhaps you haven't noticed?" A loud "Cut" came from the man in charge of the cameras, and a quiet voice from another whilst looking daggers at the speaker, said quietly, "Let's do that again shall we?" and so we did.

This was the forerunner of many occasions when Television and Radio were used to advertise a Course or some other public event. Mrs Anderson's Husband, now retired from his job as Station Manager at Yarm, was an enthusiastic supporter St. George's Church, a little way from my home and, of course, it wasn't long before the question of a fund-raising Flower Festival was suggested, and duly carried-out in 1970. It proved to be an excellent exercise, not only for the full-time students, but all the part-time ones too, even the 'Owners and Managers' added their help when possible, as the whole theme was executed in traditional English flower-arranging with Pedestals, Windows, Font, Lectern, Pulpit, and anywhere else that could be enhanced, to make sure that all students had the opportunity to join in, and all were delighted when over £500 was raised for the Church.

Since childhood I, like my Brother Geoff, had an urge to paint with water-colours, making gift cards etc. during the long evenings in winter, whilst Elijah, who also did water-colour painting and whose real talent was for drawing, particularly animals, such as Deer and Stags, always won first prize in the annual show. Throughout the years I had been too busy to spend time on painting, but in 1972 whilst watching Yvonne practising for her 'O' Level exams, I got the urge to start again, this time using oils that I had not before attempted and also had to practise. A huge tube of white paint was the starting point, with smaller tubes of various colours with which to use my imagination, and to 'Get the feel' of paint. My canvas was 12"x 9", my favourite Painter was Constable, so Clouds, Waves and all things natural were in my head to be transferred to canvas. With a loaded brush I started, continued, clouds like Constable's floating in the sky, waves of water rolling across the lower half of my canvas, until I had a picture with paint about a quarter of an inch thick covering the canvas, with colours from the sky reflecting in the water, and an empty paint tube!

It took weeks for that picture to dry, was never hung, but remains one of my better memories. I had been bitten by the 'Bug' and continued painting. The first, 'A walk through Clumber', was still wet when Arthur arrived on his annual visit, but taken back to the States, and still sits proudly on his lounge wall.

I became really smitten, packing-in a two-week painting holiday in Heidelberg in 1977 and two weeks in Cannon, just over the border in Scotland, and finally won first prize at Totley Show for a painting of the Sheep-dip at Ashford in the Water, the village in Derbyshire where my Sister-in-law Nancy lived before marrying my Brother Elijah. It was made for, and given to her at Christmas 1986. Unfortunately, after moving from Whitley Bay to Totley in 1988 there has been no time for painting, to the great disappointment of Elijah, who often said, "Stop doing that gardening, or writing, or whatever was the current occupation, and get back to your painting." I often wish I had!

In 1970 Yvonne and I paid our first visit to America for a three-week holiday with Arthur in Miami when we spent the middle week touring in one of his cars through Florida, Georgia, South and North Carolina, New York State, to Niagara, where we stayed for the night in a large Hotel, next day travelling west through Illinois, Indiana, Nebraska, Wisconsin, South Dakota and Rapid City, again staying overnight, this time in a very small 'Hotel' where Wyatt Earp was shot, his chair still hanging from a rope overhead. We left next morning for South Dakota, passing Keystone, where Yvonne wanted a trip in the helicopters flying overhead, an experience left until next day, now I was intent in travelling up Gravity Hill, where the sensation is of going up when, because of the strange terrain you are actually going down. Finally we reached the black hills of South Dakota and experienced our first trip in a helicopter where the pilot played a little game, high in the air one minute to show us the black trees from above, next minute zooming down almost hitting the top of 'Old Baldy' (the top of a huge dead Pine tree), finally arriving to marvel at the huge faces of the four Presidents carved out of the top of the mountain. A full report of all the wonderful things we saw on this, our first visit to America, would fill a whole book, so I'd better move on back to North Tyneside and College.

In order to show what a College of Education had to offer, not only for school-leavers but also for Adults, with the co-operation of the Principal, an assembly of teachers from all departments was arranged to be held in a large Marquee in North Shields. So far as numbers were concerned it was a huge success, particularly for familiar occupations known to everybody; for those not so enlightened it was another matter, as when a young girl, accompanied by her Mother, popped the question "What is Floristry?", and after a detailed explanation another questioner asked "Why is it in a College?". Another explanation brought forth the final question, "What do you pay?" which could be answered only by explaining to the poor unenlightened girl, with her Mother standing by listening, what Colleges were for. This was brought to mind by me three years later when the first local girl to pass the Senior Examination was told that a super job was waiting for her with a top Florist in London her Mother said "No" because she would get all sorts of "Grand ideas, not for such as us". Sadly, this was a continuing obstacle that deprived many girls of wonderful careers not only in Great Britain but also in many other countries.

All Technical Colleges have their roots in the old Mechanics' Institutes, and South East Northumberland's were in the one in Wallsend where the Shipyard Welders were trained. Consequently the Engineering and Welding Department at S.E.N.T.E.C was a Major and important part of the whole curriculum, where the Head of Department was a wonderful man Mr Handsford. One morning in

555

the winter of 1970-71 he came up to my classroom full of enthusiasm and ideas that his Welders needed refining a bit, bring 'em out o' their rough and ready ways, and what they needed was a bit o' female company. "So", he continued, "How about your lasses joining my Lads on a skiing weekend at Allendale Field Centre, refine 'em a bit, don't you think?" I did think, although I couldn't see myself staying upright on skis, as proved correct; what's more I couldn't get up when I fell, and I never wanted to see another ski for the rest of my life. Yvonne, now age 16, went with us and at the time felt pretty much the same way, but she persevered all next day, whilst I took a walk exploring Allendale village and enjoyed that immensely. The verdict from Mr Handsford was "A resounding success, the lads are 'Full of it', never stopped talking about it, and the 'Lasses'"!

It was not compulsory for the teachers in Colleges of Further Education to possess a Teaching Certificate, only the highest qualification in their own subject, of which mine was the Diploma of The Society of Floristry. However in 1968, because there was a serious shortage of teachers in day-schools, the Education Authority issued an order to the effect that all Teachers should obtain the Ministry Teaching Certificate to allow them in emergency to teach in day-schools. Four teachers went from S.E.N.T.E.C for two weeks to Huddersfield Teacher Training College, part of Leeds University which supplied the teachers, after which they attended Durham Technical College one day each week for two years. Various tests were undertaken, essays, lesson plans, making visual-aids, and two days on an exercise towards understanding the first computers that were fed by punched cards. These were made by punching holes into white cards, which delivered information according to the subject of the lesson, by light passing through the holes to produce the desired information. Each student had to produce one card when marks were given for the success, or otherwise, of the exercise, which was more like understanding how computers worked rather than their use! The final and most important test at the end of the two years was Teaching test held in the Student's own college under the critical eye of a University examiner.

My turn came next in 1970, but was turned down because I had no 'A Levels'. I was angry and very upset that, after all my efforts to become educated, I was considered 'Not qualified'. Having received a similar letter, Mr Garside was furious and contacted the Minister of Education in Newcastle; "How the hell do you think a fifty-four year old can have A Levels?", he shouted, "She's my best teacher and deserves this chance to qualify." Of course the Minister agreed, the same old story, they act by the rules and never think about the consequences!

So, in 1972 I found myself at Huddersfield Teacher Training College for two weeks where I found what I had heard was true, that there was more gallivanting going on than learning; men away from their wives, women loving the chance to flirt and do what loose women do. One evening a bus was ordered to take us to a local pub for what was supposedly to be just a quiet relaxation from so much studying, but in fact was a drinking 'Orgy' whilst being entertained by a dubious comedian whose whole programme was a series of obscenities. After a few minutes the two hairdressers, the Teacher from Chester-le-Street and myself all walked out in disgust and took a taxi back to College.

For the next two years the rest of the classes were held at Durham Technical College ending with an actual Teaching Test in our own Colleges, which, for me was in my own classroom, with my own class, and ten teachers acting as students, but really helping with the assessment by asking relevant questions and taking notes. By this time the Floristry Dept. had grown and now offered, as well as the Full-time class, a two-year one day a week day-time class for Shop-assistants, an evening class for those who had passed both first and second year exams towards taking the Intermediate examination after two years actual shop experience.

This system was soon terminated when the work of organising and examining became too demanding for the Members of The Society of Floristry who had done it on a voluntary basis and City and Guilds took over the first and second year examinations, the Intermediate was terminated, the Diploma remaining with The Society of Floristry. Later years changed all this in 1980 when City

557

and Guilds introduced the N.V.Q. for all practical subjects, through which students learned the theory and practice, but, like all N.V.Q. Courses since, do not have to pass a practical examination, which I considered, and still do, a very backward step when seeing the results today, after over fifty years of voluntary work towards raising the standard expected from well-trained Craftsmen/women. The evening class was continued, but was redesigned for those who wished to take the Society of Floristry Diploma, but was soon abandoned when the young florists of today and their employers plus the young Brides of today, who have known no other, are content with the garden bunches which pass for bouquets, and arrangements with no thought to the rules of design, nor artistic merit.

In 1970, I don't really know how, Mrs Anderson heard that I was a student of Ikebana, Japanese Flower arranging, an ancient art handed down from India, via China to Japan through a Japanese Emissary to China, called Ono-No-Imoco, Cousin of the Emperor who, on his return to Japan, introduced the Art of 'Putting living things in water', when branches, plants and flowers, were used to make huge arrangements depicting nature for display in the Temples. Over the years, these were adapted, added-to, altered and improved, according to the occasions and seasons, by the Founders and Teachers of the many Schools which sprang-up over the centuries, each with its own methods of interpretation, that were displayed in every home in a special place called the Tocanoma, an alcove, its base at floor level, in front of which the visitor knelt, or bowed, in acknowledgment of the message it portrayed.

It had never been taught in Colleges and was not one of the qualifications submitted during my initial interview, also, pointing out that I was not qualified to teach Ikebana beyond the stage of the student's demonstrating capability. The next question was "What do you do to qualify?" to which the answer was, "I have to take and pass the first examination of the Teacher's Course and progress through the second third stage to the fourth, if I were still working, but as my Mother was now living with me and was my main priority, little time would be available for further study. I explained that I would have to go to London, take a Refresher Course with my

Teacher and demonstrate to a panel of Judges headed by Stella Coe, the founder and head of Ikebana in England. "Well, why don't you do just that?" came the surprising statement from my persistent Head of Dept., adding, "You can take whatever time-off you need, so do what's necessary."

So I found myself in London in the house in Governor Road where, years before, I had learned and passed the tests to bring me to where I was now, and to meet once more my Teacher, wife of the Ceylonese (now Sri Lanka) Ambassador to England, who welcomed me with open arms just as she always did. After a week of intense talking, demonstrating, questioning, and helpful criticism, I faced the panel of Judges in fear and trepidation in the huge basement of the house in Pimlico of Mrs Stella Coe. The test took just over an hour, during which I gave a teaching demonstration whilst explaining all the essential points of the exercise, answering questions from the examiners that never seemed to stop, and finally bringing to an end the ordeal amidst a smiling resounding clapping, with the news from Stella that I had Passed.

This exercise was repeated in 1974 and 1979 from which I can proudly display the Certificates on my computer-room wall. I officially retired in 19 July 1980, although I continued for another year until another Floristry Lecturer took over and I finally retired in July 1981; consequently there was little point in taking the next test.

Of course, the result of all this was a class of Ikebana students towards which Mrs Anderson had arranged for an interview and demonstration of Ikebana on Tyne Tees Television. Bearing in mind the last episode with the Crew, I was on my guard as to the reception and response. I had been to the Television Studios before for an interview-cum-demonstration to advertise a pending Course in Flower Arranging, and once on Tyne-Tees Radio for a similar exercise to explain some of the points that listeners had been asking, so I was not too perturbed by the latest advertising performance.

As usual there was more talking than demonstrating, but I managed just enough to enthuse 16 applicants to the first class, before which I had pointed out to Mrs Anderson that the class would take five years for the final students to qualify and that the rules were strict. Ikebana had never before been taught in a College and I couldn't pass anybody who didn't reach the standard of the essential tests just to keep the usual minimum of 12 students. This she understood and perhaps used a bit of persuasion on the Principal and the Director of Education to let it run.

Whatever was arranged, the Class continued without question until there were only five students left and I was told that the class in College must close, but there was an alternative. If I agreed, I could take time out, whatever I wanted, if I could carry on for the last term at home. So, it transpired that 15 Queen's Road Whitley Bay became an annex to South-east Northumberland Technical College one half-day a week for the next ten months, when four out of the five qualified as Demonstrators in the art and practice of Ikebana.

What happened to the fifth student, you might well ask. Well, there's always one who doesn't quite toe the line, and that was the student who always rebelled with a "Why?" attitude, as if she already knew it all, but who did just enough to keep her place in the class, under sufferance when she was actually a 'Pain in the neck' and was only kept in the class because she was always sufficiently careful so as not to fail. The curriculum had been designed to allow for theory lessons and for tuition and practice in demonstrating from behind the arrangement instead of the usual way in front, which viewers appreciate because they can see the actual placing of the material. Constance Spry used this method of demonstrating herself, but I never saw it practised by any other demonstrator. The unruly student knew, of course, that this was not actually on the curriculum and made it clear that she wasn't going to do it. I told her that it was part of this course and if she didn't attend she would fail to qualify. Defiant, she left, contacted the nearest Teacher over the border in Scotland, told her who her Teacher was, and was granted a pass as her own student. I took this as a compliment to my teaching and never heard of her again.

The most satisfying result was from the student who throughout the whole five years had shown the most interest and dedication to the subject. She lived at Whitburn near Washington where there was a great deal of interest in the Japanese due to the recently opened Nissan Car Factory at Sunderland, and Ikebana through the Television appearances, but also because May, already learned in their Art, designed and made the Japanese arrangements in the entrance to the Factory on the occasions of the monthly Festivals in Japan, and when important people from Japan were visiting. With the approval of Kasumi (The Grand Master since the death of her Father Sofu Teshigahara the previous Master and Founder of the Sogetsu School), May started a Study Group that I visited twice in the early days, which proved very successful encouraging May herself to study towards the Tests that would lead her also to the grade of 'San yo' as I had done. Sadly, in 2007 I received a letter from her Sister telling me that she had died, a very sad moment for all who knew her. However, the Study Groups have survived and over the years have multiplied, and I am proud of the fact that, in small way, have had a hand in the spreading of Ikebana from the north east to the north west of England and is still surviving. The last time I attended a meeting of the Ikebana Teachers' Association in London, Tacashe, the Chief Representative from Tokyo at the time, was the Demonstrator, after which I was asked to give the Vote of Thanks at the end of his demonstration, an honour which surprised me, but made me very proud. Sadly, due to lack of new teachers, or lack of new students I know not, the Ikebana Teacher's Association was disbanded in 2002.

In 1973-74, St. John's church at North Shields had undergone a complete Overhaul and was now a very modern Church, but short of funds. In a conversation with the Vicar I suggested that a Flower Festival might bring in a few pounds, to which he readily agreed. This one, however, would be different, modern, not traditional arrangements as befitted this modern Church, with modern music, provided that I could persuade the Members of College Jazz Band, a mixture of Lecturers from five or six departments, male and female, to take part. Fortunately they were glad to do so and were a valuable addition to the success of the Flower Festival. All classes from the Floristry Dept. joined in as well as the Full-time students; Flower arranging, Day-release Floristry, Ikebana, all ages, including one lady aged 84, with her friend, a much younger lady, who said they liked traditional styles better than very modern. I suggested they take charge of the entrance porch, which was a good size and contained an old oak chest, a tall flower pedestal that was decorated each week for the usual services, and a four-foot high antique carved cupboard, all ideal for traditional arrangements. The Porch proved to be a super welcome to all the visitors as they entered the Church, and caused many excited gasps of surprise when they entered the main Church and saw the modern ones. It proved easier to control when students worked in groups, each one in charge of a particular area, or item, and prevented attacks of nerves from the less experienced had they worked alone.

The Ikebana students, now reduced in numbers, worked on a huge arrangement beneath a window in one of the aisles using large branches and flowers to achieve the proportions and positions of the early interpretive Temple arrangements. All the arrangements in the rest of the church were interpretive of their positions, i.e. the borrowed Violin that sat on the piano in the corner, with a double-base clinging to one 'leg', each decorated with flowers in mixed soft and loud hues to depict the notes of string instruments.

Similar in interpretation, yet very different, was the arrangement by two full-time students who had charge of the Lectern, where huge fully-out gladioli in several colours burst out from the base in all directions as the words of the Bible from the Reader. Bear in mind that this was now a modern Church, nevertheless it was a Church that demanded respect not least in the depiction of Christ himself. With this in mind the Sanctuary was chosen as the most appropriate place, and suitable on one side with a carved frame entrance into to a small room where a very old black carved wooden Galleon stood on an elaborately carved table. No one could explain exactly why it was there, nor from whence it came, but I, and particularly the older Students, agreed that it could be incorporated into the whole Festival design.

Hence, two adult students, using soft blue silk to depict the Sea of Galilee, and using a suitable piece of driftwood, did an excellent interpretation of Christ calming the waters. Three full-time students had the most important task which, if not done with a certain amount of sensitivity, could have gone extremely wrong, and during discussions it had been decided that the figure of Christ would be made from suitable pieces of light-coloured driftwood that we had been collecting from flower arrangers and loaned from flower-shop owners who used it in their shops, consequently we had a good supply to choose from. Three full-time Students worked together on the project, first in choosing and joining together the pieces that would most realistically form the body, arms and legs, bearing in mind that the ankles must be placed one over the other and fastened together with a nail on which an arrangement of small red flowers would be fastened to depict the wound made by the nail. Similar precautions were needed to illustrate the wounds in the hands, the three arrangements being completed by two of the students, whilst the third made the Crown of Thorns from the stems of wild roses and blackberries, using gloves of course, whilst intertwining one or two thistle heads. Not an easy task, but very effective and thought provoking with the crowned head leaning slightly forward.

The final task, with the aid of the two male teachers who had volunteered to help, was to hoist it into position and fix it to the wide carved top of the alcove. What should have been the simplest and easiest to dress was the Font, not the usual three-foot high Bowl that could have contained a modern interpretation, but a five-foot elaborate pedestal on which sat a shallow bowl that no-one below could see into, never mind arrange flowers.

In the classroom at the end of a flower arranging session, after our first viewing of the Church, we were discussing various ideas about how to dress the Font. I sat on the edge of my desk with one finger of my right hand idly playing with a piece of chicken wire poking up from the three-foot roll from which the students had prepared their containers, bBefore the days of Oasis. My finger tangled with the wire for moment and, in releasing it the middle of the roll rose and gently bent over and the idea was born. Standing up I pulled the inside of the roll higher and bent the top forward to simulate a slightly bent head. "There's the answer", I said, " John the

Baptist, the Vicar, or perhaps Jesus, standing at the Font with a little child in his arms, now whose going to do it?"

The three most capable students, whom I knew would work together, were chosen and full of enthusiasm for this unusual assignment that was to be the most talked about, the most interesting, moving and reverent interpretation in the Church. The question was, how was it to be done so that all these attributes could be portrayed without looking cruel, and just as important, be stable and safe. The top half held few problems as the bent head, shoulders and back, were draped to floor level with fine white cloth loaned by the Home Economics Dept. to use as a cloak whilst allowing fine variegated grasses to escape around the shoulders to simulate hair. The arms were comparatively easy for the student whose assignment was to moss two Spray-frames, already curved into suitable angles to represent arms; the one for the right arm being partly hidden by a fold in the cloak, the visible hand and wrist being carefully mossed and layered smoothly with cream Euphorbia leaves. The frame for the left arm was mossed and covered with similar leaves before fastening it securely to the left shoulder and curving it to the right side at waist level with a short piece of cream fabric, carefully draped from within the frame to the outside to represent the baby's shawl, and the curved inside was filled with flowers and suitable foliage to represent a baby.

Most important was that the whole 'Statue' had to be stable and safe, not an easy task, but with all hands on deck, two Students with arms around the waist holding the body rigid, whilst two others gently teased out the wire from the waist to the ground into folds and curves that were discreetly enhanced with fine grasses, trails of Ivy and Clematis presenting a realistic interpretation of a flowing gown, and also helping to hide the tub of large stones placed inside and draped with grey material to simulate an inner skirt when discreetly secured to the outer skirt with strong wires and canes should anyone through their curiosity be tempted to approach too closely.

With a small arrangement of flowers draping over the edge of the Font to complete the picture, the tired but satisfied students stood back and viewed their work with much warranted satisfaction. As morning turned to afternoon it became clear that this was not only to be a Church celebration but also one that brought S.E.N.T.E.C. (now North-Tyneside College of Further Education) and the Church together when the Principal, Mr Garside, called a halt to lessons at 3.30 p.m. when the Band left, to allow all the students to attend the Festival Service at 4.00 p.m.

With the parishioners who had been coming and going all day, there was a full Church. The Jazz Band found a position at the base of the steps to the Sanctuary and the Service began. Never before, and certainly never since, have I heard the hymn 'The old wooden Cross' sung to the rousing eight beats to a bar tones of a Jazz Band, its swinging tune producing foot-tapping and hand-clapping, yet with such reverence of the occasion that even the Vicar applauded. An hour later, on being presented with the collection so far, amounting to just over £400, and almost in tears, he said "The most wonderful experience has been to see people of all ages worshiping together, celebrating together and working together; an 84yr. old Lady working happily with a 15yr. old girl, is truly remarkable."

The Church was open all day for the rest of the week until Friday when all the arrangements were dismantled and the Church cleaned ready for the Sunday Service, when we were informed that the total collection and donations were over £600. It was now almost time for me to retire, but before that happened Mrs Anderson had one more advertising project for me to organise, an exhibition in the entrance to the College that would invite and encourage boys, girls, and adult students of all ages into whichever Department offered a subject for pleasure or a career.

The Florists were to design and construct the whole exhibit using appropriate accessories chosen by and loaned by all departments. I had no difficulty dealing with all the departments, not even the Welders, some of whom could be a little sarcastic sometimes about this 'Girlie' job of Flower arranging. This time, however, they were full of enthusiasm as were all the other departments, who loaned and carried, even helped to stage in many cases, from Hairdressing, through to Home Economics, Science, Catering, including the two Technicians, Domestic Science, Liberal Studies, Welders and Engineers, whose offer was a huge engine cleaned and polished to a fine art that challenged even the most shining new one. Thus we had a mixture of shapes and sizes with which to fire the Florists with enthusiasm and promote ideas for what was to produce a display that when finished and staging complete almost filled the Entrance-hall, leaving just sufficient space to allow the comings and goings from the front doors to the lifts and corridors.

By now I was nearing my sixtieth Birthday, retirement day, but all efforts to find a Teacher to take over were unsuccessful, two from the south pulling out at the last minute. I had been considering staying on for another five years in order to enhance my retirement pension, and this seemed the to me a signal that I should do just that. After making enquiries I learned that I would earn one and one-eighth pence per day towards an enhanced pension, which seemed at the time as a ridiculously low amount at the time but, bearing in mind that the department would close without a replacement Teacher I decided to carry on for the five years, which could be accomplished without permission from anyone; however, it was pointed out that should I wish to go further after that period, permission from the Principal would be necessary.

That rule worried me not at all, as I had no intention of working for another ten years, enhanced salary or none at all. The reaction from Mrs Anderson was rather negative because she happened to be the last of the original teachers when the College was founded in 1963, and as I came only three years later I also was considered one of the first, which was 'News to me' at the time. A few days later she asked me what benefits there were in working for another five years, and when I explained she also applied to stay on and, being two years younger than myself, was still there when my time to retire approached, but, of course, as my birthday was in November I carried on until that date much to her exasperation, for now, two months into the first term it had to continue for the whole year.

However, help was at hand in the shape of a student of five years past, who, having heard of the predicament, applied for the job. She had been a florist in Glasgow until her marriage and joined my class to learn more modern methods. Now with five more years' experience, and having heard of the vacancy, she said at her interview, "I just want to teach like Mrs Rundle taught me"; flattering you might say but she was kept well out of my way when she took over all the Floristry classes when I officially retired on my birthday in November. Whilst my teaching hours were very varied for now, as a part-time teacher with a salary to match, my work schedule was completely transformed and one of my first assignments was teaching cane-work to a group of Nursery Nurses who, I soon found, were little more intellectual than the three-to-four-year-old children they would eventually have in their charge.

Soaking cane was just a game, an opportunity to throw water over each other, and generally have fun. Discipline was just a word to be ignored; however, help was soon on the way. On the second morning with water splashing all over the floor in front of a wide open door of what was more like a kindergarten than a classroom, a passing Mrs Anderson paused in the doorway for two or three seconds, obviously saw what was going on, smiled, nodded, and went on her way. I took my cue realizing that this was normal behaviour of Nursery Nurses, who played like three-year-olds to understand three-year-olds, and let them get on with it. Obviously Cane work was just an activity to fill their curriculum, not intended to be a serious subject of learning.

At the same time another assignment to the College was quite new, probably taken on in order to earn more money for the department and because there was a spare Teacher thought capable of taking the class. A group of boys, aged between 16 and 19, all but two who were of doubtful intellectual ability, and none at all of the understanding of what the word work meant, were assigned to the College by the new 'Manpower Commission', which placed such groups, being unable or incapable of getting jobs.

They had a Supervisor, a man who knew nothing at all about gardening, but had been given £200 to spend on equipment and had bought spades, forks and hoes for work in the grounds of the big Hall that was used as an annex for the overflow of classes from the main College. They had been left to 'Mature' for 12yrs. and were knee-high in Docks, Thistles, Brambles and every kind of weed, plus overgrown ivy, privet, and other vegetation so fighting for space as to be beyond identification.

The assignment was to turn them into a garden for the production of vegetables and flowers for use in the College, but there was much to do in clearing the ground for any type of gardening, and it was raining, I mean 'RAINING', as never before, nor prolonged for the whole three months to the Christmas break. So spades and forks were temporarily assigned to the old derelict greenhouse once used when the House was a beautiful 'Lived' Hall. However, the Supervisor did what he was really responsible for, viz. the good behaviour of the students and let the teacher get on with teaching, and that demanded a whole new plan that, for the good name of the College, had to be successful.

Fortunately I had been given a small classroom on the top floor of the Annex and this was now put to good use. I had one microscope at my disposal which had been used for the floristry botany lessons and a quick trip now to the Botany Department to borrow some slides was, I hoped, sufficient to keep the lads interested until the rain stopped. First a short introduction, whilst the two intelligent Pauls stretched out on the long bench and relaxed, and the others lolled, or sat in apprehension as to what 'Miss' was doing.

I talked for a few minutes holding in my hand a piece of Privet from the grounds. "Do you know what this is?" I asked, "Wee aye Miss," said Stephen, "it's nobut a piece o' privet". "Would you like to see what it's like inside? I asked. The two Pauls jumped up and all gathered round in anticipation of what was going to happen, and when they had all had a long close look Stephen said in almost disbelief, "Wey Miss that's nobut a miracle". Having drawn their attention and, obviously their interest, I exchanged the privet leaf for that of a laurel, and invited them to have another look. None of them hesitated for a second and I was not only pleased, but certainly relieved to know how to keep them interested, and at least learn something, no matter how long it rained.

The botany sessions continued during September, interspersed with a little geography as appropriate whenever the opportunity arose, and soon it led to identification of trees, their characteristics, and why they grew in different areas of the World, ending with the Temperate Zone. One in particular that caught their interest was the Horse Chestnut, which, of course reminded them of the days when they had played 'Conkers' with the tree's fruit, the chestnuts, but during a discussion about how the tree got its common name, I showed a photograph of the 'Horse-shoe' where a branch had fallen off, there were 'Ums and Ars' from all sides and, as the lesson expanded into Geography, and an explanation about the 'Date Line', it was one of the Pauls, who sat up immediately almost shouting, "Say that again Miss", which I did, and got the response, "Wey Miss, that's Time-travel".

It was now the end of October and my thoughts were looking forward to when the rain stopped and we could start work on the grounds, and possibly start gardening and possibly produce something from the broken down greenhouse. I approached the Principal direct as he had always been co-operative and interested whatever I might have in mind, and this time was no exception. "Get the lads to clear away all the rubbish that's accumulated", which could be done even though the rain had not stopped, "and give the inside a good scrub and disinfectant spray, and I'll order some strong clear polythene to line the inside."

Now with a few old seed boxes begged on loan from the Parks Dept. in Whitley Bay and delivered by the Supervisor, who had become interested in all the activities, we could start raising our own tomato plants. Window sills anywhere can be useful, and in a little top floor classroom they can be invaluable as greenhouse benches. With all hands on deck as boxes were filled, seeds carefully sown, with relative information on composts, fertilisers, pricking out, etc. and, by the beginning of the New Year term, with help from the now involved Supervisor, we were ready to plant out our first tomato plants into our very presentable new greenhouse.

If there was one thing I learned from my years of teaching it was 'Get yourself on to their level', you'll never succeed by being pompous, or superior; try to raise their level without their knowing what you are aiming for, if possible! But occasionally get down to their level to show that you too are human, and understand their problems. This was demonstrated to me one day when, knowing that small groups are easier to control than one big one, I split them up into five groups and gave each a task as far away from the rest as possible in the area we had to cover. Two were clearing undergrowth under the trees on the boundary where I could see them, another was clearing rubbish out of the old glassless greenhouse and carrying it into a far corner out of the way until it could be disposed of, whilst a third, including the two lads who were rather slow in understanding, and incidentally ,were the two tallest in the group, were digging a deep trench ready for a long row of Sweet peas. Whilst discussing something with one group I noticed that the one preparing the trench were standing talking intensely and curious to know what the problem was I walked towards them with a rather flippant "You're all leaning on your spades like Corporation workmen, what is the problem?" Stephen, the tallest of the group, was quick to explain in his broad Geordie accent "Way Miss, it's 't' Maths Teacher, she's not very nice, she says we stink." "And do you stink?" I asked, moving nearer and sniffing at Stephen's jacket. "Whey noo Miss" he replied. "Well Stephen," said I, "and all of you, it is not my place to criticise another Teacher, and if you are sure that you don't stink, then ignore it and get on with your work here, or you'll never be able to pick a bunch of sweet peas to take home to Mother, will you?" "Whey noo Miss," was his rather humble reply, "but you understand, cos yo'r one-o-us." I had no answer to that!

Christmas passed and New Year came, when clearing the grounds could be completed ready for the new garden that fortunately could be completed without my help for I had one more appointment to fulfil. When I was visiting my Daughter, Yvonne, an Army nurse at Rinteln in Germany, I met a Colonel's Wife who had lived near Catterick Camp where she had met and married a young Army Officer. Now in charge of organizing leisure activities, in

570

conversation with Yvonne after I left, she asked if I would do a Demonstration tour to the Army wives, and so I found myself once more in Germany in February 1981, being met by an Army Officer, Son of the Scottish Lady Macmillan, and spent the first night at an informal party as their Guest.

This was the beginning of one of the most interesting, nerve-testing three days I have ever had, from being transported to flower markets by Officers' wives with unlimited money to spend on flowers etc. and transferred from one house to another by Officers of all ranks, to my third demonstration at Reindahlen, and the final journey on the fourth morning, to Dusseldorf by a General, who escorted me through the airport and onto the Plane to carry me home, with a suitcase full of ornaments and trinkets that I had been allowed to choose as payment from the stalls set out by the Dresden, Minton and other producers of fine art at each Flower club meeting.

Two days later I was back in the garden, now completely cleared of the overgrown shrubs etc. and gradually looking like a real garden with a bed of young spring cabbage plants, potatoes in their earthed-up trenches, spring lettuce in a frame made from a few bricks and an old window frame by the now 'Hooked' Supervisor. Things progressed through the next three months including a visit to the Parks Dept. in Whitley Bay to see the range of plants in the huge glasshouses that supplied the Council with plants and flowers for the hanging baskets, beds and borders in this small seaside town, and potted plants to decorate the town's Civic Offices.

In the middle of July the College year ended and I finally retired, with cries of "You'll come and see us sometimes, won't you Miss?" and myself answering "Of course I will", fulfilling my promise three days before the College opened again in September to cries of "It's Miss, it's Miss", as they left what they were doing and made a rush towards the gate, shaking my hand, patting me on the back and almost hugging me, with cries of "Come an' see our cabbages, Miss, come an see our tomatoes," adding proudly, "and we've got two trays o' lettuce on't winda-sill as t'Bossses, thill come before them outside."

571

The really good news was that one of the boys had shown such interest in all the activities during our visit to the Parks Dept. Nurseries that he had been offered a job there to start in the New Year. There was even better news when I noticed that the two Pauls were missing and a proud Supervisor told me how the attitudes had changed and both of them, with a little encouragement from him and the Rep. from the Manpower Commission, had obtained temporary jobs in the offices of a firm of Solicitors and one of Architects with a view to becoming Articled Apprentices.

Now it was time for me to leave, but not before the rest of them had loaded me with samples of the produce they had raised. "Miss would you like some cabbages?" and although I could see that they were not really large enough for the pot, the Supervisor nodded and a good helping was wrapped in paper and put in my hand, next it was a generous handful of lettuce, and a few potatoes of usable size, and finally a humble Stephen asked, "Miss would you like a bunch o' sweet peas?" I watched as he carefully cut the stems of about a dozen flowers and noticed the look of pride on his face as he handed them to me, and as I turned towards the gate they followed, said "Goodbye" and with very mixed feelings I turned and waved goodbye.

Chapter 17

In 1975, my Mother, then almost blind, and after many discussions, came to live with me at Whitley Bay and settled in very quickly, although as time went on she grew very unhappy when none of the family came to visit. For me it was a complete change when, instead of a lunch in the Catering Dept. of the College, or the Staff Room it meant a rush home to a partly prepared lunch for Mum and myself, and back again to the classroom in time for the next lesson. However, as time went on we settled into a routine that had advantages for both of us when I realised that what she liked most was to talk, and to this end, as soon as Dinner was over and washing-up out of the way, I settled on the three-seater, part of a suite I had bought at the Auction-rooms in Whitley Bay when I knew that she was coming, so that I could relax in the dining-room in comfort, instead of the lounge where the Television 'lived', and which she disliked intensely.

Settling down with a file resting on my knees and a pen in my hand, all I needed to do was ask one question, "Whose son was John?" or "When was Samuel born?" and the talking began. My pen raced to get every word down on paper and sometimes I was thankful to have had a bit of experience in being the secretary of one club or another, and developed the habit of writing three letters and drawing a line the length of the spoken word. This was the real beginning of my research a few years later into eight of our 'Family Trees' as I gradually became more curious. As the years went by this proved to be a good idea which, occasionally required a certain amount in planning, as when I had to go to London for a City & Guild's Meeting or to a College, usually in the North of England or in Scotland as Chief Examiner with two or three other examiners from the North or

Midland areas. Fortunately Mrs Mulholland the owner of the Residential Home at the end of Queen's Road, put me in touch with one of her semi-retired nurses who was able to come early in the morning before I left and stay until I returned. This, as it turned out, was an excellent arrangement, as it gave Mum a chance to talk, talk, talk, to another human being, which I knew she loved to do, in fact I think she rather enjoyed my occasional absences.

Then, in 1981, I finally retired, my teaching career at an end, no more getting-up at 6.30 a.m., early breakfasts and dashing off to market at 7.30 a.m., all in the past. Gradually a different routine developed, partly to spend more time with Mum, partly to prevent me from getting bored, but also to prevent Mum feeling guilty by preventing me doing some of the things I wanted to do. She need not have worried for I was quite happy to sit listening and writing and learning about our various Family Trees and occasionally arranging for the nurse to stay with her until I returned from where I happened to have to go, be it to London for a City and Guild's meeting, or a trip to one of the Archives for further information for the Family Trees, and, of course, retirement meant that daytime was free as well as evenings and whenever the weather was good we went on days out in Northumberland, to Seahouses to see the kipper-smoking sheds, to hear about and see the boat of Grace Darling who saved the life of the sailors, to Bamborough Castle once the Seat of Government, or to Lindisfarne to read about and hear the history of Saint Cuthbert.

However, I had no intention of allowing my brain to grow addled and having learned a little about both French and German languages from television programmes I decided to take two hours on two days a week for six weeks and, hopefully reach R.S.A standard. That would keep my brain from growing addled! One evening a week I would take the evening off and go Sequence dancing at North Shields where a well-known Teacher of Dancing held dancing evenings, which was not what I wanted, so I made arrangements to go to his classes and do the job properly. This led to eight years of learning and training after which I had not only passed all the tests for Waltz, Foxtrot, Quickstep, and all the other forms of dancing, but had taken the tests and become a qualified Teacher of

Dancing; not that I ever intended to do such a thing, but it pleased me somewhat to know that my brain and body were not quite addled.

So life with Mum was very pleasant for a few years, although her ailments, particularly her feet, were a constant worry and if ever I saw a pair of shoes that would suit her painful feet I would buy them, try them and, usually, they would last a few weeks until her feet started 'Grumbling' again. The biggest and most upsetting of her problems was her failing eyesight, the final reason for her accepting to leave 'The Leylands' and live with me. I knew what a big wrench it was to leave the rest of her family, the boys whom she had been so proud of since the days they were born and, had they visited more often, the parting would not have been so great, but they had families and for various reasons would not or could not have her, usually because they wouldn't do the same for their wives' Mothers, so couldn't do it for their own. I was not concerned at all, I knew that I would rather have her with me than me having to visit her at their homes.

The end was not pleasant and I have had regrets over my handling of it ever since. As do most very old people as they grow older, they fall down, no matter what is done to try to prevent it, and Mum did sometimes fall down during the night no matter how many times I told her to shout, even once provided her with a hand-bell, which she wouldn't use as it would wake me up! Once on the floor there was nothing for it to get help because her stiff leg and deadweight were too much for me to handle and I blessed the Whitley Bay Ambulance Men who, no matter what time, day or night needed only one call and they were with us in a few minutes; until the last time when, during the fall her head hit the corner of a kitchen cupboard that I had recently bought from the Auction Rooms on Park view. (The house had no kitchen except for a very small area just large enough to house a Sink, the Cooker and Clothes washer, hence my use of the space in the room that had been the Maid's room with a fairly modern fireplace, an off-shot Toilet, a small modern table and chairs, and a big bay window looking out onto the rear garden, with plenty of space for Mum's bed on the other side of the fireplace near the door to the Hall.)

575

She had often fallen down and usually I could lift her myself with a little help from her, but this time there was no hope of me even attempting it, hence my call to the Ambulance Service as on some previous occasions. In a few minutes they were with us but, even before they moved her it was evident that as she fell her head had struck the edge of the end fitment creating a huge cut on the side of her head. There was nothing anyone could do except get her to the hospital fast. As they prepared her and put her on a stretcher I phoned the Doctor on Park View, only a few minutes away. He was not very pleased as he had never approved of her staying with me, and now he gloated, "This is just what I expected" was his first remark, which didn't surprise me but his next one made me very angry when he knew that she had lived with me and been looked after by me for almost ten years, when he said "She should have been in a Home". He phoned the Hospital to notify them that she was on her way there then left with the Ambulance following him.

It was December 14th and I visited her each day, although I sometimes wondered if she knew that I was there as she was so quiet and almost asleep most of the time. Mrs Mulholland, stopped me two days later on my way home from the Hospital and seemed quite concerned, but had a suggestion, "Why don't you take a break for a day or two? Your Mother is all right and you can't do anything for her in hospital," followed by a suggestion, "There's a four-day Coach trip to Berlin this week. Why don't you book yourself on it? Do you good to get away for a bit." It was very tempting and I thought, 'Why not? She's right, I can't do anything here, my Mum hardly knows I'm there and she'll be all right until I get back.' Without any more hesitation I turned around and headed for the Coach Firm's office and booked a seat on the Coach.

Three days later on my last visit to the Hospital the bombshell dropped, all patients who could be moved were to be sent home for Christmas, and my Mother was one of them; she would leave the Hospital on the day before Christmas Eve, the day the Coach was due back to Whitley Bay. Mrs Mulholland had heard about the move from a relative of one of her Residents, and contacted me immediately. "Look," she said, "You go on your trip, I'll take your

Mother in until you get back, just relax and enjoy the break." So it was that I found myself with a Coach full of people crossing the North Sea to Hamburg and across Germany on the only route into Berlin called 'The Corridor', with just one permitted stop at a Cafe about half-way, where a heel-clicking German Soldier stood guard whilst we all walked silently in for whatsoever we might find to eat and drink; a wonderful experience whilst wondering what was to come in Berlin.

It is surprising what can be achieved in two days with good planning, and the Coach firm had, as they say, 'Done us Proud'. The Hotel, when we finally arrived, served us with an evening meal that belied all the rationing, and the resident Band entertained us with tune after tune, with invitations to 'Come up and have a go at conducting', which was great fun. Next day we had our first tour around Berlin as far as we were allowed to go, still with scars of War, as it was still divided down the middle by a huge board fence covered with all kinds of notices and graffiti that divided the East and West Germans and the Allies.

In the afternoon we all opted for a visit to the East side of Berlin, through 'Check-point Charlie'. As the coach neared the crossing we were told to put out of sight all newspapers and magazines, to leave the coach and stand in a single line with open Passports held at the side of our faces, and an order not to smile or look at the Crossing-keeper when he looks at it and then at you. The a serious warning, "Whatever happens do as you are told and Don't Smile, or they'll keep us there all day". We all did as we were told, even though the situation seemed so ridiculous, and were relieved when told to get back onto the Coach. The hour-long trip around East Berlin was worth all the problems it had created, but we were all somewhat relieved when we passed through the return gate into a much more natural atmosphere.

Next day the return to Hamburg and home was uneventful and we arrived back somewhat relieved, but glad of the opportunity to see at first hand some of the things that we had often been told about. Next morning I paid my first visit to the Nursing Home to see my Mother, and to make arrangements for her to return home. Mrs

Mulholland was reluctant to let her go, "She's not well enough yet and, really should still be in Hospital, but she'll be happier here." I was a little apprehensive and suspicious, remembering what the Doctor had said, but I realised that there was nothing I could do at this stage, and with a parting "I'll come and see her tomorrow", I returned home.

From then on the daily visits continued and, as she was now sitting out and occasionally joining in the conversation, I stayed about two hours, going home for lunch and returning about two o'clock until teatime and she seemed happy to listen to gossip and all the things that were going on outside, but I knew that she wanted to come home and, although I knew that it would be more difficult than before, at least we would be together in the freedom of our own home. After a few days I grew suspicious that she was never going to be allowed to return home; whenever it was mentioned I got the same reply, "I'll see what the Doctor says".

Two weeks had now gone by and I returned each evening more unsure and unhappy about the situation as time went on. The empty house, the empty room and the empty bed haunted me every night. I missed her, I missed getting her up in the morning and struggling to get her into bed at night, and I missed her most when I saw her empty chair in between the two sideboards. If she were never coming home again I had to do something now as I knew I would never alter anything after she'd gone. First the bed must be removed as I knew that I would be very reluctant to do so in future, and the offending fixtures could be moved into that space with the wall between either removed for access from kitchen to scullery, or left as a division between the two. I hadn't far to go to find good workmen whom I knew would understand the situation and eventually do a good job, and also give good advice, as by trade the two Brothers were Bathroom Constructors and Fitters who lived in a house directly opposite mine in Queen's Road.

I was in no great hurry, but I felt a little less miserable now that I had something else to turn my mind to, considering that I had no-one to whom I could confide, or at least 'Vent my feelings'. Now, I thought, I can cope with whatever Mrs Mulholland and the Doctor can contrive to do, and continued to visit each morning and afternoon for the next few weeks, always ready to bring her home if and when they allowed it, although I knew that this was only 'Wishful thinking' on my part. January passed followed by February and every day I saw Mum getting quieter and quieter as if she had given up hope.

On one occasion she was quietly talking to her Grandma, "Come and fetch me, Come and fetch me," another when her fingers were swollen and the Doctors were cutting off her Wedding ring, and she was crying and protesting when I arrived and on seeing me shouted "Josephine, tell them to stop, they want to cut my Wedding ring off, and it's never been off my finger for seventy-four years." It took only a moment to see why, and I understood why it was thought necessary, for her finger was so swollen and blue that it had to be done. Putting my arm around her I said "Look Mum I think it is necessary, but don't worry, I'll get it made bigger and it can be put on your finger again." But it had little effect as it still had to be removed.

I don't think she ever recovered from the trauma, even though after more than two months in the Home, it would be her ninety-third Birthday on March 14th and I had made arrangements for her to have a party, and all the other patients were to be invited. For a week I prepared and cooked, a Birthday cake, iced with roses and ribbons, and a message, sandwiches, scones and an assortment of small cakes and buns, and the whole family were coming from Totley for the day so that she would have a really Happy Birthday, and it was also Jeff's Birthday so it was a double celebration. She was very quiet, even on the day, and of course it was easy to see why; she was still in a Home where she didn't want to be, and she would still be in a Home when they had all left but sadly, it didn't put that ring back on her finger, and from then on there was little hope.

The end, however was to be even worse than I had imagined, and took me back to the time when my Grandmother lived with us, always in her Wheelchair for the last few years of her life because she said, "I'm not going in a home, because they give you 'Black Jack'". We all knew what she meant, but I think, didn't believe it! A week after the party on my usual morning visit she was sitting in a quiet

579

corner on her own facing two or three people sitting opposite including Mrs Mulholland and the Doctor, who were in conversation with each other. After nodding recognition they remained there whilst I talked to my Mother, but there was no response; she just stared straight into my eyes, no expression, no blinks, just a continuous stare. I continued talking, but without any response at all, until near to lunch time, I got up, bent to give her a kiss saying "I'll come back after lunch", and left.

Returning an hour and a half later and not seeing her there, I asked where she was, and the answer was "Oh she's in her room". I knew where her room was so made my way there when to my surprise, and horror she was in bed, haggard, thin, white-faced and unrecognisable. I was so shocked at the difference from that morning when her face had been plump, even pretty, her eyes blue and although expressionless, had been pleasant. I even wondered whether she had suddenly become completely Demented and had not known me after all. I took her hand, felt her pulse which was strong, and listened to her heavy breathing. I knew that this was the end, there was nothing I could do but sit with her, hold her hand, and wait. About an hour and a half later I felt a slight change in her pulse, which grew fainter until it stopped, and with a loud noise, almost a scream, and a gurgle, she died.

Almost immediately the door burst open and Mrs Mulholland and a nurse burst through the door and to the bed, obviously to confirm that she was dead, when the Doctor walked in, said nothing to me and pronounced her dead. I was shocked, mesmerized at the whole incident and left the room. As I approached the front door, Mrs Mulholland stopped me and asked me to collect Mum's clothes etc. in the morning, but she would like me to leave them as they would be useful for the other residents to use in case of small accidents. No mention of my Mother, I expect it was 'All in the day's work'. I rang Elijah and told him that the Undertaker at North Shields would arrange everything at their end, and John Heaths would look after the Totley end; so matter of fact, but at least it helped. Mum was buried in Holmesfield Churchyard on April 5th 1985.

Life was very quiet for the next three years, I continued with my dancing lessons and eventually took all the tests and examinations and qualified as a Dancing Teacher in 1986 although I never had any intentions of becoming one, but it helped the 'Ego', and the Trophies looked quite acceptable on the shelf between the Lounge and Dining room It was rather nice when one of my students of a few years ago who had taken advantage of a chance to leave the North and work for the President of the Society of Floristry called occasionally when she was on a visit home, and took me out for lunch at a nice little secluded restaurant in Jesmond Dene, and when possible Yvonne paid a visit from Germany when Jon had some reason to come to England.

It was on one of these occasions when Tracey was about three years old and the journey from Bury St. Edmunds carrying a huge suitcase had been particularly tiring that she suggested, or begged me, to move further south. Up to then I hadn't even considered it, I was very happy at Whitley Bay, and Arthur enjoyed the North and, usually on his visits home, spent some time with his old friends from the University, and even went to Scotland, which he loved, for a few days whilst visiting me. However, once mentioned often repeated, and so, in February 1988 I got in touch with an Estate Agent in Sheffield to find out what properties were for sale in Totley, and received leaflets almost by return. I decided to drive down to Totley to view for myself, three journeys, five houses in the Bradway area during the first month, to find that they had already been sold, had offers, or were not now available, so I gave up the idea of moving, at least for now.

Then came a call to tell me that there was a house for sale at Sunnyvale Road Totley for £3,600, would I like to make an offer? I said yes but I would like to see it before I made a decision. A call back said another man, Mr Parker had offered another hundred, did I want to offer more, I said no, let him have it, sensing that this was the usual tactics in house buying. About an hour later another call, Mrs Bartholomew says you can have it for £3,600. I said I would get my Brother to come and see it, and let them know. I rang my Brother Geoff in Rowan Tree Dell, two roads away, and asked him to check it for me, which he did, and the following day he rang me to say that he thought it was alright, except that there was a screw on the front of the cooker that was loose. Readers, I bought it!

I left Whitley Bay in March 1998 to take possession on 31st March to find that all the strip-lighting had been removed leaving the wires only two inches long, much too short for my Chandeliers. Not knowing where to contact the previous owners I spent £14 for a local electrician to re-wire all the downstairs rooms whilst I stayed with my Brother on Moorwoods Lane Holmesfield for two weeks until the house was ready for us to move in, only to find that the cooker was not the only thing that had a screw loose. Workmen were in the house for nine months, mending, removing, replacing, and putting things to rights, just in time for a house-warming party on December 19th 1989. I was in the fourth year of an Open University Course, with only one more year to go as I was already a Teacher, for which one year was allowed. Yvonne was having a 'Beano' in the kitchen with the men, including cousin Tom, who was always the life and soul of any party. Still laughing as she came back into the dining room she said. "Mum leave that Open University and get that story written 'cos I can't remember all this", and that's why I am doing just that!

For the first few weeks I thought this had been a really bad move, Totley had changed during the years that I had been away; even when I visited the Church just around the corner and saw a man sitting curled-up on a chair just inside the open door, who didn't speak, nor appear to be interested as to whom the visitor might be, only to be told on my way out some fifteen minutes later that he was the Vicar. I made my mind up there and then that I would go to Holmesfield Church where I knew that I would at least find a few old friends of the past. I wasn't wrong, on my first Sunday morning attendance a group of people standing talking in the middle aisle turned their heads and cried out, "Look who's here", as two or three ran to put their arms around me in welcome.

The next ten years were the happiest years of my life, first as a Worshiper when Malcolm was the Vicar, a wonderful man with only one fault, if that is the right word, as he was a Labour Man, a fact that was sometimes clearly illustrated in his Sermons. We organised a lovely Party for him the Sunday before he left for his next

Ministry at Crawley, Surrey in mid-summer 1988, and at least two worshipers of that time still keep in touch with him. Now with no Vicar there was an Interregnum until a new one could be appointed, during which time the Speaker John Ramsden was in charge and soon the Annual General Meeting was held when the Wardens were elected, or re-elected by the newly elected committee. John Ramsden had asked me if I would allow my name to be put forward as a Warden and, although I suspected the reason why, and also that I was expected to vote for myself, I said "Yes", but I voted for Robert, one of the present Wardens who the Speaker disliked and he was duly re-elected with the other Warden. Needless to say the Speaker was very angry, and told me that he would give me a few lessons on Politics, to which I replied, "You can't tell me anything about Politics, John", and by this time I had accepted the Post of Deputy Warden.

This suited me down to the ground as not having a fixed role to play as the Wardens had, I could create my own and I loved it, making posters, notices and tickets etc on my new Computer, organising events during an eighteen-month Interregnum. Most of all I enjoyed and felt a great deal of satisfaction in visiting those who didn't come to church, for one reason or another. I printed small visiting cards that I could put through the door if any person was not at home, or having an afternoon 'Nap'. "Just called to see you, if you need anything I am here", followed by my Tel no. I figured out that they had their own reasons why they didn't come to Church, but they were citizens of the Church Parish and that was sufficient for me, so they received baskets of fruit and vegetables, and a few flowers at Harvest Festival time like those who already came to Church, and nobody objected.

The months of the Interregnum seemed to pass very quickly with concerts, an Evening of Music and Verse, the usual vicarage Garden Party and Harvest Festival. This was a special time in the history of our Church, which was believed to have been founded as a small wooden hut about the year 900 during a visit by Saint Aiden whilst spreading the Gospel from Lindisfarne, and there is still the broken stone pillar on the grass verge outside the front door that is believed to be the remains of the Cross from which Saint Aiden preached to the local people at that time. One particular item that I had suggested was the installation of a Corner Unit in which to house the figure of St. Swithin who had been sitting on a radiator since he was rescued from the Loft two years previously, and also to provide a small alcove below in which a flower arrangement could be displayed in memory of a friend or member of the Choir or Congregation. It would also be a recognition of the thousands of worshipers who had supported the Church for over nine hundred years so that we today could celebrate. We had no problem in finding a Cabinet-maker who could produce such a unit for there was one already in Hill Crest, Baslow Road Totley, and in order to fund the project I decided to go on a 'begging tour' around the Village and surprisingly had no problems in raising the £1,500 quoted.

Towards the end of the summer of 1999 there were three applicants for the post of Vicar and, as Deputy Warden, I had the honour of joining the Archdeacon and other Dignitaries on the Interviewing Panel who bore the responsibility of choosing our next Vicar, who joined us in late November 1999. It wasn't easy going during the first few weeks, although we all liked him so far as vicars were concerned, and progressively even more so, but he had a strong feeling about Catholicism and when the statue of St. Swithin was put into the alcove from the radiator on which he had been standing since his rescue from the loft, he immediately took him out and placed him on the nearest window-sill: why? because that's what the Catholics do! No matter how many times someone replaced him, he was removed, until he disappeared altogether, whether up into the loft again is not known.

Since then the Corner unit, so I am told, is known as 'Josie's Unit' even though a framed printed page explained that it was in thanks and memories of all those worshipers who had kept the Church throughout the thousand years since St. Aiden had preached there, the first wooden Church had been built, and the remains of the stone Cross still stood on the grass outside the Church Door. I still have a copy of the reason for the Unit which was on display even during the decoration of the Church for the annual St. Swithin's festivities in July 2000.

MILLENNIUM CORNER UNIT
November 21st 1999

The Installation and Dedication of the Memorial Corner Unit took
place today to commemorate the Millennium of
St. Swithin's Parish Church Holmesfield.
By donations raised from the congregation and friends of
St. Swithin's Church, in grateful acknowledgement of all those who
have worshiped in and worked for St Swithin's Parish Church
during a thousand years on this ancient mound.

NAMES FOR THE LOG BOOK
In alphabetical order

Marjorie Adshead
Bessie Adlington
Susan & Glyn Adlington
Geoff. & Margaret Artindale
Alan Beryl Bamber
Brian & Terry Bell
Eric & Betty Booker
Doreen Buckley
Jean & Dave Burgon
Margaret Campsall
Terry & Christine Chapman
Julie Coles
Winifred A Cook
Alison & Jack Copeland
Mr & Mrs Corker
Ian & Angela Corker
A. Duffield
D. Dickinson
Howard & Kate Fisher
Margaret Ford
Mr & Mrs Fitzgerald
Kevin & Tina Gage

Charlotte Victoria Hall
Sally Hall
Sophie Clarissa Hall
Jessie Hassall
Bob & Sandra Hastings
Jill & Maurice Hastings
Christine & Richard Hibberd
Wng Cmdr J.A. Hill Belgium
Mrs Yvonne Lucille Marie Hill
Grenville & Eleanor Hinton
John & Christine Hunt
Pauline Machin
Brian & Valerie Meadows
Val Oglesby
Roy & Elin Owen
Peter & Marjorie Pearson
Andrew & Karen Price
L Robins
Dr. Arthur S Rundle
Josephine Rundle
Elijah Salt
Mrs Winifred Senior
Muriel & Ken Simmons
Alison Smith
Mrs G. Smith
John & Christine Smith
Richard & Sue Shepley
Mr & Mrs Stevenson
Pamela Stocks
Mrs Sutcliffe
May & Bill Taylor
Peggy Taylor
Kath Teal
Norma Thompson
John & Thelma Wade
Kenneth & Jean Tudor

Barry & Val Wheat
David & Maisie Wortley
Winifred Mary Wragg
Ms. Ashley Wright Ft. Drum NY, USA

So, you see, dear readers, this is not really Josie's Unit, it is a tribute paid for by donations given generously, without begging, by the residents of Holmesfield, whether churchgoers or not, who agreed with the sentiments behind the project. and were only too willing to support it. Consequently, with very little help from me, the amount of £1,560 was raised in only one day, a surprise, even for me. Remember, it is meant as a tribute to all those who have gone before us, and I hope a lasting tribute to those of to-day, and all who will follow.